This book comes with access to more content online.

Quiz yourself, track your progress,
and score high on test day!

Register your book or ebook at
www.dummies.com/go/getaccess.

Select your product, and then follow the prompts
to validate your purchase.

You'll receive an email with your PIN and instructions.

ACT® 2022

by Lisa Zimmer Hatch, MA,
and Scott A. Hatch, JD

A Wiley Brand

ACT® 2022 For Dummies®

Published by: **John Wiley & Sons, Inc.**, 111 River Street, Hoboken, NJ 07030-5774, www.wiley.com

Copyright © 2021 by John Wiley & Sons, Inc., Hoboken, New Jersey

Published simultaneously in Canada

No part of this publication may be reproduced, stored in a retrieval system or transmitted in any form or by any means, electronic, mechanical, photocopying, recording, scanning or otherwise, except as permitted under Sections 107 or 108 of the 1976 United States Copyright Act, without the prior written permission of the Publisher. Requests to the Publisher for permission should be addressed to the Permissions Department, John Wiley & Sons, Inc., 111 River Street, Hoboken, NJ 07030, (201) 748-6011, fax (201) 748-6008, or online at http://www.wiley.com/go/permissions.

Trademarks: Wiley, For Dummies, the Dummies Man logo, Dummies.com, Making Everything Easier, and related trade dress are trademarks or registered trademarks of John Wiley & Sons, Inc., and may not be used without written permission. ACT is a registered trademark of ACT, Inc. All other trademarks are the property of their respective owners. John Wiley & Sons, Inc., is not associated with any product or vendor mentioned in this book.

LIMIT OF LIABILITY/DISCLAIMER OF WARRANTY: WHILE THE PUBLISHER AND AUTHOR HAVE USED THEIR BEST EFFORTS IN PREPARING THIS BOOK, THEY MAKE NO REPRESENTATIONS OR WARRANTIES WITH RESPECT TO THE ACCURACY OR COMPLETENESS OF THE CONTENTS OF THIS BOOK AND SPECIFICALLY DISCLAIM ANY IMPLIED WARRANTIES OF MERCHANTABILITY OR FITNESS FOR A PARTICULAR PURPOSE. NO WARRANTY MAY BE CREATED OR EXTENDED BY SALES REPRESENTATIVES OR WRITTEN SALES MATERIALS. THE ADVICE AND STRATEGIES CONTAINED HEREIN MAY NOT BE SUITABLE FOR YOUR SITUATION. YOU SHOULD CONSULT WITH A PROFESSIONAL WHERE APPROPRIATE. NEITHER THE PUBLISHER NOR THE AUTHOR SHALL BE LIABLE FOR DAMAGES ARISING HEREFROM.

For general information on our other products and services, please contact our Customer Care Department within the U.S. at 877-762-2974, outside the U.S. at 317-572-3993, or fax 317-572-4002. For technical support, please visit https://hub.wiley.com/community/support/dummies.

Wiley publishes in a variety of print and electronic formats and by print-on-demand. Some material included with standard print versions of this book may not be included in e-books or in print-on-demand. If this book refers to media such as a CD or DVD that is not included in the version you purchased, you may download this material at http://booksupport.wiley.com. For more information about Wiley products, visit www.wiley.com.

Library of Congress Control Number: 2021938612

ISBN 978-1-119-81152-7 (pbk); ISBN 978-1-119-81153-4 (ebk); ISBN 978-1-119-81154-1 (ebk)

Manufactured in the United States of America

SKY10027529 061221

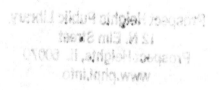

Contents at a Glance

Table of Contents

Introduction

Welcome to *ACT 2022 For Dummies*. This is a nondiscriminatory, equal-opportunity book. You're welcome to participate whether you're a genius or (like us) you need a recipe to make ice. Besides, the book's title is not a slam at you. You're not the dummy; the test is (and we've heard it called worse, believe us — especially on the Friday night before the exam).

The goal of this book is to show you exactly how to survive the ridiculous situation called the ACT. No matter how excellent your high school teachers are (or were), they've prepared you for the real world, a world that, alas, has very little connection to the ACT. High school teachers can give you a good foundation in grammar, reading, science, and math skills (the areas tested on the ACT), but you may want to think of them as the friendly old GPs, the general practitioners whose job it is to keep you well and handle the little day-to-day problems. What do you do when you have a crisis, like the ACT, that's making you really sick? We like to think of *ACT 2022 For Dummies*, as a loony but gifted specialist you can call when your situation becomes desperate.

No one wants to deal with the eccentric specialist for too terribly long. The goal of this book, just like the goal of the expert, is to come in with the Code Blue crash cart, deal with the situation, and then leave rapidly with as few lives destroyed as possible. This book has one goal: to prepare you for the ACT — period. We're not here to teach you every grammar rule ever created or every math formula that Einstein knew. We don't include any extra "filler" material to make this book look fat and impressive on bookstore shelves. If you want a thick book to use as a booster seat for the vertically challenged, go find *War and Peace.* If you're looking for something that you can use to prepare you for the ACT as quickly and painlessly as possible, again we say to you, welcome to *ACT 2022 For Dummies.*

About This Book

You likely can't escape the ACT. Many colleges require you to take this entrance exam before they'll even look at your application. Virtually every college accepts scores from either the ACT or the SAT. (Wiley just so happens to publish *SAT For Dummies* as well, should you choose to take that exam.) Many students decide to take both tests to see which one results in a better score. Is that a good idea? Absolutely. Even better, take practice tests for both (you can download a free full-length ACT from www.act.org and eight complete SATs from www.collegeboard.org) to see which one suits you best and then concentrate on just that test.

Many colleges emphasize ACT scores to compensate for grade inflation. That is, some high schools may give you an A for doing the same level of work that would gain you a C at other high schools. Because the ACT is the same for everyone (students all over the world take the exact same exam), colleges can use the scores to get inside your head and see what's really there. Think of this test as an opportunity, not a crisis: A good ACT score may help offset a low GPA. In just a few hours one fine Saturday morning, you can make up a little for a few mishaps in school.

In *ACT 2022 For Dummies,* you find out what types of questions are on the exam, which questions you should work on carefully, and which ones you're better off guessing at quickly. (Good news: The ACT has no penalty for wrong answers, so guess on absolutely every question you don't know.) We also help you figure out which approach to use for each type of question, and, perhaps most importantly, we show you some traps that are built into each question style. We've been test-prep tutors for many years and have developed a list of the "gotchas" that have trapped thousands of students over the years. We show you how to avoid being trapped, too.

This book is also full of the substantive information that you need to know, including grammar rules and geometry, algebra, and arithmetic formulas. Occasionally, we include some truly sick humor on the principle that, as you're groaning at our jokes, you won't notice that you're suffering from the questions. (Hey, as the mushroom said to his friends, "Of course, everyone likes me. I'm a fun-gi!")

Note to nontraditional students: The days of high school may be just a fading memory for you (along with your thin waistline and full head of hair). We recognize that not everyone taking the ACT is a high school junior or senior. Maybe you took a few years off to build your career or to nurture a family (or to pay your debt to society) and are now having to go back and review what you thought you had left behind years ago. It can be totally frustrating to have to deal with proper punctuation or quadratic equations all over again. Postpone your nervous breakdown. Things aren't as dismal as they look. You'll probably be surprised how quickly material comes back to you as you go through this book.

Foolish Assumptions

Although you could've picked up this book just because you have an insatiable love for English, math, reading, and science, we're betting you picked it up because you have to take the ACT. (Isn't it good to know at the outset that your authors have a remarkable grasp of the obvious?) And because we weren't born yesterday, we figure that you're taking the ACT in anticipation of applying to college. How exciting for you!

Because we've rarely met a person who actually looks forward to taking standardized entrance exams, we're lumping you into the category of "readers who are going into the ACT kicking and screaming." Okay, maybe we're being overly dramatic, but we've got a hunch that you're not especially excited about the prospect of spending four hours of precious sleeping-in time sitting in a stark classroom, darkening endless ovals on a bubble sheet under the watchful eye of a heartless proctor who continues to yell "Time!" before you've finished the section. Call us crazy!

Nevertheless, you picked up this book, so we assume that getting the best ACT score you can is important to you and that you care enough to sacrifice some of your free time to achieve that goal. Good for you!

Here are the other assumptions we've made about you while writing this book:

>> You're a high school student, and, like most high school students, you carry a full course load, participate in a number of extracurricular activities, may even have a job, and prefer to carry on a social life. Or you may have already graduated from high school and may hold down a career and tend to a family. Either way, you don't want us to waste your time with a bunch of stuff that isn't on the ACT. For instance, as much as we enjoy creating vocabulary flashcards, we don't share those with you in this book because you don't need to memorize word meanings to ace the ACT.

» You're not all work and no play. We want to make studying for the ACT as painless as possible, so we've tried to lighten things up a bit with a few jokes. Forgive us, please. Some are really lame.

» Because you're college-bound, you've spent some years engaged in a college-prep curriculum that includes algebra, geometry, and likely a little algebra II and trigonometry. We're pretty sure you've had your fair share of English, social studies, and science classes, and you've written an essay or two. Therefore, we don't bore you too much with the elementary stuff. (We do, however, cover the basic math and grammar concepts that you may have forgotten.)

Icons Used in This Book

Some information in this book is really, really important. We flag it by using an icon. Here's a list of the icons we use and details about what they mean:

TIP

Follow the arrow to score a bull's-eye by using the tips we highlight with this icon.

REMEMBER

Burn this stuff into your brain or carve it into your heart; it's the really important material. If you skip or ignore the Remember icons, you won't get your money's worth out of this book.

EXAMPLE

This icon marks sample problems.

WARNING

Pay heed to this advice and avoid the potential pitfall.

Beyond the Book

In addition to what you're reading right now, this book comes with a free access-anywhere Cheat Sheet that includes tips to help you prepare for the ACT. To get this Cheat Sheet, simply go to www.dummies.com and type "ACT For Dummies Cheat Sheet" in the Search box.

You also get access to all the full-length online practice tests and dozens of flashcards. To gain access to the online practice, all you have to do is register. Just follow these simple steps:

1. **Register your book or ebook at Dummies.com to get your PIN. Go to www.dummies.com/go/getaccess.**

2. **Select your product from the dropdown list on that page.**

3. **Follow the prompts to validate your product, and then check your email for a confirmation message that includes your PIN and instructions for logging in.**

If you do not receive this email within two hours, please check your spam folder before contacting us through our Technical Support website at http://support.wiley.com or by phone at 877-762-2974.

Now you're ready to go! You can come back to the practice material as often as you want — simply log on with the username and password you created during your initial login. No need to enter the access code a second time.

Your registration is good for one year from the day you activate your PIN.

Where to Go from Here

You've probably heard the joke about the student who was debating whether to buy a book at the bookstore. The sales clerk, eager to make his commission, proclaims, "Buy this book — it'll do half the work for you!" The student brightens up and exclaims, "Great! I'll take two!"

As much as we wish we could simply transfer test-taking material into your brain in one dump, we realize that learning it takes effort on your part. Meet us halfway. We've done our job by showing you what to study and how to go about it; now it's your turn. We suggest two ways to use this book:

>> **Fine-tune your skills.** Maybe you're already a math whiz and just need help with the English grammar. Go right to the English review we provide in Part 2. If, on the other hand, you're a grammar guru who wouldn't know a nonagon if you met one in a dark alley, turn to the math review we offer in Part 3.

>> **Start from scratch.** Grab a sack of food and some sharpened pencils, lock yourself in your room, and go through this book word for word. Don't worry; it's not as bad as it seems. Actually, starting from scratch is the preferred method. Many students make what we call the "mediocre mistake": They're good at one section, mediocre at a second, and dismal at the third. They spend all their time in their worst section and barely look at the sections that they're mediocre or good in. Big mistake! If you spend two hours studying something that's totally incomprehensible to you, you may improve your score a few points. If you spend two hours studying your mediocre material, you may improve your score by one or two points. A couple of points that you gain in your mediocre section are just as valuable as — and a heck of a lot easier to gain than — the same number of points you gain in your weakest section. Humor us and read the book from cover to cover. You'll pick up some great material.

Regardless of whether you hunt and peck your way through the chapters or approach the first six parts consecutively, absolutely take the three practice tests in Part 7. How you choose to use the full-length practice tests is entirely up to you. However, may we suggest two tried-and-true methods?

>> **Diagnostic:** Take the first practice exam to see how you score. Then devour the subject reviews and advice we provide in the first six parts of the book. Finish by taking the other two practice tests to see how much your score has improved.

>> **Pure practice:** Devour the reviews and advice first and use the three full-length exams to practice and reinforce what you've learned in the rest of the book.

Either way, you may choose to save one of the exams to practice on during the days right before you take the ACT. That way, you can walk into the test site with the test questions fresh in your brain.

After you've covered the information in this book, you may discover that you need more in-depth English or math review. Or maybe you just can't get enough of this stuff! Several Wiley publications are available to accommodate you; just search for the most recent editions. Dig more deeply into the rules of Standard English in *English Grammar For Dummies* and find tons of grammar practice in the *English Grammar Workbook For Dummies* both by Geraldine Woods. Those of you who are math challenged will find these books helpful: *ACT Math For Dummies* and *SAT Math For Dummies* by Mark Zegarelli; *Algebra I For Dummies* and *Algebra II For Dummies* by Mary Jane Sterling; and *Geometry For Dummies* by Mark Ryan (all by John Wiley & Sons, Inc.).

Figuring Out How Long All This Studying Will Take

In the real world, you have classes, family obligations, community service projects, sports practices, work, and, if you're lucky, a social life. How on earth are you going to fit reviewing this book and studying for the ACT into your schedule? The answer is that you have to commit to this project and make it a priority. How many hours should you carve out of your schedule? Here's what we suggest.

Reading the ACT overview in the first three chapters shouldn't cut out too much of your free time, no more than 30 minutes. Other parts require more of an investment.

The five parts of the book that review English, math, writing, reading, and science contain one or more chapters that explain how to approach the subject at hand and one short chapter full of practice questions. Soaking up the information in the explanations and taking the short practice tests should take you about an hour or two per test subject.

Additionally, the English Test part features a very important grammar review that we strongly suggest you spend at least an hour or two studying. Even if you're good at grammar, this section features all sorts of persnickety grammar rules, just the type that (with your luck) you'd get caught on during the ACT. Finally, the Math Test part features a pretty comprehensive math review — number basics, geometry, algebra, coordinate geometry, and trigonometry — that should take you about three hours to fully absorb.

And don't forget the three full-length practice tests, of course. Each of the tests takes 2 hours and 55 minutes to complete (a half hour longer with the Writing Test), not including breaks. Give yourself about an hour to review the answer explanations for each exam. That should be enough time for you to review the answer explanations to every question and to take advantage of the opportunity to see shortcuts you may not have noticed or traps you luckily avoided. So taking and reviewing each exam should take you about 4 or 5 hours. Here's the final timetable:

Activity	Time
Reading the ACT overview	30 minutes
Reviewing the approaches to the five test topics and working through the practice questions at 1.5 hours per topic	7.5 hours
Absorbing the four math review chapters at 1 hour per chapter	3 hours
Engrossing yourself in the grammar review chapter at 2 hours	2 hours
Enjoying the three full-length practice exams at 4 hours per exam	12 hours
Groaning in pain at the authors' lame jokes	15 minutes
Firing off letter complaining about authors' lame jokes (or sending along better ones!)	15 minutes
TOTAL TIME	26 hours

Fear not: You don't have to do it all in a day. The last thing we advocate is sleep deprivation! This book is designed so that you can start any part at any time. You don't have to have finished the general math chapter, for example, before you go through the general reading chapter.

Okay, are you ready? Are you quivering with anticipation, living for the moment when you can pick up your yellow No. 2 pencil and hold on for the thrill of a lifetime? (Or are you thinking, "These authors need to get a life!"?) Listen, you're going to take the ACT anyway, so you may as well have a good time learning how to do so. Laughing while learning is the whole purpose of this book. Take a deep breath, rev up the brain cells, and go for it! Good luck. Just remember that for you, ACT can come to stand for Ace Conquers Test!

1

Coming to Terms with Reality: An Overview of the ACT

Get cozy with the format and content of the ACT and develop a checklist of the items to take with you to the exam (and leave home). Find out how your efforts will be scored and when it's a good idea to take the ACT for a second, or even third, time.

Develop a plan to beat stress during the test and learn other ways to avoid messing up your performance so that you can achieve your best possible score.

Benefit from the advice of seasoned college counselors to help you answer the question, "What do colleges want from me?"

Chapter **1**

Getting Your ACT Together: ACT 101

Are you the type of person who jumps into the cold water all at once instead of dipping your toe in a little at a time? If so, do we have a table for you! Table 1-1 gives you an overview of the ACT and shocks you with the entire kit and caboodle all at once.

TABLE 1-1   **ACT Breakdown by Section**

Test	Number of Questions	Time Allotted
English	75	45 minutes
Mathematics	60	60 minutes
Reading	40	35 minutes
Science	40	35 minutes
Writing (optional)	1	40 minutes

If you add up the numbers, you find that you have 216 multiple-choice questions to answer in 215 minutes; 215 minutes is 3 hours and 35 minutes, or just over 3.5 hours. You get one 10-minute break between the second and third tests (the Mathematics and Reading Tests). You may also encounter an extra 20-minute section after the Science Test that the ACT will use to determine the difficulty of questions for later exams. If you choose not to take the optional Writing Test, you get to walk out right after that. If you include the time in the classroom spent giving out the tests, explaining the directions, checking IDs, answering the Interest Inventory questions, and so on, your whole morning is shot. You may as well figure on giving up 4 to 4.5 hours for this test.

THE COMPUTER-BASED ACT

If you take the ACT in a country other than the United States, your exam is offered on computer rather than on paper. This computerized option has been available for several years and is becoming more common at testing sites in the United States.

The question types, numbers of questions, and scores are the same for both tests; the difference is in the method of delivery. The computer-based ACT, or CBT, provides handy tools that allow you to approach it in much the same way you would for the paper test:

- **Highlighter and line reader:** Use these tools to focus on important data and sentences.

- **Answer eliminator and masker:** Use these tools to help you mark out wrong answers.

- **Magnifier:** This tool allows you to read the fine print for charts and graphs in the science questions.

You also have a timer to keep track of your time and the ability to move between questions and mark them for later review.

The ACT has plans to expand the digital version of the ACT and make it more widely available throughout the United States.

What to Take to the ACT

If you can't borrow the brain of that whiz kid in your calculus class for the day, you're stuck using your own. To compensate, be sure that you have the following with you before you leave for the ACT test center:

» **Admission ticket:** You receive your ticket immediately after you register online. Be sure to print it out so you have it for test day.

» **Pencils:** Take a bunch of sharpened No. 2 pencils with you. You may also want to take good erasers (nothing personal — everyone makes mistakes). Mechanical pencils aren't allowed.

» **Map or directions:** Go to the test center a few days before the actual exam to scope out your driving route and parking area. Often, the ACT is given at high schools or colleges that have parking lots far, far away from the test rooms. Drive to the location a few days in advance, park your car, and see just how long it takes you to get to the room. You don't need the stress of having to run to the test room at the last minute on test day.

» **Clothing:** Schools that host the ACT often turn off the heat for the weekend (the ACT is usually offered on a Saturday), and the test room can be freezing cold. Alternately, in the summer, schools turn off the air conditioning, making the room boiling hot. Dress in layers and be prepared for anything.

» **Photo ID:** Showing the birthmark your boyfriend or girlfriend thinks is so cute isn't going to cut it with the test proctor. You need to upload a photo when you register for the test and bring a photo ID (student ID, driver's license, passport, military ID, FBI Most Wanted mug shot, whatever) to the exam. If you don't have a photo ID, you can bring a letter of identification. The form is available on the official ACT website (act.org).

» **Eyeglasses:** Students taking the ACT frequently forget their reading glasses at home and then squint for the four long hours of the test. The ACT is enough of a headache on its own; you don't need eyestrain, as well. If you wear contacts, be sure to bring cleaning/wetting solution in case you have to take the lenses out and reinsert them during the break. (Hey, all those tears can really mess up your lenses!)

>> **Snack:** True, you get only one ten-minute break between the Math and Reading Tests, but that's enough time to gobble down something to jump-start your brain. We often suggest taking an energy bar or some peanuts, something with protein and carbohydrates. Scarfing down a candy bar is actually counterproductive; your sugar levels rise only momentarily and then drop down below where they were before you had your chocolate fix.

>> **Watch:** Keeping track of time on your own timepiece is more efficient than wasting precious seconds seeking out the clock on the testing site wall. Place your watch on the desk where you can refer to it easily throughout the exam. Digital watches may not be allowed. Stick with ones that have faces and hands. Your watch can't make any sounds either. If the proctor hears so much as a beep from your watch, she will not-so-politely request that you leave the building and cancel your test.

>> **Calculator:** The ACT gurus allow you to use a calculator only on the Mathematics Test. Although the ACT information bulletin has an entire quarter page detailing which calculators you can and cannot use, generally, you can use any calculator (yes, even a graphing calculator) as long as it doesn't make a noise or have a computer algebra system. Make sure the one you bring has at least a square root function and, ideally, basic trigonometry functions. You may not use a laptop computer (don't laugh; you'd be surprised by how many students want to bring one to the test!).

What Not to Take to the ACT

Do not, we repeat *do not*, take any of the following items with you to the ACT test room:

>> **Cellphones and other electronic devices:** Leave your cellphone in the car. You aren't allowed to bring it into the test room. One student we know was dismissed from the test because he accidentally left his cellphone in his pocket, and it rang during the exam. The same goes for other electronics, such as iPads, PC tablets, or anything else that can access the Internet or make a sound.

>> **Books and notes:** Take it from us: Last-minute studying doesn't do much good. So leave all your books at home; you aren't allowed to take them into the test room with you. (Just be sure to fill your parents in on this rule. We once had a student whose mother drove all the way to the test center with her daughter's ACT prep book, thinking the girl needed it for the test. The mom actually pulled the girl out of the test to give her the book, resulting in the girl's nearly being disqualified from the test.)

>> **Scratch paper:** You may not bring your own scratch paper to the paper-based test, and you don't receive any scratch paper during the exam. Fortunately, the exam booklet has plenty of blank space on which you can do your calculations.

What to Do If You Have Special Circumstances

Not everyone takes the ACT under the same conditions. You may have a special circumstance that can allow you to change the date of the ACT or the way you take your exam. Here are a few of the special circumstances that may affect how you take the ACT:

>> **Learning disabilities:** If you have a diagnosed learning disability (LD), you may be able to get special accommodations, such as more time to take the test. However, you must specifically request such accommodations way in advance. Prepare your requests for fall tests by the prior

June and for spring tests by the prior September. Please note that in order to be eligible for special testing on the ACT, your LD must have been diagnosed by a professional, and you should have a current individualized education plan at school that includes extended test time. Talk to your counselor for more information. Note that you can only request special accommodations in conjunction with a test registration.

>> **Physical disabilities:** If you have a physical disability, you may be able to take a test in a special format — in Braille, large print, or on audio. Go to the official ACT website (act.org) for complete information about special testing.

>> **Religious obligations:** If your religion prohibits you from taking a test on a Saturday, you may test on an alternate date. The ACT registration website specifies dates and locations in each state.

>> **Military duty:** If you're an active military person, you don't complete the normal ACT registration form. Instead, ask your Educational Services Officer about testing through DANTES (Defense Activity for Nontraditional Educational Support).

Guessing for Points to Maximize Your Score

Scoring on the ACT is very straightforward:

>> You get one point for every answer you get right.

>> You get zero points for every answer you omit.

>> You get zero points for every answer you get wrong.

The ACT doesn't penalize you for wrong answers. Therefore, guessing on the ACT obviously works to your advantage. Never leave any question blank. We suggest that you save a couple of seconds at the end of each section just to go through the test and make sure that you've filled in an answer for every single question.

REMEMBER

Your Number's Up: Scoring on the ACT

We once had a frustrated student tell us that the scores on the ACT looked a lot like measurements to him: 34, 29, 36. However, the ACT has four scores, which makes for a very strange set of measurements! The ACT scores are nothing like high school scores based on percentages. They're not even like the familiar SAT scores that range from 200 to 800. Instead, they range from 1 to 36. Scoring on the ACT works like this:

>> Each required test (English, Mathematics, Reading, and Science) receives a *scaled score* between 1 (low) and 36 (high).

>> The *composite score* is the average of the four required test-scaled scores.

>> If you take the ACT Plus Writing (which is the official title for the ACT with the optional Writing Test), you receive a Writing score that ranges from 2 (low) to 12 (high). The score is the sum of the average of each of the four subscores you receive from each of the two people who grade your essay. The Writing Test score is completely separate from your composite ACT score.

» A *percentile score* tells you where you rank in your state and nationwide.

Look at the percentiles. Just knowing that you got a 26 doesn't tell you much. You need to know whether a 26 is in the 50th percentile, the 75th percentile, or the 99th percentile. If you get a 36, you have documented lifetime bragging rights because that's a perfect score!

» You may see additional readiness indicators. A STEM Score represents overall performance on the math and science sections. An English Language Arts Score combines your performance on the English, Reading, and Writing Tests. The Progress Toward Career Readiness Indicator measures your progress toward career readiness for a variety of careers. The Understanding Complex Tests indicator tells you whether you're sufficiently understanding text material for college and career level reading. Colleges will see these scores, but they aren't combined in any way with your ACT composite.

The ACT website (act.org) provides a sample score report and scoring information that shows you what all these scores look like when you and your colleges of choice receive them.

What the ACT Expects You to Know

The ACT tests the following subjects:

» **English:** The ACT expects you to know the fundamentals of grammar, usage, punctuation, diction, and rhetorical skills. For example, you must understand sentence construction — what makes a run-on and what makes a fragment. You need to know how to distinguish between commonly confused words, like *affect* and *effect* or *principal* and *principle.* You must be able to use the proper forms of words, distinguishing between an adjective and an adverb, and you must know the difference between a comma and a semicolon. Part 2 addresses the English portion of the test.

» **Mathematics:** The ACT requires basic skills in arithmetic, geometry, and algebra. If you've had two semesters of algebra, two semesters of geometry, and a general math background, you have the math you need to answer about 90 percent of the questions. The ACT also tests algebra II and trigonometry. Oh, and you don't have to know calculus. The ACT has no calculus questions. Happy day! Refer to Part 3 for more.

» **Reading:** The ACT expects you to be able to read a passage in a relatively short amount of time and answer questions based on it. Your reading skills are probably pretty set by now. However, this fact doesn't mean you can't improve your ACT Reading score. Chapter 13 shows you a few tricks you can use to improve your speed and tells you how to recognize and avoid traps built into the questions.

» **Science:** You don't have to have much specific science background to ace the Science Test. The passages may test chemistry, biology, botany, physics, or any other science, but you don't have to have had those courses. The test gives you all the information you need to answer most of the science questions in the passages, diagrams, charts, and tables. Head to Part 5 for more about the Science Test.

» **Writing (optional):** The ACT folks added this optional section to test your writing ability. Don't worry! You've been writing for years, and the ACT people know that you can't possibly write a perfect essay in a measly 40 minutes. They're not focusing on perfection; instead, they're looking at your thesis, organization, and ability to support your thoughts. The ACT doesn't require you to write the essay, and few colleges require or even recommend the essay. The essay portion of the ACT may be eliminated from the test entirely in future administrations. Part 6 gives you the lowdown on the Writing portion of the ACT.

Repeating the Test for a Better Score

Are you allowed to repeat the ACT? Yes. Should you repeat the ACT? Probably. Other than the additional cost (both financial and emotional) required to test again, there is no real downside to retesting. Decide whether you want to repeat the ACT based on your answers to the following questions:

>> **What errors did I make the first time around?** If your mistakes were from a lack of knowledge, that is, you just plain didn't know a grammar rule or a math formula, you can easily correct those mistakes with studying.

>> **Why do I want to repeat the test?** Is your ego destroyed because your best friend got a better score than you did? That's probably not a good enough reason to retake the ACT. Do retake the exam if you're trying to get a minimum qualifying score to enable you to get into a college or earn a scholarship.

>> **Can I go through this all over again?** How seriously did you take studying the first time around? If you gave it all you had, you may be too burned out to go through the whole process again. On the other hand, if you just zoomed through the test booklet and didn't spend much time preparing for the test, you may want a second chance to show your stuff.

>> **Were my mistakes caused by factors that were not my fault?** Maybe you were in a fender-bender on your way to the exam, or perhaps you stayed up late the night before in an argument with your parents or your best friend. If you just weren't up to par when you took the exam, definitely take it again, and this time be sure to get a good night's sleep the night before.

REMEMBER

The ACT may allow students to retake individual sections in the near future. For example, If you want to improve your Science score but are happy with your other section scores, you can use a digital version of the test to take just the Science section. The ACT had scheduled the release of section testing for September 2020 but postponed its plans indefinitely to focus on the testing challenges presented by the COVID-19 pandemic. We predict that section testing will become available in 2021, likely in September, but the release date is currently unknown. When the time comes, keep in mind these considerations:

>> Section retesting will be available on Saturday national exam dates at locations that provide digital (computerized) testing. For more about the computer-based ACT, see the sidebar in this chapter.

>> You may retest only if you've already taken the full ACT at least once.

>> The ACT will provide a score report with your highest section scores and include a new composite score (called a *superscore*) calculated from the average of those scores, but whether colleges prefer to use the traditional score report or the report with the superscore results will be up to each individual college.

>> Section retakes will be offered only by computer, and scores will likely be available within two business days of testing.

The ACT doesn't automatically send colleges the scores for every time you take the test. It gives you the option of deciding which set of scores you want colleges to see. If you don't want to report the results of all your tests, keep these issues in mind:

>> **The ACT automatically sends scores to the colleges you list on your test registration form.** If you want to wait until after you see your report to decide whether certain colleges can see your scores for a particular test administration, don't list those colleges with your ACT registration.

>> **Many colleges figure your ACT composite score by averaging the highest scores you get in each section across all administrations of the test.** They refer to this practice as *superscoring* the ACT. If you get a 24 in English, a 21 in Math, a 23 in Reading, and a 25 in Science the first time you take the ACT and a 25, 20, 24, and 24, respectively, the second time, these colleges will figure your composite score by averaging your higher 25 English score, 21 Math score, 24 Reading score, and 25 Science score. Your composite score for each administration would be 23, but the composite score the colleges calculate would be 24. Therefore, you may want the colleges to get reports from all the times you take the ACT so that they can superscore your highest section scores. When the ACT institutes section retesting and the superscore report, your highest section scores will appear on one report, and (if colleges allow), you'll only have to send (and pay for) one report.

>> **A handful of colleges require you to report your scores from every test date.** Check with the admissions committee at the colleges to which you're applying to make sure they allow you to withhold score reports from particular test dates.

REMEMBER

A growing number of colleges allow you to self-report your ACT scores. Those colleges consider the ACT scores you list on your college applications or report within the college's online portal, depending on the policies of the individual school, to make admissions decisions. You only send an official score report after you've been admitted to and have decided to attend that particular college. Self-reporting allows you to save the money you'd have spent to send official score reports to every college on your application list. If you're able to take advantage of the self-reporting option, be sure to follow the college's procedures exactly and report your scores accurately. A discrepancy between the scores you report on your application and the scores that appear on your official report could be ground for rescinding your college acceptance.

Chapter **2**

Succeeding on the ACT

On the wall of our office, we have a padded cushion that's imprinted with the words, "BANG HEAD HERE!" We've found that most of our students use it either to reduce stress (we guess one headache can replace another!) or — much more commonly — to express their exasperation over unnecessary, careless (we're trying not to say it, but okay — dumb!) mistakes. Going through the material in this chapter about how to relax before and during the ACT and how to recognize and avoid common mistakes can prevent you from becoming a head-banger later.

Surviving the ACT with Four Stress-Busters

Most people are tense before a test and often feel butterflies dancing in their stomachs. The key is to use relaxation techniques that keep your mind on your test and not on your tummy. To avoid becoming paralyzed by a frustrating question during the test, we suggest that you develop and practice a relaxation plan (perhaps one that includes the techniques we describe in the following sections). At the first sign of panic, take a quick timeout. You'll either calm down enough to handle the question, or you'll get enough perspective to realize that it's just one little test question and not worth your anguish. Mark your best guess and move on. If you have time, you can revisit the question later.

TIP

Practice a quick relaxation routine in the days before you take the exam so that you know just what to do when you feel panicky on test day.

Inhaling deeply

Stressing out causes you to tighten up and take quick breaths, which doesn't do much for your oxygen intake. Restore the steady flow of oxygen to your brain by inhaling deeply. Feel the air go all the way down to your toes. Hold it and then let it all out slowly. Repeat this process again several times.

Stretching a little

Anxiety causes your muscles to get all tied up in knots. Combat its evil effects by focusing on reducing your muscle tension while breathing deeply. If you feel stress in your neck and shoulders, also do a few stretches in these areas to get the blood flowing. You can shrug your shoulders toward your ears, roll your head slowly in a circle, stretch your arms over your head, or even open your mouth wide as if to say "Ahhh." (But don't actually say it out loud.)

Thinking positive thoughts

Any time you feel yourself starting to panic or thinking negative thoughts, make a conscious effort to say to yourself, "Stop! Keep positive." For example, suppose you catch yourself thinking, "Why didn't I study this math more? I saw that formula a hundred times but can't remember it now!" Change the script to, "I got most of this math right; if I leave my subconscious to work on that formula, maybe I'll get it, too. No sense worrying now. Overall, I think I'm doing great!"

REMEMBER

The ACT isn't the end-all, be-all of your life. Cut yourself some slack on test day. You probably won't feel comfortable about every question, so don't beat yourself up when you feel confused. If you've tried other relaxation efforts and you still feel frustrated about a particular question, fill in your best guess and mark it in your test booklet in case you have time to review it at the end, but don't think about it until then. Put your full effort into answering the remaining questions. Focus on the positive, congratulate yourself for the answers you feel confident about, and force yourself to leave the others behind.

Practicing POE

You may think that acing the ACT requires that you find correct answers to the questions, and essentially you're right. But facing the challenge of staring down a set of four answer choices in the hope that the correct one will reveal itself can be daunting. Change your perspective. Instead of searching for the one correct answer in the bunch, focus on wrong answers. You'll usually have an easier time finding something wrong with an answer. The key to a successful process of elimination (POE) lies in making sure you're rejecting choices based on careful analysis rather than a gut feeling.

Usually, two of the four (or for math questions, three of the five) answer choices will be relatively easy to identify as wrong. They will obviously be off topic or contain specific information that the passages or questions don't address. When you're deliberating between the two remaining options, look for problems with one of the answers. Sometimes just one word will make the answer incorrect. The correct answer is the one left standing after you've found problems with the others.

REMEMBER

Tap your pencil on every word as you read through an answer choice to make sure you carefully consider all components before you eliminate or select that answer choice.

Avoiding a Few Dumb Mistakes That Can Mess Up Your ACT

Throughout this book, you discover techniques for doing your best on the ACT. We're sorry to say, however, that there are just as many techniques for messing up big-time on this test. Take a few minutes to read through these techniques in the following sections to see what dumb things people do to blow the exam totally. By being aware of these catastrophes, you may prevent them from happening to you. And no — the student who makes the greatest number of these mistakes doesn't receive any booby prize.

Losing concentration

When you're in the middle of an excruciatingly boring reading passage, the worst thing you can do is let your mind drift off to a more pleasant time (last night's date, last weekend's soccer game, the time that you stole your rival school's mascot and set it on the john in the principal's private bathroom — you get the point). Although visualization (picturing yourself doing something relaxing or fun) is a good stress-reduction technique to practice *before* the exam, it stinks when it comes to helping your ACT score during the test. Even if you have to pinch yourself to keep from falling asleep or flaking out, stay focused. Taking the ACT requires only four or five hours of your life. You've probably had horrible blind dates that lasted longer than that, and you managed to survive them. This, too, shall pass.

Panicking over time

Every section on the ACT begins with directions and a line that tells you exactly how many questions are in the section and, therefore, how many minutes you have per question. The ACT is no big mystery. You can waste a lot of time and drive yourself crazy if you keep flipping pages and counting up how many more questions you have to do. You can do what you can do; that's all. Looking ahead and panicking are counterproductive and waste time.

Messing up on the answer grid

Suppose that you decide to postpone doing Question 11, hoping that inspiration will strike later. But now you accidentally put the answer to Question 12 in the blank for Question 11 . . . and mess up all the numbers from that point on. After you answer Question 40, you suddenly realize that you just filled in Bubble Number 39 and have one bubble left — *aaargh!* Stroke City! It's easy to say, "Don't panic," but chances are that your blood pressure will go sky-high, especially when you eyeball the clock and see that only one minute remains.

If you have a good eraser with you (and you should), the wrong answers on the answer grid should take only a few seconds to erase. But how on earth are you going to re-solve all those problems and reread and reanswer all the questions? You're not; you're going to thank your lucky stars that you bought this book and took the following advice: When you choose an answer, *circle that answer in your test booklet first* and *then* fill in the answer on the answer grid. Doing so takes you a mere nanosecond and helps you not only in this panic situation but also as you go back and double-check your work.

Rubbernecking

Rubbernecking is craning your neck around to see how everyone else is doing. Forget those bozos. You have too much to do on your own to waste precious seconds checking out anyone else. You don't want to psych yourself out by noticing that the guy in front of you is done with his section and is leaning back whistling while you're still sweating away. Maybe the guy in front of you is a complete moron and didn't notice that the booklet has yet another page of problems. After you have the exam booklet in front of you, don't look at anything but it and your watch until time is called.

Cheating

Dumb, dumb, *dumb!* Cheating on the ACT is a loser's game — it's just plain stupid. Apart from the legal, moral, and ethical questions, you can't predict what types of grammatical mistakes will show up in the questions; what are you going to do, copy a textbook on the palm of your hand? All the math formulas that you need can't fit onto the bottom of your shoe.

Worrying about previous sections

Think of the ACT as five separate lifetimes. You're reborn four times, so you get four more chances to "do it right." Every time the proctor says, "Your time is up. Please turn to the next test and begin," you get a fresh start. The ACT rules are very strict: You can't go back to a previous section and finish work there or change some of your answers. If you try to do so, the proctor will catch you and you'll be in a world of hurt.

Worrying about the hard problems

The ACT contains a few incredibly hard questions. Forget about 'em. Almost no one gets them right, anyway. Every year, a ridiculously small number of students receive a score of 36, and if you get into the 30s, you're in a superelite club of only a few percent of the thousands and thousands of students who take the ACT annually. Just accept the fact that you either won't get to or can't answer a few of the hard questions and learn to live with your imperfection. If you do go quickly enough to get to the hard questions, don't waste too much time on them. See if you can use common sense to eliminate any answers. Then mark your best guess from the remaining choices. Keep reminding yourself that every question counts the same in a section, whether that question is a simple $1 + 1 = 2$ or some deadly word problem that may as well be written in Lithuanian.

Forgetting to double-check

Mark in your test booklet questions you're unsure about as you work through a section. If you finish a test early, go back and double-check the *easy* and *medium* marked questions. Don't spend more time trying to do the hard questions. If a question was too time-consuming for you five minutes ago, it's probably still not worth your time. If you made a totally careless or dumb mistake on an easy question, however, going back over the problem gives you a chance to catch and correct your error. You're more likely to gain points by double-checking easy questions than by staring open-mouthed at the hard ones.

REMEMBER

Every question counts the same. A point you save by catching a careless mistake is just as valuable as a point you earn, grunting and sweating, by solving a mondo-hard problem.

really want from you

» **Masterminding the right mix of academics, sports, and extracurricular activities**

» **Preparing for the all-important essay and interview**

» **Eliminating the biggest mistake most anxious applicants make**

Chapter 3

Surviving the College Admissions Process

At this point in your life, you may be asking yourself, "What do I need to know about the college admissions process?" To help you out, we took this issue to a group of experts — members of the Higher Education Consultants Association (HECA; hecaonline.org). HECA members are experienced independent college consultants from all over the world who have helped thousands of students get into the schools that best meet their needs and fulfill their dreams. They visit dozens of colleges every year, talk with the admissions officers, and know what's important to them. This chapter offers you the responses we got from a handful of HECA members when we asked them about the issues that concern you most.

What's the Main Thing Colleges Look For?

"Colleges look for genuine applicants who submit genuine responses to the questions they ask. You wouldn't believe how far honesty goes in this process. Yes, curriculum, grades, and scores are important — this is an academic competition, after all. That said, you'd be surprised at how quickly a canned or generic essay response will move your application directly to the wait-list pile (even when all else is right on-target).

"It's hard to put yourself in the admissions officer's shoes, but imagine reading a lot of the same exact stuff — things spit right back at you from the college's website — to the point that you are literally reading the same phrases and responses over and over again. That's not compelling! What *is* compelling is seeing an essay that reflects the kind of student who fits well at your college and shows a genuine interest in, and knowledge about, your school. It's that kid colleges want to admit and who colleges think will come to their campus and contribute in a meaningful way. So think carefully about your response to those 'Why here?' supplemental essays and avoid a canned response." — Bari Norman, PhD, expertadmissions.com

How Do Higher ACT Scores Increase My Scholarship Chances?

"In addition to increasing your chances of admission, higher ACT scores have another meaningful impact: larger scholarships. Most colleges engage in a strategy called *enrollment management*, which, in simple terms, means that colleges use 'academic,' 'merit,' or 'leadership' scholarships to attract students that they deem desirable. Many schools try to elevate the average test scores of their incoming freshman class, so they use these scholarships to attract students with higher test scores. This, in turn, will help the school increase its ranking. With a little research ahead of time, you can determine if a small investment of time in improving your score will provide you with a four-year financial reward . . . . (R)aising your ACT composite score by 2 points (at some public universities) could equate to more than $4,000 a year for four years. Enough to make the hours spent preparing for the test seem more than worth it." — James Maroney, www.collegetreasure.com

"Higher ACT scores may well result in a preferred financial aid package (more grants than loans) and/or a very attractive merit scholarship offer. Keep in mind that several hundred colleges now use enrollment management and financial aid leveraging techniques to attract the students they want. Typically, those who have achieved high grades and high test scores are more attractive and, thus, will receive preferential treatment when it comes time for grants and scholarships. Despite what you may have heard, families with no financial need are able to get scholarship aid at many fine colleges and universities if the student's grades and ACT scores are high enough." — Todd Fothergill, www.strategiesforcollege.com

Do Schools Care Whether I Repeat the ACT?

"Most schools are happy to have you repeat the ACT. It allows them to consider the results of your best work. A growing list of schools *superscore* results across multiple test dates. This means that they cherry-pick your highest subtest scores from different ACT sittings and use these to compute a new composite score." — Helane Linzer, PhD, www.ivymaven.com

What Classes Should I Take in High School?

"There are no specific courses that all students should take. Instead, you should take the most challenging college preparatory curriculum that you can succeed in. For graduation, most high schools require four years of English, three or four years of math, including geometry and two years of algebra, two or three years of science that includes at least one lab-based course, and two or three years of history or social science. Some colleges and universities expect to see additional coursework — four years of math or courses in fine or performing arts.

"Some students strive to boost their GPA by taking easier courses hoping for higher grades, but that strategy can sometimes backfire if the colleges they're applying to look closely at the difficulty level of their chosen curriculum. You need to consider the selectivity of the colleges you're applying to and plan accordingly. The most selective colleges want to see that you've taken the highest level of each subject offered at your school and then look at how well you've performed in those courses. Again, it's important to balance challenge with the ability to succeed. Not all students can be successful at the highest levels of all subjects, so you should consult with your teachers and school counselors to make the best course decisions for your situation." — Kimberly Davis, CEP, www.daviscollegeconsulting.com

How Helpful Are Sports and Charity?

"Colleges like to admit smart, interesting students. How do you show that you're interesting? By the activities you're involved with. Colleges don't generally care what activities you participate in, so you should choose those that you find most enjoyable. Contrary to popular belief, you don't need to be involved in a sport unless that is something that interests you. Volunteering, however, is always good to be involved with because it shows that you have an interest in others.

"The longer you do a particular activity, the better a college likes it. You should focus more on being really involved with a small number of activities than dabbling in a bunch of activities. If you can get a leadership position in an activity, that really helps you stand out when you apply to college." — Todd Johnson, www.collegeadmissionspartners.com

What Should I Say on the College Essay?

"When deciding on what you should write about for your college essay, be sure you're passionate about the topic. Don't worry about pleasing other people. Your topic needs to come from your heart, and if it does, it will read as an authentic and unique essay. If you try to write about something you're not passionate about or something you think will sound good, it will come across as cold and disconnected. The essay needs to reveal something about you and your character. Topics can range from an incident you witness — such as a bag boy at the supermarket being humiliated by a supervisor — to the plight of the homeless. Be sure to demonstrate the ability to think critically.

"Whatever your topic, approach the essay within the limits of your writing capabilities. There's nothing wrong with writing an expository essay where the thesis is clearly stated; just be sure to demonstrate your writing skills by focusing on a single topic and supporting your topic with clear and relevant details. Admissions people want to see that you can communicate your thoughts through writing and, at the same time, reveal something unique about yourself." — James E. Long, Long Range Success

What Will They Ask Me in the Interview and What Should I Say?

"An admissions officer, a campus-trained student, or alumni of the school can do college interviews. They can be either informational or evaluative, but either way, interviews count in your favor. By making the effort to arrange an interview, you're showing serious interest in the school and helping them get to know you as a person rather than a list of grades, scores, and activities. This is your chance to shine! Don't wear jeans, sneakers, or a hat. Don't chew gum, and do put your phone away. Remember to smile, shake hands with confidence, make eye contact, speak clearly, and sit up straight. Come prepared to ask a few specific questions that are not easily answered by looking at the college website. Always send a thank-you note or email within 24 hours.

"Interview questions generally fall into three categories, so if you can answer these questions, you'll be prepared:

>> What do you have to offer the school academically, artistically, socially, athletically?

>> What does the college have to offer you? How will it meet your needs?

>> Open-ended questions where you have to answer WHY?

This is where they find out what kind of person you are. Practice coming up with three reasons for these types of questions. Why do your friends like you? Why do you like playing a particular sport? What has been your biggest disappointment? What's your favorite book?" — Colleen Reed, www.americancollegeconsulting.ca

How Do I Decide Which School Is Best for Me?

"Choosing the college that is best for you is the most important decision you've faced yet. With so many options and so many factors to consider, the college decision can cause more stress than all your previous choices combined! Luckily for you, you already have the skills you need to make this important decision.

"Consider this. How have you chosen your friends throughout the years? While choosing a friend is often a subconscious decision, you nonetheless start with a personal expectation for what a friend should be. Maybe the most important aspect of friendship is the ability to have fun together. Or maybe the most important aspect is loyalty. Whatever you prioritize in friendship, you have chosen your own friends accordingly.

"The college choice employs the same strategy. The most important question to start with is, 'What do you expect out of college?' After you have listed between ten and fifteen personal expectations for college, rank them according to how important they are to you. If you listed *fun*, you must ask yourself what will make college fun for you. If you listed *challenging*, think about what type of courses will offer the challenge you seek. Information about colleges is easy to find through school websites, campus tours, email correspondence with the school, guidebooks, and word of mouth. If you take some time first to define what will make a college compatible to you, you will be able to search for the exact information you need from the schools you are considering." — Erin McKenzie, Enroute College Consulting

What's the Biggest Mistake Most Students Make in College Planning?

"As students approach the planning process for college, there are two broad areas that often trip them up. One has to do with academics while the other has to do with putting together a college list. A key to academic opportunity rests with the high school core curriculum. The more years you stick with English, science, math, history, and a foreign language, the greater your access will be to more colleges. (Some college systems recognize visual and performing arts as part of the core, and others don't.) Ditching core classes too soon or opting for a less rigorous senior year places you at risk, especially when vying for competitive colleges.

"The second big mistake that students make is how they put together a college list. Most focus on the *reach schools,* those easy-to-love colleges always on the radar of their friends and family. I believe it's important to build a college list from the bottom up, to create a solid foundation that supports the weight of the others. I call these *anchor schools.* Look first for the colleges that would love to have you apply, the ones that readily recognize your ability and talents. It's easy to fall in love with a number of colleges if you're willing to focus on the unique opportunities and passionate and knowledgeable teachers found on most campuses. A balanced college list is a key ingredient to successful college planning." — Gael M. Casner, www.collegefindedu.com

"The biggest mistake students make in their college planning is to presume that high school settings and resources are equal to collegiate ones. They are literally two different worlds. Consider this:

>> "High schools provide very structured experiences where most students attend a day that has been compartmentalized for them into class periods and activities, and they are grouped with the same students year after year. Imagine high school as a buffet table that has only one or two types of offerings on it, and in order to serve yourself, you need to ask permission. Now imagine a room full of multiple buffet tables, each with diverse and unlimited offerings with so many new people to meet, all in one spot. This is college life, where feeding your interests and intellect has unlimited possibilities, all of which you choose for yourself. This is how the two institutions differ from each another.

>> "The resources available to students in high school are more limited than to those connected to the college experience so the assumption by many students when looking at the college picture is that they'll need the same expanded setting (such as a large city) to broaden their experience. The limitations of high school can sometimes lead you to believe that a college must be located in a thriving metropolis or be large. However, *all* schools, large and small, urban or rural, have a thriving life to them, teeming with opportunities to choose.

"Don't rule out the possibility of attending a smaller college in a smaller city based only on your high school experiences. Find out all that a smaller institution has to offer. You may be surprised!" — Diane Lomonaco, LCP, CEP, collegexroads.com

How Do I Make My Final Decision?

"For some students, making the final decision of where to attend college is the toughest part of the admissions process. If you find yourself struggling with your choice, stay as calm as possible. Take a step back and spend some time thinking about your individual goals, needs, personality, and what truly matters most to you in a college experience. Then evaluate each college individually based on those criteria. Keep in mind that there really is no perfect college; every school has pluses and minuses. Yet, there are happy, successful students at every college. After you've evaluated the colleges separately, compare them with each other, narrowing down the list to the one that seems to be the best match. Unfortunately, sometimes you'll have to make some tough choices, and we all have a tendency to mourn the 'one that got away.' Be careful not to let that cloud your vision about the great options you do have! Finally, remember that while deciding where to go is the last step in the long and tiring college application process, it's actually the first step in the next exciting phase of your life: attending college! Go forth confident that your choice is a good one." — Carolyn Z. Lawrence

2

Serving Your "Sentence": The English Test

Introduce yourself to the appearance of and approach to the ACT English Test. Learn the types of questions you'll encounter and tips for handling each question format.

Take a trip down memory lane as you review important punctuation rules, define parts of speech, and structure sentences.

Pick up on punctuation, pronoun, and possessive formatting errors. Evaluate underlined verbs and adverbs. Recognize sentence fragments and problems with parallelism. Remove redundancies and learn how to approach other questions that test your knowledge of what makes for good writing.

Strut your stuff on a short version of the real deal. Practice answering questions in a one-passage quick quiz that tests your knowledge of grammar, usage, and effective writing skill.

Chapter **4**

Mastering the English Test

W hen you open your ACT booklet, the first thing you see is the English Test. Your still-half-asleep brain and bleary eyes encounter 5 passages and 75 questions. Somehow, you're to read all the passages and answer all the questions within 45 minutes. That may seem like a lot of questions in a little bit of time, but the English questions really aren't super time-consuming. You'll be fine. Just take a deep breath, and read on to discover everything you need to know to succeed on the English Test.

Figuring Out What the English Questions Want You to Know

The questions on the English Test fall into the following three categories:

» **Conventions of Standard English (CSE):** A little more than half of the questions cover the ever-popular English topics of usage and mechanics. These questions include sentence structure (whether a sentence maintains parallel structure and properly positions the descriptive words and phrases), grammar and usage (just about everything most people think of as English, such as pronoun use, verb tense, subject/verb agreement, possessive form, and so on), and punctuation (don't worry — this isn't super hard once you've mastered the few commonly tested rules). In Chapter 5 we review the foundational concepts you need to know to master usage and mechanics questions.

» **Knowledge of Language (KLA):** The questions that ask you to eliminate unnecessary or redundant expressions comprise about 15 percent of the English Test. With practice, you'll spot repetitive language almost instinctively.

» **Power of Writing (POW):** About a quarter of the questions test writing skills, such as organization and relevance (reordering the sentences or adding sentences to the passage), style (which expression, slang or formal, is appropriate within the passage or which transition properly joins two thoughts), and strategy ("Which answer most specifically conveys what Grandpa likes to eat for supper?").

Chapter 6 provides the tips and techniques you need to identify and ace all question types.

REMEMBER

Some questions are much more doable than others. For example, most students would agree that a simple grammar question asking about a pronoun reference or verb tense is easier to answer than an organization question expecting you to reposition a paragraph within the entire passage.

Seeing Is Believing: The Test's Format

The ACT English Test passages look like standard reading-comprehension passages — you know, the kind you've seen on tests for years. The difference is that these passages have many underlined portions. An underlined portion can be an entire sentence, a phrase, or even just one word. (You may want to take a quick look right now at the practice passage and questions in Chapter 7 to get an idea of what an English Test passage looks like. We'll wait.)

Okay, you're back. Here are the details about what information you get on the English Test and what you're expected to do with it.

The passages

The five passages cover a variety of topics. You may get a fun story that's a personal anecdote — someone talking about getting a car for his 16th birthday, for example. Or you may encounter a somewhat formal scientific passage about the way items are carbon-dated. Some passages discuss history; some, philosophy; others, cultural differences among nations. One type of passage is not necessarily more difficult than another. You don't need to use specific reading techniques for these passages (as you do with standard reading-comprehension passages). Just read and enjoy — and be prepared to answer the questions that accompany the passages (see the next section for details).

REMEMBER

Although these English passages aren't reading-comprehension passages per se, you do need to pay at least a little attention to content instead of just focusing on the underlined portions. Why bother? Because a few of the questions are reading-comprehension–type questions that ask you about the purpose of the passage or what a possible conclusion might be. More about those appears in Chapter 6.

The question types

The English Test has few questions in the standard interrogatory form. You won't see anything like "Which of the following is an adjective?" or "The purpose of the subjunctive is to do which of these?" Instead, you analyze underlined portions of passages and choose the answer that presents the underlined words in the best way possible. Thrown into the mix are several standard questions that ask you for the best writing strategy or the best way to organize sentences or paragraphs.

Analyzing answer choices

Most of the test is about examining answer choices and then choosing which answer fits best in the place occupied by underlined words in a sentence. Your job is to determine what type of error the question tests and which of the choices provides the correct expression. Consider that the underlined answer is no more correct or incorrect than any of the other three alternate answer choices. The answer choices are (A), (B), (C), and (D) for the odd-numbered questions and (F),

(G), (H), and (J) for the even-numbered questions. Choices (A) and (F) are often *NO CHANGE.* You select that choice if the original is the best of the versions offered. Occasionally, Choice (D) or (J) says, *DELETE the underlined portion.* Choose that answer when you want to dump the whole underlined portion and forget that you ever saw it. (And no, you can't do that with the entire test!)

Approach these types of questions methodically:

1. Look at the answer choice options listed in the right column for clues to the type of error the question tests.

Chapter 6 summarizes the kinds of errors to look for, such as pronoun or punctuation problems, word choice issues, redundancy, and subject/verb agreement mistakes.

2. Eliminate answer choices that contain errors.

Chapter 6 shows you which choices to examine first, depending on the tested error type.

3. Reread the sentence with the answer you've chosen inserted.

Don't skip this step. You may overlook a problem with your answer until you see how it works in the complete sentence.

Here's an example to demonstrate how to use this approach.

EXAMPLE

A full case of juice boxes, when opened by a horde of thirsty athletes who have been running laps, <u>don't go</u> very far.

(A) NO CHANGE

(B) do not go

(C) doesn't go

(D) doesn't get to go

The answer choices contain a verb. Problems with verbs usually involve tense or subject/verb agreement. All the answers are in present tense, so the issue is probably subject/verb agreement. Find the subject that goes with "don't go." When you sift through the clauses and prepositional phrases, you see that the subject is *case.* Because *case* is singular, it requires the singular verb *doesn't.* Eliminate Choices (A) and (B) immediately because they don't contain singular verbs. Choices (C) and (D) correct the verb problem, but Choice (D) adds unnecessary words and makes the sentence seem silly. So Choice (C) is correct.

TIP

Did you see the trap in this sentence? Some students think that *boxes, athletes,* or *laps* — each of which is plural — is the subject of the sentence. (*Laps* is especially tricky because it's right next to the verb.) In that case, they think the verb has to be plural, too, and choose Choice (A). You didn't fall for that cheap trick, did you?

Dealing with "yes, yes, no, no" questions

A few of the questions in the English Test ask you to strategize about content, style, and organization. These questions usually come right out and ask you a question about the passage. The best way to approach these questions is by eliminating answer choices that can't be right.

Sometimes the answer to a question is a simple yes or no. Two of the answer choices provide the yes option; the other two give you the no option. First, you decide whether the answer to the question is yes or no. Then you choose the answer that provides the best reason for the yes or no answer.

Here's an example. Say that this question appears in an excerpt from a stuffy scientific journal article. Most of the passage is written in third person, but one paragraph suddenly switches to first person.

EXAMPLE

Given the topic and the tone of the passage, was the author's use of the pronoun *I* in this paragraph proper?

(F) Yes, because the only way to express an opinion is by using first person.

(G) Yes, because he was projecting his personal feelings onto the topic.

(H) No, because the use of *I* is inconsistent with the rest of the passage.

(J) No, because using *I* prevents the readers from becoming involved with the topic.

In this case, you're expected to get a feel for the tone of the passage as a whole. You may think the best way to approach this question is to determine whether the answer is yes or no, but it may be easier to eliminate answers based on the because statements. Get rid of any choices that are outright false. Usually two of them obviously are wrong. In this case, Choices (F) and (J) can't be right; it's simply not true that using first person is the only way to express an opinion and that using first person prevents readers from getting involved.

Now you have a 50 percent chance of answering the question correctly. Examine the statements in Choices (G) and (H). Because most of the passage is in third person, the one paragraph in first person probably isn't right. So the answer to the question is most likely no. Thus, the correct answer is (H).

Their Pain, Your Gain: Looking Out for Traps That Others Fall into

We've taught the ACT for a couple of decades now. By this point, we've seen students fall for every trap the test makers have thought of — and some they probably never considered! Watch out for these most commonly tumbled-into traps:

- » **Forgetting the NO CHANGE option:** Because the first answer choice — Choice (A) for odd-numbered questions, Choice (F) for even-numbered questions — may be NO CHANGE, students tend to gloss over it. Don't forget that the answer in the passage has the same potential to be right as the other three options.

- » **Automatically choosing DELETE each time it shows up:** Although you may be tempted to shorten this section by screaming, "Dump it! Just dump the whole stupid thing!" every chance you get, don't fall into that habit. When you see the DELETE answer — usually either Choice (D) or Choice (J) — realize that it has the same one-in-four chance of being right as the other answers have. Consider it, but don't make it a no-brainer choice.

- » **Automatically selecting the answer with a word or grammar rule you don't know well:** When you see *who* in a sentence, you're often tempted to change it immediately to *whom* simply because you aren't sure how to use *whom*. (Don't worry. We tell you how in Chapter 6.) Apply the process of elimination and employ the knowledge you gain in Chapters 5 and 6, and you'll be fine.

- » **Wasting time on the time-consuming questions:** Some questions, like the mission ones ("Which answer most specifically conveys the type of snacks Jimbo prefers?"), can be quite simple. But others, such as the ones that ask you to reposition sentences, can seem incredibly time-wasting and frustrating. You may have to read and reread a paragraph, changing and rearranging the sentences again and again. You may be able to get the question right, but at what price? How much time do you chew up? How many more of the easy questions could you have gotten right in that time?

TIP

» **Ignoring the big picture:** Some questions are style questions. A style question expects you to sense the overall picture, to know whether the tone of the passage is friendly so that you can appropriately use a slang expression (for example, *totally lame*) or whether you need to be a bit more formal (*useless* rather than *totally lame*). If you focus on only the underlined portions and don't consider the passage as a whole, you can easily miss this type of question.

Even if a question doesn't seem to expect you to understand the entire passage, you may need to read a few sentences ahead of the question. For example, whether you add a new sentence to the passage may depend on the topic of the entire paragraph.

Chapter **5**

Getting a Grip on Grammar and Usage

The ACT English Test tests Standard written English. In the real world, you can use slang and casual English and still communicate perfectly well with your buddies, but on the ACT, you have to use the formal English that you learned in school. When you knock on a friend's door, for example, you call out, "It's me!" Right? Well, on the ACT, you have to say, "It is I." The ACT English Test focuses on two types of questions: those that test grammar and usage and those that require you to make decisions about the best way to construct sentences. Chapter 6 gives you the skinny on how to recognize and efficiently answer both types of questions.

This chapter gives you a basic grammar review that brings back those thrilling days of yesteryear when you learned the various uses for commas or perhaps fills in the gaps for English stuff you never actually covered in class. The review starts off with the really easy stuff, but don't get too bored and drop out. The harder, picky stuff comes later, and chances are that's the stuff you really need to review.

REMEMBER

Only teachers care about the technical names for all this grammar stuff. All you need to know is how to use the right rules, so don't worry about what to call things. We're very careful to use technical terms sparingly throughout this material.

The rules of grammar are really pretty logical. After you understand the basic rules regarding the parts of speech and the elements of a sentence, you have the hang of it. The following sections cover what you need to know to do well on grammar and usage questions. Bear with us as we run through the grammar basics. We promise to get through them as quickly as possible and highlight the concepts that are most important to acing the ACT English Test.

TIP

If you're a grammar guru, you may be able to skim or skip this chapter and focus on Chapter 6. If you encounter any confusing concepts or terms when you get there, come back to this chapter for some explanation.

Reviewing the Parts of Speech

Most of the English Test questions ask you to evaluate sentences. Every word in a sentence has a purpose, known as its *part of speech*. The parts of speech you should know for the ACT are verbs, nouns, pronouns, adjectives, adverbs, conjunctions, and prepositions. We're here to help you as we explain them in these chapters.

Getting in the action with verbs

A sentence must have a *verb* to be complete. For the ACT, make sure you know these concepts about verbs:

» **The difference between an action verb and a linking verb:** *Action verbs* state what's going on in a sentence. *Linking verbs,* such as the verb *to be,* link one part of the sentence to the other, sort of like the equals sign in an equation.

» **The distinction between a verb's infinite form, conjugated form, and participle form:**

   ● The *infinitive* is the basic form — to + the verb: To run or to be.

   ● The *conjugated* verb is the form that alters depending on its subject: He runs; they run; he is; they are; I am.

   ● A *participle* is the form a verb takes when it helps out other verbs as part of a verb phrase: He is running; they have run; he has been.

   A verb in its participle form, such as *being* or *given,* can't work as verb by itself. It must be paired with a helper, such as a conjugated form of "to be" or "to have" to function as verb.

REMEMBER

» **The types of verb tenses:** The most important verb tenses to know for the test are present, past, future, present perfect, and past perfect tenses. Table 5-1 gives you a quick overview of these tenses and shows you an example of how to use them.

TABLE 5-1   **Verb Tenses**

Verb Tense	Purpose	Examples
Present	Shows an action or a condition that happens right now	Steve studies grammar every day. The dog is asleep.
Past	Shows an action or a condition that was completed in the past	Steve studied grammar in high school. The dog was asleep when I came in.
Future	Shows an action or a condition that hasn't happened yet but will happen	Steve will study grammar in college, too. The dog will be asleep when the guests arrive.
Present perfect	Shows an action or a condition that's already started and may continue or that happened at an undefined time	Steve has studied grammar for the exam. The dog has been sleeping for several hours.
Past perfect	Shows an action or a condition that happened before another one did	Steve had studied grammar for many weeks before he took the exam. The dog had been sleeping for several hours when the cat awakened him.

Identifying the culprit with nouns

You've undoubtedly heard *nouns* defined as persons, places, things, or ideas. They provide information about what's going on in a sentence and who or what is performing or receiving the action, such as the italicized nouns in this sentence: The social studies *teacher* gave the *students* five *pages* of *homework* regarding *countries* in *Europe* and asked them to write an *essay* on the political *consequences* of *joining* the *European Union*. Nouns can be subjects (teacher), direct objects (pages, essay, European Union), indirect objects (students), objects of prepositions (homework, countries, Europe, consequences, joining), and predicate nouns.

Avoiding repeating yourself with pronouns

Pronouns rename nouns and provide a way to avoid too much repetition of nouns in a sentence or paragraph. To answer English Test questions on the ACT, get familiar with these types of pronouns:

>> **Personal pronouns rename specific nouns.** They take several forms: subjective, objective, possessive, and reflexive.

  - The *subjective pronouns* are *I, you, he, she, it, we, you* (plural), and *they*, and (surprise, surprise) you use them as subjects in the sentence.

  - The *objective personal pronouns* are *me, you, him, her, it, us*, and *them*. You use them as objects in a sentence.

  - The *possessive pronouns* are *my, mine, your, yours, his, her, hers, its, our, ours, their*, and *theirs*. None of the personal pronouns form their possessives with an apostrophe.

  - The *reflexive pronouns* are *myself, yourself, himself, herself, itself, ourselves, yourselves*, and *themselves*.

>> **Demonstrative pronouns point to nouns.** Words like *some, many, both, that, this, those*, and *these* when they're not paired with a noun can also serve as pronouns. (*That* is my favorite book.)

>> **Relative pronouns connect descriptions to nouns.** Relative pronouns include *that, which*, and *who* (the subjective form), *whom* (the objective form), and *whose* (the possessive form). These pronouns are the subjects of descriptive clauses; *who* is subject of clauses that describe persons, and *which* and *that* refer to entities that aren't people. Clauses that start with *which* are always nonessential (and therefore are set off with commas), and clauses that start with *that* are essential.

Defining nouns with adjectives

Adjectives describe and clarify nouns. In the sentence "The putrid odor in the lab resulted in a bunch of sick students," *putrid* defines the kind of odor and *sick* describes the condition of the students. Without the adjectives, the sentence takes on a different and ridiculous meaning: The odor in the lab resulted in a bunch of students.

TIP

When you check a sentence on the exam for errors, make sure the adjectives are in the correct places so that each adjective describes the word it's supposed to.

Clarifying the questions with adverbs

Adverbs give extra information about action verbs, adjectives, and other adverbs. They include all words and groups of words (called *adverb phrases*) that answer the questions where, when, how, how much, and why. In the sentence "The chemistry students gradually recovered from smelling the very putrid odor," *gradually* explains how the students recovered.

Many adverbs end in *lee,* but not all of them do. You know a word is an adverb if it answers the question where, when, how, how much, or why in the sentence.

You may see a question that asks for the best placement of an adverb. The most logical position for an adverb in the sentence is cozied up to the action verb it describes.

Joining together with conjunctions and prepositions

Conjunctions and *prepositions* link the main elements of a sentence. These often seemingly inconsequential words can play a major role in English Test questions. Here is what you need to remember:

>> **Conjunctions join words, phrases, and clauses.** The three types of conjunctions are *coordinating, correlative,* and *subordinating.* Don't worry about memorizing these terms; just know that they exist.

- The seven coordinating conjunctions — *and, but, for, nor, or, so,* and *yet* — are the ones you probably think of when you think of conjunctions. Some English teachers refer to these by their mnemonic — FANBOYS.

- Correlative conjunctions always appear in pairs: *either/or, neither/nor,* and *not only/but also.*

- Subordinating conjunctions introduce dependent clauses and connect them to independent clauses. *Although, as, because, before, if, since, unless, when,* and *while* are common examples of subordinating conjunctions. (For more on clauses, see the later section, "Phrases and clauses.")

>> **Prepositions join nouns to the rest of the sentence.** We'd need several pages to list all the prepositions, but common examples are *about, above, by, for, over,* and *with.* Prepositions always appear in prepositional phrases, which also include a noun. Prepositional phrases usually describe a noun (the students *in the band*) or a verb (the football player ran *down the field*).

Piecing Together the Parts of a Sentence

The parts of speech we describe in the preceding section work together to form sentences. Every sentence has at least a subject and a verb, but most add a little bit (or a lot) more information.

Subjects and predicates

Every sentence and clause has two parts: the subject and the predicate. The subject is the main actor in the sentence; it's the noun that's doing the action in the sentence or whose condition the sentence describes. The predicate is the verb and pretty much everything else in the main idea of the sentence that isn't part of the subject. The part of the predicate that isn't the verb is called the *complement*. The complement can be an adjective, predicate noun, direct object, or indirect object.

Phrases and clauses

A sentence usually contains single words, phrases, or clauses that convey more information about the sentence's main message. *Phrases* and *clauses* are groups of words that work together to form a single part of speech, like an adverb or adjective. The difference between phrases and clauses is that clauses contain their own subjects and verbs; phrases don't.

The two types of clauses are independent and dependent:

>> **Independent clauses express complete thoughts and can stand as sentences by themselves.** The sentence "Jeff opened the door, and the cat slipped out" contains two independent clauses.

>> **Dependent clauses express incomplete thoughts and are, therefore, sentence fragments if left by themselves.** "Although the cat slipped out" is an example of a dependent clause. To convert any dependent clause into a complete sentence, you must add an independent clause, as in "Although the cat slipped out, Jeff caught it before it could run away."

REMEMBER

Here's how to distinguish between a phrase and a clause and between an independent and a dependent clause:

>> If a group of words has a subject and a verb, it's a clause, not a phrase.

>> If a group of words has a subject and a verb and doesn't begin with a subordinating conjunction (see the section, "Joining together with conjunctions and prepositions," for examples of subordinating conjunctions), then it's an independent clause, not a dependent clause.

Understanding the difference between independent and dependent clauses helps you recognize a bunch of errors, such as sentence fragments, reference issues, and punctuation problems. (To understand how to spot these errors, see Chapter 6.)

Keeping Track of Punctuation Rules for Every Occasion

You use periods, commas, semicolons, and other forms of punctuation all the time when you write. But are you using them correctly? The ACT English Test gives you questions to make sure you know how. Punctuation rules are pretty straightforward. After you have them down, you can be sure you're practicing proper punctuation.

Periods and question marks

The ACT rarely tests marks that end the sentence, but just in case, here's what you need to know about periods and question marks. Periods end sentences that aren't questions (like this one). Periods also follow initials, as in *J. K. Rowling*, and abbreviations, such as *etc.* But you don't use periods for initials in agency names, such as *ROTC* and *YMCA*, or for commonly used shortened forms, such as *ad* or *memo*, but the ACT rarely tests these rules.

Question marks end direct questions, like "When will dinner be ready?" However, you never put a question mark at the end of indirect questions, such as "Pam asked me when dinner would be ready."

Semicolons

The semicolon links two independent clauses in one sentence. Using semicolons is appropriate in the following instances:

>> **To join two independent yet closely related clauses without a conjunction:** For example, the sentence "It's almost the weekend; I can finally relax" has two independent clauses that are closely related, so they appear together in the same sentence separated by a semicolon.

>> **To begin a second clause with a conjunctive adverb:** Clauses that begin with conjunctive adverbs (such as *accordingly, also, besides, consequently, furthermore, hence, however, indeed, likewise, moreover, nevertheless, otherwise, similarly, so, still, therefore,* and *thus*) use a semicolon to separate them from another clause. Here's an example: "I should relax this weekend; otherwise, I'll be tired all week." Note that a comma comes after the conjunctive adverb.

>> **To provide clarity in complex sentences:** Semicolons appear in sentences that have a numbered series or when using commas would be confusing. See what we mean in this sentence: "The secretary's duties include (1) creating, sending, and filing documents; (2) making and organizing appointments; and (3) scheduling and planning meetings." The ACT rarely tests this use for semicolons.

Colons

Colons have several functions. You can use them in place of periods to separate two independent clauses (although semicolons usually fill this role). You can also use them to relate the introductory clause in a sentence to a relevant list of specifics, a long appositive or explanation, or a quotation. Here's an example: "Megan will be finished with her homework when she completes these three tasks: a rough outline for an essay, a worksheet of math problems, and the final draft of her chemistry report." For the ACT, the only rule you need to consider when evaluating colons is that they must be preceded by a complete independent clause.

REMEMBER

If the words before the colon don't form a complete sentence, then you've used the colon incorrectly, as in this wrong construction: "Megan will be finished with her homework when she completes: a rough outline for an essay, a worksheet of math problems, and the final draft of her chemistry report." Deleting the colon fixes the problem.

Commas

The comma is perhaps the most misused punctuation mark in the English language. Whenever you see an underlined comma in the English Test, evaluate its purpose. Here are a couple of important general rules to keep in mind when you encounter commas on the ACT:

>> **Don't put a comma in a sentence just because you think it needs a pause.** Pausing is subjective; comma rules for the ACT aren't. You may pause between *cow* and *on* in this sentence to emphasize just how whacky the image is: *I saw a cow, on a bike!* But the ACT

wouldn't agree with you. That comma is wrong. Use the rules that follow in this section (not your ears) to justify whether a comma is placed properly.

>> **Remember that a single comma *never* separates a subject from its verb or a verb from the rest of the predicate.** A comma never comes between a prepositional phrase and the noun it describes. You may see *a pair* of commas between the subject and verb, but not a lone comma without a comma buddy.

Remember these comma uses to take the guesswork out of placing commas:

>> **Series:** In a series of three or more expressions joined by one conjunction, put a comma after each expression except the last one, as in the sentence "Rachel, Bryan, and Tyler bought sandwiches, fruit, and doughnuts for the picnic." Notice that no comma comes after *Tyler* and no comma comes before *doughnuts.*

TIP

The ACT won't test whether you put a comma before the *and* in a series because there isn't a firm rule about that.

>> **Omitted *and*:** Use a comma to replace an omitted *and* from a sentence in certain circumstances.

- The comma stands in for the omitted *and* that joins coordinate adjectives (those that precede and describe the same noun): Henry adores his slick, speedy bike. If there isn't an omitted *and* joining the adjectives, don't stick a comma between them: Henry adores his shiny red bike.

- The comma replaces an omitted *and* that joins two like phrases: I studied with Jerry yesterday, with Pam today.

>> **Separation of clauses:** Use commas to join together clauses in these situations:

- Put a comma before a coordinating conjunction that joins two independent clauses. Here's an example: The polka-dot suit was Sammie's favorite, but she didn't wear it when she was feeling shy.

- Use a comma to set apart a beginning dependent clause from the rest of a sentence, as in "When Sammie feels shy, she doesn't wear her polka-dot suit." But don't put in a comma when the dependent clause comes after the independent clause: Sammie doesn't wear her polka-dot suit when she feels shy.

REMEMBER

>> A run-on sentence happens when a sentence with two or more independent clauses has improper punctuation. Here's an example: I had a college interview yesterday morning and I'm pretty sure I knocked the interviewer's socks off.

>> "I had a college interview yesterday morning" and "I'm pretty sure I knocked the interviewer's socks off" are independent clauses because both have subjects (I) and verbs (*had* and *am*) and neither begins with a subordinating conjunction such as *while* or *although.* You can't just stick a conjunction or comma between these two independent clauses to make a sentence. However, you have other options:

- Put a comma before the *and:* I had a college interview yesterday morning, and I'm pretty sure I knocked the interviewer's socks off.

- Replace *and* with a semicolon: I had a college interview yesterday morning; I'm pretty sure I knocked the interviewer's socks off.

- Create two separate sentences by putting a period after *morning* and taking out the *and:* I had a college interview yesterday morning. I'm pretty sure I knocked the interviewer's socks off.

- Change one of the clauses so it's no longer independent: During my college interview yesterday morning, I'm pretty sure I knocked the interviewer's socks off.

» **Nonessentials:** When a sentence includes information that's important but not crucial to the meaning of the sentence, you set off that information with commas on both sides (unless the nonessential info begins or ends a sentence — then you just use one comma). Sometimes determining whether an expression is essential is difficult, but following these guidelines can help:

- *Asides* consist of words such as *however, in my opinion,* and *for example* and are set apart from the rest of the sentence. Here's an example: In my opinion, Sammie looks smashing in her polka-dot suit.

- *Appositives* provide additional information about a noun that isn't critical to understanding the main idea of the sentence: The polka-dot swimsuit, the one that Sammie wears only when she isn't feeling shy, contains pink dots on a black background. In the sentence "The science teacher, Ms. Paul, scheduled a meeting with her top students," *Ms. Paul* lets you know the science teacher's name. Yet without that information, the sentence still retains its meaning. When a name is part of a title, as in the sentence "Professor Paul requested a meeting" or "Science teacher Ms. Paul won an award," don't use commas.

- *Titles and distinctions* that follow a name are enclosed in commas. Case in point: Georgia White, RN, is the first speaker for career day.

- *Abbreviations,* such as *etc., e.g.,* and *i.e.,* are enclosed in commas. Here's an example: Tyler pulled out the sandwiches, drinks, doughnuts, etc., from the picnic basket.

- *Dates and place names* contain what can be considered nonessential information and are, therefore, punctuated with commas. For example, "Mike attended school in Boulder, Colorado, from September 1, 2008, to May 23, 2011." Notice that commas appear on both sides of the state name and on both sides of the year in the date.

- *Nonrestrictive clauses* are by definition nonessential. Because nonrestrictive clauses always provide information that doesn't affect the meaning of a sentence, commas always set them apart from the rest of the sentence. The second clause in the sentence "The meeting took place in Ms. Paul's classroom, which is just down the hall from the library" provides important information, but the meaning of the sentence wouldn't change if that information were left out.

- A *restrictive* clause provides essential descriptive information, so commas don't separate it from the rest of the sentence: The meeting took place in the classroom that is just down the hall from the library.

  You begin nonrestrictive clauses with *which,* restrictive clauses with *that.* (Notice in that last sentence we used a comma to replace the omitted and that joined the two similarly-constructed phrases.) If a clause describes a person, begin it with *who* regardless of whether it's restrictive or nonrestrictive.

REMEMBER

Dashes

Dashes work like colons to introduce long appositives or like commas to designate nonessential information. They can separate a beginning series from the rest of a sentence and signal abrupt breaks in the continuity of a sentence. Here's an example: A state championship, a college scholarship, and a Super Bowl ring — such were the dreams of the high school quarterback.

Apostrophes

Apostrophes have two purposes — creating contractions and forming possessives. The apostrophe takes the place of the missing letter or letters in a contraction. Think *they're* (they are), *can't* (cannot), *here's* (here is), and so on.

To show ownership of one noun by another, use an apostrophe. For example, a dog owned by a girl is "the girl's dog" and an opinion of a judge is "a judge's opinion." Here are some rules for forming possessives:

>> **Most possessives are formed by adding *'s* to the end of a singular noun or a plural noun that doesn't end in *s*.** Here are three examples: "Betty's car," "children's teacher," and "the committee's decision."

>> **If the possessive noun is plural and ends in *s*, only add the apostrophe.** Some examples include "the four boys' bikes" and "the neighbors' front porch."

TIP

Whenever you see one noun immediately followed by another, you're almost certainly dealing with possessive form. The first noun possesses the other, so you format it appropriately.

REMEMBER

None of the possessive pronouns contains an apostrophe. (*It's* is a contraction of *it is*, not the possessive form of *it*.) But indefinite pronouns do contain apostrophes, as in the sentence "Somebody's dog chewed my carpet."

Chapter **6**

Spotting Usage Errors and Ripping through Rhetorical Questions

About half of the ACT English Test questions test what most people lump together in the general category they call English: punctuation, sentence structure, and basic grammar, including diction, subject/verb agreement, modifiers (adjectives and adverbs), and so on. That's the stuff you probably forget (or intentionally purge from your brain) ten minutes after being tested on it. The other half cover rhetorical skills, which test general writing style and organization — in other words, the stuff you use every time you pick up a pen or turn on your word-processing program. Chapter 5 provides the foundation for the grammar and structure basics you need to know to do well on the English Test. In this chapter, we identify the errors and concepts that continually crop up on the ACT and show you exactly what to focus on to deal with them.

Spotting Questions That Test Standard English Conventions

The ACT tests a bunch of writing errors. This section highlights some of the usage errors that appear most frequently so that you're prepared to spot 'em without breaking a sweat.

Properly placing punctuation marks

A preponderance (or huge number) of English Test questions require you to evaluate the proper way to punctuate one sentence or more. This section reviews the types of punctuation errors the ACT tests the most and pinpoints the clues to look for when you're choosing the best mark for the job.

When you consider an underlined portion of an English passage, first look for a comma, semicolon, or other kind of punctuation. Chances are the underlined punctuation mark is the focus of the question, especially if you glance at the answer options and all contain similar words with different punctuation options. Choose the best answer based on your keen knowledge of the rules (see Chapter 5) rather than a subjective feeling.

Semicolons and periods

Underlined semicolons and periods are easy to evaluate. The two marks essentially have the same purpose: they separate independent clauses. Periods punctuate sentences, and the primary job of a semicolon is to join independent clauses in the same sentence. So just follow these steps when you see a period or semicolon in a potential answer choice:

1. **Read the words that come before the period or semicolon.**

   If the group of words doesn't contain a subject and a verb, or does but begins with a subordinating conjunction or relative pronoun, it isn't an independent clause and the period or semicolon can't be right. If the words have a subject and verb and don't begin with a subordinating conjunction, the clause is independent and the period or semicolon may be proper. Check Step 2.

2. **Read the words after the period or semicolon.**

   If they don't create an independent clause, the period or semicolon doesn't work. If they do make an independent clause, however, the period or semicolon is probably appropriate. If an answer follows a semicolon with a coordinating conjunction such as *and*, *but*, or *or*, that answer is incorrect. It's never appropriate to place a semicolon before a clause that begins with a coordinating conjunction.

If your answer choices include an option with a period and another option with a semicolon and everything else in the two answers is exactly the same (except for the capitalized word after the period), then you can likely eliminate both answers. Because both punctuation marks serve a similar function and you can't have two right answers, both options must be wrong.

Try the steps on a sample sentence:

<u>The pond dried up after the year-long drought; the wildlife that</u> previously fed on the fish and insects had to find resources elsewhere.

(A) NO CHANGE

(B) The pond dried up after the year-long drought; and the wildlife that

(C) The pond dried up after the year-long drought, the wildlife that

(D) When the pond dried up after the year-long drought; the wildlife that

The underlined part contains a semicolon, so check first for punctuation. If the semicolon joins two independent clauses, the answer is likely Choice (A). The words to the left of the semicolon make up an independent clause. They contain a main subject *pond* and verb *dried* and don't begin with a subordinating conjunction. So far so good. The stuff that comes after the semicolon is also an independent clause. There's a main subject *wildlife* and verb *had* and no beginning subordinating conjunction. The semicolon in Choice (A) is likely the correct answer. (For more on how to approach English Test questions, see Chapter 4.)

Choice (B) places a conjunction after the semicolon and that makes the semicolon wrong. Choice (C) creates the dreaded comma splice. It's never proper to join independent clauses with a comma and no coordinating conjunction. Choice (D) sticks the subordinating conjunction *when* ahead of the first clause, making it dependent instead of independent. You separate a beginning dependent clause with a comma instead of a semicolon. The sentence is right the way it is.

Colons

When the underlined part or possible answer choices contain a colon, concentrate on the words that come before the colon. If they create an independent clause that doesn't continue after the colon, the colon is likely okay. If the beginning is a phrase or dependent clause, the colon can't be right.

REMEMBER

Although the colon has to be preceded by an independent clause, any format (a list, phrase, or clause) can come after it as long as it elaborates on the information in the beginning independent clause before the colon.

Dashes

To figure out whether a single dash is proper, determine whether it could be replaced by a colon. When you see two dashes in a sentence, ask yourself whether they could be exchanged with two commas designating nonessential information. If the answer is "yes" in either situation, the dashes work just fine.

Commas

The ACT mainly tests the use of the comma for designating nonessential information and separating phrases and clauses. If a question gives you four choices with the same wording but different comma positions, you're likely applying the rules for separating out nonessential stuff. A pair of commas (or a comma paired with a period) work together to designate nonessential information, such as asides and descriptive clauses that begin with *which*. See Chapter 5 for the types of detail that aren't essential and information about the rules. Basically, if the main idea doesn't change when you take out the words between the commas, then that information is likely nonessential.

Other comma questions likely concern the rules for separating phrases and clauses. Eliminating wrong answers for both situations requires you to perform a little detective work. Don your tweed cape, Sherlock style, and answer these questions to solve the Case of the Perfectly Placed Comma:

>> **Does a single comma appear anywhere between the subject and verb?** If the answer is "yes," the comma isn't perfectly placed. So you know that the comma in this sentence doesn't work because it appears by itself between the subject *pond* and the verb *provided*: The pond that dried up last year, formerly provided a viable habitat for local wildlife.

>> **Does a single comma come between the verb and the rest of the predicate?** If so, the comma isn't placed perfectly. This comma is wrong because it separates the verb *provided* from its object *what*: The little pond provided, what many would consider to be a viable habitat for the local wildlife.

>> **Does a single comma separate a prepositional phrase from the noun it describes?** If so, the comma isn't correct. This faulty comma comes between the prepositional phrase *for the local wildlife* and the noun it describes *habitat*: The pond provides a viable habitat, for the local wildlife.

>> **Does the comma separate two independent clauses without the help of a conjunction?** If it does, the comma isn't correctly placed. Check the words that precede the comma to see whether they make up an independent clause (which has a main subject and verb and no beginning subordinating conjunction). Then check the words that come after the comma. If they also create an independent clause, the comma is wrong. The comma in this example is improper because it joins two independent clauses: The pond that dried up last year provided a viable habitat for local water fowl, now those birds must find another resource.

The options to correct this comma splice vary. Here are some of the options the ACT may provide:

- **Add a coordinating conjunction.** The pond that dried up last year provided a viable habitat for local water fowl, but now those birds must find another resource.

- **Replace with a semicolon.** The pond that dried up last year provided a viable habitat for local water fowl; now those birds must find another resource.

- **Create two sentences.** The pond that dried up last year provided a viable habitat for local water fowl. Now those birds must find another resource.

- **Change one of the clauses so that it's no longer independent.** The pond that dried up last year provided a viable habitat for local water fowl, birds that now must find another resource.

REMEMBER

Notice that the questions don't include "Does the sentence need a pause?" Pauses are subjective, so evaluate commas based on the rules rather than whether you think the sentence could use a break.

Picking up on pronoun errors

If you see a pronoun in the underlined part of a sentence, you're likely being tested on issues with the pronoun reference (the noun the pronoun refers to) or using the proper form. Here are some tips on what to look for when you see a pronoun in the underlined part:

>> **An underlined *this*, *that*, *which*, *these*, *those*, *it*, or *they*, may indicate a faulty reference.** Whenever you see one of these pronouns in the underlined part, check the sentence or prior sentence for the noun the pronoun renames. If the noun is plural, the pronoun must be plural; if it's singular, the pronoun must be singular.

The pronoun reference in this sentence is faulty: You can determine the ripeness of citrus by handling them and noting their color. *Citrus* is a singular noun, so using a plural pronoun such as *them* to refer to it is wrong. To correct this sentence, change it to this: You can determine the ripeness of citrus by handling it and noting its color.

>> **An underlined *this*, *that*, *some*, *which*, *these*, *those*, *it*, or *they*, or other personal, relative, and demonstrative pronouns may indicate an unclear reference problem.** If you can't easily find the noun a pronoun renames (we mean actually be able to point your finger to it) the reference is unclear and must be clarified. Usually you correct these problems by replacing the pronoun with a specific noun. Look for a noun in the answer choices.

This sentence contains an unclear reference: Smart growers make sure they supply the ripest fruits possible so they will buy again. The second *they* in the sentence has an ambiguous reference. The only nouns the pronoun could rename are *growers* and *fruits*. Neither of these would buy from growers again. To correct the problem, replace the second *they* with the actual noun that designates the buyer: Smart growers make sure they supply the ripest fruits possible so consumers will buy again.

>> **An underlined *who* or *whom* is likely testing proper form.** You use *who* as a subject and *whom* as an object. So it's "the man who gives the gift" and "the man to whom the gift is given."

To figure out whether *who* or *whom* is better, substitute *he* and *him*. If *him* works better, choose *whom*; if *he* is a better substitute, choose *who*: He gives the gift, but the gift is given to him. Usually *whom* is only proper when the pronoun follows a preposition.

The next time your grammar teacher asks you to name two pronouns, you can be a smart aleck and shout out, "Who, me?"

>> **Evaluate whether an underlined reflexive pronoun is proper.** The ACT hardly ever tests you on whether you use the subjective or objective forms of personal pronouns other than who, but it may test you on when the reflexive form is proper.

Use reflexive pronouns only when the receiver and the doer of an action are the same. The sentence "Please return the forms to the secretary and myself" is wrong because you aren't the doer of the action of returning the forms; you're telling someone else to give the forms to you and your secretary. The correct version of this sentence is "Please return the forms to the secretary and me." Note that a sentence such as "He came up with the idea all by himself" is accurate because the doer and the receiver of the action are the same person.

>> **An underlined *its*, *it's*, *they*, or *they're* usually indicates a question that tests you on the possessive form of personal pronouns.** No personal pronoun uses an apostrophe to form the possessive, so *it's* and *they're* are contractions of "it is" and "they are" rather than the possessives of *it* and *they*. This sentence demonstrates the proper use of both forms: It's an indication of happiness when a dog wags its tail.

To test whether *it's* or *its* is proper, replace the pronoun with "it is." If "it is" sounds right, the proper form is *it's*; if "it is" doesn't work, the proper form is *its*.

The form of *its'* doesn't exist in the English language, so an answer that includes *its'* is never correct.

REMEMBER

>> **Underlined relative pronouns may test whether you know what pronoun goes with what kinds of nouns.** Use *who* to refer to people. On the ACT, *which* and *that* refer to animals and things. So it's better to say, "There's the police officer who pulled me over yesterday" than "There's the police officer that pulled me over yesterday." Though we can't think of a time when we would be happy to make either statement!

Forming possessives

Whenever you see an underlined part that includes two nouns smack dab next to each other, you're likely dealing with the possessive form of the first noun, especially if the answer choices show you a variety of formats with apostrophes. These questions require you to determine whether the possessive form is necessary, and then if it is, to apply it correctly. Here's an example question to show you how:

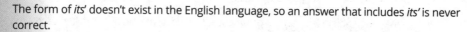

The parents made sure that their bags included several of the <u>babies colorful toys</u> to amuse them during the car trip.

EXAMPLE

(A) NO CHANGE

(B) babies' colorful toys

(C) baby's colorful toys

(D) babies fully colored toys

To answer this question, first check the answers. Notice that two of the four contain apostrophes — a good clue that you're dealing with possessive form. Check to see whether you have two nouns right next to each other. Almost always, seeing two nouns together indicates that the first should be in possessive form. The rule is true even when an adjective that describes the second noun comes between the two nouns. The noun *babies* precedes *colorful*, an adjective. But that adjective describes the noun *toys* right after it, so the simplified form would be "babies toys." Because *babies* is a noun and *toys* is a noun, you must put *babies* in the proper possessive form.

You can double-check by flipping the nouns and adding an "of the" like this: "toys of the babies." If the "of the" test works, you can be absolutely sure you're dealing with the possessive form.

TIP

So eliminate Choices (A) and (D) because neither is in possessive form. (The *fully colored* is just there in Choice (D) to try to distract you from the real error.) The remaining two choices provide either the singular possessive or the plural possessive. Figuring out which is correct on the ACT is usually easy. Look for clues in the sentence. The toys are supposed to amuse them, and *them* is plural, so the correct answer is the plural possessive in Choice (B) where the apostrophe follows the ending *s*. For more on how to form possessives, check out Chapter 5. To review the possessive forms of personal pronouns, see "Picking up on pronoun errors" earlier in this chapter.

Evaluating verbs

When you see an underlined verb, check for two potential errors in this order:

1. **Make sure the verb agrees in number (plural or singular) with its subject.**

   Okay, so subjects and verbs don't actually fight, but they do sometimes disagree. To bring peace to the situation, you must pair plural subjects with plural verbs and singular subjects with singular verbs. If you see a verb in the underlined portion of the English Test, find the subject it goes with and make sure they agree.

   When the subject isn't simple or obvious, finding it may be difficult. Just take a look at this sentence: Terry's continual quest to embellish his truck with a ton of amenities make it hard for him to stick to a budget. The subject is *quest* (a singular noun), but the interjection of "to embellish his truck with a ton of amenities" between the subject and verb may confuse you into thinking that *amenities* (a plural noun) is the subject. However, *amenities* can't be the subject of the sentence because it's the object of a preposition, and a noun can't be an object and a subject at the same time.

   TIP

   To spot subject/verb agreement errors in a complex sentence, focus on the main elements of the sentence by crossing out nouns that function as objects (especially those in prepositional phrases). Then check the subjects and verbs to make sure they agree. When you remove all the objective noun forms from the sentence "Terry's continual quest to embellish his truck with a ton of amenities make it hard for him to stick to a budget," you get "Terry's quest make it hard." Now the problem is obvious! The singular noun *quest* requires the singular verb *makes.*

   TIP

   You don't need to check for subject/verb agreement when the verb in question is a past tense action verb. Action verbs in the past tense don't have a plural and singular form.

2. **Check for proper verb tense.**

   After you've made sure that the verb agrees with the subject, check the tenses of underlined verbs. Verb forms must be in the proper tense for a sentence to make sense. Review the purpose for each verb tense in Chapter 5 to help you spot incorrect tenses. For example, you know that using future perfect tense in "Yesterday, I will have read 300 pages" is incorrect because *yesterday* is in the past, and you don't use future tense to refer to past events.

   The other verbs in the same sentence and usually the same paragraph give you clues to what tense a particular verb should be in. Generally, all verbs in a sentence should be in the same tense. For example, the sentence "I had read 300 pages in the book when my friends invite me to see a movie" must be incorrect because *had read* is past perfect tense and *invite* is present tense. You can correct the sentence by changing *invite* from present tense to past tense *(invited).*

   TIP

   In recent tests, the ACT has included at least one question that gives you the option to choose one of these tenses: *must of, may of, might of, could of, should of, would of,* and so on. These questions are easy to answer correctly because **of isn't a verb.** It's a preposition. The proper constructions are *must have, may have, might have, could have, should have,* and *would have* or their contractions, for example, *would've.* There will never ever be a time when one of these verb + *of* constructions will be the right answer. You just added a point to your raw score by reading this chapter!

Whenever you see a verb in a usage question, check subject/verb agreement first. The ACT will often throw a bunch of different tenses in the answer choice options to distract you from the real issue of subject/verb agreement.

Calling out sentence fragments

Sentence fragments are incomplete sentences. They usually show up on the ACT either as dependent clauses that pretend to convey complete thoughts or as a bunch of words with something that looks like a verb but doesn't act like one.

Always keep the following in mind:

>> **Dependent clauses by themselves are fragments because they don't provide complete thoughts.** "Although the stairs are steep . . ." is far from a complete thought.

>> **Phrases that contain verb participles (one part of a verb phrase such as a word that ends in *ing* or *ed*) don't express complete thoughts even though the participles look like verbs.** The ACT most commonly offends with the participle *being*. *Being* all by itself isn't a verb. So this phrase isn't a sentence: "The project being quite complicated." To correct the problem, look for an answer choice that converts the *ing* word to its conjugated form. For the sample sentence, you'd look for an *is* or a *was* to replace *being*.

Whenever you see *being* in the underlined part or the answer choices, run from it like the plague. An answer that contains *being* is almost always wrong.

Identifying problems with parallelism

All phrases joined by conjunctions should be constructed in the same way. For example, the following sentence has a problem with parallelism: "Ann spent the morning taking practice tests, studying word lists, and she read a chapter in a novel." Not all the elements joined by the *and* in this sentence are constructed in the same way. The first two elements are phrases that begin with a gerund (or *ing* form); the last element is a clause. Changing *read* to a gerund and dropping *she* solves the problem: "Ann spent the morning taking practice tests, studying word lists, and reading a chapter in a novel."

When you see a sentence with a list of any sort, check for a lack of parallelism. Items in a series may be nouns, verbs, adjectives, or entire clauses. However, nonparallel verbs are the items that most commonly have errors. When a clause contains more than one verb, watch out for this particular error.

Recognizing misplaced modifiers

The ACT will surely test how well you can spot errors in modification. *Modifier* is a fancy term for words or phrases, such as adjectives and adverbs, that give more information about other words, usually nouns and verbs. Errors occur when modifiers are too far away from the words they modify and when what they're modifying is unclear.

Keep the following guidelines in mind whenever you're dealing with modifiers:

>> **Modifiers must be as close to the words they modify as possible.** The sentence "Sam set down the speech he wrote on the desk" is incorrect because of a misplaced modifier. It sounds

like Sam wrote the speech on the desk! The sentence "Sam set down his speech on the desk" is much better. The ACT tests adjectives and adverbs in two general ways:

- **The English Test may give you four constructions and ask you to pick the one that pairs the proper parts of speech.** So you need to be able to recognize the best construction of paired words such as these:

  blind admiration

  blindly admiration

  blind admire

  blind admiringly

  The first pair is correct because it has an adjective *blind* describe a noun *admiration.* The other three are wrong because they incorrectly have an adverb *blindly* describe a noun *admiration,* an adjective *blind* describe a verb *admire,* and an adjective *blind* describe an adverb *admiringly.*

- **It may ask you to position an underlined part of speech — usually an adverb.** Whenever a question asks you to position an underlined portion in a sentence, first determine the part of speech of the underlined part. Underlined adverbs or adverb phrases should be near a verb. Underlined adjectives or adjective phrases or clauses should go next to the noun they describe.

» **Beginning participle phrases must have a clear reference.** A beginning participle phrase in a sentence always modifies the subject of the sentence, so the sentence has to be constructed in a way that relates the phrase to the subject. If it doesn't, the sentence contains a dangling participle. For a definition of a participle, read "Calling out sentence fragments" earlier in this chapter.

Consider this sentence: "Driving down the road, a deer darted in front of me." If you read this sentence literally, you may believe the *deer* drove down the road because the beginning phrase "driving down the road" refers to the subject of the sentence, which is *deer.* To make it clear that the driver — not the deer — drove down the road, you need to change this phrase to a clause: "As I was driving down the road, a deer darted in front of me." Alternatively, you may need to rewrite the sentence to change the subject: "Driving down the road, I spotted a deer darting out in front of me."

TIP

Because the test makers tend to focus on modification errors involving beginning phrases, be sure to check for this error every time you see a sentence with a beginning phrase.

» **Place *not only* and *but also* in parallel positions within a sentence.** People often place *not only* and *but also* incorrectly. Here's an example of a wrong way to use these expressions: "Angelique *not only* was exasperated *but also* frightened when she locked herself out of the house."

See the problem? The phrase *not only* comes before the verb was, but the phrase *but also* comes before the adjective frightened. Correct it so that both elements come before adjectives: "Angelique was *not only* exasperated *but also* frightened when she locked herself out of the house."

Checking for Proper Production of Writing

The other types of English Test questions, Power of Writing (POW) and Knowledge of Language (KLA), deal with general writing and language skills, which is a fancy way of saying they test the best way to structure and word a piece of writing. For these questions, you generally seek answers that reflect the clearest, most precise constructions. Most of these questions change up the standard answer choice format by presenting you with actual questions about an underlined part or even the whole passage. Some — including those that test redundancy, proper transitions, and diction — stick to the customary underlined part with the NO CHANGE option and three other possible answers. For more about the question formats, see Chapter 4.

Eliminating superfluous words

Sentences that say the same idea twice or that use more words than necessary may be grammatically correct but still need fixing. The ACT wants you to notice and get rid of superfluous language. For example, saying "The custodian added an additional row of desks that were brown" is silly. The construction of "added an additional" is needlessly repetitive and the desks can be described more efficiently. The sentence reads better as "The custodian added a row of brown desks."

The good news is that once you realize how much the ACT loves to test repetition and wordiness, you'll spot the problems easily. Here are some keys to recognizing these questions:

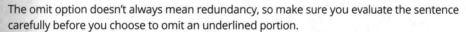

>> **Check the choices for a one-word (or the shortest) answer.** When you encounter an underlined portion containing several words and three of the answer choices are similar in length but one answer is considerably shorter, you're likely dealing with a redundancy problem, and the correct option is almost always the shorter answer. The extra stuff in the other answer choices usually restates information that's already conveyed elsewhere. Here's an example of a redundant construction: The essay contains numerous redundancies that create lots of repetition. The definition of redundancy is that it creates repetition, so you should eliminate the ending relative clause, "that create lots of repetition."

>> **Check the answers for an omit option.** Often an option to omit the underlined portion signals redundant or otherwise unnecessary information. Check the sentence and surrounding sentences for whether the underlined part repeats an idea or is irrelevant. If it does or is, choose the answer that gets rid of the underlined part altogether.

REMEMBER

The omit option doesn't always mean redundancy, so make sure you evaluate the sentence carefully before you choose to omit an underlined portion.

>> **Check for adjectives and adverbs that have the same meaning as the words they describe or two or more describing words that mean the same.** Describing someone as an "intelligent genius" or as a "smart, intelligent leader" doesn't add new information because geniuses are by their nature intelligent and *smart* and *intelligent* have pretty much the same meaning. Find the answer that eliminates the repetition.

>> **When the answer choices say roughly the same thing, choose the one that contains the fewest words.** So "story's moral" is better than "the moral of the story" (sorry Aesop), and "flawed reasoning" is more succinct than "reasoning that is fallacious."

TIP

Usually the shortest answer choice for questions that test wordiness is the correct one as long as the short answer doesn't contain an additional error.

>> **If you're given a choice between active voice and passive voice, choose active voice.** Passive voice isn't wrong, but it's weak and vague. It beats around the bush to make a point. The passive voice in the following sentence hides who's doing the action: "The speech was heard by most of the students." The sentence isn't technically incorrect, but it's better said this way: "Most of the students heard the speech." Notice also that the sentence in active voice uses fewer words.

Completing the mission

We call questions that ask you for an answer that accomplishes a certain goal *mission questions*. The mission question gives you a task, and your job is to find the choice that best completes this task. Something like this: "The author wishes to convey a high level of urgency in extricating the clown from the packed Volkswagen. Which of the following choices best accomplishes this goal?"

The key to finding the correct answer to a mission question is to remember what you aren't looking for. You aren't evaluating whether the answer choices contain usage errors or sentence structure problems; you aren't choosing the best-constructed answer. Your only focus is on the answer that fulfills the mission.

Here are some tips for answering mission questions:

>> Read the question carefully to find the one or two qualifications the correct answer must fulfill. In the clown car example, you're looking for great urgency and getting the clowns out.

>> Circle the qualifications in the question so you can find them easily as you read through the answer choices.

>> Eliminate answers that don't meet the qualifications.

>> From the remaining, choose the most specific correct answer — the one that provides the most vivid images. So an answer such as "carnival workers rushed to wrench the terrified clowns from the flaming car" is better than "carnival workers urgently pulled the clowns out of the car." The second option tries to entice you with its inclusion of *urgently*, but its language isn't as powerful as the words in the first.

Determining the function of a deletion

The ACT may underline or otherwise designate a word, phrase, or clause and then ask you what would happen to the text if the indicated part were deleted. These questions are easier to answer if you concentrate on the role the proposed deletion serves in the sentence before you look at the answer choices.

So you may be asked what this sentence would lose if its underlined part were deleted: "The floral arrangement contained a variety of blooms <u>of vivid oranges, brilliant blues, and sunny yellows</u>." The underlined part gives you specific detail. Without it you wouldn't know the flowers' colors. You then check the answer choices for one that clarifies that the sentence would lose visual details.

Often a deletion question provides you with an answer option that suggests the underlined part contains irrelevant information. That answer is hardly ever correct. Although the ACT frequently tests you on whether details are necessary, it doesn't usually use deletion questions for this task.

Pondering an addition

To test relevance (and sometimes redundancy), the ACT presents you with phrases and clauses and asks you whether they should be added to the paragraph. The overwhelming consideration is whether the information is relevant. Skim the entire paragraph that would contain the proposed addition to answer these two questions:

>> **What is the paragraph's topic?** If the addition relates to that topic, it's likely relevant and should be included. If the addition's topic is unrelated, it shouldn't be inserted.

>> **Does the paragraph already state the information in the addition?** Even if the proposed addition is relevant, it shouldn't be added if it repeats information that's already there.

Addition questions are usually formatted as "yes, yes, no, no." (See Chapter 4 for details on this question format.) If the answer to the first question is *yes* and the second question is *no*, choose between the two *yes* answer options based on which provides the best justification for the *yes*. If the answer to the first question is *no* or the answer to the second question is *no*, choose between the two *no* options. Usually the two *no* options will give you a "no because it's irrelevant" or a "no because it's redundant." Choose the one that fits.

Creating smooth transitions

There are two types of transition questions: one that asks you to choose the best transition word or phrase to introduce a clause and one that asks you for the best first or last sentence of a paragraph. In both cases, check for clues in the elements that precede and follow the transition.

Transition words

The first type looks like a regular usage question. The transition is underlined in the sentence, and your answers give you a NO CHANGE and three possible replacements. To figure out the best answer, examine the events in the sentence, or sentences, that come before the transition and the sentence that contains the transition. Then choose the word or words that best relate the two events.

REMEMBER

Transitions show three main relationships between events:

>> **Similarity:** If the events are similar, choose transitions such as *likewise, additionally, similarly,* and so on, or choose no transition at all.

>> **Contrast:** If the events oppose each other, choose transitions such as *however, in contrast, on the contrary,* and so on.

>> **Cause and effect:** If one event causes the other, choose transitions such as *therefore, because, as a result,* and so on.

TIP

Whenever you see two answer choices that provide the same transition type (for example, *in contrast* and *on the other hand*), you can eliminate both of them. They can't both be right, so they must both be wrong.

Transition sentences

Questions that seek the best transition sentences may resemble mission questions, something like "Which of the following sentences would best conclude this paragraph and introduce the next one?" or "Which of the following sentences would best introduce the topic of this paragraph?" Or they may simply underline the first sentence of a paragraph and ask you to choose the best option. In all cases, you're looking for an answer that relates the topic of the second paragraph to elements of the preceding paragraph. Attack them in two steps:

1. **Eliminate answers that don't relate to the second paragraph — the one that comes after if you're dealing with a concluding sentence or the one that contains a first sentence.**

Read the entire paragraph to determine its main topic. If an answer doesn't somehow set up that topic, it's likely wrong.

2. **From the remaining answers, choose the one that harkens back to an element in the first paragraph — the one that contains a concluding sentence or precedes an introductory sentence.**

TIP

If two of the answers provide the same transition, such as *thus* and *therefore*, then both must be wrong because both can't be right.

Transition questions can be tricky if you try to answer them too quickly. Take the time to carefully examine the stuff that precedes and follows the transition, and the correct answer will become clear.

Organizing and positioning elements

The ACT will ask you to position words, sentences, and even whole paragraphs. Questions that require placing words in a sentence are usage questions. We discuss these in an earlier section "Recognizing misplaced modifiers." In this section, we cover what to do with the sentences and paragraphs. Positioning questions are easy to spot because the answer choices are usually just a list of numbers that refer to numbered sentences or paragraphs.

TIP

Some students get overwhelmed by positioning questions and the time it takes to answer them. Remember, though, the ACT must supply obvious clues to the correct position because it has to be able to justify its correct answers, so these questions really aren't that time-consuming. Here are some tips to help you spot the clues and become a star at perfectly proper placement:

>> **Before you examine the paragraphs and passages for clues, check the answer options.** Put a pencil mark on your booklet to highlight for yourself the four possible placements. So if an answer gives you "before Sentence 3," find Sentence 3 in the paragraph and put a pencil dot or check before it. Do the same for the other three choices. Then you don't have to keep checking the answer choices to see your options. And you won't waste time considering positions that aren't included in the answer choices.

>> **When you place sentences in paragraphs, look for pronouns in the sentence you're placing or in the paragraph it fits into.** Almost always, there'll be one. Remember that pronouns refer back to the nouns they rename, so you'll position the sentence so the pronoun comes in after the noun it refers to.

>> **Check the paragraphs you position for key, but sometimes subtle, clues.** For example, it's customary in essays and articles to introduce people by their first and last names and after that refer to them by just their last names. So don't put a paragraph that calls a person by last name before a paragraph that contains both the first and last name.

>> **When you place a sentence or paragraph, determine whether it contains mostly details or mostly general information.** Details generally follow general information. Also, note the transition words that initiate sentences and paragraphs. They'll tip you off. For example, a sentence or paragraph that begins with *finally* will conclude others in a list.

Seeing the big picture

Questions that ask you about the passage as a whole come in several varieties. The most common are really just mission questions. They ask you whether the passage fulfills a particular goal. The answers are presented in "yes, yes, no, no" format. Often, the easiest way to determine the main purpose of a passage is to read its title. Compare the title to the answer choices; if you find a similarity, you've likely found the answer. If you're still not sure whether the answer is *yes* or *no*, read the reasons given by each answer choice. Usually, you can eliminate two choices because the reasons they give are so off base. Examine the remaining answers carefully to choose the most true and relevant reason.

Sticking to appropriate vocabulary and standard expressions

The ACT includes questions that ask for the best choice of words. You may have to determine the best vocabulary for a particular context or tone, or you may need to recognize proper idiomatic expressions. English speakers use certain words in certain ways for no particular reason other than because that's the way it is. It's called proper diction. But sometimes even native English speakers fail to use idiomatic expressions correctly. It's common to hear people use *further* instead of *farther* when they mean distance or *less* instead of *fewer* when they refer to the number of countable items. Memorizing all of the standard forms is impossible, but thankfully you'll be able to figure out the answers to most of the diction questions by using your ear. Check out Table 6-1 to see a few of the expressions that may be less obvious.

TABLE 6-1 Commonly Tested Words and Expressions

Word or Expression	Rule	Correct Use
among/between	Use among for comparing three or more things or persons and between for comparing two things or persons.	Between the two of us there are few problems, but among the four of us there is much discord.
amount/number	Use amount to describe singular nouns and number to describe plural nouns.	I can't count the number of times I've miscalculated the amount of money I've spent on groceries.
as . . . as	When you use as in a comparison, use the construction as . . . as.	The dog is as wide as he is tall.
better/best worse/worst	Use better and worse to compare two things; use best and worst to compare more than two things.	Of the two products, the first is better known, but this product is the best known of all 20 on the market.
different from	Use different from rather than different than.	This plan is different from the one we implemented last year. (Not this: This plan is different than last year's.)
effect/affect	Generally, use effect as a noun and affect as a verb.	No one could know how the effect of the presentation would affect the client's choice.
either/or neither/nor	Use or with either and nor with neither.	Neither Nellie nor Isaac wanted to go to either the party or the concert.
er/est	Use the er form (called the comparative form) to compare exactly two items; use the est form (called the superlative form) to compare more than two items.	I am taller than my brother Beau, but Darren is the tallest member of our family.
farther/further	Use farther to refer to distance and further to refer to time or quantity.	Carol walked farther today than she did yesterday, and she vows to further study the benefits of walking.
good/well	Good is an adjective that modifies a noun. Well is an adverb that usually answers the question how.	It's a good thing that you're feeling so well after your bout of the flu.

(continued)

TABLE 6-1 *(continued)*

Word or Expression	Rule	Correct Use
if/whether	If introduces a condition. Whether compares alternatives.	If I crack a book this summer, it will be to determine whether I need to study more math for the ACT.
imply/infer	To imply means to suggest indirectly. To infer means to conclude or deduce.	I didn't mean to imply that your dress is ugly. You merely inferred that's what I meant when I asked you whether you bought it at an upholstery store.
less/fewer	Use less to refer to quantity (things that can be counted) and fewer to refer to number (things that can't be counted).	That office building is less noticeable because it has fewer floors. That glass has less water and fewer ice cubes.
less/least	Use less to compare two things and least to compare more than two things.	He is less educated than his brother is, but he isn't the least educated of his entire family.
like/as	Use like before nouns and pronouns; use as before phrases and clauses.	Like Ruth, Steve wanted the school's uniform policy to be just as it had always been.
many/much	Use many to refer to number and much to refer to quantity.	Many days I woke up feeling much anxiety, but I'm better now that I'm reading Catholic High School Entrance Exams For Dummies.
more/most	Use more to compare two things and most to compare more than two things.	Of the two girls, the older is more generous, and she is the most generous person in her family.

TIP

The ACT often contains diction questions that involve prepositions. When you see an underlined preposition in a question, make sure the preposition works with the elements it joins. For example, "we drove *across* the country" is correct, while "we drove *on* the country" is incorrect.

The ACT may apply what we call the "least/not" format to test many diction questions. These questions ask for the "least appropriate" or "not appropriate" answer. Consider these to be a game of "one of these things is not like the other." Here is how to approach these questions:

>> **Circle the LEAST or NOT in the question so you remember you're looking for the answer that doesn't work.** The words will be capitalized, but you'd be surprised how many students still miss them.

>> **Compare each answer choice to another.** Ask yourself whether the two have similar meanings. If they do, lightly cross out both answers with your pencil. Then compare one of the remaining two answers with the ones you just penciled through. If the answer has a similar meaning, cross it out too and choose the other.

Least/not questions almost always test word meanings, but every once in a while the ACT uses them to test usage errors. Generally, though, when you see this format, think diction.

TIP

The "least/not" format may become one of your favorites. Questions asked in this manner are easy to answer once you master the approach and remind yourself to pay attention to the capitalized words.

Chapter **7**

It's Not What You Say but How You Say It: English Practice Questions

You didn't think that we crammed those grammar, punctuation, and sentence structure rules into your head just so you could lord your perfect speech over your friends, did you? Here we show you just how knowing the stimulating rules we cover in Chapters 5 and 6 comes in handy for the ACT. This practice chapter has one passage and 15 questions. Multiply that by 5 for the real ACT English Test. After you complete each question, you can review your answer by reading the explanation that follows.

Directions: Following are four paragraphs containing underlined portions. Alternate ways of stating the underlined portions follow the paragraphs. Choose the best alternative. If the original is the best way of stating the underlined portion, choose NO CHANGE. You also see questions that refer to the passage or ask you to reorder the sentences within the passage. These questions are identified by a number in a box. Choose the best answer.

Marian Anderson: Groundbreaking Singer and Friend of First Ladies

[1] Marian Anderson possibly <u>will have</u> <u>the greatest</u> influence opening doors and gaining
                          1   2

well-deserved opportunities for other African American singers than anyone else to date <u>so far</u>.
                                                                                    3

[2] Anderson, born in Philadelphia, Pennsylvania, had an early interest in music. [3] She <u>learns</u>
                                                                                        4

to play the piano and was singing in the church at the age of six. [4] She gave her first concert

at age eight, <u>when she was still a young child</u>.
                      5

[5] In 1925, Anderson won a concert hosted by the New York Philharmonic, beating out <u>no less than</u> 300 singers. [6] <u>It launched her career but,</u> America was not quite ready for her
6   7
fantastic voice, personality, or racial heritage.

In 1936, the White House <u>asking her</u> to give a performance. She confessed that this occa-
8
sion was <u>different than</u> other concerts because she was very nervous. She and Eleanor Roosevelt
9
became <u>close friends, but</u> this friendship <u>between she and the First Lady became</u> evident when
10   11
Anderson was snubbed by the Daughters of the American Revolution (DAR). The DAR refused to let Anderson perform in Constitution Hall <u>in 1939, the White House</u> made arrangements for
12
Ms. Anderson to sing on the steps of the Lincoln Memorial instead. [13]

In 1977, First Lady Rosalynn Carter presented Marian Anderson with a Congressional Gold <u>Medal, making Ms. Anderson the first African American</u> to receive such an honor. Later she was
14
inducted into the Women's Hall of Fame in Seneca Falls, New York. [15]

1. **(A)** NO CHANGE

   (B) has had

   (C) has

   (D) is having

Because Marian Anderson's influence has already been felt, future tense isn't appropriate. Ms. Anderson has influenced and continues to influence. The verb tense that shows past action that continues or may continue into the present and beyond is present perfect, so the correct answer is (B). (See Chapter 5 for more information on verb tenses.)

2. **(F)** NO CHANGE

   (G) a greater

   (H) one of the greatest

   (J) a great

You need to read the entire sentence before deciding on an answer. If you read "the greatest influence" all by itself, it sounds correct. However, if you continue to read the sentence, you find the comparative *than*. You cannot say "the greatest influence than" but rather "a greater influence than." The correct answer is (G).

REMEMBER

Be very careful to read the entire sentence. You may save a few seconds by reading only the underlined portion, but you'll sacrifice a lot of points.

3. **(A)** NO CHANGE

   (B) dating so far

   (C) so far dated

   (D) OMIT the underlined portion.

To date and *so far* are redundant; they mean the same thing. You can use one or the other but not both. (Quick! Notify the Department of Redundancy Department!) The correct answer is (D).

4. **(F)** NO CHANGE

   (G) has been learning

   (H) learned

   (J) is learning

Because Marian Anderson is no longer six years old, the sentence requires the past tense, *learned*. **Hint:** If you aren't sure of the tense, check out the rest of the sentence. You're told that Ms. Anderson "was singing," meaning the situation occurred in the past. So the correct answer is (H).

5. **(A)** NO CHANGE

   (B) still a young child

   (C) still young

   (D) DELETE the underlined portion and end the sentence with a period.

A person who is eight is still a young child — duh! The underlined portion is superfluous, unnecessary. Eliminate it. The period is necessary to finish the sentence. The correct answer is (D).

6. **(F)** NO CHANGE

   (G) less than

   (H) fewer than

   (J) no fewer than

Use *fewer* to describe plural nouns, as in fewer brain cells, for example. Use *less* to describe singular nouns, like less intelligence. Because *singers* is a plural noun, use *fewer* rather than *less*. The correct answer is (J).

REMEMBER

If you picked Choice (H), you fell for the trap. You forgot to reread the sentence with your answer inserted. The meaning of the whole sentence changes with the phrase "fewer than 300 singers." In that case, you're diminishing the winner's accomplishment. The tone of the passage is one of respect. The author is impressed that Ms. Anderson beat out "no fewer than 300 singers." Keep in mind that you must make your answers fit the overall tone or attitude of the passage. If a passage is complimentary, be sure that your answers are, too.

7. **(A)** NO CHANGE

   (B) Launching her career,

   (C) The win launched her career, but

   (D) Upon launching it,

TIP

Be very suspicious of that two-letter rascal *it*. Always double-check *it* out because *it* is so often misused and abused. It must refer to one specific noun: "Where is the book? Here it is." In Question 7, *it* doesn't have a clear reference. It could mean that winning the concert launched her career, or it may seem that the New York Philharmonic launched her career. Another problem with Choice (A) is that pesky comma. It belongs before *but*, not after *it*. Choices (B) and (D) sound as if America launched Ms. Anderson's career: "Upon launching it . . . America was not quite ready . . . ." A beginning phrase always describes the sentence's subject. Be sure to go back and reread the entire sentence with your answer inserted. Because Choice (D) clarifies exactly what launched Anderson's career and changes the beginning phrase to a dependent clause, it is the correct answer.

8. (F) NO CHANGE

   (G) asked her

   (H) was asking her

   (J) asking

The original is a fragment, an incomplete sentence. It tries to fool you into thinking that *asking* is the verb, but *ing* words all by themselves with no helping verbs to assist them can't work as verbs. The remedy is to change *asking* to the simple past verb *asked*. Because the sentence gives you a specific date, you know that the event happened at one point in the past. Therefore, Choice (H) is wrong. The White House wasn't in a continuous state of asking Ms. Anderson. So the correct answer is (G).

9. (A) NO CHANGE

   (B) different from

   (C) differed from

   (D) more different than

Standard English says *different from* rather than *different than.* Choice (D) adds more to the sentence to try to make *than* sound like a proper comparison term, but its addition also changes the meaning of the sentence. The White House concert wasn't more different than other concerts. It was simply different from other concerts that weren't as anxiety-provoking. The correct answer is (B).

REMEMBER

Choice (C) changes *than* to *from,* but it introduces another verb into a sentence that already has a verb. You may not notice the problem if you don't reread the sentence with Choice (C) inserted. Always reread the sentence with your answer choice inserted before you mark the answer on your sheet to make sure you haven't missed something important.

10. (F) NO CHANGE

   (G) close friends, and

   (H) close friends — which

   (J) close and friendly,

The clause "but this friendship . . . became evident . . ." makes no sense in the context. Use *but* only to indicate opposition or change; use a comma and the word *and* to add to and continue a thought. The correct answer is (G).

11. (A) NO CHANGE

   (B) between the First Lady and she became

   (C) between her and the First Lady became

   (D) OMIT the underlined portion.

The pronoun is the problem in this question. *Between* is a preposition, which means that the pronoun and noun that come after it are objects of the preposition. Therefore, the pronoun has to be in objective form. The objective form of *she* is *her.* You can't omit the underlined words because the resulting clause has no verb. The correct answer is (C).

REMEMBER

Many students tend to choose "OMIT the underlined portion" every time they see it, reasoning that it would not be a choice unless it were correct. Not so. If you decide to omit the underlined portion, be especially careful to reread the entire sentence. Often, omitting the underlined portion makes nonsense out of the sentence.

12. **(F)** NO CHANGE

   (G) in 1939; however, the White House

   (H) in 1939 but the White House

   (J) in 1939. Although the White House

To answer this question, you must correct the comma splice in the original sentence. You can't use a comma all by itself to join two independent clauses (complete sentences) in one sentence. You could separate them by putting a period after 1939 and capitalizing *the*. The answers don't give you that option, though. Choice (J) separates the clauses with a period, but adding *although* makes the second sentence a fragment. Another way to join two independent clauses together is with a semicolon. Choice (G) changes the comma to a semicolon and adds *however* for a smooth transition to the next thought. It properly places a comma after *however*, too. Choice (H) lacks a necessary comma before *but*. The correct answer is (G).

13. The author is considering inserting a sentence that presents a short list of other venues where Marian Anderson performed during her career. Would that insertion be appropriate here?

   (A) Yes, because the primary purpose of this paragraph is to emphasize the great number of places where Marian Anderson performed.

   (B) Yes, because it's always better to include many specific examples to advance an idea.

   (C) No, because the paragraph is about the obstacles that Marian Anderson had to overcome rather than the number of concert halls she performed in.

   (D) No, because providing a list of examples is never appropriate in an essay about a person's life.

When you see one of these "yes, yes, no, no" questions on the English Test, figure out the short answer to the question. Would a list of venues be appropriate? Probably not. (Please. The test is boring enough without having to read through a list of concert venues.) Ignore the yes answers for now and focus on the no choices. The paragraph seems to focus on the racial prejudice Anderson experienced rather than the number of places she performed in. So the correct answer is (C).

REMEMBER

You can be pretty certain that Choices (B) and (D) are wrong. Both of them contain debatable words, such as *always* and *never*, that should raise a red flag for you. If you're thinking of choosing an answer that contains one of these all-encompassing words that leaves no room for exception, first make sure that the position is justified.

14. **(F)** NO CHANGE

   (G) Medal, being the first African American

   (H) Medal; the first African American

   (J) Medal, the first African American

The original is okay the way it's written. The other choices make it sound like the medal was the first African American to receive such an honor. Choice (H) adds insult to injury by using a semicolon to do a comma's job. Note that the job of the semicolon is to separate two independent sentences; each sentence could stand alone. The correct answer is (F).

Don't forget that the sentence doesn't have to have an error. About 20 percent of the time the underlined portion requires NO CHANGE.

15. If the author of this passage were to add the following lines to the article, where would they be most logically placed?

It was an era of racial prejudice, a time when people were still legally excluded from jobs, housing, and even entertainment merely because of their race. Thus, the early promise of success seemed impossible until something amazing for the times happened.

(A) After Sentence 2

(B) After Sentence 6

(C) After Sentence 3

(D) After Sentence 5

You know from the answer options to look only in the first two paragraphs. Because the first sentence of the addition talks about racial prejudice, look in the beginning of the passage for something that mentions Marian Anderson's race. That topic is specifically discussed only in Sentence 6. So the correct answer is (B).

Be sure to go back to the passage and reread the entire paragraph with the new lines inserted to make sure that they make sense.

If you find yourself wasting too much time on a question like this one, your best bet is to eliminate answers if you can, guess, and move on. *Remember:* The ACT doesn't penalize you for wrong answers. Marking a guess for any question that has you stumped is to your advantage.

3

Don't Count Yourself Out: The Math Test

Review number basics, such as absolute value, the number line, and other math concepts you may not have seen since fourth grade. We don't insult you by starting too far back ("here are the multiplication tables you must know . . ."), but we do cover the rules that trip up many students, such as how to subtract a negative number.

Remember how to work with right triangles and apply the rules regarding corresponding angles created by parallel lines crossed by a transversal. Dust off that old SOHCAHTOA and review how to solve geometry and trigonometry problems on the ACT.

Harken back to middle school with a refresher on factoring and solving for *x*. Refer to the table of logarithm rules and take a flight on the coordinate plane to make sure you've memorized commonly-tested algebra and coordinate geometry formulas.

Move through the Mathematics Test more quickly with tips on how to use the answer choices to focus and translate English word problems into math formulas. Find out how you can benefit from plugging in real values for variables to solve theoretical problems and learn how to answer easiest questions first to save time.

Practice old and new math skills and approaches with 12 mini test questions. Read through the answer explanations to formulate a solid approach to the ACT Mathematics Test.

IN THIS CHAPTER

» Figuring out fractions, decimals, and percentages

» Reasoning through ratios, proportions, and exponents

» Finding order in operations and calculating the mean, median, mode, and range

» Considering units and measurements

» Exploring variables and attacking algebra

Chapter **8**

Number Nuts and Bolts

You've seen them before. They crop up everywhere: your high school math tests, those dreaded achievement tests, and now your college entrance exam. Yes, we're talking about multiple-choice math questions. Take heart! Many of the math questions on the ACT cover the basics.

Even though you may already know most of the math that we discuss in this chapter, it never hurts to refresh your memory. After all, the questions on the ACT that ask about the basic math topics we cover here tend to be the easiest, so they offer you the best chance for getting correct answers. Brush up on your elementary and middle school math, and you're sure to improve your score on the ACT Math Test.

The Wonderful World of Numbers

You're probably not surprised to find out that the math problems on the ACT involve numbers, but you also probably haven't thought about the properties of numbers in a long time. That's why we offer you a fairly complete number review here. (You can thank us later.)

Keeping it real: Types of numbers

Numbers fall under a hierarchy of classifications (see Figure 8-1) and are defined as such:

- » **Complex:** All numbers you can think of.

- » **Imaginary:** Represented by the variable *i*, the value of the square root of a negative number. Every once in a while, the ACT spits out a question that deals with an imaginary number. Just keep in mind that $i^2 = -1$ and $i = \sqrt{-1}$.

- » **Real:** All complex numbers that aren't imaginary.

- » **Irrational:** Numbers that can't be written as fractions, such as π and $\sqrt{2}$.

- » **Rational:** All real numbers that aren't irrational and therefore include fractions and decimal numbers that either end or repeat. For example, the fraction $\frac{1}{6}$ is a rational number. It can also be expressed as $0.1\overline{6}$.

- » **Integers:** All the positive and negative whole numbers, plus zero. Integers aren't fractions or decimals or portions of a number, so they include –5, –4, –3, –2, –1, 0, 1, 2, 3, 4, 5, and continue infinitely on either side of zero. Integers greater than zero are called *natural numbers* or *positive integers;* integers less than zero are called *negative integers.*

REMEMBER

Tread carefully when working with zero. It's neither positive nor negative.

- » **Whole:** All the positive integers and zero.

- » **Natural:** All the positive integers, excluding zero.

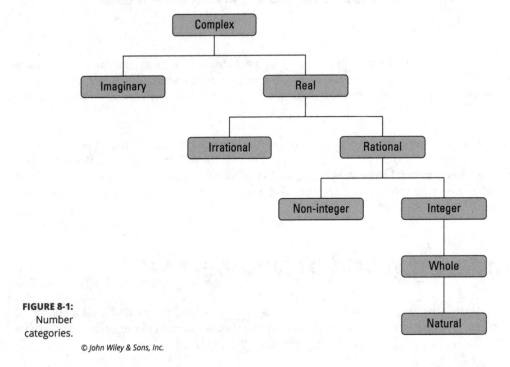

FIGURE 8-1:
Number
categories.

© *John Wiley & Sons, Inc.*

So when a question tells you to "express your answer in real numbers," don't sweat it. That's almost no constraint at all, because nearly every number you know is a real number.

Lining things up along the number line

You may have an easier time visualizing numbers if you see them on a number line. The *number line* shows all real numbers. Zero holds a place in the middle of the line. All positive numbers carry on infinitely to the right of zero, and all negative numbers extend infinitely to the left of zero, like this:

Understanding absolute value

The concept of absolute value crops up quite a bit on the ACT. The *absolute value* of any real number is that same number without a negative sign. It's the value of the distance a particular number is from zero on a number line (see the preceding section). For example, the absolute value of 1 is written mathematically as $|1|$. Because 1 sits one space from zero on the number line, $|1| = 1$. But because -1 also sits one space away from zero on the number line, $|-1| = 1$.

REMEMBER

Absolute value relates only to the value that's inside those absolute value bars. If you see a negative sign outside the bars, the value of the result is negative. For example, $-|-1| = -1$. You must always perform operations within the absolute value signs before you make the value positive: $-|-1| = -1$

Equations with a variable inside absolute value signs usually have two solutions: the one when the value within the signs is positive and the one when the value is negative.

$$|-3 + x| = 12$$
$$-3 + x = 12$$
$$x = 15$$
$$|-3 + x| = 12$$
$$-(-3 + x) = 12$$
$$3 - x = 12$$
$$x = -9$$

Getting familiar with prime numbers and factorization

The ACT expects you to know about *prime numbers*, which are all the positive integers that can be divided only by themselves and 1. A number that can be divided by more numbers than 1 and itself is called a *composite number*. Here are some other facts you should know about prime numbers:

» 1 is neither prime nor composite.

» 2 is the smallest of the prime numbers, and it's also the only number that's both even and prime. (See the section, "Working with odds/evens and positives/negatives," for more on even numbers.)

» 0 can never be a prime number because you can divide zero by every number in existence, but it's not considered to be a composite number either.

TIP

You don't need to memorize all the prime numbers before you take the ACT (yikes!), but do keep in mind that the lowest prime numbers are 2, 3, 5, 7, 11, 13, 17, 19, 23, and 29.

When you know how to recognize prime numbers, you can engage in *prime factorization*, which is just a fancy way of saying that you can break down a number into all the prime numbers (or *factors*) that go into it (refer to Figure 8-2). For instance, 50 factors into 2 and 25, which factors into 5 and 5, giving you 2, 5, and 5 for the prime factors of 50:

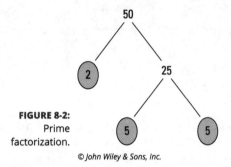

FIGURE 8-2:
Prime
factorization.

© *John Wiley & Sons, Inc.*

Minor Surgery: Basic Math Operations

You don't have to be a brain surgeon to perform the basic mathematical operations of addition, subtraction, multiplication, and division, but you do have to train your brain to do these simple calculations without error. The following sections go over these basic operations so you don't miss questions because of silly calculation mistakes.

Adding and subtracting

Addition is when you combine two or more numbers to get an end result called the *sum*.

No matter what order you add a bunch of numbers in, you always end up with the same sum: $(2+3)+4=9$ and $2+(3+4)=9$; $2+3=5$ and $3+2=5$.

When you *subtract* one number from another, you take one value away from another value and end up with the *difference* (the answer to a subtraction problem). So if $4+5=9$, then $9-5=4$.

REMEMBER

Unlike addition, order *does* matter in subtraction. You get completely different answers for $20-7-4$ based on what order you subtract them: $(20-7)-4=9$, but $20-(7-4)=17$. For another example, $2-3=-1$ doesn't give you the same answer as $3-2=1$.

Multiplying and dividing

Think of *multiplication* as repeated addition with an end result called the *product*. The multiplication problem 3×6 is the same as the addition problem $6+6+6$. Both problems equal 18.

REMEMBER

Multiplication is like addition in that the order in which you multiply the values doesn't matter: $2\times3=3\times2$ and $(2\times3)\times4=2\times(3\times4)$.

Another property of multiplication you need to know is the *distributive property.* You can multiply a number by a set of added or subtracted values by distributing that number through the values in the set values, like so:

$$2(3+4)=$$
$$(2\times3)+(2\times4)=$$
$$6+8=14$$

Of course, you can solve this problem by adding the numbers in parentheses $(3+4=7)$ and multiplying the sum by 2 $(7\times2=14)$. But when you start to add variables to the mix (see the later section, "Variables 101"), you'll be glad you know about distribution.

Division is all about dividing one value into smaller values; those smaller values, or end results, are called *quotients.* Consider division to be the reverse of multiplication:

$$2\times3=6$$
$$6\div3=2$$
$$6\div2=3$$

Working with odds/evens and positives/negatives

The ACT may ask questions that require you to know what happens when you perform operations with odd and even numbers, as well as positives and negatives. *Even numbers* are numbers that are divisible by 2 (2, 4, 6, 8, 10, and so on), and *odd numbers* are numbers that aren't divisible by 2 (1, 3, 5, 7, 9, 11, and so on). The easiest way to figure out operations with odds and evens is to try them with sample odd and even values.

To perform basic math operations with positive and negative numbers, remember these rules:

>> When you multiply or divide two positive numbers, the answer is positive.

>> When you multiply or divide two negative numbers, the answer is also positive.

>> When you multiply or divide a negative number by a positive number, you get a negative answer.

You also have to know a thing or two (or three, actually) about adding and subtracting positive and negative numbers:

>> When you add two positive numbers, your answer is positive: $3+5=8$.

>> When you add two negative numbers, your answer is negative: $-3+-5=-8$.

>> When you add a negative number to a positive number, your answer can be positive or negative: $-3+5=2$ and $3+(-5)=-2$.

Focusing on Fractions, Decimals, and Percentages

Fractions, decimals, and percentages all represent parts of a whole. The ACT asks you to manipulate these figures in all sorts of ways.

Converting fractions, decimals, and percentages

Because fractions, decimals, and percentages are different ways of showing similar values, you can change pretty easily from one form to another. Here's what you need to know:

» To convert a fraction to a decimal, just divide: $\frac{3}{4} = 3 \div 4 = 0.75$.

» To convert a decimal back to a fraction, first count the number of digits to the right of the decimal point. Then divide the number in the decimal over a 1 followed by as many zeros as there were digits to the right of the decimal. Finally, simplify the fraction (see the section, "Simplifying fractions," for details): $0.75 = \frac{75}{100} = \frac{3}{4}$.

» To change a decimal to a percent, just move the decimal two places to the right and add a percent sign: $0.75 = 75\%$.

» To turn a percent into a decimal, move the decimal point two places to the left and get rid of the percent sign: $75\% = 0.75$.

Working with fractions

Fractions tell you what part a piece is of a whole. The *numerator* is the top number in the fraction, and it represents the piece. The *denominator* is the bottom number of the fraction, and it indicates the value of the whole. If you cut a whole apple pie into 8 pieces and eat 5 slices, you can show the amount of pie you eat as a fraction, like so: $\frac{5}{10}$.

In the following sections, we show you how to do basic math operations with fractions. As a bonus, we also explain how to simplify fractions and work with mixed numbers.

Simplifying fractions

The ACT expects all fraction answers to be in their simplest forms. To simplify a fraction, first find the largest number you can think of that goes into both the numerator and denominator (called the *greatest common factor*). Then just divide the numerator and denominator by that number. For example, if you end up with $\frac{5}{10}$, you must simplify it further by dividing the numerator and denominator by 5: $\frac{5}{10} = \frac{1}{2}$.

Multiplying and dividing fractions

Multiplying fractions is easy. Just multiply the numerators by each other and then do the same with the denominators. Then simplify if you have to. For example,

$$\frac{3}{4} \times \frac{2}{5} = \frac{3 \times 2}{4 \times 5} = \frac{6}{20} = \frac{3}{10}$$

Always check whether you can cancel out any numbers before you begin working to avoid having to deal with big, awkward numbers and having to simplify at the end. In the preceding example, you can reduce the 4 and cancel the 2, leaving you with

$$\frac{3}{_2 \cancel{4}} \times \frac{\cancel{2}^1}{5} = \frac{3 \times 1}{2 \times 5} = \frac{3}{10}$$

You get to the right solution either way; canceling in advance just makes the numbers smaller and easier to work with.

REMEMBER

Dividing fractions is pretty much the same as multiplying them except for one very important additional step. First, find the *reciprocal* of the second fraction in the equation (that is, turn the second fraction upside down). Then multiply (yes, you have to multiply when dividing fractions) the numerators and denominators of the resulting fractions. For example,

$$\frac{1}{3} \div \frac{2}{5} = \frac{1}{3} \times \frac{5}{2} = \frac{5}{6}$$

Adding and subtracting fractions

Adding and subtracting fractions can be a little tricky, but you'll be fine if you follow these guidelines:

>> **You can add or subtract fractions only if they have the same denominator.** Add or subtract just the numerators, like so:

$$\frac{1}{3} + \frac{4}{3} = \frac{5}{3}$$

$$\frac{3}{8} - \frac{2}{8} = \frac{1}{8}$$

>> **When fractions don't have the same denominator, you have to find a common denominator.** To find a common denominator, you can multiply all the denominators, but doing so often doesn't give you the lowest common denominator. As a result, you end up with some humongous, overwhelming number that you'd rather not work with.

REMEMBER

To find the lowest (or least) common denominator, think of multiples of the highest denominator until you find the one that all denominators go into evenly. For instance, to solve $\frac{4}{15} + \frac{1}{6}$, you have to find the lowest common denominator of 15 and 6. Sure, you can multiply 15 and 6 to get 90, but that's not the lowest common denominator. Instead, count by fifteens — because 15 is the larger of the two denominators — $15 \times 1 = 15$. But 6 doesn't go into 15. Moving on, $15 \times 2 = 30$. Hey! Both 15 and 6 go into 30, so 30 is the lowest common denominator.

Here's another example. To find the lowest common denominator for 2, 4, and 5, count by fives. What about 5? No, 2 and 4 don't go into it. How about 10? No, 4 doesn't go into it. Okay, 15? No, 2 and 4 don't go into it. What about 20? Yes, all the numbers divide evenly into 20.

TIP

You can use your graphing calculator to find the lowest common denominator (also known as the least common multiple, or LCM) for two or more numbers. Apply the *lcm* function, enter the set of numbers, and press Enter.

TIP

Here's a trick for working with fractions with variables (see the later section, "Variables 101," for more about variables). Multiply the denominators to find the lowest common denominator. Then cross-multiply to find the numerators (see the later section, "Proportions," for details on cross-multiplying).

Say you're asked to solve this problem:

$$\frac{a}{b} - \frac{c}{d} = ?$$

Find the common denominator by multiplying the two denominators: $b \times d = bd$. Then cross-multiply:

$$a \times d = ad$$
$$c \times b = cb$$

Put the difference of the results over the common denominator:

$$\frac{ad - cb}{bd}$$

Mixing things up with mixed numbers

A *mixed number* is a whole number with a fraction tagging along behind it, such as $2\frac{1}{3}$. To add, subtract, multiply, or divide with mixed numbers, you first have to convert them into *improper fractions* (fractions in which the numerator is larger than the denominator). To do so, multiply the whole number by the denominator and add that to the numerator. Put the sum over the denominator. For example,

$$2\frac{1}{3} = \frac{(2 \times 3) + 1}{3} = \frac{7}{3}$$

Pondering percentages

In terms of percentages, the ACT usually asks you to find a percentage of another number. When you get a question like "What is 30% of 60?" evaluate the language like so:

>> *What* means ? or x (the unknown) or what you're trying to find out.

>> *Is* means = (equals).

>> *Of* means × (multiply).

Your job is to convert the words into math, like so: $? = 30\% \times 60$.

To solve this problem, convert 30% to a decimal (0.30) and multiply by 60. Tada! The answer is 18. Or, if you prefer, you could convert 30% to a fraction and multiply, like so:

$$? = \frac{30}{100} \times \frac{60}{1} = \frac{180}{100} = 18$$

Sometimes a problem asks you to figure out what percent one number is of another. For example, the number 20 is what percent of 80? To solve this type of problem, just apply a little translation to the question to get a math equation you can work with.

The *number 20* is, of course, 20. You know that *is* means =. *What* gives you the unknown, or x, and *of* means multiply. Put it all together and you get this expression: $20\% \times 80$. Now all you have to do is solve for x. Divide both sides by 80, and you get $\frac{20}{80} = x\%$, or $\frac{20}{80} = \frac{1}{4} = 0.25$. Convert 0.25 to a percent by multiplying by 100 (or moving the decimal point two places to the right), and you have your answer: $0.25 = 25\%$. (See the later section, "Solving simple equations," for more details on how to solve for x and other variables.)

Here's a sample question to test what you know about parts of a whole.

EXAMPLE

What is 25% of $5\frac{3}{4}$?

(A) $\frac{37}{130}$

(B) $5\frac{3}{4}$

(C) $1\frac{7}{16}$

(D) $2\frac{3}{16}$

(E) 12

First, you don't need to do any calculation to eliminate Choices (B) and (E). Twenty-five percent of $5\frac{3}{4}$ can't be $5\frac{3}{4}$ or 12. Then notice that the answer choices are in fraction rather than decimal form, so work the problem with fractions. When you convert 25% to a fraction, you get $\frac{1}{4}$. *Of* means multiply. So your equation is $\frac{1}{4} \times 5\frac{3}{4} = ?$. Convert the second fraction and multiply: $\frac{1}{4} \times \frac{23}{4} = \frac{23}{16} = 1\frac{7}{16}$. The correct answer is (C).

TIP

Some questions ask you to find a percentage of a value and then increase or decrease that value by the percentage. You can perform each of these tasks in one step:

>> To increase a number by a particular percentage of that number, multiply the number by 1 and the percentage. So, to find the total purchase amount of a $9.50 item with 6% tax, multiply 9.50 by 1.06: $9.50 \times 1.06 = 10.07$.

>> To decrease a number by a particular percentage of that number, multiply the number by the percentage you get when you subtract the original percentage from 100. So, to find the sale price of a $9.50 item that has been discounted by 6%, multiply 9.50 by 94% (100 – 6%): $9.50 \times .94 = 8.93$.

Eyeing Ratios and Proportions

When you know the tricks we show you in this section, ratios and proportions are some of the easiest problems to answer quickly. We call them *heartbeat problems* because you can solve them in a heartbeat. Of course, if someone drop-dead gorgeous sits next to you and makes your heart beat faster, you may need two heartbeats to solve them.

Ratios

Here's what you need to know to answer ratio problems:

TIP

>> A *ratio* is written as $\frac{of}{to}$ or of:to. The ratio *of* sunflowers *to* roses = $\frac{sunflowers}{roses}$. The ratio *of* umbrellas *to* heads = umbrellas:heads.

When you see a ratio written with colons, rewrite it as a fraction. It's easier to evaluate ratios when they're written in fraction form because you can more easily set up proportions or see that you need to give ratios common denominators to compare them.

>> A *possible total* is a multiple of the sum of the numbers in the ratio. For example, you may be given a problem like this: At a party, the ratio of blondes to redheads is 4:5. Which of the following could be the total number of blondes and redheads at the party? Mega-easy. Add the numbers in the ratio: $4 + 5 = 9$. The total number of blondes must be a multiple of 9, such as 9, 18, 27, 36, and so on.

>> When a question gives you a ratio and a total and asks you to find a specific term, do the following:

1. Add the numbers in the ratio.

2. Divide that sum into the total.

3. Multiply that quotient by each term in the ratio.

4. Add the answers to double-check that their sum equals the total.

Confused? Consider this example: Yelling at the members of his team, who had just lost 21–0, the irate coach pointed his finger at each member of the squad and called every player either a wimp or a slacker. If there were 3 wimps for every 4 slackers and every member of the 28-person squad was either a wimp or a slacker, how many wimps were there?

First, add the ratio: $3 + 4 = 7$. Divide 7 into the total number of team members: $\frac{28}{7} = 4$. Multiply 4 by each term in the ratio: $4 \times 3 = 12$; $4 \times 4 = 16$. Make sure those numbers add up to the total number of team members: $12 + 16 = 28$.

Now you have all the information you need to answer a variety of questions. There are 12 wimps and 16 slackers. There are 4 more slackers than wimps. The number of slackers that would have to be kicked off the team for the number of wimps and slackers to be equal is 4. The ACT's math moguls can ask all sorts of things about ratios, but if you have this information, you're ready for anything they throw at you.

REMEMBER

Be sure that you actually do Step 4 — adding the terms to double-check that they add up to the total. Doing so catches any careless mistakes that you may have made.

Proportions

The ACT may toss in a few proportion problems, too. A *proportion* is a relationship between two ratios where the ratios are equal. Just like with fractions, multiplying or dividing both numbers in the ratio by the same number doesn't change the value of the ratio. So, for example, these two ratios make up a proportion: 2:8 and 4:16, which you may also see written as $\frac{2}{8} = \frac{4}{16}$.

REMEMBER

Often, you see a couple of equal ratios with a missing term that you have to find. To solve these problems, you *cross-multiply*. In other words, you multiply the terms that are diagonal from each other and solve for *x*. For example, to solve this equation $\frac{3}{8} = \frac{6}{x}$, follow these steps:

1. **Identify the diagonal terms: 3 and *x*; 6 and 8.**

2. **Multiply each set of diagonal terms and set the products equal to each other.**

   $3 \times x = 3x$
   $6 \times 8 = 48$
   $3x = 48$

3. **Solve for *x*.**

   $x = 16$

   For more on how to solve for *x*, go to the later section, "Solving simple equations."

Here's a sample ratio problem for you to try.

EXAMPLE

Trying to get Willie to turn down his stereo, his mother pounds on the ceiling and shouts up to his bedroom. If she pounds seven times for every five times she shouts, which of the following could be the total number of poundings and shouts?

(F) 75

(G) 57

(H) 48

(J) 35

(K) 30

Add the numbers in the ratio: $7 + 5 = 12$. The total must be a multiple of 12 (which means it must be evenly divisible by 12). Here, only 48 is evenly divisible by 12, so the correct answer is (H).

Covering Your Bases: Exponents

Many ACT questions require you to know how to work with bases and exponents. Exponents represent repeated multiplication. For example, 5^3 is the same as $5 \times 5 \times 5 = 125$. When you work with exponents, make sure you know these important concepts:

>> The *base* is the big value on the bottom. The *exponent* is the little value in the upper-right corner.

>> In 5^3, 5 is the base and 3 is the exponent.

>> The exponent tells you how many times to multiply the base times itself.

>> A base to the zero power equals one. For example, $5^0 = 1; x^0 = 1$.

>> A base to a negative exponent is the reciprocal of itself.

This concept is a little more confusing. When you have a negative exponent, just put the base and exponent under a 1 and make the exponent positive again. For example, $5^{-3} = \frac{1}{5^3}$. Keep in mind that the resulting number is not negative. When you flip it, you get the reciprocal, and the negative just sort of fades away.

>> You can rewrite a fractional exponent as a radical. The denominator in the exponent tells you the type of radical, the numerator is the exponent that remains with the base, and the base and exponent are placed underneath the radical sign. For example, $5^{\frac{2}{3}} = \sqrt[3]{5^2}$.

>> **To multiply like bases, add the exponents.** For example, $5^4 \times 5^9 = 5^{4+9} = 5^{13}$.

You can't multiply *unlike* bases. Think of it as trying to multiply dogs and cats — it doesn't work. All you end up with is a miffed meower and a damaged dog. You actually have to work out the problem: $5^2 \times 6^3 \neq 30^5; 5^2 \times 6^3 = 5^2 \times 6^3$.

REMEMBER

WARNING

>> To divide like bases, subtract the exponents. For example, $5^9 \div 5^3 = 5^{9-3} = 5^6$.

Did you think that the answer was 5^3? It's easy to fall into the trap of dividing rather than subtracting, especially when you see numbers that just beg to be divided, like 9 and 3. Keep your guard up.

>> **Multiply the exponents of a base inside and outside the parentheses.** That's quite a mouthful. Here's what it means: $\left(5^3\right)^2 = 5^{3 \times 2} = 5^6$.

>> **To add or subtract like bases that are variables that have like exponents, add or subtract the numerical coefficient of the bases.**

The *numerical coefficient* (a great name for a rock band, don't you think?) is simply the number in front of the base. So the numerical coefficient in $5x^2$ is 5. Notice that it is *not* the little exponent in the right-hand corner but the full-sized number to the left of the base. Here are two examples of adding and subtracting bases that are variables that have like exponents:

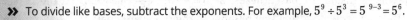
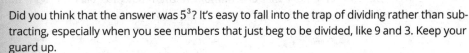

$37x^3 + 10x^3 = 47x^3$
$15y^2 - 5y^2 = 10y^2$

The numerical coefficient of any variable on its own is $1 : x = 1x$.

WARNING

You can't add or subtract like bases with different exponents: $13x^3 - 9x^2 \neq 4x^3, 4x^2,$ or $4x$. The bases and exponents must be the same for you to add or subtract the terms. For more about working with variables, go to the later section, "Variables 101."

Smooth Operator: Order of Operations

When you have several operations (addition, subtraction, multiplication, division, squaring, and so on) in one problem, you must perform the operations in the following order:

1. Parentheses.

Do what's inside the parentheses first.

2. Exponent.

Do the squaring or the cubing (whatever the exponent is).

3. Multiply or divide.

Do multiplication and division left to right. If multiplication is to the left of division, multiply first. If division is to the left of multiplication, divide first.

4. Add or subtract.

Do addition and subtraction left to right. If addition is to the left of subtraction, add first. If subtraction is to the left of addition, subtract first.

An easy *mnemonic* (memory device) for remembering the order of operations is *PEMDAS*: Parentheses, Exponents, Multiply, Divide, Add, Subtract.

Here's a sample problem:

$$10(3-5)^2 + \left(\frac{30}{5}\right)^0 =$$

First, do what's inside the parentheses: $3 - 5 = -2$ and $\frac{30}{5} = 6$. Next, do the power: $-2^2 = 4$ and $-2^2 = 4$. (Did you remember that any number to the 0 power equals 1?) Next, multiply: $10 \times 4 = 40$. Finally, add: $40 + 1 = 41$.

Dealing with Average, Median, Mode, and More

Don't be surprised if the ACT asks you a few basic statistics questions (it contains more advanced probability and statistics problems, too, but we cover those in Chapter 10). Most of these questions ask about average (also known as *average mean* or just *mean*), but you may see a few that deal with other related concepts, which is where the following sections come in.

Doing better than average on averages

To perform above average on questions about averages, you need to know how to apply the following formula for finding the average value of a set of numbers:

$$\text{Average} = \frac{\text{Sum of the numbers in the set}}{\text{Amount of numbers in the set}}$$

For example, to find the average of 23, 25, 26, and 30, apply the formula and solve, like so:

$$\text{Average} = \frac{23+25+26+30}{4} = \frac{104}{4} = 26$$

You can use given values in the average formula to solve for the other values. In other words, if the exam gives you the average and the sum of a group of numbers, you can figure out how many numbers are in the set by using the average formula.

For example, Jeanette takes seven exams. Her scores on the first six are 91, 89, 85, 92, 90, and 88. If her average on all seven exams is 90, what did she get on the seventh exam? To solve this problem, apply the formula:

$$90 = \frac{Sum}{7}$$

Because you don't know the seventh term, call it x. Add the first six terms (which total 535) and x:

$$90 = \frac{535+x}{7}$$

Cross-multiply:

$$90 \times 7 = 535 + x$$
$$630 = 535 + x$$
$$95 = x$$

The seventh exam score was 95.

Weighing in on weighted averages

In a *weighted average*, some scores count more than others. Here's an example to help you see what we mean:

Number of Students	Score
12	80
13	75
10	70

If you're asked to find the average score for the students in the class shown in the preceding table, you know that you can't simply add 80, 75, and 70 and divide by 3, because the scores weren't evenly distributed among the students. Because 12 students got an 80, multiply 12 and 80 to get 960. Do the same with the other scores and add the products:

$$13 \times 75 = 975$$
$$10 \times 70 = 700$$
$$960 + 975 + 700 = 2635$$

Divide not by 3 but by the total number of students, which is 35 $(12+13+10=35)$:

$$\frac{2635}{35} = 75.29$$

Mastering medians

The *median* is the middle value in a list of several values or numbers. To find out the median, list the values or numbers in order, usually from low to high, and choose the value that falls exactly in the middle of the other values. If you have an odd number of values, just select the middle value. If you have an even number of values, find the two middle values and average them (see the previous section on averages). The outcome is the median.

Managing modes

The *mode* is the value that occurs most often in a set of values. For example, you may be asked what income occurs most frequently in a particular sample population. If more people in the population have an income of $45,000 than any other income amount, the mode is $45,000.

Getting ready for range

The *range* is the distance from the greatest to the smallest. In other words, just subtract the smallest term from the largest term to find the range.

WARNING

The only trap you're likely to see in these basic statistics questions is in the answer choices. The questions themselves are quite straightforward, but the answer choices may assume that some people don't know one term from another. For example, one answer choice to a median question may be the mean (the average). One answer choice to a range question may be the mode. In each question, circle the word that tells you what you're looking for to keep from falling for this trap.

Try a sample statistics problem for yourself.

EXAMPLE

Find the range of the numbers 11, 18, 29, 17, 18, −4, 0, 11, 18.

(A) 33

(B) 29

(C) 19

(D) 0

(E) −4

Ah, did this one fool you? True, 33 is not one of the numbers in the set. But to find the range, you subtract the smallest from the largest number: $29 - (-4) = 29 + 4 = 33$. So the correct answer is (A).

Abracadabra: Elementary Algebra

Algebra is the study of properties of operations carried out on sets of numbers. That definition may sound like mumbo-jumbo, but, bottom line, algebra is just arithmetic in which symbols — usually letters — stand in for numbers. You study algebra to solve equations and to find the values of variables. The ACT gives you all sorts of opportunities to "solve the equation for *x*," so this chapter's here to review the basics of problem-solving.

Variables 101

As you probably already know, you encounter a lot of variables in algebra problems. *Variables* are merely symbols that stand in for numbers. Usually the symbols take the form of the letters x, y, and z and represent specific numeric values. True to their name, variables' values can change depending on the equation they're in.

Constants, on the other hand, are numbers that don't change their values in a specific problem. In algebra, letters can refer to constants, but they don't change their values in an equation like variables do. To distinguish constants from variables, the ACT generally designates constants with the letters a, b, or c.

Think of variables as stand-ins for concrete things. For example, if a store charges a certain price for apples and a different price for oranges and you buy two apples and four oranges, the clerk can't just ring up your purchase by adding $2 + 4$ to get 6 and then applying one price. If he did, he'd be incorrectly comparing apples and oranges! In algebra, you use variables to stand in for the price of apples and oranges, something, for instance, like a for apple and o for orange. When you include variables, the equation to figure out the total price of your order looks something like this: $2a + 4o = $ total cost.

The combination of a number and a variable multiplied together is called a *term*. In the case of your fruit shopping spree, $2a$ and $4o$ are both terms. The number part of the term is called the *coefficient*. When you have a collection of these terms joined by addition and/or subtraction, you've got yourself an *algebraic expression*.

Terms that have the same variable (and the same exponents on those variables), even if they have different coefficients, are called *like terms*. For example, you may see an expression that looks something like this:

$$5x + 3y - 2x + y = ?$$

$5x$ and $-2x$ are like terms because they both contain an x variable; $3y$ and y are also like terms because they both contain the y variable.

If a variable doesn't have a coefficient next to it, its coefficient is 1; so y really means $1y$. To combine the like terms, add or subtract their coefficients. In this example, you combine the x terms by adding 5 and -2. To combine the y variable terms, you add the coefficients of 3 and 1. Your original expression with four terms simplifies to two: $3x + 4y$.

On the ACT, you work with variables to perform some basic algebraic procedures. We walk you through these procedures in the following sections.

Trivia Question: Where was algebra supposedly invented? *Answer:* Muslim scholars invented Algebra in Zabid, Yemen. See? You can't blame the Greeks for everything!

Solving simple equations

One of the first algebraic procedures you need to know is how to solve for x in an equation. To solve for x, follow these steps:

1. **Isolate the variable.**

   In other words, get all the x's on one side and all the non-x's on the other side.

2. **Add or subtract all the x's on one side; add or subtract all the non-x's on the other side.**

3. **Divide both sides of the equation by the number in front of the x.**

Try out this procedure by solving for x in this equation: $3x + 7 = 9x - 5$.

1. **Isolate the variable.**

Move the $3x$ to the right by subtracting it from both sides. In other words, *change the sign* to make it $-3x$.

WARNING

Forgetting to change the sign is one of the most common careless mistakes that students make. To catch this mistake on the ACT, test makers often include trap answer choices that you'd get if you forgot to change the sign.

Move the -5 to the left, changing the sign to make it $+5$. You now have $7 + 5 = 9x - 3x$.

2. **Add the x's on one side; subtract the non-x's on the other side.**

$12 = 6x$

3. **Divide both sides by the 6 that's next to the x.**

$2 = x$

TIP

If you're weak in algebra or know that you often make careless mistakes, plug the 2 back into the equation to make sure it works:

$$3(2) + 7 = 9(2) - 5$$
$$6 + 7 = 18 - 5$$
$$13 = 13$$

If you absolutely hate algebra, see whether you can simply plug in the answer choices. If this were a problem-solving question with multiple-choice answers, you could plug 'n' chug to get the answer.

EXAMPLE

$3x + 7 = 9x - 5$. Solve for x.

(A) 7

(B) $5\frac{1}{2}$

(C) 5

(D) $3\frac{1}{2}$

(E) 2

Don't ask for trouble. Keep life simple by starting with the simple answers first, and begin in the middle with Choice (C). That is, try plugging in 5. When it doesn't work, don't bother plugging in $3\frac{1}{2}$. That's too much work. Go right down to 2. The correct answer is (E).

TIP

If all the easy answers don't work, go back to the harder answer of $3\frac{1}{2}$, but why fuss with it unless you absolutely have to?

Adding and subtracting expressions

If a question asks you to add together two or more expressions, you can set them up vertically like you would for an addition problem in arithmetic. Just remember that you can combine only like terms this way. Here's an example:

$$3x + 4y - 7z$$
$$2x - 2y + 8z$$
$$\underline{-x + 3y + 6z}$$
$$4x + 3y + 7z$$

To subtract expressions, distribute the minus sign throughout the second expression and then combine the like terms. (To review the distributive property of multiplication, go to the earlier section, "Minor Surgery: Basic Math Operations.") Here's an example of how to subtract two expressions:

$$\left(2x^2 - 3xy - 6y^2\right) - \left(-4x^2 - 6xy + 2y^2\right) = 2x^2 - 3xy - 6y^2 + 4x^2 + 6xy - 2y^2 = 6x^2 + 3xy - 8y^2 =$$

WARNING

Notice that distributing the minus sign changes the signs of all the terms in the second expression. Make sure you keep the signs straight when you subtract expressions.

Multiplying and dividing expressions

When you multiply a term by a *binomial* (an expression with two terms), you have to multiply the number by each term in the binomial, like so:

$$4x(x - 3) = 4x(x) - 12x = 4x^2 - 12x$$

To divide a binomial, just divide each term in the binomial by the term, like so:

$$\frac{16x^2 + 4x}{4x} = \frac{16x^2}{4x} + \frac{4x}{4x} = 4x + 1$$

An easy way to multiply *polynomials* (expressions with many terms) is by stacking the two numbers to be multiplied on top of each other. Say you're asked to multiply these expressions: $\left(x^2 + 2xy + y^2\right)(x - y)$. Don't pass out! First of all, the ACT rarely asks you to perform this task. Second, you can calculate this expression just like an old-fashioned arithmetic problem. Just remember to multiply each term in the second line by each term in the first line, like so:

$$x^2 + 2xy + y^2$$
$$\underline{x - y}$$
$$x^3 + 2x^2y + xy^2$$
$$\underline{-x^2y - 2xy^2 - y^2}$$
$$x^3 + x^2y - xy^2 - y^2$$

TIP

Line up your numbers during the first round of multiplication so that like terms match up before you add your first two products together.

Curses! FOILed again

When you have to multiply two binomials, use the FOIL method. *FOIL* stands for *First, Outer, Inner, Last* and refers to the order in which you multiply the variables in parentheses when you multiply two expressions. The result is a quadratic expression. You can practice FOILing by using the equation $(a + b)(a - b) = ?$ and following these steps.

1. Multiply the *First* variables: $a(a) = a^2$.

2. Multiply the *Outer* variables: $a(-b) = -ab$.

3. Multiply the *Inner* variables: $b(a) = ba$ (which is the same as *ab*).

Remember that you can multiply numbers forward or backward, such that $ab = ba$.

4. **Multiply the *Last* variables:** $b(b) = b^2$.

5. **Combine like terms:** $-ab + ab = 0ab$.

The positive and negative ab cancel each other out. So you're left with only $a^2 - b^2$.

Try another one: $(3a + b)(a - 2b) = ?$.

1. **Multiply the *First* terms:** $3a(a) = 3a^2$.

2. **Multiply the *Outer* terms:** $3a(-2b) = -6ab$.

3. **Multiply the *Inner* terms:** $b(a) = ba$ (which is the same as ab).

4. **Multiply the *Last* terms:** $b(-2b) = -2b^2$.

5. **Combine like terms:** $-6ab + ab = -5ab$.

The final answer is $3a^2 - 5ab - 2b^2$.

TIP

You need to out-and-out *memorize* the following three FOIL problems. Don't bother to work them out every time; know them by heart. Doing so saves you time, careless mistakes, and acute misery on the actual exam.

» $(a + b)^2 = a^2 + 2ab + b^2$

You can prove this equation by using FOIL to multiply $(a + b)(a + b)$.

» **Multiply the *First* terms:** $a(a) = a^2$.

» **Multiply the *Outer* terms:** $a(-b) = -ab$.

» **Multiply the *Inner* terms:** $b(a) = ba$.

» **Multiply the *Last* terms:** $b(b) = b^2$.

» **Combine like terms:** $ab + ab = 2ab$.

The final solution is $a^2 + 2ab + b^2$.

» $(a - b)^2 = a^2 - 2ab + b^2$

You can prove this equation by using FOIL to multiply $(a - b)(a - b)$.

Notice that the b^2 at the end is positive, not negative, because multiplying a negative times a negative gives you a positive.

» $(a - b)(a + b) = a^2 - b^2$

You can prove this equation by using FOIL to multiply $(a - b)(a + b)$.

Note that the middle term drops out because $+ab$ cancels out $-ab$.

Extracting by factoring

Now that you know how to do algebra forward (by distributing and FOILing), are you ready to do it backward? In this section, we show you how to switch to reverse gear and do some factoring.

Factors are the terms that make up a product. Extracting common factors can make expressions much easier to deal with. See how many common factors you can find in this expression; then extract, or *factor*, them out:

$$-14x^3 - 35x^6$$

First, you can pull out −7 because it goes into both −14 and −35. Doing so gives you $-7\left(2x^3 + 5x^6\right)$.

Next, you can take out the common factor of x^3 because x^3 is part of both terms. The simplified result is $-7x^3\left(2 + 5x^3\right)$.

You also need to know how to factor quadratic equations, which you accomplish by using FOIL in reverse. Say that the test gives you $x^2 + 13x + 42 = 0$ and asks you to solve for x. Take this problem one step at a time:

1. **Draw two sets of parentheses.**

$(\ )(\ ) = 0$

2. **To get x^2, the *First* terms have to be x and x, so fill those in first.**

$(x\ )(x\ ) = 0$

3. **Look at the *Outer* terms.**

You need two numbers that multiply together to get +42. Well, you have several possibilities: 42 and 1, 21 and 2, or 6 and 7. You can even have two negative numbers: –42 and –1, –21 and –2, or –6 and –7. You can't be sure which numbers to choose yet, so go on to the next step.

4. **Look at the *Inner* terms.**

You have to add two values to get +13. What's the first thing that springs to mind? Probably 6 + 7. Hey, that's one of the possible combinations of numbers you came up with in Step 3 for the *Outer* terms! Plug them in and multiply.

$$(x+6)(x+7) =$$
$$x^2 + 7x + 6x + 42 =$$
$$x^2 + 13x + 42 =$$

5. **Solve for x.**

If the whole equation equals 0, then either $(x+6) = 0$ or $(x+7) = 0$. After all, any number times 0 equals 0. Therefore, when you solve for x for either of these possibilities, x can equal –6 or –7.

The ACT tests your ability to factor quadratic equations in a variety of ways. Here's a sample problem:

Which of the follow is a possible sum of the two solutions for the equation, $x^2 - 11x + 30 = 0$?

(A) −17

(B) −11

(C) −1

(D) 1

(E) 11

You find the solutions for a quadratic equation by finding its binomial factors and setting both equal to 0. The two values whose product is 30 and whose sum is −11 are −6 and −5: $-6 \times -5 = 30$ and $-5 + (-6) = -11$. So the binomial factors are $(x-5)$ and $(x-6)$. Set both equal to 0 and solve for x:

$$x - 5 = 0$$
$$x = 5$$
$$x - 6 = 0$$
$$x = 6$$

So the two solutions are 5 and 6. Their sum is 11, which is Choice (E). If you pick Choice (B), you've missed a step. You've forgotten to set the factors equal to zero and solve for x. The signs for the solutions to a quadratic are the opposite of those of the values within the binomial factor.

TIP

Whenever you see an ACT problem that includes a quadratic equation, you can pretty much bet you're going to have to perform some factoring. Make sure you're familiar with the steps because factoring problems crop up frequently. Or you can use your graphing calculator to factor quadratic equations. If your calculator doesn't already contain the program, you can find ways to add the program on the Internet.

Solving a system of equations

Suppose you have two algebraic equations with two different variables. For example, an ACT question may ask you to solve for x when $4x + 5y = 30$ and $y + x = 2$. You're dealing with a *system of equations*. By themselves, there could be an infinite number of values for x and y. However, when considered together, there is only one value for x and one value for y as long as the two equations aren't equal.

There are two ways to solve for a variable in simultaneous equations: substitution or elimination.

Here's how substitution works. Because you're solving for x, you need to get rid of the y variable. Find a value for y in one equation and substitute that value for y in the other equation.

For the preceding sample equations, it takes fewer steps to solve for y in the second equation. You get $y = 2 - x$.

All you really have to do then is substitute $2 - x$ for the value of y in the first equation and solve for x:

$$4x + 5(2 - x) = 30$$
$$4x + 10 - 5x = 30$$
$$10 - x = 30$$
$$-x = 20$$
$$x = -20$$

An easier way to solve for x, especially for more complex equations, may be by elimination — stacking the equations and manipulating them in a way that allows you to eliminate one variable and solve for the other.

Here's how it's done for this problem. You need to get rid of the y variable, which you can do if you change y in the second equation to $-5y$. You can accomplish this feat by multiplying every term in the second equation by -5: $(-5)y + (-5)x = (-5)2$. It's legal to change the equation as long as you perform the same operation with each of its terms. The resulting equation is $-5y - 5x = -10$. Just change the order of the first equation so the like terms match up, stack the two equations, and solve for x:

$$5y + 4x = 30$$
$$\underline{-5y - 5x = -10}$$
$$0 - x = 20$$
$$x = -20$$

Either method gives you the same result: $x = -20$.

If an ACT question tells you that a system of equations has no solutions or unlimited solutions, the two equations are equal. To solve it, create equal equations. So, the ACT may give you the following equations, tell you that there are no solutions for the system, and ask you to solve for a.

$$5y + 4x = 30$$
$$-15y - 12x = -10a$$

You just need to recognize that the second equation is the same as the first with each term multiplied by -3. Therefore, the value for a that would make the third term equal to 30×-3 is 9: $30 \times -3 = -10(9)$.

So don't get discouraged if you see two equations with two similar variables. You have several tools for dealing with them. They're not as hard to work with as you think!

» Identifying the ins and outs of triangles and similar figures

» Centering in on polygons and circles

» Applying SOH CAH TOA and other trigonometric identities

» Working with the unit circle

Chapter **9**

Getting into Shapes: Geometry and Trig Review

Geometry may seem like one of the areas that can mess you up on the ACT. But it's easy when you take the time to memorize some rules. This chapter provides a lightning-fast review of the major points of geometry so that you can go into the test equipped to tackle the geometry questions with ease.

Toeing the Line

You don't need to memorize the following definitions for the ACT, but you do need to be familiar with them. Here are the common terms about lines that may pop up on your test:

» **Line segment:** The set of points on a line between any two points on that line. Basically, a line segment is just a piece of a line from one point to another that contains those two points and all the points in between. See line segment *CD* in Figure 9-1.

» **Midpoint:** The point halfway (an equal distance) between two endpoints on a line segment. In Figure 9-1, point *D* is the midpoint between points *A* and *B.*

FIGURE 9-1:
Line and line segment.

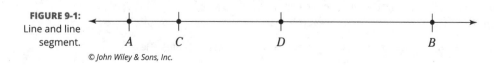

A   *C*   *D*   *B*

© John Wiley & Sons, Inc.

>> **Intersect:** To cross. Two lines can intersect each other much like two streets cross each other at an intersection.

>> **Vertical line:** A line that runs straight up and down. Figure 9-2 shows you an example of a vertical line as well as the following three kinds of lines.

>> **Horizontal line:** A line that runs straight across from left to right (refer to Figure 9-2).

>> **Parallel lines:** Lines that run in the same direction and keep the same distance apart. Parallel lines never intersect one another (refer to Figure 9-2).

>> **Perpendicular lines:** Two lines that intersect to form a square corner. The intersection of two perpendicular lines forms a right, or 90-degree, angle (refer to Figure 9-2).

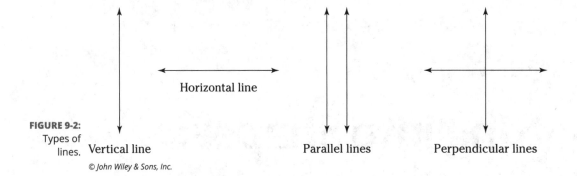

FIGURE 9-2:
Types of
lines.

Horizontal line

Vertical line

Parallel lines

Perpendicular lines

© John Wiley & Sons, Inc.

Analyzing Angles

Angle problems make up a big part of the ACT geometry test. Fortunately, understanding angles is easy when you memorize a few basic concepts. After all, you don't have to do any proofs on the test. Finding an angle is usually a matter of simple addition or subtraction.

Here are a few things you need to know about angles to succeed on the ACT:

>> **Angles that are greater than 0 but less than 90 degrees are called *acute angles*.** Think of an acute angle as being a *cute* little angle (see Figure 9-3).

>> **Angles that are equal to 90 degrees are called *right angles*.** They're formed by perpendicular lines and indicated by a box in the corner of the two intersecting lines (refer to Figure 9-3).

WARNING

Don't automatically assume that angles that look like right angles are right angles. Without calculating the degree of the angle, you can't know for certain that an angle is a right angle unless one of the following is true:

- The problem directly tells you, "This is a right angle."

- You see the perpendicular symbol ⊥, indicating that the lines form a 90-degree angle.

- You see a box in the angle, like the one in Figure 9-3.

>> **Angles that are greater than 90 degrees but less than 180 degrees are called *obtuse angles*.** Think of obtuse as obese; an obese (or fat) angle is an obtuse angle (refer to Figure 9-3).

>> **Angles that measure exactly 180 degrees are called *straight angles*.** (Refer to Figure 9-3.)

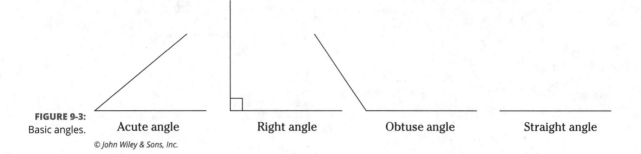

FIGURE 9-3:
Basic angles.

Acute angle   Right angle   Obtuse angle   Straight angle

© John Wiley & Sons, Inc.

» **Angles that total 90 degrees are called *complementary angles.*** Think of *C* for corner (the lines form a 90-degree corner angle) and *C* for complementary (see Figure 9-4).

» **Angles that total 180 degrees are called *supplementary angles.*** Think of *S* for supplementary (or straight) angles. Be careful not to confuse complementary angles with supplementary angles. If you're likely to get them confused, just think alphabetically: *C* comes before *S* in the alphabet; 90 comes before 180 when you count (refer to Figure 9-4).

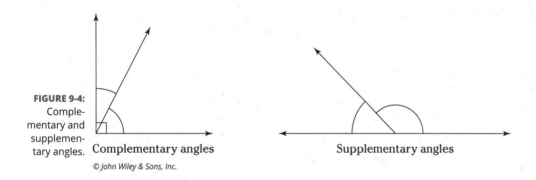

FIGURE 9-4:
Complementary and supplementary angles.

Complementary angles   Supplementary angles

© John Wiley & Sons, Inc.

» **Angles that are greater than 180 degrees but less than 360 degrees are called *reflex angles.*** (See Figure 9-5 for an example.)

320°

FIGURE 9-5:
Reflex angle.

© John Wiley & Sons, Inc.

» **Angles around a point total 360 degrees.** (See Figure 9-6.)

» **The exterior angles of any figure are supplementary to the two opposite interior angles and always total 360 degrees.** (Refer to Figure 9-6.)

» **Angles that are opposite each other have equal measures and are called *vertical angles.*** Just remember that vertical angles are *across* from each other, whether they're up and down (vertical) or side by side (horizontal). (Figure 9-7 shows two sets of vertical angles.)

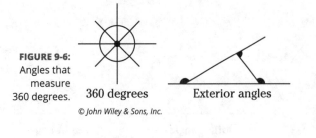

FIGURE 9-6:
Angles that
measure
360 degrees.

360 degrees   Exterior angles

© John Wiley & Sons, Inc.

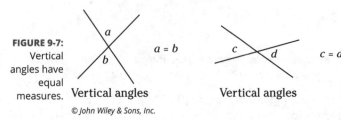

FIGURE 9-7:
Vertical
angles have
equal
measures.

$a = b$ $c = d$

Vertical angles   Vertical angles

© John Wiley & Sons, Inc.

> » **Angles in the same position around two parallel lines and a transversal are called** *corresponding angles* **and have equal measures.** (Figure 9-8 shows two sets of corresponding angles.)

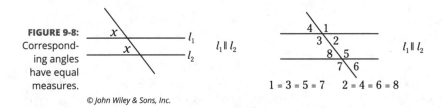

FIGURE 9-8:
Corresponding angles
have equal
measures.

$l_1 \parallel l_2$ $l_1 \parallel l_2$

$1 = 3 = 5 = 7$ $2 = 4 = 6 = 8$

© John Wiley & Sons, Inc.

TIP

When you see two parallel lines and a *transversal* (that's the line going across the parallel lines), number the angles. Start in the upper-right corner with 1 and go clockwise. For the second batch of angles, start in the upper-right corner with 5 and go clockwise. (See the second figure in Figure 9-8 for an example.) Note that in Figure 9-8, all odd-numbered angles are equal and all even-numbered angles are equal.

Be careful not to zigzag back and forth when numbering. If you zig when you should have zagged, you can no longer use the tip that all even-numbered angles are equal to one another and all odd-numbered angles are equal to one another.

Triangle Trauma

Many of the geometry problems on the ACT require you to know a lot about triangles. Remember the facts and rules about triangles in this section, and you're on your way to acing geometry questions.

Classifying triangles

Triangles are classified based on the measurements of their sides and angles. Here are the types of triangles you may need to know for the ACT:

» **Equilateral:** A triangle with three equal sides and three equal angles (see Figure 9-9).

» **Isosceles:** A triangle with two equal sides and two equal angles. The angles opposite equal sides in an isosceles triangle are also equal (refer to Figure 9-9).

» **Scalene:** A triangle with no equal sides and no equal angles (refer to Figure 9-9).

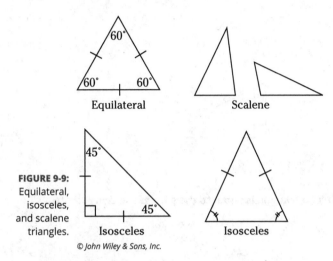

FIGURE 9-9: Equilateral, isosceles, and scalene triangles.

Equilateral   Scalene

Isosceles   Isosceles

© John Wiley & Sons, Inc.

Sizing up triangles

When you're figuring out ACT questions that deal with triangles, you need to know these rules about the measurements of their sides and angles:

» **In any triangle, the largest angle is opposite the longest side.** (See Figure 9-10.)

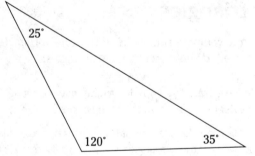

FIGURE 9-10: The largest angle is opposite the longest side.

© John Wiley & Sons, Inc.

» **In any triangle, the sum of the lengths of two sides must be greater than the length of the third side.**

In other words, $a + b > c$, where a, b, and c are the sides of the triangle (see Figure 9-11).

» **In any type of triangle, the sum of the interior angles is 180 degrees.** (See Figure 9-12.)

FIGURE 9-11:
The sum of the lengths of two sides of a triangle is greater than the length of the third side.

$3 + 3 > 3$

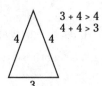

$3 + 4 > 4$
$4 + 4 > 3$

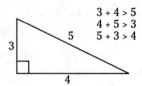

$3 + 4 > 5$
$4 + 5 > 3$
$5 + 3 > 4$

© John Wiley & Sons, Inc.

FIGURE 9-12:
The sum of the interior angles of a triangle is 180 degrees.

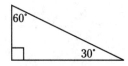

© John Wiley & Sons, Inc.

>> **The measure of an exterior angle of a triangle is equal to the sum of the two remote interior angles.** (See Figure 9-13.)

FIGURE 9-13:
The measure of an exterior angle is equal to the sum of the two remote interior angles.

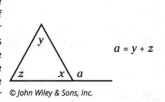

$a = y + z$

© John Wiley & Sons, Inc.

Zeroing in on similar triangles

Several ACT math questions require you to compare similar triangles. *Similar triangles* look alike but are different sizes. Here's what you need to know about similar triangles:

>> Similar triangles have the same angle measures. If you can determine that two triangles contain angles that measure the same degrees, you know the triangles are similar.

>> The sides of similar triangles are in proportion. For example, if the heights of two similar triangles are in a ratio of 2:3, then the bases of those triangles are also in a ratio of 2:3 (see Figure 9-14).

FIGURE 9-14:
Similar triangles have proportionate sides.

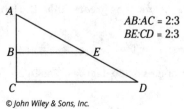

$AB{:}AC = 2{:}3$
$BE{:}CD = 2{:}3$

© John Wiley & Sons, Inc.

Don't assume that triangles are similar on the ACT just because they look similar to you. The only way you know two triangles are similar is if the test tells you they are or you can determine that their angle measures are the same.

REMEMBER

Figuring out area and perimeter

To succeed on the Mathematics Test, you should be able to figure out the area and perimeter of triangles in your sleep. Memorize these formulas:

» **The area of a triangle is $\frac{1}{2}$ base × height.**

The height is always a line perpendicular to the base. The height may be a side of the triangle, as in a right triangle (see Figure 9-15a). But the height may also be inside the triangle. In that case, it's often represented by a dashed line and a small 90-degree box (see Figure 9-15b). The height may also be outside the triangle. You can always drop an altitude. That is, put your pencil on the tallest point of the triangle and draw a line straight from that point to where the base would be if it were extended (see Figure 9-15c).

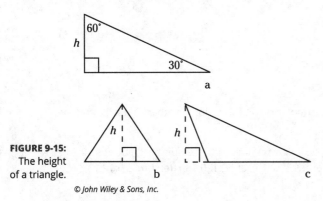

FIGURE 9-15: The height of a triangle.

© John Wiley & Sons, Inc.

» **The perimeter of a triangle is the sum of the lengths of its sides.** (See Figure 9-16.)

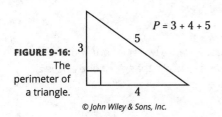

FIGURE 9-16: The perimeter of a triangle.

© John Wiley & Sons, Inc.

Taking the shortcut: Pythagorean triples and other common side ratios

In any right triangle, you can find the lengths of the sides by using the *Pythagorean theorem*, which looks like this:

$$a^2 + b^2 = c^2$$

In this formula, a and b are the sides of the triangle and *c* is the hypotenuse. The *hypotenuse* is always opposite the 90-degree angle and is always the longest side of the triangle.

Keep in mind that the Pythagorean theorem works only on right triangles. If a triangle doesn't have a right — or 90-degree — angle, you can't use any of the information in this section.

Having to work through the whole Pythagorean theorem formula every time you want to find the length of a right triangle's side is a pain in the posterior. To make your life a little easier, memorize these Pythagorean triples and other common right-triangle side ratios:

» **Ratio 3:4:5.** If one side of the triangle is 3 in this ratio, the other side is 4 and the hypotenuse is 5 (see Figure 9-17).

Because this is a ratio, the sides can be in any multiple of these numbers, such as 6:8:10 (two times 3:4:5), 9:12:15 (three times 3:4:5), or 27:36:45 (nine times 3:4:5).

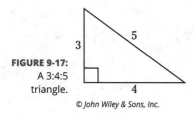

FIGURE 9-17:
A 3:4:5 triangle.

© John Wiley & Sons, Inc.

» **Ratio 5:12:13.** If one side of the right triangle is 5 in this ratio, the other side is 12 and the hypotenuse is 13 (see Figure 9-18).

Because this is a ratio, the sides can be in any multiple of these numbers, such as 10:24:26 (two times 5:12:13), 15:36:39 (three times 5:12:13), or 50:120:130 (ten times 5:12:13).

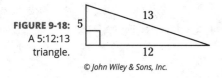

FIGURE 9-18:
A 5:12:13 triangle.

© John Wiley & Sons, Inc.

» **Ratio $s : s : s\sqrt{2}$, where *s* stands for the side of the figure.** Because two sides are equal, this formula applies to an isosceles right triangle, also known as a 45:45:90 triangle. If one side is 2, then the other side is also 2 and the hypotenuse is $2\sqrt{2}$ (see Figure 9-19).

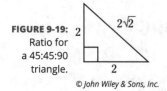

FIGURE 9-19:
Ratio for a 45:45:90 triangle.

© John Wiley & Sons, Inc.

TIP

This formula is great to know for squares. If a question tells you that the side of a square is 5 and wants to know the diagonal of the square, you know immediately that it is $5\sqrt{2}$. Why? A square's diagonal cuts the square into two isosceles right triangles (*isosceles* because all sides of the square are equal; *right* because all angles in a square are right angles). What is the diagonal of a square of side 64? $64\sqrt{2}$.

You can write this ratio another way. Instead of writing $s : s : s\sqrt{2}$, write $\frac{s}{\sqrt{2}} : \frac{s}{\sqrt{2}} : s$, where s still stands for the side of the triangle, but now you've divided everything in the ratio by $\sqrt{2}$. Why do you need this complicated ratio? Suppose you're told that the diagonal of a square is 5. That's enough information to figure out the area of the square and its perimeter.

If you know the ratio $\frac{s}{\sqrt{2}} : \frac{s}{\sqrt{2}} : s$, you know that s stands for the hypotenuse of the triangle, which is also the diagonal of the square. If s = 5, then the side of the square is $\frac{5}{\sqrt{2}}$ and you can figure out the area or the perimeter. After you know the side of a square, you can figure out just about anything.

>> **Ratio $s : s\sqrt{3} : 2s$.** This special formula is for the sides of a 30:60:90 triangle (see Figure 9-20).

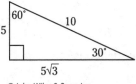

FIGURE 9-20: Ratio for a 30:60:90 triangle.

© John Wiley & Sons, Inc.

This type of triangle is a favorite of test makers. The important thing to keep in mind here is that the hypotenuse is twice the length of the side opposite the 30-degree angle. If you get a word problem that says, "Given a 30:60:90 triangle of hypotenuse 20, find the area" or "Given a 30:60:90 triangle of hypotenuse 100, find the perimeter," you can do so because you can find the lengths of the other sides (see Figure 9-21 for details).

FIGURE 9-21: Using the ratio for a 30:60:90 triangle to find the lengths of the triangle's sides.

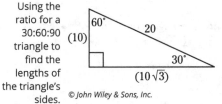 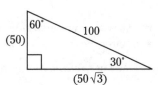

© John Wiley & Sons, Inc.

Thanks 4 Nothing: A Quick Look at Quadrilaterals

Another favorite figure of the ACT test-making folks is the *quadrilateral*, which is the fancy label mathematicians give shapes with four sides. Here's a summary of the four-sided figures you may see on the ACT:

>> **A *quadrilateral* is any four-sided figure.**

The interior angles of any quadrilateral total 360 degrees. You can cut any quadrilateral into two 180-degree triangles (see Figure 9-22).

FIGURE 9-22: A quadrilateral.

© John Wiley & Sons, Inc.

>> **A *square* is a quadrilateral with four equal sides and four right angles.**

The area of a square is s^2 (or base × height) or $\frac{1}{2}d^2$, where d stands for the *diagonal* (see Figure 9-23).

$A = s^2$

$A = \frac{1}{2}d^2$

FIGURE 9-23: A square.

© John Wiley & Sons, Inc.

>> **A *rhombus* is a quadrilateral with four equal sides and four angles that are not necessarily right angles.** A rhombus often looks like a drunken square, tipsy on its side and wobbly.

The area of a rhombus is $\frac{1}{2}d_1d_2$ or $\frac{1}{2}\text{diagonal}_1 \times \text{diagonal}_2$ (see Figure 9-24).

All squares are rhombuses, but not all rhombuses are squares.

REMEMBER

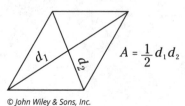

$A = \frac{1}{2}d_1d_2$

FIGURE 9-24: A rhombus.

© John Wiley & Sons, Inc.

>> A *rectangle* is a quadrilateral with four right angles and two opposite and equal pairs of sides. That is, the top and bottom sides are equal, and the right and left sides are equal.

The area of a rectangle is $\text{length} \times \text{width}$, which is the same as $\text{base} \times \text{height}$ (see Figure 9-25).

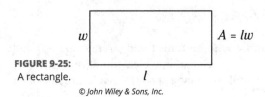

FIGURE 9-25: A rectangle.

© John Wiley & Sons, Inc.

>> A *parallelogram* is a quadrilateral with two opposite and equal pairs of sides. The top and bottom sides are equal, and the right and left sides are equal. Opposite angles are equal but not necessarily right (or 90 degrees).

The area of a parallelogram is $\text{base} \times \text{height}$. Remember that the height is always a perpendicular line from the tallest point of the figure down to the base (see Figure 9-26). Diagonals of a parallelogram bisect each other.

All rectangles are parallelograms, but not all parallelograms are rectangles.

REMEMBER

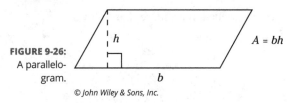

FIGURE 9-26: A parallelogram.

© John Wiley & Sons, Inc.

>> A *trapezoid* is a quadrilateral with two parallel sides and two nonparallel sides.

The area of a trapezoid is $\frac{1}{2}\left(\text{base}_1 + \text{base}_2\right) \times \text{height}$. We like to think of it as the average of the two bases times the height. It makes no difference which base you label base_1 and which you label base_2, because you're adding them together (see Figure 9-27).

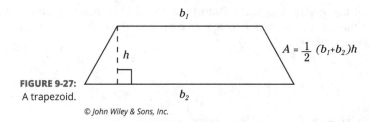

FIGURE 9-27: A trapezoid.

© John Wiley & Sons, Inc.

Keep in mind that some quadrilaterals, like the one in Figure 9-28, don't have nice, neat shapes or special names.

WARNING

If you see a strange shape, don't immediately say that you have no way of finding its area. You may be able to divide the quadrilateral in Figure 9-28 into two triangles, find the area of each triangle, and then add them together.

FIGURE 9-28:
Not all
quadrilater-
als have
special
names.

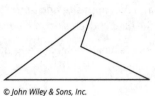

© John Wiley & Sons, Inc.

Knowing how to find the area of quadrilaterals (those with both neat and strange shapes) and other figures can help you solve *shaded-area* or *leftover* problems, in which you have to subtract the unshaded area from the total area. Here's an example of what a shaded-area figure may look like on the ACT:

Shaded areas can often be unusual shapes. Your first reaction may be that you can't possibly find the area of that shape. Generally, you're right, but you don't have to find the area directly. Instead, be sly, devious, and sneaky; in other words, think the ACT way! Find the area of the total figure, find the area of the unshaded portion, and subtract.

What is the area of the shaded portion of the circle inscribed in a square that follows?

EXAMPLE

(F) 64

(G) 16π

(H) $64 - 16\pi$

(J) $48 - 16\pi$

(K) 48

First, you have to find the area of the square. You know that the radius of the circle is 4, so the diameter of the circle, as well as the side of the square, is 8. $8 \times 8 = 64$. Therefore, the area of the square is 64. Next, find the area of the circle:

$$A = \left(4^2\right)\pi$$
$$A = 16\pi$$

Then just subtract to find the shaded area: $64 - 16\pi$. The answer is Choice (H).

Missing Parrots and Other Polly-Gones (Or Should We Say "Polygons"?)

Triangles and quadrilaterals are probably the most commonly tested polygons on the ACT. What's a polygon? A *polygon* is a closed-plane figure bounded by straight sides.

Measuring up polygons

Here's what you need to know about the side and angle measurements of polygons:

» **A polygon with all equal sides and all equal angles is called _regular_.** For example, an equilateral triangle is a regular triangle, and a square is a regular quadrilateral.

The ACT rarely asks you to find the areas of any polygons with more than four sides.

» **The _perimeter_ of a polygon is the sum of the lengths of all the sides.**

» **The _exterior angle measure_ of any polygon, also known as the sum of its exterior angles, is 360 degrees.** (An _exterior angle_ is the angle formed by any side of the polygon and the line that's created when you extend the adjacent side.)

» To find the _interior angle measure_ of any regular polygon, also known as the sum of its interior angles, use the formula $(n-2)180°$, where n stands for the number of sides. For example, to find the interior angle measure for a pentagon (a five-sided figure), just substitute 5 for n in the formula and solve:

$$(5-2)180° = 3 \times 180 = 540°$$

So the sum of the interior angles of a pentagon is 540°.

Solving for volume

The volume of any polygon is area of the base × height. If you remember this formula, you don't have to memorize any of the following specific volume formulas. If you take the time to memorize specific formulas, though, you'll use fewer steps to work out volume problems and you'll save some precious time.

» **Volume of a cube** $= e^3$

A _cube_ is a three-dimensional square. All of a cube's dimensions are the same; that is, length = width = height. In a cube, these dimensions are called _edges_ (see Figure 9-29).

FIGURE 9-29:
Volume of a cube.

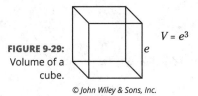

$V = e^3$

© John Wiley & Sons, Inc.

» **Volume of a rectangular solid** $= lwh$

A _rectangular solid_ is a box. The base of a box is a rectangle, which has an area of length × width. Multiply that by the height to fit the original volume formula: Volume $= ($area of base$) \times$ height, or $V = lwh$ (see Figure 9-30).

FIGURE 9-30:
Volume of a rectangular solid.

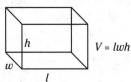

$V = lwh$

© John Wiley & Sons, Inc.

>> **Volume of a cylinder =** $\left(\pi r^2\right)h$

Think of a *cylinder* as a can of soup. The base of a cylinder is a circle. The area of a circle is πr^2. Multiply that by the height of the cylinder to get the volume. Note that the top and bottom of a cylinder are identical circles. If you know the radius of either the top base or the bottom base, you can find the area of the circle (see Figure 9-31). (See the section, "Running Around in Circles," for more on circles.)

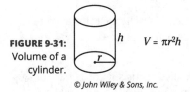

FIGURE 9-31:
Volume of a
cylinder.

$V = \pi r^2 h$

© John Wiley & Sons, Inc.

Running Around in Circles

Did you hear about the rube who pulled his son out of college, claiming that the school was filling his head with nonsense? As the rube said, "Joe Bob told me that he learned πr^2. But any fool knows that *pie* are round; *cornbread* are square!"

Circles are among the least complicated geometry concepts. To excel on circle questions, you must remember the vocabulary and be able to distinguish an arc from a sector and an inscribed angle from a central angle. Here's a quick review of the basics:

>> **A circle's *radius* goes from the center of the circle to its *circumference* (or perimeter).** (See Figure 9-32.)

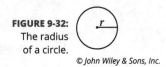

FIGURE 9-32:
The radius
of a circle.

© John Wiley & Sons, Inc.

>> **A circle gets its name from its *midpoint* (or center).**

For example, the circle in Figure 9-33 is called circle *M* because its midpoint is *M*.

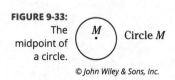

FIGURE 9-33:
The
midpoint of
a circle.

Circle *M*

© John Wiley & Sons, Inc.

>> **A circle's *diameter* connects two points on the circumference of the circle, goes through the circle's center, and is equal to two radii (which is the plural of *radius*).** (See Figure 9-34.)

>> **A *chord* connects any two points on a circle.** (See Figure 9-35 for two examples.)

The longest chord in a circle is the diameter.

>> **The area of a circle is πr^2.** (See Figure 9-36.)

>> The circumference of a circle is $2\pi r$ or πd because two radii equal one diameter.

TIP

On the Math Test, you may encounter a wheel question in which you're asked how much distance a wheel covers or how many times a wheel revolves. Or you may be asked to figure out the distance that a minute hand travels around a clock. The key to solving these types of questions is knowing that one rotation of a wheel or minute hand equals one circumference of that wheel or clock.

>> **A *central angle* has its endpoints on the circumference of the circle and its center at the center of the circle.**

The degree measure of a central angle is the same as the degree measure of its intercepted arc (see Figure 9-37). (Keep reading to find out what an arc is.)

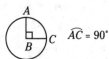
>> **An *inscribed angle* has both its endpoints and its center on the circumference of the circle.**

The degree measure of an inscribed angle is half the degree measure of its intercepted arc (see Figure 9-38).

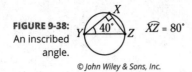

FIGURE 9-38: An inscribed angle.

© John Wiley & Sons, Inc.

Thales's theorem tells you that the endpoints of an inscribed angle in a semicircle create a right triangle. If *YZ* in the figure is the diameter of the circle, ∠*YXZ* is a right angle and △*YXZ* is a right triangle.

>> **When a central angle and an inscribed angle have the same endpoints, the degree measure of the central angle is twice that of the inscribed angle.** (See Figure 9-39.)

FIGURE 9-39: Central and inscribed angles with the same endpoints.

© John Wiley & Sons, Inc.

>> **The degree measure of a circle is 360.**

>> **An *arc* is a portion of the circumference of a circle.**

The degree measure of an arc is the same as its central angle and twice its inscribed angle (see Figure 9-40).

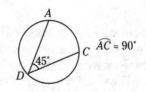

FIGURE 9-40: An arc on a circle.

© John Wiley & Sons, Inc.

To find the *length* of an arc, follow these steps:

1. **Find the circumference of the entire circle.**

2. **Put the degree measure of the arc over 360 and then reduce the fraction.**

3. **Multiply the circumference by the fraction.**

4. **A *sector* is a portion of the area of a circle.**

The degree measure of a sector is the same as its central angle and twice its inscribed angle.

To find the *area* of a sector, follow these steps:

1. **Find the area of the entire circle.**

2. **Put the degree measure of the sector over 360 and then reduce the fraction.**

3. **Multiply the area by the fraction.**

Finding the area of a sector is very similar to finding the length of an arc. The only difference is in the first step. Whereas an arc is a part of the circumference of a circle, a sector is a part of the area of a circle.

>> A *tangent line* is one that intersects (or touches) the circle at just one point.

A tangent line is always perpendicular to the radius at the point on the circumference where the line touches the circle. (See Figure 9-41.)

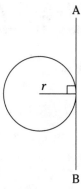

FIGURE 9-41:
Tangent line.

© John Wiley & Sons, Inc.

A pair of lines drawn from an external point and both tangent to different points on the circumference of a circle are congruent. So, lines *BC* and *CD* in Figure 9-42 are the same length, and triangle *BCD* is isosceles. The angles formed by the lines and radii at points *B* and *C* are right angles.

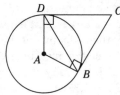

FIGURE 9-42:
Two tangent
lines from
one external
point.

© John Wiley & Sons, Inc.

Here are a few examples of how the ACT may test you about circles.

EXAMPLE

What is the area of a circle whose longest chord is 12?

(A) 144π

(B) 72π

(C) 36π

(D) 12π

(E) Cannot be determined from the information given

The diameter of this circle is 12, which means its radius is 6 because a diameter is twice the radius. The area of a circle is πr^2, and $6^2 \pi = 36\pi$. The correct answer is Choice (C).

WARNING

Choice (E) is the trap answer. If you know only that a chord of the circle is 12, you can't solve the problem. A circle has many different chords. You need to know the length of the longest chord, or the diameter.

A child's wagon has a wheel with a radius of 6 inches. If the wagon wheel travels 100 revolutions, approximately how many feet has the wagon rolled?

(F) 325

(G) 314

(H) 255

(J) 201

(K) 200

One revolution is equal to one circumference: $2\pi r$, which is approximately 12(3.14) or 37.68 inches. Multiply that by 100 to get 3,768 inches. Then divide by 12 to get 314 feet. The correct answer is Choice (G).

Find the sum of $a + b + c + d + e$.

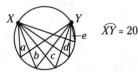

$\widehat{XY} = 20°$

Note: Figure not drawn to scale.

(A) 65 degrees

(B) 60 degrees

(C) 55 degrees

(D) 50 degrees

(E) 45 degrees

Although this figure looks a lot like a string picture you made at summer camp, with all sorts of lines running every which way, answering the question that goes along with it isn't as complicated as you may think. To get started, take the time to identify the endpoints of the angles and the center point. Each angle is an inscribed angle; it has half the degree measure of the central angle, or half the degree measure of its intercepted arc. If you look carefully at the endpoints of these angles, you see that they're all the same. They're all along arc XY, which has a measure of 20 degrees. Therefore, each angle is 10 degrees, for a total of 50. The correct answer is Choice (D).

Find the length of arc AC in Circle B, shown here.

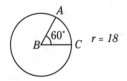

$r = 18$

(F) 36π

(G) 27π

(H) 16π

(J) 12π

(K) 6π

Take the steps one at a time. First, find the circumference of the entire circle: $C = 2\pi = 36\pi$. Don't multiply π out; problems usually leave it in that form. Next, put the degree measure of the arc over 360 and simplify. The degree measure of the arc is the same as its central angle, which is 60 degrees.

$$\frac{60}{360} = \frac{1}{6}$$

The arc is $\frac{1}{6}$ of the circumference of the circle. Multiply the circumference by the fraction:

$$36\pi \times \frac{1}{6} = 6\pi$$

The correct answer is Choice (K).

After you get the hang of these, they're kinda fun. Right?

Find the area of sector ABC in Circle B, shown here.

$r = 8$

Angle $ABC = 90°$

(A) 64π

(B) 36π

(C) 16π

(D) 12π

(E) 12π

First, find the area of the entire circle:

$$A = \pi r^2$$
$$A = 64\pi$$

Second, put the degree measure of the sector over 360. The sector is 90 degrees, the same as its central angle: $\frac{90}{360} = \frac{1}{4}$.

Third, multiply the area by the fraction:

$$64\pi \times \frac{1}{4} = 16\pi$$

The correct answer is Choice (C).

Trying Your Hand at Trigonometry

Many of our students cringe when they hear that the ACT has trigonometry questions. If you're cringing right now, too, relax and stand tall. The ACT has only a few trig questions, and this section covers what you need to know to answer most of those few, even if you've never stepped foot in a trigonometry classroom.

Dealing with trigonometric functions is about all you need to know for most of the trig questions. A few may deal with more advanced trig concepts.

Introducing trigonometric functions

ACT trigonometry questions concern trigonometric functions. *Trigonometric functions* express the relationships between the angles and sides of a right triangle in terms of one of its angles. You can answer almost every ACT trig question if you remember the mnemonic for the three basic trigonometric functions, SOH CAH TOA.

SOH CAH TOA stands for

$$\text{Sine} = \frac{\text{opposite}}{\text{hypotenuse}}$$

$$\text{Cosine} = \frac{\text{adjacent}}{\text{hypotenuse}}$$

$$\text{Tangent} = \frac{\text{opposite}}{\text{adjacent}}$$

Are you scratching your head now and asking, "Opposite? Opposite *what?*" Take a look at this right triangle and consider the guidelines that follow it.

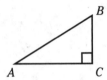

Side *AB* is the *hypotenuse* of the triangle. In relation to the angle at point *A*, side *BC* is the *opposite* side. The other side, the one that's not the hypotenuse or opposite angle *A*, is the *adjacent* side.

>> **To find sin *A* (in other words, the sine of angle *A*), all you need to do is find the length of opposite side *BC* and divide it by the length of the hypotenuse (or *AB*).**

$$\sin A = \frac{\text{opposite } A}{\text{hypotenuse}}$$

$$\sin A = \frac{\overline{BC}}{\overline{AB}}$$

Sine is usually abbreviated as *sin*; the terms mean the same thing.

>> **To find cos *A* (the cosine of angle *A*), find the length of adjacent side *AC* and use the CAH part of SOH CAH TOA.**

$$\cos A = \frac{\text{adjacent } A}{\text{hypotenuse}}$$

$$\cos A = \frac{\overline{AC}}{\overline{AB}}$$

Cosine is usually abbreviated as *cos*; they mean the same thing.

>> To find tan *A* (the tangent of angle *A*), use the TOA part of SOH CAH TOA.

$$\tan A = \frac{\text{opposite } A}{\text{adjacent } A}$$

$$\tan A = \frac{\overline{BC}}{\overline{AC}}$$

Yes, *tangent* is usually abbreviated as *tan*; they mean the same thing.

When you work with cosine and sine, keep these very simple but very important rules in mind:

>> No side in a right triangle can be greater than the hypotenuse, so you can never have a sine greater than 1.

>> Because the adjacent side can't be greater than the hypotenuse, you can never have a cosine greater than 1.

>> The sum of sine squared and cosine squared for an angle is 1, and therefore the following equations are true:

- $\sin^2\theta + \cos^2\theta = 1$
- $\sin\theta = \sqrt{1 - \cos^2\theta}$
- $\cos\theta = \sqrt{1 - \sin^2\theta}$

Additional trig functions appear less frequently on the ACT, so if you've had about all you can stand of trig, you can ignore them and still be okay on exam day. For those of you who can't get enough, review Table 9-1 for the reciprocal trig functions.

TABLE 9-1   ## Reciprocal Trigonometric Functions

Trig Function	Definition	Ratio
secant (sec)	reciprocal of sine: $\sec\theta = \dfrac{1}{\cos\theta}$	$\dfrac{hypotenuse}{opposite}$
cosecant (csc)	reciprocal of cosine: $\csc\theta = \dfrac{1}{\sin\theta}$	$\dfrac{hypotenuse}{adjacent}$
cotangent (cot)	reciprocal of tangent: $\cot\theta = \dfrac{1}{\tan\theta}$	$\dfrac{adjacent}{opposite}$

Occasionally, the ACT may spring inverse trig functions on you. Arcsine ($\sin^{-1}$), arcosine ($\cos^{-1}$), and arctangent (tan^{-1}) are the inverse functions of sine, cosine, and tangent, respectively. When you know the inverse of a function, you can calculate the corresponding angle measurement. So if you're told that $tan^{-1} = 1.192$, you could plug that value into your calculator to determine that the angle in question measures 50°. The likelihood of your encountering an inverse trig function question on the ACT is slim.

Here's an example of a common question that tests your knowledge of SOH CAH TOA.

A right triangle has an angle with a degree measure of 45. Find tan 45°.

(A) $\sqrt{2}$

(B) $\frac{\sqrt{2}}{2}$

(C) $\frac{1}{\sqrt{2}}$

(D) 0

(E) 1

First draw a 45:45:90 triangle. Remember that the ratio of the sides of this triangle is $s:s:s\sqrt{2}$, where *s* stands for the length of the side. (We discuss this ratio in an earlier section, "Taking the shortcut: Pythagorean triples and other common side ratios.")

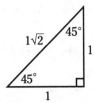

Then figure out the tan by using the TOA part of SOH CAH TOA.

$$\tan 45° = \frac{\text{opposite } 45°}{\text{adjacent } 45°}$$

$$\tan 45° = \frac{1}{1}$$

$$\tan 45° = 1$$

The answer is Choice (E). If you picked Choice (A), you tried to find the ratio of the hypotenuse to one of the other sides, which isn't one of the three main trig ratios. Choice (B) is what you'd get if you were asked to find the sine or cosine of the 45-degree angle.

REMEMBER

You know that Choice (C) can't be correct, because you can't have a radical in the denominator. If you were asked to find the sine or cosine of the 45-degree angle, you would have to rationalize the final answer: $\frac{1}{\sqrt{2}} \times \frac{\sqrt{2}}{\sqrt{2}} = \frac{\sqrt{2}}{2}$.

Circumventing the unit circle

A picture is worth a thousand words, and trigonometric functions are no exception. Once you see how trigonometric functions show up on a graph, you have a far better understanding of the repeating nature of these functions. They're called repeating functions, or *periodic functions*, because they repeat themselves in cycles over and over again.

One way to visualize this periodic trait is by looking at the *unit circle*, which is simply a circle on the coordinate plane with its center at the origin, and having a radius of 1. The unit circle is a great way to define and graph the sine and cosine functions in terms of that radius. Figure 9-43 shows to some extent how this circle graphically displays these two functions.

From the vantage point of the unit circle, you can see how the sine and cosine are related to one another. You know that these two functions are the measurements of complementary angles. When one of the acute angles in the triangle gets bigger, the other acute angle gets smaller, and vice versa. So, the sine and cosine of an angle vary directly with each other.

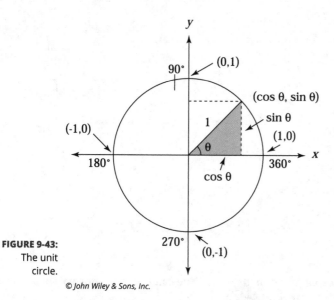

FIGURE 9-43:
The unit
circle.

© John Wiley & Sons, Inc.

The sine and cosine have some important properties about their positive and negative signs when the $\angle\theta$ increases on the unit circle in a counter-clockwise manner.

>> Any angle between 0° and 90° (Quadrant I) has a positive sine and a positive cosine.

>> Any angle between 0° and 180° (Quadrant II) has a positive sine and a negative cosine.

>> Any angle between 90° and 270° (Quadrant III) has a negative sine and a negative cosine.

>> Any angle between 270° and 360° (Quadrant IV) has a negative sine and a positive cosine.

The unit circle shows the repeating nature of trig functions. The measure of the sine at 0° is equal to 0 and the cosine measures 1. If you move the angle around the circle and come back to the beginning, the measure of the angle is now 360°, but the sine and cosine have the same measurement at this new angle as they had when the angle was 0°. The angle looks the same, even though it has a difference of 360°. All that work for nothing!

Measuring in radians

You may be asked a question that tests your knowledge of *radians* instead of degrees as a way of measuring angles. The *radian measure* of an angle on the unit circle is the ratio of the length of the arc to the radius. The radian measure is unit-free — that is, it doesn't matter if you measure the radius of the circle in inches or miles; it's still simply a proportionate measure of the arc to the angle.

The circumference of a circle is equal to $2\pi r$, so the total radian measurement of a circle is 2π radians, and the radian measurement of a semicircle is π radians. You can have a little over 6 radians in a circle. Figure 9-44 compares radian and degree measurements of angles in a circle.

You can see that because there is a total of 2π radians in a circle, each increment of 30° is equal to $\frac{1}{6}\pi$, or length = width = height radians. Each 90° angle is $\frac{\pi}{2}$ radians. So Quadrant I is between 0 and $\frac{\pi}{2}$ radians, Quadrant II is between $\frac{\pi}{2}$ and π radians, Quadrant III is between π and $\frac{3\pi}{2}$ radians, and Quadrant IV is between $\frac{3\pi}{2}$ and 0 radians.

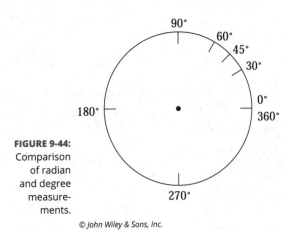
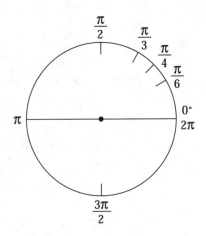

FIGURE 9-44:
Comparison
of radian
and degree
measure-
ments.

© John Wiley & Sons, Inc.

When you're working in radians, keep in mind that $\pi = 180°$. You can use that information to convert from radians to degrees if you're ever confused.

TIP

Graphing trig functions on a coordinate plane

The ACT may require you to recognize the graph of a trigonometric function on a coordinate plane. The graph of a trig function on a coordinate plane looks a bit like the unit circle, but it's easier to see the repeating nature of trig functions on the coordinate plane. Typically, on the coordinate plane, the x-axis becomes a numerical measure of the angle, which is usually measured in radians.

Figure 9-45 shows the graph of $y = \cos x$ on the coordinate plane. The pattern goes on forever in both directions. Because sine and cosine vary indirectly and proportionately with each other, the graph of $y = \sin x$ looks very similar, except that for $y = \sin x$, the curve begins at $y = 0$ instead of $y = 1$ for $y = \cos x$.

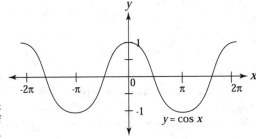

FIGURE 9-45:
Graph of
$y = \cos x$.

© John Wiley & Sons, Inc.

To answer ACT questions about the graphs of periodic functions, make sure you're familiar with these two terms:

>> **Amplitude:** The simple definition is the point where the function is farthest from the origin on the y-axis. In Figure 9-45, the amplitude is 1. You know this because the function is $y = (1)\cos x$. If the function were $y = 2\sin x$, the amplitude would be 2. The value of the amplitude precedes sin and cos in sine and cosine functions.

>> **Period**: This is the horizontal length of the function's complete cycle (also known as *interval*) from one maximum or minimum amplitude to another. In Figure 9-45, the function moves horizontally from $-\pi$ to π in one cycle, so the period is 2π. Generally, sine and cosine functions have periods of 2π, which equals 360°.

The graph of tangent functions look different, as you can see in Figure 9-46.

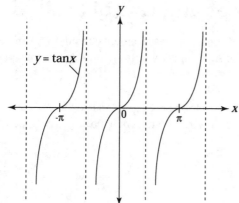

FIGURE 9-46:
Graph of
tangent
functions.

© John Wiley & Sons, Inc.

Tangent functions are also periodic functions, but their shapes are different from sine or cosine graphs. The tangent function has a period of only π radians, because it repeats itself twice as often as the sine and cosine. Also, you'll notice that it goes on forever upward and downward, but each cycle of the tangent has a limit on the x-axis. In Figure 9-46, the dotted vertical lines are *asymptotes* — that is, they are values of x where the function does not exist. The asymptote lines represent values that the tangent function approaches but never quite touches.

The main thing to remember about these graphs is that you should be able to recognize the function when you see it on the ACT.

TIP

Here's an example of one of the more advanced trig questions that may appear on the ACT.

If $\sin 25° = \cos\theta$, then $\angle\theta$ could equal

EXAMPLE

(A) −335°

(B) −295°

(C) −115°

(D) 25°

(E) 395°

The unit circle shows you that the sine and cosine form complementary angles, one of which measures 90°. So if the original angle is $\sin 25°$, then the complementary angle is 65° because $90° - 25° = 65°$. Now, it's child's play to find any angle in your choices that results when you add or subtract a multiple of 360° to or from 65°. The obvious choice here is Choice (B), or −295°, because $65° - 360° = -295°$.

TIP

You would have chosen Choice (A) as your answer if you subtracted only 180° and if you took it away from the wrong angle of 25° instead of subtracting from the complementary angle 65°. If you picked Choice (C), you subtracted from the correct angle, but you again subtracted only 180°. If you picked Choice (D), then you simply picked the wrong angle to begin with and didn't add or subtract anything to or from it. And if you ended up with Choice (E), you added 360° to the wrong angle. Not much better for your result.

Applying the Law of Sines and Law of Cosines

You can also use trig functions to help you figure out measurements of sides and angles on irregular, or *oblique*, triangles. Questions on the ACT expect you to memorize the formulas for these two laws and know when and how to apply them:

> » The *Law of Sines* shows that the sides of any triangle are proportional to the sines of their opposite angles. The sides are indicated by lowercase letters and the angles by uppercase letters, as shown in Figure 9-47.
>
> $$\frac{\sin A}{a} = \frac{\sin B}{b} = \frac{\sin C}{c}$$

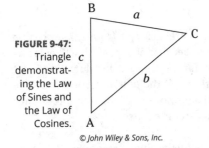

FIGURE 9-47: Triangle demonstrating the Law of Sines and the Law of Cosines.

© John Wiley & Sons, Inc.

> » The *Law of Cosines* indicates that the square of the length of any one side of a triangle equals the sum of the squares of the lengths of the other two sides less twice the product of these two sides and the cosine of their included angle.
>
> $$c^2 = a^2 + b^2 - 2ab\cos C$$

After you're familiar with the formulas, you'll need to know when to use them.

The Law of Sines comes in handy when you want to find out measurements of a triangle and you already know the following:

> » One side and two angles

> » Two sides and an angle opposite from one of them

The Law of Cosines comes in handy when you know the following:

> » Three sides of a triangle

> » Two sides of a triangle and their included angle

The questions that involved these two laws are usually simple after you know how to use them.

Find the equation that gives you the measure of one side in $\triangle ABC$ where the shortest side of the triangle measures 8 units, the longest side measures 13 units, and the angle opposite the unknown side measures 65°.

(A) $\dfrac{\sin A}{13} = \dfrac{\sin C}{c}$

(B) $\dfrac{\sin A}{8} = \dfrac{\sin B}{13}$

(C) $c = \sqrt{8^2 + 13^2}$

(D) $c = \sqrt{8^2 + 13^2 - 2(8)(13)\cos 65°}$

(E) $c = \sqrt{8^2 - 13^2 + 2(8)(13)\cos 65°}$

Here's how to solve:

1. **Draw a picture and label the parts you know, something like this:**

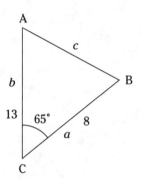

2. **Browse your answer choices.**

Choices A and B apply the Law of Sines, Choice C uses the Pythagorean theorem, and Choices D and E look like the Law of Cosines. The question doesn't indicate that the triangle contains a 90° angle, so Choice C must be wrong. That formula works for right triangles only. Because the question gives you two side lengths and the measure of the angle that includes those two sides, you can use the Law of Cosines.

3. **Eliminate Choices A and B.**

The Law of Sines would work only if the problem also gave you information about one of the angles across from the longest and shortest sides. When you examine the remaining two rearrangements of the Law of Cosines, notice that Choice E contains the wrong operators. The proper form for the Law of Cosines is to add and then subtract $(a^2 + b^2 - 2ab\cos C)$, not subtract and then add. Choice D is the answer.

Chapter **10**

Algebra and Other Sleeping Aids

The ACT tests your knowledge of core high school subjects, and most high schools require students to study algebra. We cover elementary algebra in Chapter 8, so this chapter reviews more advanced algebra concepts, including dealing with inequalities, radicals, functions, and even logarithms. We also outline what you need to know to work with questions that cover the coordinate plane.

Suffering Inequalities

Mathematical expressions don't always involve equal sides. You may in fact see a few *symbols of inequality*, or signs that mean values aren't equal to each other or that one value is greater or less than another.

Mathematics applies standard symbols to show how the two sides of an equation are related. You're probably pretty familiar with these symbols, but a little review never hurts. Table 10-1 gives you a rundown of the more commonly used algebra symbols that signify inequality. Expect to see them crop up here and there on the ACT.

TABLE 10-1 ## Mathematical Symbols for Inequality

Symbol	Meaning
$\neq$	Not equal to
$>$	Greater than
$<$	Less than
$\geq$	Greater than or equal to
$\leq$	Less than or equal to

When you use the greater than or less than symbols, always position the wide side of the arrow toward the bigger value, like so: $5 > 2$ or $2 < 5$.

TIP

Think of the greater than or less than symbols as sharks and the numbers as fish. The shark's open mouth always heads for the bigger fish, which just so happens to be the bigger value.

You can solve for x in simple inequalities the same way you do in equations. Just add or subtract the same number to or from both sides of the inequality, and multiply or divide both sides by the same number. Here's an example:

$$x + 6 \leq 0$$
$$x \leq -6$$

REMEMBER

When you multiply or divide both sides of an inequality by a negative number, you have to reverse the direction of the inequality symbol. For example, when you simplify $-2x < 6$ by dividing both sides by -2 to isolate x, you must switch the symbol so that the final answer is $x > -3$:

$$-2x < 6$$
$$x > -3$$

You can also use inequalities to show a range of numbers instead of just one single value. For example, the ACT may show the range of numbers between -3 and $+2$ as an inequality, like so: $-3 < x < 2$. This expression, called a *compound inequality*, means that x could be -2, -1, 0, and 1 or any number that falls between -3 and 2.

To show the range of -3 to $+2$ including -3 and $+2$, use the $\leq$ sign: $-3 \leq x \leq 2$. Now numbers represented by x include -3 and 2 in the possibilities.

The following example problem shows you how inequalities may appear on the ACT.

EXAMPLE

If $3 > x > -1$ and x is an odd integer, what does x equal?

(A) 2

(B) 0

(C) 1

(D) -1

(E) -2

Use the process of elimination to narrow down your choices. The problem says that x is odd, so you know that Choices (A), (B), and (E) are wrong; 2, -2, and 0 aren't odd. Because x is greater than -1, it can't equal -1. Consequently, Choice (D) is also out. The answer must be Choice (C) because you know that x is between 3 and -1. Therefore, the possible integers for x are 2, 1, and 0. The only odd integer in that list is 1.

Using Your Imagination: Complex Numbers

Imaginary numbers (expressed by the variable i) are downright difficult to imagine. In fact, they don't appear on a traditional number line. The fundamental concept to remember is that i represents the value that, when squared, results in -1 ($i^2 = -1$). Besides that mind-blowing equation, here are the other rules regarding imaginary numbers that you need to know for the ACT:

» $i = \sqrt{-1}$: If $i^2 = -1$, it stands to reason that $i = \sqrt{-1}$.

» **There are only four possible results for taking i to a power**: $\sqrt{-1}$, -1, $-\sqrt{-1}$, and 1. $i^1 = \sqrt{-1}$, $i^2 = -1$, $i^3 = -\sqrt{-1}$, $i^4 = 1$. Then it repeats: $i^5 = \sqrt{-1}$, $i^6 = -1$, and so on.

» **To add imaginary numbers, just add them as you would any other variable:**
$$(3i - 4) + (5i - 6) = 8i - 10$$

» **When you multiply imaginary numbers, replace i^2 with -1:**

$$(3i - 4)(5i - 6) =$$
$$15i^2 - 18i - 20i + 24 =$$
$$15i^2 - 38i + 24 =$$
$$15(-1) - 38i + 24 =$$
$$-15 - 38i + 24 =$$
$$-38i + 9 =$$

» **Eliminate an imaginary number in the denominator:**

- **For one complex term, multiply both the numerator and denominator by that term:**

$$\frac{(3i - 4)}{5i} =$$
$$\frac{(3i - 4)}{5i} \times \frac{5i}{5i} =$$
$$\frac{-15i^2 - 20i}{25i^2} =$$
$$\frac{15 - 20i}{-25} =$$

- **For complex binomial terms, multiply both the numerator and denominator by the conjugate:**

$$\frac{(3i - 4)}{(5i - 6)} =$$
$$\frac{(3i - 4)}{(5i - 6)} \times \frac{(5i + 6)}{(5i + 6)} =$$
$$\frac{-38i + 9}{25i^2 + 30i - 30i - 36} =$$
$$\frac{-38i + 9}{25(-1) - 36} =$$
$$\frac{-38i + 9}{-61} =$$

Too Hip to Be Square: Roots and Radicals

ACT math questions require you to know how to work with roots and radicals. For the purposes of the ACT, the two terms mean the same thing. The *square root* of a value is the number you multiply by itself to get that value. In other words, the square root of 9 (or $\sqrt{9}$) is 3 because you multiply 3 by itself to get 9. A cube root of a value is the number you multiply by itself 3 times to get that value. So the cube root of 27 (or $\sqrt[3]{27}$) is 3 because $3 \times 3 \times 3 = 3^3 = 27$. To simplify working with square roots or cube roots (or any other roots), think of them as variables. You work with them the same way you work with x, y, or z.

Adding and subtracting radicals

Adding and subtracting radicals is easy to do as long as you remember a couple of guidelines:

>> **To add or subtract like radicals, add or subtract the number in front of the radical.**

$$2\sqrt{7} + 5\sqrt{7} = 7\sqrt{7}$$
$$9\sqrt{13} - 4\sqrt{13} = 5\sqrt{13}$$

>> **You *can't* add or subtract unlike radicals (just as you cannot add or subtract unlike variables).**

$$6\sqrt{5} + 4\sqrt{3} = 6\sqrt{5} + 4\sqrt{3}$$

You can't add the terms and get $10\sqrt{8}$.

REMEMBER

Don't glance at a problem, see that the radicals aren't the same, and immediately assume that you can't add the two terms. You may be able to simplify one radical to make it match the radical in the other term. For example,

$$\sqrt{52} + \sqrt{13} = ?$$

Begin by simplifying. Take out a perfect square from the term:

$$\sqrt{52} = \sqrt{4} \times \sqrt{13}$$

Because $\sqrt{4} = 2$, $\sqrt{52} = 2\sqrt{13}$.

So you can add the two original terms:

$$\sqrt{52} + \sqrt{13} = 2\sqrt{13} + \sqrt{13} = 3\sqrt{13}$$

Here's another example:

$$\sqrt{20} + \sqrt{45} = x$$
$$\left(\sqrt{4} \times \sqrt{5}\right) + \left(\sqrt{9} \times \sqrt{5}\right) = x$$
$$2\sqrt{5} + 3\sqrt{5} = x$$
$$5\sqrt{5} = x$$

Multiplying and dividing radicals

When you multiply or divide radicals, the motto is "just do it." All you do is multiply or divide the numbers and then pop the radical sign back onto the finished product. For example,

$$\sqrt{5} \times \sqrt{6} = \sqrt{30}$$
$$\sqrt{15} \div \sqrt{5} = \sqrt{3}$$

If you have numbers in front of the radical, multiply them as well. Let everyone in on the fun. For example,

$$6\sqrt{3} \times 4\sqrt{2} = \left(6 \times 4\right)\left(\sqrt{3} \times \sqrt{2}\right) = 24\sqrt{6}$$

REMEMBER

When you express the division of a radical as a fraction, you have to be careful. A fraction with a radical in the denominator is an irrational number (for more on irrational numbers, review Chapter 8). The ACT won't credit any answer choice with a radical in the denominator. Whenever your calculations result in a fraction with a square root in the denominator, you have to rationalize your answer. (That doesn't mean you justify to the teacher how on earth you came up with that answer; it means you get rid of the root in the denominator.) Don't worry. Rationalizing is easy. Just multiply both the top and the bottom by the square root in the denominator, like so: $\frac{1}{\sqrt{2}} \times \frac{\sqrt{2}}{\sqrt{2}} = \frac{\sqrt{2}}{2}$.

EXAMPLE

Find the value of $37\sqrt{5} \times 3\sqrt{6}$.

(F) $40\sqrt{11}$

(G) $40\sqrt{30}$

(H) $111\sqrt{11}$

(J) $111\sqrt{30}$

(K) $1,221$

This problem calls for straightforward multiplication: $37 \times 3 = 111$ and $\sqrt{5} \times \sqrt{6} = \sqrt{30}$. The correct answer is Choice (J).

Working from the inside out

When you see an operation inside the radical, do it first and then take the square root. For the following example, first solve the equation inside the radical using the common denominator of 360:

$$\sqrt{\frac{x^2}{40} + \frac{x^2}{9}}$$

$$\sqrt{\frac{9x^2}{360} + \frac{40x^2}{360}}$$

$$\sqrt{\frac{49x^2}{360}}$$

Now take the square roots of both the numerator and denominator: $\sqrt{49x^2} = 7x$ (because $7x \times 7x = 49x^2$) and $\sqrt{360} \approx 18.97$. Did you say that $\sqrt{360} = 6$? Nope! $\sqrt{36} = 6$, but $\sqrt{360} \approx 18.97$. Beware of assuming too much; doing so may lead you down the path to temptation.

Your final answer is $\frac{7x}{18.97}$. Of course, you can bet that the answer choices will include $\frac{7x}{6}$.

Thinking Exponentially: Logarithms

The ACT may include one or two questions that present you with a *logarithm,* which is essentially the number of times you multiply the base times itself to get the big number. The definition of a logarithm can be boiled down to taking this equation, $x = a^y$, and rearranging it to become $y = \log_a x$. It's just another way of saying y is the log to the base a of x.

So $\log_4 256$ is the number of times you multiply 4 (the base) by itself to get 256 (the big number, to use the technical term). In this case, $\log_4 256 = 4$.

If the ACT asks you to find the value for x in $\log_x 16 = 4$, you know what to do. Find which base to a power of 4 equals 16. The answer is 2 because 2^4 is 16.

Log rules

The ACT may include a question that asks you to apply logarithm rules, so make sure you memorize the information in Table 10-2.

TABLE 10-2 Logarithm Rules

Logarithm Rule Name	Rule
Logarithm product rule	$log_b(xy) = log_b(x) + log_b(y)$
Logarithm quotient rule	$log_b\left(\dfrac{x}{y}\right) = log_b(x) - log_b(y)$
Logarithm power rule	$log_b(x^y) = y \times log_b(x)$
Logarithm base switch rule	$log_b(c) = \dfrac{1}{log_c(b)}$
Logarithm of 1 = 0	$log_b(1) = 0$
Logarithm of the base = 1	$log_b(b) = 1$

Natural logarithms

A certain irrational number is very useful in calculating compounded interest on savings, the natural decay of radioactive material, and other scientific measures such as atmospheric pressure at various altitudes. This versatile value is represented by *e* and is called a *natural logarithm*. The natural logarithm of a positive number *x* (written as ln*x* and pronounced "ell enn" *x*) is a logarithm to the base *e* of *x*, where *e* = 2.71828 . . . .

Natural logarithms can be expressed in several different ways:

» $\ln a = x$

» $log_e a = x$

» $e^x = a$

Natural log problems are rare on the ACT and straightforward when they appear. What's more, you can use the *ln* function on your graphing calculator to solve them. You use the *log* key for base 10 common logs.

TIP

If logarithms make your head spin, don't worry. You won't get too dizzy on the ACT because you're not likely to see more than one of them on the Mathematics Test.

Barely Functioning with Functions

If you've never studied functions, don't worry. The ACT doesn't ask you a lot of function questions. And the ones that do appear are relatively easy. You're essentially just applying substitution. For example, you may see a problem like this one:

$f(x) = (2x)^2$

Solve for $f(2)$.

The function shows the relationship between x and y. $f(x) = y$, and x is the x-coordinate you plug into the function to solve for y. So, the $f(2)$ supplies the x-value (2) you input into the function. The output is the y-value that results when you input the 2 into the function and solve. In other words, just plug in the 2 where you see an x in the equation to find the corresponding value for y, or $f(x)$:

$$f(2) = (2 \times 2)^2 = 4^2 = 16$$

You may also need to find functions of variables. Treat them exactly the same way that you do actual values. So if you're given $f(x) = (2x)^2$ and asked to find $f(x+y)$, you solve by following the same steps:

1. **Substitute all the stuff in the parentheses $(x + y)$ for x in the original function:**
$$f(x+y) = \left[2(x+y)\right]^2$$

2. **Distribute the 2:**
$$f(x+y) = (2x+2y)^2$$

3. **Square the binomial expression:**
$$f(x+y) = (2x+2y)(2x+2y)$$
$$f(x+y) = 4x^2 + 4xy + 4xy + 4y^2$$
$$f(x+y) = 4x^2 + 8xy + 4y^2$$

Regardless of what's inside the parentheses of the function, you substitute that for x in the original function.

Taking a Flight on the Coordinate Plane

Quite a few questions on the ACT cover coordinate geometry, which involves working with points on a graph that's officially known as the *Cartesian coordinate plane*. This perfectly flat surface has a system that allows you to identify the position of points by using a pair of numbers. The following sections take a closer look at the coordinate plane.

Defining the coordinate plane

Here are some terms you need to know to answer the ACT's coordinate geometry questions. Figure 10-1 shows you these terms on a coordinate plane.

>> **x-axis:** The x-axis is the horizontal axis on a coordinate plane, where values or numbers start at the intersect point that has a value of 0. Numbers increase in value to the right of this point and decrease in value to the left of it. All points along the x-axis have a y-value of 0.

>> **y-axis:** The y-axis is the vertical axis on a coordinate plane, where values or numbers start at the intersect point that has a value of 0. Numbers increase in value going up from this point and decrease in value going down from it. All points along the y-axis have an x-value of 0.

>> **Origin:** The origin is the point (0, 0) on the coordinate plane; it's where the x- and y-axes intersect.

» **Quadrant:** The intersection of the *x*- and *y*-axes forms four quadrants on the coordinate plane, which just so happen to be named Quadrants I, II, III, and IV, as shown in Figure 10-1.

» **Ordered pair:** An ordered pair is made up of two coordinates, which describe the location of a point in relation to the origin. The horizontal (*x*) coordinate is always listed first, and the vertical (*y*) coordinate is always listed second. Point *A* in Figure 10-1 designates (2, 3).

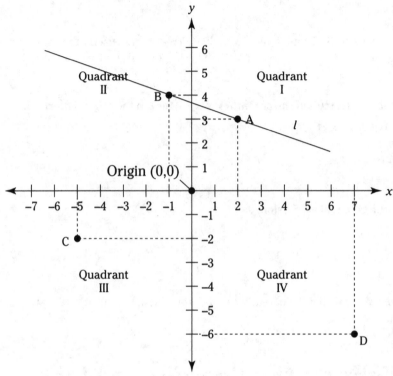

FIGURE 10-1:
The coordinate plane.

Knowing which formulas you need to guide your flight

When working with elements on the coordinate plane, keep these rules in mind:

» **A line connecting points with the same *x*- and *y*-coordinates — (1, 1), (2, 2), and (3, 3), for example — forms a 45-degree angle (see Figure 10-2).**

» **To locate the middle point of a line, use the *midpoint formula*:**

$$M = \left(\frac{x_1 + x_2}{2}, \frac{y_1 + y_2}{2} \right)$$

For example, to figure out the midpoint of a line that ends at points *A* (2, 3) and *B* (–1, 4) in Figure 10-1, use the formula:

$$M = \left(\frac{2 + (-1)}{2}, \frac{3 + 4}{2} \right)$$

$$M = \left(\frac{1}{2}, \frac{7}{2} \right)$$

$$M = \left(\frac{1}{2}, 3\frac{1}{2} \right)$$

TIP

To help you remember the midpoint formula, think of it as the average of the two x-coordinates and the average of the two y-coordinates.

>> **To find the distance between two points, use the *distance formula*:**

$$\sqrt{\left(x_2 - x_1\right)^2 + \left(y_2 - y_1\right)^2}$$

For example, you can figure the distance between points A (2, 3) and B (–1, 4) in Figure 10-1 by using this formula:

$$D = \sqrt{\left(-1-2\right)^2 + \left(4-3\right)^2}$$
$$D = \sqrt{\left(-3\right)^2 + \left(1\right)^2}$$
$$D = \sqrt{9+1}$$
$$D = \sqrt{10}$$

>> *Slope* **measures how steep a line is.** It's commonly referred to as *rise over run*. Think of slope as a fraction. A slope of 4 is really a slope of $\frac{4}{1}$.

- A line with a negative slope goes down from left to right (its left side is higher than its right side).

- A line with a positive slope goes down from right to left (its right side is higher than its left side).

- A horizontal line has a slope of 0.

- A vertical line has an undefined slope.

- Parallel lines have the same slope.

>> **One way to find the slope of a line is to locate two of its points and apply the formula for slope:**

$$Slope = \frac{y_2 - y_1}{x_2 - x_1}$$

You can calculate the slope of line l in Figure 10-1 using Points A and B, like so:

$$\frac{4-3}{-1-2} = \frac{1}{-3} = -\frac{1}{3}$$

>> **The *equation of a line* (or slope-intercept form) is** $y = mx + b$**.** The m is the slope of the line, and the b is where the line crosses the y-axis (called the y-intercept). So a line with an equation of $y = 4x + 1$ has a slope of $\frac{4}{1}$ and a y-intercept of 1.

You can draw a line on the plane if you know its equation. Find the y-intercept on the y-axis. Then use the slope to create the line. Go up by the slope's numerator and across by the slope's denominator.

TIP

Whenever you get an equation for a line that doesn't fit neatly into the slope-intercept form, go ahead and play with the equation a little bit (sounds fun, doesn't it?) to get it into the $y = mx + b$ format. That way, you can either solve the problem or get a visual idea of the graph of the line. For instance, if you see the equation $\frac{1}{3}y - 3 = x$, all you have to do is manipulate both sides of the equation until it looks like the slope-intercept form that you know and love:

$$\frac{1}{3}y = x + 3$$
$$y = 3x + 9$$

>> *Voilà!* You now know the slope of the line (3) as well as the y-intercept (9) by using some basic algebra. Pretty tricky!

FIGURE 10-2:
A line
connecting
points with
the same
x- and y-
coordinates.

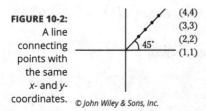

© *John Wiley & Sons, Inc.*

Here's a sample question that tests your knowledge of the equation of a line.

EXAMPLE

What is the equation of a line with a slope $-\frac{2}{3}$ and a y-intercept of 7?

(F) $3x + 2y = 21$

(G) $-2x + 3y = 14$

(H) $2x - 3y = 21$

(J) $2x + 3y = 14$

(K) $2x + 3y = 21$

When you look at the answer choices, you see that they all have the same format: $ax + by = c$.

You need to convert the equation to that format as well. Because the equation of a line is $y = mx + b$, you know that m is the slope and b is the y-intercept. So what are you waiting for? Plug in the values:

$$y = \left(-\frac{2}{3}\right)x + 7$$
$$3y = -2 + 21$$
$$2x + 3y = 21$$

The correct answer is (K).

Graphing more functions

Occasionally, the ACT may ask you more complex questions about the coordinate plane. While not every ACT includes the following concepts, they're definite possibilities for test questions, so make sure you're familiar with them.

>> **Graphing a linear inequality is almost exactly the same as graphing the equation for a line, except a linear inequality covers a lot more ground on the coordinate plane.** While the graph of an equation for a line simply shows the actual line on the coordinate plane, the graph of a linear inequality shows everything either above or below the line on the plane. The graph appears as a shaded area to one side of the line. Figure 10-3 shows the graphs of several inequalities.

>> **When you graph a quadratic equation, it appears as a *parabola*, a curve shape that opens either upward or downward.** A parabola is a figure on a plane where every point on the figure is the same distance from a fixed point called the *focus* and a fixed line called a *directrix*. Following are some important properties of parabolas.

- **The axis of symmetry:** This is the vertical line that bisects the parabola so that each side is a mirror image of the other.

- **The vertex:** This is the rounded end of the parabola, which is the lowest point on a curve that opens upward and the highest point on a curve that opens downward. It's where the parabola crosses the axis of symmetry.

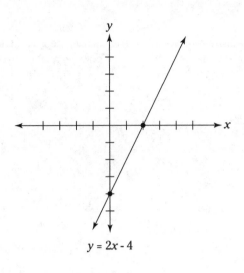

$y = 2x - 4$

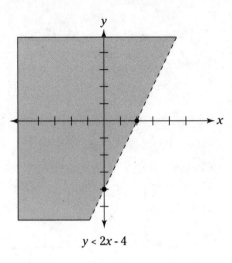

$y < 2x - 4$

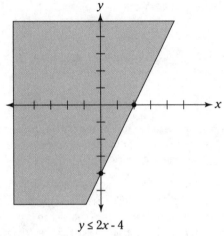

$y \leq 2x - 4$

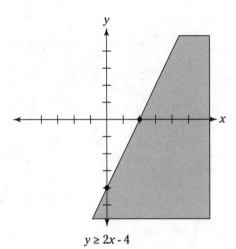

$y \geq 2x - 4$

FIGURE 10-3:
Graphing
lines and
inequalities.

© John Wiley & Sons, Inc.

» **The *standard form* equation of a parabola is** $y = a(x - h)^2 + k$ **(where** $a \neq 0$**).** The coordinate point (h, k) is the vertex. The vertical line $x = h$ is the axis of symmetry. If a is a positive number, the parabola opens upward. If a is negative, the parabola opens downward. When a is less than 1 but greater than –1, the curve widens; when a is greater than 1 or less than –1, the curve narrows.

» **The *general form* equation is** $y = ax^2 + bx + c$ **(where** $a \neq 0$**).** When $y = 0$, the solutions for x tell you where the parabola crosses the x-axis. The coordinate point $(0, c)$ represents the y-intercept of the parabola. The axis of symmetry is the line $x = -\dfrac{b}{2a}$, and the x-coordinate of the vertex is $-\dfrac{b}{2a}$. When you apply the *discriminant* $(-b^2 - 4ac)$ to the general form, you learn the following:

- If the value of the discriminant is 0, the parabola touches the x-axis at only one point, which means that the vertex is on the x-axis.

- If the value of the discriminant is positive, the parabola intersects the x-axis at two points.

- If the value of the discriminant is negative, the parabola doesn't intersect the x-axis at any point.

Figure 10-4 shows the graph of several parabolas and their formulas. In the graph of $y = x^2$, the values for h and k are 0, so the vertex is at the origin. The parabola opens upward because a is 1, a positive number. A change in the constant h moves the parabola sideways along the *x*-axis. No *h* in the equation (that is, if *h* = 0) indicates that the vertex lies on the *y*-axis. The constant *k* determines whether the vertex of the parabola moves up or down in relation to the *y*-axis. No *k* in the equation (that is, if *k* = 0) means the vertex of the parabola is on the *x*-axis.

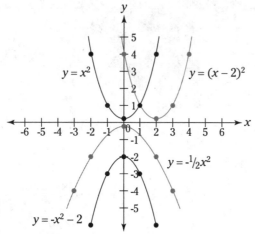

$y = x^2$

$y = (x-2)^2$

$y = -\frac{1}{2}x^2$

$y = -x^2 - 2$

FIGURE 10-4:
Graphs of parabolas.

© John Wiley & Sons, Inc.

» **The equation of a circle is** $(x-h)^2 + (y-k)^2 = r^2$, **where the center of the circle is point** **(*h*, *k*) and *r* is the circle's radius.** If the origin is the center of the circle, the equation will be $x^2 + y^2 = r^2$.

» **An *ellipse* contains all points on a plane that are located the same distance from the** **sum of two points called *foci*.** The long distance across the ellipse is called the *major axis*. The short distance across the ellipse is called the *minor axis*. The *center* of the ellipse is the midpoint of the two foci, and the *vertices* are the two points furthest from the center, the points on the ellipse that intersect with the major axis. Figure 10-5 shows an ellipse and its components. The formula for the area of an ellipse is πab, and the standard equation of an ellipse is

$$\frac{(x-h)^2}{a^2} + \frac{(y-k)^2}{b^2} = 1$$

The value of *a* in the formula is equal to half the length of the horizonal axis, and the value of *b* is half the length of the vertical axis. Points *h* and *k* refer to the coordinates at the center of the ellipse.

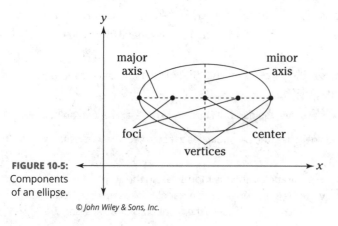

major axis

minor axis

foci

center

vertices

FIGURE 10-5:
Components of an ellipse.

© John Wiley & Sons, Inc.

>> A *hyperbola* contains all points in a plane where the difference of the distance between two fixed points is constant. Figure 10-6 shows a hyperbola as basically two mirror-image parabolas: the positive branch and the negative branch. The *asymptote lines* are imaginary lines that run alongside the two branches. The curve of the hyperbola comes very close to but never touches these lines. The standard form equation for a hyperbola is

$$\frac{(x-h)^2}{a^2} - \frac{(y-k)^2}{b^2} = 1$$

The center of the hyperbola is the coordinate point (*h*, *k*). The *a* and *b* represent the respective distances from the fixed points. If the term with the *x* is negative, the hyperbola opens upward and downward. If the term with the *y* is negative, the hyperbola opens to the left and right.

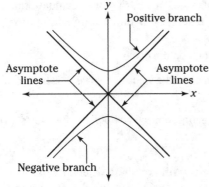

FIGURE 10-6:
Components
of a
hyperbola.

© John Wiley & Sons, Inc.

You can try a couple of practice questions to see how some of these concepts may appear on the ACT.

EXAMPLE

What is the vertex of the graph of the equation $y = -2(x-3)^2 + 4$?

(A) (−3, −4)

(B) (3, 4)

(C) (3, −4)

(D) (−3, 4)

(E) (−6, −4)

Remember the equation of a parabola: $y = a(x-h)^2 + k$. The vertex of the parabola is (*h*, *k*). The *h* value in the equation is 3 and the *k* value is 4. So the vertex of the graph of the equation in the question is (3, 4). The correct answer is Choice (B).

Choice (D) is a trap answer. Note that the value of *h* is 3 and not −3. The only way that the value of *h* could be −3 is if the original equation were $y = -2\left[x-(-3)\right]^2 + 4$. Then you'd have to switch the sign to put the equation into the correct form for the equation of a parabola.

EXAMPLE

What is the equation of a circle with the coordinate point (5, −1) as its center and a radius of 6?

(F) $(x-5)^2 + (y+1)^2 = 6$

(G) $(x-5)^2 + (y-1)^2 = 36$

(H) $(x-5)^2 + (y+1)^2 = 36$

(J) $(x+5)^2 + (y-1)^2 = 12$

(K) $(x-5)^2 - (y+1)^2 = 36$

The answer choices look so similar that you definitely need to know the details of the formula for a circle if you have any hope of getting this one right: $(x-h)^2 + (y-k)^2 = r^2$.

Because you know the radius is 6, you also know the radius squared is 36, which means you can easily eliminate Choices (F) and (J). Choice (K) is obviously incorrect because you know that you have to add the two terms together in the formula for the circle; Choice (K) subtracts the two terms. That leaves you with Choices (G) and (H). Choice (G) would be okay if the center had the coordinate point of (5, 1), but in your question, the y-coordinate of the center is negative. So you switch the sign around when you plug it into the equation. The correct answer is (H).

Evaluating graphs of functions

Every function has a distinct y-value for every x-value. So any graph on the coordinate plane that meets this criteria is the graph of a function. The ACT may ask you to evaluate functions on the coordinate plane. Here are a few preliminary considerations for accomplishing this:

>> The function's input is the x-coordinate of a point on the plane.

>> The output — the value that results when you input the value and solve — is the y-coordinate of that point on the plane.

>> Using the x-and y-coordinates indicated by the function, you can plot the function's points on the coordinate plane.

Say a test question tells you to find $f(3)$ on the coordinate plane when $f(x) = 2x^2 + 7$. The input (or x-coordinate) is 3. Plug 3 into the function to find the output (or y-coordinate):

$$f(3) = 2(3)^2 + 7$$
$$f(3) = (2 \times 9) + 7$$
$$f(3) = 18 + 7$$
$$f(3) = 25$$

In graphing terms, you know the x-coordinate is 3 (because the question tells you so), and the y-coordinate is 25. If you were to graph this point on a coordinate plane, the ordered pair would be (3, 25). It's that simple.

Here are some more concepts to remember when you encounter function questions:

>> The *domain* of a function is the set of all possible numbers for the input (x) of the function, usually all real numbers. An imaginary x-value or one that would create a zero denominator wouldn't be included in the domain for that function.

>> The *range* of a function is the set of possible numbers for an output (y) of the function.

>> The *root* of a function is the solution you get when the equation equals 0, a point where the graph of the equation or function intersects with the x-axis. In other words, the roots are the x-values when $y = 0$.

>> The *degree* of a function is the highest power (exponent) of any variable or term that occurs in the function. The degree of the function indicates the highest possible roots for that function. These roots may be distinct or the same. To have distinct roots, the polynomial function needs

to have separate and distinct solutions to the function. The polynomial function $g(x) = x^3 - 4x^2 - 3x + 18$ has three roots (its highest power) but only two distinct roots or solutions ($x = 3$ and $x = -2$) because its factors are $(x-3)^2 (x+2)$.

The degree can also indicate the shape of the function:

- A first-degree function has no exponents and is a straight line.

- A second-degree function has a highest power of 2, as in a quadratic formula, which forms a parabola. Second-degree functions have a low point or high point, also known as the *extremum*. In a parabola, the extremum is the vertex.

- A third-degree function has a highest power of 3 and no more than two extrema, a fourth-degree function has a highest power of 4 and no more than three extrema, and so on. The extrema for these functions are called *local minimums* and *local maximums*. You can get information about the degree of a function from its graph. Figure 10-7 illustrates what could be at least a fourth-degree function because it has three extreme values: two local minimums and a local maximum. It also has four distinct zeroes (four points where the function crosses the *x*-axis, indicating that it likely has four distinct solutions.)

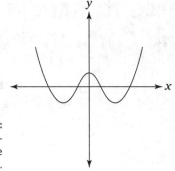

FIGURE 10-7:
Fourth-
degree
function.

© John Wiley & Sons, Inc.

Occasionally, the test makers may ask you to find a *piecewise function*, which is a function that's broken into pieces, or different rules. It's not much different from a "normal" function. You determine the function depending on how you define the possible values of the domain. Here's an example:

$$f(x) = \begin{cases} 2x-1, \ x \le 1 \\ x+4, \ x > 1 \end{cases}$$

Notice that the function is split into pieces. The value of *x* determines the value of *y* just as it does in normal functions, but the *y*–value of a piecewise function follows a different pattern depending on which of the two rules *x* falls under.

So, if *x* = 0 in the preceding function, it's less than 1, which means the first rule applies. Plug in 0 for *x*: $2(0) - 1 = -1$. The point on the coordinate plane would be (0, –1). If $x = 1$, $y = 2(1) - 1$, or 1, and the point would be (1, 1). You can graph these points on the coordinate plane and draw the line between them. Just remember that the line is limited to *x*–values that are equal to or less than 1.

If $x = 2$, then the second rule governs, and the corresponding y-coordinate is $2 + 4$, or 6. When $x = 3$, y is $3 + 4$, or 7. The points are (2, 6) and (3, 7). You can draw this line on the plane, too. A picture of these two functions on the coordinate plane would look something like this:

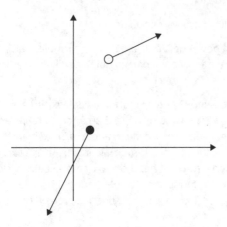

Picking Your Way through Percent Increase, Probability, Permutations, and Combinations

In addition to traditional algebra and arithmetic, the ACT may also test your knowledge of how to deal with percent increase/decrease, probability, and more advanced statistics. Plan to see several of these question types on your Mathematics Test.

Managing the ups and downs

You may see a problem that asks you what percent increase or decrease occurred in the number of games a team won or the amount of commission a person earned.

To find a percent increase or decrease, use this formula:

$$\% \text{ increase or decrease} = \frac{\text{number increase or decrease}}{\text{original whole}}$$

In basic English, to find the percent by which something has increased or decreased, you take two simple steps:

1. **Find the number (amount) by which the thing has increased or decreased.**

For example, if a team won 25 games last year and 30 games this year, the number increase was 5. If a salesperson earned $10,000 last year and $8,000 this year, the number decrease was $2,000. Make that number the numerator (the top part) of the fraction.

2. **Find the original whole.**

This figure is what you started out with before you increased or decreased. If a team won 25 games last year and won 30 games this year, the original number was 25. If the salesperson earned $10,000 last year and $8,000 this year, the original number was $10,000. Make the number you started out with the denominator (the bottom part) of the fraction.

You now have a complete fraction. Divide the fraction to convert to a decimal and multiply by 100 to make it a percentage.

EXAMPLE

In 2010, Coach Denges won 20 prizes at the county fair by tossing a basketball into a bushel basket. In 2011, he won 25 prizes. What was his percent increase?

(F) 100

(G) 30

(H) 25

(J) 20

(K) $16\frac{2}{3}$

The number by which his prizes increased, from 20 to 25, is 5. That's the numerator. The original whole, or what he began with, is 20. That's the denominator. So your fraction looks like this:

$$\frac{5}{20} = \frac{25}{100} = 25\%$$

The correct answer is Choice (H).

Practicing probability

Probability questions are usually word problems. They may look intimidating, with so many words that make you lose sight of where to begin, but they aren't impossible to solve. In fact, by using the two simple rules we explain in the following sections, you can solve the simple probability problems the ACT tosses at you.

TIP

No matter what kind of probability problems you face, remember that probability can only be 0, 1, or a number in between 0 and 1. You can't have a negative probability, and you can't have a probability greater than 1, or 100 percent.

Finding the probability of one event

To find a probability, use this formula to set up a fraction:

$$P = \frac{\text{Number of possible desired outcomes}}{\text{Number of total possible outcomes}}$$

The denominator is the easier of the two parts to begin with because it's the total possible number of outcomes. For example, when you're flipping a coin, you have two possible outcomes, giving you a denominator of 2. When you're tossing a die (one of a pair of dice), you have six possible outcomes, giving you a denominator of 6. When you're pulling a card out of a deck of cards, you have 52 possible outcomes (a deck of cards contains 52 cards), giving you a denominator of 52. When 25 marbles are in a jar and you're going to pull out one of them, you have 25 possibilities, giving you a denominator of 25. Very simply, the denominator is the whole shebang — everything possible.

The numerator is the total number of the outcomes you want. If you want to see heads when you toss a coin, you have exactly one desired outcome because the coin has only one head side, giving you a numerator of 1. Your chance of tossing heads, therefore, is $\frac{1}{2}$ — one possible heads and two possible outcomes altogether. If you want to roll a 5 when you toss a die, the numerator is 1 because the die has exactly one 5 on it. The probability of tossing a 5 is $\frac{1}{6}$ — one possible 5 out of six possible outcomes altogether.

If you want to draw a jack from a deck of cards, you have four chances because the deck contains four jacks: hearts, diamonds, clubs, and spades. Therefore, the numerator is 4. The probability of drawing a jack out of a deck of cards is $\frac{4}{52}$ (which reduces to $\frac{1}{13}$). If you want to draw a jack of hearts, the probability is $\frac{1}{52}$ because the deck contains only one jack of hearts.

EXAMPLE

A jar of marbles has 8 yellow marbles, 6 black marbles, and 12 white marbles. What is the probability of drawing out a black marble?

(A) $\frac{1}{6}$

(B) $\frac{3}{13}$

(C) $\frac{4}{13}$

(D) $\frac{6}{13}$

(E) 1

Use the formula. Begin with the denominator, which is all the possible outcomes: $8+6+12=26$. The numerator is how many outcomes result in what you want: 6 black marbles. The probability is $\frac{6}{26}$, which you can reduce to $\frac{3}{13}$, which is Choice (B).

If you came up with Choice (C) or (D), you figured out the probability of choosing a yellow or white marble, respectively. You know that Choice (E) can't be right. A probability of 1 means that there's a 100 percent chance that you'll pick a black marble.

Finding the probability of multiple events

You can find the probability of multiple events by following several rules. Table 10-3 lists and describes each rule, shows the corresponding formula, and provides an example of when you'd use it.

TABLE 10-3 **Finding the Probability of the Occurrence of Multiple Events**

Rule	Circumstance	Formula	Example
Special Rule of Addition	The probability of the occurrence of either of two possible events that are mutually exclusive	$P(A \text{ or } B) = P(A) + P(B)$	The probability of rolling a 5 or 6 on one roll of one die
General Rule of Addition	The probability of the occurrence of either of two possible events that can happen together	$P(A \text{ or } B) = P(A) + P(B) - P(A \text{ and } B)$	The probability of drawing a playing card that displays a club or a queen
Special Rule of Multiplication	The probability of the occurrence of two events at the same time when the two events are independent of each other	$P(A \text{ and } B) = P(A) \times P(B)$	The probability of rolling a 5 and a 6 on one roll of two dice
General Rule of Multiplication	The probability of the occurrence of two events when the occurrence of the first event affects the outcome of the second event	$P(A \text{ and } B) = P(A) \times P(B/A)$ (The line between the B and A stands for "B given A"; it doesn't mean divide.)	The probability of first drawing the queen of clubs from a pack of 52 cards, keeping the queen of clubs out of the pack, and then drawing the jack of diamonds on the next try

EXAMPLE

A candy machine contains gumballs: three blue, two red, seven yellow, and one purple. The machine distributes one gumball for each dime. A child has exactly two dimes with which she will purchase two gumballs. What is the chance that the child will get two red gumballs?

(A) $\frac{2}{169}$

(B) $\frac{1}{13}$

(C) $\frac{2}{13}$

(D) $\frac{1}{156}$

(E) $\frac{1}{78}$

TIP

You need to treat getting the two red gumballs as two events. The occurrence of the first event affects the probability of the second event because after the child extracts the first red gumball, the machine has one fewer gumball. So you apply the general rule of multiplication.

The chance of getting a red gumball with the first dime is 2 (the number of red gumballs) divided by 13 (the total number of gumballs in the machine), or $\frac{2}{13}$. If the child tries to get the second gumball, the first red gumball is already gone, which leaves only 1 red gumball and 12 total gumballs in the machine, so the chance of getting the second red gumball is $\frac{1}{12}$. The probability of both events happening is the product of the probability of the occurrence of each event:

$$P(A \text{ and } B) = P(A) \times P(B/A)$$
$$P(A \text{ and } B) = \frac{2}{13} \times \frac{1}{12}$$
$$P(A \text{ and } B) = \frac{2}{156}$$
$$P(A \text{ and } B) = \frac{1}{78}$$

Choice (E) is the correct answer. Choice (A) is $\frac{2}{13} \times \frac{1}{13}$, which would look right if you didn't subtract the withdrawn red gumball from the total number on the second draw. Choice (B) is the chance of drawing one red gumball from a machine with 13 gumballs and only one red gumball. In this problem, $\frac{1}{13}$ is also the chance of drawing the purple gumball. If you picked Choice (C), you found the chance of drawing the first red gumball.

Calculating outcomes and orderings

A few questions in each Mathematics Test will ask for the possible number of outcomes, either combinations or orderings for particular events. Some of these problems are easy; you just need to apply the *counting principle*. Others may require you to dust off the chapter on factorials from math classes past.

Combinations

When a question asks for the total possible outcomes given two or more events and order isn't an issue, you're dealing with a *combination*. Apply the counting principle. The counting principle just means that you multiply the number of possibilities for one event by the number of possibilities for the other event. Say you go to an ice cream social that offers three flavors of ice cream, five kinds of toppings, and four different-patterned bowls to put them in. To determine the number of different combinations you could pick for one ice cream flavor, one topping, and one bowl, you just multiply $3 \times 4 \times 5$. That's 60 different combinations to choose from!

Calculations become a little more complex when you must create combinations with a smaller number of members than the original pool. For example, say you want to know how many possible five-number lock combinations you can create from the ten possible 1-digit numbers when the order of the lock combination doesn't matter and no number is repeated. Here's where factorials come into the picture.

The *factorial function* designates the product of descending whole numbers. Its symbol is the exclamation point, !. So $4! = 4 \times 3 \times 2 \times 1$. The formula for finding the number of possible combinations of fewer elements drawn from a greater pool is this:

$$\frac{n!}{r!(n-r)!}$$

The n signifies the total number options to draw from, and the r stands for the number in the groups you're putting together.

So for the lock scenario, you set up the formula like this:

$$\frac{10!}{5!(10-5)!}$$

In the formula, n is 10 because there are ten digits to choose from (0, 1, 2, 3, 4, 5, 6, 7, 8, 9); r is 5 because you seek to create five-number combinations from the ten total digits.

To calculate the number of combinations, expand the formula:

$$\frac{10 \times 9 \times 8 \times 7 \times 6 \times 5 \times 4 \times 3 \times 2 \times 1}{5 \times 4 \times 3 \times 2 \times 1(5!)} = C$$

The $5 \times 4 \times 3 \times 2 \times 1$ in the numerator and denominator cancel to give you this:

$$\frac{10 \times 9 \times 8 \times 7 \times 6}{(5)!} = C$$

You can then calculate the answer like this:

$$\frac{10 \times 9 \times 8 \times 7 \times 6}{(5)!} = C$$

$$\frac{10 \times 9 \times 8 \times 7 \times 6}{5 \times 4 \times 3 \times 2 \times 1} = C$$

$$\frac{30,240}{120} = C$$

$$252 = C$$

There are 252 possible five-number lock combinations from all ten digits when order doesn't matter and no digits are repeated.

Permutations

Permutations problems ask you to determine how many arrangements of numbers are possible given a specific set of numbers and a particular order for the arrangements. For example, figuring out the number of possible seven-digit telephone numbers you can create is a permutation problem. And the answer is huge (10^7) because you have ten possible values (the integers between 0 and 9) to fill each of the seven places.

REMEMBER

Order matters when you set up permutations. Even though two different phone numbers may have the same combination of numbers, such as 345-7872 and 543-7728, the numbers ring two different phones because you input them in a different order. Rely on factorials to figure out permutations.

Suppose a photographer wants to know how many different ways she can arrange five people in a single row for a wedding photo. The number of possible arrangements of the five-person wedding party is 5! or $5! = 5 \times 4 \times 3 \times 2 \times 1 = 120$.

As you can see, more possible arrangements exist as the number of objects in the arrangement increases.

Permutations get a little more challenging when you have a fixed number of objects, n, to fill a limited number of places, r, and you care about the order the objects are arranged in.

For example, consider the predicament of the big-league baseball coach of a 20-member team who needs to determine the number of different batting orders that these 20 ball players can fill in a nine-slot batting lineup. The coach could work this permutation out by writing all the factors from 20 back nine places (because 20 players can fill only nine slots in the batting order), like this:

$$20 \times 19 \times 18 \times 17 \times 16 \times 15 \times 14 \times 13 \times 12 = x$$

But this time-consuming process isn't practical in the middle of a game. Luckily, the coach can rely on the permutation formula for n objects taken r:

$$_nP_r = \frac{n!}{(n-r)!}$$

Apply the formula to figure out the possible number of batting orders:

$$_nP_r = \frac{n!}{(n-r)!}$$

$$_nP_r = \frac{20!}{(20-9)!}$$

$$_nP_r = \frac{20!}{11!}$$

That's all there is to it. Now you can apply the outcome formulas to a sample problem.

EXAMPLE

Alice received a bracelet with four distinct removable charms. How many different ways can she arrange the four charms on her new bracelet?

(A) 4

(B) 8

(C) 24

(D) 100

(E) 40,320

Because the bracelet has four charms, the number of arrangements or permutations is 4!: $4 \times 3 \times 2 \times 1$.

Then just multiply the numbers to get the number of possible arrangements (the order you multiply them in doesn't matter). Because $4 \times 3 \times 2 \times 1 = 24$, the correct answer is Choice (C).

Setting Up Sequences

A sequence is a set of ordered values. Every ACT Math Test is likely to contain at least one question that deals with sequences. Commonly tested sequences on the ACT can be one of two kinds:

>> **Arithmetic sequences are formed by adding a common value (called the common difference) to each term.** The following sequence has a common difference of 3: {0, 3, 6, 9}. This sequence has a common difference of –2: {8, 6, 4, 2, 0}. Both sequences are formed by adding the common difference to one term to get the next term.

>> **Geometric sequences are formed by multiplying each term by a common value (called the common ratio).** This geometric sequence has a common ratio of 3: {3, 9, 27, 81}. A geometric sequence with a common ratio of $\frac{1}{3}$ could look like this: {81, 27, 9, 3}.

ACT math questions may ask you to find specific terms in or the sum of a sequence of values. To answer these questions, keep in mind some important rules:

>> **To find the nth term of an arithmetic sequence, apply the following rule, where n represents the position of the term in the sequence, a_1 is the first term, and d is the common difference between the terms.**

$$a_n = a_1 + d(n-1)$$

>> **To find the nth term of a geometric sequence, apply the following rule, where n represents the position of the term in the sequence, a_1 is the first term, and r is the common ratio.**

$$a_n = a_1 r^{(n-1)}$$

>> **To find the sum of a sequence of numbers, apply the following rule, where n represents the number of terms in the sequence, a_1 is the first term, and d is the common difference between the terms.**

$$Sum = \frac{n}{2}\left[2a_1 + d(n-1)\right]$$

Managing Matrices

The ACT test makers may slip a matrix question into the Mathematics Test. If you see these questions, don't panic. They'll be easy to deal with once you review the following approach.

A matrix is simply an array of values. Although you can perform several operations with matrices, the ACT will likely ask you to multiply them. Here are some considerations for working with matrices:

>> **When multiplying matrices, the number of columns in the first matrix must equal the number of rows in the second matrix as you move from left to right.** So, you can multiply a set of matrices if the first one has two columns of numbers and the second one has two rows, but you can't multiply a set where the first matrix has two columns of numbers and the second matrix has three rows, even if the second matrix also has two columns.

» When you multiply the values in a one-row matrix and a one-column matrix, you add the first number in the first matrix to the first number in the second matrix and then add the product of the second value in the first and second matrices, to which you then add the product of the third values in each of the matrices:

$$\begin{vmatrix} 6n & 7n & 5 \end{vmatrix} n \times \begin{vmatrix} 1 \\ 2 \\ 3 \end{vmatrix} = (6 \times 1) + (7 \times 2) + (5 \times 3) = 6 + 14 + 15 = 35$$

» When you work with matrices with more than one row and one column, you apply the same process but several times:

$$\begin{vmatrix} 6 & 7 & 5 \\ 3 & 2 & 1 \end{vmatrix} n \times \begin{vmatrix} 1 & 4 \\ 2 & 3 \\ 3 & 2 \end{vmatrix} = \begin{vmatrix} 35 & 55 \\ 10 & 20 \end{vmatrix}$$

Here are the steps for arriving at the solution:

1. Add the products of the first row of the first matrix and the first column of the second matrix, as we demonstrated here, to get the first value in the matrix product (35).

2. Add the products of the first row in the first matrix and the second column of the second matrix to find the second value in the matrix product (55):

$$(6 \times 4) + (7 \times 3) + (5 \times 2) = 24 + 21 + 10 = 55$$

3. Add the products of the second row of the first matrix and the first column of the second matrix to find the third value in the matrix product (10):

$$(3 \times 1) + (2 \times 2) + (1 \times 3) = 3 + 4 + 3 = 10$$

4. Add the products of the second row of the first matrix to the second column of the second matrix to find the fourth value in the matrix product (20):

$$(3 \times 4) + (2 \times 3) + (1 \times 2) = 12 + 6 + 2 = 20$$

To find the determinant of a two-column, two-row matrix $\begin{vmatrix} a & b \\ c & d \end{vmatrix}$, apply the formula: $ad - bc$.

» Taking a common-sense approach to the Math Test

» Speeding things up with some timing tips

» Knowing what to do — and what not to do — on the Math Test

Chapter **11**

Numb and Number: Acing the Mathematics Test

Okay, you math whiz, here's a question for you. Quick, without your calculator, answer this question: How many seconds are there in a year? Answer: Exactly 12: January 2nd, February 2nd, March 2nd . . .

You can't escape the ACT Mathematics Test, no matter how hard you try. One of the four tests of the ACT is the one-hour Mathematics Test, whose questions, alas, aren't quite as much fun as the ones we ask here. But don't worry. This chapter tells you what you need to know to ace the test.

What You See Is What You Get: The Format and Breakdown of the Math Test

No, the "breakdown" in the preceding heading doesn't refer to *your* (nervous) breakdown, but rather to the breakdown of the number and types of problems in the Mathematics Test. This 60-minute test features 60 questions (which makes figuring out your average time per problem convenient, no?). The questions fall into pretty standard categories.

In the ACT bulletin and in many ACT study books, you may have to slog through incredibly detailed analyses of the exact number of each question type on the test: 14 plane geometry questions, 4 trigonometry questions, blah, blah, blah. We refuse to put you to sleep with that sort of detail. The truth is that the number of questions of each concept varies from test to test. And it's not as if you have any control over the distribution of questions, right? (We can just see the letter: "Dear ACT: Please be sure that I have more geometry and fewer algebra problems — thanks . . . .")

The following is the short 'n' sweet version of the kinds of math questions you encounter in the dark alleyways of the ACT:

» **Pre-algebra:** (Normal people refer to this as *arithmetic.*) Quite a few questions cover basic arithmetic, including such concepts as fractions, decimals, and subtracting negative numbers.

» **Elementary algebra:** You learn this type of material in your first semester or two of algebra. These questions test your ability to work with variables, set up algebraic formulas, solve linear equations, and do the occasional FOIL problem.

» **Intermediate algebra/coordinate geometry:** Fewer than half of the questions cover more difficult quadratic problems, as well as inequalities, bases, exponents, radicals, basic graphing (finding points on an x, y–coordinate graph), and functions.

» **Probability and statistics:** A few of the questions expect you to know how to solve problems involving average/mean, median, combinations, permutations, and probability.

» **Plane geometry and trigonometry:** Many questions cover plane figures (what you think of as "just plain figures," like triangles, circles, quadrilaterals, and so on), and trigonometry. The trig questions make up no more than 10 percent of the test, so if you haven't had trig yet, don't despair. At least half of the trig questions are very basic, covering trig ratios and basic trigonometric identities. Confused? Don't worry about the exact number of questions. Just remember two important points:

» You have 60 minutes to do 60 questions.

» About one-third of the questions are arithmetic, one-third are algebra, and one-third are geometry.

Absence Makes the Heart Grow Fonder: What Isn't on the Math Test

Instead of obsessing over how awful the ACT Mathematics Test is, focus on a few of its good points — namely, what isn't on the test:

» **Calculus:** The ACT does not — we repeat, *does not* — test calculus. You don't even have to know how to pronounce *calculus* to get a good ACT Mathematics Test score. It helps to be familiar with foundational trigonometry concepts, and a little pre-calculus experience may help you work more quickly through one or two questions. Yes, about 10 percent of the test covers trig concepts, but if you answer the other questions correctly, we're happy, you're ecstatic, and your math score is outta sight.

» **Traps:** Many standardized math exams are full of nasty old traps. The ACT is not. It's not out to get you like other tests. Here, the questions really test your math knowledge, not your patience. You don't have to be quite as paranoid on the ACT as you do on some other exams.

Getting into the Grind: The Approach

You've done multiple-choice math problems all your life. In fact, you probably don't have much more to learn about doing multiple-choice math questions. However, the following common-sense steps can help you stay focused as you move quickly through the Math Test:

1. Identify the point of the question.

Yes, even the stupid word problems have a point. Each question is trying to get you to supply a specific piece of information. It helps to read the end question first to determine what you're solving for. Does the question ask you to find the circumference or an area? Do you have to state the value of *x* or of 2*x*? Circle precisely what the question asks for. After you finish the problem, go back and double-check that your answer provides the circled information.

REMEMBER

We just said that the ACT is not out to trap you — but that doesn't mean you can't trap yourself. Among the answer choices are answers that you get by making careless errors. Suppose, for example, that the problem asks for the *product* of numbers, and you find the *sum*. Your answer will undoubtedly be there with the other wrong answers (and the one right one, of course). If the question asks for one-half of a quantity and you solve for twice the quantity, that answer will also likely be there. Because these types of answer choices are available to you, it's especially important that you identify *exactly* what the problem asks for and supply only that information.

TIP

To help you focus, especially on word problems, read the final lines of the question first. Knowing what you're solving for as you read the rest of the question saves time. As you read through the rest of the question, circle numbers and variables to help you focus on the information the question provides to figure out the answer.

2. Budget your time and brain strain: Decide whether the problem is worth your time and effort.

You don't have to do every math problem in order, you know. Read the question and then predict how time-consuming it will be to solve. If you know you have to take several steps to answer the question, you may want to skip the problem, mark it, and go back to it later. If you're not even sure where to start the problem, don't sit there gnawing at your pencil as if it were an ear of corn (unless you're Pinocchio, wood really isn't brain food). Guess and go.

REMEMBER

Guess, guess, guess! The ACT has no penalty for wrong answers. You're going to (or already have) read that statement hundreds of times throughout this book. We say it every chance we get to remind you that you can guess without fear of reprisal. Whenever you skip a problem, choose an answer, any answer, mark it on your answer sheet, and hope that you get lucky. Put a big arrow in the margin of the test booklet next to the question (not on the answer sheet, because it may mess up the computer grading) to remind yourself that you made a wild guess. But if you run out of time and don't get back to the question, at least you have a chance of guessing the answer right.

3. Look before you leap: Preview the answer choices.

Look at the answer choices before you begin doing any pencil-pushing. Often, the choices are variations on a theme, like 0.5, 5, 50, 500, and 5,000. If you see those answers, you know you don't have to worry about the digit, only the decimal. Maybe the answers are very far apart, like 1, 38, 99, 275, and 495. You probably can make a wild estimate and get that answer correct. But if you see that the answers are close together (like 8, 9, 10, 11, and 12), you know you have to invest a little more time and effort into being extra careful when solving the problem.

We'd be wealthy if we had a nickel for every student who groaned and complained as he or she looked at the answer choices, "Man, I didn't really have to work that whole problem out. I could've just estimated from the answer choices." Absolutely true.

4. **Give yourself a second chance: Use your answer to check the question.**

Think of this step as working forward and backward. First, work forward to come up with the answer to the question. Then plug the answer into the question and work backward to check it. For example, if the question asks you to solve for *x*, work through the equation until you get the answer. Then plug that answer back into the equation, and make sure it works out. This last step takes less time than you may think and can save you a lot of points.

Not all the math questions on the ACT contain only one sentence or request that you simply "solve for x." In fact, many math questions require you to sift through a bunch of information to figure out what the real question is. These word problems, as they're called, require you to translate words into numbers and then arrange them in a way that makes mathematical sense. You know what we're talking about — those problems that tell you how fast Train A travels and what speed Train B moves at and then expect you to figure out exactly what hour the two trains will collide. Watch out!

Don't worry; we're here to help you make sense of all these words. Several words translate nicely into mathematical expressions, and many types of word problems lend themselves perfectly to specific formulas or strategies.

Translating English into Math

When you see a word problem on the Math Test, you may feel a little lost at first. Straightforward math equations seem so much more, well, straightforward. Even though word problems are written in English, they may seem like they're written in a foreign language. To help you with the translation, Table 11-1 provides you with some of the more common words you encounter in word problems and tells you what they mean (and look like!) in math terms.

TABLE 11-1 **Common Words and Their Math Counterparts**

Plain English	Math Equivalent
More than, increased by, added to, combined with, total of, sum of	Add (+)
Decreased by, diminished by, reduced by, difference between, taken away from, subtracted from, less than, fewer than	Subtract (–)
Of, times, product of	Multiply (×)
Ratio of, per, out of, quotient	Divide (÷ or /)
Percent	÷100
Is, are, was, were, becomes, results in	Equals (=)
How much, how many, what, what number	Variable (*x, y*)

REMEMBER

Subtraction phrases such as "taken away from," "subtracted from," "less than," and "fewer than" require you to switch the order of the quantities you're subtracting. For example, "Ten decreased by six" means 10 – 6 (which equals 4), but "Ten subtracted from six" means 6 – 10, or –4.

As you read through a word problem, analyze its language to determine what math operations it involves. Keep this general process in mind:

1. Determine what you're supposed to solve for, specifically what the *x* is in the equation.

2. Analyze the rest of the information to figure out how to arrange the equation to solve for *x*.

Many of the word problems on the ACT, like the following example, concern percentages.

EXAMPLE

To pay for college expenses, Ms. Bond takes out a loan in the amount of $650 with a simple interest rate of 8%. What is the total amount of the loan with interest?

(A) $658

(B) $52

(C) $702

(D) $1,170

(E) $1,300

The problem asks for the total amount (that's the x) of Ms. Bond's loan with (which means +) interest, so you have to add what she owes in interest to the original amount of the loan. Before you add the interest amount, you must find out what the amount of interest is. The language of the problem tells you that Ms. Bond has to pay an interest rate of (meaning ×) 8% (which means you divide 8 by 100). Written with numbers rather than words, the problem looks something like this:

$$\frac{8}{100} \times 650 + 650$$

Perform the operation in parentheses first (as we explain in Chapter 8) to get 0.08. Next, multiply $650 by 0.08 to get $52. Ms. Bond pays $52 in interest. Add the interest amount to the loan amount to get your final answer: $650 + $52 = $702. The correct answer is Choice (C).

If you picked Choice (A), you added 8 to $650, which isn't the proper way to determine interest. Choice (B) is the correct interest amount but not the total amount of the loan plus the interest. If you opted for Choice (D), you incorrectly divided 8 by 10 rather than by 100 to come up with the interest amount. And Choice (E) is just $650 doubled.

Time Flies When You're Having Fun: Timing Tips

The most common complaint we hear from students about the Mathematics Test is, "There's just not enough time. If I had more time, I could probably ace every single question, but I always run out of time." True enough. Although having one minute per question (60 math questions, 60-minute section) sounds good, you'll be surprised how fast time goes by. We have a few suggestions to help you make the best use of your time.

Skim for your favorite questions

We think of this technique as eating dessert first (something we always do). Go for the chocolate cake first (the easy questions) to make sure time doesn't run out before you get to the good stuff. Leave the green beans (the harder problems) for the end. If you run out of time (which happens to many test takers), at least you'll have finished the questions that you had the best chance of answering correctly.

In fact, consider approaching the last 20 questions in the Math Test (traditionally the hardest) in two passes. When you get to about question 35 or 40, follow these steps:

1. **Skim the problem to discover the answer to these two questions:**

   - Is the concept tested one I feel comfortable with?

   - Will it take me less than one minute to solve it?

2. **If the answer is yes to both questions, go for it!** Answer the question, mark your answer on your answer sheet and move on.

3. **If the answer to either question is no, skip it!** Draw a big X next to the question in your test booklet and check out the next question.

4. **Answer the remaining questions in the same way, never spending more than about 30 seconds on any one question and marking questions you skip.**

   If a question you first think will be easy turns out to be time-consuming, skip it, mark it, and move on.

5. **When you've seen all 60 questions, go back to the ones you've marked.**

   The point is to make it all the way through the section because some of the later questions in the section can be really easy. You would hate to miss them because you've spent too much time on one or two dumb questions.

6. **Make sure you've marked answers for every question on your answer sheet.**

   If you decide to skip a question in any section on the ACT, make sure you mark an answer for it on your answer sheet before you move on. You won't receive a penalty for wrong answers, so make sure you've bubbled in an answer for every question in the section before the proctor calls time. You can always erase the guess later and replace it with the answer you've selected.

REMEMBER

Backsolve when the answers are actual values

On many problems, you can simply plug in the answer choices to see which one fits. This technique is call *backsolving*. If you find yourself thinking that there must be some sort of equation you can come up with to solve a complex problem, but you can't actually come up with that formula or you know what to do but the computations will be super time-consuming, try plugging in the answers. This will only work if the answers contain no variables, of course, and will work best if the answers are all integers.

The ACT arranges answer choices from greatest to least or least to greatest, so unless there's some other compelling reason to start with another answer choice, begin with Choice (C), the middle value.

For example, suppose that the question is something like this:

EXAMPLE

Given the equation, $x + \frac{1}{2}x + \frac{1}{3}x = 110$ what is the value of x?

(A) 95

(B) 90

(C) 72

(D) 60

(E) 30

Yes, you can use a common denominator and actually work through the problem to find x directly. But it may be quicker and easier to use your calculator to plug in the answer choices. Start with the middle choice, Choice (C). If $x = 72$, then $\frac{1}{2}x = 36$ and $\frac{1}{3}x = 24$. But $72 + 36 + 24 = 132$, not 110. Because the sum is too big, you know the number you plugged in is too big as well. Go down the list, plugging in the smaller numbers. Try Choice (D). Let $x = 60$: $60 + 30 + 20 = 110$. That works! (See Chapter 8 for more on working with common denominators and variables like x.)

Plug in values for variables

When you encounter a question that's mostly variables with possible answer choices that are expressions with mostly variables, this is a job for *plugging in*! Make up values to substitute for the variables to make solving these questions much easier. Here's how:

1. **Make up easy-to-work-with values for each of your variables.**

   Make sure your values follow the guidelines provided by the question. For instance, if the question tells you that x is an even integer, pick a simple even integer like 2 to substitute for x.

2. **Substitute the values for the variables in the problem to come up with an actual value the expression should equal.**

3. **Plug the values you've created into each of the answer choices to find which one results in the amount you come up with in Step 2.**

This simple example shows you what these steps look like in action.

EXAMPLE

The entrance fee for Great Mountains National Park is $10 for vans and $5 for cars. In one summer the park collected x van fees and y car fees. Which of the following is an expression for the total amount in dollars that the park collected for the entire summer?

(A) $10x + 5y$

(B) $10x + 5x$

(C) $15(x + y)$

(D) $10(x + y) + 5(x + y)$

(E) $50xy$

You may recognize the correct answer immediately, but bear with us and learn the approach so you'll be prepared for trickier questions later.

1. **Give your variables values.**

   Say $x = 2$ and $y = 4$. Don't worry that 2 van fees and 4 car fees in a whole summer doesn't make a lot of sense in real life. The goal is to keep your calculations quick and easy breezy.

2. **Substitute the values for the variables to figure out the total dollar amount that would be collected for 2 vans and 4 cars:**

   2 van fees at $10 is $20 and 4 car fees at $5 is $20. So the total amount collect is $40.

3. **Plug 10 for v and 5 for y in each answer choice to see which one results in $40.**

Check Choice (A). $10(2) + 5(4) = 40$. That's your answer! You could try the others just to be sure, but you'll see that no other answer results in $40.

Kindly refrain from showing off everything you know

Some of the ACT problems have extraneous information. For example, a geometry problem may list all sorts of numbers, including lengths of sides and measures of interior angles. If you read the question first and it asks you to find the area of a trapezoid, you know you need just the numbers for base and height. (Remember the formula? The area of a trapezoid is $A = \frac{1}{2}\left(\text{base}_1 + \text{base}_2\right)h$.) Extra red-herring info can make you waste a lot of time. We already know that you're brilliant (you bought this book, didn't you?); you don't need to prove it by doing more than you're asked during the test. If you convert every problem into two or three new problems, you'll never finish the Math Test on time.

Put aside two minutes to fill in the remaining ovals

The ACT assesses no penalty for guessing. We like to say that over and over and over again until you're so exasperated that you want to cut off our air supply. It's critical to remember that you don't lose points for wrong answers; always keep in mind that wild guesses are worth making. Nothing is worse than that sinking feeling you get when the proctor calls time and you still have five problems you haven't even looked at. If you save a few minutes at the end, you can wildly fill in answers for those last ten problems. Choose one column of answers (all A/F, B/G, C/H, D/J, or E/K). You have a good chance of getting at least two of the ten correct.

REMEMBER

The proctor is *supposed* to tell you when you have only five minutes left in the test. Before the test actually begins, you may want to remind your proctor to do so. Also, be sure to wear a wristwatch so you're in control of your own pacing. Don't own one? Buy one now and practice with it!

Do's, Don'ts, and Darns: What to Do and Not Do on the Math Test

Although the math questions are pretty straightforward, a few basic do's and don'ts are worth noting here.

Do get the lead out

Give your pencil a workout. If you have to solve a geometry problem, jot down the formula first and then just fill in the numbers. If you have the formula staring at you, you're not as likely to make a careless mistake as you would be if you tried to keep everything in your head. If the geometry problem has words, words, words, but no picture, draw the picture yourself. When you plug in the answer choices or make up your own numbers to substitute for variables, write down what you plugged in and tried. We see students redoing the same things over and over because they forgot what they'd already plugged in. Doodle away. You get no scratch paper for the ACT, but the test booklet has plenty of white space.

Don't start working until you've read the entire problem

So you read the first part of a problem and start trying to solve for the area of the triangle or the circumference of the circle. But if you read further, you may find that the question asks only for a *ratio* of the areas of two figures, which you can figure out without actually finding the precise areas. Or you may solve a whole algebraic equation, only to realize that the question didn't ask for the variable you found, but for something else entirely. Reading the question first can prevent this messiness. As we say in the "Getting into the Grind: The Approach" section, earlier in this chapter, read the last line or two of the problem first and circle the part of the problem that specifies exactly what you're solving for.

Do reread the problem with your answer inserted

Very few students take this last critical step. Most test-takers are so concerned with finishing on time that they solve the problem and zoom on to the next question. Big tactical error. Rereading the question in light of your answer can show you some pretty dumb mistakes. For example, if the question asks you for the average of 5, 9, 12, 17, and 32 and your answer is 75, you can immediately realize that you found the sum but forgot to divide by the number of terms. (And of course, 75 is one of the answer choices.) Maybe the question asks you to find one interior angle of a figure, and your answer is 190. If you look at the angle and see that it is *acute* (less than 90 degrees), you've made a mistake somewhere.

Don't strike out over a difficult question early on

Most standardized exams put their questions in order of difficulty, presenting the easy ones first, then the medium ones, and finally the hard ones. Things aren't as cut and dried on the ACT Mathematics Test. You may find a question that you consider pretty tough very early in the exam. Although *easy* and *hard* are subjective, many of our students over the years have been furious with themselves because they never looked at the last several questions — reasoning that if they couldn't get the earlier ones right, they obviously couldn't get the later ones at all. Wrong. We've seen some relatively simple questions, especially basic geometry questions, close to the end of the exam.

Chapter **12**

More Fun than a Root Canal: Mathematics Practice Questions

You've had so much fun reviewing algebra, geometry, and trigonometry that you simply can't wait to jump right in and practice what you know, right? Well, we don't want you to have to wait any longer to strut your stuff. Here's a set of a dozen math practice questions; give 'em your best shot!

Directions: Each of the following questions has five answer choices. Choose the best answer for each question.

1. $\dfrac{\left(a^{4} \times a^{3}\right)^{2}}{a^{4}} =$

   (A) a^{36}

   (B) a^{10}

   (C) a^{9}

   (D) a^{6}

   (E) a^{4}

First, do the operation inside the parentheses. When you multiply like bases, you add the exponents: $a^{4} \times a^{3} = a^{7}$. When you have a power outside the parentheses, you multiply the exponents: $\left(a^{7}\right)^{2} = a^{14}$. Finally, when you divide by like bases, you subtract the exponents: $a^{14} \div a^{4} = a^{14-4} = a^{10}$. The correct answer is Choice (B).

If you picked Choice (D), you fell for a trap answer. If you said $a^4 \times a^3 = a^{12}$ and $a^{(12)(2)} = a^{24}$, you may have divided a^{24} by a^4 and gotten a^6. If you chose Choice (A), you fell for another trap. You may have reasoned that $a^4 \times a^3 = a^{12}$. Because 12 squared is 144, you may have thought that $a^{(12)^2} = a^{144}$ and that $a^{144} \div a^4 = a^{36}$.

All these trap answers are intentional, put there to test whether you know how to perform operations with exponents. If you're still confused about how to multiply and divide like bases, turn to Chapter 8.

2. The ratio of knives to forks to spoons in a silverware drawer is 3:4:5. Which of the following could be the total number of knives, forks, and spoons in the drawer?

(F) 60

(G) 62

(H) 64

(J) 65

(K) 66

The total number of utensils must be a multiple of the sum of the numbers of the ratios. In other words, add $3 + 4 + 5 = 12$. The total must be a multiple of 12. Only one answer choice, 60, divides evenly by 12, so you know the correct answer is Choice (F).

If you're confused about ratios (supposedly one of the easiest portions of the exam), check out Chapter 8.

3. An usher passes out 60 percent of his programs before the intermission and 40 percent of the remainder after the intermission. At the end of the evening, what percent of the original number of programs does the usher have left?

(A) 60

(B) 40

(C) 24

(D) 16

(E) 0

Whenever you have a percentage problem, plug in 100 for the original total. Assume that the usher begins with 100 programs. If he passes out 60 percent of them, he has passed out 60, leaving him with 40. Now comes the tricky part. After the intermission, the usher passes out 40 percent of the remaining programs: 40 percent of 40 is 16 ($0.4 \times 40 = 16$) and $40 - 16 = 24$. So the correct answer is Choice (C).

Did you fall for the trap answer in Choice (E)? If you thought the usher first passed out 60 programs and then passed out the remaining 40, you believed that he had no programs left at the end of the evening. The word *remainder* is the key to this problem. The usher didn't pass out 40 percent of his original total, but 40 percent of the remaining programs.

If you chose Choice (D), you made a careless mistake. The number 16 represents the percentage of programs the usher passed out after the intermission. The question asks for the percent of programs the usher had left. We suggest that you circle the portion of the question that tells you what you're looking for. When you double-check your work, review this circled portion first.

4. A salesman makes a commission of $1.50 per shirt sold and $2.50 per pair of pants sold. In one pay period, he sold 10 more shirts than pairs of pants. If his total commission for the pay period was $215, what was the total number of shirts and pairs of pants he sold?

(F) 40

(G) 50

(H) 60

(J) 110

(K) 150

Let x be the number of pairs of pants the salesman sold. The number of shirts is $x+10$ (because the problem tells you that the salesman sold 10 more shirts than pairs of pants). Set up the following equation:

$$\$1.50(x+10)+\$2.50(x)=\$215$$

Now just follow these steps to solve for x:

1. **Multiply:** $1.50x+15+2.50x=215$

2. **Combine like terms:** $4.00x+15=215$

3. **Isolate the x on one side:** $4.00x=215-15$

4. **Subtract:** $4.00x=200$

5. **Divide:** $x=200\div4$, or $x=50$

WARNING

If you answered with Choice (G), you fell for the trap answer (after all that hard work)! Remember to go back and reread what the question is asking for. In this case, it wants to know the total number of pants and shirts sold. So you're not done working yet. If x (which equals 50) is the number of pairs of pants, then $x+10$ (which is 60) is the number of shirts sold. (Note that 60 is a trap answer as well.) Combine $50+60$ to get the right answer, 110. The correct answer is Choice (J).

5. Kim and Scott work together stuffing envelopes. Kim works twice as fast as Scott. Together they stuff 2,100 envelopes in four hours. How long would Kim, working alone, take to stuff 175 envelopes?

(A) 20 minutes

(B) 30 minutes

(C) 1 hour

(D) 3 hours

(E) 6 hours

The ratio of Kim's work to Scott's work is 2:1. In other words, she does two out of every three envelopes. Scott does one out of every three envelopes, for a total of 700 envelopes ($2,100\div3$). Scott stuffs 700 envelopes in four hours, and Kim stuffs 1,400 ($2,100-700=1,400$) in four hours. Divide 1,400 by 4 to find that Kim produces 350 stuffed envelopes per hour. 175 is one-half of 350. Therefore, in one half-hour (or 30 minutes), Kim can stuff 175 envelopes. The correct answer is Choice (B).

TIP

When you encounter a word problem like this one, don't start thinking about equations immediately. Talking through the problem may help you more than creating a bunch of equations.

6. If $DC = 6$ and point O is the center of the circle, what is the shaded area in the figure?

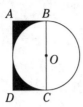

(F) $72 - 18\pi$

(G) $72 - 36\pi$

(H) 9π

(J) $36 - 18\pi$

(K) $36 - 36\pi$

A *shaded area* is the leftover portion of a figure. To find a shaded area, you usually find the total area and the unshaded area and then subtract. In this figure, the shaded area is the total area of rectangle $ABCD$ less the area of half the circle. If the side DC is 6, the radius of the circle is also 6.

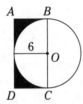

The area of a circle is πr^2; therefore, the area of this circle is $\pi 6^2$ or 36π. Be careful to remember that you're working only with a semicircle. The shaded area subtracts only half the area of the circle, so you know you have to subtract 18π. That immediately narrows the answers to Choices (F) and (J).

Next, find the area of the rectangle. (The area of a rectangle equals length × width.) The width of DC is 6. Because the radius of the circle is 6, the diameter of the circle is 12. So BC, the diameter of the circle, is the same as the length of the rectangle. To find the area of the rectangle, simply multiply: $6 \times 12 = 72$. Finally, subtract: $72 - 18\pi$. The correct answer is Choice (F).

Shaded area questions should be one of the easiest types of questions to get correct. If you got confused on this problem, flip to Chapter 9.

7. When $5a^2 + (5a)^2 = 120$, what is the value of a?

(A) 2

(B) 3

(C) 4

(D) 5

(E) 6

First, deal with the parentheses: $(5a)^2 = 5a \times 5a$, which is $25a^2$. Then add like terms: $25a^2 + 5a^2 = 30a^2$. Finally, solve the equation for a:

$$5a^2 + \left(5a\right)^2 = 120$$
$$30a^2 = 120$$
$$a^2 = 120 \div 30$$
$$a^2 = 4$$
$$a = 2$$

The correct answer is Choice (A).

WARNING

Choice (C) is the trap answer. If you divided 120 by 30 and got 4, you may have picked Choice (C), forgetting that 4 represented a^2, not a.

Of course, you also could simply plug in each answer choice and work backward to solve this problem. Start with the middle value in the answer choices. If $a = 4$, then

$$5\left(4\right)^2 + \left(5 \times 4\right)^2 =$$
$$5\left(16\right) + 20^2 =$$
$$80 + 400 = 480$$
$$480 \neq 120$$

The value of Choice (C) is too great, so try Choices (A) and (B), which are smaller numbers.

8. Three times as much as $\frac{1}{3}$ less than $3x$ is how much in terms of x?

   (F) $9x$

   (G) $8x$

   (H) $6x$

   (J) x

   (K) $\frac{1}{3}x$

   Working backward in this type of problem is usually the easiest way to solve it. One-third less than $3x$ is $2x$. You can calculate it this way: $3x - \frac{1}{3}(3x) = 3x - x = 2x$. Then just multiply by 3: $3 \times 2x = 6x$. The correct answer is Choice (H).

9. The following chart shows the weights of junior high school students. What is the sum of the mode and the median weights?

Weight in Pounds	Number of Students
110	4
120	2
130	3
140	2

   (A) 230 pounds

   (B) 235 pounds

   (C) 250 pounds

   (D) 255 pounds

   (E) 258 pounds

This question tests vocabulary as much as it tests math. The *mode* is the most frequently repeated number. In this case, 110 is repeated more often than any other term. The *median* is the middle term when the numbers are arranged in order. Here you have 110, 110, 110, 110, 120, 120, 130, 130, 130, 140, 140. Of these 11 numbers, the sixth one, 120, is the median. And $110 + 120 = 230$, so the correct answer is Choice (A).

Don't confuse *median* with *mean.* The *mean* is the average. You get the mean by adding all the terms and then dividing by the number of terms. If you confused median with mean, you'd really be in a quandary, because the sum of the mean and the mode is 232.73 and that answer isn't an option. If you picked Choice (B), you fell into a different trap. You found that 125 was the median by adding the first and last terms and dividing by 2. Sorry. To find the median, you have to write out all the terms from least to greatest (all four 110s, both 120s, and so on) and then locate the middle term.

10. Points E, D, and A are colinear. The ratio of the area of $\triangle EBD$ to $\triangle ABD$ is

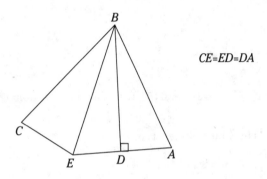

$CE = ED = DA$

(F) 3:2

(G) 3:1

(H) 2:1

(J) 1:1

(K) 1:2

The area of a triangle is $\frac{1}{2}bh$. The base of EBD is ED. ED is equal to AD, which is the base of $\triangle ABD$. The bases of the two triangles are equal. The heights are equal, as well. By definition, the height of a triangle is a line from the tallest point perpendicular to the base. If the triangles have the same base and the same height, the ratio of their areas is 1:1. So the correct answer is Choice (J).

11. Given this equation $\begin{array}{r} 95c5 \\ +3cbd \\ \hline ab3a2 \end{array}$, solve for the sum of $a + b + c$.

(A) 15

(B) 14

(C) 13

(D) 12

(E) 11

If you're rushed for time, this problem is a good one to skip and come back to later. Mark a guess on your answer sheet, put a big checkmark next to the questions in your test booklet, and evaluate the question after you've finished the last math question. Remember that the ACT doesn't assess a penalty for wrong answers. Never leave an answer blank. Even a wild guess is worthwhile. However, if you do a few of these practice problems, you'll be surprised at how quickly you can get them right.

Don't panic. This problem is much easier than it appears. Start with the right-hand column, the ones or units column: $5 + c = $ a number that ends in 2. You know that the 2 must be a 12 instead of just a 2 because you can't add a positive number to 5 and get 2, which means $c = 7$. Jot down $c = 7$.

When you carry the 1 to the tens column, you get $1 + 7$, which is 8, and $8 + b = a$. You don't know a yet . . . or do you? Go to the far-left column (the thousands column). If the answer is $ab3\ a2$, the variable a must equal 1. You can't add two four-digit numbers and get 20,000-something. The most you can get is 10,000-something (for example, $9,999 + 9,999 = 19,998$). Now you know that a is 1. Jot down $a = 1$.

Go back to the tens column: $1 + 7 = 8$ and $8 + b = 11$ (it can't be 1; it must be 11). Therefore, $b = 3$. Carry the 1 to the hundreds column: $1 + 5 = 6$ and $6 + c$ (which is 7) $= 13$. Yes, this is true — a good check. Carry the 1 to the next column: $1 + 9 = 10$ and $10 + 3$ is 13, which is what we said ab was in the first place. Therefore, $c = 7$, $b = 3$, $a = 1$, and $7 + 3 + 1 = 11$. The correct answer is Choice (E).

REMEMBER

The most common mistake that students make on this type of problem is forgetting to carry the 1 to the next column. Double-check that you have done so.

12. $a\beta b = \dfrac{1}{a} + \dfrac{1}{b}$ What is the value of $\dfrac{2}{15}\beta\dfrac{2}{18}$?

(F) 14

(G) 14.5

(H) 15

(J) 16

(K) 16.5

This problem is a symbolism problem, one that you should think through in words instead of heading for an equation. The symbol β indicates that you add the reciprocals of the two numbers. For example, the reciprocal of a is $\dfrac{1}{a}$, and the reciprocal of b is $\dfrac{1}{b}$. Therefore, add the reciprocals of $\dfrac{2}{15}$ and $\dfrac{2}{18}$. $\dfrac{15}{2} + \dfrac{18}{2} = \dfrac{33}{2} = 16.5$. The correct answer is Choice (K).

REMEMBER

The β has this meaning for this problem only. The meanings of symbols vary from problem to problem; always read the problems carefully.

4

Time to Read the Riot ACT: The Reading Test

Chapter **13**

This, Too, Shall Pass(age): Sailing through the Reading Test

After working through an ACT Reading Test, a student said, "If I'd known it would end up like this, I never would have let my first-grade teacher show me how to read!" Now, that's just silly. If he hadn't learned to read, he'd be lost on the ACT and other sources of fine entertainment. The first day you spent with your ABCs prepared the way for this chapter, which explains the approach to the third section of the ACT — the Reading Test.

In this chapter, you find out what types of passages to expect and what the questions look like. After you know the ins and outs of excelling on the Reading Test, you'll be glad you learned to read.

Facing 40 Questions: The Reading Test

The Reading Test consists of four passages, each with 10 questions, for a total of 40 questions. Each passage is supposed to be similar in difficulty to materials you encounter during your freshman year of college. The test contains one passage on each of the following topics:

>> **Prose fiction:** The first passage in the section is a fiction passage from a novel or a short story. Some of the fiction passages are very fun to read. But don't expect that you'll have read them before. In all the years we've been preparing students for the ACT, we've had only one student tell us she remembers having read the passage before in a novel. The ACT test makers obviously don't want to test you on what you're already familiar with (and maybe even have discussed in class); they want to test you on how well you evaluate a passage that's new to you.

- **Social studies:** The social studies passage comes after the prose fiction piece and covers sociology, anthropology, history, geography, psychology, political science, and economics. That's an incredibly wide range of topics when you think about it. The history passages are generally easier to understand; some of the psychology ones can be intense.

- **Humanities:** The third passage can be about music, dance, theater, art, architecture, language, ethics, literary criticism, and even philosophy. Most students tend to like the humanities passages because (believe it or not) they're actually interesting.

- **Natural sciences:** The last passage is what most people think about when they hear the word *science*. The natural sciences passage can cover chemistry, biology, physics, and other physical sciences.

  Are you panicking right now, screaming, "I haven't taken physics! No fair!"? Not to worry. The questions don't require you to know any particular subjects. Everything you need to answer the questions is right there in the passages, and you can go back to the passages as often as you like.

Timing

The Reading Test is 35 minutes long. Assuming you live to the average age of around 80, the Reading Test is only about 0.000000008 percent of your life. Now that doesn't seem so bad, does it? Because the test includes 40 questions, you need to spend just a little less than a minute per question. Remember that a little less than a minute includes reading the passage as well as working through the questions.

TIP

When you're finished with the prose fiction passage, glance at the clock. You should be no more than nine minutes into the section. If you've taken significantly more time than that to finish the first passage, you need to work more wisely (and quickly!) on the remaining passages.

Scoring

You get three reading scores. One is the total score, based on all four passages and 40 questions. Colleges pay the most attention to this score. Then you get two subscores: one in natural sciences/social studies (based, obviously, on the natural sciences and social studies passages) and one in arts/literature (based on the prose fiction and humanities passages). Though you may be interested to see which passages you did better on, colleges rarely put much emphasis on your reading subscores.

Getting Prepared: Reading Strategies

You've probably been reading since you were about 5 years old. It's a little late for us to teach you the basics. But we can tell you how to make the best use of your time in this test. To do your best on this 35-minute test, follow these guidelines for skimming through the passages and focus on the questions.

Preview the passages

You're naturally going to like one type of passage more than the others. Look for it and read it first, being extremely careful to shade in the correct bubbles on your answer grid as you answer the questions.

TIP

What happens if your brain takes a little vacation and you suddenly find you've filled in the bubbles all wrong? Maybe you started off by reading Passage 2, with Questions 11–20, but you filled in the bubbles for Questions 1–10? Hey, you laugh now, but mixing up the bubbles is easy to do, especially when you skip around. The first reaction usually is panic; first you erase all your answers, and then you try to remember what they were. Bad move. Here's how to handle this problem: As you answer a question, first circle the correct response in your booklet and then fill in the bubble for that response on the answer grid. That way, if you mess up and have to erase your answer grid, you can just glance at your answer booklet and find the right answers again.

Decide on an approach

Some students do well under time pressures and can finish all four passages and the questions in the allotted 35 minutes. Those students often don't have to read slowly and carefully, getting every little morsel the passages have to offer; instead, they can read quickly to get the overall idea. Other students get so totally nervous if they have to rush, they mess up completely. If you're one of these students, a better strategy for you may be to concentrate on reading three of the passages carefully and answering all (or almost all) the questions correctly on them. Here are the steps to success if you apply the *three-passage approach*:

1. **Pick the passage you like the least and mark guesses for all ten of its questions on your answer sheet.**

   Choose the same answer, all As/Fs, Bs/Gs, Cs/Hs, or Ds/Js, for the ten questions. It's highly likely that the correct answer for at least two of the ten questions will pop up in one column. Consider that passage answered and done.

2. **Gravitate to the passage type you like best.**

   Devote a little more than 11 minutes to carefully answer its ten questions. The key to success with this approach is to be super accurate. Mark your answers on the sheet.

3. **Do the same for your second favorite passage.**

4. **End with your third favorite.**

   Make sure you mark answers for all 40 questions in the Reading Test.

TIP

The three-passage approach works best when you commit to concentrating on only three passages. Don't even entertain the idea that you may get to the fourth passage. Otherwise, you'll be tempted to rush and risk missing more questions than you would if you pretend that the section has only three reading opportunities.

Generally, the highest reading score you can achieve with the three-passage approach is a 27. And that's if you get some lucky guesses on the passage you skip and correctly answer almost all of the other 30 questions.

Skim the passage effectively

Save time by skimming — not reading — the ACT passages before you tackle the questions. When you practice reading questions, set a timer for 60 seconds on your phone. When the timer buzzes, stop reading and move to the questions. Here are some tips on how to accomplish that feat:

>> **Know how paragraphs are organized.** Most writers (except writers of literature) pay attention to the maxim, "Tell 'em what you're gonna tell 'em; tell 'em; and tell 'em what you told 'em."

- **The first sentence of a paragraph presents its main topic.** Read the first several lines to get a glimpse of what the paragraph is about.

- **The middle sentences provide supporting evidence or examples for its main idea.** You can pretty much skip these lines on your first reading. Save reading this stuff for when you encounter a question that asks about supporting details.

» **Don't memorize.** We see some students stop reading, gaze out into the distance, and mutter to themselves, counting off on their fingers. These students are obviously trying to memorize facts from the passage: "Let's see, the three basic elements that make up Kleinschwab's Elixir are . . .." Stop! You don't have to memorize anything; in fact, doing so can be counterproductive. Although you naturally want to remember some of what you read, you can always go back to the passage as often as you want. When you go to the passage for information, you'll find it more quickly if you summarize (not memorize!) as you read.

» **Summarize.** As you read each paragraph's topic sentence, think about what you're reading and summarize it in your own words. Don't make things complicated. A simple "This paragraph is about the way the Greeks looked at nature and the next paragraph covers the way the Romans looked at nature" helps to focus your thoughts and keep track of where information occurs in the passage.

- *Question:* Should you underline or outline as you go?

- *Answer:* Other than a quick circling of a paragraph topic, don't spend time underlining or outlining during your first read of the passage. When you go back into the passage to answer questions, you may want to keep track of information to help you answer other questions. Highlight key words (especially things like dates, proper names, unusual vocabulary, lists of examples, key transition words, and anything that really confuses you). Occasionally jotting a note in the margin to summarize a paragraph is particularly helpful. For example, next to Paragraph 1, you may write, "Need for elixir." Next to Paragraph 2, you may write, "Failed experiments." By Paragraph 3, you may write, "Success; uses of elixir." You get the idea. You're allowed to refer to the passages as often as you want; having an idea of what is where in the passage can save you precious seconds.

» **Look for relationships and connections.** If the author contrasts two or more concepts, ask yourself what makes one idea different from the others. When a passage compares and contrasts theories, ideas, or techniques, keep track of which explanations apply to each and pay attention to which of the theories, ideas, or techniques the author seems to favor. Perhaps you're given thoughts in sequence. Try to keep track of what comes first, next, and last. For passages that talk about cause and effect, determine how one thing impacts another.

- *Question:* Should you read the questions before you read the passages?

- *Answer:* The large number of questions that accompany each ACT passage make it tricky to get helpful information from skimming through the questions first. You may find it helpful to completely skip the passage and jump right into answering the questions.

Identifying Reading Question Types

Although you may encounter many different types of reading questions on the ACT, most fall into one of the following general types. Each of these question types requires a slightly different approach.

>> *Big picture questions* ask you about the passage as a whole.

>> *Direct statement questions* ask you to regurgitate information straight from the passage.

>> *Inference questions* require you to make logical assumptions about the passage details.

The next sections break down each of these question types and explain how to answer them correctly.

Big picture questions

Big picture questions are almost always the first questions in the set of ten questions for a passage. A question may ask, "Which of the following is the main idea of the passage?" or "The primary purpose of Paragraph 3 is to do which of these?" You've likely tackled big picture questions like these on other exams. As you answer them on the ACT, keep in mind these three characteristics of the overall idea:

>> **The big picture is broad and general.** It covers the entire passage (or the entire paragraph, if the question asks about a paragraph). Be sure not to choose a "little" answer. The mere fact that a statement is true doesn't mean it's the main idea. Suppose you have a question that asks you for the main idea of a passage about high school education. One answer choice says, "The ACT gives students the heebie-jeebies." No one can argue with that statement, but it isn't the main idea of the passage.

>> **The answer to a big picture question may repeat the topic sentence or key words.** If the passage is about Asian philosophy, the correct answer may have the words *Asian philosophy* in it. Don't immediately choose any answer just because it has those words, but if you're debating between two answers, the one with the key words may be the better choice.

>> **The answer to a big picture question is always consistent with the tone of the passage and the attitude of the author.** If the passage is positive and the author is impressed by the philosophy, the main idea will be positive, not negative or neutral. If the author is criticizing something, the main idea will be negative.

REMEMBER

The best answer to a big picture question is general rather than specific. If an answer choice for a big picture question contains information that comes from just one part of the passage, it probably isn't the best answer. Here are some other ways to eliminate answer choices for main-idea questions:

>> **Avoid answer choices that contain information that comes only from the middle paragraphs of the passage.** These paragraphs probably deal with specific points rather than the main theme.

>> **Cross out any answer choices that contain information that the passage doesn't cover.** These choices are irrelevant.

>> **See whether you can eliminate answer choices based on just the first words.** For example, if you're trying to find the author's main point in a natural science passage with an objective tone, you can eliminate answers that begin with more subjective words, like *argue* or *criticize*.

Direct statement questions

The *direct statement question* covers one particular point, not the passage as a whole. This question is one of the easiest to get correct, especially when the question gives you a line reference. You just go to the passage and find the specific answer. Clues that you're dealing with direct statement questions are in the verbs they contain. Questions that ask for what the author or passage *states*, *claims*, *indicates*, and so on are usually direct statement questions. And they're often the ones that start with "According to the passage." Some examples include "According to the passage, James confronted Gary about the business when which of the following occurred?" or "The author states that the results of the experiments were considered unacceptable because. . . ."

The key to answering detail questions is knowing where the information is in the passage so you can get to it quickly. (Here's where summarizing the main point of each paragraph as you skim comes in handy; see the earlier section "Skim the passage effectively" for more info.) Read the question carefully, and keep in mind that the right answer may paraphrase the passage instead of providing a word-for-word repeat.

If you're running short of time or your brain cells are about ready to surrender, look for this type of question and answer it first. You can often answer detail questions correctly even if you haven't read the entire passage. Find a key word in the question (such as, say, *elixir*) and skim the passage for that word.

The passage provides you with the correct answer to a direct statement question. Eliminate any answer choices that require you to make an assumption or inference that the passage doesn't specifically present. If you miss one of these questions, you've probably not read enough of the passage to locate the answer and have resorted to guessing.

Inference questions

Inference questions ask you about information that a passage implies rather than states directly. Specifically, they test your ability to draw conclusions from the information that's actually in the passage. You may have to read between the lines a little to find the answers to these questions. For instance, suppose you read a passage about hummingbirds. Information in one paragraph may state that hummingbirds fly south for the winter. Information in another paragraph may say that the Speckled Rufus is a kind of hummingbird. From this information, you can infer that the Speckled Rufus flies south in the winter.

You can usually spot inference questions because they contain words such as *infers*, *suggests*, or *implies*. An example could be this: "The passage suggests which of the following about Gary's response to John."

When you face an inference question, look for the choice that extends the information in the passage just a little bit. Answer choices that make inferences that you can't support with what's stated in the passage are incorrect. Don't choose an answer that requires you to come up with information that isn't there. Sometimes knowing a lot about a passage's topic can throw you off because you may be tempted to answer questions based on your own knowledge rather than the passage.

Figuring Out Reading Question Formats

Sometimes an ACT reading question's format gives you clues on how to best answer it. Almost every Reading Test (but not every passage) contains at least a couple of questions in the common formats covered by the following sections.

Vocabulary in context

You may have to determine the meaning of a word by its use in context. These questions, creatively called *vocabulary-in-context questions*, are pretty easy to answer correctly because you can use the passage to figure out what the word in the question means. They give you a word or phrase (usually italicized or in quotations) and its line reference and ask you what that word means as it's used in the passage.

The key to finding the best answer for a vocabulary-in-context question is to substitute the answer choices for the word in the passage. The answer choice that replaces the vocabulary word and makes sense within the context of the sentence and sentences around it is the right answer.

The only potentially tricky part about these questions is that they may test you on unfamiliar definitions of words that you know the meanings of. Sometimes, ACT passages use common words in uncommon ways. For example, the author may mention that, "Lawrence was unable to cow Michael, despite his frequent threats." Although *cow* usually refers to a four-footed bovine, in this case, the word is used as a verb, meaning to intimidate or frighten. (Don't let the ACT cow you!)

If a set of questions has a vocabulary-in-context variety, answer it first. You don't have to know a lot about the passage to answer these babies, and the question tells you exactly where to go to answer it.

Most nearly means

Occasionally, you see an ACT reading question worded this way: "When the author says that Gary was 'cleverly incommunicative,' she most nearly means that his response is which of these?" A question that asks for what a passage or an author most nearly means or suggests by quoted or italicized portions of a paragraph may be easily answered by simply examining the possible answer choices. Usually the correct answer provides a definition or description of the quoted material and doesn't require you to check out the passage at all. For example, the answer to the question about Gary's response could be "Gary wisely chooses to refrain from responding to Jack's confrontation."

Exception questions

Most questions ask you to choose the one correct answer, but some questions are cleverly disguised to ask for the one answer that isn't true. We call these beauties *exception questions*. You can recognize them by the presence of a negative word (usually *except* or *not*) in the question: "The passage lists all of the following as reasons that Gary objected to the new model EXCEPT:" When you see questions worded this way, you know you're looking for the one answer choice that isn't true.

Exception questions aren't that difficult if you approach them systematically. Determining which answer choice doesn't appear in the passage takes time because you may think you have to look in the passage for the choice and not find it. But we have a better way to find the right (or should we say wrong?) answer. Instead of determining whether an answer *isn't* true, just eliminate the three true answers. Doing so leaves you with the one false (and therefore correct) answer. Identifying choices that are true according to the passage is much easier than determining the one choice that isn't. Take your time, and you'll do exceptionally well on exception questions.

Approaching Comparative Passages

One of the passages in the Reading Test will consist of a set of comparative passages. You see two passages on the same general topic followed by ten questions. The set of passages may appear in any of the four passage types. The questions are grouped into three categories: those about the first passage, those about the second one, and those about both of them. So, you may see two shorter humanities passages instead of one long one. Some of the ten questions ask you about just one of the two passages. The others require you to compare ideas in the two passages.

When you see one of these comparison exercises on your test, treat the first two-thirds of the ten questions (the ones about each of the individual passages) the same way you do the one-passage format. Pay attention to the wording in the question to be sure you're answering it based on the appropriate passage.

The last several questions require you to compare two passages, asking you how they're different, on which points they agree, or how one author would respond to the opinion of the other author.

TIP

The trick to answering the comparison questions is to eliminate answer choices based on one passage at a time.

>> **For questions that ask you how passages are different, first eliminate answers that are untrue for one passage.** If any answers remain, eliminate those that are untrue for the other passage. The answers to these questions are usually worded like this: "Passage A focuses on Gary's side of the story while Passage B favors John's version." You know this answer is untrue if Passage A doesn't focus on Gary or if Passage B doesn't favor John. The minute you find one thing wrong with an answer, the entire answer has to be wrong.

>> **For questions that ask you for a point on which the authors would agree, eliminate answers that are untrue for either passage.** You can usually dismiss answers that clearly summarize one passage's position. Usually the correct answer to these questions reflects a general point of agreement rather than a strong opinion held by one author or the other.

TIP

The ACT isn't an especially tricky exam. However, these basic tips can prevent you from falling for the few traps that do exist . . . or from creating traps of your own.

>> **Try leaping before you look.** For many students, the best way to save time and focus on what's important is to jump straight into the questions without even looking at the passage first. This strategy feels very uncomfortable at first, but with practice it can be a real time-saver. Here are the steps to follow to make the most of this approach:

1. **Read the short bolded blurb at the beginning of the passage.**

   This short intro may give you a general idea of the passage's topic.

2. **Skim the questions to find the one that appears easiest to answer first.**

   Choose direct statement questions with line or paragraph references or those that contain elements such as dates, capitalized words, or proper names that are easy to skim for.

3. **As you read the passage parts to answer one question, initial, underline, or circle important info that may help you with subsequent questions.**

4. **When you've exhausted the question with easy references, tackle the big picture question if there is one.**

   You may need to answer several questions before you have enough information to find the passage's main idea. Check the last paragraph for clues.

5. **Work on questions whose answer choices contain elements that are easy to look for.**

6. **Save the inference questions for the end.**

To master this approach, be willing to leave a question if you spend more than 30 seconds searching for the answer. Eliminate obviously incorrect answers and take on another question in the set. Often when you go back to the question, you can answer it based on work you've done on other questions.

» **You don't have to work in order.** Start with the passage you like best. If you're a science buff, answer questions 31–40 first. Then go to the other three passages. There's no good reason to leave your best chance for success for the end of the test when you're running out of time. Likewise, answer the questions in a set in the order that makes the most sense. Start with questions that refer you to particular parts of the passage or that ask you for definitions. Save more challenging questions for the end of the set when you've spent more time in the passage.

You can use information you glean from answering some questions in a set to help you answer other questions in the set.

REMEMBER

» **Know how to eliminate wrong answers.** Using the process of elimination helps you weed out distracters and focus on the right answer. Sometimes you have to choose the best choice out of three pretty great choices. Other times you must choose from four really crummy options. Common wrong answers to reading-comprehension questions include the following:

- **Choices that contain information that the passage doesn't cover:** Even if the information in these choices is true in real life, you can't pick them because the passage needs to be the source of the information. Eliminate these choices no matter how tempting they may be.

- **Choices that contradict the passage's main point, author's tone, or specific details:** After you've read the passage, you should be able to quickly eliminate most of the choices that contradict what you know about the passage.

- **Choices that don't answer the question:** Paying careful attention to the wording of each question can help you narrow down your answer options. For example, a question may ask about a disadvantage of something discussed in the passage. If one of the answer choices lists an advantage rather than a disadvantage, you can eliminate that choice without thinking twice.

- **Choices that contain debatable words.** *Debatable words* are words that leave no room for exception, such as *all, always, completely, never, every, none,* and so on. The rest of the answer may look pretty good except for that unrelenting word.

  Don't automatically throw out every answer that has one of these words. But if your answer contains a debatable word, make absolutely sure that information in the passage justifies the presence of that strong position.

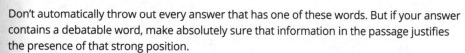
REMEMBER

» **Don't read more into the passage than what's there.** Many questions are based on information that the passage specifically states. Other questions are based on information that the passage implies. Don't take matters to extremes or bring in background information that you happen to have. Suppose that the passage talks about the fall of communism in the Soviet Union and its satellite countries. You can't automatically assume the author also believes that communism will fail in China. Don't choose the answer that takes the reasoning too far.

One final word: Try to enjoy the passages. We know; that's easy for us to say. But believe it or not, some of this reading material is very interesting. If you approach it with a negative attitude, your mind is already closed to it, making the material much more difficult to comprehend and remember. If you at least pretend that you're going to have a good time getting through it, you're much more likely to put things in perspective, get a better handle on the material, and maybe even learn something new.

Chapter **14**

Where Are SparkNotes When You Need Them? Reading Practice Questions

On the actual ACT, the Reading Test consists of four full-length passages, each with about 750 words. Ten questions follow each passage. You have only 35 minutes to read the four passages and answer all 40 questions. This abbreviated practice exam (we want to ease you into this stuff slowly) has four shorter passages and a total of eight questions. Use it to practice your approach to the reading questions. Don't worry about timing now. Think about what type of passage you're dealing with (prose fiction, social science, humanities, or natural science) and identify each question type. A short explanation of the answer follows each question. See Chapters 19, 21, and 23 for the complete tests, and check out Chapter 13 for everything you need to know about the Reading Test.

Directions: Answer each question based on what is stated or implied in the passage.

Passage 1 — Prose Fiction

This passage is adapted from the Robert Louis Stevenson novel *Kidnapped.*

Meanwhile such of the wounded as could move came clambering out of the fore-scuttle and began to help; while the rest that lay helpless in their bunks harrowed me with screaming and begging to be saved.

The captain took no part. It seemed he was struck stupid. He stood holding by the shrouds, talking to himself and groaning out aloud whenever the ship hammered on the rock. His brig was like wife and child to him; he had looked on, day by day, at the mishandling of poor Ransome; but when it came to the brig, he seemed to suffer along with her.

All the time of our working at the boat, I remember only one other thing; that I asked Alan, looking across at the shore, what country it was; and he answered, it was the worst possible for him, for it was a land of the Campbells.

We had one of the wounded men told off to keep a watch upon the seas and cry us warning. Well, we had the boat about ready to be launched, when this man sang out pretty shrill: "For God's sake, hold on!" We knew by his tone that it was something more than ordinary; and sure enough; there followed a sea so huge that it lifted the brig right up and canted her over on her beam. Whether the cry came too late or my hold was too weak, I know not; but at the sudden tilting of the ship I was cast clean over the bulwarks into the sea.

I went down, and drank my fill; and then came up, and got a blink of the moon; and then down again. They say a man sinks the third time for good. I cannot be made like other folk, then; for I would not like to write how often I went down or how often I came up again. All the while, I was being hurled along, and beaten upon and choked, and then swallowed whole, and the thing was so distracting to my wits, that I was neither sorry nor afraid.

Presently, I found I was holding to a spar, which helped me somewhat. And then all of a sudden I was in quiet water, and began to come to myself.

It was the spare yard I had got hold of, and I was amazed to see how far I had traveled from the brig. I hailed her indeed; but it was plain she was already out of cry. She was still holding together; but whether or not they had yet launched the boat, I was too far off and too low down to see.

While I was hailing the brig, I spied a tract of water lying between us, where no great waves came, but which yet boiled white all over, and bristled in the moon with rings and bubbles. Sometimes the whole tract swung to one side, like the tail of a live serpent; sometimes, for a glimpse, it all would disappear and then boil up again. What it was I had no guess, which for the time increased my fear of it; but I now know it must have been the roost or tide race, which carried me away so fast and tumbled me about so cruelly, and at last, as if tired of that play, had flung me and spare yard upon its landward margin.

1. The narrator compares the ship to the captain's wife and child to:

   (A) lament the captain's long separation from his family.

   (B) demonstrate the difficulty the captain has keeping focused on his job.

   (C) predict the captain's future madness.

   (D) show the depth of the connection the captain has to his ship.

The focus of the second paragraph is on how the captain is upset by the condition of his ship. To compare his ship to his wife and child is to show how much he loves the ship and, thus, to emphasize the deep attachment he has to the vessel. So the correct answer is Choice (D).

2. By saying that he "got a blink of the moon" in the fifth paragraph, the narrator most nearly means that he:

   (F) he foresaw his own demise.

   (G) he saw the sky as he came up out of the water to get air.

   (H) he was hallucinating as he was drowning.

   (J) a barely perceptible quarter moon hung low in the sky.

In the first line of the fifth paragraph describes the narrator's dunking and near drowning. He was bobbing up and down in the water, going under the sea and then coming up for air, at which point he saw the moon. Make sure you answer the question in the context in which you find the statement; don't use your own common sense. And if you picked Choice (J), you chose an answer that provided too much unjustifiable detail to be right. The correct answer is Choice (G).

Multinational corporations frequently have difficulty explaining to politicians, human rights groups, and (perhaps most important) their consumer base why they do business with, and even seek closer business ties to, countries whose human rights records are considered very bad by United States standards. The CEOs say that in the business trenches, the issue of human rights must effectively be detached from the wider spectrum of free trade.

Discussion of the uneasy alliance between trade and human rights has trickled down from the boardrooms of large multinational corporations to the consumer on the street who, given the wide variety of products available to him, is eager to show support for human rights by boy-cotting the products of a company he feels does not do enough to help its overseas workers.

International human rights organizations also are pressuring the multinationals to push for more humane working conditions in other countries and to, in effect, develop a code of busi-ness conduct that must be adhered to if the American company is to continue working with the overseas partner.

The President, in drawing up a plan for what he calls the "economic architecture of our times," wants economists, business leaders, and human rights groups to work together to de-velop a set of principles that the foreign partners of United States corporations will voluntarily embrace. Human rights activists, angry at the unclear and indefinite plans for implementing such rules, charge that their agenda is being given low priority by the State Department. The President strongly denies their charges, arguing that each situation is approached on its merits without prejudice, and hopes that all the groups can work together to develop principles based on empirical research rather than political fiat, emphasizing that the businesses with experi-ence in the field must initiate the process of developing such guidelines. Business leaders, while paying lip service to the concept of these principles, secretly fight against their formal endorse-ment as they fear such "voluntary" concepts may someday be given the force of law. Few busi-ness leaders have forgotten the Sullivan Principles, in which a set of voluntary rules regarding business conduct with South Africa (giving benefits to workers and banning apartheid in the companies that worked with U.S. partners) became legislation.

3. Which of the following best states the central idea of the passage?

(A) Politicians are quixotic in their assessment of the priorities of the State Department.

(B) Multinational corporations have little, if any, influence on the domestic policies of their overseas partners.

(C) Disagreement exists between the desires of human rights activists to improve the working conditions of overseas workers and the practical approach taken by the corporations.

(D) It is inappropriate to expect foreign corporations to adhere to American standards.

The main idea of the passage is usually stated in the first sentence or two. The first sentence of this passage discusses the difficulties that corporations have in explaining their business ties to certain countries to politicians, human rights groups, and consumers. From this statement, you may infer that those groups disagree with the policies of the corporations. So the correct answer is Choice (C).

TIP

Did you pick Choice (A) just because of the hard word, *quixotic?* It's human nature (we're all so insecure) to think that the hard word we don't know must be the right answer, but it isn't always so. Never choose an answer just because it has a word you can't define unless you're sure that all the answers with words you can define are wrong. *Quixotic* means idealistic, impractical (think of the fictional character Don Quixote tilting at windmills). The President's belief is not the main idea of the passage.

REMEMBER

Just because a statement is (or may be) true doesn't necessarily mean that it's the correct answer to a question. Many of the answer choices to a big picture question in particular often are true or at least look plausible. To answer a main-idea question, pretend that a friend of yours just came up behind you and said, "Hey, what'cha reading there?" Your first response is the main idea: "Oh, I read this passage about how corporations are getting grief from politicians and other groups because they do business with certain countries." Before you look at the answer choices, predict in your own words what the main idea is. You'll be pleasantly surprised how close your prediction is to the correct answer (and you won't be confused by all the other plausible-looking answer choices).

TIP

Choice (D) is a moral value, a judgment call. Who's to say what's appropriate and what's inappropriate? An answer that passes judgment, one that says something is morally right or morally wrong, is almost never the correct answer on the ACT.

4. Which of the following statements about the Sullivan Principles can best be inferred from the passage?

(F) They had a detrimental effect on the profits of those corporations doing business with South Africa.

(G) They represented an improper alliance between political and business groups.

(H) They placed the needs of the foreign workers over those of the domestic workers whose jobs would therefore be in jeopardy.

(J) They will have a chilling effect on future adoption of voluntary guidelines.

Choice (F) is the major trap here. Perhaps you assumed that because the companies seem to dislike the Sullivan Principles, they hurt company profits. However, the passage doesn't say anything about profits. Maybe the companies still made good profits but objected to the Sullivan Principles on principle. The companies just may not have wanted such governmental intervention even if profits didn't decrease. If you picked Choice (F), you read too much into the question and probably didn't read the rest of the answer choices.

In Choice (J), the phrase "chilling effect" means a negative or discouraging effect. Think of something with a chilling effect as leaving you cold. Because few corporations have forgotten the Sullivan Principles, you may infer that these principles will discourage the companies from agreeing to voluntary principles in the future. Thus, the correct answer is (J).

TIP

To get this question correct, you really need to understand the whole passage. If you didn't know what was going on here, you'd be better off just to guess and move on. An inference question usually means you have to read between the lines; you can't just go back to one specific portion of the passage and get the answer quickly.

Passage 3 — Humanities

Many people believe that the existence of lawyers and lawsuits represents a relatively recent phenomenon. The opinion that many hold regarding lawyers, also known as attorneys, is that they are insincere and greedy. Lawyers are often referred to as "ambulance chasers" or by other pejorative expressions.

Despite this negativity, lawyers are also known for their fights for civil rights, due process of law, and equal protection. Lawyers were instrumental in desegregating the institutions in our society and in cleaning up the environment. Most legislators at the local, state, and federal level of government are lawyers because they generally have a firm understanding of justice and the proper application of statutory and case law.

Lawyers are traditionally articulate public speakers, or orators, too. One of the finest legal orators was Marcus Tullius Cicero, who was an intellectually distinguished, politically savvy, and incredibly successful Roman lawyer. Cicero lived from 143–106 B.C. and was one of only a few Roman intellectuals credited with the flowering of Latin literature that largely occurred during the last decades of the Roman republic.

Cicero's compositions have been compared to the works of Julius Caesar. Their writings have customarily been included in the curriculum wherever Latin is studied. Cicero was a lifelong student of government and philosophy and a practicing politician. He was a successful lawyer whose voluminous speeches, letters, and essays tend to have the same quality that people usually associate with pleading a case. His arguments are well structured, eloquent, and clear. Cicero perfected the complex, balanced, and majestic sentence structure called "periodic," which was imitated by later writers from Plutarch in the Renaissance to Churchill in the 20th century.

5. *Pejorative*, as it appears in the last line of the first paragraph, most nearly means:

   (A) comic.

   (B) dishonest.

   (C) self-serving.

   (D) uncomplimentary.

Get clues for answering this question from the information around the word. The passage classifies "ambulance chaser" as a pejorative expression. In the next sentence, the author uses the phrase "this negativity" to refer to the act of using pejorative statements for attorneys. Therefore, *pejorative* must have a negative connotation. You can eliminate Choice (A) — even though the thought of an overweight attorney running after a screaming ambulance may make you laugh. Plug the remaining choices into the sentence to see which one makes the best substitute for *pejorative.* The obvious answer is *uncomplimentary.* So the correct answer is Choice (D).

If you picked Choice (B) or (C), you were probably thinking of words that describe the way that the author says many people think of attorneys. *Dishonest* is a synonym for *insincere,* and *self-serving* has a meaning that's similar to *greedy.* Trap answers like Choices (B) and (C) are why you must read your answers in the context of the sentence. By doing so, you see that *pejorative* describes the expressions that others give to attorneys, not the attorneys themselves.

6. Which of these, according to the author, is a way that lawyers have positively contributed to society?

   (F) They have fought legislation designed to clean up the environment.

   (G) They have proposed laws to make "ambulance chasing" illegal.

   (H) They have taught public speaking skills to disadvantaged youth.

   (J) They have advocated for integration of public institutions.

The author covers the positive attributes of lawyers in the second paragraph, which mentions their contributions to cleaning up the environment and promoting integration. The passage doesn't say anything about the legalization of "ambulance chasing" or teaching public speaking, so you can eliminate Choices (G) and (H). Choice (F) is a little tricky if you don't read it carefully. Because Choice (F) says that attorneys have fought rather than promoted cleaning up the environment, it says just the opposite of what the passage states. So Choice (J) is the correct answer.

Passage 4 — Natural Science

Biomes are the major biological divisions of the earth. Biomes are characterized by an area's climate and the particular organisms that live there. The living organisms make up the "biotic" components of the biome, and everything else makes up the "abiotic" components. The density and diversity of a biome's biotic components is called its "carrying capacity." The most important abiotic aspects of a biome are the amount of rainfall it has and how much its temperatures vary. More rain and more stable temperatures mean more organisms can survive. Usually, the wetter a biome is, the less its temperature changes from day to night or from summer to winter. Biomes include deserts, rain forests, forests, savannas, tundras, freshwater environments, and oceans.

Deserts are areas that get less than 10 inches of rain per year. Most deserts are hot (like the Sahara), but some are actually cold (like parts of Antarctica). Therefore, the thing that distinguishes deserts is their extreme dryness. The organisms that live in a desert need to be able to survive drastic temperature swings along with dry conditions, so the desert's carrying capacity is extremely low. Desert animals include reptiles like lizards and snakes and some arachnids like spiders and scorpions.

Freshwater environments and oceans are also biomes. The freshwater biome includes elements like rivers, lakes, and ponds. These areas are affected by temperature swings, the amount of available oxygen, and the speed of water flowing through them. All of these are affected by the larger climate area the freshwater biome is in, which also affects the biotic components. Algae, fish, amphibians, and insects are found in freshwater biomes. Oceans cover about 70 percent of the earth's surface, so they comprise the biggest biome. Temperature swings aren't nearly as wide in the oceans as they are on land, and there's plenty of water to go around. Therefore, the carrying capacity of the oceans is huge. The density and diversity of organisms isn't quite as high as in the tropical rain forest, but the total number of organisms in the oceans is much bigger than all of the terrestrial biomes put together.

7. According to the passage, an accurate definition of "carrying capacity" of a biome would be:

   (A) the number and variety of living organisms it has.

   (B) the type of abiotic features it has.

   (C) its level of humidity.

   (D) how much its temperatures vary.

The first paragraph defines "carrying capacity" as the density and diversity of a biome's components. A good paraphrase for this definition is the number and variety of organisms, or Choice (A). The other answers refer to other characteristics of a biome that appear in the passage but don't define carrying capacity.

Don't immediately pick an answer choice just because you see it mentioned in the passage. The correct answer must apply specifically to the question being asked.

8. According to the passage, all of these elements affect the quality of a freshwater environment EXCEPT:

   (F) oxygen levels.

   (G) swings in temperature.

   (H) the larger climate in which it exists.

   (J) the policies of the country in which it exists.

The answer to this exception question comes straight from the passage. Lines 17–18 say that freshwater biomes are affected by temperature swings, the amount of available oxygen, and the speed of water flowing through them, so you can eliminate Choices (F), (G), and (H). The passage doesn't cover issues that are unrelated to the natural environment, so the correct answer is Choice (J).

The best way to answer exception questions is to turn the wording around a bit. For example, you can approach this question by asking yourself to choose the answer that states something that *doesn't* affect the quality of a freshwater environment.

5

Studying Brain Defects in Laboratory Rats: The Science Test

Chapter **15**

From Frankenstein to Einstein: Excelling on the Science Test

Return your brain to the full upright and locked position. You don't have to use it as much as you may fear for the ACT Science Test.

So relax, unclench your hands, and take a few deep breaths. You are not, repeat *not*, expected to be able to remember the entire periodic table or to know the difference between the substantia nigra and a Lorentz transformation. After all, your grades in science classes appear on your transcript for the admissions officers to read if they really want to assess your science knowledge. The point of the Science Test (which aptly enough used to be called *Science Reasoning*) is to demonstrate that you have an important collegiate skill: the ability to approach novel information, sort it out, and draw conclusions from it. In other words, you don't have to know what a scientist knows, but you do need to be able to think as a scientist thinks.

REMEMBER

The fastest way to improve your science score is by repeating this mantra to yourself as you make your way through the test: Science questions are easier than they seem; almost everything I need to know to answer them is right in front of me.

Examining the Science Test's Format

The Science Test consists of 40 questions that are based on six passages (six or seven questions per passage). You have 35 minutes to answer these questions, which means you have about 6 minutes per passage. That's not a lot of time.

TIP

To save precious minutes, *don't read the passage before you view the questions.* Jump into the questions right away. Most of the information you need comes right out of the charts and graphs (we cover how to evaluate those in the section, "Analyzing Tables, Graphs, and Diagrams," later in this chapter), and the details in the paragraphs can be more confusing than enlightening. Get direction on where to look for the answers from the questions and answer choices. Only a few questions actually require you to do much reading from the text. You'll likely have to do some reading for questions based on passages with significantly more text than charts and graphs and for questions that ask you about experimental procedure.

Plan on allotting yourself a little less than 1 minute per question. Some of the questions will be so easy that you'll answer them in a heartbeat and build up a reservoir of time, which you can then spend on the harder questions. But, of course, some of the questions may seem so impossible that you'll want to sue your brain for nonsupport. We show you how to approach these brain-busters, but if you can't answer a question within a minute, take a guess and move on. Mark it because you may have a chance to tackle it later.

Classifying Passage Format

Although the passages tend to increase in difficulty as you move through the section, the change won't be sharply obvious. The questions may become a bit more challenging as you move through each individual passage, so the first question or two in a passage may be more easily and quickly answered than the last two. If you get hung up on the last question of a passage, mark your best guess and move on to the easier questions in the next passage.

The following sections discuss the three basic types of science passages that cover a variety of science topics including:

>> **Data representation:** Of the six passages in a typical science test, two or three are this type.

>> **Research summaries:** Two or three are research summaries.

>> **Conflicting viewpoints:** One is this type.

Although these passage formats present information in slightly different ways, the general approach is the same regardless of the passage type:

TIP

>> Read through the answer choices before you read the questions to determine the question type and where to focus.

>> Match information in the questions and answers to corresponding information in the passage.

Data-representation passages

Passages that represent data tend to emphasize tables and graphs. They usually begin with a short paragraph that introduces the passage topic and defines terms followed by one or more tables, graphs, or diagrams that are chock-full of result data. For these passages, you focus primarily on reading and evaluating the data in the tables and graphs (see the section, "Analyzing Tables, Graphs, and Diagrams," later in this chapter) and only read the text if you need clarification of terms. Here's an example of a data-representation passage:

EXAMPLE

Using different quantities of microshels, scientists studied the prehistorical bird species known as *Braisia idioticus* to discover the effect that variations in paraloxin had on the rate in rics per second of samanity in the species as a whole. The results are summarized in Table 15-1:

TABLE 15-1: **Effect of Paraloxin Variation on Samanity Rate in *Braisia Idioticus***

Paraloxin (microshels)	Samanity Rate (rics/sec)
0	14
1	18
2	23
3	25
4	27
5	89
6	90
7	34
8	29
9	24

Don't worry if you've never heard of paraloxin or samanity rate; we made them up! We examine how to handle this sample passage in the section, "Considering Question Types," later in this chapter.

Research summaries

Research-summary passages usually also include one or more tables and/or diagrams, so they require the same data-interpretation skills. These passages include two or three separate experiments or studies to test one scientific topic. Each experiment or study has its own introductory text that conveys its specific setup. Make sure you focus on these paragraphs because these passages often contain questions that examine the relationship between two studies and compare and contrast their experimental design. We cover how to handle study comparison questions in the section, "Considering Question Types," later in this chapter. Here is an example of a simple research summary:

EXAMPLE

Researchers tested the travel distance of a rubber ball based on launch angle θ and launch velocity *V*. They designed a catapult that could be adjusted to propel the rubber ball at various angles and at various speeds as shown in Figure 1. They then used the apparatus to conduct two experiments.

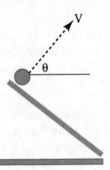

FIGURE 1: ACT format.

Experiment 1

The researchers set the catapult to propel the rubber ball at a constant velocity of 15 *m/s* and then launched it at several angle measures. For each launch, they measured the distance between the launching point of the catapult and point at which the rubber ball landed on the ground. They recorded these distances in Figure 2 in meters (*m*).

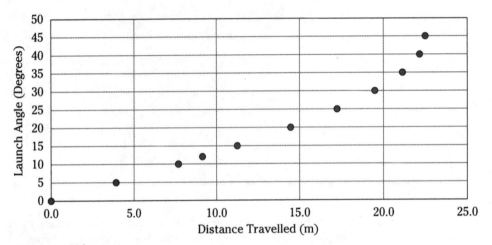

FIGURE 2: ACT format.

Experiment 2

The researchers then set θ on the catapult at 45° and varied the velocity in *m/s* at which they launched the same rubber ball. They again measured the distance from the catapult to the point at which the rubber ball landed on the ground for each launch and recorded the results in Figure 3.

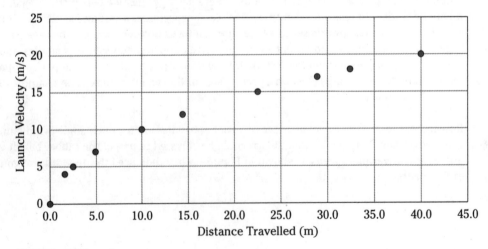

FIGURE 3: ACT format.

Conflicting viewpoints

Each Science Test has one conflicting-viewpoints passage with seven questions. The conflicting-viewpoints passage is easy to recognize because it usually begins with an introduction followed by two, three, four, or more major portions of text with headings like "Student 1," "Student 2," and "Student 3" or "Scientist 1" and "Scientist 2." These headings designate different ways of interpreting the information presented in the introduction. Most frequently, the opinions come from inexperienced students and therefore may contain information that contradicts known scientific truths.

TIP

Although some conflicting-viewpoints passages may contain as many charts and graphs as the other two passage types, these passages are usually primarily text-based, and all the data is contained with the paragraphs.

Here is a plan of attack for approaching the traditional text-based conflicting-viewpoints passage.

1. **Jump right into answering the questions.**

That way you only read those portions of the passage you need to answer each question.

2. **If you absolutely can't resist the temptation to read the passage before you answer the questions, don't spend more than about 30 seconds on your skimming.**

Just note the highlights:

- **Skim the introduction.** Glance long enough to determine what phenomenon the viewpoints are considering. Maybe several students discuss whether objects can travel faster than the speed of light or a couple of scientists examine data to determine whether other planets in the solar system could support life.

- **Read the first and maybe last sentence of each viewpoint to get a rough idea of the students' main points and how they are the same and different.** These main ideas express the students' positions on the situation discussed in the passage's introduction. Read just enough to get the gist and note how the opinions are organized.

3. **Use clues from the questions and answer choices to direct you to the portions of the passage where you'll likely find the answers.**

- **If the first question or so asks for an answer "according to the passage," search first in the introductory information that precedes the viewpoints.** The answers to these questions often involve the background information and aren't particular to any one opinion.

- **Use the answers to help you focus.** Key words in the answers can direct you to the opinions that hold the answer. The ACT often organizes the opinions so that the same type of information appears in the same sentence of each opinion. So, if Student 1 describes in the first sentence what happens to Chemical 1 when it reacts with iron, Student 2's first sentence likely contains an opinion on the same reaction.

- **Focus on data points in the questions and opinions.** If a question asks what happens when liquid reaches 102 degrees, search for degree information in the opinion paragraphs.

- **If the question asks what's true for Scientist 1, concentrate on the section containing Scientist 1's viewpoint and find what's true for Scientist 2 in the Scientist 2 portion.** Doing so may seem obvious, but in the heat of the test moment, you may lose focus. When searching for the correct answer, concentrate primarily on the opinion's main idea — the stuff in the first and maybe last sentence.

Don't get involved in the messy and often confusing middle-of-the-paragraph details unless a question makes you. When a question asks about a particular detail, such as the effect of gamma rays on man-in-the-moon marigolds, search both viewpoints specifically for language that relates to gamma rays or marigolds.

When you're dealing with a conflicting-viewpoints passage, your job is to follow the logic of each viewpoint. Don't try to decide which viewpoint is correct. No one cares — not the ACT, not the college admissions office, and certainly not you. In fact, the ACT sometimes presents a viewpoint that's clearly false. For example, one student may claim that evolution takes place as a result of the inheritance of *acquired* characteristics. You know that this viewpoint is wrong. Think about it: If you gnaw your fingernails down to the bone worrying about the ACT, it doesn't follow that someday your children will be born with no fingernails! Again, worry only about the logic of the viewpoint, not whether it's right or wrong.

Here is an example of a simple passage with conflicting viewpoints:

A teacher presented three students with four test tubes containing four liquids: two clear and two caramel-colored. She explained that Liquid 1 was tap water, Liquid 2 was distilled water, Liquid 3 was coffee brewed with Liquid 1, and Liquid 4 was coffee brewed with Liquid 2. She then provided the students with four pH strips with results for the four liquids. Strip A indicated a pH of 7, Strip B indicated a pH of 6.5, Strip C indicated a pH of 4.9, and Strip D indicated a pH of 5.1. She asked each student to determine which pH result corresponded to each liquid and provide an explanation.

Student 1

Because Liquid 2 is distilled water, it has a neutral pH and must be associated with Strip A. Coffee is more acidic than water, so Liquid 3 and Liquid 4 must be associated with the strips with the lowest pH readings. Because Liquid 1 has a lower pH than Liquid 2, it must contain fewer bicarbonates than Liquid 2 and therefore must be more acidic than distilled water but not as acidic as coffee, so its pH must be the one indicated in Strip B. Therefore, Liquid 3 has to be more acidic than Liquid 4 because it was mixed with the more acidic water. Liquid 3 is associated with Strip C, and Liquid 4 is associated with Strip D.

Student 2

Student 2 is correct about the pH of distilled water, but, because Liquid 1 has a lower pH than Liquid 2, it must contain more bicarbonates than Liquid 2. The combination of liquids and corresponding strips is as follows: Liquid 1 to Strip B, Liquid 2 to Strip A, Liquid 3 to Strip C, and Liquid 4 to Strip D.

Student 3

Because Liquid 2 is distilled water, it has a low pH and must be associated with Strip C. Coffee is more acidic than water, so Liquid 3 and Liquid 4 must be associated with the strips with the highest pH readings. Because Liquid 1 has a higher pH than Liquid 2, it must contain fewer bicarbonates than Liquid 2 and therefore must be more acidic than distilled water but not as acidic as coffee, so its pH must be the one indicated in Strip D. Liquid 3 is associated with Strip B, and Liquid 4 is associated with Strip A.

Analyzing Tables, Graphs, and Diagrams

Most passages test your ability to read and extract information from tables, graphs, or diagrams. In fact, data analysis is a primary assessment of the Science Test. We start with general guidelines for analyzing data:

TIP

>> **Examine the table, diagram, or graph as a whole.** Identify what the graphic is displaying (for example, drug dosages, reaction times, kinetic energy, or astronomical distances). You may need to skim the text immediately preceding the table or figure to get a full understanding of what's going on.

>> **Pay attention how the table or figure is labeled.**

>> **Note the units of measurement.** Tables and figures always present units of measurement very clearly. The axes on graphs are usually labeled, legends typically accompany diagrams, and column and row headings usually include the units.

>> **Look for trends in the data, noting any significant shifts.** The ACT Science Test frequently tests how data is related. Generally, a table or graph provides you with a clear picture of whether data is related directly or inversely or not at all.

   ● **Direct or positive correlation:** When two pieces of data increase at the same time or decrease at the same time, they are related directly.

   ● **Inverse or negative correlation:** When one piece of data increases at the same time another decreases or decreases at the same time another increases, those data points have an inverse relationship.

   ● **No correlation:** Data have no relationship or correlation when they act independently of one another.

>> **Observe corresponding data across multiple tables and figures in the passage.** Sometimes science questions require you to use data from one graph or table to draw conclusions about a data piece on another table or graph. Look for matching wording in the labels (column headings in tables and axis labels in graphs) to find where data from different tables and graphs may intersect with overlap.

Tackling tables

Tables in passages may be simple (like Table 15-1) or complex with multiple columns and subcolumns. To examine even the most complex table most efficiently, focus on the column headings. As you read through the questions and their answer options, locate key words and terms that match the table's column designations. For example, if a question associated with Table 15-1 referenced microshels, you likely need to examine the first column of the table to answer the question.

To determine relationships in data provided in tables, isolate the columns that display the data in question and observe what happens to the data in one column as the other increases or decreases. For example, in Table 15-1, you see that as paraloxin increases, samanity rate gradually increases until paraloxin reaches 4 microshels. Then it hits a sharp peak when paraloxin rises to 5 and 6 microshels and then falls to levels comparable to those obtained when paraloxin was lower.

Grappling with graphs

Graphs on the ACT mostly contain lines or bars. They may be simple, displaying just two variables on the *x* and *y* axes, or they may be more complex, displaying multiple lines or bars or containing more than one variable on the vertical axes. More complex graphs are usually accompanied by a key. Figure 15-1 is a simple graph displaying plant height in *cm* as it relates to an amount of added growth factor in *mg*.

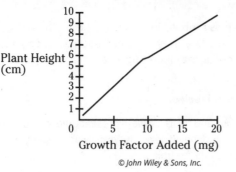

FIGURE 15-1:
Example of a graph you may see on the Science Test.

© John Wiley & Sons, Inc.

To keep the data straight, concentrate on the labels:

» The horizontal and vertical axis designations and their increments

» The wording in the keys, if provided

» Any explanatory details offered at the bottom of the graph

Avoid making assumptions about the data. Read carefully, noting, for instance, whether the numbers on the vertical axis are expressed as totals or averages, in kilograms or grams or whether the time designation on the horizontal axis is in days, hours, minutes, or seconds.

To evaluate data relationships on graphs, follow the trends as indicated usually by lines or bars. When the value of one variable moves along a graph in the same direction as the value of another variable, those variables have a direct relationship and the line on the graph has a positive slope. In the sample graph in Figure 15-1, plant height and the amount of growth factor added have a positive correlation; as one increases, the other increases also, and line has a general positive slope. A positive correlation can also apply to decreasing values; as one decreases, the other variable also decreases. Variables with an inverse relationship (when one increases as the other decreases and vice versa) create a line with negative slope.

Dissecting diagrams

Passages may also contain pictures in addition to tables and graphs. These diagrams usually display a visual representation of an element of the experiment's setup. You likely won't need to refer to these pictures too often. In fact, you can ignore them for answering most science questions. For example, you likely don't need the picture of the catapult in the sample research summary (see the section, "Research summaries," earlier in the chapter) to understand the overall experiment. Every now and again, however, diagrams are integral to understanding how an experiment is constructed and therefore to successfully answering questions about it. To see what we mean, check out this introduction to a particular experiment and its accompanying diagram.

EXAMPLE

A student constructs a circuit using a battery, switches, resistors, and an electric motor. The current flows from the battery through one of the switches when the switch is closed. The current then proceeds through the resistor to the motor. See Figure 1.

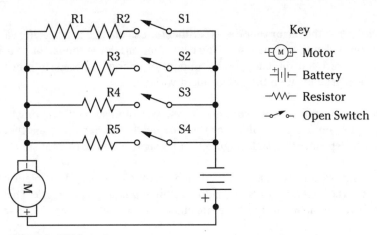

FIGURE 1: ACT format.

To answer questions about this experiment, you need to examine the diagram to find out that the circuit involves four switches and five resistors and that the flow moves from bottom right up through the switches and resistors to the motor at the bottom left. This picture provides you with a better understanding of how the student constructed the circuit than the explanatory paragraph alone does.

Examining Experimental Procedures

In addition to having a general understanding of how to analyze a passage's tables and figures, you also need to know a little about experimental procedural to excel on the science questions. Here are the basics:

REMEMBER

>> **Purpose of the study:** Every experiment has a purpose. You may be very familiar with identifying the goal of the project or the purpose of the study as you have probably done so on every lab write-up you've turned in since kindergarten. The ACT is kind enough to do your work for you by stating or implying the purpose in the introductory paragraph.

The ACT expects you to understand some key principles of why the researchers created the experiment in the first place. But don't worry! Identifying the purpose of the experiment takes only a few seconds. Usually, the purpose is to examine what effect x has on y. You can usually pick up on the purpose as you answer the questions and evaluate the charts.

>> **Experimental design:** The passage tells you how the researchers have set up and controlled the experiment or study and provides information such as what apparatus they've used and which variables they've held constant.

>> **Results:** Ultimately, an experiment or study needs to convey the collected data. These results are usually presented in a table or graph.

REMEMBER

You don't have time to analyze procedures in depth. Most of what you pick up about purpose and design results from answering the questions. Don't try to understand the research before you start examining the questions.

Independent and dependent variables

The Science Test assumes you know enough about experimental setup to distinguish independent variables and dependent variables.

REMEMBER

An *independent variable* is the factor that the experimenter can change to a specific value, such as the amount of water added to a plant's soil. The *dependent variable* is the factor that isn't under the experimenter's direct control, such as the amount of energy released. In other words, the dependent variable is dependent on the independent variable.

The most typical relationship between columns, rows, axes, and so on is one in which one column, row, axis, and so on presents values for the independent variable and another one shows what happens to the dependent variable. Figure 15-1 presents a classic relationship.

Here, the amount of growth factor added is the independent variable, and the plant height is the dependent variable. The experimenters can't directly manipulate plant height. They can add a certain amount of growth factor but then have no choice but to wait and see what happens to the plant height.

A proper experiment systematically varies the factor that is the possible cause and holds all other factors constant. For example, if scientists want to investigate what effect having the flu has on one's ability to perform multiplication problems, a proper experiment would compare people who have the flu with those who don't, while keeping the groups equal in terms of such factors as age, mathematical ability, and the presence of psychological disorders. If the groups differ in one or more of these other factors, the researchers can't be certain that any observed difference in multiplication performance was a result of the flu. For instance, what would you think if the nonflu group, which consisted of 12-year-olds, did better on multiplication than the flu group, which consisted of 8-year-olds? You couldn't be certain whether age or the flu virus accounted for the difference.

REMEMBER

The ability to distinguish the independent variable from the dependent variable is essential for answering many procedure questions. You may even get a question directly asking about this distinction.

The control

Most proper experiments have a *control*. Essentially, the control is an experimental element that is kept constant throughout the experiment to allow experimenters to compare results to what happens when the independent variable isn't applied. For example, the experimenters in the plant growth factor study whose results are conveyed in Figure 15-1 would likely prepare a plant with no added growth factor added to determine what happens to plant height in the absence of growth factor.

TIP

ACT science questions may ask you to come up with the experiment's control. Identify the independent variable and then find the elements of the experiment that test what occurs in the absence of that variable.

REMEMBER

Defective experimental designs, in which experimenters don't include proper controls, produce limited results. By their very nature some studies can't adhere to an ideal experimental design. For example, if a scientist suspected that 2-year-olds who had been vaccinated for measles got more colds than 2-year-olds who hadn't been vaccinated, a proper design would be to give one group the vaccine and to withhold it from another group. However, the experimenters can't just keep one group of kids unvaccinated (mothers tend to get cranky when you make their kids sick "in the best interests of science"). Instead, the experimenters would have to try to collect data on how frequently the children came down with colds before they were immunized (children aren't immunized against measles until they're at least 1 year-old) and perhaps collect data about children who haven't been vaccinated from kids whose parents have voluntarily kept them from vaccinations because of religious beliefs or allergies.

Immersing Yourself in Answer Choices

The ACT science questions may include extraneous information designed to distract you and make you overthink the question. The trick is to focus on one bit of the question at a time rather than the whole enchilada. And one of the best ways to focus your approach is to consider the answer options.

The answer choices may give you more clues than the actual questions. The answers show you what you need to figure out and where to find it in the passage, so always read through the answers before you read the question. That way, you read only the parts of the question that are necessary to eliminate wrong answers. Usually two answers are obviously incorrect. Look for those first so you can concentrate on the difference between the remaining two answers. Sometimes you can eliminate three answers easily without reading the questions at all.

Take a look at this somewhat silly sample question for a passage regarding plant experiments to see what we mean:

EXAMPLE

A new study is conducted under the same conditions as the original study on dandelion plants and Venus Fly Trap plants except that scientists applied Chemical B to the Venus Fly Trap plants for six weeks instead of three weeks. Based on the original study data, is it likely that the Venus Fly Trap plants in the new study will grow human hair after six weeks?

(A) Yes, because in the original study dandelion plants exposed to Chemical B for more than three weeks showed evidence of human hair growth.

(B) Yes, because in the original study Venus Fly trap plants exposed to Chemical B for more than three weeks showed evidence of human hair growth.

(C) No, because in the original study dandelion plants exposed to Chemical B for more than three weeks showed no evidence after six weeks of human hair growth.

(D) No, because in the original study Venus Fly trap plants exposed to Chemical B for more than three weeks showed no evidence of human hair growth.

Don't freak out because you're unfamiliar with the chemical components of Chemical B or because you failed the botany section of AP Biology. Knowing specifics about plants isn't required to answer an ACT science question. Before you begin to tear out your own hair, leap right into the answer choices. Notice the answers reveal that you have to evaluate only two pieces of data in the original study:

>> Whether the original study shows that dandelion plants exposed to Chemical B for more than three weeks grew hair.

>> Whether the original study shows that Venus Fly Trap plants exposed to Chemical B for more than three weeks grew hair.

Eliminate answer choices that aren't true. If the original study showed no hair growth in dandelion plants after three weeks, you can cross out Choice (A) because it isn't true based on the data in the passage. If the original study showed hair growth in Venus Fly Trap plants after three weeks, Choice (D) must be wrong because the data doesn't support it. Now the question is much easier. The answer has to be either Choice (B) or (C), and because Choice (C) deals with what didn't happen to dandelions instead of what did happen to Venus Fly Traps, Choice (B) is likely the right answer.

REMEMBER

Follow the path of least resistance. Don't make the questions harder than they are. For more on answering questions with answers formatted like this one, see the nearby sidebar.

Considering Question Types

Ultimately, your Science Test score is based on the number of questions you answer correctly. In this section, we discuss the types of questions you can expect and how to answer them.

You may find yourself lamenting one of the following as you become embroiled in a science question:

>> If only I had a calculator . . .

>> If only I had paid more attention in biology, physics, chemistry, earth science, and so on . . .

When you entertain either one of these thoughts, you're overthinking the question. Relax and remind yourself to look for the obvious answer. The ACT can't test super-specific science knowledge because not all high school students follow the same science curriculum. Though several questions in each Science Test may check your knowledge of basic science concepts and vocabulary that aren't included in the passage content, this information is usually limited to foundational concepts you should have learned in middle school. We provide a set of flashcards in the online content for you to use to brush up on commonly tested science concepts and terms.

Science Test questions come in two general categories:

>> **Those that ask for results:** These questions ask you to interpret the results of a study or series of studies. For these, you focus strictly on reading data from charts and graphs, and you read text only when you need to define information contained in the tables and figures.

>> **Those that ask about experimental procedures:** The second category of questions may ask you for the control, independent variable, or steps of an experiment or experiments. These questions require you to focus on the text rather than the charts and graphs. Look for the answers in the setup paragraphs, even if the questions reference a particular figure.

The following sections take a closer look at these two categories and provide you some examples.

Questions about results

Results questions appear in data-representation passages and research summaries and some conflicting-viewpoints passages that contain tables or graphs. The easiest way to spot results questions is to look for numbers in your answer choices, but other question formats test your ability to evaluate tables and graphs, too. The following sample questions show several ways the ACT may do that.

When you encounter a data results on the test, we suggest that you use the following approach to get through it quickly and painlessly:

1. **Ignore the passage at first and jump right to the first question.**

No use wasting precious time reading or reviewing the passage details. There's plenty of time for careful examination of the passage as you answer the questions.

2. **Examine the question for clues to where in the passage you'll find the answer.**

Sometimes the clues will be obvious: "According to Table 1, when is samanity rate greater?" Other times, you'll know which table or graph to check based on the specific data referenced in the question. For instance, if you encounter a question that asks for the relationship between microshels and ric/sec, you know that Table 15-1 is your chart.

3. **Read the table and chart carefully (see the section, "Analyzing Tables, Graphs, and Diagrams," earlier in the chapter).**

Reading data

Many results questions simply require you to carefully read tables and graphs.

EXAMPLE

According to the information in Figure 15-1, what was the plant height when 5 mg of plant growth factor was applied?

(A) 1 cm

(B) 3 cm

(C) 7 cm

(D) 10 cm

Find 5 mg along the horizontal axis, and draw a vertical line at the 5 mg mark parallel to the y-axis. Note where the line you've drawn intersects the data on the graph. Check your answer options. The intersection point obviously isn't as high as 7 or 10 cm, so Choice (C) and (D) are wrong. The point is closer to 3 cm than 1 cm, so the answer is Choice (B). Notice that you don't have to know anything about plants. You just have to look at what's in front of you.

EXAMPLE

According to the information in Figure 15-1, what range of added growth factor in mg resulted in the greatest change in plant height in cm?

(A) between 1 mg and 10 mg

(B) between 10 mg and 11 mg

(C) between 11 mg and 15 mg

(D) between 15 cm and 20 mg

Examine the data line on the graph. The line is steeper before plant height reaches about 6 cm, which corresponds to about 10 mg of growth factor. After that, the line's slope flattens a bit. Eliminate any answers that suggest that greatest rate of height change occurs at a level of added growth factor of 10 mg. Choice (A) is the best answer.

According to the information in Table 15-1, as Paraloxin in microshels increased, samanity rate:

(A) increased only

(B) decreased only

(C) increased then decreased

(D) decreased then increased

What? You don't know what paraloxin, samanity, rics, or microshels are? You've never heard of the ferocious flying *Braisia idioticus*? We're not surprised, considering that we just made them up. We're babbling here to make the point that you can get an idea of what the passage is discussing *without* having a clue about what all the terms mean. As you read the preceding table, say to yourself, "When this thing called paraloxin is changed, samanity rate, whatever it is, may also change. I need to take a closer look at the data to see what happens. The weird units simply measure paraloxin and samanity rate."

Check the column for Paraloxin. The data increases as you move from the top of the column to the bottom. As you move down the column for samanity rate, the numbers increase, so eliminate Choices (B) and (D). Don't stop, though. As Paraloxin increases from 6 to 9 microshels, the number for samanity rate goes down. Choice (C) is the best answer.

Use the example passage from the section, "Research summaries," earlier in this chapter to answer the next two questions. The first one is an example of a question that displays answers in columns, and the second shows you that analyzing data in tables and graphs can help you eliminate more complicated answer choices, too.

Which of the following combinations of launch angle and launch velocity resulted in the greatest distance travelled?

	Angle in degrees	Velocity (m/s)
(A)	5	5
(B)	45	10
(C)	5	20
(D)	45	20

Check the answer options and consider each column one at a time. The options for the first left column are 5 degrees and 45 degrees. Angle launch information is in Figure 2, and the question asks for the greatest distance, so you can eliminate Choices (A) and (C) because a 5-degree launch angle results in a shorter distance than a 45-degree launch angle does. You can also eliminate a velocity of 5 from consideration because Choice (A) is out. The remaining velocity choices in the right column are 10 and 20. Figure 3 indicates that a high velocity results in a longer distance, so Choice (D) is correct.

EXAMPLE

According to the results of Experiment 1 in the catapult study, does a wider launch angle increase or decrease the distance the rubber ball travelled?

(A) Increase, because distance travelled (m) at 15 degrees was longer than distance travelled at 30 degrees

(B) Increase, because distance travelled (m) at 15 degrees was shorter than distance travelled at 30 degrees

(C) Decrease, because distance travelled (m) at 15 degrees was longer than distance travelled at 30 degrees

(D) Decrease, because distance travelled (m) at 15 degrees was shorter than distance travelled at 30 degrees

Often, you can eliminate at least two answers in these "yes, yes, no, no" question formats before you even read the question. Read the explanation in each answer choice and eliminate answers that contradict the data. To determine what happens to distance as a result of angle width, examine Figure 2 in the passage because it records the launch angle data.

The distance travelled at 15 degrees was a little more than 10 meters, and the distance the ball travelled at 30 degrees was about 20 meters. The explanations in Choices (A) and (C) contradict the data in Figure 2, so eliminate them. At this point, you can check the question to see whether the correct answer is "increase" or "decrease" based on the fact that a 30-degree angle resulted in a longer distance than the 15-degree angle. Because a 30-degree angle is wider than a 15-degree angle, the answer must be Choice (B).

Extending data through intrapolation and extrapolation

What if a question asks you about a point or value that isn't actually plotted (or given) on the graph or table? You can still answer the question. You *interpolate* by looking at the two closest values; in plain English, you just insert an intermediate term by estimating.

EXAMPLE

According to Table 15-1, the samanity rate when Paraloxin is 1.5 is most likely:

(A) less than 18 rics/sec.

(B) between 18 and 23 rics/sec.

(C) between 23 and 27 rics/sec.

(D) greater than 27 rics/sec.

Draw a horizontal line between 1 and 2 microshels of Paraloxin. Given that the samanity rates increase in this area of the table and because the samanity rate is 18 when Paraloxin is 1 and 23 when Paraloxin is 2, the samanity rate when paraloxin is 1.5 is probably between 18 and 23. Choice (B) is the correct answer. In addition to interpolation, you may have to deal with *extrapolation*. As the *extra* in its name implies, extrapolation asks you to come up with a value that's beyond the range depicted in the table or graph.

EXAMPLE

Suppose the researchers added a growth factor of 25 mg to a plant tested in the experiments whose data is reflected Figure 15-1. The plant height in cm for this plant will be closest to:

(A) 8 cm

(B) 10 cm

(C) 12 cm

(D) 15 cm

In the plant growth graph shown in Figure 15-1, you probably safely predict that the straight upward line will continue at a constant rate for a while as growth factor moves past 20 mg, the last number presented in the horizontal axis. Therefore, you can safely eliminate answers that are equal to or less than 10 mg. Choices (A) and (B) are wrong. Height increased 2 mg when the level of growth factor increased from 15 mg to 20 mg, so it's reasonable to extrapolate that plant height will increase another 2 cm when growth factor is increased another 5 mg. Even when the plant height increased at a higher rate for lesser growth factor amounts, the rate was never as high as 5 cm over a 5 mg increase in growth factor, so Choice (D) is justified. Choice (C) is the correct answer.

REMEMBER

Another way the ACT may test your ability to extrapolate is by asking you how the results of one study may have an effect on another study. When you come up against a question like the next example that presents you with a new set of results from a different but related experiment, your job is to determine how these new results fit into what you already know.

EXAMPLE

Suppose the researchers in the catapult experiment in the section, "Research summaries," earlier in this chapter conduct a third experiment in which they repeat Experiment 2 with a 30-degree launch angle. Compared to the rubber ball in Experiment 2, the rubber ball in Experiment 3 most likely travelled:

(A) a lesser height at each velocity tested

(B) a lesser distance at each velocity tested

(C) the same distance at each velocity tested

(D) a greater distance at each velocity tested

Experiment 2 was originally carried out at a 45-degree launch angle. You know from Experiment 1 that decreasing the launch angle decreases the distance travelled. From this information you can logically deduce that the distance travelled will be less for each velocity tested. Choice (B) is the correct answer.

TIP

Questions that begin with "suppose" and answer options that have you choose among "less than a certain value," "between two values," "two other values," and "greater than a certain value" usually signal a question that asks you to extrapolate.

Questions about procedure

You can spot a procedure question because it asks about information that sets up or happens during the experiment rather than about what happened as a result of an experiment. Although you'll find some procedure questions in data-representation passages, they appear most often in research summaries. These questions can cover a variety of elements of experiment design.

REMEMBER

You don't have time to analyze procedures in depth. Most of what you pick up about purpose and design results from answering the questions. Don't try to understand the research before you start examining the questions.

The questions test your ability to follow the logic of the experimental design itself. Why or how was the experiment designed? What was the purpose of choosing one variable or one control?

TIP

Experiment-design questions are some of the few question types for which you may need to read the text portion of a science passage. Usually, you find the answers to these questions in the introductory paragraph for each experiment. Often experiments build on each other, so the foundational setup for Experiment 3 may be in the introduction to Experiment 1. Read carefully to be sure you're setting up the right experiment.

Distinguishing between dependent and independent variables and identifying the control

The Science Test frequently tests your ability to identify the components of an experiment. Consider these two examples:

EXAMPLE

Which of the following is the dependent variable in Experiment 1 in the catapult passage introduced in the section, "Research summaries," earlier in this chapter?

(A) Distance travelled

(B) Launch angle

(C) Velocity

(D) Catapult design

The dependent variable is the value that changes based on the independent variables set up by the researchers. The researchers control the velocity and launch angle, so they're independent variables instead of dependent variables. Choices (B) and (C) are wrong. Catapult design doesn't vary, so it's neither an independent nor a dependent variable. Choice (D) is wrong. The dependent variable (the variable being measured) was the distance travelled by the tennis ball. Choice (A) is the best answer. For more on the difference between independent and dependent variables, see the section, "Independent and dependent variables," earlier in the chapter.

EXAMPLE

Students test the boiling points of three chemical substances when they are mixed with a solution. The students add the solution to each of four test tubes. They then add Chemical A to Tube 1, Chemical B to Tube 2, and Chemical C to Tube 3. The students then heat each tube and record the boiling point for each liquid in the test tubes. Which of the test tubes serves as the experimental control?

(A) Tube 1

(B) Tube 2

(C) Tube 3

(D) Tube 4

The way to identify the control is to note what the procedure description doesn't say. The students use four test tubes but only add chemicals to three of them. The tube without the chemical must be the control to determine the boiling point of the solution without the addition of one of the chemicals. Choice (D) is the answer. For more on the experiment control, see the section, "The control," earlier in this chapter.

Comparing studies

Passages with more than one study may have a question that asks you to compare the setup of each. Save time on these questions by reading the setup for the second experiment. It's usually contained in the paragraph right before the results data (graph or table). That paragraph almost always tells you how the second experiment is the same as or different from the first.

These sample questions show a couple ways the ACT may compare the studies in the catapult passage that we introduce in the section, "Research summaries," earlier in the chapter.

Which of the following expresses the difference between Experiment 1 and Experiment 2 in the catapult passage? In Experiment 2:

(A) the researchers varied launch angle and kept launch velocity constant while in Experiment 1, the researchers varied launch velocity and kept launch angle constant.

(B) the researchers varied both launch velocity and launch angle while in Experiment 1, the researchers varied launch velocity and kept launch angle constant.

(C) the researchers kept both launch angle and launch velocity constant while in Experiment 1, the researchers varied both launch angle and launch velocity.

(D) the researchers varied launch velocity and kept launch angle constant while in Experiment 1, the researchers varied launch angle and kept launch velocity constant.

The set-up paragraph for Experiment 2 clearly states that the researcher kept launch angle constant and varied launch velocity. Read just the first part of each answer choice, and eliminate any answers that state that researchers varied launch angle. Choices (A) and (B) both state that the researchers varied launch angle, so eliminate them. Choice (C) states that researchers in Experiment 2 kept launch velocity constant, so it's wrong. You didn't even need to read what the answers say about Experiment 1 to know that Choice (D) is the right answer.

Which of the following is a way in which the two experiments in the study were the same?

   I. The studies propelled rubber balls from a catapult.

   II. The catapult was set at an angle of 45 degrees.

   III. The studies varied the speed of the rubber ball as it travelled from the catapult.

(A) I only

(B) III only

(C) I and II only

(D) I, II, and III

Both studies launched a rubber ball from the catapult, so the right answer has to contain I. Eliminate Choice (B). Experiment 1 didn't vary the velocity, so the answer won't include III; eliminate Choice (D). You just need to determine whether both studies set the angle at a 45-degree angle. Clearly, Experiment 2 did. The set-up paragraph tells you that. Check Experiment 1. There is a point on the graph associated with an angle degree measure of 45, so the researchers must have set the catapult at 45 degrees for that experiment, too. Choice (B) is correct.

Questions with Roman numerals are almost always procedure questions or questions that test your knowledge of basic science terms.

Testing your science knowledge

The ACT tests your knowledge of science with Roman numerals and in other ways. The ACT expects you to know just the fundamentals, information you likely learned in middle school science classes. This example is based on the catapult passage from the section, "Research summaries," earlier in this chapter.

EXAMPLE

Which of the following expresses the difference between Experiment 1 and Experiment 2 in the catapult passage? In Experiment 2:

(A) the researchers varied launch angle and kept launch velocity constant while in Experiment 1, the researchers varied launch velocity and kept launch angle constant.

(B) the researchers varied both launch velocity and launch angle while in Experiment 1, the researchers varied launch velocity and kept launch angle constant.

(C) the researchers kept both launch angle and launch velocity constant while in Experiment 1, the researchers varied both launch angle and launch velocity.

(D) the researchers varied launch velocity and kept launch angle constant while in Experiment 1, the researchers varied launch angle and kept launch velocity constant.

The set-up paragraph for Experiment 2 clearly states that the researcher kept launch angle constant and varied launch velocity. Read just the first part of each answer choice, and eliminate any answers that state that researchers varied launch angle. Choices (A) and (B) both state that the researchers varied launch angle, so eliminate them. Choice (C) states that researchers in Experiment 2 kept launch velocity constant, so it's wrong. You didn't even need to read what the answers say about Experiment 1 to know that Choice (D) is the right answer.

EXAMPLE

Was the potential or kinetic of the rubber ball greater immediately before the ball was launched from the catapult?

(A) Potential energy, because the ball was not in motion immediately before it was launched from the catapult

(B) Potential energy, because the ball was already in motion immediately before it was launched from the catapult

(C) Kinetic energy, because the ball was not in motion immediately before it was launched from the catapult

(D) Potential energy, because the ball was already in motion immediately before it was launched from the catapult

You can answer this by focusing on the choice between potential and kinetic energy or by focusing on the truth of the explanation in each answer. Immediately before the ball was launched from the catapult, the ball wasn't in motion, so you can eliminate Choices (B) and (D). Kinetic energy is the energy an object has while it is in motion, so the ball in prelaunch stage must have more potential energy than kinetic energy. Choice (A) is correct.

TIP

You can use the online flash cards included with this edition of *ACT 2022 For Dummies* to drill the science information commonly tested in the Science Test.

Finding purpose

Another way the ACT may test experimental design is by asking you to identify the reason experimenters set up a study. Here's an example using the catapult passage from the section, "Research summaries," earlier in the chapter.

EXAMPLE

The catapult study was designed to answer what question?

(A) Is it possible to launch a rubber ball from a catapult?

(B) What is the farthest distance a rubber ball can travel when it is launched from a catapult?

(C) What effect does the angle from which an object is propelled and the velocity with which it is propelled have on the distance an object travels?

(D) How long does it take a rubber ball to travel a distance of 45 meters when it is launched from a catapult at the greatest velocity and widest launching angle?

Find answers to eliminate. The study doesn't calculate time, so Choice (D) is unrelated. Although the study did reveal that a rubber ball could be launched from a catapult, that revelation wasn't the intended reason for the study, so Choice (A) is out. The study does test the distance the rubber ball travelled, but there's no indication that the study produced, or intended to produce, the farthest distance the ball could travel. Choice (B) isn't right, so Choice (C) is correct.

Questions about viewpoints

The questions in the conflicting-viewpoints passages are similar to those in the other two passage types. If the scientific viewpoints relate to charts and graphs, the questions will ask you to analyze them. If the viewpoints regard interpretations of a particular experiment, you'll see questions about the way the experiment is designed and be asked to evaluate the results from the perspective of a particular student or scientist. For more information about conflicting-viewpoints passages, see the section, "Conflicting viewpoints," earlier in this chapter. The conflicting-viewpoints passage contains some question types that don't appear in the other passages, though. We cover the two most common ones in this section.

Comparing viewpoints

If a question asks you to compare and contrast viewpoints, focus on the main point of each opinion and eliminate answers based on one viewpoint at a time. Note the similarities and differences between viewpoints. The evidence used in the second viewpoint may be different from the evidence used in the first viewpoint, but it may also be the same. The key difference lies in how the second opinion interprets the evidence. Here is an example of a question that asks you to compare viewpoints based on the pH study passage from the section, "Conflicting viewpoints," earlier in the chapter.

EXAMPLE

Which of the students would agree that the presence of bicarbonates in water lowers pH levels?

(A) Student 2 only

(B) Students 1 and 3

(C) Student 3 only

(D) Students 1, 2, and 3

Find where Student 1 discusses bicarbonates. Student 1 clearly states in the third sentence that lower pH indicates fewer bicarbonates. Therefore, Student 1 associates bicarbonates with a higher pH level. Eliminate Choices (B) and (D). Read the same sentence for Student 2. Student 2 states the opposite; low pH indicates more bicarbonates. Student 2 must be in the correct answer, so Choice (C) is out. The answer has to be Choice (A). If you check Student 3, you see that this student agrees with Student 1. Choice (A) is confirmed.

Supporting or weakening conclusions

Some questions ask you to support or weaken a particular viewpoint. The best way to strengthen a viewpoint is to come up with evidence that confirms that the opinion's assertions are valid. The best way to weaken a viewpoint is to present evidence that casts doubt on the assertions. For example, suppose a student claims that pandas are carnivores based on evidence that bears are carnivores. That pandas are carnivores because bears are carnivores is strengthened if pandas are bears. But it's weakened if pandas aren't bears.

WARNING

Keep in mind exactly which of the viewpoints you need to support or weaken for each question. Some of the wrong (trap!) answer choices deal with another viewpoint and, as a consequence, won't answer the question.

The answer choices for a supporting or weakening question usually follow a predictable pattern. One choice, the correct answer, supports or weakens the correct viewpoint. One incorrect choice deals with the correct viewpoint but has the wrong effect on it (strengthens when you want to weaken, or vice versa). Another incorrect choice deals with the other viewpoint. Usually this choice strengthens the other viewpoint, so it's there to test your ability to keep the viewpoints straight. Occasionally, this incorrect choice weakens the other viewpoint. Such a choice is tough to eliminate, but remember that weakening (or strengthening) one viewpoint doesn't automatically strengthen (or weaken) the other. The third incorrect choice likely presents irrelevant evidence.

Because supporting/weakening the conclusion questions may be unfamiliar to you, here's an example of how to work through the answer choices for one.

EXAMPLE

Suppose you have a passage about whether smoking cigarettes causes cancer. Scientist 1 says that it does, citing the fact that smokers have a higher incidence of cancer than nonsmokers do. Scientist 2 says that smoking cigarettes doesn't cause cancer, claiming that there's no proof that smoking causes the uncontrolled growth seen in cancer. Scientist 2 explains the association between smoking and cancer as a result of the fact that some people have a certain body chemistry that leads to both a smoking habit and cancer.

Which of the following strengthens Scientist 1's viewpoint?

(A) Nicotine, a major cigarette ingredient, has been shown to cause cancer in laboratory rats.

(B) Smokers invariably eat a lot of fatty foods, which have been shown to cause cancer.

(C) Injecting rats with Chemical ABC caused them to seek out tobacco and also produced cancer cells.

(D) Lack of exercise causes heart disease.

Choice (B) weakens Scientist 1's point of view by suggesting that another cause is at work. Choice (C) goes right along with Scientist 2's suggestion. Choice (D) is irrelevant. It discusses neither cigarettes nor cancer. The best answer is Choice (A); it supports Scientist 1's theory.

REMEMBER

You don't care whether the answer choice's statement is actually true or false in the real world. For example, Choice (D), which claims that lack of exercise causes heart disease, may very well be true. So what? It has nothing to do with supporting Scientist 1's statement that smoking cigarettes causes cancer.

Chapter **16**

Faking Atomic Ache Won't Get You out of This: Science Practice Questions

Question: What happened to the band director when he stuck his finger into an electrical outlet? Answer: Nothing. He was a bad conductor!

If your store of science knowledge is so low that you don't even understand this joke, don't worry. You don't need much specific science knowledge to do well on the Science Test. Nearly everything you need to answer the questions is stated or implied in the passages provided. (If you get the joke but don't laugh, maybe your standards are higher than our comedic ability!)

This chapter gives you a Science Test passage with twice the usual number of questions. On the actual ACT, the passages have only 6 or 7 questions, not 12 as in this chapter. We give you double the usual number to give you practice in the various ways the ACT can test the same basic points. For now, don't worry about the format or the timing. Review the material in Chapter 15; then apply that material to the questions in this chapter.

Directions: Based on the following science passage, answer the 12 questions.

Don't forget to read all the answer explanations after you're done!

Passage

By using electrical recording devices, scientists have shown that many cells in the part of the brain involved with processing visual information respond only to lines of a certain orientation. For example, some brain cells fire when vertical lines are present but do not respond to horizontal lines. Animals that rely on vision must have an entire set of cells so that at least some part of their brains responds when lines of a given orientation are present in their environment.

Scientists conducted several studies on *R. norvegicus domestica* (a species of rat commonly used in laboratory experimentation) to explore how much brain organization is affected by the animal's environment and investigate the role that environment plays in the development of rat vision. Over a period of six weeks, scientists exposed rat pups of various ages to a variety of visual environments: continuous exposure to vertical lines, continuous exposure to horizonal lines, continuous exposure to lines of both horizontal and vertical orientations, and continuous exposure to complete darkness. They then observed the subjects' behavior in mazes with horizontal and vertical obstacles and monitored and measured electrical activity from the visual part of the subjects' brains. The rat pups that were 6 weeks and 6 months old at the beginning of the study had been raised in *normal* environments (environments with uncontrolled exposure to various stimuli and light and dark patterns) from birth until that time. The results of the series of studies is provided in Table 1, which shows the study number, age of *R. norvegicus domestica* at the beginning of the study, the type of environmental factors imposed during the study, the corresponding percentage of brain activity when the subjects were exposed to horizonal and vertical stimuli after the study, and the subjects' ability to navigate obstacles in mazes.

TABLE 1

Study	Age of *R. norvegicus domestica*	Imposed Environmental Factor			% Brain Activity		Maze Navigation	
		Horizontal Line Exposure	Vertical Line Exposure	Complete Darkness	Horizontal Stimuli Exposure	Vertical Stimuli Exposure	Collide with Horizontal Obstacles	Collide with Vertical Obstacles
1	Newborn	yes	Yes	no	50	50	No	no
2	6 weeks	yes	Yes	no	50	50	No	no
3	Newborn	No	No	yes	5	5	Yes	yes
4	Newborn	no	yes	no	0	75	Yes	no
5	Newborn	yes	No	no	75	0	No	yes
6	6 months	No	No	yes	50	50	No	no
7	6 months	No	Yes	no	50	50	No	no
8	6 months	yes	No	no	50	50	No	no

Initial Analysis

This passage presents you with a short introduction and a single table that reports both procedure details and study results. You may be tempted to read through all that mess before you tackle the questions. Don't waste your time! All passages are best approached by skipping the passage and jumping right into answering the questions.

TIP

Use the information in the questions to direct you to the part of the passage you need to go to find the answers. If the question confuses you, get guidance from reading the answer choices. They can tell you what elements to focus on.

Questions

1. On the basis of Study 1, can newborn rat pups see vertical lines?

   (A) No, because the newborn rat pups did not collide with vertical obstacles.

   (B) No, because the newborn rat pups collided with horizontal obstacles.

   (C) Yes, because the newborn rat pups collided with horizontal obstacles.

   (D) Yes, because the newborn rat pups did not collide with vertical obstacles.

   This "yes, yes, no, no" question type concerns Study 1. A quick glance at the answer choices tells you that the only data you need to consider is whether the pups collided with vertical and horizontal obstacles. Focus your attention on Table 1's last columns. The table clearly shows that the pups avoided collisions with both horizontal and vertical obstacles. Examine your answer choices more thoroughly. You can immediately eliminate Choices (B) and (C) because they're not true. The pups in Study 1 avoided the horizontal obstacles.

   Now all you have to figure out is whether colliding with vertical obstacles indicates whether the pups can see vertical lines. Don't overthink this one. You don't have to worry that some ground-breaking study in Sweden may have revealed that the eye actually sees horizontal objects as vertical, and vice versa. The pups avoided the vertical objects, so they likely saw them. The best answer is Choice (D).

REMEMBER

Take the path of least resistance. Pick the most logical answer given the data in the passage and your own knowledge of the world.

2. Scientists place a 3-week-old rat pup that had been raised in an environment with both horizontal and vertical visual stimuli in a maze of vertical and horizontal obstacles. Which of the following is the most likely result?

   (F) The rat pup collides with horizontal obstacles but avoids vertical obstacles.

   (G) The rat pup collides with vertical obstacles but avoids horizontal obstacles.

   (H) The rat pup collides with both vertical and horizontal obstacles.

   (J) The rat pup avoids both vertical and horizontal obstacles.

   If a newborn pup can get around the maze and a pup raised in an environment with exposure to both horizontal and vertical stimuli for six weeks can get around the maze, then you can logically conclude that a pup raised in a normal environment for three weeks would also be able to do so. Only Choice (J) has a pup that doesn't need a crash helmet, so it's your winner.

REMEMBER

Did you have Smart Students' Disease on this question and read more into the question? If you said, "Yeah, but what if . . ." and started imagining all sorts of horrible and unlikely possibilities ("Maybe the rat OD'd on cheese and staggered around . . ."), you made this problem much harder than it really was. Keep it simple, okay?

3. Scientists place a 6-month-old rat that had been raised in a normal environment in a maze of vertical and horizontal obstacles. Which of the following is the most likely result?

   (A) The rat makes no attempt to get around the obstacles.

   (B) The rat negotiates around both vertical and horizontal obstacles.

   (C) The rat bumps into horizontal obstacles but gets around vertical obstacles.

   (D) The rat bumps into vertical obstacles but gets around horizontal obstacles.

Did you try to answer this question based on Studies 1 and 2? Doing so worked for the previous question because it spoke of an age, 3 weeks, that was between newborn (Study 1) and 6 weeks (Study 2). Check the question for details. In this question, the rat is older than the oldest pup in Studies 1 and 2, meaning that you can't be sure that the present trend continues. (Common sense tells you that the trend probably will continue, but you must be able to distinguish between what will probably happen and what will necessarily happen.)

Skim the studies for ones that provide a more definitive answer. In Studies 6, 7, and 8, scientists took rats that had previously been exposed to a normal environment for six months and exposed them to a different environment for six weeks. Because the rat in this question didn't have to endure a different experience and the vision of the rats that were exposed to the different environments turned out okay, the rat that wasn't placed in such an environment should also be okay. So the correct answer is Choice (B).

TIP

If you were really lost on this problem, you could eliminate Choice (A) right away because it's much too extreme. Answers with words like *rarely* and *infrequently* are right much more often than their dramatic counterparts like *no* and *never*. Because nothing indicates a favoring of vertical over horizontal lines, or vice versa, you can eliminate Choices (C) and (D) as well.

4. Which of the following was not under the direct control of the experimenters?

   (F) the length of time that the rat spent in a controlled environment

   (G) the percentage of measured brain activity in response to exposure to horizontal lines

   (H) the age at which the rat was tested for visual response

   (J) the types of obstacles placed in a maze

This is an experiment set-up question, which means you may need to read a little of the introductory material to answer it. When an experimental factor, or *variable*, is under the direct control of the experimenters, the experimenters can decide exactly how much (or what type) of that factor to use without having to depend on any intervening process. Choice (F) is clearly under the control of the experimenters. The experimenters can let the rat out of the maze (the environment) any time they want. Choice (J) is just as clear. The experimenters can throw in more vertical or horizontal obstacles at will.

Choice (H) is a little tougher to eliminate. You may think that the rat's age is up to the rat (or at least up to its parents), but the experimenters can decide exactly how old the rats have to be in order to be used in a certain part of the experiment.

By process of elimination, Choice (G) is correct. The experimenters can try to affect brain activity by changing the environment, but exactly how many brain cells respond depends on physiological factors outside the experimenters' control.

TIP

The basic science info covered in Question 4 comes into play in many different passages. *Independent variables* — Choices (F), (H), and (J), in this case — are those that experimenters can manipulate independently of any other factor. For example, the experimenter can change the time spent in the dark environment from six weeks to five weeks without changing the type of obstacles in the maze. A *dependent variable* — Choice (G) in this case — depends on what else was done in the experiment.

5. What is the relationship between Study 6 and Study 3?

(A) An examination of the results of Study 6 and Study 3 shows that the effects of six weeks in darkness may depend on the rat's age at the time scientists place the subjects in complete darkness.

(B) The rats in Study 3 were exposed to a different experimental environment that those in Study 6.

(C) Study 6 extends the findings of Study 3 by showing that longer periods of darkness also change brain-cell activity.

(D) Study 6 contradicts the findings of Study 3 by showing that, when rats are placed in darkness for a longer period of time, the maze navigation results found in Study 3 are altered.

You can dump Choices (B), (C), and (D) because they aren't true. The two studies imposed the same environmental condition, complete darkness, so Choice (B) is wrong. The other two answers are wrong because Study 6 used older rats (ones that have been alive for a longer period of time), but these rats, as well as those of Study 3, were in darkness for only six weeks.

Often, three answer options for science questions are obviously wrong. The only answer left is Choice (A), which is correct.

6. Some humans who have suffered brain injuries have been able to recover a lost brain function by having the brain reorganize itself. On the basis of all the rat-vision studies, which of the following humans would be most likely to recover a lost function through brain reorganization?

(F) a 50-year-old man who suffers a stroke (lack of oxygen to a certain region of the brain)

(G) an 80-year-old woman who suffers a stroke

(H) a 30-year-old combat soldier who suffers a bullet wound in the brain

(J) a baby who has had part of the left side of his brain surgically removed along with a tumor

Calm down, calm down — no one expects you to know exactly how each of these brain traumas affects brain functioning. Everything you need to answer this question is there in the passage. Plus, you can rely on what you know from your world experience to eliminate less logical answers to science questions. The key is to pick up on the ages. Which rats showed a change from the ordinary response pattern when the environment changed? The young rats. Similarly, a young human's brain is likely to be more flexible than that of an older human. Haven't you always pointed out to your parents not to be so narrow-minded and set in their ways? Choice (J), which features the youngest human, is the correct answer.

If you're almost having a stroke right now arguing with us, you probably didn't notice how carefully the question was worded: "Which of the following humans would be *most likely* to . . . ?" True, you don't know for sure that the baby would have some lost brain function, but all you're asked is which of the answer choices is the most likely (and, no, "a student studying for the ACT" wasn't among them).

7. Scientists exposed a 1-year-old rat that was raised in a normal environment and had normal vision to only horizontal lines. Which of the following is the most reasonable prediction?

(A) After three weeks, the cells in the visual part of the rat's brain fail to respond to vertical lines.

(B) After six weeks, the cells in the visual part of the rat's brain fail to respond to vertical lines.

(C) After six weeks, the cells in the visual part of the rat's brain respond to vertical lines.

(D) After six months, the cells in the visual part of the rat's brain respond to vertical lines.

Study 8 shows that 6-month-old rats exposed to only horizontal lines for six months still have brain cells capable of responding to vertical lines. This info knocks out Choices (A) and (B). After six months, the wiring in the rat's visual part of the brain seems to be fixed, so you can assume that the 1-year-old rat's brain has fixed wiring.

Be careful of Choice (D). You can't say for sure what effects an exposure longer than six weeks will have. Choice (C) is a much safer (and correct!) choice.

TIP

Have you been noticing throughout these answer explanations how often you can narrow the answers down to two choices very quickly? If you're in a hurry or if you're confused, make a quick guess. Remember that the ACT doesn't penalize you for wrong answers.

8. Suppose the researchers subjected *R. norvegicus domestica* that were 6 weeks old at the beginning of the study to six weeks of complete darkness. Based on information in the table, the level of brain activity in response to horizontal stimuli that the researchers measured in these subjects at the end of the study was most likely:

(F) less than 5 percent

(G) between 5 percent and 60 percent

(H) between 60 percent and 75 percent

(J) greater than 75 percent

To answer this question, examine the results in the column that shows the brain response to horizonal stimuli for studies that exposed rats to complete darkness for six weeks, Study 3 and Study 6. The newborn rats in Study 3 displayed 5 percent activity when exposed to horizontal stimuli, and the 6-month-old rats in Study 6 displayed 50 percent activity when exposed to horizontal stimuli. This comparison indicates that rats that were older at the beginning of the study responded better to horizontal stimuli than the newborn subjects.

Therefore, there is no reason to believe that rats that were 6 weeks old at the beginning of the study would show less brain activity than the newborns, so Choice (F) is incorrect. Nor does the table suggest any reason to believe that the younger rats would register a higher percentage of brain activity in response to horizontal activity than the older rats in Study 6. Therefore, Choices (H) and (J) must be wrong. The rats in the new study most likely had brain activity that measured above the 5 percent indicated for newborns, most likely closer to the 50 percent indicated for the older rats in Study 6. So the correct answer is Choice (G).

9. Which study best shows or studies best show that a particular environmental stimulus can lead to a change in the way the cells in the visual part of a rat's brain respond?

(A) Study 4 only

(B) Study 4 and Study 5 only

(C) Study 5 and Study 8 only

(D) Study 1, Study 5, and Study 8 only

First, notice that the answer choices only concern Studies, 1, 4, 5, and 8. Don't waste time evaluating Studies 2, 3, and 7.

Study 1 was performed with newborn rat pups that received a variety of stimuli and weren't subjected to complete darkness. Because this study didn't isolate one particular controlled environmental stimulation, it doesn't best indicate how one environmental component affects the brain. You can eliminate Choice (D).

Study 4 looks good. It isolates one controlled environmental stimulus. Exposure to only vertical lines caused a loss of cells able to respond to horizontal lines and a gain of cells able to respond to vertical lines. Because the correct answer must have Study 4 in it, eliminate Choice (C).

Study 5 is very similar to Study 4 in that it tests what happens to the rats when exposed to just one controlled stimulus. Study 5 shows a loss of cells able to respond to vertical lines and a gain of cells able to respond to horizontal lines. So the correct answer is Choice (B).

Notice that by using process of elimination you can avoid examining Study 8 altogether. What a fantastic time-saver! If you want to be absolutely sure, go ahead and verify that Study 8 doesn't work. Study 8 shows that the controlled environment for 6-month-old rats didn't alter their brain activity or ability to navigate horizontal and vertical obstacles. Their results were the same as those for newborn and 6-week-old rats that received a variety of stimuli. This study, taken by itself, suggests little support for an environmental contribution.

10. If Study 4 is conducted but Studies 3 and 5 are not, can the scientists conclude that all cells in the visual part of a rat pup's brain require stimulation in order to function?

(F) Yes, because Studies 3 and 5 test what happens when brain cells are not exposed to vertical lines.

(G) Yes, because Study 4 tests both vertical and horizontal-responding cells.

(H) No, because Study 4 only tests whether brain cells respond to vertical lines.

(J) No, because Study 4 does not test whether vertical-responding cells require stimulation.

This "yes, yes, no, no" question tests whether you understand that experimental results are limited when only certain conditions are tested. Notice that the answer choices indicate that you're focusing on whether the studies tested responses to horizontal and vertical lines. Eliminate Choices (G) and (H) because they're not true. Study 4 didn't test responses to vertical lines.

Choices (F) and (J) provide true statements, but only Choice (J) pinpoints the limitations of Study 4 — that it doesn't test vertical-responding cells. Studies 3 and 5 did test the vertical factor and allow for a more general conclusion regarding brain cells and environmental input, so they're necessary to understand the role of all cells. So the answer has to be Choice (J). Study 4 is inadequate by itself.

11. On the basis of all the studies, which of the following best summarizes the role of the environment in the development of a rat's visual brain-cell responses?

(A) The environment has no effect on the development of a rat's visual brain-cell responses.

(B) Environmental input early in a rat's life contributes to the continuation of normal brain-cell responses to stimuli.

(C) Environmental input can change the pattern of brain-cell responses throughout a rat's life.

(D) The environment is the only factor that influences brain-cell responses.

If Choice (A) were true, the pups in Studies 3, 4, and 5 would have normal visual responses. Eliminate Choice (A). If Choice (C) were true, the rats in Studies 6, 7, and 8 would show a change in response patterns. Choice (D) is at odds with Study 1. If the environment is the only factor, why do newborn rats show responses to all types of stimuli? This reasoning leaves only Choice (B), which is correct.

TIP

Are you noticing and using the wording in the questions and choices to help you choose and eliminate answers? The conservative language ("contributes to the continuation" rather than "directly determines") reinforces Choice (B) as the answer. Notice how easily you can contradict Choice (A), which contains the word *no*, Choice (C), which says *throughout*, and Choice (D), which includes *only*.

12. Which of the following studies would probably add the most new information to the work done in this set of experiments?

   (F) A study identical to Study 3, except that the pups are in the dark environment for seven weeks.

   (G) A study identical to Study 6, except that the rats are in the dark environment for five weeks.

   (H) A study identical to Study 6, except that the study uses 1-year-old rats.

   (J) A study identical to Studies 4 and 5, except that the rats are exposed only to diagonal lines.

Study 3 shows that six weeks of darkness almost entirely wipes out the cells' ability to respond. Perhaps seven weeks would cause a complete cessation of responding, but the point made from Study 3 (namely, that lack of visual stimulation leads to impaired brain-cell responding) has already been established. Therefore, the study mentioned in Choice (F) won't add much.

Study 6 strongly suggests that the response patterns in the visual part of a rat's brain are fixed enough at six months so that six weeks of an abnormal environment have no noticeable effect. If six weeks have no noticeable effect, why would five weeks be any different? Eliminate Choice (G). If the brain-cell responses are fixed by the time a rat is 6 months old, you can reasonably expect that a 1-year-old rat would show the same responses. Eliminate Choice (H).

The study mentioned in Choice (J) would help because it would show what happens to cells that respond to lines that are oriented both vertically and horizontally. This study would add some information regarding how precise the brain cells are in regard to lines in the environment. For example, is a diagonal line close enough to a vertical line that the exposure only to diagonal lines still allows the rat to respond to vertical lines? The answer to this question may increase understanding of how the environment interacts with the visual part of a rat's brain.

6

Writing Rightly: The Optional Writing Test

Chapter **17**

Excelling on Your Essay: The Writing Test Review

The ACT provides an optional Writing Test in addition to the other four multiple-choice sections. Its importance in the college application process is dwindling, and most colleges don't require or even recommend it. If you need to write the essay to enhance your application, make sure you present your best effort.

Writing a great essay is totally different from writing a really great ACT essay. A great essay is one you plan and think about for days, write for days, and edit for even more days. The whole process usually takes a considerable amount of time. But on the ACT, you have to cram all that planning, thinking, writing, and editing into only 40 minutes, and, trust us, that's not enough time to write something worthy of a literary award. But don't fret! All you need to do is figure out what the test makers are looking for; then you can give them exactly that.

What to Expect From the ACT Writing Test

If you want to write an ACT essay that pleases your readers, make sure you do all of the following:

» **State and develop a perspective.** Establishing a perspective requires you to explain your thoughts using examples, reasons, and details.

» **Evaluate and analyze the perspectives given.** Use them to help you form your thesis and add depth to your discussion, but don't think you need to analyze each perspective in your essay.

» **Consider the relationship between your perspective and at least one other.** This analysis demonstrates that you thoroughly understand a complex issue.

» **Maintain focus.** Staying focused requires you to stay on topic and make sure you don't add thoughts that aren't related to the prompt question.

- » **Back your ideas with detailed supporting information.** Rely on anecdotes and examples from your own experience.

- » **Organize ideas.** Organizing your thoughts and ideas requires you to present your ideas in a logical way, using transitional words and phrases and sequencing your ideas so that they build on each other.

- » **Communicate clearly.** Communicating clearly requires you to use a variety of sentence structures and vocabulary, and it requires you to spell correctly and make sure your grammar and punctuation are right.

To relieve your anxiety and help you manage the short amount of time you have to write the essay, we break down the essay into manageable chunks. If you follow the steps and advice we outline in this chapter, writing the essay will be much easier than you think.

Making the Grade: How the ACT Folks Score Your Essay

You'll be happy to know that you personally get not one, but two — yes, two — trained readers who score your essay. And if the first two don't agree, you get a third — yes, a third — reader all to yourself. Don't you feel special? The ACT folks sure think you are.

Here's the skinny on how you get your final Writing Test score: Two readers read your essay, and each one assigns it a numerical grade from 1 to 6. The sum of those ratings is your Writing Test subscore (2 to 12). When you choose to write the essay, the ACT people also report an English and Language Arts (ELA) score based on the results of your English Test and Writing Test performance. If you choose not to take the Writing Test, you get only the English Test score. The absence of the Writing Test score doesn't affect your ACT score in any other area, and neither your Writing Test nor your ELA score affects your ACT composite score in any way.

Examining the Prompt and Creating a Thesis

Responding to the ACT Writing Test prompt is somewhat like taking part in a debate. You'll read a consideration concerning a pertinent issue and then view three different perspectives. Your job is to get in on the action and form an opinion of your own.

The prompt may overwhelm you or bore you. It may include information that seems irrelevant. But no matter what, it poses a question worthy of careful consideration. Your first step is to review the information provided in the introduction and consider the three alternative positions that follow, and your second step is to form an opinion of your own. You don't really have to believe it yourself; you just need to write about it with confidence. The ACT people don't know you, and they certainly won't go to your house to ask you to explain yourself further. The key to starting a strong essay is taking a strong position right away. Here's what you need to do first:

1. **Read the question.**

   Here's the sample prompt (we refer to it throughout the rest of this chapter):

In some high schools, many teachers and parents have encouraged the school to require school uniforms that students must wear to school. Some teachers and parents support school uniforms because they think their use will improve the school's learning environment. Other teachers and parents do not support requiring uniforms because they think it restricts individual freedom of expression. It is worth considering the impact created by introducing a school uniform requirement.

- **Perspective 1:** Schools should indeed require all students to wear school uniforms to improve the overall learning environment. Doing so will reduce distractions and problems that arise from students being judged by how they look and dress, and will also make it harder for cliques to establish themselves.

- **Perspective 2:** Requiring uniforms in public schools is yet another way to muffle our students' freedom of expression. Uniforms also perpetuate the idea that in order to coexist, we must all conform to the same standard.

- **Perspective 3:** Requiring students to wear school uniforms helps level the playing field in terms of socioeconomic status. Kids will no longer be judged by how cheap or expensive their attire is, and families won't feel pressured to dress their school-age children in clothes they can't afford.

2. **Pay attention to the first paragraph.**

Typically, the first sentence of the prompt describes the issue. The following two sentences provide the position of its proponents and the view of the opposition. Can you identify the issue in the prompt in Step 1? The first sentence tells you that the issue is whether uniforms should be required. The second sentence tells you the reasoning behind those who favor uniforms: improvement in the school's learning environment. The third sentence gives the case of the opposition: uniforms restrict freedom of expression. And the last sentence provides the consideration. Read this sentence carefully because it reveals the crux of the issue — in this prompt, the impact of requiring uniforms.

The prompt's second paragraph requests the following:

Write a unified, coherent essay in which you evaluate multiple perspectives as to whether high school students should be required to wear school uniforms. In your essay, be sure to do the following:

- Clearly state your own perspective on the issue and analyze the relationship between your perspective and at least one other perspective.

- Develop and support your ideas with reasoning and examples.

- Organize your ideas clearly and logically.

- Communicate your ideas effectively in standard written English.

3. **Develop your own perspective regarding the question being posed by the prompt.**

Do you think schools need to have uniforms? Or do you think students should come to school naked (just needed to wake you up here — did it work?). Don't just start writing before you decide your position.

4. **Compare your perspective with those already provided.**

Maybe your perspective is very similar to one of the three provided, or maybe it's entirely different. Your essay only has to contain elements of one perspective; you aren't required to analyze all three.

Putting Up Your Dukes: Defending Your Perspective

By now you've read the prompt and all three perspectives, and you probably identify with one or two of them more than the others. Even if you don't, the time has come to put your own feelings about the issue down on paper. Remember that the ACT folks don't care what you really feel; they just want an essay, and they want one pronto!

REMEMBER

Here are two "nevers" to remember as you begin your essay:

>> Never tell the ACT folks the reasons why you agree or disagree with the prompt and perspectives in the first sentence.

>> Never straddle both sides of an issue without coming out with a clear opinion.

Throwing a Good First Punch: The Hook

Now that you've considered all perspectives and taken a stance of your own, you need to expand your first paragraph. Getting the reader's attention is key to keeping it throughout your essay. You must *hook* (grab the attention of) your reader right from the beginning. Think of the first paragraph as a funnel going from large thoughts to smaller ones.

>> **The first sentence needs to capture the overall debate of the prompt.** For example, if your prompt is about school uniforms, you may want to write something like this:

The appropriateness of uniforms is the subject of widespread debate.

Although you haven't yet stated your position, you've let the reader know that the essay is going to be about uniforms. You haven't given up your hand yet, which makes the reader want to continue reading your essay. Good job!

>> **The second sentence needs to express both sides of the argument.** Representing both sides is easier than you think, because the original prompt gives you both sides of the debate. Reread the second and third sentences in the prompt. Reword them in your own voice and stick those thoughts right after your first sentence.

For example, you may write the following sentence about the uniform prompt:

Although some people believe uniforms will improve the learning environment, others argue that uniforms may restrict individual freedom of expression.

Even though you may favor one view over another, you should mention both in your introduction to show that you recognize both sides of the argument. The ACT graders are sticklers for this point. Your score will be low if you fail to address the counterargument(s) at some point in your essay.

>> **The third sentence establishes and expands on your position.** To establish your position, you merely have to state the points that you'll cover in your essay to support your side and then state your side. These points eventually turn into your essay's three body paragraphs (see the section "The Proof Is in the Pudding: Defending Yourself" for details on writing the body paragraphs.)

For example, you may write the following sentence to take the position for uniforms in high schools:

> Because certain types of clothing can distract students, lead to school violence, and interfere with a student's ability to fit in, I believe that high schools should require uniforms for students.

Alternatively, you could vary your sentence structure by presenting your thesis separate from the sentence that presents your three points that will become your three body paragraphs:

> It's apparent to me that certain types of clothing can distract students, lead to school violence, and interfere with a student's ability to fit in. Therefore, I believe that high schools should require uniforms for students.

Your first paragraph is now complete:

> The appropriateness of dress codes is the subject of widespread debate. Although some people believe uniforms will improve the learning environment, others argue that uniforms may restrict individual freedom of expression. Because certain types of clothing can distract students, lead to school violence, and interfere with a student's ability to fit in, I believe requiring school uniforms will positively impact the high school experience.

TIP

The *thesis* should be the last sentence of your introduction paragraph. Don't give up your hand too early and don't neglect building the suspense.

Another way to hook your reader is to begin your essay with a story. If you're advocating for school uniforms, you may introduce your position by recounting the embarrassment your best friend experienced when a group of mean girls pointed out in the middle of chemistry class that her jeans clearly lacked a designer label.

The Proof Is in the Pudding: Defending Yourself

To create a great ACT essay, you must use specific examples, reasons, and details that prove your position on the prompt, and help refute counterarguments made by others. The ACT folks are looking for two things here, which we discuss in the following sections:

» Specific examples

» Variety of examples

Using specific examples

To get a handle on how specific your examples should be, consider the last time your parents questioned you about your Saturday night activities. We'll bet their questions included all the old stand-bys: Where did you go? Who was there? Why are you home so late? Who drove? How long has he had his license? You know that vague answers never cut it.

This skill that you've been practicing for years is going to come in handy when you take your ACT Writing Test, because you're already great at giving the specifics (or making them up). Really good examples discuss extremely specific details, events, dates, and occurrences. Your goal is to write in detail and to try not to be too broad and loose. For example, say that you're trying to find examples to support uniforms. You can conclude that allowing students to wear whatever they want leads to distraction among the students. Great, but you need to be more specific. You need to give an example from your life when you witnessed this distraction, or site a relevant article you've read. In other words, give dates, mention people, rat on your friends! Just choose examples that you know a lot about so that you can get down to the nitty-gritty and be extremely specific.

Mixing things up with a variety of examples

Over the past few years, you may have had to come up with a variety of excuses for breaking curfew — the car broke down, traffic was horrendous, the movie ran late, you forgot the time, you fell asleep . . . you know the routine. Again, thank your parents for helping you with yet another skill you can apply to the ACT Writing Test. Coming up with specific examples about how you feel about uniforms just from your personal life is easy, but it's also boring.

REMEMBER

Use a broad range of examples from different areas, such as literature, cultural experiences, your personal life, current events, business, or history. If you spend just a few moments thinking about the topic, you can come up with great examples from varied areas.

So, to answer the question, "Should schools require students to wear uniforms?" you may strengthen your own perspective by using examples like these:

>> **Personal life:** A scenario where you saw a girl wearing a short skirt and teeny top and noticed how it interfered with other students' ability to concentrate

>> **Current events:** An example from a magazine article you read about a high school shooting that explains how the boys who fired guns in their school were trying to hurt the kids who looked and dressed like jocks

>> **Cultural experience:** The concern regarding wearing gang-related colors and logos and the potential implications doing so may have regarding violence in the schools

A nice variety of examples like these definitely gets the attention of the ACT folks and helps you sound like the smart writer that you are.

Forming logical arguments

The ACT Writing Test provides you with an issue and three perspectives and expects you to examine the whole to create a logical thesis. Accomplishing this task is easier when you know a little about how to form arguments.

A logical argument consists of premises and a conclusion. The *premises* give the supporting evidence that you can draw a conclusion from. You can usually find the *conclusion* in the argument because it's the statement that you can preface with "therefore." The conclusion is often, but not always, the argument's last sentence. For example, take a look at this simple deduction:

All gazelles are fast. That animal is a gazelle. Therefore, that animal is fast.

The premises in the argument are "All gazelles are fast" and "that animal is a gazelle." You know this because they provide the supporting evidence for the conclusion that that animal is fast. The perspectives in the Writing Test prompt are unlikely to be so obvious as to include a conclusion designated by a "therefore," but you can form your own "therefore" statement to determine the conclusion.

In *deductive reasoning*, you draw a specific conclusion from general premises as we did for the earlier gazelle argument. With *inductive reasoning*, you do just the opposite; you develop a general conclusion from specific premises. Consider this example of an inductive argument:

Grace is a high school student and likes spaghetti. (Specific premise)

Javi is a high school student and likes spaghetti. (Specific premise)

Gidget is a high school student and likes spaghetti. (Specific premise)

Manny is a high school and likes spaghetti. (Specific premise)

Therefore, it is likely that all high school students like spaghetti. (General conclusion)

Because an inductive argument derives general conclusions from specific examples, you can't come up with a statement that "must be true." The best you can say, even if all the premises are true, is that the conclusion can be or is likely to be true. The perspectives you see in the Writing Test will be based on inductive reasoning.

Inductive reasoning often relies on three main methods. Knowing these ways of reaching a conclusion can help you analyze perspectives and effectively draw your own conclusions:

>> **Cause-and-effect arguments:** This argument concludes that one event is the result of another. These types of arguments are strongest when the premises prove that an event's alleged cause is the most likely one and that there are no other probable causes. For example, after years of football watching, you may conclude the following: "Every time I wear my lucky shirt, my favorite team wins; therefore, wearing my lucky shirt causes the team to win." This example is weak because it doesn't take into consideration other, more probable reasons (like the team's talent) for the wins.

>> **Analogy arguments:** This argument tries to show that two or more concepts are similar so that what holds true for one is true for the other. The argument's strength depends on the degree of similarity between the persons, objects, or ideas being compared. For example, in drawing a conclusion about Beth's likes, you may compare her to Alex: "Alex is a student, and he likes rap music. Beth is also a student, so she probably likes rap music, too." Your argument would be stronger if you could show that Alex and Beth have other similar interests that apply to rap music, like hip-hop dancing or wearing bling. If, on the other hand, you show that Alex likes to go to dance clubs while Beth prefers practicing her violin at home, your original conclusion may be less likely.

>> **Statistical arguments:** These arguments rely on numbers to reach a conclusion. These types of arguments claim that what's true for the statistical majority is also true for the individual (or, alternately, that what's true of a member or members of a group also holds true for the larger group). But because these are inductive reasoning arguments, you can't prove that the conclusions are absolutely true. When you analyze statistical arguments, focus on how well the given statistics apply to the conclusion's circumstances. For instance, if you wanted people to buy clothing through your website, you may make this argument: "In a recent study of consumers' preferences, 80 percent of shoppers surveyed said they prefer to shop online; therefore, you'll probably prefer to buy clothes online." You'd support your conclusion if you could show that what's true for the majority is also true for an individual.

Hamburger Writing: Organizing Your Essay

Ever taken a bite of a big, juicy hamburger from a fast-food restaurant? Well, okay, we don't blame you for not wanting to see what's really lurking between the buns (even though it tastes darn good). But if you're feeling adventurous (and want to ace the essay part of the ACT), you may want to follow along as we dissect the classic fast-food burger and match each ingredient with a specific part of your essay. Yes, you heard right. Every great essay is organized like a big, juicy hamburger.

No matter your prompt's topic, the ACT graders want to see a specific format to your writing. In other words, they don't want all the ingredients thrown in any old way. By following the organization we outline in the next few sections, you can give the test graders a supersized essay worthy of a supersized score.

The top bun: Introduction

The top bun includes the funnel of information that leads to your thesis. We show you how to write it in the previous sections. Now you can move on to the essay's body paragraphs.

The three meats: Example paragraphs

Think of your supporting arguments in terms of three different kinds of meat — perhaps two beef patties and some bacon or a chicken club with turkey and bacon. Each meat represents a separate paragraph in your essay, the purpose of which is to add specific examples that help prove the position that you state in your top bun. (Are you getting hungry yet?)

Each meaty paragraph needs to include the following elements:

>> Three to five sentences

>> A solid topic sentence that relates directly to your position (remember, you already wrote your ideas in the top bun — your thesis)

>> A variety of reasons, details, and examples that illustrate that specific topic

In the thesis, we wrote about the uniform prompt, and we said that clothing can be distracting (see the section, "Throwing a Good First Punch: The Hook," for more on this sample thesis). You can use that thought as the topic sentence for your first meat paragraph. For example, you may open your first body paragraph with something like this:

Uniforms should be required because a variety of clothing choices can be very distracting in the learning environment.

Now you have to write a few sentences that prove that clothing can be distracting. Make sure that you use specific and clear examples from a variety of sources, including personal experience, history, culture, and literature. Don't stray off topic, or in this case, begin writing about anything other than the fact that clothing can be distracting. In other words, don't get distracted when writing about distraction!

Here's a sample meat paragraph that you (and the graders) can really sink your teeth into:

> Uniforms should be required because a variety of clothing choices can be very distracting in the learning environment. Social media and advertisements flash images of young girls wearing practically nothing, for example, a fashion that most teenagers try to emulate *(culture reference)*. However, wearing skimpy clothes and showing body parts can make some people look and react, which may interrupt an important part of class. That can be quite distracting when you're trying to learn the Pythagorean theorem *(personal experience reference)*. Furthermore, paying attention to the teacher is difficult when you hear people discussing another student's $150 Dolce and Gabbana jeans *(cultural reference)*. A uniform does away with these distractions by enforcing a more conservative style of clothing, allowing the focus in the classroom to remain on education rather than fashion.

Sounds good, right? Well, your essay isn't full, yet, even after a meaty paragraph like this one. You still have two more meats to gobble down! Lucky for you, you've already decided which topics you're going to discuss in the next two meaty paragraphs: You mentioned distractions, school violence, and fitting in as part of your essay's introduction (see the section, "Throwing a Good First Punch: The Hook," for details). You just wrote about distractions in the first meat paragraph, so your second meat is about school violence and your third is about fitting in. Don't get so caught up in your own argument that you forget the task at hand, though, and that includes careful consideration of the other perspectives provided. Pepper your paragraphs with nods to the opposition. Maybe you're refuting the points made by others, or maybe you're agreeing — but you do need to acknowledge them and consider their merits, if any.

To make things easier, structure the second and third examples by including the following elements:

>> A solid topic sentence that defends your position

>> A few sentences in which you give reasons, details, and examples that support the topic of this paragraph or refute a counterargument

>> A variety of examples taken from different areas, such as literature, culture, personal experience, and history

You'll want to acknowledge arguments you don't agree with (the three perspectives provide examples, but you can come up with your own, too), and then show why they're not strong enough to change your position. For example, you could point out that the clothes you wear aren't the only form of personal expression and that the lack of distractions created by uniforms may actually make it easier to express yourself in other areas, such as art, music, and writing.

The lettuce, tomato, and special sauce: Transitions

Like the sandwich, your essay needs to taste good (that is, read well) as a whole. Transitions serve as the special sauce and other burger fixin's that help smooth out the differences between your paragraphs. You must include transitions between your first and second, and second and third meat paragraphs. The most obvious way to do so is by using transitional words, such as *secondly, finally, another idea, another example, furthermore,* and *in addition,* just to name a few. Using these obvious transitions will be good enough to earn a score of 5, but to achieve the perfect 6, your transitions will need to be subtler. For example, you may transition from one paragraph to another by alluding in the second paragraph to a concept mentioned in the first one.

The bottom bun: Conclusion

No matter how full of this essay you are by the time you add your three meaty paragraphs and all the saucy transitions, you need to consume the bottom bun before you're done. Ideally, the bottom bun or conclusion of your essay should include the following two elements:

>> A restatement of your position

>> An expansion of your position that looks to the future

You can address both elements in three to four sentences. Just make sure you include your position, references to your meat topics, and one sentence that pulls everything together. Here's an example:

> Implementing a uniform policy would be beneficial *(restatement of your position)*. Requiring uniforms has the potential to limit distractions in the classroom, reduce school-related violence, and help students find more creative ways to fit in *(references to your meat topics)*. School uniforms would direct the appropriate focus back on education rather than keep it fixated on an adolescent fashion show *(looking toward the future)*.

Wielding the Red Pen: Editing and Proofing

With the finish line directly in front of you, all you have left to do is to make a quick sprint (or should we say edit?) to the end of your essay. You absolutely must make time to proof your masterpiece. If you don't, your essay score will reflect your hasty goodbye. You're not finished until you've double-checked (and corrected) your writing. This section gives you five quick editing and proofreading techniques that can keep you from tripping before you cross the finish line.

TIP

Chapter 5 reviews the basic rules of grammar and sentence structure and reminds you of simple things to watch for when you check your sentences. Being the wonderful student that you are, you've probably already studied that chapter and are now ready to launch straight into editing.

Using the touch method to look for spelling mistakes and ghost words

Your brain is smarter than you think it is. When you proofread, your brain may see your writing the way you intended it to be rather than the way it really is. Your sentences may be missing just a few little words here and there, but, without them, your paragraphs and essay fail.

TIP

Use your pencil to quickly touch every single word that you wrote. Doing so helps you find words that you omitted, catch simple spelling errors, and locate places where you've repeated words or thoughts. The smallest errors are often the most costly. The three easiest mistakes to catch are misusing *there, their,* and *they're; your* and *you're;* and *it's* and *its.* Touching the words as you proofread helps you outsmart your brain and catch these simplest of mistakes.

Calling all action verbs: Be descriptive

You can't score your best if readers fall asleep in the middle of your essay. Wake them up by forcing them to read caffeine-filled words. In other words, use bold action verbs rather than mild-mannered, wimpy verbs. For example, instead of writing, "He ran to the store quickly," replace *ran* with *bolted*, *sprinted*, or *flew*. These words express more action and give the sentence movement. *Ran* is boring. Replacing boring verbs with verbs that create vivid pictures definitely improves your essay.

Avoiding problems with punk-tu-a-tion: Punctuate properly

Rebellion against authority may be your motto on most days, but you can't rebel against grammar and punctuation rules on the ACT essay. They always win. Here are the questions you need to ask yourself when you edit your essay for punctuation and other common grammar mistakes:

» Did I use the correct periods, exclamation points, and question marks?

» Did I capitalize the first words of my sentences and proper nouns?

» Do my subjects agree with my verbs?

» Did I use commas correctly?

» Are any of my sentences run-ons or fragments?

» Are my words spelled correctly?

Handwriting check: Write legibly

You need to get into med school before you can start writing like a doctor. If the ACT graders can't read your essay, how will they know how brilliant it is? Illegible writing is an easy error to catch as you proofread your essay. If *you* can't read your writing, erase what you can't read and rewrite it. Pencils with good erasers — what a useful invention!

Writing Don'ts

Relax. You've been writing since the first grade, you have something to say, and this test is your way to prove it. All you need is a quick refresher on the basics of essay writing, which, lucky for you, we cover in the following sections. Avoid the pitfalls we describe here, and you'll be well on your way to a winning essay.

Writing before you think

If you have no destination, you're bound to get lost. The most important part of writing your essay is having a strong structure and a clear idea of where you're going. If you put your pen to the paper without knowing what the heck you're going to say, you can bet your bottom dollar that the ACT folks won't know what you're saying either.

REMEMBER

Make a quick plan before you start writing, and you'll avoid an essay that wanders aimlessly.

Panicking about time

Writer's block — when you simply can't think of anything to put down — often occurs in stressful situations and is frequently the result of a time crunch. You have 40 full minutes to complete the writing portion of the ACT. That's plenty of time to read the question, organize your thoughts, write your essay, and do a quick edit.

TIP

To get the most out of your 40 minutes, we suggest you break them down like this:

>> 5 minutes to read the question and organize your thoughts

>> 5 minutes to write your thesis and outline

>> 25 minutes to write the bulk of your essay

>> 5 minutes to edit and proofread

Notice that we don't include any time for panicking. Panicking takes 40 minutes just to get over, and by then, your time's up!

Referring to the perspectives by number

The ACT really doesn't want you to provide a thorough analysis of each of the perspectives. You need only contain an element of one of the perspectives in your essay. And you aren't expected to give the perspective titles or even reference them at all. Merely including an idea from one of them as you support your own opinion is enough to meet the goal of considering the perspectives.

Sticking to the status quo

The ACT Writing Test gives you a *prompt,* or topic, to write about. The prompt requires you to form an opinion on an issue and support it with compelling evidence from your own experience. You may think you're confined to a traditional five-paragraph expository exercise, but if you think you can pull it off, the ACT rewards a creative approach. If you're a good storyteller, you may want to use a personal anecdote that illustrates your position. You can use that story as a way of engaging the reader and making your point through imagery and action. If you're a financial whiz kid, you may want to dazzle the readers with a statistical analysis that shows the economic feasibility of your position or the financial impossibility of the opposition.

Of course, if you're more comfortable with the standard introductory paragraph, three supporting paragraphs, and conclusion, then by all means stick to the standard. Just make sure you produce an organized, well-thought-out essay that answers the question that they asked with the most specific, unique evidence you can think of.

Using words you don't know

Nobody can be Shakespeare, especially in 40 minutes — not even Bill himself. When writing your essay for the ACT, you don't have the thesaurus button on your word processor in front of you — which actually may be a good thing. One of the worst mistakes you can make is using words that you think sound good but aren't absolutely sure how to use. Instead of trying to use words that you don't know, impress the ACT readers with your thoughts and your ability to communicate clearly. Using words you don't know or understand completely may give the ACT graders a laugh, but you won't be laughing when you see your score.

Being overly critical of yourself

Nobody writes the perfect essay in 40 minutes. Nobody! The graders know that, and you need to, as well. Trying to be obsessively perfect does you more harm than good. If you spend too much time critiquing yourself, the ACT graders won't have anything to critique. Fortunately, you don't have to be perfect to get a high score. You can get a good score in 40 minutes if you follow the suggestions and format described in this book. Simply watch your time, stay organized, and express yourself clearly (and in your own words).

Writing like you speak

Everyone knows that speaking is much easier than writing. However, this test is neither the time nor the place to impress the test makers with your street vocabulary. Whatever you do, don't drop it like it's hot, don't think you're too cool for school, don't think you're kinda-like the, like, greatest, or like "ohmygod" this is so cool, or else it's your bad. In other words, you're not texting, you're not talking to your best friends, and you're not trying to communicate on the playground. You're writing for a bunch of old fogies who have no idea what the latest slang means. Stick to words that your grandparents understand.

Repeating yourself over and over again

One of the biggest mistakes that you can make on the ACT Writing Test is saying the same thing again and again in different words. Don't try to lengthen your essay by repeating yourself. The test graders get it the first time. If you find yourself repeating sentences for lack of things to say, then you didn't spend enough time planning the essay.

REMEMBER

The way to avoid too much repetition is by organizing your thoughts and coming up with specific and different examples to prove your thesis before you start writing.

Failing to edit your essay

One of the most embarrassing things that can happen to you on a perfect first date is having toilet paper stuck to your shoe and having your date tell you about it! Date over. To counteract a potential faux pas like this one, make sure that you double-check your shoes before leaving the bathroom — a skill that you can also apply to finishing your ACT essay. (At last, a real-world skill you can finally use.)

REMEMBER

Leave yourself time to proofread and check your essay for any obvious sentence structure errors, spelling mistakes, lack of clarity, missing or wrong punctuation, repetition, and illegible handwriting. By doing so, you eliminate any embarrassing toilet paper that's stuck to your writing before your date — or should we say your test grader — notices.

Reviewing Some Example Essays and Their Scores

The ACT essay receives a score from 1 to 6 from one of two readers in four areas: quality of analysis, strength of development, clarity of organization, and quality of writing. The lowest score you can receive from one reader in each area is — get this — a 1, and the highest score is a 6.

One of the best ways to avoid the common mistakes associated with receiving lower scores is to read examples of essays that have garnered different scores, which is where this section comes into play. Here we explain what you need to do to get the highest possible score on your essay by beginning with an example of an essay worthy of each score and then explaining why the sample deserves that particular score. Feel free to laugh at the ones with lower scores. We did. After reading these examples, you'll have a much better idea of what to avoid in your writing. To see the prompt for these essays, read the section, "Examining the Prompt and Creating a Thesis," earlier in this chapter.

1 — 1 is the loneliest number: How not to be a 1

Like Perspective 1 says, kids should where uniforms. Then I wouldn't have to see all the gangsters walking around with there pants around there knees. But the girls should be able to where whatever they want, because no one minds when the show off there stomachs. Student and principles should both where uniforms. Its only fair.

Being number 1 may be great for high school football, but it isn't great on your ACT test. This writer chooses a side to some degree, but she doesn't support or back up her thesis. Not only does she fail to support her position, but she also wanders throughout the "essay." Her lack of focus, irreverent examples, and writing style merit a score of 1 in each area. Oh, and by the way, the number of spelling and word errors distracts the reader from her ideas and negatively influences the way the graders look at her essay.

2 — 2 little 2 late: Steering clear of coming in second

I don't agree with the teachers and parents in Perspectives 1 and 3 who think we should have uniforms. Our style of dress is what makes us individuals and sets us apart form each other.

At my school students who dress in certain ways find others who are like them. You always know who is interested in the same stuff as you by what they wear. Imposing a uniform doesn't allow us to make friendships with people you are like ourselves.

Uniforms would make people mad. Teachers would find it hard to control all their students because students would want to rebel. Kids wouldn't be able to find friends who are like them and this would cause them to rebel.

These are just a few reasons why we should not have a uniform at school. There are many more reasons then just these but these are the most important.

This writer takes a stance and shows that he can support his point of view, but his lack of organization leaves readers' heads spinning. He also appears to be agreeing with the second perspective, but fails to mention the parallel between his own opinion and this perspective. The writer has paragraph structure in this essay, with an introductory paragraph and conclusion, but he's missing clear transitions between the two body paragraphs. His simple sentence structure and spelling errors let everyone know that his writing skills are not as sophisticated as they should be. A score of 2 may be better than a 1, but it isn't a score you should strive for.

3 — Still finding yourself on the wrong side of the tracks

In my opinion, kids should not have a uniform because it takes away freedoms that they should have. There are some clothing styles that teenagers wear that are not appropriate like tight revealing clothes. But to make students buy certain clothes like blue pants and white shirt infringes on their rights.

In America freedom of expression is very important and by forcing us to wear certain things schools are taking away one of our rights. If they start taking away this right, they might start taking away other ones too.

Uniforms are unfair because some families cannot afford them. Many kids would need a whole new wardrobe and their families would have a hard time buying this for them. Not only would they need clothes, but they also need clothes for outside of school. For poorer families this would be hard.

A uniform would take away some of our freedom of expression and it would be a financial strain for poorer families. I think that there should be no uniforms.

A score of 3 is almost a reason for celebration. Almost. This writer states her own perspective and advances her argument. The essay maintains a semblance of structure. She presents a clear point of view with two supporting points that address the language presented in the prompt. Her sentences are more complex than the ones written by most eighth-graders, and she presents a clear conclusion that sums up her points.

However, her overall writing style and propensity for rambling sentences leave something to be desired. When you add the average 3 scores from each reader, you get an overall score of 6. But a 7 is the lowest score you can receive and still be considered "college ready" in writing.

The ACT readers recognize her developing skill, but she still has room for improvement. Her essay would be better if she discussed counterarguments and more fully developed her ideas. Her paragraphs aren't complete, and she doesn't include transitions to link her ideas and increase the essay's flow. Plus, she makes numerous punctuation mistakes. With a little work, this essay could make it to the right side of the tracks.

4 — Reaching 4 a better score

I believe that it would be a good idea for our schools to adopt uniforms. Some people argue that it would restrict student's freedom of expression, but I do not agree with this position. It is important that we have a right to express ourselves, but our society does not allow us to have unrestricted freedoms like this all the time. It is important to learn discipline, show respect for other's feelings and learn how to be successful operating in the real world. School uniforms create a better learning environment and also helps students prepare for their futures.

The most important benefit of imposing dress codes would be creating a better school environment. Students who are trying to concentrate and learn would be unfocused because of inappropriate clothing. Small clothing, tight tops, and sagging pants might be okay for after school but not appropriate for the classroom. Certain types of people might find profanity and obscene images offensive. Art and creative writing are better ways to express your creativity rather than on your clothing. Less distractions in the classroom would help a student to get a better education.

Another important benefit of having uniforms would teach students how to dress properly for different occasions. Clothes that you would wear to a party would not be appropriate for a dinner with your boyfriends parents. Likewise, you wouldn't wear your work clothes on a date. Some jobs in society require people to wear uniforms. Uniforms in schools help students to realize what the world is like and get ready to enter it.

Another important concern for students is trying to fit in. Uniforms take the emphasis off what you look like and put more emphasis on learning.

In conclusion, it is important for schools to require uniforms. Getting an education is the most important thing about school and uniforms take away distractions. Learning how to dress for the real world is also important. And it helps with the pressures of trying to fit in.

A score of 4 would make anyone want to run and frolic through green pastures because the ACT folks think you have writing skills that are adequate for college. You may not be the most eloquent writer, but at least you're clear and organized. Your respectable score reflects your ability. This writer takes a stance, backs it up using both points made in the prompts and some entirely new ones, and acknowledges counterarguments. He maintains focus throughout the essay, and he supports each idea in well-defined paragraphs with specific examples to make the graders happy. This writer demonstrates a simple organizational structure that works; the essay properly includes an introduction that sets up what the writer talks about in the body paragraphs and a conclusion that sums up his points without word-for-word repetition. This essay shows that the writer has learned adequate writing skills in school, even though he hasn't mastered perfect punctuation or impeccable word choice. (In the second paragraph, *less distractions* should be *fewer distractions*, and switching back and forth between third and second person isn't stylistically pleasing.)

5 — Shining brightly: A 5-star winner

There is a debate now amongst parents and teachers about whether a school uniform should be required. Mandating uniforms would positively impact the learning environment in our schools and significantly improve the excellence of our education. First, students would be able to focus on academics rather than the social facet of school. Second, the appearance of the school would improve. And third, students would be better prepared for the working world.

The most crucial benefit of requiring uniforms would be to significantly reduce the distractions in the classroom. For students to be successful in the future, it is important that we concentrate on the material being taught in the classroom. It is difficult to do this when you overhear students whispering about their newest Gucci purse or admiring their best friend's Prada shoes. Young people place such an emphasis on style and image rather than substance. In addition, students see school as a social venue rather than a learning environment.

Secondly, when students and faculty are well groomed, the aesthetic appeal of the school is improved. Formal attire is not necessary to achieve this. For example, requiring long pants and a collared shirt would be sufficient. Not only would the school look more professional, it would change the character of the school. Holding students to a higher standard would require them to do it for themselves. It would improve their maturity level as well.

Finally, sporting uniforms would prepare today's youth for the work of their future. A majority of jobs require uniforms or a standard dress code. I think it is important for schools to not only prepare students academically for their future, but also in proper conduct and grooming. Just because someone has impressive qualifications doesn't mean they'll be hired if they look like they just rolled in from the beach. Allowing students to dress however they choose might eventually be harmful to their future success.

The notion that uniforms would hinder a student's freedom of expression is valid, but I still think a dress code is a good idea. A dress code addresses the important issues at hand while at the same time allowing the student to find more appropriate ways of expression. You can express individuality through art, music, speech, and other means regardless of your clothing.

In conclusion, I strongly support the idea of enforcing a school uniform. Not only would uniforms improve our learning environment, but they would also improve the character of the school and ready its students for a successful future.

A score of 5 gets you a gold star on the blackboard! It isn't ACT perfection, but it's close. This writer is able to effectively state her position by clearly answering the question and addressing counterarguments. She presents a well-organized and fluid essay with a variety of specific examples drawn from both the prompts and her own perspective. She develops the ideas in each paragraph and uses them to support her argument. This writer explores a cultural component that shows advanced critical-thinking skills and displays a mastery of vocabulary and precise word choice. Some problems with sentence structure and changing from third to second person within the same sentence keep this essay from receiving a perfect score.

6 — Unlocking the code to a perfect score

The trend of inappropriate dress in our schools is causing alarm in our parents and educators. This population argues that wearing inappropriate clothes is distracting in the classroom and interferes with the learning environment. They believe that requiring uniforms would provide a reasonable solution to the problem. Although those opposed to uniforms believe that enforcing them would hinder the student's freedom of expression, I believe that the advantages far outweigh this potential disadvantage.

When freedom of expression begins to interfere with appropriate and meaningful education in the classroom, we must address this serious dilemma. The current lack of uniforms is not working. We are not breaking new ground when we suggest that the fashion that is spewed upon our youth in the mass media is riddled with sexual undertones. Examples can be seen in every teen magazine, youth-oriented television program, and in the most popular music videos. Further, clothing that advertisers would consider benign, stimulates and raises the hormone levels of every young male and promotes distractions in the classroom. The only solution to help create an environment where learning takes precedence is to adopt school uniforms. Obviously, a uniform policy would be easier to enforce a dress code and would bring many advantages to the entire academic population.

First and foremost, uniforms would help students to fight the materialistic world's values. Our society feels that designer labels, such as Joe's Jeans, Elizabeth and James, and Zoe Couture, create self-worth and that without these, a person is open to cruel comments and non-acceptance. Many students cannot afford to "buy" their self-worth and are required to rise above the standards our society and media feeds them. As a teenager, acceptance is the most crucial aspect of their daily lives, and school uniforms take away the financial burden that our society imposes upon them. Although uniforms must be purchased, this is a minimal financial burden compared to overly high-priced current designer wear that students ask for.

Uniforms could also help curb gang-related violence that occurs in many of our nation's schools. Specific colors, logos, and signs have been adopted into the lifestyle of gang members and each carries its own significance. What was once an ordinary red shirt could now be considered an intentional bullet fired in a gang battle. Uniforms decrease the division lines between gangs as well as protect students who are ignorant to the unwritten laws that govern gangs.

For myself, uniforms would dramatically decrease the amount of time I spend preparing for my day. No longer would I need to delve into the bottom of my closet to find an outfit that I haven't worn this week. I do not need to worry that my best friends might come to school in the same outfit as mine, because uniforms ensure that they will! Uniforms give me extra time to finish the homework I haven't done rather than spend time worrying about my wardrobe.

Some may argue that uniforms prevent creative expression, but those who agree with this opinion are limiting their notion of creativity to fashion. There are many other ways to express creativity. In fact, requiring uniforms may actually encourage freedom of expression. Without the distraction created by questionnable clothing, students may be better able to express themselves in art class, through scientific research, and with literary exploits. Uniforms help to ensure a learning environment that is free from distractions and fosters creative expression in areas that are important.

I highly value the worth of uniforms and feel they should be enforced throughout the entire school district. Solving problems in the entire district would help ensure a safer community, save money, encourage better learning, and give students a little extra time in the morning.

The secret to perfection on the ACT Writing Test is garnering a 6, and with an essay like this, you can likely earn it. The ACT graders are practically drooling over this writer's style because it recognizes the complexity of the issue, analyzes the provided perspectives, develops the author's own position, and then describes the relationships among all points. He supports the reasons for his position with specific, well-thought-out, and varied examples. His structure and organization are logical, and he includes smooth but subtle transitions between his paragraphs. His writing displays his own unique wit and personality, and he concludes his essay with a reference to an anecdote from a prior paragraph. Given the time limits, this essay is nearly perfect, and the occasional misplaced comma and misspelling of *questionable* won't concern the graders.

Chapter 18

Practicing Promptly with Practice Prompts: Essay Practice Questions

In Chapter 17, you do a lot of reading about writing. But you'll never get better at writing without actually writing — which is why you've turned to this chapter. Here, we give you two sample prompts to practice with, and we suggest that you time yourself so that you get a sense of what 40 minutes of writing feels like. Practicing like this helps you avoid panicking when you take the real test.

Directions: Follow the guidelines in Chapter 17 and create an essay on each of the following two prompts. You don't have enough space to write your essay in this chapter, so grab some extra pieces of paper. One to one and a half pages for each essay should do the trick. (Just make sure you don't peek at our writing tips that follow each prompt until after you're done writing!)

Be sure to give yourself a good, long break in between essays. When you're done with each one, read through the tips we give you for writing each essay topic and assess your effort. Or, better yet, have your parents or English teacher read your essays for feedback.

Writing Prompt 1

Many successful people believe that a competitive environment fosters high achievement. In high schools, some parents and teachers think that competition among students encourages them to strive toward higher academic potential. Others think that academic competition negatively affects students' performance by causing undue stress and feelings of failure. Should high schools encourage or discourage a competitive academic atmosphere?

Read and carefully consider these perspectives. Each suggests a particular way of thinking about the benefits and drawbacks of a competitive school atmosphere.

Perspective 1: For today's students, school is their training ground for real life. In real life, they will find themselves in constant competition. Whether for jobs, the affections of another, or a day on the golf course, students will not be able to avoid competition, so they may as well train for and get used to it in high school.

Perspective 2: Today's high school students are under enough pressure without being faced with increased academic competition while at school. Peer pressure, pressure to excel in sports, and pressure to succeed in their parents' eyes is more than enough stress for students of high school age to deal with.

Perspective 3: Academic competition among students should be encouraged to a point. Healthy competition gives our students a valuable opportunity to excel and gain self-esteem and gives all students a reasonable chance of winning. Unhealthy competition is that which either implicitly or explicitly rewards stronger students in a way that allows these students to exploit their perceived superiority over those students whose accomplishments have not been recognized.

Write a unified, coherent essay in which you evaluate multiple perspectives as to whether high schools should encourage competition. In your essay, be sure to do the following:

» Clearly state your own perspective on the issue and analyze the relationship between your perspective and at least one other perspective.

» Develop and support your ideas with reasoning and examples.

» Organize your ideas clearly and logically.

» Communicate your ideas effectively in standard written English.

Your perspective may be in full agreement with any of the others, in partial agreement, or wholly different.

In this prompt, you're tasked with assessing the strengths and weaknesses of a competitive high school environment. The question doesn't have a right or wrong answer; what's important is that you clearly evaluate the perspectives provided, state and develop one of your own, and explain how your own perspective relates to those given.

Say, for example, that you support the concept of competition. In that case, you may begin your essay with a thesis statement about how fostering a competitive learning environment at the high school level is necessary to provide students with a taste of what's to come when they enter the real world. Your introduction may point out that the real world is very competitive and that the purpose of high school is to provide students with a foundation for success, as is stated by Perspective 1. Subsequent paragraphs may argue that many students thrive in a competitive environment and that measures like grading on a curve may encourage students to study more thoroughly and learn more in an effort not to fall behind. You must support your argument with examples, such as a quick summary of Darwin's Survival of the Fittest theory or the fact that the entire college admissions process is one big competition.

Be sure to consider the opposing side and the other perspectives provided. For example, you may explain how some people, like the author of Perspective 2, believe that an increasingly competitive environment in schools creates unnecessary stress at a time when students are still learning and becoming familiar with their own strengths and abilities and that high school is a time in students' lives when they should be able to hone their skills at their own pace, in whatever manner they learn most efficiently. To address this opposing side, point out that students who require extra time and attention may work with a tutor or log additional study hours in order not to be left behind . . . a luxury they're unlikely to see once they enter the far more cutthroat post-school job market.

Your closing paragraph is your last opportunity to make an impression on the reader. Use this paragraph to tie together the key points you made earlier in the essay. Present a succinct conclusion that brings the discussion full circle, perhaps by mentioning that more competitive high school students may become the leaders that help America compete with other nations worldwide.

Alternatively, you may choose to write against fostering a competitive environment at the high school level, as is done in Perspective 2, choosing instead to write about how the high school years are the last chance students have to focus on learning by whatever methods are most effective for them as individuals. The rest of life can be likened to a competition, and, as most high school students have yet to reach adulthood, many of them simply are not ready to excel in a highly competitive environment. You may argue that the adolescent and teen years are stressful and emotionally taxing enough without the added stress of competition in the classroom, something most people become more equipped to handle as they enter adulthood.

When you address the opposing arguments, you can say that while it's true that the future holds much competition, students will develop an ability to deal with that competition in college. You may note that students aren't required to apply for an education (although they may be in the case of private schools) until they reach the college level, and with good reason: They're simply not mentally and emotionally prepared for that level of competition in early adolescence.

REMEMBER

You don't need to (and likely shouldn't) refer to the provided perspectives in your essay; address the ideas contained in the opinions but don't mention them by number. Whether you identify with a perspective already provided or have created a perspective of your own that's entirely different isn't as important as using solid examples and concise arguments to argue and support your case.

Writing Prompt 2

The prevailing attitude in many countries is that civic leaders must maintain the highest ethical and moral standards. Some people think that this attitude sets a good example for a country and its citizens. Others argue that leaders who show normal human flaws connect them with those they lead and thereby enable progress and growth. It is important to consider the role that ethical standards play in evaluating our leaders.

Read and carefully consider these perspectives. Each one suggests a particular way of thinking about the role of ethics in leadership.

Perspective 1: Why do we vote for our civic leaders if we want them to be just like everyone else? There are millions of people in this country, and we choose one to represent us all. Leaders should indeed be held to higher moral and ethical standards because all eyes, young and old, are on them at all times. We want the person in a position of power to be someone our children can look up to.

Perspective 2: People will be more likely to embrace and respect their political and civic leaders if they feel they are human and easy to identify with. Look at Bill Clinton – he clearly made errors and showed poor judgment, but is still one of the most beloved ex-presidents in our nation's history.

Perspective 3: If we do not hold our political and civic leaders to a higher standard, how are we supposed to garner the respect of other countries? For many nations, our leaders are all they know of America. We want to gain their respect and admiration, and the best starting point for doing so is electing individuals of strong moral and ethical stature.

Write a unified, coherent essay in which you evaluate multiple perspectives as to whether leaders should be held to higher moral and ethical standards than the general population. In your essay, be sure to do the following:

>> Clearly state your own perspective on the issue and analyze the relationship between your perspective and at least one other perspective.

>> Develop and support your ideas with reasoning and examples.

>> Organize your ideas clearly and logically.

>> Communicate your ideas effectively in standard written English.

Your perspective may be in full agreement with any of the others, in partial agreement, or wholly different.

In this prompt, you may argue for or against holding leaders to a higher moral and ethical standard than the common citizen. Say that you agree with the author of Perspective 1 that leaders should be more accountable for their actions than the average person. Your thesis paragraph may state that leaders are leaders for a reason — because they embody the ideals of a given population and because anyone could be a leader if leaders shared the same flaws as everyone else.

Your subsequent arguments may cite examples of elected officials whose poor or lack of judgment resulted in problems for those they governed. For example, you may mention a politician who misused his power or access to government funds to help further his own agenda. You may note that a leader is inherently in a position to serve as a role model and should, therefore, be expected to act accordingly at all times while in the public eye.

You may choose to address the opposing side offered by the author of Perspective 2 by stating that, while it's true that all humans are flawed by nature, leaders become leaders because of something exemplary about them. People elect and choose them because they aren't just like everyone else. Therefore, it's acceptable to hold them to a higher standard.

To wrap things up, your closing paragraph needs to echo, not directly repeat, the key points you make in the essay to support your initial argument and whether you agree with the perspectives given.

Should you choose to support the opposing side, you may formulate your thesis around the idea that great leaders are a representation of the population they rule, flaws and all. They were chosen for a leadership role based on their ability to relate and identify with the people they govern, and this ability enables them to effectively make decisions in the best interests of their people. Strengthen your argument with real-life examples, such as citing a politician whose moral character is undeniably questionable (like the Bill Clinton example provided in Perspective 2) and yet who is still revered as one of the best and most effective leaders of our time. Or offer a similar example of a leader whose questionable ethics didn't interfere with his or her ability to effectively rule a given population.

Providing inspirational examples of leaders who have been effective despite their character flaws has the added benefit of addressing the concerns of the opposition. You may point out that character flaws don't necessarily weaken a leader's accomplishments and may actually enhance the effectiveness of leaders who acknowledge their weaknesses. Perhaps leaders who are more representative of the common man may inspire others who work to overcome character flaws that they, too, may one day land a position of power and decision making. Plus, people are more likely to see flawed leaders as relatable, approachable figures who are more likely to have the general public's best interests at heart.

Conclude with a few lines that summarize the key arguments you make in your essay and draw a final conclusion as to why moral and ethical equals are the best choice for leadership roles.

7

Putting It All Together with Three Full-Length Practice ACTs

Chapter **19**

Practice Exam 1

Here's your chance to test what you know on an ACT sample test. The following exam consists of five tests: a 45-minute English Test, a 60-minute Mathematics Test, a 35-minute Reading Test, a 35-minute Science Test, and a 40-minute Writing Test.

To make sure you replicate the torturous climate of the real experience, take this test under the following normal exam conditions:

>> Sit where you won't be interrupted or tempted to use your cellphone or binge serial TV shows.

>> Use the answer sheet provided to give you practice filling in the dots.

>> Set your timer for the time limits indicated at the beginning of each test in this exam.

>> Don't go on to the next test until the time allotted for the test you're taking is up.

>> Check your work for that test only; don't look at more than one test at a time.

>> Don't take a break during any test.

>> Give yourself one ten-minute break between the Math Test and the Reading Test.

TIP

When you finish this practice exam, turn to Chapter 20. There you can check your answers using an abbreviated answer key and read more detailed explanations of how to approach every question. Go through the answer explanations to all the questions, not just the ones that you missed. Intertwined in the explanations are reviews of important concepts from the previous chapters and tips for improving the efficiency of your approach.

Note: The ACT Writing Test is optional. If you register to take the Writing Test, you'll take it after you've completed the other four tests. For details about the optional Writing Test, see Part 6.

Answer Sheet

Begin with Number 1 for each new test.

English Test

1. (A) (B) (C) (D)	51. (A) (B) (C) (D)
2. (F) (G) (H) (J)	52. (F) (G) (H) (J)
3. (A) (B) (C) (D)	53. (A) (B) (C) (D)
4. (F) (G) (H) (J)	54. (F) (G) (H) (J)
5. (A) (B) (C) (D)	55. (A) (B) (C) (D)
6. (F) (G) (H) (J)	56. (F) (G) (H) (J)
7. (A) (B) (C) (D)	57. (A) (B) (C) (D)
8. (F) (G) (H) (J)	58. (F) (G) (H) (J)
9. (A) (B) (C) (D)	59. (A) (B) (C) (D)
10. (F) (G) (H) (J)	60. (F) (G) (H) (J)
11. (A) (B) (C) (D)	61. (A) (B) (C) (D)
12. (F) (G) (H) (J)	62. (F) (G) (H) (J)
13. (A) (B) (C) (D)	63. (A) (B) (C) (D)
14. (F) (G) (H) (J)	64. (F) (G) (H) (J)
15. (A) (B) (C) (D)	65. (A) (B) (C) (D)
16. (F) (G) (H) (J)	66. (F) (G) (H) (J)
17. (A) (B) (C) (D)	67. (A) (B) (C) (D)
18. (F) (G) (H) (J)	68. (F) (G) (H) (J)
19. (A) (B) (C) (D)	69. (A) (B) (C) (D)
20. (F) (G) (H) (J)	70. (F) (G) (H) (J)
21. (A) (B) (C) (D)	71. (A) (B) (C) (D)
22. (F) (G) (H) (J)	72. (F) (G) (H) (J)
23. (A) (B) (C) (D)	73. (A) (B) (C) (D)
24. (F) (G) (H) (J)	74. (F) (G) (H) (J)
25. (A) (B) (C) (D)	75. (A) (B) (C) (D)
26. (F) (G) (H) (J)	
27. (A) (B) (C) (D)	
28. (F) (G) (H) (J)	
29. (A) (B) (C) (D)	
30. (F) (G) (H) (J)	
31. (A) (B) (C) (D)	
32. (F) (G) (H) (J)	
33. (A) (B) (C) (D)	
34. (F) (G) (H) (J)	
35. (A) (B) (C) (D)	
36. (F) (G) (H) (J)	
37. (A) (B) (C) (D)	
38. (F) (G) (H) (J)	
39. (A) (B) (C) (D)	
40. (F) (G) (H) (J)	
41. (A) (B) (C) (D)	
42. (F) (G) (H) (J)	
43. (A) (B) (C) (D)	
44. (F) (G) (H) (J)	
45. (A) (B) (C) (D)	
46. (F) (G) (H) (J)	
47. (A) (B) (C) (D)	
48. (F) (G) (H) (J)	
49. (A) (B) (C) (D)	
50. (F) (G) (H) (J)	

Mathematics Test

1. (A) (B) (C) (D) (E)	31. (A) (B) (C) (D) (E)
2. (F) (G) (H) (J) (K)	32. (F) (G) (H) (J) (K)
3. (A) (B) (C) (D) (E)	33. (A) (B) (C) (D) (E)
4. (F) (G) (H) (J) (K)	34. (F) (G) (H) (J) (K)
5. (A) (B) (C) (D) (E)	35. (A) (B) (C) (D) (E)
6. (F) (G) (H) (J) (K)	36. (F) (G) (H) (J) (K)
7. (A) (B) (C) (D) (E)	37. (A) (B) (C) (D) (E)
8. (F) (G) (H) (J) (K)	38. (F) (G) (H) (J) (K)
9. (A) (B) (C) (D) (E)	39. (A) (B) (C) (D) (E)
10. (F) (G) (H) (J) (K)	40. (F) (G) (H) (J) (K)
11. (A) (B) (C) (D) (E)	41. (A) (B) (C) (D) (E)
12. (F) (G) (H) (J) (K)	42. (F) (G) (H) (J) (K)
13. (A) (B) (C) (D) (E)	43. (A) (B) (C) (D) (E)
14. (F) (G) (H) (J) (K)	44. (F) (G) (H) (J) (K)
15. (A) (B) (C) (D) (E)	45. (A) (B) (C) (D) (E)
16. (F) (G) (H) (J) (K)	46. (F) (G) (H) (J) (K)
17. (A) (B) (C) (D) (E)	47. (A) (B) (C) (D) (E)
18. (F) (G) (H) (J) (K)	48. (F) (G) (H) (J) (K)
19. (A) (B) (C) (D) (E)	49. (A) (B) (C) (D) (E)
20. (F) (G) (H) (J) (K)	50. (F) (G) (H) (J) (K)
21. (A) (B) (C) (D) (E)	51. (A) (B) (C) (D) (E)
22. (F) (G) (H) (J) (K)	52. (F) (G) (H) (J) (K)
23. (A) (B) (C) (D) (E)	53. (A) (B) (C) (D) (E)
24. (F) (G) (H) (J) (K)	54. (F) (G) (H) (J) (K)
25. (A) (B) (C) (D) (E)	55. (A) (B) (C) (D) (E)
26. (F) (G) (H) (J) (K)	56. (F) (G) (H) (J) (K)
27. (A) (B) (C) (D) (E)	57. (A) (B) (C) (D) (E)
28. (F) (G) (H) (J) (K)	58. (F) (G) (H) (J) (K)
29. (A) (B) (C) (D) (E)	59. (A) (B) (C) (D) (E)
30. (F) (G) (H) (J) (K)	60. (F) (G) (H) (J) (K)

Reading Test	Science Test
1. Ⓐ Ⓑ Ⓒ Ⓓ	1. Ⓐ Ⓑ Ⓒ Ⓓ
2. Ⓕ Ⓖ Ⓗ Ⓙ	2. Ⓕ Ⓖ Ⓗ Ⓙ
3. Ⓐ Ⓑ Ⓒ Ⓓ	3. Ⓐ Ⓑ Ⓒ Ⓓ
4. Ⓕ Ⓖ Ⓗ Ⓙ	4. Ⓕ Ⓖ Ⓗ Ⓙ
5. Ⓐ Ⓑ Ⓒ Ⓓ	5. Ⓐ Ⓑ Ⓒ Ⓓ
6. Ⓕ Ⓖ Ⓗ Ⓙ	6. Ⓕ Ⓖ Ⓗ Ⓙ
7. Ⓐ Ⓑ Ⓒ Ⓓ	7. Ⓐ Ⓑ Ⓒ Ⓓ
8. Ⓕ Ⓖ Ⓗ Ⓙ	8. Ⓕ Ⓖ Ⓗ Ⓙ
9. Ⓐ Ⓑ Ⓒ Ⓓ	9. Ⓐ Ⓑ Ⓒ Ⓓ
10. Ⓕ Ⓖ Ⓗ Ⓙ	10. Ⓕ Ⓖ Ⓗ Ⓙ
11. Ⓐ Ⓑ Ⓒ Ⓓ	11. Ⓐ Ⓑ Ⓒ Ⓓ
12. Ⓕ Ⓖ Ⓗ Ⓙ	12. Ⓕ Ⓖ Ⓗ Ⓙ
13. Ⓐ Ⓑ Ⓒ Ⓓ	13. Ⓐ Ⓑ Ⓒ Ⓓ
14. Ⓕ Ⓖ Ⓗ Ⓙ	14. Ⓕ Ⓖ Ⓗ Ⓙ
15. Ⓐ Ⓑ Ⓒ Ⓓ	15. Ⓐ Ⓑ Ⓒ Ⓓ
16. Ⓕ Ⓖ Ⓗ Ⓙ	16. Ⓕ Ⓖ Ⓗ Ⓙ
17. Ⓐ Ⓑ Ⓒ Ⓓ	17. Ⓐ Ⓑ Ⓒ Ⓓ
18. Ⓕ Ⓖ Ⓗ Ⓙ	18. Ⓕ Ⓖ Ⓗ Ⓙ
19. Ⓐ Ⓑ Ⓒ Ⓓ	19. Ⓐ Ⓑ Ⓒ Ⓓ
20. Ⓕ Ⓖ Ⓗ Ⓙ	20. Ⓕ Ⓖ Ⓗ Ⓙ
21. Ⓐ Ⓑ Ⓒ Ⓓ	21. Ⓐ Ⓑ Ⓒ Ⓓ
22. Ⓕ Ⓖ Ⓗ Ⓙ	22. Ⓕ Ⓖ Ⓗ Ⓙ
23. Ⓐ Ⓑ Ⓒ Ⓓ	23. Ⓐ Ⓑ Ⓒ Ⓓ
24. Ⓕ Ⓖ Ⓗ Ⓙ	24. Ⓕ Ⓖ Ⓗ Ⓙ
25. Ⓐ Ⓑ Ⓒ Ⓓ	25. Ⓐ Ⓑ Ⓒ Ⓓ
26. Ⓕ Ⓖ Ⓗ Ⓙ	26. Ⓕ Ⓖ Ⓗ Ⓙ
27. Ⓐ Ⓑ Ⓒ Ⓓ	27. Ⓐ Ⓑ Ⓒ Ⓓ
28. Ⓕ Ⓖ Ⓗ Ⓙ	28. Ⓕ Ⓖ Ⓗ Ⓙ
29. Ⓐ Ⓑ Ⓒ Ⓓ	29. Ⓐ Ⓑ Ⓒ Ⓓ
30. Ⓕ Ⓖ Ⓗ Ⓙ	30. Ⓕ Ⓖ Ⓗ Ⓙ
31. Ⓐ Ⓑ Ⓒ Ⓓ	31. Ⓐ Ⓑ Ⓒ Ⓓ
32. Ⓕ Ⓖ Ⓗ Ⓙ	32. Ⓕ Ⓖ Ⓗ Ⓙ
33. Ⓐ Ⓑ Ⓒ Ⓓ	33. Ⓐ Ⓑ Ⓒ Ⓓ
34. Ⓕ Ⓖ Ⓗ Ⓙ	34. Ⓕ Ⓖ Ⓗ Ⓙ
35. Ⓐ Ⓑ Ⓒ Ⓓ	35. Ⓐ Ⓑ Ⓒ Ⓓ
36. Ⓕ Ⓖ Ⓗ Ⓙ	36. Ⓕ Ⓖ Ⓗ Ⓙ
37. Ⓐ Ⓑ Ⓒ Ⓓ	37. Ⓐ Ⓑ Ⓒ Ⓓ
38. Ⓕ Ⓖ Ⓗ Ⓙ	38. Ⓕ Ⓖ Ⓗ Ⓙ
39. Ⓐ Ⓑ Ⓒ Ⓓ	39. Ⓐ Ⓑ Ⓒ Ⓓ
40. Ⓕ Ⓖ Ⓗ Ⓙ	40. Ⓕ Ⓖ Ⓗ Ⓙ

English Test

TIME: 45 minutes for 75 questions

DIRECTIONS: Following are five passages with underlined portions. Alternate ways of stating the underlined portions come after the passages. Choose the best alternative; if the original is the best way of stating the underlined portion, choose NO CHANGE.

The test also has questions that refer to the passages or ask you to reorder the sentences within the passages. These questions are identified by a number in a box. Choose the best answer and shade in the corresponding oval on your answer sheet.

Passage 1

Personal Trainers Help Drop Pounds

When it comes <u>to losing weight fast; some</u>
<u>methods are</u> more effective than others. For those
___1___
who are serious about slimming down in a short
amount of time, <u>one of the easiest ways being</u> to
___2___
hire a personal trainer.

Because there's no standard of licensure
for the <u>profession, it's critical</u> that you do your
___3___
homework prior to hiring <u>one.</u>⑤ Seek out a certified
___4___
fitness professional — ideally, someone who is
<u>capable</u> and able to communicate <u>well and clearly.</u>
___6___   ___7___
You also may want to pick someone whose physique mirrors one that you <u>would have wanted</u> for
___8___
yourself. <u>For example,</u> if you're inspired by your
___9___
trainer, you're more likely to stay on track and less
likely to skip out on workout sessions.

<u>It's also a good idea to select someone with</u>
<u>whom you connect, at least to some extent, on</u>
<u>a personal level.</u> Not all personalities mesh
___10___
well together. Some people thrive off positive
<u>reinforcement, others fare better</u> when faced with
___11___
constructive criticism. ⑫

<u>To decide, whether a potential trainer will be</u>
___13___
<u>a good fit,</u> ask questions about training style and
fitness philosophy. Weight loss and physical fitness
<u>starts</u> with effective training methods, and a
___14___
personal trainer can be the perfect person to get
you on track toward a new and better you. ⑮

1. **(A)** NO CHANGE
   (B) losing weight fast, some methods are
   (C) losing weight fast: some methods are
   (D) losing weight fast — some methods are

2. **(F)** NO CHANGE
   (G) one of the easiest ways to be
   (H) one of the easiest ways is
   (J) the easiest way being

3. **(A)** NO CHANGE
   (B) profession, its critical
   (C) profession, its' critical
   (D) profession; it's critical

4. **(F)** NO CHANGE
   (G) them
   (H) a coach
   (J) it

5. At this point, the author is considering adding the following statement:

This might include asking friends, family, or coworkers, or reading online reviews or testimonials.

Should the writer make this addition here?

(A) Yes, because it provides specific ways the reader may accomplish the prior suggestion offered in the passage.

(B) Yes, because it further explains the benefits of using a personal trainer.

(C) No, because it contains information that has been stated previously in the passage.

(D) No, because it does not emphasize how easy it is to find a personal trainer.

6. Which of the following alternatives to the underlined portion is LEAST acceptable?

(F) competent

(G) useful

(H) experienced

(J) skilled

7. (A) NO CHANGE

(B) clearly

(C) well and clear

(D) in a clear manner

8. (F) NO CHANGE

(G) want

(H) wanted

(J) had wanted

9. (A) NO CHANGE

(B) However,

(C) To illustrate,

(D) Delete the underlined portion and capitalize if.

10. Which of the following choices best guides the reader from the preceding paragraph and introduces this new paragraph?

(F) NO CHANGE

(G) Always check a trainer's credentials before you sign on.

(H) Some trainers offer better gym facilities than others.

(J) Missing workout sessions may cause you to give up on your training altogether.

11. (A) NO CHANGE

(B) reinforcement, others fare best

(C) reinforcement, but others fare better

(D) reinforcement, and, others fare best

12. Which of the following sentences, if added here, would most effectively conclude this paragraph and introduce the topic of the next?

(F) Trainers who may seem tough at first are eventually the most effective.

(G) If you don't like your trainer, you're unlikely to be happy with your results.

(H) Finding a trainer whose teaching style meshes with your learning style will likely give you the best results.

(J) Similarly, when you like the taste of healthy foods, you're more likely to eat them.

13. (A) NO CHANGE

(B) To decide whether a potential trainer will be a good fit,

(C) To decide whether, a potential trainer, will be a good fit

(D) To decide whether a potential trainer, will be a good fit,

14. (F) NO CHANGE

(G) begins

(H) starting

(J) start

GO ON TO NEXT PAGE ➤

15. Suppose the author's intent was to create an essay that highlights some of the best ways to lose weight. Would this essay successfully achieve that goal?

(A) Yes, because the essay shows that hiring a trainer is a helpful way to lose weight.

(B) Yes, because the essay highlights the importance of creating and sticking to a workout regimen.

(C) No, because the essay does not reveal that hiring a trainer may actually lead to weight gain from increased muscle mass.

(D) No, because the essay focuses on only one method for losing weight.

Passage 2

The Pitching Machine

[1]

Known as <u>Americans pastime, and to many</u>
                        16
<u>baseball</u> means much more. Hitting baseballs is a
  17
major part of many a <u>childhood and using</u> a
                              18
pitching machine can be a great resource for ball
players at any level to fine-tune <u>their</u> skills behind
                                      19
the plate.

[2]

Among the more popular pitching machine
models are circular-wheel machines and arm-
action machines. If you're looking to buy one, look
for a variety that closely <u>simulates</u> the pitches
                              20
you'll experience during real game play. You
should also look for a machine that simulates an
assortment of different release points. Machines
that <u>have thrown</u> an array of different pitches
        21
allow players to work on hitting while <u>improving</u>
<u>hand-eye coordination.</u>
        22

[3]

When choosing a machine, take into account
the age of the player. [23] Players who are just
starting out will likely benefit most from a pitching
machine that releases balls <u>slower</u>, allowing the
                                24
players to familiarize themselves with the basics of
batting.

[4]

More advanced players <u>who hit at more</u>
                                    25
<u>elevated levels</u> may favor a fast-pitch machine.
Featuring many customizable options, <u>a hitter can</u>
<u>adjust the amount of time that passes between the</u>
<u>release of each baseball and set the machines at</u>
                                                26
<u>different heights.</u>

[5]

Baseball is a wonderful sport <u>to take part in,</u>
                                        27
and these pitching machines can prove tremen-
dously effective for players of all skill levels. [28]
The device is a home run for players who <u>want to</u>
<u>and are interested in maximizing</u> their skills at the
                        29
plate. [30]

16. (F) NO CHANGE
(G) America's pastime
(H) the pastime of American's
(J) Americas pastime

17. (A) NO CHANGE
(B) but, to many, baseball
(C) to many baseball
(D) DELETE the underlined portion.

18. (F) NO CHANGE
(G) childhood. Therefore, using
(H) childhood, but using
(J) childhood, using

19. (A) NO CHANGE
   (B) they're
   (C) there
   (D) its

20. Which of the following alternatives to the underlined portion is LEAST acceptable?
   (F) copies
   (G) mimics
   (H) imitates
   (J) fakes

21. (A) NO CHANGE
   (B) throw
   (C) throwing
   (D) threw

22. (F) NO CHANGE
   (G) improving hand-eye coordination at the same time
   (H) also improving hand-eye coordination
   (J) improving, at the same time, hand-eye coordination

23. The author is considering adding the following phrase to the end of the preceding sentence:

to improve safety and maximize the effectiveness of the machine.

Should the writer make this addition here?
   (A) Yes, because it clarifies the reasons for selecting a particular type of pitching machine.
   (B) Yes, because it implies that younger players may not experience the same benefits from pitching machines as older players.
   (C) No, because it distracts the reader from the main topic of the paragraph.
   (D) No, because it repeats a point made earlier in the essay.

24. (F) NO CHANGE
   (G) more slow
   (H) more slowly
   (J) more slower

25. (A) NO CHANGE
   (B) who hit at elevated levels
   (C) hitting at elevated levels
   (D) DELETE the underlined portion.

26. (F) NO CHANGE
   (G) adjustments may be made to the amount of time that passes between the release of each baseball and the machines' height settings.
   (H) time between baseballs may be adjusted and heights changed.
   (J) the machines may be adjusted to change their height and the amount of time that passes between the release of each baseball.

27. Which of the following is LEAST acceptable?
   (A) NO CHANGE
   (B) in which to take part
   (C) of which to take part
   (D) DELETE the underlined portion.

28. The writer is considering adding a comma and the following point after "levels" in the preceding sentence: but mostly for younger hitters

Should the writer make this addition?
   (F) No, because it contradicts the author's point that pitching machines are equally effective for players of all skill levels.
   (G) No, because professional players likely benefit more from pitching machines than do little league players.
   (H) Yes, because it furthers the author's argument that young players benefit more from pitching machines than older ones.
   (J) Yes, because it builds upon the point made in the fourth paragraph.

29. (A) NO CHANGE
   (B) have an interest and desire in maximizing
   (C) want to maximize
   (D) aspire and endeavor to maximize

GO ON TO NEXT PAGE ▶

30. For the sake of logic and coherence, Paragraph
    5 should be placed:
    (F) where it is now.
    (G) before Paragraph 1.
    (H) after Paragraph 2.
    (J) after Paragraph 3.

Passage 3

Teddy Roosevelt: A Political Maverick

No figure better represents the Progressive Era than Theodore "Teddy" Roosevelt. Born into a wealthy New York family, Roosevelt <u>has risen</u> to
<u>   31</u>
national <u>prominence</u> rather quickly. Early in his
          32
career, Roosevelt served as commissioner of the New York City Police Department before becoming the Assistant Secretary of the Navy. In the Spanish-American War, Roosevelt gained notoriety for leading his military volunteer unit, <u>the "Rough</u>
<u>Riders" to victory in the Battle of San Juan Hill</u>
                        33
in Cuba. In 1900, Roosevelt became Republican William McKinley's vice-presidential candidate. McKinley was assassinated in 1901. [34] Roosevelt became the <u>most youngest</u> President of the United
                    35
States at age 42.

"TR," as he came to be known, <u>exuded</u> an
                                 36
active, vibrant personality. Roosevelt was intelligent, well read, and <u>knows a great deal</u> about the
                          37
environment, history, and naval strategy. He demonstrated his love for sports and competition by participating in boxing, <u>being a big-game hunter</u>,
                                38
and other outdoor pursuits. His dynamic lifestyle carried over into his presidency, which lasted from 1901 to 1909, and he became one of the <u>most active</u>
                                              39
<u>and busy</u> presidents in the history of the United States. <u>Among the topics he tackled were trusts,</u>
                                        40
railroads, safety in the food industry, and the environment.

Roosevelt demonstrated his distaste for trusts during the coal strike crisis of 1902. No fewer than 50,000 coal miners went on strike, demanding better working conditions and higher pay. Roosevelt intervened, inviting the union representatives and mine owners to the White House to try to find a solution. <u>Therefore,</u> the owners refused to speak
          41
with the union representatives. Roosevelt was infuriated by this rebuff, and he threatened to send federal troops to operate the mines. At the urging of J.P. Morgan (the renowned financier who formed the U.S. Steel Corporation), the owners backed down and gave the miners shorter workdays (9 hours) and better wages (10% wage increases). [42]

Railroad reform was another of Roosevelt's important contributions to the progressive cause. <u>During</u> the beginning of the 20th century, railroad
 43
companies controlled the prices of their services. Roosevelt believed that this system gave private companies too much power, which ultimately hurt consumers. <u>For example,</u> he supported the Hep-
              44
burn Railroad Act, which gave the Interstate Commerce Commission the power to regulate the prices of railroad rates and audit railroad <u>company's</u> financial records. Congress passed the
   45
Hepburn Railroad Act, and Roosevelt signed it into law in 1906. Roosevelt proved that he would not hesitate to challenge the powers and abuses of big business.

31. **(A)** NO CHANGE
    (B) rises
    (C) rose
    (D) has rose

32. **(F)** NO CHANGE
    (G) infamy
    (H) obscurity
    (J) anonymity

33. **(A)** NO CHANGE
    (B) the "Rough Riders," to victory in the Battle of San Juan Hill
    (C) the "Rough Riders" to victory, in the Battle of San Juan Hill
    (D) the "Rough Riders," to victory in the Battle of San Juan Hill,

34. The author is considering inserting a few lines about what led to McKinley's assassination and who was responsible. Would that insertion be appropriate here?
    (F) Yes, because it would clarify how Roosevelt came to assume the presidency.
    (G) Yes, because it contains important clarifying information about McKinley.
    (H) No, because the focus of the passage is Roosevelt, not McKinley.
    (J) No, because this information should appear earlier in the passage.

35. **(A)** NO CHANGE
    (B) younger
    (C) most young
    (D) youngest

36. Which of the following substitutes for the underlined word would be the LEAST appropriate?
    (F) infused
    (G) conveyed
    (H) radiated
    (J) emanated

37. **(A)** NO CHANGE
    (B) had known quite a bit
    (C) knowledgeable
    (D) he knew

38. **(F)** NO CHANGE
    (G) was a big-game hunter
    (H) engaging in big-game hunting
    (J) big-game hunting

39. **(A)** NO CHANGE
    (B) most active
    (C) most active and lively
    (D) DELETE the underlined portion.

40. **(F)** NO CHANGE
    (G) Among the topics that were tackled were trusts,
    (H) Among the tackled topics was trusts,
    (J) Trusts were among the tackled topics along with

41. **(A)** NO CHANGE
    (B) However,
    (C) Finally,
    (D) As a result,

42. The author is considering deleting the preceding sentence. Without the sentence, the paragraph would primarily lose:
    (F) details that summarize one of Roosevelt's specific accomplishments.
    (G) interesting but irrelevant information.
    (H) foreshadowing of an event detailed in the next paragraph.
    (J) general observations about Roosevelt's achievements.

GO ON TO NEXT PAGE

43. (A) NO CHANGE
   (B) At
   (C) After
   (D) Through

44. (F) NO CHANGE
   (G) Nevertheless,
   (H) On the contrary,
   (J) Thus,

45. (A) NO CHANGE
   (B) companies
   (C) companies'
   (D) companys'

Passage 4

Remote Computer Repair

[1]

In today's fast-paced world, the multifaceted virtues of the World Wide Web enables our fingers
46
to access virtually anything simply, with the easy
touch of a button. While this facility has eased a
47
good bit of how we do things in the modern
working world, what it has failed to accomplish, is
48
the prevention of a crisis when a computer suddenly crashes. So, remote computer repair provides
49
a great resource for anyone that conducts a
50
business in front of a computer screen.

[2]

If your computer experiences crashes, viruses,
51
needs a tune-up, or requires hardware or software
installation, remote computer repair can get you
up and running again quickly. Rather than wait
days or even weeks without your machine, consider
52
having a trained professional perform repairs
remotely so that you can avoid lost time or wages
as a result from your damaged equipment.
53

[3]

Remote computer repair is done by a professional logging into your computer using a highly
secure Internet connection. Rather than paying you
54
an actual visit. It can be a great option for people
who cannot be without they're computer for long
55
or for those who cannot get to a repair shop.
Remote repair can get your laptop or PC in working
order again in a matter of hours or even minutes,
depending on the severity of the problem. 57
56

[4]

Whether you need to remove viruses, fixing a
frozen screen, install a home or business office
58
network, or need help with any number of other
issues, a remote computer repair person should be
your first call when you need your machine up and
running as quickly as possible. 60
59

46. (F) NO CHANGE
   (G) World Wide Web is enabling
   (H) World Wide Web enable
   (J) Internet enables

47. (A) NO CHANGE
   (B) simply and without difficulty
   (C) simply and easily with our hands
   (D) simply

48. (F) NO CHANGE
   (G) what, it has failed to accomplish
   (H) what it has failed, to accomplish
   (J) what it has failed to accomplish

49. (A) NO CHANGE
   (B) However,
   (C) On the other hand,
   (D) For instance,

50. **(F)** NO CHANGE

    (G) anyone, which conducts

    (H) anyone who conducts

    (J) anyone, who conducts

51. **(A)** NO CHANGE

    (B) crashes: viruses,

    (C) crashes, is prone to viruses,

    (D) crashes, or viruses,

52. **(F)** NO CHANGE

    (G) wait days, or even weeks without your machine,

    (H) wait days or, even weeks, without your machine

    (J) wait days or even weeks, without your machine,

53. **(A)** NO CHANGE

    (B) with

    (C) as

    (D) of

54. **(F)** NO CHANGE

    (G) connection rather

    (H) connection, and rather

    (J) connection; rather

55. **(A)** NO CHANGE

    (B) his or her

    (C) their

    (D) there

56. The author of the passage is considering deleting the underlined phrase from the sentence and ending it with a period. If the author were to delete this content, the sentence would primarily lose:

    (F) a minor detail about remote repair.

    (G) an example of the type of repair that can be accomplished remotely.

    (H) an explanation for a time difference.

    (J) a foreshadowing of the topic in the following paragraph.

57. Which of the following sentences would best conclude Paragraph 3?

    (A) More severe issues take longer than simple ones.

    (B) Remote computer repair can prove tremendously helpful for those who cannot be without their computers.

    (C) Calling a remote technician will also save you traveling time to and from the repair shop.

    (D) When computer issues arrive, your first call should be to a remote computer repair specialist.

58. **(F)** NO CHANGE

    (G) removing viruses, fixing a frozen screen, installing a home

    (H) removing viruses or fixing a frozen screen or install a home

    (J) remove viruses, fix a frozen screen, install a home

59. Which of the following would be the LEAST suitable replacement for the underlined portion?

    (A) immediately

    (B) right away

    (C) promptly

    (D) DELETE the underlined portion.

60. To make this passage a coherent whole, Paragraph 4 should be:

    (F) placed where it is now.

    (G) placed before Paragraph 1.

    (H) placed after Paragraph 2.

    (J) deleted entirely.

GO ON TO NEXT PAGE

Competition for Niches

[1]

Competing for a limited number of resources, such as nutrients, energy, and territory, an organism's characteristics and behaviors evolve to **61** compensate. [2] Darwin's theory states that competition for resources are what drives evolu- **62** tion, so most characteristics and behaviors have evolved in order to improve its ability to compete **63** and survive in the ecosystem. [3] Over the genera- tions, each species in the ecosystem will settle into its own way of carving out a living. [4] A niche **64** includes the species' diet, its territory, its behav- iors, its roles in the nutrient cycles, and anything else that helps define its lifestyle. [5] Another way to describe this is to say that each species estab- lishes its own "niche" in the ecosystem. 65

[2]

Every niche has two types of components: abiotic and biotic. "Abiotic" means nonliving. This **66** category includes elements such as the physical terrain of the area, what its average yearly rainfall is, and average daily temperature. "Biotic" means **67** living; this part of the niche includes all of the other species in the community — the predators, prey, parasites, competitors, and so on — with whom the particular species is likely to interact **68** during its life.

Whenever the niche of a species overlap with **69** **70** another, such as when two species occupy the same space or eat the same food, that species is automatically in competition with the other. Competition in the wild can take many forms and only occasionally involves direct combat. A species can win a competition by being faster, more effi- cient, smarter, or more colorful. In the end, only **71** three possible results of a competition exist: win, lose, or compromise. One species may win the competition and take over that part of the niche, they may lose and be forced to retreat from that part, **72** or two species may find a way to divide that part of the niche so that they can coexist peacefully. 73

[4]

In addition to interspecific competition, competition between individuals of the same species, called *intraspecific competition*, also occurs. This competition can lead to the development of unusual qualities, such as, vibrant coloring. **74** Sometimes only the prettiest, the smelliest, or the loudest are able to win the competition and pass on their lovely, stinky, or noisy genes. 75

61. (A) NO CHANGE

(B) amount of resources, such as nutrients, energy, and territory, an organism's characteristics and behaviors evolve

(C) number of resources, such as nutrients, energy, and territory, results in the evolution of an organism's characteristics and behaviors

(D) amount of resources, such as nutrients, energy, and territory, causes an organism's characteristics and behaviors to evolve

62. (F) NO CHANGE

(G) is

(H) have been

(J) were

63. (A) NO CHANGE

(B) a life form's

(C) it's

(D) their

64. Which of the following substitutes for the underlined word would be the LEAST appropriate?

(F) securing

(G) making

(H) forging

(J) capturing

65. For the sake of logic and coherence in Paragraph 1, Sentence 5 should be placed:

(A) where it is now.

(B) before Sentence 2.

(C) before Sentence 3.

(D) before Sentence 4.

66. Which of the following substitutes for the underlined portion would NOT be acceptable?

(F) components, and they are abiotic and biotic

(G) components that are abiotic and biotic

(H) components, abiotic and biotic

(J) components — abiotic and biotic

67. (A) NO CHANGE

(B) an area's physical terrain, average yearly rainfall, and average daily temperature

(C) the physical terrain of an area, the area's average yearly rainfall, and what its average daily temperature is

(D) its physical terrain, average yearly rainfall, and average daily temperature

68. (F) NO CHANGE

(G) through whom

(H) with which

(J) that

69. (A) NO CHANGE

(B) Although

(C) Whether

(D) Often,

70. (F) NO CHANGE

(G) overlaps,

(H) are overlapping,

(J) was overlapping,

71. (A) NO CHANGE

(B) For example,

(C) On the other hand,

(D) Finally,

72. (F) NO CHANGE

(G) it may

(H) or they may

(J) DELETE the underlined portion.

73. Which of the following additions here provides the best conclusion for Paragraph 3?

(A) Otherwise, the species are more likely to engage in direct combat.

(B) Competition between species is inevitable.

(C) Those that fit the niche best are most likely to survive within it.

(D) Each species generally occupies its exclusive niche.

GO ON TO NEXT PAGE

74. (F) NO CHANGE

    (G) qualities such as:

    (H) qualities; such as

    (J) qualities such as

75. To maintain the logical consistency of the passage, Paragraph 4 should be placed:

    (A) where it is now.

    (B) before Paragraph 1.

    (C) after Paragraph 1.

    (D) after Paragraph 2.

Mathematics Test

TIME: 60 minutes for 60 questions

DIRECTIONS: Each question has five answer choices. Choose the best answer for each question and shade the corresponding oval on your answer sheet.

1. What is the value of $y \times 2^x$ if $x = 3$ and $y = 2$?

(A) 8

(B) 16

(C) 12

(D) 10

(E) 64

2. The first four terms of a geometric sequence are .75, 1.5, 3, and 6. What is the fifth term?

(F) 12

(G) 9

(H) 18

(J) 11.25

(K) 36

3. In the following figure, A, B, and C are collinear. The measure of $\angle ABD$ is three times that of $\angle DBC$. What is the measure of $\angle ABD$?

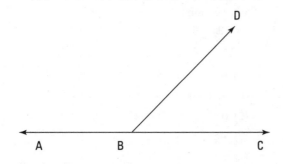

(A) 135°

(B) 120°

(C) 67.5°

(D) 60°

(E) 45°

4. Which of the following is equivalent to $\dfrac{3}{\frac{3}{8}}$?

(F) 3

(G) 24

(H) $\frac{9}{8}$

(J) $\frac{1}{8}$

(K) 8

5. What is the measure of angle b in the following figure where lines C and D are parallel?

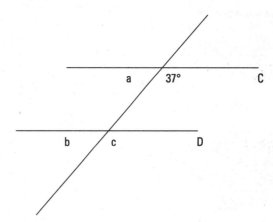

(A) 37°

(B) 53°

(C) 127°

(D) 143°

(E) 180°

GO ON TO NEXT PAGE

6. Ross has 2 black socks and 2 white socks lying in his drawer. If he blindly selects two socks from the drawer, what is the chance that he will select the black pair?

(F) $\frac{1}{6}$

(G) $\frac{1}{4}$

(H) $\frac{1}{2}$

(J) $\frac{5}{6}$

(K) $\frac{3}{4}$

7. A triangular ramp from the ground to the bed of a truck that stands 6 feet off the ground has a base of 8 feet. How long in feet is the length of the bottom of the ramp?

(A) 5 feet

(B) 5.29 feet

(C) 8 feet

(D) 10 feet

(E) 100 feet

8. What is the solution to $\frac{1}{6} + \frac{1}{2} + \frac{1}{3}$?

(F) $\frac{1}{11}$

(G) $\frac{3}{11}$

(H) $\frac{1}{2}$

(J) 1

(K) $\frac{37}{36}$

9. Which is the correct factoring of $4x^2 - 4x - 3$?

(A) $(2x-1)(2x+3)$

(B) $(4x+1)(x-3)$

(C) $(2x+1)(2x-3)$

(D) $(4x-1)(x+3)$

(E) $(4x-1)(4x+3)$

10. At what point does $7x + 4y = 28$ intersect the y-axis in the standard (x, y) coordinate plane?

(F) (4, 0)

(G) (7, 0)

(H) (0, 4)

(J) (0, 7)

(K) (28, 0)

11. Simplify $\left(\frac{3x}{y}\right)\left(\frac{x^3 y^2}{6}\right)$.

(A) $\frac{x^4 y}{2}$

(B) $\frac{x^4 y^3}{2}$

(C) $\frac{x^2 y^3}{2}$

(D) $\frac{3x + x^3 y^2}{y + 6}$

(E) $\frac{3x + x^3 y^2}{6y}$

12. Jacob is making cupcakes for his friend Jack's birthday party. The only supplies he needs to buy are x pounds of flour at $3.50 per pound, s pounds of sugar at $4.50 per pound, and 3 cupcake pans at $6 per pan. Which of the following expresses Jacob's total cost, in dollars, of providing the cupcakes for Jack's birthday party?

(A) $(x + \$3.50)(s + \$4.50) + \$18.00$

(B) $x + \$3.50 + s + \$4.50 + \$18.00$

(C) $\$3.50x + \$4.50s + \$18.00$

(D) $\$3.50s + \$4.50x + \$6.00$

(E) $(\$3.50x)(\$4.50s) + \$18.00$

13. What is the value of y in the following system of equations?

$2x + 3y = 6$

$x - y = 8$

(A) 6

(B) 2

(C) 0

(D) −6

(E) −2

14. Which of the following is equal to 1.54×10^{-3}?

(A) 1,540

(B) 154

(C) 0.0154

(D) 0.00154

(E) 0.000154

15. Tickets to a movie cost \$8 for adults and \$5 for children. If 40 tickets are sold for a total of \$251, how many adult tickets were sold?

(A) 15

(B) 17

(C) 20

(D) 23

(E) 25

16. Which of the following functions is represented on the standard (x, y) coordinate plane shown here?

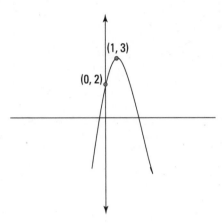

(F) $y = (x+3)^2 - 1$

(G) $y = -(x+3)^2 + 1$

(H) $y = -(x+1)^2 + 3$

(J) $y = (x-1)^2 + 3$

(K) $y = -(x-1)^2 + 3$

17. Which of the following represents the possible x-solutions to the inequality $4x - 5 < 9x + 2$?

(A) $x < -\dfrac{7}{5}$

(B) $x > -\dfrac{7}{5}$

(C) $x < \dfrac{7}{5}$

(D) $x > \dfrac{7}{5}$

(E) $x > \dfrac{9}{4}$

18. Which of the following could be the equation of line m graphed in the standard (x, y) coordinate plane shown here?

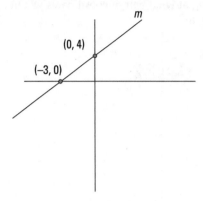

(F) $3x - 4y = 12$

(G) $4x - 3y = 12$

(H) $4y - 3x = 12$

(J) $3y - 4x = 12$

(K) $3y + 4x = 12$

19. Which of the following values for x makes $\log_6 9 + \log_6 x = 2$?

(A) $\dfrac{1}{3}$

(B) $1\dfrac{1}{3}$

(C) 3

(D) 4

(E) 27

20. What is the volume in cm^3 of a circular cylindrical soda can whose diameter is 10 cm and height is 15 cm?

(F) 10π

(G) 150π

(H) 375π

(J) 625π

(K) $15{,}000\pi$

GO ON TO NEXT PAGE

21. If in the standard (x, y) coordinate plane the quadrilateral ABCD shown here were reflected over the line $y = 2$ to form quadrilateral $A_1B_1C_1D_1$, at what pair of coordinates would point A_1 lie?

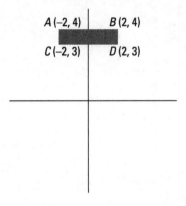

A (−2, 4)   B (2, 4)

C (−2, 3)   D (2, 3)

(A) (−2, 0)

(B) (6, 4)

(C) (2, 4)

(D) (−2, −4)

(E) (−2, 2)

22. Which of the following expresses all values of x that make the solution of $x^2 + x - 20$ positive and nonzero?

(F) $x > 20$

(G) $-5 < x < 4$

(H) $x > 20$ and $x < 0$

(J) $x < -5$ and $x > 4$

(K) $x > 4$

23. Klaus decided to give 20% of the money he got for his birthday to his favorite charity and put the rest in the bank. If he put $280 in the bank, how much money did he receive for his birthday?

(A) $56

(B) $70

(C) $350

(D) $336

(E) $375

24. If it costs $50 to fill up a 20-gallon tank of gas, how much would it cost to fill up a 16-gallon tank of gas?

(F) $37.50

(G) $62.50

(H) $46

(J) $48

(K) $40

25. In the right triangle shown here, what is cos C?

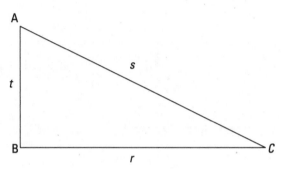

(A) $\frac{t}{r}$

(B) $\frac{s}{r}$

(C) $\frac{t}{s}$

(D) $\frac{r}{s}$

(E) $\frac{s}{t}$

26. What coordinate point is the midpoint of the line segment that goes from point (−1, 3) to point (5, −5) in the standard (x, y) coordinate plane?

(F) (−3, 4)

(G) (2, −1)

(H) (3, −1)

(J) (2, 4)

(K) (−1, −5)

27. For all pairs of real numbers x and y where $x = 3y + 8$, what does y equal?

(A) $\frac{x}{3} - 8$

(B) $x - \frac{8}{3}$

(C) $3y + 8$

(D) $\frac{x - 8}{3}$

(E) $x - 8$

28. On the following number line, the distance between A and D is 28 units. The distance between A and C is 15 units. The distance between B and D is 18 units. What is the distance in units between B and C?

A _____ B ____ C _____ D

(F) 5

(G) 6

(H) 8

(J) 10

(K) 13

29. It takes Emma 40 minutes in her car traveling at 45 miles per hour to drive the same distance as it takes Nadine to drive in one hour. How fast is Nadine driving in miles per hour?

(A) 53.3

(B) 65

(C) 30

(D) 67.5

(E) 35

30. What is the perimeter of the following polygon whose angles each measure 90°?

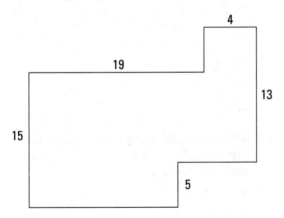

(F) 56

(G) 74

(H) 77

(J) 79

(K) 82

31. What is the circumference of a circle whose area is 16π?

(A) 8π

(B) 4

(C) 4π

(D) 8

(E) 16π

32. The following stem-and-leaf plot shows all of the test scores Cydney received in her algebra course this year. Each test score reflects the number of points received out of a possible 100 points. What was Cydney's median math test score for the year?

Scores that Cydney Received on All Math Tests this Year	
7	8 9 9
8	2 3 4 5 5 6 7 7 9 9 9
9	1 4 6 6 9

(F) 86

(G) 87

(H) 89

(J) 86.5

(K) 88

33. If $f(x) = x - 3$, what is $f(2x + 2)$?

(A) $-x - 2$

(B) $3x - 1$

(C) $2x - 1$

(D) $3x - 4$

(E) $2x - 4$

34. A car's starting velocity is 10 meters per second as it enters a ramp to the freeway. The physics equation for velocity is $v = at + v_0$ where t stands for time and v_0 is the initial velocity. What is the car's acceleration (a) in meters per square second if it takes 10 seconds to reach 30 meters per second and it accelerates uniformly?

(F) 3

(G) 13

(H) 7

(J) 2

(K) 130

GO ON TO NEXT PAGE

35. A license plate in the fictional state of Greenwood has two digits followed by two letters. How many different license plate combinations can Greenwood create if digits can be repeated but letters cannot?

(A) 60,840

(B) 65,000

(C) 67,600

(D) 71

(E) 72

36. On a recent math test, Caroline scored 99, Stephanie scored 97, Julie scored 92, and Amanda scored 88. Courtney was the only other person who took the test and the average of the five scores was a 91. What was Courtney's score?

(F) 79

(G) 88

(H) 91

(J) 94

(K) 99

37. The floor of a 14-foot-wide rectangular room has an area of 672 square feet. What is the length, in feet, of its diagonal?

(A) 25

(B) 45.913

(C) 48

(D) 50

(E) 2,500

38. For what values of x does $x^4 - 5x^2 + 4 = 0$?

(F) 1 and 4 only

(G) −1 and −4 only

(H) 1, 4, −1, and −4 only

(J) 5 only

(K) 1, 2, −1, and −2 only

39. Sam has 3,600 cubic centimeters of peanut butter to make nine sandwiches for her softball team. The bread measures 10 centimeters by 10 centimeters. If she spreads the peanut butter evenly over the bread, how high will the peanut butter reach on each sandwich?

(A) 2 cm

(B) 4 cm

(C) 3.6 cm

(D) 9 cm

(E) 36 cm

40. What would be the slope of any line perpendicular to line *m* in the following figure?

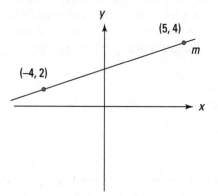

(F) $\frac{9}{2}$

(G) $\frac{2}{9}$

(H) $-\frac{2}{9}$

(J) −1

(K) $-\frac{9}{2}$

41. Which of the following would express the 31st term of the geometric sequence represented by 2, 4a, . . .?

(A) $(2a)^{31}$

(B) $2^{31}a^{30}$

(C) $2^{30}a^{31}$

(D) $2a^{30}$

(E) $4a^{31}$

42. What is the measure in degrees of ∠DBC in the following diagram if polygon ABCD is a trapezoid?

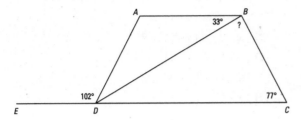

(F) 102

(G) 45

(H) 33

(J) 147

(K) 70

43. There is a straight 65-mile road between Denver and Boulder. If Jackson leaves Boulder at 3:15 PM traveling 40 mph and Emily leaves Denver at the same time traveling 60 mph, how many miles from Denver will the two pass each other?

(A) 20

(B) 26

(C) 32.5

(D) 36

(E) 39

44. What is the distance in the standard (x, y) coordinate plane between the points (−6, 1) and (2, 7)?

(F) $\sqrt{52}$

(G) $\sqrt{28}$

(H) 10

(J) 8

(K) 6

45. The 337 cars on the lot at Madi's Auto Dealership come in a variety of colors. About $\frac{2}{3}$ of the cars on the lot are blue. Of those, about $\frac{1}{4}$ are royal blue and $\frac{3}{4}$ are navy blue. About how many cars are navy blue?

(A) 56

(B) 169

(C) 253

(D) 225

(E) 84

46. For all $x \neq 0$ and $y \neq 0$, $\dfrac{\left(3x^3y^2\right)^2}{3xy^{-3}} = ?$

(F) x^5y^7

(G) $3x^5y^7$

(H) x^5y

(J) $3x^5y$

(K) $3x^4y^7$

47. What is the largest possible sum of two integers that have a product that ranges between −8 and 0 exclusive?

(A) 4

(B) 5

(C) 6

(D) 8

(E) There is no limit to the value of the sum of the two integers.

48. Austin wants to open up a barbershop because there seems to be an insufficient number of them in the area. First, however, he needs to determine whether he will be running a profitable business. He has found a space to rent for $600 per month and his monthly supplies will cost about $200. If he has to pay 10 barbers $12 per hour to cut hair, the barbers are working 120 hours per month, and he can sell 1,200 haircuts for $15 apiece, will his business make a profit after the first month?

(F) No, his business will lose $4,400 in the first month.

(G) No, his business will lose $2,800 in the first month.

(H) Yes, his business will make a profit of $2,800 in the first month.

(J) Yes, his business will make a profit of $4,400 in the first month.

(K) Yes, his business will make a profit of $18,000 in the first month.

GO ON TO NEXT PAGE

49. If $0° \leq x \leq 90°$ and $\cos x = \frac{7}{25}$, then what is $\tan x$?

(A) $\frac{24}{7}$

(B) $\frac{24}{25}$

(C) $\frac{7}{24}$

(D) $\frac{15}{7}$

(E) $\frac{25}{7}$

Use the following information to answer questions 50 – 52.

The following figure maps in the standard (x, y) coordinate plane the locations that Becca frequents most often in her small town of Larkspur. Most weekday mornings, Becca walks from her house to school. After school, she stops at the library to study before she walks to the diner to begin her 3-hour shift as a server.

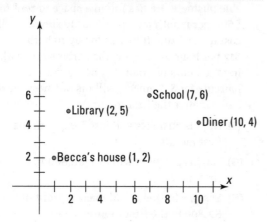

50. What is the slope of the straight line that marks the shortest distance Becca walks from the library to the diner?

(F) -8

(G) $-\frac{1}{8}$

(H) $\frac{1}{8}$

(J) $\frac{4}{3}$

(K) 8

51. Which of the following represents the equation of a circle that is tangent to the x-axis and whose center is the point that marks Becca's house?

(A) $(x-2)^2 + (y-1)^2 = 1$

(B) $(x+2)^2 + (y+1)^2 = 4$

(C) $(x-1)^2 + (y-2)^2 = 4$

(D) $(x+1)^2 + (y+2)^2 = 2$

(E) $(x-1)^2 + (y-2)^2 = 2$

52. Which of the following is closest to the shortest distance, to the nearest mile, that Becca could walk between her house and the school if each unit in the coordinate system is equivalent to 2 miles?

(F) 5

(G) 11

(H) 14

(J) 17

(K) 18

53. $\frac{2}{5}$ of a number is equal to $\frac{1}{4}$ of 21 more than that number. What is the number?

(A) 28

(B) 35

(C) 42

(D) 56

(E) 140

54. If $y = 7x - h$ and $x = h + 7$, then what is the value of y expressed in terms of x?

(F) $y = 6h + 49$

(G) $y = 6x - 7$

(H) $y + h = 7x$

(J) $y = 6x + 7$

(K) $y = 7xh + 49x - h$

55. A circle whose radius is 7 cm is circumscribed inside a square. What is the area of the part of the square that is not taken up by the circle?

(A) 49π

(B) $49 - 14\pi$

(C) $49 - 49\pi$

(D) $196 - 49\pi$

(E) $196 - 14\pi$

56. What is the area in square units of the following rectangle?

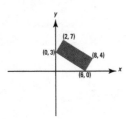

(F) 11.18

(G) 24

(H) 30

(J) 56.33

(K) 900

57. Which one of the following graphs best represents the inequality $y \le \sin(x) + 2$?

(A)

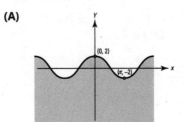

(B)

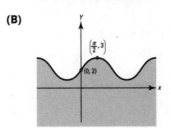

(C)

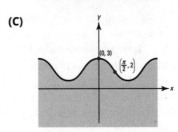

(D)

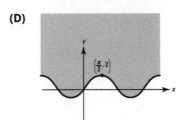

(E)

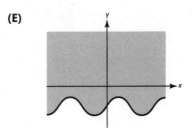

GO ON TO NEXT PAGE

58. What is the length to the nearest tenth of side *a* on the following triangle?

Note: The law of cosines states that
$c^2 = a^2 + b^2 - 2ab\cos C$.

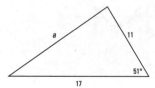

(F) $a = \sqrt{410 - (374\cos 51°)}$

(G) $a = 410 - (374\cos 51°)$

(H) $a = \sqrt{36\cos 51°}$

(J) $a = \sqrt{410 - (374\cos 129°)}$

(K) $a = \sqrt{36\cos 129°}$

59. Jamie conducted a poll to show her classmates' favorite genres of music. Of all the students in her class, 20% chose not to participate in the poll. Of those students who responded, 25% said Rock, 37.5% picked Pop, 20% picked Hip Hop, and 17.5% picked Country. If seven students picked Country, how many students are in her class?

(A) 40

(B) 50

(C) 48

(D) 32

(E) 30

60. Jordyn has $600 in a savings account that earns 5% in interest compounded biannually, which means that she earns 5% of her existing money twice per year. The money she makes through interest is then added to the amount of money she already has in her savings account. After a year and a half, Jordyn moves $210 to a checking account that doesn't earn interest to buy a camera. How much money to the nearest cent does Jordyn have in her savings account after two years?

(F) $720.00

(G) $729.30

(H) $508.80

(J) $504.00

(K) $484.58

DO NOT TURN THE PAGE UNTIL TOLD TO DO SO STOP DO NOT RETURN TO A PREVIOUS TEST

Reading Test

TIME: 35 minutes for 40 questions

DIRECTIONS: Each of the four passages in this section is followed by ten questions. Answer each question based on what is stated or implied in the passage and shade the corresponding oval on your answer sheet.

Passage I — Prose Fiction

This passage is adapted from the novel, *Song of the Lark*, by Willa Sibert Cather.

Line

"And it was Summer, beautiful Summer!" Those were the words of Thea's favorite fairy tale, and she thought of them as she ran one Saturday morning in May, her music book under her arm.
(05) She was going to the Kohlers' to take her lesson, but she was in no hurry.

It was in the summer that one really lived. Then all the little overcrowded houses were opened wide, and the wind blew through them with sweet, earthy
(10) smells of garden-planting. People were out painting their fences. The cottonwood trees were a-flicker with sticky, yellow little leaves, and the feathery tamarisks were in pink bud. With the warm weather came freedom for everybody. The very old people,
(15) whom one had not seen all winter, came out and sunned themselves in the yard. The double windows were taken off the houses, the tormenting flannels in which children had been encased all winter were put away in boxes, and the youngsters felt a plea-
(20) sure in the cool cotton things next their skin.

Thea had to walk more than a mile to reach the Kohlers' house. On a little rise of ground that faced the open sandy plain, was the Kohlers' house, where Professor Wunsch lived. Fritz Kohler
(25) was the town tailor, one of the first settlers. He had moved there, built a little house and made a garden, when Moonstone was first marked down on the map. He had three sons, but they now worked on the railroad and were stationed in dis-
(30) tant cities. One of them had gone to work for the Santa Fe, and lived in New Mexico.

Mrs. Kohler seldom crossed the ravine and went into the town except at Christmastime, when she had to buy presents to send to her old friends
(35) in Freeport, Illinois. As she did not go to church, she did not possess such a thing as a hat. Year after year she wore the same red hood in winter and a black sunbonnet in summer. She made her own dresses; the skirts came barely to her shoe-tops,
(40) and were gathered as full as they could possibly be

to the waistband. She preferred men's shoes, and usually wore the cast-offs of one of her sons. She had never learned much English, and her plants and shrubs were her companions. She lived for her
(45) men and her garden. Beside that sand gulch, she had tried to reproduce a bit of her own village in the Rhine Valley. She hid herself behind the growth she had fostered, lived under the shade of what she had planted and watered and pruned. Shade, shade;
(50) that was what she was always planning and mak- ing. Behind the high tamarisk hedge, her garden was a jungle of verdure in summer. Above the cherry trees and peach trees stood the windmill, which kept all this verdure alive. Outside, the sage-
(55) brush grew up to the very edge of the garden.

Everyone in Moonstone was astonished when the Kohlers took in the wandering music-teacher. In seventeen years old Fritz had never had a crony, except the harness-maker and Spanish Johnny. This
(60) Wunsch came from God knew where, and played in the dance orchestra, tuned pianos, and gave lessons. When Mrs. Kohler rescued him, he was sleeping in a dirty, unfurnished room over one of the saloons, and he had only two shirts in the world. Once he was un-
(65) der her roof, the old woman went at him as she did at her garden. She sewed and washed and mended, and made him so clean and respectable that he was able to get a large class of pupils and rent a piano. As soon as he had money, he sent to the Narrow Gauge
(70) lodging-house, in Denver, for a trunkful of music which had been held there for unpaid board. With tears in his eyes the old man—he was not over fifty, but sadly battered—told Mrs. Kohler that he asked nothing better of God than to end his days with her,
(75) and to be buried in the garden, under her linden trees. They were not American basswood, but the European linden, which has honey-colored blooms in summer, with a fragrance that surpasses all trees and flowers and drives young people wild with joy.

(80) Thea was reflecting as she walked along that had it not been for Professor Wunsch she might have lived on for years without ever knowing the Kohlers, without ever seeing their garden or the inside of their house.

GO ON TO NEXT PAGE ➤

(85)   Professor Wunsch went to the houses of his other pupils to give them their lessons, but one morning he told Mrs. Kronborg that Thea had talent. Mrs. Kronborg was a strange woman. That word "talent," which no one else in Moonstone
(90) would have understood, she comprehended perfectly. To any other woman, it would have meant that a child must have her hair curled every day and must play in public. Mrs. Kronborg knew it meant that Thea must practice four hours a day.
(95) A child with talent must be kept at the piano, just as a child with measles must be kept under the blankets.

1. Which of the following examples best parallels the analogy that Mrs. Kronborg made in the final paragraph?

   (A) A student with good writing skills must work harder on math.

   (B) A young girl with beauty must be kept under close watch.

   (C) A person with outdoor allergies must be kept indoors.

   (D) A child with learning differences may benefit from tutoring.

2. The author associates all of the following with the onset of summer EXCEPT:

   (F) seeing new neighbors

   (G) the blossoming of cottonwood trees

   (H) home dwellers painting their fences

   (J) children wearing cool clothing instead of warm

3. The use of the word crony at line 58 most likely means:

   (A) elder.

   (B) buddy.

   (C) enemy.

   (D) teacher.

4. When the author says, "the old woman went at him like she did her garden" (lines 65–66), she most nearly means Mrs. Kohler:

   (F) determined to rid Professor Wunsch of his less desirable qualities.

   (G) tried in vain to improve his appearance.

   (H) spruced him up with care and attention.

   (J) tried to mold him into her idea of perfection.

5. The author makes all of the following assertions regarding Mrs. Kohler's personal style, EXCEPT:

   (A) she wore a black hood in the wintertime.

   (B) she wore a black sunbonnet in the summertime.

   (C) Mrs. Kohler preferred men's shoes over women's.

   (D) Mrs. Kohler made her own dresses.

6. The best way to describe the way Professor Wunsch feels toward Mrs. Kohler is:

   (F) indifferent.

   (G) amorous.

   (H) grateful.

   (J) bitter.

7. Mrs. Kohler's garden is best described as a:

   (A) haven where she hid, planned, and found purpose.

   (B) reminder of her homeland, filled with hedges, fruit trees, and sage-brush.

   (C) barren sand gulch that she fled to when she was lonely.

   (D) verdant paradise fed by Moonstone's frequent rainfall.

8. The author makes which of the following assertions about Mr. Kohler?

   (F) He played in the dance orchestra.

   (G) He had only three friends.

   (H) He had a son who lived in Santa Fe.

   (J) He was one of the first men to live in Moonstone.

9. The author would most likely say that Thea differed from other children in that she:

   (A) had few friends and attended few social gatherings.

   (B) studied music with Professor Wunsch.

   (C) was particularly fond of fairy tales.

   (D) was musically gifted.

10. Thea's attitude in the first paragraph can best be described as:

(F) cheerful.

(G) eager.

(H) combative.

(J) restless.

Passage A

This passage is adapted from *Posttraumatic Stress Disorder: Issues and Controversies*, edited by Gerald M. Rosen (2004).

Line   Controversy has haunted the diagnosis of post-traumatic stress disorder (PTSD) ever since its first appearance in the third edition of the *Diagnostic and Statistical Manual of Mental Disorders* (*DSM-III*).
(05) At the outset, psychiatrists opposed to the inclusion of the diagnosis in the *DSM-III* argued that the problems of trauma-exposed people were already covered by combinations of existing diagnoses.

       Ratifying PTSD would merely entail cobbling
(10) together selected symptoms in people suffering from multiple disorders (for example, phobias, depression, and personality disorders) and then attributing these familiar problems to a traumatic event. Moreover, the very fact that the movement
(15) to include the diagnosis in the *DSM-III* arose from Vietnam veterans' advocacy groups working with antiwar psychiatrists prompted concerns that PTSD was more of a political or social construct rather than a medical disease discovered in nature.

(20)   Although the aforementioned two concerns have again resurfaced in contemporary debates about PTSD, additional issues have arisen as well. For example, the concept of a traumatic stressor has broadened to such an extent that, today,
(25) the vast majority of American adults have been exposed to PTSD-qualifying events. This state of affairs is drastically different from the late 1970s and early 1980s, when the concept of trauma was confined to catastrophic events falling
(30) outside the perimeter of everyday experience. Early 21st-century scholars are raising fresh questions about the syndromic validity of PTSD.

Passage B

This passage is adapted from *Post-Traumatic Stress Disorder*, edited by Dan J. Stein MD, PhD, Matthew J. Friedman, MD, and Carlos Blanco, MD, PhD (2011).

       Of the many diagnoses in the *Diagnostic and Statistical Manual of Mental Disorders* (*DSM-III*), very few invoke an aetiology in their diagnostic criteria: (35) (i) organic mental disorders (caused, for example, by a neurological abnormality); (ii) substance-use disorders (caused, for example, by psychoactive chemical agents); (iii) post-traumatic stress disorder (PTSD); (iv) acute stress disorder (ASD); (40) and (v) adjustment disorders (ADs). The latter three are all caused by exposure to a stressful environmental event that exceeds the coping capacity of the affected individual. The presumed causal relationship between the stressor and PTSD, ASD, (45) and AD is complicated and controversial. Controversy notwithstanding, acceptance of this causal relationship has equipped practitioners and scientists with a conceptual tool that has profoundly influenced clinical practice over the past 30 years. (50)

       PTSD is primarily a disorder of reactivity rather than of an altered baseline state, as in major depressive disorder or general anxiety disorder. Its psychopathology is characteristically expressed during interactions with the interpersonal or (55) physical environment. People with PTSD are consumed by concerns about personal safety. They persistently scan the environment for threatening stimuli. When in doubt, they are more likely to assume that danger is present and will react (60) accordingly. Avoidance and hyper-arousal symptoms can be understood within this context. The primacy of traumatic over other memories (for example, the re-experiencing symptoms) can also be understood as a pathological exaggeration of an (65) adaptive human response to remember as much as possible about dangerous encounters in order to avoid similar threats in the future.

GO ON TO NEXT PAGE ➡

11. According to Passage A, psychiatrists opposed to PTSD's inclusion in the *Diagnostic and Statistical Manual of Mental Disorders (DSM-III)* based their arguments on the following points, EXCEPT:

(A) Today's definition of catastrophic trauma is a far cry from what it was in the late 1960s and early 70s.

(B) PTSD sufferers could already be grouped into one or more existing diagnosis categories.

(C) What qualifies as a "stressor" by today's definition has become far too broad.

(D) PTSD is more of a social and political construct than a legitimate affliction.

12. The author's attitude in Passage A can best be described as:

(F) contemplative.

(G) indecisive.

(H) explanatory.

(J) argumentative.

13. The author of Passage A refers to the 1970s and 1980s in order to:

(A) show how far American medicine has come over time.

(B) highlight a time that saw numerous catastrophic events.

(C) compare the number of PTSD sufferers between then and now.

(D) reveal how America's definition of "trauma" has changed over time.

Questions 14 – 16 pertain to Passage B

14. *Aetiology*, as it appears in the first sentence of Passage B, most likely means:

(F) that which creates controversy.

(G) the cause, manner, or set of causes that lead to a disease or condition.

(H) the study of the origin of words.

(J) an abnormality.

15. Which of the following sentences best summarizes the main idea of Passage B?

(A) PTSD is controversial, but it has had a profound impact on both sufferers and the medical profession as a whole over the years.

(B) PTSD is a legitimate, debilitating condition that deserves additional research and financial resources.

(C) PTSD was given a name largely because medical professionals needed a way to categorize veterans suffering from various mental conditions after returning from war.

(D) PTSD is no longer an accurate diagnosis, because the world has come to accept any number of situations as "stressors" that might set it off.

16. The author of Passage B makes all of the following assertions about PTSD EXCEPT:

(F) that it is caused by exposure to a particularly stressful environmental factor that is more than the affected individual can handle.

(G) that PTSD is a disorder that results from an altered baseline state.

(H) that PTSD sufferers frequently search their surroundings for anything that might be viewed as a threat.

(J) that clinical practice over the years has been largely influenced by the acceptance of a causal relationship between a stressor and the onset of PTSD.

Questions 17 – 20 pertain to both Passage A and Passage B

17. Which of the following best demonstrates the different perspectives between the psychiatrists and scholars mentioned in Passage A and the author of Passage B?

(A) The psychiatrists in Passage A think that the definition of PTSD has become too broad, while the author of Passage B feels it is a legitimate condition that has played an important role in clinical practice.

(B) The psychiatrists and scholars in Passage A believe that PTSD is a genuinely debilitating condition, while the author of Passage B believes today's doctors are too quick to offer up a PTSD diagnosis.

(C) The psychiatrists and scholars in Passage A believe that PTSD is simply a combination of other existing conditions, while the author of Passage B feels that PTSD is a disorder of an altered baseline state.

(D) The psychiatrists and scholars in Passage A believe that social conditions led to the theory behind PTSD, while the author of Passage B believes it was politics.

18. The authors of both passages are most likely to agree on which of the following statements?

(F) PTSD is a disorder of reactivity.

(G) The use of the PTSD diagnosis is highly political.

(H) PTSD sufferers are overly concerned with personal safety.

(J) PTSD is a highly controversial condition.

19. The authors of either Passage A or Passage B make all of the following assertions about the *Diagnostic and Statistical Manual of Mental Disorders (DSM-III)* EXCEPT:

(A) that few diagnoses listed also list causes.

(B) that psychiatrists initially did not want PTSD listed in the publication.

(C) that PTSD appeared in its third edition.

(D) that the information it contains about PTSD is wholly insufficient.

20. Which of the following statements is consistent with information contained in both passages?

(F) PTSD is caused by stressful factors that exceed one's ability to cope, and scientists and medical professionals are often too quick to make the proper diagnosis.

(G) PTSD is an increasingly prevalent problem in America, and years of research must be devoted to its causes and treatment.

(H) The PTSD diagnosis is a controversial one, and scientists and medical professionals have differing opinions on its causes and its inclusion in the *Diagnostic and Statistical Manual of Mental Disorders (DSM-III)*.

(J) Scientists and medical professionals disagree over which stressors are sufficient to lead to PTSD.

Passage III — Humanities

Adapting literature for the screen can be daunting. To increase one's chances of creating a successful adaptation, Linda Seger suggests choosing original works with a good story. In her book, *The Art of Adaptation*, Seger goes on to (05) clarify that a good story contains three elements: a goal, a problem or an issue, and a life-altering journey.

Almost every aspect of life is touched by change. Outer physical change is readily apparent: (10) Babies grow into adults, winter becomes spring, natural structures build up and erode. Less tangible but not less important are the inner changes that human beings experience. Just as a disruption of normal physical growth is unhealthy, so is a lack of (15) inner growth. Although inner growth and change is healthy and exciting, it also requires courage and discernment. Journeying from a familiar state to a different one means sacrificing what is known and comfortable for something that is unknown and (20) uncertain, and this transformation involves risk. Inner growth comes at a price, and humans face a fundamental dilemma: To change requires a sacrifice of the old and familiar, but to remain static is to sacrifice a chance at new life. (25)

GO ON TO NEXT PAGE ▶

Experiencing myth and ritual in film may assist people with this universal dilemma. According to Joseph Campbell in his book The Hero with a Thousand Faces, the purpose and effect of myth
(30) and ritual ". . . was to conduct people across those difficult thresholds of transformation that demand a change in the patterns not only of conscious but also of unconscious life." Myth serves to draw people into and through the important transfor-
(35) mation journey.

Through an examination of myths and rituals, Campbell distinguishes what he called the mono-myth, a heroic quest for an immensely precious treasure at high personal cost. The hero of the
(40) monomyth endures a series of trials and even death or a death-like experience that liberates the hero from the past limitations of his old existence and renews life's possibilities. Mythology not only documents the transformation process of a mythic
(45) hero but also provides a means for other people to experience the hero's transformation.

Campbell claims it is "the prime function of mythology and rite to supply the symbols that carry the human spirit forward, in counteraction to
(50) those other constant human fantasies that tend to tie it back." Myth may carry out this function by providing a vicarious heroic journey for the one who encounters myth in film adaptations of literary works. As viewers experience the transfor-
(55) mations of film characters, they may gain insight into possibilities for their own heroic quests and, through contact with the stories of others, may embark on their own transformational journeys into more mature human beings.

21. The author's primary purpose in writing this passage is most likely to:

(A) establish that to create a well-executed screen adaptation, one should choose a story modeled on a mythological journey.

(B) show that positive change is not possible without taking risks.

(C) warn that screenwriters should not attempt to adapt literary works that do not contain a mythic journey.

(D) reveal that a good film adaptation contains a series of trials and a near-death experience.

22. The author of the passage suggests that inner growth requires:

(F) an unhealthy forfeiture of established patterns of living and an acceptance of necessary risks.

(G) viewing film adaptations of literary works.

(H) courage to remain constant in changeable and unfamiliar environments.

(J) sacrifice of one's comfortable fantasies and the exploration of uncharted territory.

23. Which of the following would the author of the passage be most likely to include in the list along with ". . . babies grow into" (line 11)?

(A) Taste preferences change to include a wider appreciation of foods.

(B) Young adults in their twenties make wiser decisions that adolescents.

(C) Brown hair thins and turns to gray.

(D) Best friends become strangers.

24. In saying "to change requires a sacrifice of the old and familiar, but to remain static is to sacrifice a chance at new life" (Line 25), the author most likely means that:

(F) sacrifice is inevitable.

(G) change of any kind is better than no change at all.

(H) a life-altering journey is ultimately more fulfilling than the actual change one achieves as a result.

(J) being resistant to change requires a more substantial risk than does facing the unknown.

25. The primary purpose of the second paragraph is to:

(A) outline some of the ways humans may achieve inner growth.

(B) offer a more detailed description of one of the components of a good story.

(C) encourage the reader to risk inner growth by journeying from familiar to unfamiliar circumstances.

(D) provide examples of some physical alterations humans may experience throughout their lives.

26. With which of the following statements would the author of the passage most likely agree?

(F) Mythology provides a way for others to benefit from the hero's metamorphosis.

(G) The three main elements of a good story are a life-altering journey, a serious problem, and a protagonist with whom the reader can empathize.

(H) Outer change is less significant but easier to achieve than inner change.

(J) Widely loved stories, if done well, produce remarkably successful screen adaptations.

27. Each of the following is a characteristic of Campbell's monomyth EXCEPT:

(A) liberation from past limitations.

(B) great personal risk.

(C) constant human fantasies.

(D) a search for treasure.

28. According to Campbell, the purpose of ritual is to:

(F) transform a person's unintentional patterns.

(G) give people the tools to help others cross difficult thresholds in their lives.

(H) force people to break bad habits.

(J) promote a rich fantasy life.

29. When the author refers to "this universal dilemma" (line 27), she most likely means:

(A) deciding whether to experience myth and ritual in films.

(B) choosing between conscious and unconscious thoughts.

(C) forgoing comfortable patterns to take on new challenges.

(D) engaging in activities that promote physical growth.

30. Based on information in the passage, Linda Seger is most likely which of the following?

(F) Mythic hero

(G) Film script consultant

(H) Book critic

(J) Psychologist

Passage IV — Natural Science

This passage is adapted from *Reading the Weather*, by T. Morris Lonstreth.

If there is anything that has been overlooked more than another it is our atmosphere. But it absolutely cannot be avoided, because if it were not for the atmosphere this earth of ours would be a wizened and sterile lump. (05)

To be sure the earth does not loom very large in the eye of the sun. It receives a positively trifling fraction of the total output of sunheat. So negligible is this amount that it would not be worth our mentioning if we did not owe our existence to it. It (10) is thanks to the atmosphere, however, that the earth attains this (borrowed) importance. It is thanks to this thin layer of gases that we are protected from that fraction of sunheat which, however insignificant when compared with the (15) whole, would otherwise be sufficient to fry us all in a second. Without this gas wrapping, we would all freeze (if still unfried) immediately after sunset. The atmosphere keeps us in a sort of thermos globe, unmindful of the burning power of the great (20) star, and of the uncalculated cold of outer space.

GO ON TO NEXT PAGE

Yet, limitless as it seems to us, our invaluable atmosphere is a small thing after all. Half of its total bulk is compressed into the first three and a half miles upward. Only one sixty-fourth of it lies above the twenty-one mile limit. Compared with the thickness of the earth this makes a very thin envelope.

Light as air, we say, forgetting that this stuff that looks so inconsequential weighs fifteen pounds to the square inch. The only reason that we don't crumble is because the gases press evenly in all directions, thereby supporting this crushing burden. A layer of water thirty-four feet thick weighs just about as much as this air-pack under which we feel so buoyant. But if these gases get in motion we feel their pressure.

As it blows along the surface of the earth this wind is mostly nitrogen, oxygen, moisture, and dust. The nitrogen occupies nearly eight-tenths of a given bulk of air, the oxygen two-tenths, and the moisture anything up to one-twentieth. Five other gases are present in small quantities. The dust and the water vapor occupy space independently of the rest. As one goes up mountains the water vapor increases for a couple of thousand feet and then decreases to the seven mile limit after which it has almost completely vanished. The lightest gases have been detected as high up as two hundred miles and scientists think that hydrogen, the lightest of all, may escape altogether from the restraint of gravity.

At first glance the extreme readiness of the atmosphere to carry dust and bacteria does not seem a point in its favor. In reality it is. Most bacteria are really allies of the human race. They benefit us by producing fermentations and disintegrations of soils that prepare them for plant food. It is a pity that the few disease breeding types of bacteria should have given the family a bad name. Without bacteria the sheltering atmosphere would have nothing but desert rock to protect.

Further, rain is accounted for only by the dust. Of course this sounds very near the world's record in absurdities. But it is a half-truth at least, for moisture cannot condense on nothing. Every drop of rain, every globule of mist must have a nucleus. Consequently each wind that blows, each volcano that erupts is laying up dust for a rainy day. Apparently the atmosphere is empty. Actually it is full enough of dust-nuclei to outfit a full-grown fog if the dew point should be favorable. If there were no dust in the air all shadows would be intensest black, the sunlight blinding.

But the dust particles fulfill their greatest mission as heat collectors — they and the particles of water vapor which have embraced them. It is in reality owing to these water globules and not to the atmosphere that supports them that we are enabled to live in such comfortable temperatures.

So it comes about that the heavy moist air near the earth is the warmest of all. So high altitudes and low temperatures are found together. But after the limit of moisture content has been reached the temperature gets no lower according to reliable investigations. Instead a monotony of 459° below zero eternally prevails –459° is called the absolute zero of space.

The vertical heating arrangements of the atmosphere appear somewhat irregular. But horizontally it is in a much worse way. The surface of the globe is three quarters water and one quarter land and irregularly arranged at that. The shiny water surfaces reflect a good deal of the heat which they receive, they use up the heat in evaporation and what they do absorb penetrates far. The land surfaces, on the contrary, absorb most of the heat received, but it does not penetrate to any depth. As a consequence of these differences, land warms up about four times as quickly as water and cools off about four times as fast. Therefore, the temperature of air over continents is liable to much more rapid and extreme changes than the air over the oceans.

31. The primary purpose of the passage is to:

(A) explain why the earth's temperatures rise and fall.

(B) highlight the role of dust particles in determining the weather.

(C) explore the many roles of bacteria.

(D) describe the role of the earth's atmosphere.

32. The author makes all of the following assertions about dust EXCEPT:

(F) dust plays a larger role in producing warm temperatures than the atmosphere.

(G) dust accounts for only rain.

(H) particles of dust form the nucleus of rain droplets.

(J) volcanic eruptions and blowing winds are some of the sources of dust layers.

33. According to the author, the wind, as it blows along the surface of the earth, is comprised of all the following EXCEPT:

(A) dust particles.

(B) nitrogen gas.

(C) bacteria.

(D) hydrogen.

34. According to the passage, what does the author consider dust's most important role?

(F) Serving as a heat collector.

(G) Forming the basis of rain.

(H) Minimizing the sun's glare.

(J) Providing a thick layer of protection around the earth.

35. Which of the following does the author consider one of the world's absurdities?

(A) Without dust, sunlight would be blinding.

(B) The irregularly configured surface of the earth is made up of three quarters water and one quarter land.

(C) Air temperatures over vast expanses of land are prone to much more rapid and extreme changes than the temperatures over oceans.

(D) No other factors but dust account for the presence of rain.

36. The main point of the last paragraph is that:

(F) air over water and air over land are subject to different heating and cooling patterns.

(G) the earth's vertical heating arrangements are better than its horizontal heating arrangements.

(H) land surfaces absorb most of the heat received by the sun.

(J) deficiencies in the earth's atmosphere create dangerously extreme variances in temperature.

37. According to the author, the element that prevents humans from burning under the sun's heat is:

(A) a small fraction of sunheat.

(B) the uncalculated cold of outer space.

(C) a thin layer of gases weighing just about fifteen pounds to the square inch.

(D) a thick layer of gases that forms a sort of thermos globe.

GO ON TO NEXT PAGE

38. The word *trifling* in line 7 most likely means
    (F) shallow.
    (G) insignificant.
    (H) silly.
    (J) novel.

39. The author mentions all of the following EXCEPT:
    (A) the fraction of the atmosphere that lies above the 21-mile (above the earth's surface) limit.
    (B) the temperature referred to as the absolute zero of space.
    (C) the amount of nitrogen in any given bulk of air.
    (D) atmospheric differences in the Northern and Southern Hemispheres.

40. When the author claims that "dust and water vapor occupy space independently of the rest" (lines 43–45), he most likely means:
    (F) gases become lighter as one climbs higher into the atmosphere.
    (G) dust and water make up more of the air's atmosphere than nitrogen does.
    (H) moisture and dust exert more atmospheric pressure than gases.
    (J) the properties of dust and water vapor are not determined by the other components of the atmosphere.

Science Test

TIME: 35 minutes for 40 questions

DIRECTIONS: Following are seven passages and then questions that refer to each passage. Choose the best answer and shade in the corresponding oval on your answer sheet.

Passage I

A conductivity meter measures the electrical conductivity in a solution and is used to measure the number of impurities in freshwater. One way to purify water is to remove ions. A solution with a higher ion content has a higher conductivity than a solution with fewer ions. A group of scientists studied water solution samples from 3 different sites from which they took 3 separate measurements — temperature in degrees Celsius, conductivity ($\mu S / m$), and species richness (number of invertebrate species found) — 10 different times. Site 1 was located 5 kilometers upstream of the city center, Site 2 was located in the city center, and Site 3 was 5 kilometers downstream of the city center.

Temperature and conductivity were measured with a conductivity meter. Species richness was collected, and invertebrates were placed in 98% ethanol to preserve the specimens. The collection was taken to the lab and dissecting microscopes were used to count and identify the invertebrate species. The results are shown in Table 1.

1. Based on Table 1, in Site 1, as the temperature of the solution increased, conductivity:

   (A) increased only.

   (B) decreased only.

   (C) stayed the same.

   (D) varied with no general trend.

TABLE 1

Site 1: Upstream			Site 2: City Center			Site 3: Downstream		
Temperature (Celsius)	Conductivity ($\mu S/m$)	Species Richness	Temperature (Celsius)	Conductivity ($\mu S/m$)	Species Richness	Temperature (Celsius)	Conductivity ($\mu S/m$)	Species Richness
23	200	10	25	900	1	22	655	5
23	155	12	24	800	2	23.5	599	4
24	220	11	23	821	1	22.5	621	6
23.5	185	9	23	906	3	25	632	4
24	188	10	24	855	2	25	588	5
22.5	190	11	22	899	1	24	612	7
25	203	14	23	865	4	23	641	6
24	253	12	24	845	1	23	625	5
23	211	10	22	933	2	23.5	598	4
25	177	8	23	865	2	24	600	3
23.7	198.2	10.7	23.3	868.9	1.9	23.6	617.1	4.9

GO ON TO NEXT PAGE

2. The scientists' research suggests that the collection site or sites whose water solution contains the greatest number of impurities is/are:

(F) Site 1

(G) Site 2

(H) Site 3

(J) Site 1 and Site 3

3. The conductivity of typical drinking water ranges between 50 and 500 $\mu S/m$. Based on the results of the scientists' research, which of the three sites contain(s) water solutions that may be safe to drink?

(A) Site 1 only

(B) Site 3 only

(C) Site 1 and Site 2

(D) Site 2 and Site 3

4. Suppose an additional study was conducted in the same manner at a site located in rural pastureland several miles upstream from Site 1. The average conductivity of this site was measured to be 500 $\mu S/m$. The average species richness of this new site would most likely be:

(F) less than 1.9.

(G) between 1.9 and 4.9.

(H) between 4.9 and 10.7.

(J) greater than 10.7.

5. Based on the results of the research, which abiotic factor generally correlated to species richness?

(A) Only temperature correlated to species richness.

(B) Only conductivity correlated to species richness.

(C) Both temperature and conductivity correlated to species richness.

(D) No abiotic factors correlated to species richness.

6. The scientists most likely used which of the following to collect the data necessary to determine species richness?

(F) Balance

(G) pH meter

(H) Nets

(J) Thermometer

Passage II

Convict cichlids are highly aggressive freshwater fish that are found in streams and rivers in Central America. Their aggression allows them to protect their breeding territory from intruders that enter and consume their offspring. Both males and females are aggressive, and aggressiveness is also related to size.

Experiment 1

Researchers collected 30 males and 30 females and separated them into 3 categories based on size: small (50–69 mm), medium (70–89 mm), and large (90–109 mm). They allowed one fish (the focal fish) to claim a territory in an aquarium tank for 5 days. On day 6, they placed an intruder of equal size to and of the same sex as the focal fish into the aquarium and watched the aggressive behaviors for 30 minutes. Aggressive behaviors viewed were lateral displays, frontal displays, biting, mouth wrestling, and chasing. All behaviors were lumped together and the total time spent in these behaviors was averaged for each group. Table 1 records the findings of average number of minutes within 30-minute time periods that the convict cichlid fish exhibited acts of aggression based on size and sex.

TABLE 1

	Small (50–69 mm) Focal Fish & Intruder	Medium (70–89 mm) Focal Fish & Intruder	Large (90–109 mm) Focal Fish & Intruder
Males	12	18	23
Females	6	10	14

Experiment 2

Researchers repeated Experiment 1 but varied the size of the intruder they introduced into the tank on day 6. In the study, 10 females and 10 males received an intruder that was 20 mm smaller than the focal fish, 10 females and 10 males received an equal-sized intruder, and 10 males and 10 females received an intruder that was 20 mm larger than the focal fish. All intruders were the same sex as the focal fish. The same types of aggressive behaviors as those in Experiment 1 were observed for 30 minutes and recorded. Behaviors were grouped together, and the total time spent in these behaviors was averaged for each group. Table 2 records average number of minutes of aggression within a 30-minute time period in convict cichlid fish based on intruder size and sex.

TABLE 2

	Intruder 20 mm Smaller than Focal Fish	Equal-Sized Intruder	Intruder 20 mm Larger than Focal Fish
Males	12	20	11
Females	6	11	5

7. The two experiments were likely designed to answer which of these questions?

(A) Are highly aggressive fish more likely to exist in fresh or saltwater?

(B) What are the most common types of aggressive behaviors exhibited by convict cichlids?

(C) Is size or gender a better indicator of the potential for aggression in convict cichlids?

(D) How does the relative size of an intruder fish affect the number of aggressive behaviors exhibited by a focal fish?

8. According to Experiment 1, which of the following is the correct order of cichlids from highest to lowest aggression?

(F) Large female, large male, medium female, small male.

(G) Large male, large female, medium male, small female.

(H) Large male, medium male, large female, small male.

(J) Large male, medium male, small male, large female.

9. Based on Experiment 1 and Experiment 2, male cichlids exhibited:

(A) about half as much aggression as female cichlids.

(B) about twice as much aggression as female cichlids.

(C) about the same amount of aggression as female cichlids.

(D) about half as much aggression as female cichlids in Experiment 2 and about twice as much aggression as female cichlids in Experiment 1.

10. Experiment 1 and Experiment 2 differed in that Experiment 2 varied which independent variable?

(F) Gender of the intruder.

(G) Relative size of the intruder to focal fish.

(H) Level of aggression in the intruder.

(J) Number of days provided for the focal fish to establish its territory.

11. In Experiment 2, the recorded amount of aggression was influenced primarily by:

(A) the gender and size of the focal fish.

(B) only the gender of the focal fish.

(C) only the size of the intruder.

(D) the gender of the focal fish and the size of the intruder.

12. The scientists who conducted the research wanted to use the lab data to determine which combination of two cichlids would be the best protectors of their offspring. Based on the results of the two experiments, which of the following pairs was the one the scientists likely concluded was the best?

(F) Medium male paired with a large female.

(G) Large male paired with a small female.

(H) Medium male paired with a medium female.

(J) Small male paired with a small female.

13. Where solid bars represent male cichlids and patterned bars represent female cichlids, which of the following graphs provides the most accurate representation of the results of Experiment 2?

(A)
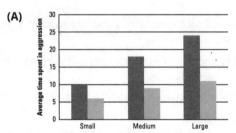

(B)
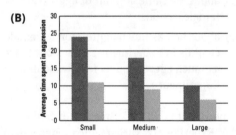

(C)
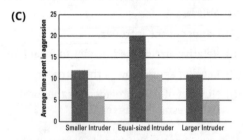

(D)
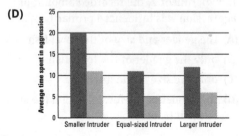

Passage III

Genetically modified organisms (GMOs) are any organisms that are modified with respect to their genetics. A wide range of methods exist for producing GMOs, from procedures as simple as selective breeding (which has been conducted for thousands of years) to the more recent technology of inserting genes of one organism into those of another organism. GMOs have been used to produce medical advances such as creating insulin for people with diabetes. However, more recently there have been debates over the role GMOs should play in foods.

Two researchers present their opinions.

Researcher 1

GMO foods were first designed in an attempt to control pests without using pesticides. Traditional pesticides can be harmful to the environment, so reducing pesticides would provide significant environmental benefits. In addition, GMO foods are thought to increase crop yields. Given that our world population continues to grow exponentially, food may become a limited resource and using genetically modified foods may assist in the sustenance of an exploding global population. GMOs have been a part of food production for several decades, and no scientific evidence exists to support the view that the nutritional value of GMOs is less than that of food that has not been genetically modified. Nor does evidence suggest that GMOs cause harm to the organisms that consume them. Some studies have reported minor increases in food allergies associated with GMOs, but that information is likely correlational, not causational.

Researcher 2

Genetically modified foods may have been first implemented to replace pesticides, but recent data shows that pests become resistant to the GMO plants more quickly than to plants that have not been genetically modified and are treated with pesticides. Reducing pesticides benefits the environment, but this reduction can be achieved without resorting to producing GMOs. Planting a variety of species instead of monocultures and using natural pest repellants (e.g., lady bugs) would reduce pesticide use in a better way than GMOs. Not all GMOs yield higher crops, and other options to combat limited food production, such as home and community gardening, exist. Placing the burden of food production on individuals would reduce the strain on big corporations. Recent efforts in urban areas include converting spaces on rooftops to community farms. Although current studies show no direct correlation between GMOs and health problems in humans, GMOs have not been studied long enough to rule out the possibility of long-term effects. The nutritional value of GMOs may be similar to that of organically grown food, but the taste and overall quality are not. Anyone who has eaten both organic foods and GMOs will attest to the former's superiority. The last problem with GMOs is that cross contamination can occur. Plant pollen can travel long distances and GMO plants can hybridize with organic crops.

14. According to Researcher 1, what are the benefits of GMOs?

(F) They reduce pesticide use and increase crop yields.

(G) They increase pesticide use and decrease crop yields.

(H) They increase the nutritional value of food and do not cause harm to organisms.

(J) Researcher 1 sees no benefits of GMOs.

15. According to the passage, with which of the following statements would both researchers agree?

(A) Increasing pesticide use would be good for the environment.

(B) There is no direct correlation between GMOs and health problems in humans.

(C) GMO foods have improved taste and quality.

(D) GMO foods increase food allergies in many of the humans who consume them.

16. According to Researcher 2, a major disadvantage of GMOs is that:

(F) their pollen can travel long distances.

(G) their use decreases the number of naturally occurring pest reducers.

(H) their use increases the prevalence of harmful pesticides.

(J) they are directly correlated with health problems in humans.

17. According to Researcher 1, a harmful effect that may be correlated to GMO foods is:

(A) pesticide resistance.

(B) production of tumors in consumers.

(C) decreased nutritional value.

(D) increased food allergies in consumers.

18. According to Researcher 2, the use of pesticides may be reduced by all of the following EXCEPT:

(F) replacing only some organically grown crops with GMOs.

(G) planting a variety of species instead of monocultures.

(H) using ladybugs as repellants.

(J) increasing the number of community farms.

19. According to Researcher 2, GMOs have been linked to which of the following?

(A) An increase in the number of pesticides.

(B) An increase in the number of home and community gardens.

(C) Inferior food quality.

(D) A larger burden placed on food-producing corporations.

GO ON TO NEXT PAGE

20. Which of the following graphs is consistent with Researcher 1's view but not Researcher 2's?

(F)

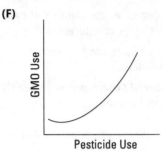

(G)

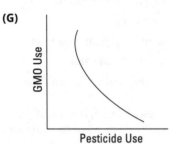

(H)

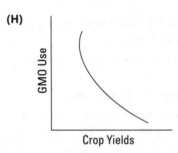

(J)

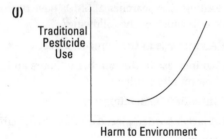

Plants need several elements to grow, such as light, water, and nutrients. The most important nutrients are nitrogen (N), phosphorus (P), and potassium (K). These inorganic nutrients are converted from organic nutrients during the process of decomposition. Certain organisms, called *decomposers*, help speed up the process of decomposition. Researchers wanted to test whether applying decomposers in the form of compost or synthetic fertilizers were better for growing plants. In addition, the researchers wanted to determine the optimal light conditions for plant growth. The researchers conducted the following two experiments, where the amount of water applied in each case was kept at a constant.

Experiment 1

The three researchers set up three treatment groups. In each contained environment, the researcher planted 20 pea seeds. The first treatment group contained sandy soil with nothing else added. The second treatment group contained sandy soil to which was added a compost mixture by earthworm decomposers. The third group contained potting soil that was enriched with synthetic fertilizers. Once planted, the seeds received 12 hours of sunlight per day and were watered once a day for eight weeks. After eight weeks, each plant stem was measured from the top of the soil to the top of the main stem. The researchers recorded the measurements in Figure 1.

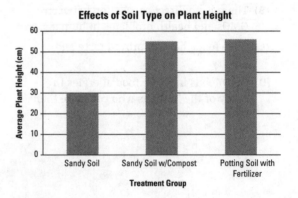

FIGURE 1

Experiment 2

The same experiment was conducted using only the sandy soil mixed with earthworm-generated compost for all 60 plants. Each treatment group received different amounts of daily exposure to sunlight. One group received 6 hours, another 10 hours, and the other 14 hours of sunlight. Each group received 20 seeds that were planted at the same time and were watered once a day for 8 weeks. After 8 weeks, each plant stem was measured from the top of the soil to the top of the main stem. The results are displayed in Table 1.

TABLE 1

Hours of Daily Sunlight	Plant Height (cm)
6	40
10	50
14	59

21. Which of the following is an independent variable in the two experiments?

    I.   Type of soil

    II. Plant height

    III. Hours of sunlight

    (A) I only

    (B) II only

    (C) I and III only

    (D) I, II, and III

22. According to the results of the two experiments, the environment that would produce the greatest amount of plant growth would be:

    (F) sandy soil and at least 12 hours of daily sunlight.

    (G) sandy soil with compost and at least 10 hours of daily sunlight.

    (H) Potting soil and at least 6 hours of daily sunlight.

    (J) Potting soil and at least 14 hours of daily sunlight.

23. Which of the following best describes the difference between the two experiments?

    (A) In Experiment 1, light length per day was varied; in Experiment 2, the soil type was varied.

    (B) In Experiment 1, light length per day was constant; in Experiment 2, the soil type was varied.

    (C) In Experiment 1, the soil type was varied; in Experiment 2, light length per day was varied.

    (D) In Experiment 1, the soil type was varied; in Experiment 2, the amount of daily water was varied.

GO ON TO NEXT PAGE

24. If the researchers set up a third experiment similar to Experiment 2 where they tested the effect of the amount of daily sunlight on seeds grown in the potting soil, then based on the results of Experiments 1 and 2, they could reasonably predict which of the following about the average height of the resulting plants in Experiment 3?

(F) For all hours of sunlight exposure, plant height after eight weeks in Experiment 3 would be taller than plant height after eight weeks in Experiment 2.

(G) For all hours of sunlight exposure, plant height after eight weeks in Experiment 3 would be shorter than plant height after eight weeks in Experiment 2.

(H) For all hours of sunlight exposure, plant height after eight weeks in Experiment 3 would be similar to plant height after eight weeks in Experiment 2.

(J) Plant height for seeds exposed to ten hours of daily sunlight after eight weeks in Experiment 3 would be shorter than plant height of those grown in only sandy soil after eight weeks in Experiment 1.

25. If the researchers plot the results of Experiment 2 on a line graph with plant height on the y-axis and hours of daily sunlight on the x-axis, what would be true about the line that connects the plot points?

(A) The line would be horizontal.

(B) The line would increase gradually and then decrease.

(C) The slope of the line would be negative.

(D) The line would have a positive slope.

26. After conducting Experiments 1 and 2, researchers drew the conclusion that if pea seeds grown in sandy soil with compost were provided 16 hours of daily sunlight under the same conditions as the prior two experiments, their plant height after 8 weeks would measure no more than 65 cm. Is this conclusion reasonable based on the results of the two experiments?

(F) Yes, because the ratio of plant height to number of daily hours of sunlight decreased as the researchers increased the amount of daily sunlight exposure.

(G) Yes, because the ratio of plant height to number of daily hours of sunlight increased as the researchers increased the amount of daily sunlight exposure.

(H) No, because the ratio of plant height to number of daily hours of sunlight decreased as the researchers increased the amount of daily sunlight exposure.

(J) No, because the ratio of plant height to number of daily hours of sunlight increased as the researchers increased the amount of daily sunlight exposure.

27. Which of the following conclusions about plant growth is justified based on the two experiments?

(A) Plant height is increased when seeds receive a combination of increased nutrients, greater exposure to sunlight, and large amounts of water.

(B) Exposure to sunlight has a greater effect on plant height than soil type.

(C) Soil type influences plant height more significantly than either exposure to sunlight or water.

(D) Nutrients in the form of compost and synthetic fertilizers affect plant height similarly.

On a scale of 0 to 14, pH measures how acidic or alkaline a solution is. Most living aquatic organisms live at or near pH 7. Scientists from the United States Geological Survey (USGS) confirmed reports of increasing numbers of dead fish in small lakes and ponds within a 3,500 square km area of land over a six-month period, and no known pollutants had entered the affected area. The scientists checked the water quality of the ponds to determine the cause of the mass fish kills.

Experiment 1

The scientists took samples from 10 of the ponds that had experienced increased fish deaths (contaminated ponds) and another 10 ponds in the same area where increased numbers of deaths were not evident (healthy ponds).

Water samples were extracted from each of the 20 ponds for three consecutive mornings at the same time each day. Each sample was tested for temperature and pH levels. The results of the two measurements for the three samples were averaged for each site. The results for the 10 contaminated ponds were then averaged, and separate averages were calculated for the 10 healthy ponds. The averages for both were represented in Figures 1 and 2.

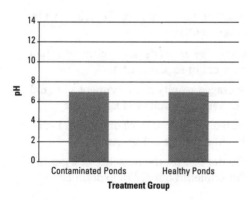

FIGURE 1

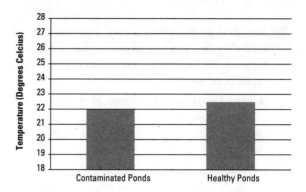

FIGURE 2

Experiment 2

High levels of nitrogen and phosphorus from fertilizer runoff can cause algae blooms, which may indicate increased decomposition and result-ant decreases in oxygen (O_2). The scientists conducted a second experiment in which they tested water samples from the same 20 ponds for nitrates (NO_2) and dissolved oxygen (O_2). As in Experiment 1, the measures were averaged and the results were recorded in Figure 3.

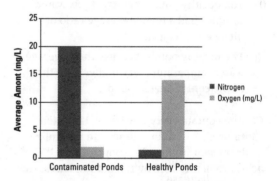

FIGURE 3

28. In Experiment 1, which of the following was true about the contaminated ponds as compared to the healthy ponds?

(F) The pH of the contaminated ponds was higher.

(G) The temperature of the contaminated ponds was higher.

(H) Both pH and temperature were higher in the contaminated ponds.

(J) Neither pH nor temperature was higher in the contaminated ponds.

GO ON TO NEXT PAGE

29. Based on the two experiments, which of the following best expresses the relationship between pH levels and O_2 levels in the two types of ponds?

(A) Pond water with low levels of O_2 had high levels of pH.

(B) Pond water with low levels of O_2 had low levels of pH.

(C) Pond water with high levels of O_2 had pH levels that were more alkaline than acidic.

(D) There is no apparent relationship between pH levels and O_2 levels in the two types of ponds.

30. Based on the information in the passage, which of the pond types likely had more algae blooms?

(F) The contaminated ponds, because their water samples had a higher average ratio of nitrogen to oxygen.

(G) The contaminated ponds, because their average water temperature was higher than that of the healthy ponds.

(H) The healthy ponds, because their water samples had a higher average ratio of nitrogen to oxygen.

(J) The healthy ponds, because their average water temperature was higher than that of the contaminated ponds.

31. Granite contains very few bases. Limestone contains bases. Natural bases can neutralize acids present in the rain, snow, or soil. If the acids are neutralized by the natural bases, the pH of the lake will remain about the same. If the scientists determined that runoff from snowmelt that feeds the ponds in the area has a pH lower than 7, based on information in the passage, which of the following is most likely regarding the composition of the rocks in the two types of ponds?

(A) The contaminated ponds contain more granite-based rock, and the healthy ponds contain more limestone-based rock.

(B) Both types of ponds contain limestone-based rock.

(C) Both types of ponds contain mostly granite-based rock.

(D) The contaminated ponds contain more limestone-based rock, and the healthy ponds contain more granite-based rock.

32. Rapidly moving water tends to contain more dissolved oxygen than do more stagnant bodies of water. Based on this information, which of the following was most likely?

(F) Water in the contaminated ponds moved more slowly than the water in the healthy ponds.

(G) Water in the healthy ponds moved more slowly than the water in the contaminated ponds.

(H) Water in the two pond types moved at about the same speed.

(J) The water depth of the contaminated ponds was greater than the water depth of the healthy ponds.

33. A scientist hypothesized that the large number of fish deaths was caused by acid rain in the area of the tested ponds. Do the results of the experiments justify this hypothesis?

(A) Yes, because the contaminated ponds contained low levels of nitrates.

(B) Yes, because the healthy ponds contained higher levels of dissolved oxygen than did the contaminated ponds.

(C) No, because average pH levels were the same for both types of ponds.

(D) No, because average temperatures were similar for both types of ponds.

34. Experiment 2 differed from Experiment 1 in that the scientists:

(F) tested fewer ponds in Experiment 1 than they did in Experiment 2.

(G) averaged results in Experiment 1 but did not average results in Experiment 2.

(H) tested for the presence of a gas in Experiment 1 but not in Experiment 2.

(J) did not test for the presence of a gas in Experiment 1 but did in Experiment 2.

Passage VI

A wave is an oscillation that occurs through matter or space. A wave consists of many characteristics that define it. The wavelength (λ) is the distance between two crests or two troughs as shown in Figure 1. The period (T) is the time it takes a wave to complete one oscillation. The frequency (v) is the number of periods per unit time, measured in hertz (Hz). The wave velocity (c) is the distance traveled in a period per unit time. The period of the wave completely defines its frequency, and vice versa. The following equations are used to determine wave period and velocity.

$$T = 1/v$$
$$c = \lambda / T$$

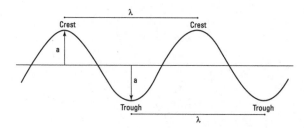

FIGURE 1

Oceanographers took 265 days' worth of data for deep-water waves in three bodies of water off the coast of the United States: the Atlantic Ocean, Pacific Ocean, and Gulf of Mexico. Table 1 charts the average wavelength and velocity for each body of water.

TABLE 1

	Velocity (c) in m/s	Wavelength (λ) in m	Frequency (v) in Hz
Atlantic Ocean	0.95	425	0.0022
Pacific Ocean	0.95	625	0.0015
Gulf of Mexico	0.86	650	0.0013

35. Compared to the average period (T) for a wave in the Pacific Ocean, the average period (T) for a wave in the Atlantic Ocean would likely be:

(A) the same, because the average velocity of waves in the Atlantic Ocean is the same as the average velocity of waves in the Pacific Ocean and the average wavelengths in both oceans are different.

(B) the same, because the average wavelength of waves in the Atlantic Ocean is the same as the average wavelength of waves in the Pacific Ocean and the average velocities of waves in both oceans are different.

(C) different, because the average wavelength of waves in the Atlantic Ocean is different from the average wavelength of waves in the Pacific Ocean and the average velocities of waves in both oceans is the same.

(D) different, because the average velocity of waves in the Atlantic Ocean is different from the average velocity of waves in the Pacific Ocean

36. According to information in the passage, which of the studied bodies of water most likely has the greatest average wave period (T)?

(F) The Atlantic Ocean has the greatest average period.

(G) The Pacific Ocean has the greatest average period.

(H) The Gulf of Mexico has the greatest average period.

(J) Both the Atlantic and Pacific Oceans have greater average periods than the Gulf of Mexico.

37. The frequency of a wave cycle in the deeper waters of another large body of water was found to be 0.0075 m/s. Based on information in the passage, its wavelength is most likely:

(A) less than 425 m.

(B) between 425 and 625 m.

(C) between 625 and 650 m.

(D) greater than 650 m.

GO ON TO NEXT PAGE

38. The amplitude (*a*) is the distance from the wave's centerline to its crest or trough. Based on information in the passage, which of the three bodies of water had the greatest average wave amplitude?

(F) Atlantic Ocean

(G) Pacific Ocean

(H) Gulf of Mexico

(J) The passage does not provide sufficient information to determine the greatest average wave amplitude.

39. For all tested bodies of water, as wavelength increased, frequency:

(A) decreased only.

(B) increased only.

(C) generally stayed the same.

(D) decreased then increased.

40. Which of the following would increase the average period for the waves of each of the bodies of water tested?

(F) Only increased velocity would increase the wave period.

(G) Only decreased wavelength would increase the wave period.

(H) Both decreased wavelength and increased wave velocity would increase the wave period.

(J) Both decreased wave velocity and increased wavelength would increase the wave period.

DO NOT TURN THE PAGE UNTIL TOLD TO DO SO **STOP** **DO NOT RETURN TO A PREVIOUS TEST**

Writing Test

TIME: 40 minutes

DIRECTIONS: Respond to the following prompt with a well-organized essay that follows the rules of Standard English. Write your essay on a separate sheet of lined paper.

Some people believe that the elderly population should be required to reapply for a driver's license and retake a driving test after they reach a particular age. As the Baby Boomer generation ages, more and more elderly drivers are taking to the roadways, and with the aging process comes a variety of issues that can lead to problems behind the wheel. Hearing loss, diminished vision, and longer reaction times are just a few of these possible concerns. Is it fair to force an entire population to reapply for something they have already earned and been using for decades? Given the increasing number of elderly drivers on the road, this is an important issue worthy of careful consideration.

Read and carefully consider these perspectives. Each suggests a particular way of thinking about whether elderly drivers should have to reapply for a driver's license once they reach a certain age.

Perspective 1: Elderly drivers should have to retake their driving tests once they reach a particular age for both their own safety and that of all others out on the roadways. Certain abilities decrease with age, and many of those abilities that do decrease are critical for maintaining safe driving practices.

Perspective 2: Forcing elderly drivers to retake their driving tests based on age, rather than a demonstrated lack of ability behind the wheel, is essentially a form of age discrimination and should not be put into practice.

Perspective 3: Requiring all elderly drivers to reapply for driver's licenses after they reach a given age puts an unnecessary strain on already limited resources in our DMVs and driving schools, and it would take attention away from the inexperienced teen population that is learning the rules of the road for the first time.

Essay Task

Write a unified, coherent essay in which you evaluate multiple perspectives as to whether elderly drivers should be forced to reapply for a driver's license once they reach a given age. In your essay, be sure to:

- Clearly state your own perspective on the issue and analyze the relationship between your perspective and at least one other perspective.

- Develop and support your ideas with reasoning and examples.

- Organize your ideas clearly and logically.

- Communicate your ideas effectively in standard written English.

Your perspective may be in full agreement with any of the others, in partial agreement, or wholly different.

DO NOT TURN THE PAGE UNTIL TOLD TO DO SO **STOP** DO NOT RETURN TO A PREVIOUS TEST

Chapter 20

Practice Exam 1: Answers and Explanations

So you've completed Practice Exam 1 in Chapter 19, and now you want to check your answers and find out your score. Well, you've come to the right place!

In this chapter, we provide detailed answer explanations for each problem on the test to help you understand why one answer is correct and the others aren't. Along the way, you find zillions of tips, traps, and other valuable information you can use when you face the actual exam on test day. So be sure to read all the explanations carefully — yes, even the ones you got right!

After the explanations, you find the scoring guide that helps you determine what score you would've received if this practice test were real. If you're short on time, skip to the end of this chapter, where we provide an abbreviated answer key.

English Test

1. **B.** The underlined part contains a semicolon, so you're likely dealing with proper punctuation. For the semicolon to be proper, the words before it and after it must express a complete thought. The words after the semicolon make up an independent clause; they have a subject *methods* and a verb *are* and don't begin with a subordinating conjunction. But the words before the semicolon begin with the subordinating conjunction *when*, so even though they have the subject and verb *it comes*, they don't form a complete thought. The semicolon is wrong and so are the colon and dash. The proper way to separate a beginning dependent clause from the rest of the sentence is with a comma. Choice (B) is correct. To review punctuation rules, flip to Chapter 5.

2. **H.** When you see *being* in an answer choice, that answer is almost always wrong. *Being* by itself doesn't function as a verb, so the sentence as provided has no verb. The same problem applies to Choice (J). The only option that gives the sentence a verb is Choice (H).

REMEMBER

When *ing* verbs such as *being* appear in sentences without the assistance of those trusty helping verbs, they can't function as verbs and complete the sentence. Always check sentences with *ing* verbs to make sure they include a helping verb to carry the load.

3. **A.** Quickly eliminate Choice (C). The form *its'* doesn't exist. Then check the pronoun *it* in the underlined portion. You know the contraction form (*it's*) is okay because you substitute *it is* for *it's* and the sentence sounds just fine. Eliminate Choice (B) because it contains the possessive form of *it*. Choice (D) has the proper form of *it*, but it improperly separates the beginning dependent clause from the rest of the sentence with a semicolon instead of a comma. Choice (A) is best.

4. **H.** The underlined word is ambiguous — *one* what? The pronouns offered by Choices (G) and (J) don't provide clarity, so the best answer is the clearly-stated noun in Choice (H).

5. **A.** The predominate question you ask yourself for an addition question is whether the proposed addition's topic is relevant to the substance of the paragraph. The paragraph is about finding a personal trainer, and the new sentence relates to that topic. So you can eliminate Choices (C) and (D). Of the two remaining answers, Choice (A) is best because the sentence offers ways to find a personal trainer rather than the benefits of using one.

6. **G.** When you encounter questions that ask for the least appropriate answer, find the option that has a different meaning from the other ones. The original word is *capable*, which means skilled or experienced. *Competent* is also a synonym. So eliminate those answers. The option that has a slightly different meaning is *useful*. To be of use isn't the same as being able. Choice (G) doesn't fit.

7. **B.** To communicate well and communicate clearly mean roughly the same thing, so Choice (A) is redundant. Choice (C) is redundant and improper because it uses the adjective *clear* to describe the verb *communicate*. Both Choices (B) and (D) eliminate the redundancy, but Choice (B) does so more precisely (think fewest words).

8. **G.** An underlined verb usually signals you to check for subject/verb agreement and verb tense issues. The verbs agree in number with *you*, so look for the proper tense. The rest of the paragraph is in present tense, which means the verb in this sentence should be too. Choice (G) is correct.

9. **D.** The underlined part is a transition. To pick the best transition, check the sentence or sentences before it and the sentence that contains it. The answer that brings the two thoughts together best is the correct transition. The idea before the transition is that you may wish to choose a trainer with a similar physique. Staying on track isn't an example of choosing someone with a similar body shape, so Choice (A) doesn't work. Choice (C) provides the same transition, so it must be wrong. Choice (B) shows contrast, and the ideas aren't opposite. The best solution is to eliminate the transition altogether.

TIP

If the answer choices contain two similar transition words, eliminate both. You can't have two right answers, so they must both be wrong.

10. **F.** To determine the best transition sentence, focus first on the paragraph it introduces. The following sentences provide information about the different personalities and styles of trainers. It's not about credentials, facilities, or missing workouts, so the best answer is Choice (F).

11. C. The underlined part creates a comma splice. The words before and after the comma both express complete thoughts. So Choice (A) is out. Choice (B) doesn't correct the punctuation problem. Rule out Choice (D) because a comma after an *and* that joins two complete thoughts is rarely proper. The answer has to be Choice (C). It fixes the comma splice by inserting a conjunction between the two independent clauses and doesn't create another punctuation error.

12. H. Choice (J) is irrelevant; nothing in the essay discusses healthy or unhealthy eating habits. Choice (F) deals with only one aspect of the preceding paragraphs, so it's not the best conclusion for the whole paragraph. Between Choices (G) and (H), Choice (H) is better. It more clearly sets up the topic of the next paragraph: deciding whether a trainer is a good fit.

13. B. The answer choices are the same but for the commas. The underlined part is a beginning prepositional phrase, so it should be separated from the rest of the sentence with a comma at the end. Choice (C) is out because it doesn't have a comma at the end of the phrase. Choice (D) sticks a comma between a subject *trainer* and its *verb will be*, so it can't be right. The comma between *decide* and *whether* in Choice (A) serves no purpose. The best answer is Choice (B); it places the comma at the end of the phrase and contains no unnecessary additional punctuation.

14. J. When you see an underlined verb, first check for subject/verb agreement. The subject of the sentence is compound: *weight loss and physical fitness*. Compound subjects take plural verbs. Don't be fooled by the ending *s*; the verb *starts* is singular. *Begins* is also singular. Choices (F) and (G) are wrong. Choice (H) tries to replace the verb with an *ing* word that can't work as a verb on its own. The answer is the plural verb *start* in Choice (J).

15. D. This big picture question actually asks you about the passage's main purpose. Focus on the exact language of the question and ask yourself whether the essay highlights some of the best ways to lose weight. It talks about one way to lose weight, but it doesn't go into any others. The correct answer likely begins with *No*. When you check Choices (C) and (D), you see that Choice (D) is the better answer. The essay only highlights one weight loss method, so it wouldn't provide much information about more than one way to lose weight.

16. G. In the underlined part, you have two nouns smack dab next to each other. Whenever you see a noun following another noun, the first noun is almost always possessive. Choice (G) puts the first noun in possessive form, so it's the right answer. Choice (H) uses the possessive form improperly.

A noun that's the object of a preposition (in this case *of*) is never possessive.

17. C. The placement of a comma before a coordinating conjunction such as *and*, *but*, or *or* is only proper when the conjunction joins two complete thoughts. *Known as America's pastime* isn't a complete thought, so beginning the underlined part with a conjunction can't be right. Eliminate Choices (A) and (B). If you omit the underlined words, the subject of the sentence becomes *known* and *means* is the verb. If that isn't bad enough, Choice (D) also separates the subject and verb with a single comma, which is never proper. Choice (C) is the answer that preserves *it* as the subject and doesn't commit any messy comma infractions.

18. G. Choices (F) and (J) contain punctuation problems, so you can eliminate them. Choice (F) is a run-on, and Choice (J) creates a comma splice. Punctuation is okay in Choices (G) and (H), so choose the better answer based on the transition it provides between the two thoughts. The cause-and-effect transition created by *therefore* makes more sense than the contrast suggested by *but*. So Choice (G) is correct.

19. A. Check the underlined possessive pronoun for proper form. *Their* renames *players*, so the plural format is proper and Choice (D) can't be right. The next step is to decide whether you need the possessive form. Because *skills* is a noun, the possessive form is necessary.

Whenever a noun immediately follows a pronoun or other noun, the first noun should be in possessive form.

20. J. All of the choices are synonyms for *simulates*, but Choice (J) doesn't fit as well as the others. The definition of *fake* implies that the pitches would be false, which isn't exactly the same as the similarity suggested by the original sentence and the other three answers.

21. B. The underlined word is a verb. Subject/verb agreement isn't an issue, so check tense. The rest of the paragraph is in present tense. Choice (B) is also in present tense, so it's the best answer.

22. F. Choices (G), (H), and (J) add unnecessary words to the original construction. *While* suggests *at the same time*, so any words or phrases that restate the simultaneous actions are redundant. Stick with the original in Choice (A).

23. A. Determine whether the addition relates to the topic of the paragraph. The paragraph is about what to consider when selecting a machine, so the phrase is relevant. The answer is likely *yes*. When you double-check the *no* options, you see that neither is true. The addition isn't distracting nor is it repetitive. So check out the *yes* options. Choice (B) is out because the passage suggests that a pitching machine is beneficial for players of *all* ages. The addition clarifies the reasons to consider the age of the player, so you can feel confident in selecting Choice (A).

24. H. Eliminate Choice (J) immediately because "more slower" creates two comparative forms, adding *more* and *er* to the adjective. The comparative form of one-syllable words is usually to add *er* to the end rather than *more* to the end, so Choice (G) is out. Choices (G), (J), and (F) are all wrong, too, because they use an adjective to describe the verb *releases*. The only answer that properly provides an adverb to describe the verb is Choice (H).

Adjectives never define active verbs. Only adverbs do.

25. D. *Advanced* and *elevated* have the same meaning, so it's redundant to use both. Eliminate Choices (A), (B), and (C) because they're repetitive and awkward. The solution is to eliminate the clause as suggested by Choice (D).

26. J. The lengthy underlined part appears in a sentence with a beginning participle (verb part) phrase. A beginning participle phrase *always* describes the subject of the sentence, so check the subject to see whether it makes sense that it would feature many customizable options. A *hitter*, *adjustments*, and *time* don't feature customizable options. Only *machines* can have customizable options. So Choice (J) is the only logical answer.

Whenever you see a lengthy underlined portion in a sentence with a participle phrase at the beginning, check for *dangling participles* — a phrase that doesn't logically describe the subject of the sentence.

27. C. Remember that you're looking for the answer that *doesn't* work. The proper preposition that fits with "to take part" is *in* not *of*. Therefore, the unacceptable answer is Choice (C).

The ACT often asks you to consider the proper use of prepositions, so when you see answer choices with different preposition options, determine which preposition fits the sentence.

28. F. If you can't quickly determine whether the proposed addition is relevant, check what comes after *because* in each answer to eliminate choices that aren't true. Choice (H) is a definite *no* because nowhere in the essay does the author stress that young players are more likely to benefit from pitching machines than older ones are. Eliminate Choice (G) because the author never claims that older players are more likely to experience the benefits of a pitching machine. Similarly, Choice (J) isn't true; the fourth paragraph doesn't contain a point that the suggested addition would build upon. Choice (F) is the best answer. The addition would contradict the author's statement in Paragraph 1 that pitching machines are a great resource for players at all levels.

29. C. Here's another redundancy error. In Choice (A), "want to" and "interest in" don't provide different information. *Interest* and *desire* have essentially the same meaning in Choice (B). To *aspire* and *endeavor* are similar verbs, so Choice (D) is also redundant. The only answer that isn't repetitive is Choice (C).

30. F. Notice *these* in the fifth paragraph. To properly reference "these pitching machines," the paragraph must follow another paragraph that introduces the machines. So Choice (G) must be wrong. The last paragraph sums up the points made elsewhere in the essay. A summary of points is usually included in the introduction or conclusion. You've already established that the paragraph can't be first, so it's best where it is now at the end of the passage.

TIP

Placing checkmarks in the essay for each of the possible positions for Paragraph 5 will save time. You won't have to continually check your answers for the potential options.

31. C. The underlined verb doesn't have a subject/verb agreement problem, so check the tense. The verb is in present perfect tense, which would indicate that Roosevelt's rising may still continue. Later you see that Roosevelt was around in 1900, so it's unlikely that he's still living, let alone rising. The correct tense is the simple past *rose*, Choice (C). Choice (D) is clearly incorrect because *has rose* isn't a proper verb construction, and Choice (B) can't be right because the other past actions in the paragraph are expressed in past tense.

32. F. To answer this question correctly, you need to know the meaning of *prominence*. *Prominence* is defined as "the state of being important or famous." While *infamy*, Choice (B), does mean "widely known," its connotation is negative, which doesn't match the tone of the passage or the author's overall impression of Teddy Roosevelt. Choices (C) and (D) are both antonyms of *prominence*, indicating that Teddy Roosevelt was not, in fact, very well known at all. The passage implies that Roosevelt was very well known, so stick with Choice (F) and leave the underlined portion as is.

33. B. Note that a comma exists before the underlined part, which means that *unit* is followed by a nonessential descriptive phrase. The element that describes *unit* is "the 'Rough Riders.'" So choose the answer that puts commas on both sides of that noun phrase. Choices (B) and (D) complete the task, but Choice (D) adds an incorrect comma after *Hill*. Choice (B) is best.

34. H. Inserting information about how and why McKinley was assassinated may be relevant to a passage about McKinley, but the passage is about Roosevelt and McKinley is not mentioned again. And how Roosevelt came to assume the presidency is not nearly as important as what he did once he had the job, so the proposed addition is irrelevant and Choices (F) and (G) are out. The passage doesn't mention McKinley elsewhere, so Choice (J) is wrong. Choice (H) is correct.

35. D. The proper way to construct the superlative form of a one-syllable word such as *young* is to add *–est* to the end. So the best answer is Choice (D).

36. F. The answer that is least like *exude* is Choice (F). All of the other choices mean something akin to "give off," but the meaning of *infuse* is slightly different. To infuse is to fill or "put in."

37. C. Don't let Choices (B) and (D) fool you. This question doesn't present a tense issue. The problem is parallelism. Each element of Roosevelt's description should be the same part of speech, and because *intelligent* and *well read* are adjectives, the correct answer must also be an adjective. Choice (C) provides parallel construction.

38. J. Note that the underlined part is an element of a series of activities Roosevelt participated in. To keep the series parallel, pick the activity expressed in Choice (J). Were you tempted by Choice (H)? Continuing the series with *engaging* seems to fit with the *-ing* construction of *participating*, but the third element doesn't begin with a gerund, so Choice (H) can't be correct.

Every element of a series should begin with the same grammatical format to maximize parallel structure.

39. B. Did you notice that *active* and *busy* have essentially the same meaning? Including both adjectives doesn't enhance the sentence, so the best answer is the more succinct Choice (B).

An omit option in the answer choices usually signals redundancy. Be careful, though. Indeed this question involves redundancy, but omitting the underlined words doesn't take care of the problem and changes the intended meaning of the sentence. The sentence isn't about Roosevelt becoming one of the presidents in the history of the United States; its point is that he was one of the busiest. If you choose to omit, reread the sentence without the underlined part to make sure it makes sense.

40. F. The original is correct. Choice (G) introduces passive voice "topics that were tackled" instead of the active "topics he tackled." Choice (H) creates a problem with subject/verb agreement. The plural *topics* needs the plural verb *were*. Choice (J) uses far too many words to convey the same idea as Choice (F). The best answer is Choice (F).

41. B. The underlined part provides a transition, so read the sentence before it and the sentence it's a part of to see how the ideas in each sentence relate. The preceding sentence states that Roosevelt invited union members and mine owners to work out a solution. The next sentence states that the owners refused to speak with the union. The two ideas suggest contrast: Roosevelt invited them, *but* the owners refused. The best answer is *however* in Choice (B). For Choice (C) to be correct, the idea that the owners refused would have to be the final step in a series, but the events continue after the sentence with the underlined words. Choices (A) and (C) create a cause-and-effect relationship, but Roosevelt's invitation didn't cause the owners to refuse. Choice (B) is best.

Questions about transition words often contain two answers that provide the same transition. Once you determine that two answers are similar, you can eliminate both. Because they can't both be right, they must both be wrong.

42. F. Consider the message in the proposed deletion. The sentence concludes a detailed example of one of Roosevelt's accomplishments. Choice (F) states this purpose clearly. Choice (J) is wrong because the sentence contains specific information rather than general observations. Choice (H) is also incorrect. The next paragraph is about railroads rather than mines, so you know that the sentence doesn't foreshadow a subsequent point. Without the last sentence, the reader wouldn't know the outcome of the incident, so Choice (G) can't be correct.

TIP

The correct answer to a deletion question is rarely that the deleted material is irrelevant or unnecessary. If you choose such an answer, make sure the deleted portion has nothing to do with the topic of the paragraph.

43. B. The underlined word and answer choices are prepositions. Choose the one that fits the meaning of the sentence. Notice that the main verb *controlled* is in simple past tense. So the event happened at one point in time. Later in the paragraph, you discover that the law designed to deal with railroad control was finalized in 1906. The railroads couldn't have controlled prices after the beginning of the 20th century, so Choice (C) is wrong. Choices (A) and (D) suggest continuation over a long period rather than a specific point in time, so they don't work. The best answer is Choice (B), which properly conveys that the control existed specifically in the first years of the 20th century.

44. J. The underlined part provides a transition between the statement that Roosevelt believed that the system gave companies too much power and hurt consumers with the information that he supported an act that regulated the railroad. Eliminate Choices (G) and (H) because they provide the same transition. They can't both be right. The remaining choices suggest an example or a cause and effect. Supporting the act isn't an example of Roosevelt's belief. Instead, his belief is the *reason* for his support of the act. The best answer is Choice (J) because this shows cause and effect.

45. C. The apostrophes in the answer choices should clue you into checking for possessive form. The underlined word is a noun followed by the noun phrase "financial records." A noun followed by another noun or noun phrase almost always indicates possessive form. So your answer will contain an apostrophe and you can eliminate Choice (B). Choice (D) is wrong because the plural of *company* is *companies*. The remaining choices require you to determine whether the noun is plural or singular. It must be plural because if it were singular, it would be preceded by an article such as *the* or *a*. The way to make *companies* possessive is to end the word with an apostrophe. Choice (C) is correct.

TIP

When you see possessive form in the ACT English test answers, the correct answer will almost always be possessive. If you pick an answer that isn't possessive, double-check to make you haven't missed something.

46. H. The subject that goes with *enables* is *virtues*, which is plural. So the verb must be the plural *enable* rather than the singular *enables*. The only answer to correct the error is Choice (H). Choice (J) is there to distract you. The verb is the issue; you don't need to give a thought to whether *World Wide Web* or *Internet* is better.

TIP

When you encounter an underlined verb, check first to see that it has the same number (plural or singular) as the subject.

47. D. The display of three long answers and one short one is usually a clue that the question tests redundancy. When you see this format, check for repetition. *Simple* and *easy* have the same meaning, so Choice (A) is wrong. Choices (B) and (C) contain similar repetition. The one-word answer to these questions is almost always right. Pick Choice (D).

48. J. Believe it or not, the subject of this sentence is the noun clause "what it has failed to accomplish." The comma after *accomplish* in Choice (F) separates the subject from the verb *is*, and a single comma is never correct when it lies between the subject and the verb. Choices (G) and (H) place a comma in the middle of the noun clause, so they can't be right. The correct punctuation is Choice (J) with no commas at all.

49. **A.** The underlined part provides a transition between the statement that computers crash and remote repair provides a great resource. The ideas aren't contrasting, so eliminate Choices (B) and (C). Repair isn't an example of a computer crash, so Choice (D) is wrong. The best solution is to leave the sentence as is; computers crash so computer repair is great. Choice (A) is correct.

50. **H.** Eliminate Choices (F) and (G) because *anyone* refers to a person and *who* is the pronoun that refers to people. The difference between the remaining answers is the comma after *anyone*. The comma indicates that the clause that begins with *who* isn't essential to the meaning of the sentence, but without it, the sentence would suggest that remote computer repair is great for *anyone* instead of *anyone who owns a business*. Choice (H) without the comma is better.

51. **C.** The issue in this sentence is parallel structure. Each element of the series begins with a verb except the second. You know the sentence isn't okay as is, so eliminate Choice (A). Choice (B) can't be right because a colon must be preceded by a complete thought. The words that come before the colon make up a dependent clause. Of the remaining two answers, only Choice (C) initiates the second element *viruses* with a verb, so it's the best answer.

52. **F.** Examine the added commas in the answer choices. Those in Choice (G) suggest that "or even weeks without your machine" is nonessential information that you can easily remove without changing the meaning of the sentence. Without the words, though, you don't know what you're waiting for. Choice (J) creates the same confusion by indicating that "without your machine" isn't essential. If you extracted "even weeks" from the sentence as suggested by Choice (H), the last part would read "wait days or without your machine," which makes no sense. It also eliminates the necessary comma after *machine* that separates the beginning phrase from the main idea of the sentence. Because Choices (G), (H), and (J) aren't correct, you know Choice (F) must be right. It suggests that you don't have to wait days or weeks if you seek remote repair.

53. **D.** To answer this question correctly, pick the preposition that goes with result. English speakers say "as a result of" rather than "as a result from," "as a result with," or "as a result as." Choice (D) is best.

TIP

An underlined preposition means you need to read the sentence very carefully to make sure you choose the answer that provides the intended meaning.

54. **G.** "Rather than paying you an actual visit" isn't a complete sentence, so it needs to be part of the sentence that comes before it. Eliminate Choice (F). Choices (H) and (J) present other ways of punctuating two complete thoughts in the same sentence, so they also can't be right. The best answer is Choice (G), which correctly completes the rest of the first sentence of this paragraph with the remainder of the description of remote computer repair. There's no need for any punctuation.

55. **C.** *They're* is the contraction of "they are" and doesn't show possession. You need possessive form because you have a pronoun *they* followed by a noun. Choice (A) is incorrect. Choice (B) is awkward and incorrect because "his or her" is singular and the renamed noun is *people*, which is plural. *There* indicates place not possession, so Choice (D) is wrong. The possessive form of *they* is *their*, so pick Choice (C).

56. **H.** Check the purpose of the underlined part. It provided additional information about the factor that determines whether a repair will take hours or minutes. That function is best described by Choice (H). The phrase isn't a detail about or example of remote repair, so Choices (F) and (G) can't be right. The next paragraph summarizes the passage, so the phrase doesn't provide foreshadowing as indicated by Choice (J).

57. **C.** Eliminate Choices (A), (B), and (D) because they're redundant. The paragraph already makes the points in Choices (A) and (B), and the idea in Choice (D) is indicated in previous paragraph statements. Choice (C) completes the description of the time benefits of remote repair, so it's the best answer.

58. **J.** This question tests your knowledge of parallel structure. All the verbs in the sequence must be written in the same form, and because the last element of the series begins with *need* and isn't underlined, the other parts of the series can't begin with an *–ing* verb. You can eliminate Choices (F), (G), and (H) because all contain gerund forms. The only answer choice that keeps the series consistent is Choice (J).

59. **D.** The underlined portion contains clarifying information, because it stresses that remote computer repair is great for someone who needs to get back to work ASAP. So, you don't want to eliminate it entirely, as Choice (D) indicates. Choices (A), (B), and (C) are all acceptable ways of saying *as quickly as possible*, so Choice (D) is the correct answer.

Don't choose the option to omit every time you see it in the answer choices. Carefully evaluate each question to make sure the deletion is appropriate.

60. **F.** To answer this question correctly, you first need to determine whether the fourth paragraph appears out of place. Given that it's the concluding paragraph and nicely summarizes the information contained in the previous paragraphs without introducing any new information, it's likely fine where it is. To be sure, check the other options. The first paragraph provides a clear introduction to the passage, so eliminate Choice (G). Choice (H) isn't logical because you wouldn't state the benefits of remote repair before you define it. Choice (F) is correct.

61. **C.** This sentence has a lot going on. Simplify your approach by first eliminating Choices (B) and (D). *Amount* refers to elements that aren't countable; *number* refers to those that are. You can count resources, so the proper word is *number*. Then carefully examine the remaining two answers. They likely sound fine, but notice that Choice (A) contains the beginning phrase "competing for a limited number of resources." Beginning phrases describe the subject, and this sentence's subject is "characteristics and behaviors." Characteristics and behaviors don't compete for resources; organisms do. So Choice (A) contains a dangling participle. Choice (C) corrects the problem by making *competing* the subject of the sentence and eliminating the beginning phrase.

62. **G.** The underlined word is a verb, so check for subject/verb agreement. The subject is the singular *competition* and not the plural *resources*, so the verb must be singular. The only singular option is Choice (G).

63. **B.** The underlined pronoun has no clear reference. The nouns that precede the pronoun are *competition, resources, evolution, characteristics,* and *behaviors*. None of these nouns logically names something that can improve its ability to compete. Because you can't point to the particular noun the pronoun renames, you don't know whether the proper form is *it* or *they*. The only possible answer is Choice (B) because it clarifies exactly what has the ability to compete.

Whenever you encounter an underlined pronoun, look for the noun it renames. If you can't point to the specific noun in the preceding sentence or two, the issue is an unclear pronoun reference. Look for the answer that replaces the pronoun with a specific noun.

64. **J.** Eliminate answers that have the same nuance of meaning as "carving out." The remaining choice will be the least appropriate. Choices (F), (G), and (H) duplicate the original idea of the organism's creating a way to live. The meaning of *capture* in Choice (J) is slightly different. It implies that the organism is taking the living from something else rather than creating it on its own.

65. **D.** Search the fifth sentence for ideas that need prior reference. The sentence refers to "this" (meaning "this statement"), so it needs to follow the sentence that contains that particular statement. The sentence in the paragraph that's most like saying that each species establishes its own niche is the third. Moving the fifth sentence after Sentence 3 also defines *niche* before it's further described in the fourth sentence. Choice (D) is best.

66. **G.** The original sentence sets up the two components of a niche using a colon. You know that a dash may replace a colon, so Choice (J) works and should be eliminated. Choice (H) properly uses a comma to designate the two types, so cross out that option. Choice (F) is okay; it creates two independent clauses and punctuates them properly with a comma and conjunction. The problem answer is Choice (G). It implies that niches have two components that are both abiotic and biotic. Because it distorts the message, Choice (G) is the least appropriate substitute and therefore, the most appropriate answer.

67. **B.** The underlined series has a problem with parallel structure. The first and third elements are noun phrases, but the second element is a clause. Choice (C) contains a similar issue by making the third element a clause. Choices (B) and (D) correct the parallel structure, but Choice (D) introduces a pronoun with an unclear reference. *Its* could refer to *niche*, but it could also refer to *category*. The answer that corrects the original without creating a new problem is Choice (B).

68. **H.** The pronoun *whom* refers only to people, so Choices (F) and (G) are wrong. Choice (J) omits the preposition that goes with *interact* and states that a species interacts predators, prey, and so on rather than interacts *with* them. The best answer is Choice (H) because it contains the proper pronoun and includes the necessary preposition.

69. **A.** Evaluating this sentence may be easier if you simplify it: Species compete whenever their niches overlap. It sounds right the way it is, but check the other possibilities to be sure. Choice (B) is incorrect; the species don't compete *although* their niches overlap. It doesn't make sense that species compete *whether* their niches overlap, so Choice (C) is wrong. Choice (D) changes the beginning dependent clause to an independent clause, so it can't be right. The best answer is Choice (A).

70. **G.** The underlined verb doesn't agree with the number of its subject. The subject *niche* is singular, so it needs the singular verb *overlaps*. All of the other options suggest plural verbs. Pick Choice (G).

71. **A.** The underlined transition joins together a sentence that presents the ways a species can win a competition with a sentence that lists the three possible results of a competition. The second sentence isn't an example of winning nor does it present an opposite position. So Choices (B) and (C) can't be right. At first, Choices (A) and (D) may seem to provide the same transition, but *finally* suggests the final element or step in a chronological list. Choice (A) provides the more precise transition by suggesting a conclusion rather than a chronological end.

72. **G.** The underlined pronoun renames "one species," which is singular. The plural *they* is incorrect, and Choices (F) and (H) must be wrong. The singular pronoun *it* corrects the problem. Choice (G) is best.

If you picked Choice (J), you fell for the trap. If you omit the underlined words, you mess with the parallel structure of the series. The elements would in essence be these: one species may win, lose and be forced to retreat, or two species may find a way. The first and third are clauses, but the second is a phrase.

REMEMBER

It's always a good idea to reread the sentence with your answer choice inserted, but especially when you've chosen to omit the underlined words.

73. **C.** Even if you don't remember that Darwin was a firm believer in "survival of the fittest," you can probably still see why Choice (C) is the best option. Choices (A) and (D) contradict the earlier statements that competition only occasionally involves direct combat and that species may occupy the same niche, so they can't be right. Choice (B) repeats an earlier point, so it isn't the best choice. Stick with Choice (C).

74. **J.** The easiest answers to eliminate are Choices (G) and (H). The words that follow *qualities* don't create a complete thought, so the semicolon in Choice (H) is wrong. The words that precede the colon in Choice (G) don't form a complete thought, so that option is punctuated improperly. The first comma in Choice (F) may be okay, but the comma following "such as" is never proper. By process of elimination, Choice (J) is best.

75. **A.** Information in the fourth paragraph directly piggybacks what is discussed in the third paragraph about competition among species. So Paragraph 4 is likely positioned properly as is, but it's a good idea to check out the other options to make sure. There's no way any passage would begin with "in addition to," so Choice (B) is out. Neither the first nor the second paragraph discusses interspecific competition. The best answer is Choice (A).

Mathematics Test

1. **B.** According to the order of operations, exponential parts of the equation always must be solved before multiplication parts of the equation. Because $x = 3$, $2^x = 8$ because $2 \times 2 \times 2 = 8$. Next, that value must be multiplied by the value of y, which is 2, giving you the final answer of 16, which is Choice (B).

   Beware of Choice (E), which mixes up the order of operations by multiplying 2 and y and then raising the resulting value of 4 to the power of x.

2. **F.** A geometric series is a series of numbers in which each number is multiplied by a common value to determine the number that comes after it. In this particular geometric series, the first number is multiplied by 2 to find the second number, which is then multiplied by 2 to find the third number, and so on, because $0.75 \times 2 = 1.5$ and $1.5 \times 2 = 3$. Find the 5th term, then, by multiplying the 4th term (6) by 2 to get Choice (F), 12.

3. **A.** To find the measure of $\angle ABD$, you can set up an equation calling the measure of $\angle ABD = 3x$ and $\angle DBC = x$. $\angle ABD$ and $\angle DBC$ combine to measure $180°$ because A, B, and C are collinear. In this case, $3x + x = 180$. Simplify this equation to $4x = 180$. When you divide both sides by 4, you get $x = 45$. Don't stop there and pick Choice (E), though. That's the measure of $\angle DBC$. Multiply 45 by 3 to get $135°$, which is the measure of $\angle ABD$.

   If you picked Choice (C), you incorrectly presumed that A, B, and C form a right angle.

4. **K.** Divide by multiplying 3 by $\frac{8}{3}$. The 3s cancel, so the answer is 8.

   Don't get caught picking Choice (J), which simplifies the 3 in the numerator and the 3 in the numerator of the denominator to equal 1. That's not the way to divide a fraction.

REMEMBER

   When you divide by a fraction, you solve by simply multiplying by the reciprocal of the second fraction.

5. **D.** Angle a and the 37° are supplementary, which means their sum measures 180°. So the measure of angle a is $180 - 37$ or 143°. Because lines C and D are parallel and crossed by a transversal, angle a corresponds with angle b, which means they have the same degree measure. So angle b also measures 143°.

6. **F.** Before you find the chance that Ross will pick two black socks, you first have to find the chance that the first sock he picks will be black. That chance is $\frac{2}{4}$ or $\frac{1}{2}$ because 2 out of 4 socks are black. Then, you have to multiply that fraction by the probability that the second sock will be black. Be careful, because the second probability isn't also $\frac{1}{2}$ because Ross has already picked a black sock from the drawer. After the first sock, only 3 socks remain in the drawer and only 1 is black. So the chance that the second sock he picks will be black is actually $\frac{1}{3}$. The chance that both socks Ross picks will be black can then be found by multiplying $\frac{1}{2}$ by $\frac{1}{3}$, which is $\frac{1}{6}$. Pick Choice (F).

7. **D.** This question concerns a simple right triangle. The following figure shows the values of the leg lengths.

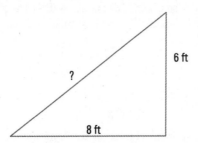

The ramp length is the hypotenuse. Memorize the 3-4-5 Pythagorean triple; ACT math questions incorporate it frequently. The lengths of the sides of this triangle are just those of the traditional 3-4-5 triangle times 2, so the missing side is 10 feet.

REMEMBER

If you don't remember Pythagorean triples, you can find the length of the ramp, which is the hypotenuse in this case, by plugging values into the Pythagorean theorem ($a^2 + b^2 = c^2$) and solving for c, but it's much faster to rely on common side ratios of right triangles.

8. **J.** To solve this expression, change the fractions so they have the same denominator. The least common denominator of this specific set of fractions is 6 because all three denominators evenly go into it. The first fraction doesn't change because its denominator is already 6, but $\frac{1}{2}$ converts to $\frac{3}{6}$ and $\frac{1}{3}$ converts to $\frac{2}{6}$. Your next task is to find the sum of $\frac{1}{6} + \frac{3}{6} + \frac{2}{6}$. When adding fractions with common denominators, just add the numerators and put the sum over the common denominator. In this case, the answer is $\frac{6}{6}$, which simplifies to 1, Choice (J).

9. **C.** Rather than attempting to factor this complex quadratic, you can work more quickly by applying FOIL to all the answer possibilities. Start with the middle answer. You just need to figure out the middle term because the first and last terms of each answer choice are the same. The product of the outer terms of Choice (C) is $-6x$; the inner terms multiply to $2x$. The sum of the outer and inner terms is $-4x$, so Choice (C) is correct.

TIP

An alternative and possibly quicker way to factor quadratic equations when the coefficient of the first term is not 1 is called the "dream method." The dream method requires you to multiply the coefficient of the x^2 term by the last term in the quadratic. In this case, you multiply 4 by -3 to get -12. Then, set up blank terms that begin with the original coefficient of the original first term multiplied by the variable, like this: $(4x+)(4x+)$. Then find the factors of −12 that add up to the coefficient of the middle term in the original expression, in this case −4. These factors are 2 and −6. Place these values in the blank terms you just created to make $(4x+2)(4x-6)$. Then reduce each term as much as you can to get your final answer of $(2x+1)(2x-3)$.

10. **J.** Make answering this question quick and simple by noticing first that the point on the x-axis that also lies on the y-axis has an x-coordinate of 0. The x-coordinate is the first number in the ordered pair. Eliminate Choices (F), (G), and (K) because they don't have x-coordinates of 0. You know the answer is either Choice (H) or (J). Substitute 0 for x in the equation and solve for y. That gives you $0+4y=28$ so $y=7$. The point that $7x+4y=28$ intersects the y-axis is (0, 7), Choice (J).

You can also approach this problem by solving the original equation for y to put it in the format of the equation of a line: $y=mx+b$, where b is the y-intercept. When you solve for y, you get $y=-\dfrac{7}{4}x+7$. So you know the y-intercept is 7. The only answer with a y-coordinate of 7 is Choice (C).

11. **A.** When simplifying expressions that involve only multiplication, you can simply combine like variables. First, multiply the numerators to get $3x^4y^2$. Then multiply the denominators to get $6y$. Divide the y terms: $\dfrac{y^2}{y}=y$. The coefficients reduce to $\dfrac{1}{2}$ to make the final answer $\dfrac{x^4y}{2}$. When you multiply the same variable raised to powers, you combine the terms by simply adding the powers. To divide the same variable raised to powers, subtract the exponents.

REMEMBER

12. **C.** The correct formula is the one that shows how much Jacob paid for the flour, sugar, and trays.

If the proper formula isn't immediately obvious to you, you could spend a whole bunch of time trying to figure it out. Or you could save some time and substitute numbers for the variables in the problem to see which answer works out. We vote for saving time!

When you're substituting numbers for variables, pick easy numbers to work with. Say that Jacob bought 10 pounds of flour for $3.50 a pound and 10 pounds of sugar for $4.50 a pound. That means that $x=10$ and $s=10$. Write this information on your test booklet. Jacob spent $35 on flour (10 times $3.50) and $45 on sugar (10 times $4.50). He also spent $18 for pans (3 times $6). The total cost is $98. Plug your made-up numbers into the answer choices to see which one equals 98.

Choice (C) is the only answer that equals $98 because $3.50(10)+$4.50(10)+$18.00=$98.00$.

13. **E.** To solve a series of equations, you must cancel out one of the variables. Because the question asks that you find y, it makes sense to cancel out x in order to isolate y. To do this, multiply the bottom equation by −2 and stack the two equations like this:

$$2x+3y=6$$
$$-6x+2y=-16$$

When you add the equations, the x terms cancel, the y terms add to $5y$, and the sum of the right side of the equation is −10: $5y=-10$. When you solve for y, you get −2.

14. **D.** When converting a number in scientific notation, the easiest trick is to just move the decimal to the right the same number of places as the power of the 10. In this case, moving the decimal to the right −3 positions is the same as moving it to the left 3 positions. Write

the number with extra zeros on each end and no decimal point in your test booklet. The number looks something like this:

00001540000

Now place the decimal in its original position between the 1 and the 5 and move it to the left 3 places to come up with the answer 0.00154. Then check your answer by moving the decimal to the right 3 places and see if you get the same number as in the original scientific notation number. You do!

15. **B.** To find the number of adult tickets sold, create a system of equations that models the given information. The equation for the total of 40 tickets sold could be $a + c = 40$, where a is the number of adult tickets sold and c is the number of children's tickets sold. The other equation is $\$8a + \$5c = \$251$ because the price of adult tickets times the number of adult tickets sold plus the price of children's tickets times the number of children's tickets sold equals the total cost of tickets sold. Because you want to find the number of adult tickets sold, it makes sense to cancel out the c variable and solve for a. First, multiply the first equation by -5 to get $-5a - 5c = -200$. Add that equation to $8a + 5c = 251$:

$$8a + 5c = 251$$
$$-2a - 5c = -200$$

Adding up these two equations, you find that $3a = 51$. When you divide both sides by 3, you find that $a = 17$.

16. **K.** First of all, you can tell from the graph that the parabola faces downward, so the x^2 term has to be negative. Right away, you can eliminate Choices (F) and (J). You can also tell that the graph has a vertical displacement of 3. Vertical displacement is indicated by the term that is added to or subtracted from the x^2 term. This means that you can get rid of Choice (G). You're down to Choices (H) and (K). The difference is that Choice (H) adds the 1 in parentheses and Choice (K) subtracts the 1. When the parabola moves in a positive direction horizontally, the number is subtracted from, not added to, x inside the parentheses. This means that the final answer is Choice (K).

You can check your answer by testing the vertex point in your equation to make sure it is valid. In this case, that point is $(1, 3)$. When you plug the point into the equation in the answers, you get $3 = -(1-1)^2 + 3$ or $3 = 3$, which is true.

17. **B.** Solve the inequality just as you would an ordinary equation. Move all the constants to the right and all the x terms to the left. When you do, you end up with $-5x < 7$. Divide both sides by 5 to get a final solution for x: $x > -\frac{7}{5}$.

REMEMBER

When you divide both sides of an inequality by a negative value, you change the direction of the sign.

18. **J.** The standard form of the equation of a line is $y = mx + b$, where m is the slope and b is the y-intercept. You can tell from the graph that the y-intercept is at $(0, 4)$ so $b = 4$. You can eliminate Choices (G) and (H) because when you solve them for y, they result in a b value of 3 instead of 4.

The next order of business is to determine the slope of the line by finding rise over run: $m = \frac{y_2 - y_1}{x_2 - x_1}$. The two given points on the graph are $(0, 4)$ and $(-3, 0)$. To find the slope, plug the coordinates into the equation: $m = \frac{0 - 4}{-3 - 0}$ or $m = \frac{4}{3}$. The only answer that results in a slope of $\frac{4}{3}$ when you solve for y is Choice (J).

19. D. When you add logs with the same base, you multiply the number being logged. So rewrite the question as $\log_6(9x) = 2$. Plug in your answer options for x. Choice (D) is correct because the product of 9 and 4 is 36, which is the value you get when you multiply 6 by itself two times.

The easiest way to solve logs is to know that the log base raised to the power of the answer equals the number being logged. In this problem, $6^2 = 9x$, so $x = 4$. Be careful to not get caught picking Choice (E), which adds rather than multiplies the numbers being logged.

20. H. Plug the values you know into the equation for volume of a circular cylinder: $V_c = \pi r^2 h$. To solve for V, you need the radius of the base and the height of the cylinder. The diameter is 10 cm, so the radius is half that, 5 cm. The height is 15 cm. The resulting solution is this:

$$V_c = (5cm)^2(15cm)\pi$$
$$V_c = (25cm)(15cm)\pi$$
$$V_c = 375\pi$$

After you memorize simple geometry formulas, questions that ask you to find the value of a shape's dimension will be some of the easiest and quickest to solve in the ACT Math section.

21. A. The original point A lies at $(-2, 4)$. Because the whole quadrilateral is reflected over the horizontal line $y = 2$, to find the reflected point A, you only need to reflect point A over the line $y = 2$. The x-coordinate of the point does not change because $y = 2$ is a horizontal line. You can eliminate Choices (B) and (C) because they don't contain x-coordinates of -2.

The original y value of point A is 4, which is 2 units above the line $y = 2$, so reflected point A is 2 units below the line $y = 2$. This makes the y value of reflected point A equal to 0 and the point $(-2, 0)$, which is Choice (A).

If you picked Choice (D), you reflected point A over the x-axis instead of the line $y = 2$.

22. J. This question is asking for all values of x that would make the quadratic equal to a number greater than 0. To solve it, factor the polynomial to give you $(x + 5)(x - 4)$. (If you need a refresher on how to factor polynomials, see Chapter 10.) So the values for x that would make the expression equal to 0 are $x = -5$ and $x = 4$.

To find the values for x that make the expression greater than 0, consider that the expression is positive when both factors equal positive values or when both factors have negative values. The first factor is positive when $x > -5$ and the second factor is positive when $x > 4$, so both factors are positive when $x > 4$. At this point, you know the answer is Choice (J) because it's the only option that includes $x > 4$ and one other set of values for when the factors are both negative. Choice (K) doesn't take into consideration that the expression will be positive when both of its factors are negative.

Another way to approach this question is by substituting answer choices into the expression. Eliminate Choices (F) and (H) because although it's true that values over 20 make the solution greater than 0, so do some values that are less than or equal to 20. Choice (G) is wrong because values greater than 4 make the expression positive and some values less than 4 (say 3) make the expression negative. To evaluate Choice (J), try 5 and -6 for x in the expression. Both make its solution greater than 0, so Choice (J) is right and Choice (K) is wrong.

23. C. First, eliminate Choices (A) and (B). If Klaus gave money away, he started out with more than $280. Then set up an equation. If Klaus gave 20% of his money and ended up with $280, that $280 is 80% of what he originally received. You can write 80% as 0.8 and *of* means multiply, so the equation is $0.8x = \$280$. To solve, divide each side by 0.8: $x = 350$. Choice (C) is correct.

Be sure not to just take 20% of the $280. Remember, the $280 already has been reduced by 20%, so 20% of that value is actually less than the amount that Klaus put in the bank.

24. **K.** This question is just a proportion in disguise! Set it up to solve for dollars. Fifty dollars for 20 gallons is the same as x dollars for 16 gallons: $\frac{\$50}{20 \text{ gal}} = \frac{x}{16 \text{ gal}}$.

Cross multiply and solve:

$$(50)(16) = 20x$$
$$800 = 20x$$
$$40 = x$$

The correct answer is Choice (K).

25. **D.** The equation you use to find cosine is $\cos = \frac{\text{adjacent}}{\text{hypotenuse}}$. When you look at the figure, the side adjacent to angle C is a and the hypotenuse of triangle ABC is side b. So $\cos C = \frac{a}{b}$.

REMEMBER

You'll for sure encounter at least a couple trig questions that require you to apply the trig identities, so memorize the acronym SOH CAH TOA. Know it cold for test day.

26. **G.** To find the midpoint of a line segment, find the average of both the x- and y-coordinates of the endpoints. The average of the x-coordinates is half of $-1 + 5$, which is 2. Eliminate any answer that doesn't have an x-coordinate of 2. That leaves you with Choices (G) and (J). Find the midpoint of the y-coordinates. Half of $3 - 5$ is -1. The answer is Choice (G).

If you picked Choice (F), you found the difference between the points instead of the sum.

27. **D.** To solve the equation for y, you must get y on its own side of the equation. First, subtract each side by 8 to get $x - 8 = 3y$. Then just divide both sides of the equation by 3 to get $\frac{x-8}{3} = y$, which is Choice (D).

If you forgot to also divide 8 by 3, you would have mistakenly selected Choice (A).

28. **F.** Label the whole line (from A to D) with a distance of 28, from A to C with 15, and from B to D with 18. It's easy to see that the distance from B to C is the overlapping portion of what you just labeled. Add the distance from A to C and the distance from B to D to get 33. Subtract 28 from 33 to get the distance of the overlap; the length between B and C is 5. Choice (F) is the answer.

TIP

Another way to solve this problem is to set up an equation. Call the distance between B and C x because that's the unknown. So the distance between A and B is $15 - x$ and the distance between C and D is $18 - x$. Set the sum of the three shorter segments equal to the longer length between A and D: $(15 - x) + x + (18 - x) = 28$. Simplify to get $33 - x = 28$ and you can see that x (the distance between B and C) equals 5.

29. **C.** To answer this question, set up a simple equation. Because Emma and Nadine both travel the same distance, you need to set up an equation where Emma's miles = Nadine's miles. Remember to convert minutes to hours because the units are in miles per hour rather than miles per minute. In hours, 40 minutes is $\frac{2}{3}$ of an hour. Multiply Emma's speed times the number of hours she spent in the car and set it equal to the number of hours Nadine spent in the car times Nadine's speed:

$$(45)\left(\frac{2}{3}\right) = (x)(1)$$
$$30 = x$$

Nadine's speed is 30 mph, which is Choice (C).

30. K. The fastest way to approach this problem is to notice that the measure of the perimeter is the same as the perimeter of a 23-by-18 rectangle. The length is $19 + 4$ or 23, and the width is $13 + 5$ or 18. So the perimeter is $(2)(23) + (2)(18)$, which is $46 + 36$ or 82. The answer is Choice (K).

31. A. To find the circumference of a circle, you need to know its radius. The question doesn't give you the radius of the circle, but you do know its area. Can you find the radius from the area? Sure! Apply the area formula: $16\pi = \pi r^2$. Divide both sides by pi to get $16 = r^2$. Find the square root of both sides to determine that the radius is 4. Then you can plug the value of the radius in the formula for circumference:

$$C = 2\pi 4$$
$$C = 8\pi$$

The answer is Choice (A).

TIP

Memorize the equations for area and circumference of a circle; you'll use them a bunch on the ACT. To refresh your memory, here they are: $A = \pi r^2$ and $C = 2\pi r$.

32. G. The median value of Cydney's math test scores is the middle score. First, put the scores in ascending order. Then determine the total number of test scores; there are 19. Because the number of test scores is odd, the median is the one value in the middle. If the total number were even, the median would be the average of the two middle values. You can then find the median by crossing off the smallest and biggest numbers on either end of the set, one by one, until you get to the middle. Or you can divide 19 by 2 to get 9.5. That tells you that there are 9 values to the left of the median and 9 to the right. Either way, the middle value is 87.

33. C. The first expression gives you the equation for the output, and the second tells you what value (the input) to substitute for x in the first. To find $f(2x+2)$, you plug in $2x+2$ for x in $x - 3$. So the output when the input is $2x + 1$ is $(2x + 2) - 3$, which simplifies to $2x - 1$. The answer is Choice (C).

TIP

When you see a function question on the ACT, get excited. These are simple substitution problems, so they're really easy!

34. J. The ACT Math test will likely have at least one question that gives you an equation in a word problem and asks you to solve for one of the variables. All you have to do is plug in the proper values for the other variables and solve.

You are given the equation $v = at + v_0$ and are asked to find the acceleration (a). Reformat the equation so you're solving for a. Subtract v_0 from both sides and then divide both sides by t. The equation to solve for acceleration is $a = \frac{v - v_0}{t}$. Now find the values for the other variables. You know that initially the car travels 10 meters per second, so plug in 10 for v_0 to get $a = \frac{v - 10}{t}$. Next, note that the time that the car accelerates is 10 seconds, so plug in 10 for t: $a = \frac{v - 10}{10}$. You're told that the final velocity is 30 meters per second, so substitute 30 for v and solve:

$$a = \frac{30 - 10}{10}$$
$$a = \frac{20}{10}$$
$$a = 2$$

The answer is Choice (J).

35. B. Digits can be repeated and there are 10 different digits from 0 to 9. Letters cannot be repeated and there are 26 possibilities in the alphabet. Apply the multiplication principle by multiplying the total possibilities for each element of the license plate. There are 10 for the first position, 10 for the second, 26 for the third, and 25 for the fourth because you can't repeat the letter in the third position. The product of 10, 10, 26, and 25 is 65,000.

If you picked Choice (A), you calculated the problem as though the digits could not be repeated, but letters could be. Choice (C) presumes that both digits and letters can be repeated.

36. F. Set up the average equation and plug in what you know. The average of the 5 scores is a 91. The sum of the scores is $99 + 97 + 92 + 88 + x$ where x represents Courtney's score. The number of scores is 5. The equation is as follows:

$$91 = \frac{99 + 97 + 92 + 88 + x}{5}$$

If you multiply both sides of the equation by 5, you end up with $455 = 376 + x$. When you solve the equation, x is 79, which is Courtney's score. The answer is Choice (F).

REMEMBER

The ACT Math section will likely have a few average questions. Make sure you know the formula like the back of your hand (but don't write it there!). By definition, an *average* equals the sum of all the scores divided by the number of scores:

$$\text{Average} = \frac{\text{Sum of scores}}{\text{Number of scores}}$$

You'll often have to find one of the numbers that makes up the sum in the numerator, so be prepared.

37. D. The diagonal is the length that extends from one vertex across the rectangle to the opposite vertex. It cuts the rectangle into two right triangles. When you know the side lengths of the rectangle, you can use what you know about right triangles to find the hypotenuse, which is also the diagonal of the rectangle.

The question gives you the rectangle's area as 672 square feet and its width as 14 feet. To find the value of the length, apply the area formula: $A = lw$. So $672 = 14l$ and $48 = l$. The sides of the right triangle with a hypotenuse that is the diagonal of the rectangle are 48 and 14. You could apply the Pythagorean theorem, but first check for a Pythagorean triple. A common factor of 48 and 14 is 2. The triangle is a 7-24-25 right triangle times 2. Multiply 25 by 2 to discover that the hypotenuse and therefore, the diagonal of the room is 50 feet, which is Choice (D).

38. K. Factor the quadratic. Find the square root of the first term. Then consider the last term, 4, and ask yourself what the factors of +4 are that have a sum of −5. Those two factors are −4 and −1, so the binomial factors of the quadratic are $\left(x^2 - 4\right)\left(x^2 - 1\right)$. If you want, you can apply FOIL to your factors to make sure you factored correctly. At this point, you may be tempted to pick Choice (F), but you aren't through; the terms can be factored further. Notice that the binomial factors are the differences of perfect squares. Finding their factors is easy. The two factors are the sum and difference of the square roots of each perfect square in the expression. So when you factor $\left(x^2 - 4\right)$, you get $\left(x + 2\right)\left(x - 2\right)$. When you factor $\left(x^2 - 1\right)$, you get $\left(x + 1\right)\left(x - 1\right)$. The fully factored quadratic is $\left(x + 1\right)\left(x - 1\right)\left(x + 2\right)\left(x - 2\right) = 0$. The expression in its entirety equals 0 when any one of these factors equals 0. Set each equal to 0, and you see that the full set of values for x that solve the equation are 1, 2, −1, and −2, which is Choice (K).

TIP

When you see a quadratic equation, your first thought should be to find its binomial factors. Once you factor, you'll likely discover the next step.

39. B. First, find the area that requires peanut butter. If one piece of bread measures 10 centimeters by 10 centimeters, the area of each piece is 100 square centimeters. So 9 sandwiches will have a total area of 900 square centimeters because 100 square centimeters 9 times is 900 square centimeters. Because Sam has a total of 3,600 cubic centimeters of peanut butter and the total area of the sandwiches is 900 square centimeters, she needs to spread peanut butter reaching a height of 4 centimeters on each sandwich because 3,600 divided by 900 is 4. The correct answer is Choice (B).

40. K. To find the slope of any line perpendicular to a given line, first find the slope of the given line. The graph shows that the given line travels through the points $(-4, 2)$ and $(5, 4)$. The slope is the rise over the run or $m = \frac{y_2 - y_1}{x_2 - x_1}$. Plug values into the slope equation to solve:

$$m = \frac{4 - 2}{5 - (-4)}$$
$$m = \frac{2}{9}$$

The slope of a perpendicular line is the opposite reciprocal of the slope of the line it intersects. So switch the sign to negative and flip the numerator and denominator to find the slope of any perpendicular line: $-\frac{9}{2}$. Choice (K) is right.

If you picked Choice (F), you forgot to switch the sign. Choice (J) results if you switched the sign and forgot to find the reciprocal.

41. B. Because the first number in this series is 2 and the next value is $4a$, the common multiplier that is used to find the next number in the geometric series is $2a$. The first term in the series is 2, and you need to find 30 more terms multiplied by $2a$: $2(2a)^{30}$. Expand the term to $2 \times 2^{30} \times a^{30}$. Combine terms by adding the exponents:

$$2^1 \times 2^{30} \times a^{30} = x$$
$$2^{31} \times a^{30} = x$$

The correct answer is Choice (B).

Choice (A) would make sense had the first term been $2a$ instead of 2. Choices (D) and (E) are wrong because they don't take into consideration the value of the coefficient.

42. K. A trapezoid has parallel bases, so line BD is a transversal that crosses parallel lines. So angle BDC and angle DBA are corresponding angles. Both equal 33 degrees. All you have to do to determine the measure of angle DBC is to add 33 and 77 and subtract the sum from 180 because the angles of a triangle total 180 degrees: $180 - (33 + 77) = 70$. Angle DBC measures 70 degrees and the answer is Choice (K).

43. E. On this question, units are the most important and tricky aspect to manage. To solve this question, set up an equation that allows you to cancel the units. Divide Jackson's distance travelled by his speed and Emily's distance travelled by her speed so that hours = hours. Assign the distance Emily travels to be x because that signifies the distance from Denver. The distance Jackson travels is $65 - x$ because the total distance is 65 miles. Your equation looks like this: $\frac{x}{60} = \frac{65 - x}{40}$. Cross multiply and solve:

$$40x = 60(65 - x)$$
$$40x = 3,900 - 60x$$
$$100x = 3,900$$
$$x = 39$$

Because x is the distance measured from Denver, the answer is 39 miles, which is Choice (E).

If you simply multiplied Jackson's distance times his speed and Emily's distance times her speed and solved the equation, you would have gotten Choice (B). Not only is this wrong mathematically, but it also doesn't make sense. If Emily is driving from Denver and drives faster than Jackson, they will pass each other more than halfway between Boulder and Denver, and the point 26 miles from Denver is closer to Denver than Boulder.

44. H. One way to solve this question is by plugging the given values into the distance formula and solving:

$$d = \sqrt{(y_2 - y_1)^2 + (x_2 - x_1)^2}$$
$$d = \sqrt{(7-1)^2 + (2-(--))^2}$$
$$d = \sqrt{6^2 + 8^2}$$
$$d = 10$$

Pick Choice (H).

If you don't remember the distance formula, don't fret! Draw the given points on a make-shift coordinate plane. Draw a line from the point $(-6, 1)$ over to the point $(2, 1)$. Then, draw a line up from the point $(2, 1)$ to the point $(2, 7)$ to make a right triangle with the two given points as vertices of the non-right angles. You can now see that the legs of the triangle are length 6 and length 8, so you know the diagonal has to be length 10 because it is a 3-4-5 right triangle.

TIP

Make sure you're familiar with the distance formula because you're almost guaranteed to see a problem that requires you to use it on the ACT.

45. B. To find the blue cars on Madi's lot, take $\frac{2}{3}$ of the 337 total. *Of* means multiply and $\frac{2}{3} \times 337$ is 225 blue cars. If $\frac{3}{4}$ of those are navy blue, multiply $\frac{3}{4} \times 225$ to find that 169 cars are navy blue. You can also solve this problem in one step by multiplying $\frac{2}{3} \times \frac{3}{4} \times 337$ to get 169.

Either way, the answer is Choice (B).

46. G. This is just a simplification question. Answer it by canceling terms. Because the whole numerator is squared, you need to square every component of the numerator before you do anything else. First, determine that 3 squared is 9. Next, find the value of $(x^3)^2$ and $(y^2)^2$ by multiplying the exponents: $(x^3)^2 = x^6$ and $(y^2)^2 = y^4$. The new expression is $\frac{9x^6 y^4}{3xy^{-3}}$. Divide the coefficients to get 3 and eliminate any answer that doesn't have a coefficient of 3. Then divide the variables by subtracting the exponents: $\frac{x^6}{x} = x^5$ and $\frac{y^4}{y^{-3}} = y^7$. Combine all of these components to get your final answer of $3x^5 y^7$. The answer is Choice (G).

Remember to subtract the negative exponent by adding 4 and 3; otherwise, you'll mistakenly pick Choice (J). If you just add rather than multiply the exponents in the first step, you'll incorrectly pick Choice (K).

47. C. Approach this problem by trying answer choices. The question asks for the largest sum, so start with the greatest answer. Consider Choice (D). Possible integers that add up to 8 are 9 and -1, but their product is -9, which doesn't fit within the given range. Try 6. The integers -7 and -1 have a sum of 6, and their product, -7, fits within the range. Once you know 6 works, pick Choice (C) and move on. Even if the other answers work, they aren't the largest options.

48. H. To determine whether Austin will make a profit, you need to find Austin's costs in the first month and subtract that amount from the total he will earn in the first month: Income − Expenses = Profit. Calculate his costs. The question states that Austin's rent and supplies will cost a flat $800 per month. Add to that the amount of money he will pay the barbers. If he pays each barber $12 per hour and they each work 120 hours per month, he will pay each barber $1,440 per month. Because there are 10 barbers, he will pay all barbers a total of $14,400 in the first month. His total monthly cost will be $14,400 + 800$ or $15,200 in the first month. Now, to find Austin's profits, multiply the number of haircuts he will sell by the price of each haircut. The problem tells you that he will sell 1,200 haircuts for $15 apiece, so his total revenue will be $18,000. The revenue will be more than the costs, so you can eliminate the *No* answers, Choices (F) and (G). When you subtract his cost from his revenue, you see his overall profit in the first month will be $2,800: $18,000 − $15,200 = $2,800$. The answer is Choice (H).

49. A. Apply SOH CAH TOA. Knowing that the cosine of the angle is $\frac{7}{25}$ tells you that the adjacent side is 7 and the hypotenuse is 25. Tangent is TOA, or opposite over adjacent. So eliminate Choices (B) and (C) because they don't have 7 in the denominator. You know two sides of the triangle, so you could apply the Pythagorean theorem to find the opposite side, but don't bother. The answer choices tell you the only other side length possibility is 24 and one of the Pythagorean triples is 7-24-25, so save some time and pick the only answer that puts 24 in the numerator, Choice (A).

50. G. The equation to find slope is $m = \frac{y_1 - y_2}{x_1 - x_2}$. Simply plug in values to answer this question. The library is at point (2, 5) and the diner is at point (10, 4). When you plug those values into the slope equation and solve, you get this:

$$m = \frac{5-4}{2-10}$$
$$m = -\frac{1}{8}$$

The answer is Choice (G).

51. C. For this problem, apply the general equation for a circle: $(x-h)^2 + (y-k)^2 = r^2$, where h and k are the x- and y-coordinates of the center of the circle and r is its radius. The radius of the circle is 2, so the correct answer has to be an equation that is equal to 2 squared or 4. Eliminate Choices (A), (D), and (E) and you're done. Choice (C) is obviously correct because Choice (B) adds rather than subtracts within the parentheses. If you picked Choice (E), you forgot to square the radius.

There is an 'equation of a circle' question on almost every ACT, so you must know the general equation.

REMEMBER

52. H. Apply the distance formula or create a right triangle with Becca's walk as the hypotenuse:

$$d = \sqrt{(y_2 - y_1)^2 + (x_2 - x_1)^2}$$
$$d = \sqrt{(6-2)^2 + (7-1)^2}$$
$$d = \sqrt{(4)^2 + (6)^2}$$
$$d = \sqrt{16 + 36}$$
$$d = \sqrt{52}$$

Multiply the distance in units by 2 to get the approximate number of miles Becca walks:

$$2\sqrt{52} = \text{miles}$$
$$2\sqrt{4 \times 13} = \text{miles}$$
$$4\sqrt{13} = \text{miles}$$

The square root of 13 is in between the square root of 9 and the square root of 16, or somewhere between 3 and 4. The product of 4 and 3 is 12; the product of 4 and 4 is 16. The only answer that falls between 12 and 16 is Choice (H). If you use the square root key on your calculator, you find that the distance is approximately 14.42 miles.

53. **B.** For this question, set up an equation that models the word problem. Use x to represent the number you're trying to find. In English/math translation, *of* means multiply, *is* means equals, and "more than" means add, so your equation is $\frac{2}{5}x = \frac{1}{4}(x + 21)$. Be careful to notice that you multiply the second fraction by the sum of x and 21; otherwise, you may incorrectly pick Choice (E).

To solve the equation, get rid of the fractions by multiplying the whole equation by 4 to come up with $(4)\frac{2}{5}x = (x + 21)$ and then again by 5. Your new equation is $8x = 5(x + 21)$. Expand the right side of the equation to get $8x = 5x + 105$. Subtract $5x$ from both sides to get $3x = 105$. When you divide both sides by 3, you know the number is 35, Choice (B).

TIP

You can also approach your answer by backsolving. Plug in the answers until you find the one that fits. $\frac{2}{5}$ of 35 is 14 and $\frac{1}{4}$ of 56 is also 14, so Choice (B) works.

54. **J.** To eliminate h, rearrange and stack the equations:

$$y = 7x - h$$
$$-7 = -x + h$$
$$y - 7 = 6x$$

Add 7 to both sides and you see the answer is Choice (J).

REMEMBER

The key to this question is to know that "y expressed in terms of x" means that the only two variables in your answer should be x and y, and y should be alone on one side of the equation.

55. **D.** Approach this question like you would a shaded area question. It may help to draw a picture. Draw a square with a circle that touches all sides in the center. Draw a radius of the circle and label it 7 cm. It's easy to see that the diameter of the circle is 14 cm and that the sides of the square are equal to the diameter of the circle. Label the sides of the square as 14 cm, like this:

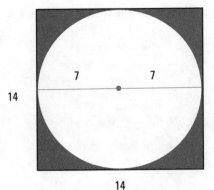

Eliminate Choice (C) because its value is negative, and the shaded area can't be negative. Find the area of the square by squaring the side length: $14^2 = 196$, so you can automatically narrow your options to Choice (D) or (E).

Apply the formula for area of a circle ($A = \pi r^2$) by substituting 7 for r. The circle's area is 49π. The answer that presents the difference between the two areas is Choice (D).

If you picked Choice (E), you applied the circumference formula rather than the area formula.

TIP

The best way to solve a shaded area problem is by finding the total area and the unshaded area and then calculating the difference between those two areas.

56. H. Use the distance formula to find the side lengths of the rectangle. Plug in the values of one of the longer lines in the rectangle and solve:

$$d = \sqrt{(y_2 - y_1)^2 + (x_2 - x_1)^2}$$
$$d = \sqrt{(0-3)^2 + (6-0)^2}$$
$$d = \sqrt{(-3)^2 + 6^2}$$
$$d = \sqrt{9 + 36}$$
$$d = \sqrt{45}$$

When you apply the formula to the shorter side of the rectangle, you get this:

$$d = \sqrt{(y_2 - y_1)^2 + (x_2 - x_1)^2}$$
$$d = \sqrt{(7-3)^2 + (2-0)^2}$$
$$d = \sqrt{4^2 + 2^2}$$
$$d = \sqrt{16 + 4}$$
$$d = \sqrt{20}$$

To find the area of the rectangle, multiply the length of the shorter side by the length of the longer side, $\sqrt{45} \times \sqrt{20} = \sqrt{900}$, which is 30. Choice (H) is correct.

57. B. Consider the equation in the question: $\sin x + 2$ is the regular sin x graph moved up 2. You can eliminate all answer choices except Choices (B) and (C) because all of the other choices have no vertical translation (they don't show a vertical movement of the $\sin x + 2$ graph). Plug in values to $\sin x + 2$ to determine which of the remaining answers is true. Try 0: $\sin 0 - 0$. So on the correct graph, when $x = 0$, the y value will be 2. This is only true for Choice (B).

58. F. The question gives you the equation you need: $A^2 = B^2 + C^2 - 2BC \cos a$. Use values from the figure to plug into this equation. The only angle measure provided is the 51° angle, which is angle a because it is opposite side A. Substitute 51° for a in the equation. Eliminate Choices (J) and (K) because they don't have the correct angle measure. It doesn't matter which side is B or C; just plug in 17 and 11 for the two side lengths. You get this solution:

$$A^2 = 17^2 + 11^2 - 1(17)(11)\cos 51°$$
$$A^2 = 289 + 121 - (34)(11)\cos 51°$$
$$A^2 = 410 - (374\cos 51°)$$
$$A = \sqrt{410 - (374\cos 51°)}$$

Choice (G) is wrong because it neglects to take the square root of the right side. If you picked Choice (H), you didn't follow the proper order of operations. You have to multiply the 374 by the cosine value before you subtract it from 410. The correct answer is Choice (F).

TIP

Whenever the ACT provides a note, pay attention. The note usually contains the formula you need to solve the problem. And a note often signals an easy question. You just need to determine which information in the question you need to plug into the formula.

59. B. The question states that 17.5% of students who responded to the poll is equal to 7 students, which gives you quite a bit to go on. You can set up a simple proportion where x is the number of students who responded to the poll and 17.5% is represented in fraction form: $\frac{17.5}{100} = \frac{7}{x}$. When you cross multiply, you get $17.5x = 700$. Divide both sides by 17.5 to discover that $x = 40$. But don't stop there and pick Choice (A). Forty is just the number of students in Jamie's class who responded in the poll, not the total number of students in her class. You know that 20%, or $\frac{1}{5}$, didn't participate in the poll. That means that 80%, or $\frac{4}{5}$, did participate. Set up another proportion where $\frac{4}{5} = \frac{40}{x}$ and x is the total number of students in Jamie's class. When you cross multiply, you get $4x = 200$. Divide both sides by 4 to find that $x = 50$. So Jamie's class has 50 students. The answer is Choice (B).

If you picked Choice (C), you didn't take into consideration the students who didn't respond to the poll.

60. H. Jordyn starts with $600 and every six months she makes 5% on her existing money. So after 6 months, Jordyn has 1.05 times the $600 she started with, which is $630. But you don't just add $30 every month because Jordyn makes 5% on what she already has in the bank account. So after one year, she makes 5% of $630, not $600. Take 1.05 times $630 to find her balance of $661.50 after one year. At a year and a half, Jordyn has 1.05 times $661.50, or $694.58. At this point, she moves $210 to a checking account, so she has a balance of $484.58.

This isn't your final answer, though! You have to compound this value one more time because the question asks how much money she has after two full years. After two years, Jordyn has 1.05 times what she had after a year and a half, which is $484.58, so she has a final balance of $508.80. Choice (H) is correct.

Reading Test

1. C. First, go to the last paragraph to find Mrs. Kronborg's analogy. It appears in the last sentence right after the statement that Mrs. Kronborg knew talent meant practicing. She compares the need for a talented child to practice in the way that a child with measles needs to sleep. So a talented child *should* practice, and a child with measles *should* sleep. The answer that provides a similar *should* statement is Choice (C). A person with outdoor allergies *should* stay indoors.

Choice (A) is unlike the analogy because it mentions two separate skills — math and writing. For Choice (B), while it's obvious why a child with measles must be kept under blankets, it is decidedly less obvious why a beautiful child should be kept under close watch. So, that's probably not the best choice, either. Choice (D) uses *may* instead of *must*. *Must*, like *should*, is an absolution, while *may* is hypothetical. You can feel confident in selecting Choice (C).

You're supposed to choose the best answer out of the four options. To determine which is the best, use that secret weapon known as *POE*, or the process of elimination. By eliminating answers you know can't be right, you help isolate the answer that fits the best.

2. **F.** The second paragraph begins "It was in the summer that one really lived," so check there first. The author mentions fence painting in the third sentence, cottonwood trees in the fourth sentence, and the shedding of warm clothes for cotton at the end. So eliminate Choices (G), (H) and (J). By process of elimination, check Choice (F). The paragraph suggests that people see their neighbors, but it doesn't specifically say the neighbors are *new*. Choice (F) is correct.

3. **B.** This vocabulary-in-context question is best answered by substituting each answer for *crony* in the fifth paragraph. Not only does it not make sense to say that Fritz had never had an elder, but the paragraph also doesn't say whether the music teacher was older than Fritz. Eliminate Choice (A). Choice (D) doesn't seem right. The author later says Fritz hasn't had a crony since "the harness-maker and Spanish Johnny." There is nothing in the passage that suggests that either of these individuals ever taught him anything. Because the passage directly states that the Kohlers took this person in to live with them, you can reasonably assume that they don't view him as an enemy — so eliminate Choice (C). If you replace *crony* with *friend*, the paragraph makes sense. Choice (B) is best.

4. **H.** Eliminate Choice (F), because the statement compares the way Mrs. Kohler treated Professor Wunsch to the way she treated her garden, and nothing in the passage suggests that there was anything undesirable about her garden. Eliminate Choice (G) because the paragraph goes on to discuss how Mrs. Kohler was successful in making the professor particularly clean and respectable — so she certainly wasn't trying in vain. Now, you're left with either Choice (H) or (J). Of the two, Choice (H) is better. The paragraph indicates that Mrs. Kohler helped get the professor in tip-top shape, but it doesn't provide clues to what would make up her idea of perfection. Stick with Choice (H).

5. **A.** Answering this question correctly requires careful attention to detail. A close reading of the fourth paragraph and its description of Mrs. Kohler's typical attire reveals the answer. The black bonnet in summer appears in the third sentence, the handmade dresses in the fourth, and the men's shoes in the fifth. Choices (B), (C), and (D) are mentioned and therefore, wrong. If you read the paragraph carefully, you notice that the hood Mrs. Kohler wore in the winter was red, not black, so Choice (A) is the correct answer.

6. **H.** The fact that Professor Wunsch says that his greatest desire was to spend the rest of his days with Mrs. Kohler and then be buried in her garden lets you know that his feelings toward her must be positive, so you can confidently eliminate Choices (F) and (J), since they are negative. Now, you're down to either Choice (G) or Choice (H). Nothing in the passage suggests he felt amorous or romantic toward her, so examine Choice (H) more closely. Does it make sense that the professor would be particularly grateful to the woman that took him in, cleaned him up, and helped him find work? Indeed it does. Choice (H) is your answer.

7. **A.** Eliminate answers that contain elements that don't fit. Although the passage describes the garden as verdant, it doesn't suggest that it's the frequent rainfall that makes it green. Notice that the third paragraph describes the Kohler property as an open, sandy plain; it's unlikely that Moonstone receives frequent rainfall, so eliminate Choice (D). You can also easily get rid of Choice (C). The garden is a jungle of verdure, so it isn't best described as a barren sand gulch. Examine the remaining two choices for clues that would help you eliminate one. Choice (B) is true all the way up to the last word. Mrs. Kohler hasn't cultivated sage-brush in her garden, so the best answer must be Choice (A). The passage states

that she hid and planned in her garden, and it's reasonable to assume that she found purpose in creating shade there.

TIP

Usually you can easily eliminate two answer choices. Then focus on the remaining two to find the one answer that contains an element that can't be justified by the passage. Eliminate that answer to discover the correct option.

8. **J.** The passage doesn't devote a lot of attention to Mr. Kohler; he's only mentioned in the third and fifth paragraphs. You can get rid of Choice (A). Professor Wunsch is the musician, not Fritz Kohler. The fifth paragraph states that Mr. Kohler was friends with the harness-maker and Spanish Johnny but doesn't mention a third crony, so Choice (G) is wrong. Examine Choice (H) carefully. The passage says that one of Mr. Kohler's sons had gone to work for the Santa Fe in New Mexico, but it means the railroad. You know that the son lived in New Mexico, but you don't know that he specifically lived in Santa Fe. Thus, Choice (H) is also wrong, and so the best answer is Choice (J). Because the passage states that Mr. Kohler was one of the first settlers in Moonstone, you can logically conclude that he was one of the first to live there. Pick Choice (J).

9. **D.** The final paragraph of the passage discusses Thea's musical talent, and since *gifted* is a synonym for *talented*, Choice (D) is likely your answer. To be sure, though, take a look at the other possibilities. While the passage suggests Mrs. Kohler doesn't get out much, it doesn't indicate the same about Thea. You can't justify Choice (A). The first paragraph states that Thea has a favorite fairy tale, but it doesn't say she was particularly fond of fairy tales in general. Choice (C) is too much of a stretch. Choice (B) is true. Thea did study music with Professor Wunsch, but so did other children. Although Choice (B) is true, it doesn't show a way that Thea differed from other children. Stick with Choice (D).

REMEMBER

Just because something in an answer choice is true doesn't necessarily mean it answers the question correctly.

10. **F.** Thea is mentioned in the first and last paragraphs. Begin by concentrating on the first because it gives more information about Thea's disposition. Nothing in the first paragraph — or the entire passage, for that matter — suggests that Thea was combative, so eliminate Choice (H). You'd have to infer more than is provided to pick Choice (J). Nowhere does it suggest that Thea is restless. The two remaining options are *cheerful* and *eager*. The first paragraph states that Thea is running, but it also says she is in no hurry to get to her music lesson. She isn't running because she's eager to get to lessons but because she's happy about the beautiful summer day. Choice (F) is better than Choice (G).

11. **A.** The last sentence of the first paragraph refers to those opposed to the inclusion of PTSD in the manual and claims that the diagnosis is already covered. Choice (B) is a reason and not an exception, so eliminate it. You can find information about the broadened concept of stressors, so Choice (C) is a reason and therefore, wrong. The last sentence of the second paragraph contains the reason in Choice (D). The only answer that doesn't appear in the passage is Choice (A).

TIP

An EXCEPT question requires you to find correct answers and then eliminate them. So, before you examine the answer choices, remind yourself to cross out "right" answers and choose the remaining "wrong" answer.

12. **H.** The opinions in Passage A are those of early 21st-century scholars and not necessarily the author. The author presents others' viewpoints without comment, so the primary tone is objective and explanatory. The best answer is Choice (H).

13. D. The "state of affairs" referred to in the author's mention of the 1970s and 80s is to the broadening scope of what constitutes trauma and not medicine or the increasing number of PTSD sufferers since those decades. You can eliminate Choices (A) and (C). Although the paragraph talks about the catastrophic events of the time, it does so to highlight that those events were extraordinary rather than numerous. Choice (B) is wrong. The main reason the author mentions the 70s and 80s is to point out that the definition of traumatic events then was different than it is currently. Choice (D) is the best answer.

14. G. Don't worry if you're unfamiliar with the word in the question. Simply substitute the answer choices for *aetiology* in the passage to see which makes the most sense in context. The examples in the first sentence of Passage B are diagnoses and not word origins, so Choice (H) doesn't make sense. Although an abnormality is mentioned in one of the examples, none of the others mention it and the rest of the paragraph isn't about abnormalities. Choice (J) is wrong. To choose between controversy and causation, provided by the remaining two answer choices, examine the context of the paragraph. It mentions controversy, but the primary purpose of the paragraph addresses the causes of the disorders, so the aetiology lacking in the manual must be Choice (G).

15. A. You can easily eliminate Choices (C) and (D) because they contain points made in Passage A and not Passage B. At first glance, Choice (B) looks promising: the author of Passage B does seem to clarify that PTSD is legitimate and debilitating. But the rest of the answer doesn't work. The passage makes no mention of further research or funding for PTSD. The whole answer has to work for it to be correct. Choice (A) is better: the first paragraph indicates that the diagnosis is controversial but that its acceptance has helped practitioners, and the second paragraph focuses on how PTSD impacts its sufferers. The best answer is Choice (A).

16. G. Read through the answer choices to find out where the passage may discuss each one. You can find choices (F) and (J) in the first paragraph. Choice (F) paraphrases the second sentence of that paragraph, and Choice (J) states the information in the last sentence. The fourth sentence of the second paragraph provides nearly the same wording as Choice (H). Because these three answer choices express information directly stated by the passage, they must not be the exception and must be wrong. The passage refers to an "altered baseline state" in the second paragraph, but the reference is designed to show what PTSD is not rather than what it is. Choice (G) is the exception and thus the right answer.

17. A. To help you focus, analyze each answer one passage at a time. The psychiatrists mentioned in Passage A don't recognize a PTSD diagnosis and therefore, wouldn't consider it to be a debilitating condition. Eliminate Choice (B). The rest of the answers seem to work for Passage A, so consider the author of Passage B. The author doesn't feel that PTSD is a disorder of an altered baselines state, nor does the author mention politics, so Choices (C) and (D) don't work. The answer that fits both passages is Choice (A).

18. J. Consider one passage at a time. Passage B doesn't talk about the politics of a PTSD diagnosis and wouldn't agree with Choice (G). Passage A doesn't refer to PTSD as a disorder of reactivity, nor does it state that sufferers are overly concerned with their safety. Choices (F) and (H) are wrong. Both passages state that PTSD is a controversial diagnosis. The best answer is Choice (J).

19. D. The author of Passage A claims that psychiatrists initially objected to the PTSD diagnosis in the third edition of the manual, so neither Choice (B) nor (C) is the exception. Passage B claims that few diagnoses in the manual listed causation, so Choice (A) is present and not an exception. Neither passage states that the manual is insufficient; the best answer is Choice (D).

20. **J.** Neither passage recommends additional research into PTSD, so Choice (G) is unlikely. Passage B isn't concerned with the speed of some professionals' PTSD diagnoses, so Choice (F) is wrong. Although both passages indicate that PTSD diagnosis is controversial, Passage B isn't concerned with its inclusion in the *DSM-III*; Choice (H) is out. Passage B states that "the presumed causal relationship between the stressor and PTSD. . .is complicated." Passage A suggests in the last paragraph that the types of stressors that could cause PTSD have broadened to a point where some medical professionals question the validity of the diagnosis. Therefore, both passages consider the exact relationship between stressors and PTSD to be controversial. Choose Choice (J).

When answering questions about the similarities and differences between two passages, examine the answer choices one passage at a time to help you focus and eliminate wrong answers more efficiently.

21. **A.** To answer this main theme question, apply the process of elimination. Rule out choices with information that is too specific. The passage discusses the idea in Choice (D) only in the fourth paragraph, so it's wrong. You should also get rid of answers that contain ideas that are too broad. Choice (B) focuses on the concept of positive change in general rather than what makes for a good screenplay. Rule out Choice (C) because it's not true. The passage contains no warnings. The best answer has to be Choice (A). It ties the initial theme of what makes for a good film adaptation to the explanation of the life-changing mythological journey included throughout the rest of the passage.

For questions that ask you for the purpose or tone of an entire passage, choose answers that apply to the whole passage, not just part of it. Eliminate ideas that appear in only one or two of the paragraphs or that concern concepts that are more general than the passage's topic.

22. **J.** This question asks for the author's suggestion, which tells you that the correct answer is implied rather than directly stated. In the second paragraph, the author makes a primary observation about inner growth and change — that it means letting go of the familiar and risking the unknown. The answer that paraphrases this idea best is Choice (J). The author states that inner growth is healthy, so you can eliminate Choice (F) based on its first two words. Even though the rest of this first answer choice seems pretty good, don't ignore its implication that inner growth is unhealthy. Read Choice (H) carefully; it actually contradicts the notion that inner growth requires change. The second paragraph says that inner growth requires courage but not the courage to stay the same. The last line of the paragraph conveys that remaining static isn't a requirement for inner growth but instead an obstacle to achieving it. Choice (G) may seem correct at first, but the passage only says that experiencing myth in film may assist with the dilemma of whether to risk change. It doesn't say inner growth requires viewing films. The answer must be Choice (J). The second paragraph states that inner growth requires sacrificing the old and familiar and risking the unknown and uncertain. The last paragraph quotes Campbell's claim that human fantasies tend to tie back to the human spirit, so you can reasonably conclude that comfortable fantasies are included in the "old and familiar," and uncharted territory is another way of alluding to the unknown.

23. **C.** The referenced list provides examples of situations where outer physical change is readily apparent. Choose the answer that provides another instance of outer physical change. Choices (B) and (D) don't express physical changes. Choice (A) is physical, but it isn't outwardly apparent. The only answer choice that expresses an outer physical change you can see is Choice (C).

24. J. The statement points out that even though making a change involves sacrifice or risk, the risk of not taking that risk is missing out on a chance at a new life. The rest of the passage clarifies the author's view that embracing this new life is better than missing it by holding on to old ways. Therefore, the best synopsis of the quote is Choice (J). Choice (F) may seem tempting, but the statement suggests the inevitability of sacrifice only as it relates to the transformation journey and not to the inevitability of sacrifice in general. The quote specifically addresses the change that comes with risk rather than change in general, so Choice (G) is wrong. Choice (H) can't be right because nowhere does the passage suggest that the journey is more fulfilling that the resulting change. Stick with Choice (J).

TIP

Sometimes you can answer questions that ask what a quote or phrase most likely means by focusing on which answer best paraphrases the quote. If you like, you can then go back into the passage to make sure it justifies your answer.

25. B. Answer this question by asking yourself why the author included the second paragraph in the essay. The paragraph focuses on what it means to undergo a life-altering journey, which is one of the elements of a good story mentioned in the first paragraph. Choice (B) offers a neat paraphrase of this objective. The essay is more explanatory than encouraging, so it's unlikely that the author specifically includes the second paragraph to persuade readers to change their lives. Cross out Choice (C). Although the paragraph does offer up some examples of physical change, this inclusion merely serves to contrast inner change and outer change and isn't the main reason for the paragraph. Choice (D) isn't correct. Because the paragraph discusses only one real way to achieve inner growth instead of several, Choice (A) isn't a better option than Choice (B). Stick with Choice (B).

26. F. Choice (F) is essentially a rephrasing of a sentence that appears in the middle of the final paragraph: "Mythology . . . provides a means for other people to experience the hero's transformation." That sounds good, but check the other answers to be sure. A protagonist people can easily identify with isn't one of the elements of a good story listed in the first paragraph, so Choice (G) is out. Eliminate Choice (H); the second paragraph contrasts the tangibility of inner and outer change but doesn't state that one is more important than the other. The first paragraph doesn't include a widely loved story as one of the criteria for a film adaptation's success, so Choice (J) is out. Choice (F) is best.

27. C. Focus on the fourth paragraph and eliminate answers that appear in the passage. The second sentence states that the hero experiences a liberation from past limitations, so eliminate Choice (A). The idea of great personal risk and quest for treasure are suggested by the reference at the end of the first sentence to a treasure quest that results in personal cost. Choices (B) and (D) are out. By process of elimination, the answer is Choice (C).

28. F. The passage references Joseph Campbell in the third paragraph, so start there. It states that the purpose of ritual is to provide transformation that demands changes in conscious and unconscious patterns. That sounds most like Choice (F). Choice (G) references difficult thresholds in general, but the reference is specifically to thresholds of transformation. The paragraph doesn't suggest that ritual forces anything, nor does it mention fantasy. So Choices (H) and (J) are wrong, and the best answer is Choice (F).

29. C. The sentence refers to *this* universal dilemma, so look in the prior paragraph for clues. The last sentence mentions two sacrifices: one that results from changing and one that results from not changing. Find the answer that states this dilemma best. Choice (D) is out because the growth is inner, not physical. Choice (A) is wrong because the dilemma isn't relevant to just the film experience. Of the remaining answers, Choice (C) defines the dilemma better. It's about choosing to change rather than choosing between types of thoughts. Pick Choice (C).

30. G. From the first paragraph, you know that Seger is an author of a book about adaptation and that the adaptation is likely from literature to film. Therefore, she's most likely a film script consultant. Pick Choice (G).

31. D. While the roles of bacteria, or Choice (C), are indeed discussed, this discussion appears in only a small part of the passage and not until about halfway through. If bacteria were the main purpose of the passage, one could expect that they would be mentioned in the very first paragraph — so eliminate Choice (C). Similarly, while some attention is given to the earth's changing temperatures, or Choice (A), there isn't nearly enough to have temperature change be the passage's central or primary focus. So, you're down to either Choice (B) or (D). Of the two, Choice (D) is broader and more all-encompassing and better summarizes the passage in its entirety. While the author notes that "If there is anything that has been overlooked more than another it is our atmosphere," he really only devotes the first couple paragraphs to discussing why the atmosphere is overlooked. When you examine the passage in its entirety, Choice (D) is the strongest choice.

32. G. The correct answer is Choice (G). The passage claims that rain is "accounted for only by the dust," which means that the rain exists because the dust exists. You can't conclude, however, that this statement means that rain is the only element dust accounts for. Choices (H), and (J) are all mentioned by the author in Paragraph 7, and Choice (F) is mentioned in Paragraph 8.

33. C. The author begins the fifth paragraph with a discussion of the wind, where he plainly states that it is "mostly nitrogen, oxygen, moisture, and dust." So you can eliminate Choices (A) and (B). He also mentions five other gases. At the end of the paragraph, you learn that hydrogen is one of these gases, so get rid of Choice (D). He doesn't specifically say that bacteria are part of wind, so the answer is Choice (C).

TIP

There's no rule that you have to answer the questions in order. If you have trouble figuring out the answer to a question that involves much of the passage, skip it and go back after you've answered other questions. Often, something you read for one question will help you answer another.

34. F. While both Choice (G) and Choice (H) are ways in which dust affects the earth, neither is discussed in such a way that would suggest the author considers them dust's greatest role. So, your answer is either Choice (F) or (J). Choice (J) sounds like something the author might say about atmosphere rather than dust, and furthermore, the author essentially paraphrases Choice (F) at the start of Paragraph 8. Choice (F) is correct.

35. D. While Choice (A) is an assertion made by the author, he doesn't appear to consider this fact an absurdity, so go ahead and knock that one out of contention. Eliminate Choice (B) for the same reason. Take a closer look at the remaining choices. Choice (C) is indeed noted by the author in the passage's final paragraph, but it is done so in a matter-of-fact manner, suggesting that the author doesn't consider it an absurdity. Only in his discussion of rain and dust does he use the word *absurdities*, so you may confidently select Choice (D).

36. F. Not only are Choices (G) and (H) incorrect — land surfaces absorb most of the heat received, and water surfaces reflect most of it — but even if they were written correctly, these responses would be supporting points made in the final paragraph, not the *main* point. So the answer is either Choice (F) or (J). Choice (J) is actually an assertion made in the second-to-last paragraph, so give Choice (F) a closer look. Does it adequately summarize the information in the final paragraph? It does, so you may feel confident that Choice (F) is correct.

37. **C.** The author asserts in the second paragraph that it is the atmosphere that protects us from "that fraction of sunheat which, however trifling when compared with the whole, would otherwise be sufficient to fry us all in a second." Choice (A) makes no sense. The fraction of sunheat wouldn't protect humans from the sun's heat. Choice (B) isn't discussed until the end of the paragraph, long after the discussion of humans' protection from the sun's heat — so it can't be right. As for Choice (D), the author mentions that the atmosphere keeps us in a sort of thermos globe; however, the gas layer is thin rather than thick. So Choice (C) is the strongest option.

38. **G.** To answer this question correctly, look for clues in the context. The line in question states, "It is thanks to this thin layer of gases that we are protected from that fraction of sunheat which, however trifling when compared with the whole, would otherwise be sufficient to fry us all in a second." So you're likely looking for a word that means something close to "a small part." Thus, *insignificant* is the strongest answer. To be sure, though, take a look at the others. Choice (F), *shallow*, certainly doesn't mean a small part, so knock that one out of contention. Eliminate Choice (J) because *novel* means new, not small. As for Choice (H), *trifling* could mean silly, but try substituting the word *trifling* in the paragraph with *silly*. Does it make sense to say the earth receives a silly fraction of sunheat? No, so Choice (G) is correct.

39. **D.** A careful review of the passage reveals that Choice (A) appears in paragraph three, Choice (B) appears in the second-to-last paragraph, and Choice (C) in the fifth paragraph. Nowhere does the author discuss the atmospheric differences between the Northern and Southern Hemispheres, so you can feel confident in your selection of Choice (D).

40. **J.** Read the answers to see which one best paraphrases the quoted material. The *rest* refers to the other components of wind, so Choice (J) seems most logical. The passage doesn't say that dust and water are heavier or appear in greater quantities than the others. If you chose Choice (G) or (H), you made assumptions not justified by the passage. Choice (F) is about gases rather than dust and wind, so it isn't correct. Choice (J) is best.

Science Test

1. **D.** The question points you to the data for Site 1 on the table. It asks you to determine the relationship, if any, between temperature and conductivity. Don't assume that the temperatures increase as you move down the chart. Note that the first two temperatures are both 23 but the conductivity for both entries is very different. So there isn't an obvious relationship between the two and Choice (D) is the best answer.

The answer that states there's no apparent relationship or that data is insufficient is often the last answer and may be correct. So don't be afraid to pick it. Don't assume there must be a relationship.

2. **F.** The table doesn't have a category for number of impurities, so you need to read a bit of the text to determine which column gives you the information you need to assess purity. The first sentences indicate that removing ions is a way to purify water and that conductivity and ion content are directly related — the more ions a solution has, the higher its conductivity. So use the conductivity column on the table to assess the sites' relative purity. The site with the lowest conductivity is Site 1. Its average conductivity is around 200 as compared to 870 at Site 2 and 620 at Site 3. Pick Choice (F).

TIP

You know that Choice (J) can't be right because the conductivity averages for Sites 1 and 3 are very different.

3. **A.** This question provides new information — that drinking water's conductivity usually ranges between 50 and 500. Use it to evaluate the table. The only site with conductivity levels between 50 and 500 is Site 1. The answer has to be Choice (A).

TIP

This question was very similar to the second question. Don't be thrown off if you think the ACT Science questions test you more than once on the same general concept. They do it all the time.

4. **H.** To extrapolate for this question, use the table to find the average conductivity that's closest to 500. Site 2's average at about 620 is higher than 500, and Site 1's average at about 200 is much lower. The average species richness for Site 1 is 10.7 and for Site 2 is 4.9. The answer has to lie between those two values. So pick Choice (H).

5. **B.** Data are correlated when you can determine a relationship between them. Notice that for fall on three sites the temperatures were roughly the same. Yet species richness varied among the sites. So temperature isn't correlated to species richness, and you can eliminate Choices (A) and (C). Check conductivity. It appears from the average figures that lower conductivity means greater species richness, so those data are correlated. The answer is Choice (B).

6. **H.** The passage indicates that species richness was collected from freshwater sites. It then explains that based on the collection invertebrate specimens were counted and identified. The logical means of collecting invertebrates is nets, Choice (H). The passage doesn't associate temperature, pH, or weight with species richness, so the other answers must be wrong.

7. **D.** The passage doesn't test behaviors of saltwater fish, so Choice (A) is incorrect. The setup for Experiment 1 lists the types of aggressive behaviors the scientists viewed as a fact rather than a question to answer through experimentation; eliminate Choice (B). The two experiments include gender and size considerations in their setup, but the main difference between them is the relative size of the intruder fish and the focal fish. Experiment 1 established the number of aggressive behaviors presented when one intruder and focal fish are of similar size. The second experiment provides information the scientists can use to determine whether the number of aggressive behaviors changes when they vary the comparative size of intruders and focal fish for a larger number of fish. The scientists do not mix the sexes of the intruders and focal fish, so Choice (C) isn't correct. The scientists must be primarily concerned with how the relative size of the intruder affects the number of aggressive behaviors in the focal fish. Choice (D) is best.

8. **H.** The question directs you to Experiment 1, so focus on the data in Table 1. Before you do, however, take a look at the answer choices. All but the first begin with large male as the one with the highest aggression. Notice that in the column for large fish, the males have more aggressive behaviors than the females, so eliminate Choice (F). The second entry in the remaining choices is either large female or medium male. Check Table 1 to see which has more aggressive behaviors. The large female has 11 and the medium male has 18, so the male is more aggressive and Choice (G) is wrong. Choice (H) and (J) differ in the order of the last two fish. The large female has one more aggressive behavior than the small male, so based on the table, the answer has to be Choice (H).

9. **B.** Use information from both tables to answer this question. You know from answering Question 6 about Experiment 1 that male fish are generally more aggressive than female fish, so eliminate Choices (A) and (C). Check Table 2 to see whether the findings change in the second experiment. The males are generally more aggressive in the second experiment, too, so the answer has to be Choice (B).

10. **G.** To answer this question, you determine how the experiments differed based on what's true for Experiment 2. First, run through the answer choices to eliminate options that aren't true about the independent variables in Experiment 2. The number of days didn't vary in Experiment 2, so eliminate Choice (J). The researchers were testing for aggression, so Choice (H) wasn't an independent variable and must be wrong. The gender and relative size of the intruders varied in Experiment 2. The difference between the two experiments, though, was that Experiment 2 varied the comparable sizes of intruders to focal fish. This variation didn't occur in Experiment 1, so the best answer is Choice (G).

11. **D.** The columns in Table 2 vary the size of the intruder, so that element must be important in determining aggressive behavior. Eliminate Choices (A) and (B) because neither mentions size of intruder. Then you just need to determine whether the gender of the focal fish was another factor. The table rows delineate male and female data, and the text tells you that the gender of the focal fish determined the gender of the intruder. So gender must also be important, and the answer must be Choice (D).

12. **F.** Read the introductory text to discover that aggression allows the fish to protect their young. In both experiments, bigger fish meant more aggression for both genders. So the best answer is one that pairs the fish with the most aggressive behaviors. From Table 1, you learn that the medium male and large female would have about 32 aggressive behaviors between them. The large male and small female would have about 29 aggressive behaviors. So get rid of Choice (G). The other answers contain smaller males than Choice (G), so you can eliminate them as well. The answer is Choice (F).

REMEMBER

Don't overthink this question. You're choosing the best answer and are given only the number of aggressive behaviors and time spent in aggressive behaviors to evaluate. Between the two experiments, you see that the number of aggressive behaviors correlates directly with the number of minutes engaged in those behaviors. So the combination that produces the most aggressive behaviors has to be better than any other answer with a smaller number of behaviors.

13. **A.** Translate the data in the table to a bar graph. Table 2 shows the number of minutes spent in aggression. Bigger fish spent more time than smaller fish and males more than females, so pick the graph that best reflects this trend. All graphs show more time for males, so focus on size.

Eliminate answers that show higher bars for smaller intruders. So Choices (B) and (D) are out. You can also eliminate Choice (C) because it shows time for equal intruders higher than for larger intruders. The answer has to be Choice (A).

14. **F.** The question directs you to Researcher 1, so start there. Researcher 1's overall opinion on GMOs is positive, so Choice (J) is unlikely. Choice (G) doesn't describe benefits, so eliminate it. Choices (F) and (H) are benefits, but the researcher never says that GMOs increase nutritional values. The statement is that they haven't been shown to have fewer nutrients than organics, but that's not the same as having more nutritional value. Choice (F) is the best answer.

15. **B.** The first researcher is generally positive about GMOs and the second is generally negative, so they are unlikely to agree on much. Eliminate Choice (A) because both researchers say the opposite — decreasing pesticides is good for the environment. Researcher 2 states that the taste and quality of GMOs is inferior to organics, so Choice (C) is out. Researcher 1 mentions allergies, but Researcher 2 doesn't, so Choice (D) is wrong. Both researchers state that no correlation exists between health problems and GMOs, so the best answer is Choice (B).

16. **F.** Researcher 2 states directly that no correlation exists between health problems and GMOs, so Choice (J) is out. The first sentence of Researcher 2's paragraph states that pests become resistant to GMOs, but that doesn't necessarily mean that their use decreases naturally occurring pest reducers or increases the use of harmful pesticides. So Choices (G) and (H) are out, and by process of elimination, Choice (F) is correct. The last disadvantage mentioned by Researcher 2 is that plant pollen travels large distances, which means organic foods are contaminated by GMOs.

17. **D.** Choice (A) is mentioned by Researcher 2 but not Researcher 1. Choice (B) is mentioned by neither. And Researcher 1 specifically states that GMOs do not have reduced nutritional value. Eliminate Choices (A), (B), and (C). The first researcher mentions the possibility of increased allergies in the last sentence of the opinion. So the answer has to be Choice (D).

18. **F.** The second researcher mentions planting a variety of species, using natural repellants such as ladybugs, and increasing community farms as ways of reducing pesticides. Eliminate all answers but Choice (F). This researcher warns that GMOs can pollinate organic crops, so it's unlikely that he would advocate for growing some GMOs.

19. **C.** A link suggests a cause–and–effect relationship. Researcher 2 discusses the rise of community gardens as possible ways to reduce pesticide use and put less strain on food-producing corporations. Neither is necessarily linked to GMO use. Although the researcher states that pests become resistant to GMOs more quickly, he doesn't state that pesticide use increases as a result. The researcher isn't impressed with the food quality of GMOs, so the best answer is Choice (C).

20. **G.** Scan the options. The graphs show several relationships concerning GMOs and pesticide use, and you're supposed to choose the one that represents what Researcher 1 thinks. The first few sentences of Researcher 1's opinion indicate an inverse relationship between GMOs and pesticide use. As GMOs increase, pesticides decrease. So you can eliminate Choice (F). Choice (H) is out because Researcher 1 states that increased use of GMOs increases crop yields. Researcher 1 agrees that increased pesticide use creates increased harm to the environment, but so does Researcher 2, so Choice (J) is consistent with the opinions of both researchers. The best answer is Choice (G). Researcher 2 isn't convinced that GMOs directly cause a decrease in pesticide use because pests become resistant to GMO plants, which suggests that pesticides would eventually be necessary with GMOs as well.

21. **C.** An independent variable is an element that the experimenters change in the setup and execution of the experiment. The researchers tested both sandy and potting soil, so the type of soil is an independent variable. Eliminate Choice (B) because it doesn't contain I. Table 1 reveals that the researchers varied the number of hours of daily sunlight the plants received, so hours of sunlight is also an independent variable, Choice (A) must be wrong. Plant height varied based on the design of the experiment, so it was a dependent variable. Choice (D) can't be right. The answer is Choice (C).

22. **J.** More daylight creates greater plant height, and potting soil or sandy soil with compost produces taller plants than sandy soil alone. The answer with potting soil and the most sunlight is Choice (J).

23. **C.** Look at the table and figure. The table records results from Experiment 2. The column headings are hours of sunlight, so you know that the light varied in that experiment. Eliminate Choices (A), (B), and (D). Choice (C) is the only answer that states the light was varied in Experiment 2.

24. **H.** The second experiment used sandy soil with compost. Experiment 1 indicates that potting soil and sandy soil with compost have similar results, so what's true for Experiment 2 will likely also be true for Experiment 3. The answer that says this best is Choice (H).

25. **D.** Experiment 2 shows a direct relationship between hours of sunlight and plant height. The line that shows a direct relationship is one with a positive slope. Choice (D) is the best answer.

26. **F.** Read the information that follows the Yes and No in each answer. It's true that the ratio of plant height to daily number of hours decreased as researchers increased the number of hours, so keep Choice (F) in the running. But eliminate Choice (G) because the ratio decreased as the number of hours increased. For the same reason, keep Choice (H) and eliminate Choice (J). Now go back and read the question to determine whether the answer is *yes* or *no*. The conclusion is reasonable because the plant height would likely be close to 65 cm. The ratio of plant height to number of hours is decreasing as the number of hours increases. Pick Choice (F).

TIP

Approach "Yes, Yes, No, No" questions by evaluating the answers before you read the question. Usually you can eliminate answers before you even read the question. And reading the answers first shows you which information to focus on when you answer the question.

27. **D.** No experiment tested the relative effects of sunlight, soil type, or water on plant height, so you don't know which had a more significant effect. Therefore, Choices (B) and (C) are wrong. Choice (A) may appear correct, but the experiments didn't test water, so you don't know what amounts of water result in the greatest plant growth. Choice (D) is best because it is justified by the information in Figure 1 — plants grown in potting soil and sandy soil with compost grew to similar heights.

28. **J.** Focus on Figures 1 and 2 because they record results for Experiment 1. Figure 1 shows that the pH of the two types of ponds was similar, so Choices (F) and (H) are wrong. Figure 2 shows that healthy ponds had slightly higher temperatures, so Choice (G) is out. The answer is Choice (J).

29. **D.** The pH levels in the ponds were very similar, but the oxygen level in the healthy ponds was significantly higher. So there's no relationship between pH levels and oxygen levels. Pick Choice (D).

30. **F.** The introduction to Experiment 2 states that algae blooms may be caused by high levels of nitrogen. Based on Figure 3, the contaminated ponds had higher nitrogen levels, so they likely had more algae blooms. Choice (F) is best. Algae blooms aren't associated with water temperature, so Choices (G) and (J) can't be right. And Choice (H) isn't true. The healthy ponds had lower levels of nitrogen.

31. **B.** The pH of both types of ponds is the same, so the types of rocks are likely the same for both of them. Therefore, you can eliminate Choices (A) and (D). If the runoff has a pH lower than 7 but Figure 1 shows the pond water to have a pH around 7, the rocks in the pond may be neutralizing the acidity of the runoff. The question tells you that limestone contains bases and bases can neutralize acids, so the ponds are more likely to contain limestone–based rock. The granite wouldn't affect the pH. Choice (B) is a better answer than Choice (C).

32. **F.** The question doesn't concern water depth, so eliminate Choice (J). The contaminated ponds have less dissolved oxygen than the healthy ponds, so it's more likely their water is moving more slowly and the healthy pond water is moving more quickly. Choice (F) says it best.

33. **C.** Use the answers to help you focus. Choice (A) isn't true, so you can eliminate that answer. The remaining choices contain information that's borne out by the passage. Your job is to determine which is related to acid rain. The passage suggests that acidity relates to pH levels, so the best answer is Choice (C).

34. **J.** The set–up information for Experiment 2 clearly states that the ponds tested in Experiment 2 were the same as those in Experiment 1 and that the measures were averages as in Experiment 1, so Choices (F) and (G) must be wrong. Only Experiment 2 tested for the amount of oxygen in the ponds, and oxygen is a gas, so the correct answer is Choice (J).

35. **C.** Eliminate Choices (B) and (D) because their explanations are wrong. The average velocities of waves in the two oceans are the same, and the wavelengths of waves in the two oceans are different. Choice (A)'s explanation is correct: the Atlantic and Pacific Oceans have waves with similar average velocities and different average wavelengths, but similar velocities and different wavelength wouldn't produce similar periods. The passage expresses the relationship between velocity (c) and period (T) as $c = \lambda / T$, so for the T to be the same for waves in both oceans, their wavelengths would also have to be the same. The correct answer is Choice (C).

36. **H.** Table 1 provides information on the tables, but no column provides the data for wave period. Above the table is an equation that solves for T: $T = 1/v$ and v is frequency. The greatest wave period is the one with the lowest value in the denominator, so the answer is Choice (H). According to the table, the Gulf of Mexico has the shortest frequency and therefore, the greatest average wave period.

37. **A.** The table indicates an inverse relationship between wavelength values and frequency values: as wavelength increases, frequency decreases. A frequency of 0.0075 m/s is greater than the other frequencies, so the wavelength for this body of water must be less than 425 m. Pick Choice (A).

38. **J.** You know that amplitude is the distance from the centerline to the crest, but you don't know how to calculate amplitude from the data in the passage. Don't be afraid to pick Choice (J) and move on.

39. **A.** Because the relationship between wavelength and frequency is inverse, as wavelength increased, frequency decreased. Pick Choice (A).

40. **H.** The formula for c (velocity) is wavelength over average period. Eliminate Choice (F) because a higher velocity would result in a lower value for the average period. The remaining answers involve wavelength, so you need to consider the role wavelength plays in determining the average period. If you solve for T in the velocity formula, you get T = wavelength/velocity. A smaller numerator and a lower denominator in the formula for T would increase velocity. So the answer is Choice (H).

Writing Test

If you wrote the optional essay for this test, check it over and make sure your essay contains these necessary features:

> **A clear position:** Did you take a stand and stick to it? Remember that which side you take isn't a big deal. How well you support your position makes or breaks your essay. You should take only a few seconds to choose which side to argue before you start writing.

> **A clear understanding of the complexity of the issue:** Top essays include a careful analysis of possible positions to weigh the pros and cons of all and arrive at the best possible solution.

> **A strong thesis:** Did you create a thesis that answers the question posed by the prompt and sets up your essay? Try to slip in some of the wording from the prompt. Make sure your thesis introduces the two or three main points you use to back up your stand on the issue.

> **A steady focus:** Every element of your essay should be about your thesis. Make sure you didn't stray off topic.

> **Good organization:** We know it sounds boring, but your essay must have an introduction, body, and conclusion. Make sure you devote each paragraph in the body to a discussion of one of your two or three main supporting points. Check out the hamburger organization plan that we outline in Chapter 17 to help you evaluate the organization of your essay.

> **Excellent examples:** Professional essay readers really love to see creative, descriptive examples that strengthen your points. Vivid details draw readers in and endear them to your writing prowess.

> **Clear and interesting writing:** Check your essay for sentence structure variety, precise word choice, and impeccable spelling, grammar, and punctuation.

Sample response

The issue of whether elderly drivers should be forced to retake driver's tests once they reach a certain age is indeed polarizing. Studies show that drivers' ability to drive safely diminishes once they reach a particular age, but some believe that forcing drivers to reapply is offensive and a form of age discrimination. Despite the potential for offense, requiring that drivers test after a certain age is necessary to maintain public safety.

Diminished vision and decreased reaction time are common effects of the aging process, and they are also common consequences of drinking and driving. No one argues that drinking and driving is dangerous, so why would we accept the same dangerous behaviors in our elderly population? Laws are enacted to ensure public safety. People shouldn't be able to drive while impaired whether that impairment is from taking substances or advanced age.

Given the increased safety mandatory testing would ensure, issues of age discrimination don't hold up. Simply put, some things require more attention as we age. Take a mammogram, for example. Most young women aren't having them performed regularly because they aren't as likely to develop breast cancer as older women, but the procedure is a necessary step to ensure safety as women age. Discrimination is justified when the circumstances result in benefit. If forcing older populations to retest once they reach a certain age is age discrimination against the elderly, then allowing those over age 62 to receive social security benefits is discriminatory against those under 62. Allowing those over 21 to consume alcohol is not discriminatory to those who have yet to reach the age of 21. Some age discrimination is necessary when taking into consideration the different circumstances for different age groups.

People change as a result of the aging process. Creating laws that are appropriate for these changes to maintain safety is logical and justifies issues of age discrimination. Having elderly drivers reapply for driver's licenses is necessary to maximize safety and allow the greatest number of people to enjoy full, long, and healthy lives.

Score One for Your Side: The Scoring Guide

The ACT scoring may be weird (Why is 36 the high score? Why not a 21 or a 49 or a 73?), but it is very straightforward. Follow these simple directions to score your practice exam:

1. **Count the number of correct responses in each of the practice tests — English, Mathematics, Reading, and Science (see the answer key at the end of the chapter).**

   Do NOT subtract any points for questions you missed or questions you didn't answer. Your score is based only on the number of questions you answered correctly. That number is called your *raw score*.

2. **Locate your raw score in Table 20-1 and move to the left to find the *scale score* that corresponds to your raw score.**

   For example, a raw score of 50 on the English Test gives you a scale score of 21.

3. **Add your four scale scores and divide that sum by 4; the resulting average is your *composite score*.**

   Fractional averages follow standard rules for rounding up or down to the nearest integer.

   For example, say that your scale scores were 23, 31, 12, and 19; your composite score would be $85 \div 4 = 21.25$, or 21.

TABLE 20-1 **Scoring Guide**

Scale Score	Raw Scores			
	English	Mathematics	Reading	Science
1	0–1	0	0	0
2	2	–	1	–
3	3	1	2	1
4	4–5	–	3	–
5	6–7	–	4	–
6	8–9	2	5	2
7	10–11	3	6	3
8	12–13	–	7	4
9	14–16	4	8	5
10	17–19	5	9	6
11	20–22	6–7	10	7
12	23–25	8	11–12	8–9
13	26–28	9–10	13	10

Raw Scores Scale Score	English	Mathematics	Reading	Science
14	29–31	11–12	14	11–12
15	32–35	13–14	15	13–14
16	36–37	15–17	16	15
17	38–40	18–19	17	16–17
18	41–43	20–22	18–19	18–19
19	44–45	23–24	20	20–21
20	46–48	25–26	21	22
21	49–50	27–29	22	23–24
22	51–53	30–32	23	25
23	54–55	33–34	24	26–27
24	56–57	35–37	25	28
25	58–59	38–40	26–27	29
26	60–62	41–42	28	30
27	63–64	43–45	29	31
28	65–66	46–48	30	32
29	67	49–50	31	33
30	68–69	51–53	–	34
31	70	54–55	32	35
32	71–72	56	33	36
33	73	57	34	37
34	–	58	35	38
35	74	59	36	39
36	75	60	37–40	40

Answer Key for Practice Exam 1

English Test

1.	B	16.	G	31.	C	46.	H	61.	C
2.	H	17.	C	32.	F	47.	D	62.	G
3.	A	18.	G	33.	B	48.	J	63.	B
4.	H	19.	A	34.	H	49.	A	64.	J
5.	A	20.	J	35.	D	50.	H	65.	D
6.	G	21.	B	36.	F	51.	C	66.	G
7.	B	22.	F	37.	C	52.	F	67.	B
8.	G	23.	A	38.	J	53.	D	68.	H
9.	D	24.	H	39.	B	54.	G	69.	A
10.	F	25.	D	40.	F	55.	C	70.	G
11.	C	26.	J	41.	B	56.	H	71.	A
12.	H	27.	C	42.	F	57.	C	72.	G
13.	B	28.	F	43.	B	58.	J	73.	C
14.	J	29.	C	44.	J	59.	D	74.	J
15.	D	30.	F	45.	C	60.	F	75.	A

Mathematics Test

1.	B	13.	E	25.	D	37.	D	49.	A
2.	F	14.	D	26.	G	38.	K	50.	G
3.	A	15.	B	27.	D	39.	B	51.	C
4.	K	16.	K	28.	F	40.	K	52.	H
5.	D	17.	B	29.	C	41.	B	53.	B
6.	F	18.	J	30.	K	42.	K	54.	J
7.	D	19.	D	31.	A	43.	E	55.	D
8.	J	20.	H	32.	G	44.	H	56.	H
9.	C	21.	A	33.	C	45.	B	57.	B
10.	J	22.	J	34.	J	46.	G	58.	F
11.	A	23.	C	35.	B	47.	C	59.	B
12.	C	24.	K	36.	F	48.	H	60.	H

Reading Test

1.	C	9.	D	17.	A	25.	B	33.	C
2.	F	10.	F	18.	J	26.	F	34.	F
3.	B	11.	A	19.	D	27.	C	35.	D
4.	H	12.	H	20.	J	28.	F	36.	F
5.	A	13.	D	21.	A	29.	C	37.	C
6.	H	14.	G	22.	J	30.	G	38.	G
7.	A	15.	A	23.	C	31.	D	39.	D
8.	J	16.	G	24.	J	32.	G	40.	J

Science Test

1.	D	9.	B	17.	D	25.	D	33.	C
2.	F	10.	G	18.	F	26.	F	34.	J
3.	A	11.	D	19.	C	27.	D	35.	C
4.	H	12.	F	20.	G	28.	J	36.	H
5.	B	13.	A	21.	D	29.	D	37.	A
6.	H	14.	F	22.	J	30.	F	38.	J
7.	D	15.	B	23.	C	31.	B	39.	A
8.	H	16.	F	24.	H	32.	F	40.	H

Chapter **21**

Practice Exam 2

Ready to see how you do on a sample ACT? The following exam consists of five tests: a 45-minute English Test, a 60-minute Mathematics Test, a 35-minute Reading Test, a 35-minute Science Test, and a 40-minute Writing Test.

To get the most bang for your buck, take this test under the following normal exam conditions:

>> Sit where you won't be interrupted or tempted to use your cellphone or play video games (even though it seems downright cruel).

>> Use the answer sheet provided to give you practice filling in the dots.

>> Set your timer for the time limits indicated at the beginning of each test in this exam.

>> Do not go on to the next test until the time allotted for the test you're taking is up.

>> Check your work for that test only; don't look at more than one test at a time.

>> Don't take a break during any test.

>> Give yourself one ten-minute break between the Math Test and the Reading Test.

TIP

When you finish this practice exam, turn to Chapter 22, where you'll find detailed explanations of the answers as well as an abbreviated answer key. Go through the answer explanations to all the questions, not just the ones that you missed. You'll find a cornucopia of valuable information that provides a good review of everything that we cover in the other chapters of this book. We've even thrown in a few cheesy jokes to help you get through it.

Note: The ACT Writing Test is optional. If you register to take the Writing Test, you'll take it after you've completed the other four tests. For details about the optional Writing Test, see Part 6.

Answer Sheet

Begin with Number 1 for each new test.

English Test

1. Ⓐ Ⓑ Ⓒ Ⓓ	51. Ⓐ Ⓑ Ⓒ Ⓓ
2. Ⓕ Ⓖ Ⓗ Ⓙ	52. Ⓕ Ⓖ Ⓗ Ⓙ
3. Ⓐ Ⓑ Ⓒ Ⓓ	53. Ⓐ Ⓑ Ⓒ Ⓓ
4. Ⓕ Ⓖ Ⓗ Ⓙ	54. Ⓕ Ⓖ Ⓗ Ⓙ
5. Ⓐ Ⓑ Ⓒ Ⓓ	55. Ⓐ Ⓑ Ⓒ Ⓓ
6. Ⓕ Ⓖ Ⓗ Ⓙ	56. Ⓕ Ⓖ Ⓗ Ⓙ
7. Ⓐ Ⓑ Ⓒ Ⓓ	57. Ⓐ Ⓑ Ⓒ Ⓓ
8. Ⓕ Ⓖ Ⓗ Ⓙ	58. Ⓕ Ⓖ Ⓗ Ⓙ
9. Ⓐ Ⓑ Ⓒ Ⓓ	59. Ⓐ Ⓑ Ⓒ Ⓓ
10. Ⓕ Ⓖ Ⓗ Ⓙ	60. Ⓕ Ⓖ Ⓗ Ⓙ
11. Ⓐ Ⓑ Ⓒ Ⓓ	61. Ⓐ Ⓑ Ⓒ Ⓓ
12. Ⓕ Ⓖ Ⓗ Ⓙ	62. Ⓕ Ⓖ Ⓗ Ⓙ
13. Ⓐ Ⓑ Ⓒ Ⓓ	63. Ⓐ Ⓑ Ⓒ Ⓓ
14. Ⓕ Ⓖ Ⓗ Ⓙ	64. Ⓕ Ⓖ Ⓗ Ⓙ
15. Ⓐ Ⓑ Ⓒ Ⓓ	65. Ⓐ Ⓑ Ⓒ Ⓓ
16. Ⓕ Ⓖ Ⓗ Ⓙ	66. Ⓕ Ⓖ Ⓗ Ⓙ
17. Ⓐ Ⓑ Ⓒ Ⓓ	67. Ⓐ Ⓑ Ⓒ Ⓓ
18. Ⓕ Ⓖ Ⓗ Ⓙ	68. Ⓕ Ⓖ Ⓗ Ⓙ
19. Ⓐ Ⓑ Ⓒ Ⓓ	69. Ⓐ Ⓑ Ⓒ Ⓓ
20. Ⓕ Ⓖ Ⓗ Ⓙ	70. Ⓕ Ⓖ Ⓗ Ⓙ
21. Ⓐ Ⓑ Ⓒ Ⓓ	71. Ⓐ Ⓑ Ⓒ Ⓓ
22. Ⓕ Ⓖ Ⓗ Ⓙ	72. Ⓕ Ⓖ Ⓗ Ⓙ
23. Ⓐ Ⓑ Ⓒ Ⓓ	73. Ⓐ Ⓑ Ⓒ Ⓓ
24. Ⓕ Ⓖ Ⓗ Ⓙ	74. Ⓕ Ⓖ Ⓗ Ⓙ
25. Ⓐ Ⓑ Ⓒ Ⓓ	75. Ⓐ Ⓑ Ⓒ Ⓓ
26. Ⓕ Ⓖ Ⓗ Ⓙ	
27. Ⓐ Ⓑ Ⓒ Ⓓ	
28. Ⓕ Ⓖ Ⓗ Ⓙ	
29. Ⓐ Ⓑ Ⓒ Ⓓ	
30. Ⓕ Ⓖ Ⓗ Ⓙ	
31. Ⓐ Ⓑ Ⓒ Ⓓ	
32. Ⓕ Ⓖ Ⓗ Ⓙ	
33. Ⓐ Ⓑ Ⓒ Ⓓ	
34. Ⓕ Ⓖ Ⓗ Ⓙ	
35. Ⓐ Ⓑ Ⓒ Ⓓ	
36. Ⓕ Ⓖ Ⓗ Ⓙ	
37. Ⓐ Ⓑ Ⓒ Ⓓ	
38. Ⓕ Ⓖ Ⓗ Ⓙ	
39. Ⓐ Ⓑ Ⓒ Ⓓ	
40. Ⓕ Ⓖ Ⓗ Ⓙ	
41. Ⓐ Ⓑ Ⓒ Ⓓ	
42. Ⓕ Ⓖ Ⓗ Ⓙ	
43. Ⓐ Ⓑ Ⓒ Ⓓ	
44. Ⓕ Ⓖ Ⓗ Ⓙ	
45. Ⓐ Ⓑ Ⓒ Ⓓ	
46. Ⓕ Ⓖ Ⓗ Ⓙ	
47. Ⓐ Ⓑ Ⓒ Ⓓ	
48. Ⓕ Ⓖ Ⓗ Ⓙ	
49. Ⓐ Ⓑ Ⓒ Ⓓ	
50. Ⓕ Ⓖ Ⓗ Ⓙ	

Mathematics Test

1. Ⓐ Ⓑ Ⓒ Ⓓ Ⓔ	31. Ⓐ Ⓑ Ⓒ Ⓓ Ⓔ
2. Ⓕ Ⓖ Ⓗ Ⓙ Ⓚ	32. Ⓕ Ⓖ Ⓗ Ⓙ Ⓚ
3. Ⓐ Ⓑ Ⓒ Ⓓ Ⓔ	33. Ⓐ Ⓑ Ⓒ Ⓓ Ⓔ
4. Ⓕ Ⓖ Ⓗ Ⓙ Ⓚ	34. Ⓕ Ⓖ Ⓗ Ⓙ Ⓚ
5. Ⓐ Ⓑ Ⓒ Ⓓ Ⓔ	35. Ⓐ Ⓑ Ⓒ Ⓓ Ⓔ
6. Ⓕ Ⓖ Ⓗ Ⓙ Ⓚ	36. Ⓕ Ⓖ Ⓗ Ⓙ Ⓚ
7. Ⓐ Ⓑ Ⓒ Ⓓ Ⓔ	37. Ⓐ Ⓑ Ⓒ Ⓓ Ⓔ
8. Ⓕ Ⓖ Ⓗ Ⓙ Ⓚ	38. Ⓕ Ⓖ Ⓗ Ⓙ Ⓚ
9. Ⓐ Ⓑ Ⓒ Ⓓ Ⓔ	39. Ⓐ Ⓑ Ⓒ Ⓓ Ⓔ
10. Ⓕ Ⓖ Ⓗ Ⓙ Ⓚ	40. Ⓕ Ⓖ Ⓗ Ⓙ Ⓚ
11. Ⓐ Ⓑ Ⓒ Ⓓ Ⓔ	41. Ⓐ Ⓑ Ⓒ Ⓓ Ⓔ
12. Ⓕ Ⓖ Ⓗ Ⓙ Ⓚ	42. Ⓕ Ⓖ Ⓗ Ⓙ Ⓚ
13. Ⓐ Ⓑ Ⓒ Ⓓ Ⓔ	43. Ⓐ Ⓑ Ⓒ Ⓓ Ⓔ
14. Ⓕ Ⓖ Ⓗ Ⓙ Ⓚ	44. Ⓕ Ⓖ Ⓗ Ⓙ Ⓚ
15. Ⓐ Ⓑ Ⓒ Ⓓ Ⓔ	45. Ⓐ Ⓑ Ⓒ Ⓓ Ⓔ
16. Ⓕ Ⓖ Ⓗ Ⓙ Ⓚ	46. Ⓕ Ⓖ Ⓗ Ⓙ Ⓚ
17. Ⓐ Ⓑ Ⓒ Ⓓ Ⓔ	47. Ⓐ Ⓑ Ⓒ Ⓓ Ⓔ
18. Ⓕ Ⓖ Ⓗ Ⓙ Ⓚ	48. Ⓕ Ⓖ Ⓗ Ⓙ Ⓚ
19. Ⓐ Ⓑ Ⓒ Ⓓ Ⓔ	49. Ⓐ Ⓑ Ⓒ Ⓓ Ⓔ
20. Ⓕ Ⓖ Ⓗ Ⓙ Ⓚ	50. Ⓕ Ⓖ Ⓗ Ⓙ Ⓚ
21. Ⓐ Ⓑ Ⓒ Ⓓ Ⓔ	51. Ⓐ Ⓑ Ⓒ Ⓓ Ⓔ
22. Ⓕ Ⓖ Ⓗ Ⓙ Ⓚ	52. Ⓕ Ⓖ Ⓗ Ⓙ Ⓚ
23. Ⓐ Ⓑ Ⓒ Ⓓ Ⓔ	53. Ⓐ Ⓑ Ⓒ Ⓓ Ⓔ
24. Ⓕ Ⓖ Ⓗ Ⓙ Ⓚ	54. Ⓕ Ⓖ Ⓗ Ⓙ Ⓚ
25. Ⓐ Ⓑ Ⓒ Ⓓ Ⓔ	55. Ⓐ Ⓑ Ⓒ Ⓓ Ⓔ
26. Ⓕ Ⓖ Ⓗ Ⓙ Ⓚ	56. Ⓕ Ⓖ Ⓗ Ⓙ Ⓚ
27. Ⓐ Ⓑ Ⓒ Ⓓ Ⓔ	57. Ⓐ Ⓑ Ⓒ Ⓓ Ⓔ
28. Ⓕ Ⓖ Ⓗ Ⓙ Ⓚ	58. Ⓕ Ⓖ Ⓗ Ⓙ Ⓚ
29. Ⓐ Ⓑ Ⓒ Ⓓ Ⓔ	59. Ⓐ Ⓑ Ⓒ Ⓓ Ⓔ
30. Ⓕ Ⓖ Ⓗ Ⓙ Ⓚ	60. Ⓕ Ⓖ Ⓗ Ⓙ Ⓚ

Reading Test	Science Test
1. Ⓐ Ⓑ Ⓒ Ⓓ	1. Ⓐ Ⓑ Ⓒ Ⓓ
2. Ⓕ Ⓖ Ⓗ Ⓙ	2. Ⓕ Ⓖ Ⓗ Ⓙ
3. Ⓐ Ⓑ Ⓒ Ⓓ	3. Ⓐ Ⓑ Ⓒ Ⓓ
4. Ⓕ Ⓖ Ⓗ Ⓙ	4. Ⓕ Ⓖ Ⓗ Ⓙ
5. Ⓐ Ⓑ Ⓒ Ⓓ	5. Ⓐ Ⓑ Ⓒ Ⓓ
6. Ⓕ Ⓖ Ⓗ Ⓙ	6. Ⓕ Ⓖ Ⓗ Ⓙ
7. Ⓐ Ⓑ Ⓒ Ⓓ	7. Ⓐ Ⓑ Ⓒ Ⓓ
8. Ⓕ Ⓖ Ⓗ Ⓙ	8. Ⓕ Ⓖ Ⓗ Ⓙ
9. Ⓐ Ⓑ Ⓒ Ⓓ	9. Ⓐ Ⓑ Ⓒ Ⓓ
10. Ⓕ Ⓖ Ⓗ Ⓙ	10. Ⓕ Ⓖ Ⓗ Ⓙ
11. Ⓐ Ⓑ Ⓒ Ⓓ	11. Ⓐ Ⓑ Ⓒ Ⓓ
12. Ⓕ Ⓖ Ⓗ Ⓙ	12. Ⓕ Ⓖ Ⓗ Ⓙ
13. Ⓐ Ⓑ Ⓒ Ⓓ	13. Ⓐ Ⓑ Ⓒ Ⓓ
14. Ⓕ Ⓖ Ⓗ Ⓙ	14. Ⓕ Ⓖ Ⓗ Ⓙ
15. Ⓐ Ⓑ Ⓒ Ⓓ	15. Ⓐ Ⓑ Ⓒ Ⓓ
16. Ⓕ Ⓖ Ⓗ Ⓙ	16. Ⓕ Ⓖ Ⓗ Ⓙ
17. Ⓐ Ⓑ Ⓒ Ⓓ	17. Ⓐ Ⓑ Ⓒ Ⓓ
18. Ⓕ Ⓖ Ⓗ Ⓙ	18. Ⓕ Ⓖ Ⓗ Ⓙ
19. Ⓐ Ⓑ Ⓒ Ⓓ	19. Ⓐ Ⓑ Ⓒ Ⓓ
20. Ⓕ Ⓖ Ⓗ Ⓙ	20. Ⓕ Ⓖ Ⓗ Ⓙ
21. Ⓐ Ⓑ Ⓒ Ⓓ	21. Ⓐ Ⓑ Ⓒ Ⓓ
22. Ⓕ Ⓖ Ⓗ Ⓙ	22. Ⓕ Ⓖ Ⓗ Ⓙ
23. Ⓐ Ⓑ Ⓒ Ⓓ	23. Ⓐ Ⓑ Ⓒ Ⓓ
24. Ⓕ Ⓖ Ⓗ Ⓙ	24. Ⓕ Ⓖ Ⓗ Ⓙ
25. Ⓐ Ⓑ Ⓒ Ⓓ	25. Ⓐ Ⓑ Ⓒ Ⓓ
26. Ⓕ Ⓖ Ⓗ Ⓙ	26. Ⓕ Ⓖ Ⓗ Ⓙ
27. Ⓐ Ⓑ Ⓒ Ⓓ	27. Ⓐ Ⓑ Ⓒ Ⓓ
28. Ⓕ Ⓖ Ⓗ Ⓙ	28. Ⓕ Ⓖ Ⓗ Ⓙ
29. Ⓐ Ⓑ Ⓒ Ⓓ	29. Ⓐ Ⓑ Ⓒ Ⓓ
30. Ⓕ Ⓖ Ⓗ Ⓙ	30. Ⓕ Ⓖ Ⓗ Ⓙ
31. Ⓐ Ⓑ Ⓒ Ⓓ	31. Ⓐ Ⓑ Ⓒ Ⓓ
32. Ⓕ Ⓖ Ⓗ Ⓙ	32. Ⓕ Ⓖ Ⓗ Ⓙ
33. Ⓐ Ⓑ Ⓒ Ⓓ	33. Ⓐ Ⓑ Ⓒ Ⓓ
34. Ⓕ Ⓖ Ⓗ Ⓙ	34. Ⓕ Ⓖ Ⓗ Ⓙ
35. Ⓐ Ⓑ Ⓒ Ⓓ	35. Ⓐ Ⓑ Ⓒ Ⓓ
36. Ⓕ Ⓖ Ⓗ Ⓙ	36. Ⓕ Ⓖ Ⓗ Ⓙ
37. Ⓐ Ⓑ Ⓒ Ⓓ	37. Ⓐ Ⓑ Ⓒ Ⓓ
38. Ⓕ Ⓖ Ⓗ Ⓙ	38. Ⓕ Ⓖ Ⓗ Ⓙ
39. Ⓐ Ⓑ Ⓒ Ⓓ	39. Ⓐ Ⓑ Ⓒ Ⓓ
40. Ⓕ Ⓖ Ⓗ Ⓙ	40. Ⓕ Ⓖ Ⓗ Ⓙ

English Test

TIME: 45 minutes for 75 questions

DIRECTIONS: Following are five passages with underlined portions. Alternate ways of stating the underlined portions come after the passages. Choose the best alternative; if the original is the best way of stating the underlined portion, choose NO CHANGE.

The test also has questions that refer to the passages or ask you to reorder the sentences within the passages. These questions are identified by a number in a box. Choose the best answer and shade in the corresponding oval on your answer sheet.

Passage 1

Food Trends
by Joel Shapiro

Recently, it has been a current trend in the food service industry to decrease fat content and sodium. This trend, which was spearheaded by the medical community as a method of fighting heart disease, has had some unintended side effects obesity and heart disease — the very thing the medical community was trying to fight.

Fat and salt are very important parts of a diet. It is required to process the food that we eat, to recover from injury, to stay hydrated, and for several other bodily functions. Fat and salt are required parts of diet. When fat and salt are removed from food, the food tastes as though it's missing something. As a result, people will eat more food to try to make up for that missing element. Even worse, people tend to compensate by eating more junk food. Such as potato chips, soda, candy, and doughnuts, my favorite. Junk food is full of fat and salt; by eating more junk food people will get more salt and fat than they need in their diet.

There is another interesting side effect of removing salt and fat from food — less flavor. It took me several years to figure out why the food that I was getting at restaurants had lesser flavor as time went by but the food that I prepare at home continued to have strong flavors. I discover the answer in a bowl of chili. I had been making chili (my family's favorite dish and one that I serve at least once a week) with low-fat meats, following the current trend toward low-fat food. One day at the grocery, the store had run out of the low-fat meat, so I bought some meat with much higher fat content than I normally purchase. The chili I made from this meat tasted much better than the previous chili.

From that point on, I experimented, with ingredients that were not low in fat. The resulting dishes were much more satisfying than before. In addition, I found that people I served them to didn't eat as much. After talking at several, I discovered that they found the meals much more satisfying than they had in the past. Therefore, they ate less. And, as a result, ending up eating less calories than they had with the low-fat meals.

[1] Salt is a more difficult ingredient to judge. [2] If there is too much, the meal doesn't taste good, and diners will push the food aside uneaten. [3] If there isn't enough, the dish tastes like something is missing and diners will eat more food to obtain enough salt. [12]

Salt also helps bring out the flavors of the dish. The trick is to find just the right amount. I generally do this by tasting. As I cook, I taste the sauce or food that I am preparing. If it tastes like "something is missing," then I add a little salt. I stir it in, give it a few minutes and then try it again. Eventually, it <u>tastes perfectly</u>.
13

Fat and salt enhance the way foods taste and are important parts of any diet. Including an adequate amount of both of them in your meals will reduce your urge to snack between meals (often on unhealthy, empty-calorie treats) and will improve the flavor of your food. However, be careful not to go overboard. Moderation is key; it's possible to consume too much of both, <u>being not good for the</u> 14 <u>health.</u> [15]

1. (A) NO CHANGE
   (B) Recently, there has been a current trend in the food service industry
   (C) A recent trend in the food service industry has been
   (D) Recently, having trended toward in the food service industry

2. (F) NO CHANGE
   (G) effects, including obesity
   (H) affects, such as obesity
   (J) affects: obesity

3. (A) NO CHANGE
   (B) It's
   (C) Both are
   (D) They were

4. (F) NO CHANGE
   (G) Fat, and also salt, are required parts of diet.
   (H) When on a diet, fat and salt are required.
   (J) DELETE the underlined portion.

5. (A) NO CHANGE
   (B) food, including potato chips, soda, candy, and doughnuts, my favorite
   (C) food, such as potato chips, soda, candy, and, my favorite doughnuts
   (D) food, potato chips, soda, candy, and doughnuts are my favorites

6. (F) NO CHANGE
   (G) less and less
   (H) lesser and lesser
   (J) the least

7. (A) NO CHANGE
   (B) discovering
   (C) discovered
   (D) had discovered

8. (F) NO CHANGE
   (G) the previous chili's
   (H) the flavor of the previous chili
   (J) the first one's

9. (A) NO CHANGE
   (B) on; I experimented,
   (C) on, I experimented;
   (D) on, I experimented

10. (F) NO CHANGE
    (G) After talking with any number of them,
    (H) After talking to several of them,
    (J) After talking afterwards to several people,

11. (A) NO CHANGE
    (B) As a result, they are eating less food and consuming less
    (C) As a result, they consumed less
    (D) And, as a result, they consumed fewer

12. The writer wants to add the following sentence to this paragraph:

    Although it has no calories, salt can affect how much food people consume.

    This sentence would most logically be placed:
    (F) before Sentence 1.
    (G) after Sentence 1.
    (H) before Sentence 3.
    (J) at the end of the paragraph.

13. (A) NO CHANGE
    (B) tastes well
    (C) tastes perfect
    (D) perfectly tastes

14. (F) NO CHANGE
    (G) which isn't healthy
    (H) not being too healthy
    (J) and that is for the health not good

15. The author wants to emphasize the importance of having the right amounts of fat and salt and discourage against eliminating them altogether by adding this sentence to the end of the last paragraph:

    However, if you eat no salt or fat, you are likely to overeat and become obese.

    Should the author include this addition?
    (A) No, because the addition would be redundant.
    (B) No, because the sentence contradicts information that the author states in the first paragraphs of the passage.
    (C) Yes, because the sentence provides information that the reader needs to know and cannot find elsewhere in the passage.
    (D) Yes, because the paragraph does not adequately conclude the passage without the inclusion of the sentence.

Passage 2

Native American Government

[1] The question has been asked how Native American tribes, whom govern themselves do so.
                              16
[2] Most tribal governments are organized democratic, that is, with an elected leadership. [3]
                          17
The governing body is referred to as a council, it is
                                              18
composed of persons elected by vote of the eligible adult tribal members. [4] The presiding official is the chairman, although some tribes use other titles, such as principal chief, president, or gov-
                19
ernor. [5] An elected tribal council, recognized as such by the Secretary of the Interior and the people working for him, have authority to speak and act for
                                    20
the tribe and represent it in negotiations with
                      21
federal, state, and local governments. 22

Just what do tribal governments do? They generally define conditions of tribal membership, regulate domestic relations of members, prescribe rules of inheritance for reservation property not in trust status, levy taxes, regulate property under tribal jurisdiction, control conduct of members by tribal ordinances, and they administer justice.
                                  23

What role do Native Americans have in the American political system? They have the same obligations for military service as do other U.S. citizens. They have fought in all American wars
                  24
since the Revolution, they served on both sides in the Civil War. Eli S. Parker, a Seneca from New York, was at Appomattox as an aide to General Ulysses S. Grant when Lee surrendered, and the unit of

Confederate Brigadier General Stand Watie, a Cherokee, was the last to surrender. It was not until World War I <u>that Native American's demonstrating</u>
<u>25</u>
patriotism (6,000 of the more than 8,000 Native Americans who served in the war were volunteers) moved Congress to pass the Indian Citizenship Act of 1924. One reads <u>in your history books</u> about
<u>26</u>
<u>using the Navajo Marines of their language</u> as a
<u>27</u>
battlefield code, the <u>only such code</u> that the enemy
<u>28</u>
could not break. Today, one out of every four Native American men is a military veteran, and 45 to 47 percent of tribal leaders <u>is a military veteran.</u> 30
<u>29</u>

16. (F) NO CHANGE

 (G) tribes go about governing themselves

 (H) tribes who go about governing them and do so

 (J) tribes, who, governing themselves, do so

17. (A) NO CHANGE

 (B) democratically

 (C) in a way that is democratic

 (D) OMIT the underlined portion.

18. (F) NO CHANGE

 (G) council; however, it is

 (H) council, but is

 (J) council and is

19. (A) NO CHANGE

 (B) such as, principal

 (C) like principle

 (D) like, principle

20. (F) NO CHANGE

 (G) had

 (H) has

 (J) having

21. (A) NO CHANGE

 (B) be representing it

 (C) to represent them

 (D) representing them

22. The most logical and coherent location for Sentence 4 would be:

 (F) where it is now.

 (G) before Sentence 1.

 (H) after Sentence 1.

 (J) after Sentence 5.

23. (A) NO CHANGE

 (B) and administering

 (C) and administer

 (D) and to be administering

24. (F) NO CHANGE

 (G) They did fight

 (H) It has fought (the tribal)

 (J) Fighting

25. (A) NO CHANGE

 (B) when the Native Americans, who demonstrated

 (C) that the Native Americans' demonstrated

 (D) when the Native Americans'

26. (F) NO CHANGE

 (G) in history books

 (H) in their history books

 (J) in one of their history books

27. (A) NO CHANGE

 (B) the use by Navajo Marines of their language

 (C) Navajos using their Marine language

 (D) the Navajo Marines language use

28. (F) NO CHANGE

 (G) only code such

 (H) only code, such

 (J) only such code,

GO ON TO NEXT PAGE ▶

29. **(A)** NO CHANGE

   (B) is military veterans

   (C) are military veterans

   (D) is a veteran of the military

30. Given that the author was supposed to write an essay that predicts the roles Native Americans will play in future wars, does this passage fulfill this goal?

   (F) No, because the primary purpose of the passage is to explain the responsibilities of tribal governments.

   (G) No, because the passage discusses only current and past events.

   (H) Yes, because the passage is mostly about the contributions of Native Americans to the military.

   (J) Yes, because the most logical topic for the next paragraph of the passage would be how Native Americans will contribute to future wars.

Passage 3

A Trip to Lassen

Every summer, my family takes a car trip to one of this countrys great national parks. Last
                                                                              31
summer we had the pleasure of spending several days in Lassen Volcanic National Park in Northern California. As we were there, the park ranger gave
                                      32
us a lot of interesting information about the park's geology, biology, and history.

[1] Apparently, the theory of plate tectonics claim
                                                                              33
that as the expanding oceanic crust, which is the
                                                            33
thinnest of the two types, forces its way under the
                    34
continental plate margins; it pierces deeply enough
                                  35
into the hot areas of the earth to liquefy again.

[2] Compartments of molten rock (called magma)

result. [3] About half a million years ago, Mount
          36
Tehama gradually building up here throughout

countless eruptions. [4] These become the feeding
              37
chambers for volcanoes, like the one that created
                                        38
Mount Tehama. [5] Mount Tehama fell long before

Lassen Peak came into existence, but it's caldera
                                                              39
ruptured, which is why there's no big lake there

now. 40

The park's flora is a mix of species that are

native to the Sierra Nevada range from varieties
                                                      41
that emanate from the Cascade Mountains. The

result is that the park in all areas boast more than
                                                        42
700 plant species, which is amazing when you

consider that nearby Mount Shasta has less than

500. 43 Around two thirds of the species are at the

northern limit of their range in the park, which

means that about one third of the species, those

from the Cascades, are at their southern limit.

The park ranger told us that historians have a

difficult time determining what life was like for

those who occupied the Lassen area long ago. They

do know, though, that it was a meeting point for

four groups of Native Americans; Atsugewi, Yana,
                                                  44
Yahi, and Maidu. Its harsh weather conditions,

generally high elevation, and itinerate deer

populations made the Lassen area pretty much

uninhabitable in the winter months. Therefore,

Native American groups probably just lived there

during warmer months when they could better

engage in hunting and gathering. 45

31. **(A)** NO CHANGE
    (B) one of these countrys' great national parks
    (C) one of this country's great national parks
    (D) one of this country's great national park's

32. **(F)** NO CHANGE
    (G) Whenever
    (H) While
    (J) During our time while

33. **(A)** NO CHANGE
    (B) claim when
    (C) claims that whichever
    (D) claims that as

34. **(F)** NO CHANGE
    (G) crust, the thinnest of the two types of crust
    (H) crust which is the thinner type
    (J) crust, which is the thinner of the two types of crust,

35. **(A)** NO CHANGE
    (B) margins, it pierces
    (C) margins; however, it pierces
    (D) margins and piercing

36. **(F)** NO CHANGE
    (G) resulting
    (H) results
    (J) resulted

37. **(A)** NO CHANGE
    (B) was built up here, going through countless
    (C) had builded up here through uncounted
    (D) built up here through countless

38. **(F)** NO CHANGE
    (G) as
    (H) as if
    (J) likely

39. **(A)** NO CHANGE
    (B) but its caldera
    (C) and Tehama's caldera
    (D) therefore, the caldera that it had

40. To make this paragraph more logical and coherent, Sentence 4 should be positioned:
    (F) where it is now.
    (G) after Sentence 2.
    (H) before Sentence 1.
    (J) after Sentence 5.

41. **(A)** NO CHANGE
    (B) and
    (C) form
    (D) to

42. **(F)** NO CHANGE
    (G) boasts and has
    (H) boasts over
    (J) have more than

43. At this point in the essay, the author is considering adding a specific description of the kinds of plants that grow on Mount Shasta. Should the author make this addition?
    (A) No, because the essay is about Lassen Volcanic Park rather than Mount Shasta.
    (B) No, because Mount Shasta has fewer species of plant life than Mount Tehama.
    (C) Yes, because the main topic of the paragraph is a discussion of plant species.
    (D) Yes, because it is always a good idea for a writer to provide many specific details in an essay.

44. **(F)** NO CHANGE
    (G) of Native Americans: Atsugewi,
    (H) of Native Americans, these are Atsugewi,
    (J) that are comprised by Native Americans — Atsugewi,

GO ON TO NEXT PAGE

45. Which of these best describes the function of the last paragraph?

- **(A)** It summarizes the information discussed in the previous paragraphs.
- **(B)** It presents a personal opinion that contradicts information that the author presents at the beginning of the passage.
- **(C)** It introduces a topic not previously discussed in prior paragraphs.
- **(D)** It supports the author's hypothesis that the Lassen area is only inhabitable during the winter months.

Passage 4

One Boy's Role Model

As a young boy, I having dreamed of following
46
in the footsteps of explorer Richard Halliburton,

who it is fair to say has been my hero since
47
childhood. Let other boys dream of being Viking
48
warriors or knights in shining armor. I have always

wanted to be a world-famous explorer, going

places no one has ever been or returning to places

where civilization flourished long ago.

Richard Halliburton lived the life I always

wanted to live, and he wrote about it in ways that

motivated me as a youngster and still have the

power to thrill me as a man. I am especially

captivated by his stories of his trip to Pompeii,
49
which he calls the city that rose from the dead.

A few miles past Naples, Italy along the slopes of

Vesuvius, this city is found. It is much the same
50
as it was before the eruption in A.D. 79, with wine

jars still lying on the ground and ruts in the streets

from the passing chariots still visible.

[1] He calls these chilling effects the volcano's "tantrums" and mentions that, while the locals treat them casually, he himself cannot help that
51
consider what future explorers would think if they found his body, complete with tourist guide, wristwatch, and toothbrush. [52] [2] Halliburton makes his writing accessible by including familiar references that everyone can relate to, such as graffiti on the walls. [3] And describing the signboards and
53
posters in perfect condition that display announcements of gladiator contests and proclaim catchy quotations. [4] (My favorite is, "Good health to anybody who invites me to dinner.") [5] Neither
54
too wordy or too concise, the explorer's writing
55
appeals to the secret fears of all of us by mention-
56
ing that, as he sat in his hotel room that evening

and looks out over the landscape, he could see
57
flashes of red light shooting up from the summit

of it. [59] [60]
58

46. (F) NO CHANGE
- **(G)** As a young boy, I dreamed of
- **(H)** As a young boy, I am dreaming of
- **(J)** Dreaming, as a young boy, of

47. (A) NO CHANGE
- **(B)** whom, it is fair to say,
- **(C)** who, it's fair to say
- **(D)** of whom it is fair to say,

48. (F) NO CHANGE
- **(G)** Let other boy's dream
- **(H)** Dreams that other boys have
- **(J)** Other boys dream,

49. (A) NO CHANGE
(B) fascinated at
(C) captivated about
(D) apprehended with

50. (F) NO CHANGE
(G) This city is found a few miles past Naples, Italy, along the slopes of Vesuvius.
(H) Located a few miles past Naples, Italy, along the slopes of Vesuvius, you find this city.
(J) Along the slopes of Vesuvius, a few miles past Naples Italy is where this city is located.

51. (A) NO CHANGE
(B) he cannot help but
(C) he himself cannot help it that
(D) he himself cannot help but

52. The author most likely includes Halliburton's reference to a "tourist guide, wristwatch, and toothbrush" in Sentence 1 to:
(F) show how far hygienic practices have come since A.D. 79.
(G) add a touch of humor to the prospect of having Halliburton's body found in a lava flow.
(H) let the reader know what kinds of items an explorer carries with him.
(J) emphasize just how devastating the effects of Vesuvius were on Pompeii.

53. (A) NO CHANGE
(B) And like — the signboards
(C) Along with mentioning the signboards
(D) He also mentions the signboards

54. (F) NO CHANGE
(G) invite me to dinner
(H) invite him to dinner
(J) DELETE the underlined portion.

55. (A) NO CHANGE
(B) or, too, concise
(C) nor too concise
(D) nor concise enough

56. (F) NO CHANGE
(G) explorer, writing, appeals
(H) explorer and his writing appeals
(J) explorer's writing having appealed

57. (A) NO CHANGE
(B) evening and is looking out over
(C) evening, having looked over
(D) evening and looked out over

58. (F) NO CHANGE
(G) its summit
(H) their summit
(J) the summit of Vesuvius

59. To make the last paragraph more logical and coherent, Sentence 1 should be:
(A) positioned where it is now.
(B) positioned before Sentence 4.
(C) positioned after Sentence 5.
(D) DELETED, because there are no other references to volcanoes in the essay.

60. This essay on Richard Halliburton would most likely appear:
(F) in an encyclopedia entry about famous Italian explorers.
(G) on the editorial page of a small newspaper.
(H) as part of a memoir written by an older gentleman.
(J) in a geography textbook.

GO ON TO NEXT PAGE

Bird Mating Habits

The courting ritual of many birds <u>that</u> includes
61
elaborate dances and posturing. Some birds have
intricate <u>set routines that never vary,</u> patterns that
62
are repeated continuously in a dance as old as the
species itself. Other birds appear to be improvising,
making up steps as they go along and adapting
their movements to fit the situation. Some of the
dancers appear <u>more warlike than romantic</u> with
63
puffed-out chests and aggressive strutting. Some
of the dancers even charge the objects of their
affections. A type of pheasant, called the tragopan,
pops out from behind a rock to show himself to
the female. <u>While</u> one would expect the female to
64
be surprised or at least startled, more often than
not she is what one zoo curator called "amazingly
unimpressed."

Another part of the mating ritual is <u>to be</u>
<u>providing</u> an appropriately enticing home,
65
<u>often called a bower,</u> for the female. The nesting
66
areas are decorated with everything and anything
the bird can find, including twigs, feathers, small
rocks, trash bag pieces, <u>and sometimes there are</u>
<u>even broken glass shards.</u> Some experts have noted
67
that the birds with the less attractive plumage, dull
light brown birds with no exceptionally attractive
coloring, create the <u>more colorful and elaborate</u>
68
bowers, perhaps as compensation.

Not all birds are plain-colored. The male tragopan (found in southern Tibet) has a bright yellow
face and a red head. The wattled pheasant has
a dark body but a fan of snowy, almost painfully
white tail feathers. He also has a blue wattle around
the head and <u>red irises in the eye region.</u> The bird of
69
paradise can range from black to bright orange and
blue. You may know that a peacock has "eyes" on
its tail feathers, but did you know that a pheasant
<u>is with them,</u> too? The Argus pheasant can raise his
70
wing feathers, which are decorated with a pattern
that seems to resemble eyes. <u>This is why the Argus</u>
<u>pheasant got its name,</u> after Argus, the watchman
71
in Greek mythology who had a hundred eyes. Some
birds are so stunning that people who observed
them in captivity theorized that the birds must have
come from the Garden of Eden, the only place that
could possibly support such beauty.

<u>The courtship dances of birds have been</u>
<u>emulated by humans.</u> In New Guinea, <u>for example.</u>
72
<u>Warriors</u> wear large headdresses made with bird of
73
paradise feathers and dye their bodies to resemble
those of their favorite birds. 74 75

61. **(A)** NO CHANGE
    (B) which
    (C) those
    (D) DELETE the underlined portion.

62. **(F)** NO CHANGE
    (G) sets of routines, and they never vary,
    (H) routines and sets, never varying,
    (J) routines,

63. **(A)** NO CHANGE
    (B) as warlike than romantic
    (C) more warlike as romantic
    (D) as warlike as romantic

64. Which of the following substitutes for the underlined word would be the LEAST appropriate?
    (F) Although
    (G) Whereas
    (H) Because
    (J) Even though

65. **(A)** NO CHANGE
    (B) to have provision for
    (C) to have provided
    (D) to provide

66. **(F)** NO CHANGE
    (G) often called a bower —
    (H) often called, a bower
    (J) often, called a bower

67. **(A)** NO CHANGE
    (B) and even sometimes there are broken shards of glass
    (C) and, sometimes, even broken glass shards
    (D) and, sometimes, even, you find broken glass shards

68. **(F)** NO CHANGE
    (G) most colorful and elaborate
    (H) mostly colorful and elaborate
    (I) more than colorful and elaborate

69. **(A)** NO CHANGE
    (B) red irises
    (C) red in the irises region
    (D) red irises in the regions of the eye

70. **(F)** NO CHANGE
    (G) with them,
    (H) has them,
    (J) also has them,

71. **(A)** NO CHANGE
    (B) The Argus pheasant was named
    (C) This is the reason why they named the Argus pheasant
    (D) Therefore, the name is the Argus pheasant

72. **(F)** NO CHANGE
    (G) Humans have been emulating the courtship dances of birds.
    (H) The courtship dances of the bird has been emulated by humans.
    (J) Humans have emulated the courtship dances of birds.

73. **(A)** NO CHANGE
    (B) for instance; warriors
    (C) for example: Warriors
    (D) for example, warriors

GO ON TO NEXT PAGE

74. Which of these sentences is the best choice to come after the last sentence?

    (F) The costumes the men perform in are thought by some to resemble the appearance of those same birds.

    (G) Then they strut and posture in patterns that imitate the dance routines of the birds they look like.

    (H) Tragopans are commonly called horned pheasants because they have two horns that stand up during their courtship dance.

    (J) New Guinea is an island in the South Pacific and the most linguistically diverse area in the world.

75. Suppose the writer had been assigned to write an essay that includes a description of a courtship ritual of birds. Did the author complete the task successfully with this essay?

    (A) Yes, because the author describes how male pheasants attract female pheasants by building a bower.

    (B) Yes, because the author presents a theory and then provides examples of how that theory is manifested in real life.

    (C) No, because the author describes the coloring of only a few types of pheasants.

    (D) No, because the author includes a paragraph about how humans dance like birds.

DO NOT TURN THE PAGE UNTIL TOLD TO DO SO   **STOP**   **DO NOT RETURN TO A PREVIOUS TEST**

Mathematics Test

TIME: 60 minutes for 60 questions

DIRECTIONS: Each question has five answer choices. Choose the best answer for each question and shade the corresponding oval on your answer sheet.

1. Five cheerleaders and ten football players contributed to a coach's retirement party. Each cheerleader gave the same amount of money, exactly twice as much as each football player gave. If together the 15 friends donated $480, how much money did each football player give?

(A) $5

(B) $15

(C) $22

(D) $24

(E) $26

2. What is the fourth term in the arithmetic sequence 2, 5, 8 . . .?

(F) 9

(G) 10

(H) 11

(J) 12

(K) 13

3. If $x = -3$, which of the following is equal to $2x - (3y - 3x) + 4y$?

(A) $y + 15$

(B) $y + 12$

(C) $y - 12$

(D) $y - 15$

(E) $7y - 15$

4. What is the measure of angle LMX?

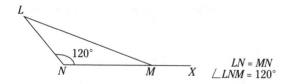

$LN = MN$
$\angle LNM = 120°$

(F) 150°

(G) 120°

(H) 100°

(J) 60°

(K) 30°

5. Jarnelle can assemble 300 widgets in an hour. To be eligible for a raise, she must be able to raise her rate of assembly by 25 percent. At the new rate, how many widgets could Jarnelle assemble in 8 hours? (Assume a steady rate with no breaks.)

(A) 6,125

(B) 3,000

(C) 375

(D) 300

(E) 75

6. To solve the following proportion, a must be which of the following?

$$\frac{3}{5} = \frac{a}{25}$$

(F) 20

(G) 18

(H) 15

(J) 12

(K) 5

7. What is the number of square units in the area of an isosceles right triangle with a hypotenuse of $5\sqrt{2}$?

(A) $2\sqrt{2}$

(B) 25

(C) $2.5\sqrt{2}$

(D) 12.5

(E) $10 + 5\sqrt{2}$

8. Which of the following is another way of expressing $6a - \left[(a - 3) - a \right]$?

(F) $4a + 3$

(G) $5a - 3$

(H) $6a - 3$

(J) $5a + 3$

(K) $6a + 3$

GO ON TO NEXT PAGE

9. Veronica buys a car on sale for 25 percent off the original price but has to pay a 5 percent luxury tax on the sale price. If the before-sale price of the car is $18,000, how much does Veronica pay for the car?

(A) $18,900

(B) $14,400

(C) $14,175

(D) $13,500

(E) $4,500

10. A floor with a length three times its width has a perimeter of 640 feet. What is its area in square feet?

(F) 100,000

(G) 19,200

(H) 14,400

(J) 8,800

(K) 6,000

11. If $a = 3$ and $b = 10$, which of the following is the closest approximation to $\dfrac{a + b(a-b)^2(a^2-b)}{b(a^2+b)}$?

(A) 10

(B) 2.5

(C) −1

(D) −2.5

(E) −8

12. Three angles, x, y, and z, share the same vertex and lie along a straight line. If $x = \frac{1}{2}y$ and $y = \frac{2}{3}z$, how much is $z - x$?

(F) 90°

(G) 85°

(H) 80°

(J) 70°

(K) 60°

13. What is the answer when $5a^3b^4 + 3a^2b^3$ is subtracted from $a^3b^4 - 2a^2b^3$?

(A) $-4a^3b^4 - 5a^2b^3$

(B) $-4a^3b^4 + a^2b^3$

(C) $6a^3b^4 + a^2b^3$

(D) $4a^3b^4 + a^2b^3$

(E) $4a^3b^4 + 5a^2b^3$

14. If a 30:60:90 triangle has a perimeter of $30 + 10\sqrt{3}$, what is its area in square units?

(F) $2000\sqrt{3}$

(G) 2,000

(H) $100\sqrt{3}$

(J) $50\sqrt{3}$

(K) $10\sqrt{3}$

15. The average scores of students on a final exam are as shown on the following chart.

Dustin	Kristiana	Leoni	Tim	Deidre
75	82	79	91	93

What is the positive difference between the mean and the median of their scores?

(A) 84

(B) 82

(C) 12

(D) 5

(E) 2

16. Rectangle $ABCD$ has a diagonal of 6 units, and one side measures 3 units. What is the perimeter, in units, of the rectangle?

(F) 24

(G) $12 + 12\sqrt{3}$

(H) $12 + 6\sqrt{3}$

(J) $6 + 6\sqrt{3}$

(K) 6

17. Which of the following is true of the pair of numbers 4 and 6?

(A) Their least common multiple is 24.

(B) Their least common denominator is 4.

(C) Neither number has any prime factors.

(D) The least prime factor of both numbers is 3.

(E) The least common multiple of both numbers is 12.

18. For all x and y, $\left(3x^2y + xy^2\right) - \left(2x^2y - 2xy^2\right) =$

(F) $x^2 - x$

(G) $x^2y - xy^2$

(H) $x^2y - 3xy^2$

(J) $5^2y - xy^2$

(K) $x^4y^2 + 3x^2y^4$

19. What is the number of square units in the total surface area of this cylinder, including both ends?

(NOTE: The formula for the total surface area of a cylinder is $2\pi r^2 + 2\pi rh$)

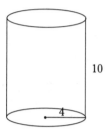

10

4

(A) 16π

(B) 40π

(C) 100π

(D) 104π

(E) 112π

20. What is the slope of a line parallel to the line $2x + 3y = 6$?

(F) $\dfrac{4}{3}$

(G) 1

(H) $\dfrac{3}{4}$

(J) $-\dfrac{2}{3}$

(K) 0

21. What is $\left(2a^2 + ab - 8\right) - \left(3a^2 - 2ab + 8\right)$?

(A) $ab + a^2$

(B) $3ab + a^2 - 16$

(C) $3ab + a^2$

(D) $3ab - a^2 - 16$

(E) $ab - a^2 - 16$

22. Jessica and Josh want an average score of 95 for five exams. Jessica's scores are 93, 92, 90, and 100. Josh's scores are 95, 97, 89, and 94. For each student to average a 95 for the five exams, how many more points does Josh need to get than Jessica on the last test?

(F) 5

(G) 4

(H) 2

(J) 1

(K) 0

23. Simplify $2y - (4 - 3y) + 3$.

(A) $-y - 12$

(B) $-y + 7$

(C) $5y - 7$

(D) $5y - 1$

(E) $5y + 1$

24. If the shaded area in the following square is $144 - 36\pi$, what is the diagonal of the square?

(F) $13\sqrt{2}$

(G) $12\sqrt{3}$

(H) $12\sqrt{2}$

(J) $6\sqrt{2}$

(K) 6

25. What is the measurement in degrees of x?

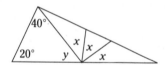

40°

20°

x

x

y

x

(A) 10

(B) 20

(C) 30

(D) 40

(E) 50

26. A machine sorts ball bearings. Due to a mechanical problem, the machine drops half the ball bearings per cycle. If the machine finishes its fifth cycle with 11 balls still remaining in the machine, how many balls were in the machine at the end of the first cycle?

(F) 704

(G) 352

(H) 176

(J) 88

(K) 44

GO ON TO NEXT PAGE

27. Five friends are going to share computer time. Each of the five will pay $22.20 for his share. If the friends want to drop their individual price paid down to under $12.00 each, how many additional friends must join in sharing the price of the computer time? (Assume all friends pay equal shares.)

(A) 8

(B) 5

(C) 4

(D) 3

(E) 2

28. If $\frac{1}{a} = 4$ and $\frac{1}{b} = 5$, how much is $\frac{1}{ab}$?

(F) $\frac{1}{20}$

(G) $\frac{1}{9}$

(H) 9

(J) 20

(K) 200

29. The circumference of Circle O is 10π units. What is the area of triangle ABC in square units?

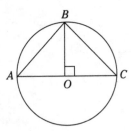

(A) 10

(B) $10 + 10\sqrt{2}$

(C) 20

(D) 25

(E) 50

30. If $4^{-x} = 64$, what is the value of x?

(F) −4

(G) −3

(H) 0

(J) 3

(K) 4

31. In the following right triangle XYZ, what is the value of tan Z?

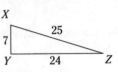

(A) $\frac{7}{25}$

(B) $\frac{7}{24}$

(C) $\frac{24}{25}$

(D) $\frac{25}{24}$

(E) $\frac{24}{7}$

32. After a slower reader increased her reading speed by 25 percent, she was still 50 percent slower than a faster reader. Before the slower reader increased her speed, the faster reader's speed was what percent of the slower reader's speed?

(F) 300%

(G) 250%

(H) 225%

(J) 200%

(K) 125%

33. The current pushes a swimmer back 2 feet for every 2 yards she swims. If she needs to cover 500 yards and each stroke takes her 5 yards, how many strokes must she take?

(A) 1,000

(B) 700

(C) 500

(D) 150

(E) 100

34. A farmer can plow x rows in y minutes. Which of the following represents the number of rows the farmer can plow in w hours?

(F) $60xyw$

(G) $\frac{x+7}{60}(w)$

(H) $\frac{w}{60}(x)$

(J) $\frac{w+x+y}{60}$

(K) $60\frac{x}{y}(w)$

35. If $f(x) = 1 + x^3$, what is $f(-5)$?

(A) 126

(B) 124

(C) −124

(D) −125

(E) −126

36. Two interior angles of an octagon sum up to 480. What is the average measure in degrees of each of the remaining interior angles in the figure?

(F) 180

(G) 175

(H) 150

(J) 125

(K) 100

37. Square *RSTU* has a perimeter of 48. If *A*, *B*, *C*, and *D* are the midpoints of their respective sides, what is the perimeter of square *ABCD*?

(A) 32

(B) $24\sqrt{2}$

(C) 24

(D) $12\sqrt{3}$

(E) $12\sqrt{2}$

38. What is the perimeter of the figure shown here?

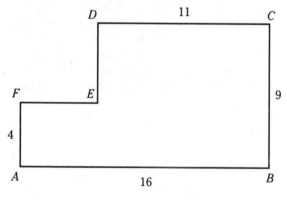

(F) 75

(G) 60

(H) 59

(J) 56

(K) 50

39. Given that *a* and *b* are integers and $a + b = 26$ and $a \neq b$, what is the largest possible value for *ab*?

(A) 169

(B) 168

(C) 165

(D) 26

(E) 13

40. Given that $x \neq 4$, simplify $\dfrac{\sqrt{x}+2}{\sqrt{x}-2}$.

(F) −1

(G) $\dfrac{x+4}{x-4}$

(H) $-\sqrt{x}-1$

(J) $\dfrac{x+4\sqrt{x}+4}{x-4}$

(K) $-\sqrt{x}+4$

41. $64^{\frac{2}{3}} = ?$

(A) 0

(B) 4

(C) 8

(D) 16

(E) 32

42. Set A = (2, 3, 4, 5, 6, 7, 8, 9)

Set B = (3, 6, 9, 12, 15)

Let *a* be a number from Set A and *b* be a number from Set B. Define *a@b* as the sum of all prime numbers from Set A and all non-prime numbers from Set B. What is the value of *a@b*?

(F) 61

(G) 60

(H) 59

(J) 51

(K) 50

GO ON TO NEXT PAGE

43. A cookie jar contains nine chocolate chip cookies, six oatmeal cookies, and four sugar cookies, and there are no other cookies in the jar. Paul pulls out and eats a chocolate chip cookie, an oatmeal cookie, a chocolate chip cookie, a sugar cookie, and an oatmeal cookie. What percent probability is there that the next time he reaches into the jar he will pull out a chocolate chip cookie?

(A) $66\frac{2}{3}$

(B) 50

(C) 40

(D) $33\frac{1}{3}$

(E) $\frac{1}{2}$

44. A street has a number of billboards. Starting at one end of the street, the billboard advertising milk is the 13th. From the other end of the street, the billboard is the 14th. How many billboards are there along the street?

(F) 24

(G) 25

(H) 26

(J) 27

(K) 28

45. The expression $x^2 + 7x - 8$ can be factored as the product of two linear factors, in the form $(a \pm b)(x \pm b)$. What is the sum of these two factors?

(A) $2x - 7$

(B) $2x + 7$

(C) $2x - 6$

(D) $2x + 6$

(E) $2x - 8$

46. $3a + 5b = 10$. Solve for b in terms of a.

(F) $5 - \frac{5}{2}a$

(G) $2 - \frac{3}{2}a$

(H) $2 - \frac{3}{5}a$

(J) $2a - \frac{3}{2}$

(K) $2a - \frac{3}{5}$

47. If $-4mx - \frac{3b}{c} = 4my$, then $x + y =$?

(A) $\frac{-3b}{4mc}$

(B) $\frac{-3b}{8mc}$

(C) $\frac{-3b}{16m^2c}$

(D) $\frac{-6b}{4m^2c}$

(E) $\frac{-3b}{c} - 4m$

48. What is the solution set for $a(a + 4) = 12$?

(F) {6, −2}

(G) {−6, 6}

(H) {−6, 2}

(J) {12, 0}

(K) {4}

49. What is the simplified form of $x\left[(3 + x)(4x) + 2\right]$?

(A) $4x^3 + 12x^2 + 2x$

(B) $2x^3 + 12x^2 + 2x$

(C) $12x^3 + 4x^2 + 2x$

(D) $4x^3 + 2x^2 + 4x$

(E) $4x^3 + 4x^2 + 12$

50. A car passed a designated point on the freeway and travelled for 2 hours at 80 m/hr. Then, in an effort to save gas, the driver slowed to 70 m/hr for 1 hour. The driver stopped for gas and lunch for 1 hour and then travelled 80 m/hr for 1 hour. The graph of the driver's distance (d) from the designated point as a function of time (t) would most resemble which of the following?

(F) d

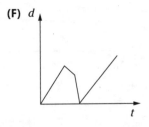

(G) d

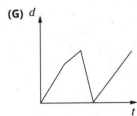

(H) d

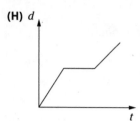

(J) d

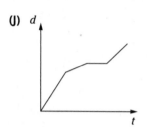

(K) d

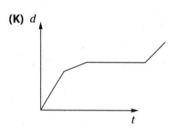

51. What is the sum of the two solutions to the equation $x^2 - 5x + 6 = 0$?

(A) -5

(B) -1

(C) 1

(D) 5

(E) 6

52. Which of the following represents the graph of the solution set of $x + 1 \le 8$?

(F)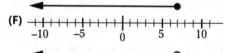

(G)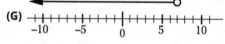

(H)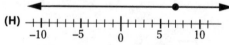

(J)

(K)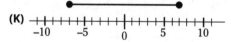

53. A line's equation is $x + 2y = 4 - (x + y)$. Its equation may also be expressed as $y = $?

(A) $\dfrac{3}{4} + \dfrac{2x}{3}$

(B) $\dfrac{4}{3} + \dfrac{2x}{3}$

(C) $\dfrac{4}{3} - \dfrac{2x}{3}$

(D) $\dfrac{1}{4} - \dfrac{2x}{3}$

(E) $\dfrac{2x}{3}$

54. Which of the following is equivalent to $\dfrac{\sin^2 \theta + \cos^2 \theta}{\sec^2 \theta}$?

(F) $\cos^2 \theta$

(G) $\sin^2 \theta$

(H) $\tan^2 \theta$

(J) $\dfrac{1}{\cos^2 \theta}$

(K) $\sin^2 \theta + 1$

55. What is the simplified form of $\dfrac{7}{2 + \sqrt{3}}$?

(A) 21

(B) $7 + \sqrt{3}$

(C) $7 - 7\sqrt{3}$

(D) $14 + 7\sqrt{3}$

(E) $14 - 7\sqrt{3}$

56. For all $a \ne 0$, what is the slope of the line passing through $(2a, -b)$ and $(-a, -b)$ in the usual (x, y) coordinate plane?

(F) 0

(G) $\dfrac{2b}{3a}$

(H) $\dfrac{3a}{2b}$

(J) $3a$

(K) undefined

57. Three painters take ten hours to paint four rooms. How many hours will 9 painters take to paint 12 rooms at the same rate?

(A) $1\dfrac{1}{3}$

(B) $3\dfrac{1}{3}$

(C) 6

(D) 10

(E) 30

GO ON TO NEXT PAGE

58. Which of the following is equal to $\dfrac{(10.8)(10^{-3})}{(400)(10^{-5})}$?

(F) $(0.027)(10^2)$

(G) $(0.0027)(10^2)$

(H) $(27)(10^{-2})$

(J) $(0.27)(10^{-2})$

(K) $(0.0027)(10^{-2})$

59. Georgia buys q quarts of milk at d dollars per quart and b boxes of cereal at $d+1$ dollar per box. Which of the following expressions represents the total amount spent?

(A) $qb+bd+1$

(B) $(q+b)(d+1)$

(C) $(q+b)(2d+1)$

(D) $d(q+b)+b$

(E) $bd(q+b)$

60. Find the area of rectangle *ACEG*.

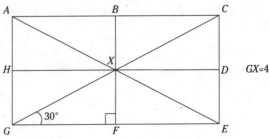

$GX=4$

(F) $8\sqrt{2}$

(G) $8\sqrt{3}$

(H) 16

(J) $16\sqrt{2}$

(K) $16\sqrt{3}$

Reading Test

TIME: 35 minutes for 40 questions

DIRECTIONS: Each of the four passages in this section is followed by ten questions. Answer each question based on what is stated or implied in the passage and shade the corresponding oval on your answer sheet.

Passage I — Prose Fiction

This passage is excerpted from the novel, *The Twelve*, by William Gladstone.

Max knew from the beginning that there was a purpose to his life and an important destiny that he had been called upon to fulfill. This understanding wasn't something tangible, however. There (05) was a voice in his head that spoke of a reason for which he had been born, yet there were no words — just colors and powerful vibrations. His inner world, this secret playground, was filled with beauty and elegance, and it made Max very happy.

(10) He seemed to be able to summon knowledge on any subject but had a particular attachment to the art of mathematics and exhibited an uncanny ability and proficiency with numbers, which constantly swirled around in his mind, vibrating in a multitude (15) of colors. Even before he could walk, he was able to multiply triple-digit numbers in his head.

And this talent adopted a three-dimensional component. He imagined boxes placed vertically and horizontally and at tangents without end. He (20) envisioned each box as the universe complete unto itself and would contemplate the shape, direction and lack of beginning or end within each box or collection of boxes.

Such exercises afforded him pleasure, as did (25) most things in life. However, there remained one constant reminder that all was not perfect.

Louis.

Despite the violence he experienced at the hands of his older brother, Max considered Louis (30) his best friend. Their uncanny link caused Max to feel great empathy for his sibling, and it seemed as if they both remembered the blissful paradise that had been the womb.

From the moment of his birth, Max accepted (35) that wherever he was, he was exactly where he was supposed to be in life and was completely at peace with the idea.

Louis, on the other hand, was angry that he had been forced to leave that perfect state of being and that the world had greeted him with a stran- (40) glehold. Thus, he had come into this world kicking and screaming and remained in a constant state of revolt.

That Max felt no such thing angered Louis even more, and he was determined to make his (45) brother's life as miserable as his own by virtue of force and fear. Even as toddlers, Louis would attack Max, pinning him to the floor and choking him, and then retreat as soon as Max started to cry. When the adults came running, he had achieved a (50) safe distance, and they never realized the level of the violence. Since Max couldn't express himself, they remained utterly ignorant.

Eventually Max learned to play dead. He found it otherwise impossible to resist, since Louis (55) was filled with such superhuman strength when enraged that it would take more than one adult to subdue him, had they even been aware of the need.

And despite his inherent inclination to be optimistic, Max found that the constant attacks began (60) taking their toll. He never felt safe at home and knew that, whatever successes he achieved at school, or in any aspect of life, he would suffer for it.

As the attacks increased, he seriously considered ending his life in order to escape his tormentor. (65)

At the age of seven, he contemplated stabbing himself in the stomach with a butter knife. While in his secret, inner world, he had seen the potential for his existence and was excited for the possibilities that lay ahead, the outer world presented him (70) with a very large, unavoidable obstacle.

His decision made, he picked up the knife.

Yet as he pushed the soft-edged blade into his tummy, he remembered the quiet, inner voice from early infancy. So he put the knife aside, realizing in (75)

GO ON TO NEXT PAGE

that moment that he had a purpose — a true mission — and even though there might be obstacles in his path, he would have the courage to face whatever came his way.

(80) Once he'd learned how to escape his brother's choke holds.

As a toddler, despite his lack of coherent speech, Max exhibited leadership qualities by taking charge of any group.

(85) As he grew, he excelled in every subject at school and had real joy in learning. He was very good in sports and at twelve years old was Westchester County's fastest runner in the fifty-yard dash. Max joked that it was running away from (90) Louis that had led him to become such a fast runner.

When he graduated from eighth grade, he was valedictorian, president of the student council and captain of the football, wrestling and baseball teams. He had an extraordinary sense of anticipat- (95) ing where the ball or opponents might be headed, he always seemed to be in the right place at the right time, and the idea of making an error never occurred to him.

He expected himself to be perfect in every- (100) thing he did . . . and so, he was. Yet these expectations didn't yield the anxiety experienced by most children.

There was no question that he was loved by his parents, and thanks to his father's success, he had (105) material abundance. So, despite the torments leveled in his direction by his brother, Max managed to survive his early adolescence.

1. Which of the following best expresses the main point of the first paragraph (Lines 1–10)?

   (A) Max lived in a constant state of optimism and positive thinking.

   (B) Max thought in colors and vibrations rather than in prose.

   (C) Max recognized that his thought process was different from others.

   (D) Max knew he was put on this earth for a reason, and while he had yet to determine exactly what that reason was, he was comforted by it.

2. The word *tangible*, as it is used in Line 4, most likely means:

   (F) vague or elusive.

   (G) concrete.

   (H) affirmative.

   (J) changeable.

3. Throughout his early adolescence, Max exhibited natural talent in all of the following areas EXCEPT:

   (A) mathematics.

   (B) track.

   (C) gymnastics.

   (D) football.

4. The following selection that best summarizes the passage as a whole is:

   (F) Max was able to overcome the most troubling obstacle in his life, his brother Louis, and become an overachiever despite the hardships he'd suffered at his brother's hands.

   (G) Max lived a life plagued by feelings of inadequacy as a result of the cruelty he suffered growing up alongside Louis.

   (H) Max's ability to hide the traumas in his home life enabled him to excel academically and through sports.

   (J) Max was intellectually superior to his peers from a very early age and suffered socially as a result.

5. The author would most likely say that Max thought about ending his life because:

   (A) his failure to be able to communicate verbally with his parents left him feeling he needed to take drastic measures to call attention to Louis's abuse.

   (B) the hardships he suffered at the hands of his brother seemed impossible to overcome despite his belief that he held a special purpose in this world.

   (C) he knew almost from birth that he was drastically different from his peers, and the thought of spending his whole life feeling like an outsider was too much to bear.

   (D) he felt that if he didn't take his own life, Louis would do so for him and he no longer could stand living in fear.

6. When the author refers to *exercises* in Line 24, he means:

(F) using his mind to position imaginary shapes.

(G) rudimentary calisthenics.

(H) multiplying six-digit numbers in his head.

(J) playing dead in front of Louis.

7. The author feels that Max exhibited leadership skills in his early years by:

(A) exhibiting a penchant for empathizing with others.

(B) showing an appreciation for those he didn't necessarily get along with, such as his unexplainable fondness for his brother Louis despite his cruel nature.

(C) approaching obstacles in his life in a calm, organized manner.

(D) demonstrating he could take charge of a group.

8. The author would most likely say that Max differed from most children his age in all but which of the following ways?

(F) He desperately yearned for the approval of his parents and teachers.

(G) He failed to speak throughout the majority of his childhood.

(H) He was unaffected by the high expectations adults placed on him.

(J) He felt from birth onward that he was exactly where he was supposed to be in life.

9. In Lines 70–71, when the author says, "the outer world presented him with a very large, unavoidable obstacle," he is most likely referring to:

(A) Louis.

(B) Max's unmatchable intellect.

(C) Max's lack of communication skills.

(D) society as a whole.

10. Which of the following best describes Max's progression throughout the passage?

(F) He spent his early years living in near-constant fear but devoted his later youth to instilling fear in others.

(G) He began life socially inept and was able to overcome struggles and excel in a variety of social situations.

(H) He lacked self-esteem throughout his early childhood but then became down-right narcissistic as the years progressed.

(J) He spent his early years in fear of his cruel older brother but was later able to capitalize on the experience.

Passage II — Social Science

This passage is adapted from *How to Develop Self-Esteem in Your Child: 6 Vital Ingredients*, by Dr. Bettie Youngs.

What is the work of childhood? Each stage of a child's development presents its own set of tasks (05) and demands, all focused on gaining self-knowledge or selfhood. The work of each stage is pretty well-defined.

Until the age of two, a child primarily views himself as part of his mother (or father, if he is the (10) primary caretaker). Upon reaching two, he develops the ability to be aware that he is really separate from her. This situation presents him with the task of establishing autonomy — separateness. The two words that best describe his new-found selfhood, (15) that he is in fact a separate person, are "no" and "mine." Possession is the tool he uses to enforce that sense of separate self.

Having realized his separateness, the three-year-old goes on to master his environment. Mas- (20) tery plays an important role in his perception of self. It influences his feelings of being capable or not capable. His need for success in his endeavors at this stage is crucial. He labors over each of his accomplishments. He is slow and methodical and (25) takes forever to do each task. Needing feedback to know if he has been successful, he strives for recognition of these achievements. ("Watch me, Mommy! Watch me, Mommy!") That he has something to offer nurtures his sense of competence and (30) proves his value.

GO ON TO NEXT PAGE ▶

Parents are the name of the game for the five-year-old. At this age, the mother is the center of the child's world. He not only wants to please her, but he also wants to be near her, wants to talk with her, wants to play with her, and wants to help her around the house. The five-year-old's adoration of his parents is unquestionably heartwarming. The result is almost totally parent-pleasing behavior.

(40) In his determination to do everything just right, he'll ask permission for the simplest thing, even when he needn't; and he will then beam with pleasure when the parent smiles and gives permission.

Age six can be described as the stage of "me-
(45) ness." Self-centeredness comes before other-centeredness. While children were in the preschool stage, they discovered that they were separate from their parents, although they still kept their parents as the center of their existence. At six, they
(50) must shift the focus from their parents to themselves. They now place themselves at the center of their world instead of parents or others. Although they may appear to be excessively self-centered and unconcerned with the needs and feelings of
(55) others, this is an important milestone in their development. They are now ready to undertake the task of being receptive to their own interests and attempting to understand them.

At age 16, it is not uncommon for a child to
(60) experience feelings of being confused, embarrassed, guilty, awkward, inferior, ugly, and scared, all in the same day. In fact, a teenager can swing from being childish and petulant to being sedate, or from acting rational to irrational, all in the same
(65) hour. It's a time of confusion and uncertainty. The goal is to experience intimacy; he needs to belong. This is a time of duality. The 16-year-old wants to be with others, yet he wants to be alone; he needs his friends, but he will sabotage them if they ap-
(70) pear to outdo him; he'll root for a friend out loud, but he'll secretly wish for his friend's failure. Age 16 is a time when he wants total independence, but he is not capable of it. He doesn't really want to live without his parents, although he believes
(75) that they are roadblocks hindering his life.

The final stage of development in childhood is establishing total independence. In changing from being dependent on others to being self-dependent, children confront some pretty big (and
(80) frightening) issues. They have three tasks. Their first task is to determine vocation. A child needs to ask what he is going to do with his life. Underlying this task is the self-esteem need to be somebody, to experience positive feelings of strength, power,

and competence. Second, he needs to establish (85) values. The goal is to sort out his own values and to decide which ones to keep and which ones to discard. Following this step is the only way that he can develop integrity. Perhaps most striking is his need to establish a workable and meaningful (90) philosophy of life. Reevaluating his moral concepts will mean searching for his own personal beliefs, complete with facing religious, ethical, and value-laden ideologies. Developing personal convictions will be influenced by his level of self-esteem, es- (95) pecially if a conflict exists among what he believes, what his family believes, and what his friends find acceptable. Third, he needs to establish self-reliance.

11. The author's primary purpose in writing this passage is to:

(A) show that early childhood learning is important because it provides the foundation for life.

(B) analyze the causes behind low self-esteem in children.

(C) denounce child psychologists.

(D) discuss the various behaviors associated with the ages of children.

12. According to the author, the ultimate goal of children is to gain:

(F) recognition.

(G) selfhood.

(H) praise.

(J) competence.

13. The author uses the comment, "Watch me, Mommy! Watch me, Mommy!" to make the point that three-year-olds:

(A) recognize that they are individuals, separate from their parents.

(B) do tasks in order to please their parents.

(C) need outside acknowledgment of their accomplishments at a specific age of development.

(D) are prone to repeating themselves.

14. Which of the following is another way of stating, "Parents are the name of the game" (Line 32)?

(F) Parents design games and activities to entertain and stimulate their children.

(G) The names parents give their children determine their sense of self-worth.

(H) Parental gamesmanship influences children's development.

(J) Parents are of prime importance to their children.

15. You may infer from the fifth paragraph (Lines 44–58) that the author considers a lack of sensitivity in six-year-olds:

(A) abnormal and rare.

(B) cute at that age but unacceptable in adults.

(C) precocious because such egotism does not usually begin until the teenage years.

(D) vital in order for children to recognize their separateness from their parents.

16. Which of the following phrases best expresses the idea of the sixth paragraph (Lines 59–76)?

(F) The goal is to experience intimacy.

(G) This is a time of duality.

(H) Age 16 is a time when a child wants total independence.

(J) A 16-year-old believes that parents are roadblocks hindering his life.

17. As used in Line 81, *vocation* means:

(A) rest and relaxation.

(B) geographical area.

(C) romance.

(D) career.

18. The author mentions all of the following as specific tasks in establishing self-dependence EXCEPT:

(F) figuring out what to do in life.

(G) determining moral concepts.

(H) developing self-reliance.

(J) avoiding conflicts between what he believes and what others believe.

19. Which of the following best describes the organization of the passage?

(A) Concepts are discussed in order from most important to least important.

(B) Discussions begin with a presentation of a theory followed by proven facts.

(C) Discussions are ordered chronologically.

(D) The author presents beliefs and then offers predictions.

20. It may be reasonably inferred from the passage that all stages of childhood have as their ultimate goal:

(F) fiscal security.

(G) recognition.

(H) independence.

(J) parental respect.

Passage III — Humanities

Passage A

El Greco received his formal art training in Crete and Italy, but he created his master works in Spain, a country known both for a heightened sense of spirituality and a feeling for the real and tangible. His formal training was a blend of Byzantine mysticism and Italian Mannerism. During his early years he learned from Cretan monks to make flat, mystical icons in the Byzantine tradition. He then studied under Jacopo Bassano and Titian in Venice, but was most influenced by his apprenticeship to Tintoretto, who introduced him to the emotion, force, and strong movement characteristic of Mannerism. (Line) (05) (10)

These early influences, coupled with a short stay in Rome where he was stimulated by the work of Michelangelo, supplied the background for the unique style El Greco achieved when he settled in Toledo to paint religious commissions for churches and convents. Not only did El Greco receive diverse artistic training, but he also received a well-rounded spiritual, historical, literary and scientific education from his early humanistic schooling and his eclectic group of friends in cosmopolitan Toledo. His paintings combined his varied artistic and intellectual influences to portray the interplay between the spiritual world and the material world. (15) (20) (25)

GO ON TO NEXT PAGE

Considered by many to be his masterpiece, *The Burial of the Count of Orgaz* reflects his forceful ability to illustrate both worlds.

(30)   Because his art was commissioned by churches and because art before the advent of photography served not only aesthetic purposes but also as a record of history, El Greco most often re-created specific religious events. *The Burial of the Count of* (35) *Orgaz* uses the burial of an esteemed and religious Spanish count, who had died over 250 years before its painting, as a means of portraying the relationship between the heavens and the earth. The brilliantly colored oil-on-canvas painting, mea- (40) suring 16 feet high and almost 12 feet wide, adorns one wall of the Church of San Tome in Toledo. The painting contains two main settings. The lower scene depicts an ornately robed Saint Stephen and Saint Augustine gently lowering the armored body (45) of Count Gonzalo Ruiz de Toledo into an unseen grave. Surrounding the saints is a group of clergy and noblemen in varying states of worship and mourning. Above this scene hover the inhabitants of heaven.

(50)   In contrast to the generally well-defined features of the figures in the lower scene, the figures in the heavens are blurred and ethereal. The dominant figure among the angels and saints is the blue-and-red-clothed Virgin Mary, who appears (55) to be taking petitions from a seemingly endless string of souls. Mary's gaze is not directed at the petitioners, however. She is gently reaching for the soul of the Count of Orgaz that floats toward her in the undefined form of a baby. Alongside Mary, (60) Saint Peter watches, holding the keys to heaven. Above and somewhat at a distance, Christ sits as Lord over the scene. The only connections between the two scenes are the flames that leap from the torches held by the noblemen to the heavenly (65) realm, the cross held by one of the clergy, and the eyes of the priest as he gazes toward the soul of the Count of Orgaz. These connections suggest that the division between heaven and earth, spiritual and material, can only be transcended by the Spirit, (70) symbolized by the flames, by Christ, symbolized by the cross, and, perhaps, through the knowledge of the priest.

Passage B

El Greco painted *The Burial of the Count of Orgaz* in Toledo, Spain, during the years 1586–88. Almost 400 years later, Joseph Beuys, a post–World War II (75) German artist, initiated his artistic career with mixed-media drawings that combined pencil with colored ink or watercolor on creased paper, one of which he entitled *Kadmon*. Although the two artists painted different subjects in different time periods, (80) in different countries, with different media and in different styles, they convey a common meaning.

Like El Greco, Joseph Beuys experienced a variety of personal and artistic influences that inspired him to portray spiritual and earthly themes (85) in his works. Beuys grew up in the tiny German town of Kleve, and his youth was influenced by the small community's predominant Catholicism and its bucolic, natural setting. Unobstructed by the limitations of church sponsorship and freed by (90) modern artistic exploration, Beuys chose more primordial subject matter for his interpretations. According to Christopher Lyon, Beuys's art grew out of his attempts to deal with the chaotic aftermath of World War II, and his early drawings portray (95) both the personal and political schisms that were created by the war's devastation. His early works reveal his vivid imagination and demonstrate what Lyon calls a "mythic approach to his life and art," a technique Beuys continued to explore more fully (100) in his studies at the Dusseldorf Academy of Art and in his unique performance art demonstrations in later years. *Kadmon*, one of Beuys's earliest works, portrays his fascination with the relationship between the mystical and the tangible. (105)

21. All of the following figures are depicted in El Greco's *The Burial of the Count of Orgaz* EXCEPT:

(A) Saint Augustine.

(B) clergy and noblemen.

(C) the Virgin Mary.

(D) Tintoretto.

22. It is reasonable to infer from Passage A that El Greco's artistic education:

(F) resulted from an intricate combination of religious and nonreligious influences.

(G) was largely a product of his formal training at the Dusseldorf Academy of Art.

(H) reached its height during his apprenticeship to Michelangelo.

(J) was more diverse and richer than the artistic educations received by other artists of his day.

23. Passage A states that El Greco painted his most accomplished works in:

(A) Italy.

(B) Crete.

(C) Spain.

(D) Germany.

24. The author of Passage A believes *The Burial of the Count of Orgaz* suggests that the separation between the spiritual and material worlds can be overcome by:

(F) Saint Peter because he holds the keys to heaven.

(G) the flame, which to the author is a representation of the Holy Spirit.

(H) wealth and power as symbolized by the torches held by the noblemen.

(J) the petitions of an endless line of souls.

25. Passage B implies that a significant influence on Beuys's art was:

(A) a blend of Byzantine mysticism and Italian Mannerism.

(B) studying the works of El Greco.

(C) growing up in a small, rural town in Germany.

(D) his Catholic school upbringing.

26. The word *schisms* in Line 96 refers to:

(F) solutions.

(G) religious beliefs.

(H) fascinations.

(J) divisions.

27. As presented in Line 77, "mixed-media drawings" most likely refers to drawings that:

(A) have been reproduced in a variety of different formats.

(B) have been created using more than one artistic technique.

(C) have been displayed in public settings and then reproduced to appear in print publications.

(D) have received mixed critical reviews in the media.

28. Based on Passage A and Passage B, El Greco and Beuys likely used different subjects to showcase the interplay between the heavens and the earth because:

(F) El Greco's vocation was supported by the church, but Beuys was not obligated to create works for a particular sponsor.

(G) Beuys's art was influenced by primeval subjects, whereas El Greco's art was inspired by his passion for history.

(H) the two had differing religious views.

(J) the two came from different socioeconomic backgrounds.

29. The two passages reveal a possible similarity between *The Burial of the Count of Orgaz* and *Kadmon*; both works:

(A) were created using a mixture of media.

(B) explored a common theme.

(C) were created based on influences from similar artists.

(D) portrayed similar subject matter.

30. Compared to Passage B, Passage A provides more information about:

(F) how the artist's work specifically portrays the relationship between the spiritual and material worlds.

(G) the shared themes portrayed in *The Burial of the Count of Orgaz* and *Kadmon*.

(H) how dealing with events in the artist's personal experience directly influences the subject matter in his artwork.

(J) the artist's various artistic influences and the materials he used.

GO ON TO NEXT PAGE

Line   Thrombosis refers to abnormal clotting that causes the blood flow in a blood vessel to become obstructed. Venous thrombosis refers to such an obstruction in a vein, often at some site of inflam-
(05) mation, disease, or injury to the blood vessel wall. The clot (thrombus) may remain fixed at the site of origin, adhering to the wall of the vein. Or the clot (or a fragment of it) may break loose to be carried elsewhere in the circulatory system by the blood.
(10) The migratory clot or fragment is then called an embolus.

     In pulmonary embolism, the clot or fragment breaks free from its site of origin, usually a deep vein of the leg or pelvis, and is carried by the blood
(15) through progressively larger veins into the inferior vena cava, a very large abdominal vein that emp-ties into the right side of the heart. The embolus is pumped through the right side of the heart and into the pulmonary artery, whose branches supply blood
(20) to the lungs. Depending on its size, the embolus may pass through the larger pulmonary branches, but may eventually enter a branch too narrow to allow it to pass. Here it lodges, obstructing blood flow to the lung tissues supplied by that vessel
(25) and its finer divisions "downstream" from the embolus.

     The clinical consequences of pulmonary em-bolism vary with the size of the embolus and the extent to which it reduces total blood flow to the
(30) lungs. Very small emboli cause so little circula-tory impairment that they may produce no clinical signs or symptoms at all. In fact, among the esti-mated 300,000 patients who experience pulmonary embolism each year, the great majority suffer no
(35) serious symptoms or complications, and the disor-der clears up without significant aftereffects.

     However, in a significant percentage of patients, the pulmonary embolism is massive, sometimes reducing total pulmonary blood flow by
(40) 50 percent or more; and the consequences may be grave: seriously strained circulation, shock, or acute respiratory failure. Massive pulmonary embolism causes some 50,000 deaths each year in the U.S.

     Certain classes of patients are more likely
(45) than others to develop venous thrombosis with its attendant risk of pulmonary embolism. Disorders that increase susceptibility include venous inflam-mation (phlebitis), congestive heart failure, and certain forms of cancer. Women are more suscep-
(50) tible during pregnancy and during recovery from childbirth than at other times, and those taking

birth control pills appear to be at slightly higher risk than are women who do not. Postoperative patients constitute a high-risk group, particularly following pelvic surgery and orthopedic procedures involving the hip. Any operations requiring that (55) the patient be immobilized for prolonged peri-ods afterward exacerbate the risk of this problem. Among patients recovering from hip fractures, for example, the incidence of venous thrombosis may run as high as 50 percent. (60)

     Venous thrombosis can sometimes be diag-nosed by the presence of a swollen extremity with some evidence of inflammation or a clot that can be felt when the affected vein is examined. But sometimes venous thrombosis produces no clear- (65) cut clinical signs so that other tests may be needed to confirm the diagnosis.

     One such test entails injecting fibrinogen tagged with a radioactive isotope of iodine into the blood. Fibrinogen has a strong affinity for blood (70) clots and is incorporated into them, carrying its radioactive label with it. The clot can then be lo-cated with a radiation-sensing device.

     Another diagnostic technique, called venog-raphy, involves injecting a dye (one that shows (75) clearly on X-rays) into the vein where obstruction is suspected. The X-ray venogram provides very detailed information on the extent and location of the obstruction.

     A third technique uses sensitive instruments (80) that measure blood flow in vessels of the extremi-ties to detect any circulatory impairment that may result from thrombosis.

     Signs of nonfatal pulmonary embolism may include sudden shortness of breath, chest pain, in- (85) creased heart rate, restlessness and anxiety, a fall in blood pressure, and loss of consciousness. But clinical symptoms may vary by their presence or absence and in their intensity, and their similarity to symptoms that may result from other disorders (90) can make the diagnosis of pulmonary embolism difficult on this basis alone.

     Pulmonary angiography (X-ray visualization of the pulmonary artery and its branches after injection of a radiopaque dye) is the most reliable (95) diagnostic technique, but it is a complex test that cannot be done routinely in all patients. A some-what simpler test involves injecting extremely fine particles of a radioactively labeled material such as albumin into a vein and then scanning the lungs (100) with a radiation detector while the particles traverse the pulmonary blood vessels.

31. The purpose of the first paragraph (Lines 1–11) is to:

(A) analyze the causes of blood clots.

(B) describe types of blood clots.

(C) predict who is most likely to get a blood clot.

(D) inform the readers of steps to take for the prevention of blood clots.

32. Which of the following best describes the difference between a thrombus and an embolus?

(F) A thrombus is in the lung; an embolus may be anywhere.

(G) A thrombus is usually fatal; an embolus is rarely fatal.

(H) A thrombus remains stationary; an embolus moves within the circulatory system.

(J) A thrombus is larger than an embolus.

33. It is reasonable to conclude from the passage that pulmonary embolism:

(A) may clear up on its own.

(B) is invariably fatal.

(C) is more severe in children than in adults.

(D) may be prevented by following a specific diet.

34. According to the passage, a common origin for a pulmonary thrombosis is in the:

(F) heart.

(G) brain.

(H) leg.

(J) arm.

35. In Line 45, the phrase "attendant risk" refers to:

(A) risks faced by those who aid others.

(B) risks that accompany something else.

(C) minimal, almost nonexistent, risks.

(D) risks that are higher for women than men.

36. The word *exacerbate* in Line 57 means:

(F) reduce.

(G) cure.

(H) exaggerate.

(J) worsen.

37. The author suggests which of the following about pulmonary angiography (Line 93)?

(A) It diagnoses a specific type of pulmonary embolism that is more complex than other types of embolisms.

(B) Its use of radiopaque dye creates severe allergic reactions in some patients.

(C) It involves the use of radioactive particles that are injected into a vein and then detected with a radiation detector.

(D) The test has properties that prevent it from being used repeatedly on some patients.

38. Which of the following is the best title for the passage?

(F) How to Cure Pulmonary Embolisms

(G) How Blood Clots Develop

(H) Means of Preventing Blood Clots and Embolisms

(J) Description and Diagnosis of Blood Clots

39. The reason that the author introduces the three tests discussed in Lines 68–83 is to:

(A) lament the high cost of diagnosis.

(B) prove that any blood clot can eventually be diagnosed.

(C) describe the means of confirming a suspected diagnosis.

(D) reject the premise that all blood clots are fatal.

40. According to the author, using clinical symptoms to diagnose pulmonary embolisms:

(F) is cheaper and more time-effective than using high-tech machinery.

(G) should be done cautiously and in conjunction with other tests.

(H) can be done only in the least acute cases.

(J) cannot be done routinely on all patients.

Science Test

TIME: 35 minutes for 40 questions

DIRECTIONS: Following are seven passages and then questions that refer to each passage. Choose the best answer to each question and shade in the corresponding oval on your answer sheet.

Passage I

In the pole vault, the pole acts to convert the energy generated by an athlete running down a runway into a force that lifts the athlete over a crossbar. The most advanced vaulters use stiff poles that quickly convert the horizontal energy into the lifting force. Beginning vaulters are not strong, fast, or skillful enough to bend a stiff pole as needed to generate substantial vertical lift. Beginning vaulters must use more flexible poles.

To test the suitability of two materials for use in poles, scientists subjected three miniature poles to two laboratory tests. Pole No. 1, made of fiberglass, is 50 cm long, with a diameter of 1 cm and a mass of 1 kg. Pole No. 2, also made of fiberglass, is also 50 cm long but has a diameter of 1.5 cm and a mass of 2.25 kg. Pole No. 3, made of carbon fiber, is 50 cm long, 1.5 cm in diameter, and has a mass of 1 kg.

Study 1

Scientists tested the three poles to determine how much force is required to bend the poles to an 85-degree angle. Table 1 shows the results.

Study 2

Scientists bent each pole to an 85-degree angle and then allowed the pole to snap back to a straight position. Table 2 shows the time required for each pole to snap back.

Table 1 — Results of Bent-Pole Test

Pole	Force in Newtons (N)
1	4.9
2	5.8
3	6.3

TABLE 2 — Results of Snap-Back Test

Pole	Time in Milliseconds (msec)
1	733
2	626
3	591

1. According to the results of the two tests, the relationship between the force required to bend a pole and the time needed for the pole to snap back to its regular position is that:
   - **(A)** the greater the force required to bend the pole, the more time required for the pole to snap back.
   - **(B)** the greater the force required to bend the pole, the less time required for the pole to snap back.
   - **(C)** for only the fiberglass poles, the greater the force required to bend the pole, the more time required for the pole to snap back.
   - **(D)** for only the fiberglass poles, the greater the force required to bend the pole, the less time required for the pole to snap back.

2. On the basis of Study 1, the relationship between pole mass and stiffness is that:
   - **(F)** poles with greater masses are stiffer.
   - **(G)** fiberglass poles with greater masses are stiffer.
   - **(H)** poles with smaller masses are stiffer.
   - **(J)** there is no relationship between pole mass and pole stiffness.

3. Which of the following is a controlled variable in this study?
   - **(A)** pole diameter
   - **(B)** force required to bend poles
   - **(C)** time for poles to return to vertical
   - **(D)** force generated when poles return to vertical

4. Kinetic energy results from the actual motion of an object, while potential energy is a measure of the energy that results if an object were to move from a certain location. During a pole vault, virtually all the energy is in the form of potential energy:

(F) when the vaulter is running down the runway.

(G) when the pole is bent.

(H) as the pole unbends and sends the vaulter upward.

(J) as the vaulter falls into the pit.

5. Ideally, vaulters like to use long poles because the poles reach closer to the crossbar. If a pole is too long, though, a vaulter has difficulty carrying it down the runway because of its mass. Given these considerations, the material that is best suited for a very long pole is:

(A) fiberglass, because it snaps back relatively slowly.

(B) fiberglass, because it has a relatively high mass-to-volume ratio.

(C) carbon fiber, because it is relatively stiff.

(D) carbon fiber, because it has a relatively low mass-to-volume ratio.

6. On the basis of the entire study, which of the following would be the most appropriate pole for the beginning pole vaulter?

(F) Pole 2

(G) Pole 1

(H) Pole 3

(J) either Pole 2 or Pole 3

7. Suppose a fourth 50-foot pole made of carbon fiber with a diameter of 1.0 cm was tested. Based on the two studies, the force required to bend the pole to an 85-degree angle and time required for this pole to snap back to a straight position from that angle would be closest to which of the following?

(A) A force less than 4.9 N and a time greater than 733 msec.

(B) A force greater than 4.9 N and a time greater than 733 msec.

(C) A force less than 6.3 N and a time greater than 591 msec.

(D) A force greater than 6.3 N and a time greater than 591 msec.

Passage II

A radioactive substance is one that contains atoms with nuclei that change into other types of atomic nuclei. For example, a uranium nucleus can lose two protons and two neutrons and become a thorium nucleus. Atoms of some radioactive substances change more frequently than others. Over time, the rate of change for any substance slows as a greater percentage of atomic nuclei change to a final, more stable state.

Devices can measure the number of atomic changes that take place at a given time. Each of these changes is commonly called a *disintegration*. Table 1 and Table 2 show the disintegration rates for two unknown substances.

TABLE 1 — Substance A Disintegrations

Time (hours)	Disintegration Rate (millicuries)
0	200
5	100
10	50
15	25
20	12.5

Table 2 — Substance B Disintegrations

Time (hours)	Disintegration Rate (millicuries)
0	2,000
4	1,000
8	500
12	250
16	125

8. As time in hours increases, the disintegration rate in millicuries:

(F) increases for Substance A and decreases for Substance B.

(G) decreases for Substance A and increases for Substance B.

(H) increases for both substances.

(J) decreases for both substances.

GO ON TO NEXT PAGE

9. It is reasonable to deduce that after 20 hours the disintegration rate for Substance B will be about:

  (A) 0 millicuries.

  (B) 12.5 millicuries.

  (C) 62.5 millicuries.

  (D) 200 millicuries.

10. If Substance A starts with 10,000,000 radioactive atoms, the number of atoms present at 15 hours will be:

  (F) 666,667.

  (G) 1,250,000.

  (H) 3,333,333.

  (J) 5,000,000.

11. The disintegration rate of Substance B is 1,500 millicuries:

  (A) at about 2 hours.

  (B) at exactly 2 hours.

  (C) at about 3 hours.

  (D) at exactly 3 hours.

12. Given that the half-life of a radioactive substance is the time it takes for half of the radioactive atoms to disintegrate, the substance with the shorter half-life is:

  (F) Substance A, because it reaches its half-life after 5 hours.

  (G) Substance A, because it will be completely disintegrated after 25 hours.

  (H) Substance B, because the disintegration rate fell to half its original value in 4 hours.

  (J) Substance B, because it was measured for 16 hours instead of 20.

13. Radioactive substances are potential health hazards because the particles emitted from radioactive substances can damage parts of the human body. Therefore, humans should take great care to limit the amount of radioactivity they are exposed to. Which of the following is safest for a human to handle?

  (A) Substance A after 5 hours

  (B) Substance A after 20 hours

  (C) Substance B after 8 hours

  (D) Substance B after 16 hours

Passage III

When sunlight heats the earth's surface, much of that energy is radiated back to the atmosphere. Although some of this re-radiated energy escapes to space, a significant amount of it is reflected back to the earth's surface by molecules in the atmosphere. These molecules — water, nitrous oxide, methane, and carbon dioxide — trap re-radiated energy in the same way that glass in a greenhouse does and warms the earth. Hence, the term "greenhouse effect" has been used to refer to the warming of the earth caused by the gases' keeping heat within the earth's atmosphere.

Scientists agree that the greenhouse effect results in higher temperatures on earth but disagree as to whether recent increases in atmospheric carbon dioxide will lead to undesirable global warming. Two scientists discuss this possibility.

Scientist 1

Ancient ice cores from Antarctica indicate that the concentration of carbon dioxide in the atmosphere and global mean temperatures have followed the same pattern of fluctuations in levels over the past 160,000 years. Therefore, the increase in atmospheric carbon dioxide concentration from 280 parts per million to 360 parts per million that has occurred over the past 150 years points to significant and detrimental climatic changes in the near future. The climate has already changed: The average surface temperature of the earth has increased 0.6°C in the past hundred years, with the ten hottest years of that time period all occurring since 1980. Although 0.6°C may not seem large, changes in the mean surface temperature as low as 0.5°C have dramatically affected crop growth in years past. Moreover, computer models project that surface temperatures will increase about 2.0°C by the year 2100, and will continue to increase in the years after, even if concentration of greenhouse gases is stabilized by that time. If the present trend in carbon dioxide increase continues, though, carbon dioxide concentration will exceed 1,100 parts per million soon after 2100, and will be associated with a temperature increase of approximately 10.0°C over the present mean annual global surface temperature.

Scientist 2

The observed increases in minor greenhouse gases such as carbon dioxide and methane will not lead to sizeable global warming. Water vapor and clouds are responsible for more than 98% of the earth's greenhouse effect. Current models that project large temperature increases with a doubling of the present carbon dioxide concentration incorporate changes in water vapor, clouds, and other factors that would accompany a rise in carbon dioxide levels. The way these models handle such feedback factors is not supported by current scientific knowledge. In fact, there is convincing evidence that shows that increases in carbon dioxide concentration would lead to changes in feedback factors that would diminish any temperature increase associated with more carbon dioxide in the atmosphere. The climatic data for the past hundred years show an irregular pattern in which many of the greatest jumps in global mean temperature were too large to be associated with the observed increase in carbon dioxide. The overall increase of 0.45°C in the past century is well under what the models would have predicted given the changes in carbon dioxide concentration. As with the temperature models, recent increases in atmospheric carbon dioxide have not risen to the extent predicted by models dealing solely with carbon dioxide levels. The rate of carbon dioxide concentration increase has slowed since 1973. Improved energy technologies will further dampen the increase so that the carbon dioxide concentration will be under 700 parts per million in the year 2100.

14. Which of the following is an assumption made by Scientist 1?

- **(F)** Feedback factors have little effect on the magnitude to which increased carbon dioxide will increase temperature.
- **(G)** Humans will not be able to limit their activities that contribute to rising carbon dioxide levels.
- **(H)** A rise in the global mean temperature of 1.0°C is not significant.
- **(J)** Temperature fluctuations will match carbon dioxide changes when carbon dioxide changes are abrupt.

15. A scientific article states that "scientists will soon develop computer models that accurately account for feedback factors." This statement is consistent with:

- **(A)** only the viewpoint of Scientist 1.
- **(B)** only the viewpoint of Scientist 2.
- **(C)** the viewpoints of both Scientist 1 and Scientist 2.
- **(D)** the viewpoint of neither Scientist 1 nor Scientist 2.

16. Which of the following is the most likely reason that the two scientists present different figures for the temperature rise that has occurred over the past hundred years?

- **(F)** It has been difficult to determine the mean global temperature with complete accuracy.
- **(G)** Scientist 2 uses figures that do not take account of the rise in atmospheric carbon dioxide.
- **(H)** Scientist 1 notes that all ten of the hottest years in the last hundred years have come since 1980.
- **(J)** It has not been established that global warming is a threat to the earth.

17. Indicative of rising temperatures, a large block of the Larson B Ice Sheet in Antarctica recently broke off, raising water levels around the world and increasing the vulnerability of coastal areas to flooding. In light of this information, which of the following predictions would be most consistent with Scientist 1's viewpoint?

- **(A)** Feedback factors will retard the future rate of ice sheet disintegration.
- **(B)** The amount of ice that will break off will double with a doubling of atmospheric carbon dioxide.
- **(C)** The breakup of the ice sheet will minimize global warming.
- **(D)** Coastal areas will be more prone to flooding in the next hundred years.

GO ON TO NEXT PAGE

18. Scientists 1 and 2 would most likely agree with which of the following statements about atmospheric carbon dioxide levels?

   (F) Increasing carbon dioxide levels affect other factors.

   (G) Humans will never be able to stabilize atmospheric carbon dioxide levels.

   (H) The rate of increase in carbon dioxide levels will rise throughout the next hundred years.

   (J) Carbon dioxide levels are directly linked to temperature.

19. Scientist 1's claim about the significance of increased global temperatures over the past hundred years is most vulnerable to the criticism that:

   (A) the carbon dioxide increases that she presents have taken place over the past 150 years.

   (B) she does not specify which years since 1980 have been hottest.

   (C) she does not specify whether the change in crop growth she cites was caused by an increase or decrease in temperature.

   (D) the figures she presents for temperature increases over the next hundred years are greater than the figure she provides for the past hundred years.

20. It is reasonable to infer from Scientist 2 that:

   (F) humans will be able to adapt to any problem produced by global warming.

   (G) a change in atmospheric water vapor could significantly affect global temperatures.

   (H) atmospheric carbon dioxide levels will never reach 1,100 parts per million.

   (J) atmospheric carbon dioxide levels will eventually stop increasing.

Passage IV

Angiosperms, or flowering plants, typically produce flowers seasonally. The various angiosperm species produce their flowers at different times of the year. For example, some flowers bloom in early spring, while others bloom in the summer. Research has shown that these flowering plants respond to changes in day length. A cocklebur, for example, does not produce flowers during the time of year that has days longer than 15.5 hours. When the length of day drops below this figure, flowering occurs. This type of flower is known as a short-day (SD) plant. Long-day (LD) plants do the opposite. These plants do not flower until the length of day exceeds a certain critical value. Plants that do not respond to changes in day length are called day-neutral (DN) plants. The following experiments investigate what aspect of changing day length is responsible for the plants' responses.

Experiment 1

Botanists raise both SD and LD plants in a greenhouse under long-day conditions. As expected, the SD plants do not flower, and the LD plants do flower. When a brief period of darkness interrupts a long day, the LD plants continue to flower.

Experiment 2

Scientists raise both SD and LD plants in a greenhouse under short-day conditions. The SD plants flower, and the LD plants do not flower. When a brief flash of light interrupts the long night, the SD plants stop flowering and the LD plants begin to flower.

Experiment 3

Experimenters perform a yearlong study in which they raise both SD and LD plants in several greenhouses. The light/dark cycle corresponds to the day-length changes that occur normally over the course of a year. Daytime temperatures differ in each greenhouse. All SD plants flower at the same time of year. As expected, all LD plants flower at a different time than the SD plants do, but the LD plants all flower at the same time when compared to one another.

Experiment 4

Conditions are identical to those of Experiment 3, except that while daytime temperatures are kept the same across all greenhouses, nighttime temperatures vary. SD and LD plants still flower at different times of the year, but the plants vary considerably as far as when each plant begins to flower. For example, SD plants in greenhouses with warmer nighttime temperatures flower at a different time than do SD plants in cooler greenhouses.

21. Experiment 4 differs from Experiment 3 in that in Experiment 4:

(A) nighttime temperatures in all greenhouses were varied while daytime temperature were kept the same.

(B) daytime temperatures in all greenhouses were varied while nighttime temperatures were kept the same.

(C) daytime temperatures and nighttime temperatures were kept the same across all greenhouses.

(D) daytime temperatures and nighttime temperatures were varied across all greenhouses.

22. On the basis of Experiments 1 and 2, the most critical factor in determining whether SD and LD plants will flower is the:

(F) total number of daytime hours.

(G) total number of nighttime hours.

(H) number of uninterrupted daytime hours.

(J) number of uninterrupted nighttime hours.

23. Cocklebur, an SD plant, and spinach, an LD plant, are both raised on an 8-hour day, 16-hour night cycle. If a brief flash of light is presented in the middle of the 16-hour night, the most likely result will be that:

(A) neither plant will flower.

(B) cocklebur will flower; spinach will not.

(C) spinach will flower; cocklebur will not.

(D) both plants will flower.

24. The variable that the experimenters do not directly control is:

(F) type of plant.

(G) flowering.

(H) amount of light.

(J) temperature.

25. Are the results of Experiments 3 and 4 consistent with the results of Experiments 1 and 2?

(A) No, because Experiments 3 and 4 use a wider variety of plants.

(B) No, because temperature does not change in Experiments 1 and 2.

(C) Yes, because both sets of experiments suggest that the plants respond to a night factor rather than a day factor.

(D) Yes, because both SD and LD plants are used in all the experiments.

GO ON TO NEXT PAGE

26. Which of the following best represents the shape of a line graph that records flowering activity as a function of day length for an LD plant that starts to flower when day length exceeds 15 hours?

(F)

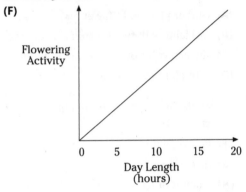

(G)

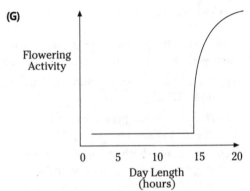

(H)

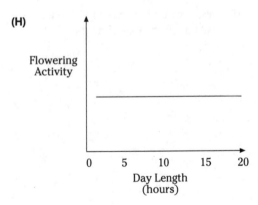

(J)

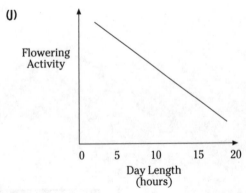

27. Near the equator, day length varies little throughout the year. That is, periods of day and night are virtually equal every 24 hours. Assuming proper soil, water, and other essential conditions, the plant that would most likely flower when grown near the equator would be:

(A) an LD plant that flowers only when the daylight exceeds 14 hours.

(B) an SD plant that flowers only when the day length falls between 6 and 11 hours.

(C) a DN plant.

(D) an SD plant that flowers only when daylight falls below 8 hours.

Passage V

Matter exists in three phases: solid, liquid, and gas. In general, these phases are defined by how far apart the particles in the substance are. Particles are typically closest together in a solid and farthest away from one another in a gas.

Temperature is clearly related to phases. As temperature rises, particles move faster and farther away from one another and matter changes from a solid to a liquid to a gas. The temperature at which matter changes from liquid to gas is called its boiling point.

Pressure also affects phases of matter. A substance that is a gas at a certain temperature and low pressure may become a liquid at the same temperature if pressure is increased.

Figures 1 and 2 summarize the relationship among temperature, pressure, and phase for both bromine and water.

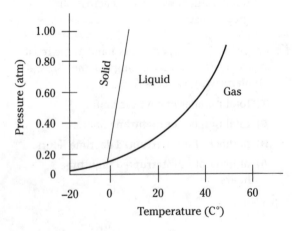

FIGURE 1: Bromine phases.

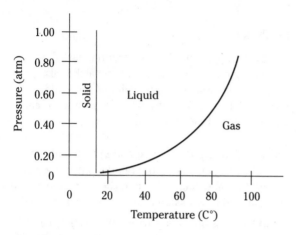

FIGURE 2: Water phases.

28. At 60°C and 1.00 atm, water is:

(F) a solid.

(G) a liquid.

(H) a gas.

(J) in the process of changing from a solid to a liquid.

29. Sublimation occurs when a solid changes to a gas without going through a liquid phase. A point at which sublimation can occur is when:

(A) bromine is at –20°C and 0.05 atm.

(B) bromine is at 0°C and 0.80 atm.

(C) water is at 0°C and 0.80 atm.

(D) water is at 80°C and 0.50 atm.

30. At 30°C, as pressure is decreased from 0.6 atm to 0.3 atm, it is true that:

(F) bromine changes from a gas to a liquid.

(G) bromine changes from a liquid to a gas.

(H) water changes from a solid to a liquid.

(J) water changes from a gas to a liquid.

31. For which of the following are the particles farthest apart?

(A) bromine at –10°C and 1.00 atm.

(B) bromine at 50°C and 0.80 atm.

(C) water at 0°C and 0.40 atm.

(D) water at 100°C and 0.60 atm.

32. At high altitudes, pressure is lower and softening spaghetti in boiling water takes longer than it does at sea level. According to the information in the passage, the most reasonable explanation for this effect is that:

(F) ice crystals form on the spaghetti.

(G) air temperature is lower at high altitudes.

(H) the boiling point is lower at lower pressure and lower temperatures are not as effective at softening spaghetti.

(J) at lower pressure, water boils at a higher temperature and reaching this temperature takes longer.

33. Based on Figures 1 and 2, at all levels of pressure, which of the following is a true statement regarding the relationship between water and bromine?

(A) Water spends more time as a liquid than bromine does.

(B) Bromine spends more time as a liquid than water does.

(C) Water changes from a liquid to a gas at a greater temperature than bromine does.

(D) Bromine changes from a liquid to a gas at a lower temperature than water does.

Passage VI

Radon is a gas that is emitted from the earth's crust in small quantities. Radon can readily be detected in wells. An accidental discovery of excessive radon emission in an earthquake-prone area led seismologists to study the association between radon emission and earthquakes. Such an association could prove valuable in perfecting ways to predict earthquakes.

Study 1

Scientists selected four sites that had experienced recent earthquakes and measured radon emissions in several wells located near the epicenter (the point on the earth's surface above the focus of an earthquake). At each well, the scientists recorded the percentage by which that well's radon emission exceeded the average radon emission found in wells throughout the world. This percentage was called the differential. These measurements are depicted in Figures 1 through 4.

Figure 1

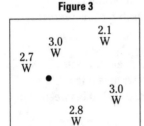

3.8
W

4.4
W

0.2
W

2.7
W

3.6
W

0.1
W

● (Epicenter)

China
Magnitude - 7.9
Average differential - 2.5

Figure 2

1.8
W

2.0
W

1.9
W

2.1
W

● (Epicenter)

1.5
W

Iran
Magnitude - 6.9
Average differential - 1.9

Figure 3

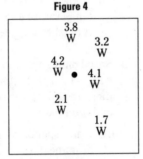

2.1
W

3.0
W

2.7
W

● (Epicenter)

3.0
W

2.8
W

California, USA
Magnitude - 7.2
Average differential - 2.7

Figure 4

3.8
W

3.2
W

4.2
W

● 4.1
W

2.1
W

1.7
W

Chile
Magnitude - 7.5
Average differential - 3.2

Legend for all figures

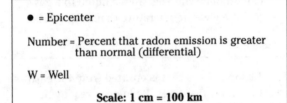

● = Epicenter

Number = Percent that radon emission is greater
than normal (differential)

W = Well

Scale: 1 cm = 100 km

Study 2

To study whether the differential varied depending on the magnitude of an earthquake, seismologists made a scatter plot of the average differential against earthquake magnitude for each site. Figure 5 shows this scatter plot.

34. Based on Figures 1, 2, 3, and 4, which of the following expresses the relationship between earthquake magnitude and the average percent that radon emissions are greater than normal?

(F) Across all sites, earthquakes with greater magnitudes produced greater average differentials.

(G) Across all sites, earthquakes with lesser magnitudes produce greater average differentials.

(H) This is no clear relationship between magnitude and average differential.

(J) Sites with greater earthquake magnitudes have more wells.

35. It is reasonable to conclude from Study 1 that:

(A) there is no correlation between earthquakes and increased radon emissions.

(B) some evidence suggests a correlation between earthquakes and increased radon emissions.

(C) radon emissions of wells more than 1,000 km from the epicenter of an earthquake do not increase.

(D) radon emissions at an earthquake's epicenter are more than 5 percent greater than normal levels for the entire earth.

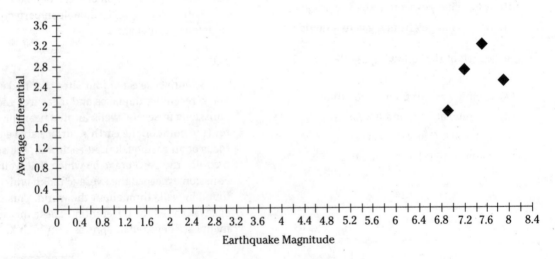

FIGURE 5: Scatter plot of average differential and earthquake magnitude.

36. Which of the following would strengthen the claim that increased radon emissions are associated with earthquakes?

   (F) Scientists measure radon emissions from wells near the epicenter of an earthquake in the Caribbean and record measurements that do not differ significantly from average radon emissions throughout the world.

   (G) For each of the locations depicted in the figures for Study 1, scientists study wells that were 500 miles from the epicenters and find that these wells had similar emission differentials to those recorded at wells near the earthquakes' epicenters.

   (H) Scientists find a location with a 7.9 magnitude earthquake and an average emission differential of 3.6.

   (J) Scientists discover more earthquake activity at the epicenters depicted in the figures for Study 1.

37. Do the findings in Study 1 support the conclusion that radon emissions cause earthquakes?

   (A) No, because the results merely suggest that earthquakes and increased radon emissions occur together.

   (B) No, because the differentials would have to exceed 4 percent at all well sites to support this conclusion.

   (C) Yes, because every well site had higher-than-normal radon emissions.

   (D) Yes, because the radon comes from beneath the earth's surface.

38. Which of the following is an important control condition that is lacking in the studies?

   (F) The studies fail to measure radon emissions from more than five or six wells from each site.

   (G) The studies do not measure radon emissions from sites that experienced earthquakes with magnitudes greater than 8.0.

   (H) The studies do not take into consideration radon emissions from sites that have not had an earthquake in more than 400 years.

   (J) The studies do not include radon emission measurements from the same sites before the earthquakes occurred.

39. A study that would provide useful information to make a determination of whether radon emissions can be used to predict earthquakes would be one that measures radon emissions:

   (A) before an earthquake takes place.

   (B) as an earthquake takes place.

   (C) around epicenters for earthquakes that have a magnitude weaker than 6.9.

   (D) around epicenters for earthquakes that have a magnitude stronger than 7.9.

40. The information in Study 2 provides:

   (F) conclusive proof that there is a correlation between earthquake magnitude and the average differential of radon emissions.

   (G) strong support for the theory that there is almost no relationship between the occurrence of earthquakes and higher radon emissions.

   (H) a visual depiction of the relationship between earthquake magnitude and the percentage that its radon emissions exceed average levels.

   (J) a visual record of the negative correlation between earthquake magnitude and average differential.

GO ON TO NEXT PAGE ➤

Writing Test

TIME: 40 minutes

DIRECTIONS: Prepare a response to the prompt below in a logical, clear, and well-organized essay that follows the rules of Standard English. Write your essay on a separate sheet of lined paper.

As an alternative to traditional fundraising, the school board is proposing to fund school activities and athletic equipment by contracting with a large soft drink company to place advertisements on school buses and gymnasium walls. The contract with the soft drink company will generate about $200,000.00 per year for the district, much more than can be raised by traditional fundraising methods like magazine sales. A parents' organization opposes the contract, stating that soft drink advertisements on school buses and inside school buildings send the message that the school endorses student consumption of soft drinks despite research that shows that soft drink consumption may lead to obesity. Given the potential ramifications of allowing the ads, versus prohibiting them, this is an important issue that deserves careful consideration.

Read and carefully consider these perspectives. Each suggests a particular way of thinking about the school board's proposed soft drink advertisements.

Perspective 1: Yes, soft drinks are bad for you, but the same can be said about refined sugar, sweetened juices and potato chips. The point is, people are going to eat what they want to eat, whether an ad on a school bus or an ad on TV is the one telling them to. The school may as well reap the financial benefits.

Perspective 2: The school day offers a clear opportunity to ingrain what is important in the minds of today's youth, and that includes instilling healthy eating habits. The school building and school buses are not the right places for ads promoting unhealthy, bad-for-you products.

Perspective 3: While it is unfortunate that the contract that will generate $200,000 for the school comes from a soft drink company, the school's need for funding trumps its need to tell students what they can and cannot eat. Until a better alternative comes along, posting the ads is the lesser of two evils.

Essay Task

Write a unified, coherent essay in which you evaluate multiple perspectives as to whether schools should enter into advertising contracts with soft drink companies to raise funds. In your essay, be sure to:

- Clearly state your own perspective on the issue and analyze the relationship between your perspective and at least one other perspective.

- Develop and support your ideas with reasoning and examples.

- Organize your ideas clearly and logically.

- Communicate your ideas effectively in standard written English.

Your perspective may be in full agreement with any of the others, in partial agreement, or wholly different.

DO NOT TURN THE PAGE UNTIL TOLD TO DO SO **STOP** DO NOT RETURN TO A PREVIOUS TEST

Chapter 22

Practice Exam 2: Answers and Explanations

You've completed the practice exam in Chapter 21, and now you can't wait to check your answers and discover your score. Well, this chapter is your key to doing just that.

Here, we go over the right and wrong answers to each question in the practice exam. As part of our explanations, we include tons of valuable information that you'll be able to use when you face the real ACT on exam day.

If you're short on time, skip to the end of this chapter, where we provide an abbreviated answer key. Be sure to check out Chapter 20 when you're done looking over this chapter; there, you'll find the scoring guide that helps you determine what score you would've received if this practice test were real.

English Test

1. **C.** You probably noticed a couple of problems with the underlined portion. Perhaps the most obvious is that *recently* and *current* have the same meaning, so having them both in the sentence is downright redundant. One of them has to go. They both still appear in Choice (B), which means you can ditch that answer. That leaves you with Choices (C) and (D). Choice (D) sounds awkward, and it makes the sentence a fragment with no verb. The answer has to be Choice (C) because it gets rid of the repetition and also takes care of the *it* in the original sentence that doesn't clearly refer to any particular noun.

2. **G.** Chapter 6 discusses the difference between *effect* and *affect*. An *effect* is a result, and you usually see it used as a noun. To *affect* is to concern or influence, and you usually see this word used as a verb. The use of *effect* is correct here. Take note: Your not knowing the distinction between these two words can adversely affect your ACT score.

   Knowing *effect* is correct enables you to narrow the answers down to Choices (F) and (G). Choice (F) is wrong because the phrase "obesity and heart disease" gives more information about the types of side effects (it sort of renames *side effects*) and, therefore, needs to be set off with commas or, in this case, a comma and a period.

3. **C.** In the sentence, the noun that the pronoun *it* renames is unclear. The reference could be fat or salt or both. Find the answer choice that clarifies the pronoun reference. Choice (B) doesn't eliminate *it*. It just changes "it is" to a contraction. With Choice (C), though, the plural pronoun *both* makes clear that both fat and salt are required. The rest of the paragraph is in present tense, so the past tense verb in Choice (D) is definitely out.

   TIP

   Whenever you see an underlined pronoun, check to make sure that its reference is definite. You should be able to point to the noun that the pronoun renames. If you can't find that particular noun, you've found the error.

4. **J.** The sentence repeats the ideas conveyed in the first and second sentences of the paragraph without adding anything new, so it has no reason for being in the passage at all. Choice (J) allows you to put an end to the needless repetition. Besides, Choices (G) and (H) create new errors that you don't want to deal with. Choice (G) has a subject/verb agreement problem, and Choice (H) contains the dreaded passive voice.

5. **B.** Well, you can't stick with Choice (A) because it creates a sentence fragment; you need a subject and verb to go with the "such as" phrase. Check the answer choices to see what you can do about the problem. Cross out Choice (D). By now you know that you can't have two sentences combined as one without bringing in some form of punctuation. Choice (C) corrects the fragment, but it creates a new error with the comma before "my favorite." For the comma to work there, you'd have to see another comma after "my favorite" to show that the words are an aside. You have to go with Choice (B) because it fixes the fragment and properly punctuates the aside.

6. **G.** The author means to imply that restaurant food is getting progressively blander. Strangely, you don't use the word *lesser* to show a gradual lessening. (You usually use it to describe people: "a lesser man would have thrown his book out the window, but I held on to mine.") The phrase "less and less" shows a progressive reduction, so Choice (G) is right. Choice (J) is wrong because *least* implies a comparison of at least three items, not the two (flavor before and flavor now) referred to here.

7. **C.** From the context of the passage, you know that the verb needs to be in the past tense. Neither Choice (A) nor Choice (B) has a past tense verb. Choice (D) sets the action in the past but uses the past perfect tense, which indicates an action that was going on in the past while something else happened. The best verb for this simple sentence is the simple past tense, *discovered.*

   TIP

   Often, to determine the tense of a verb, you need to read a little before and after the sentence with the underlined portion. The sentence for this question introduces a story about something that happened in the past. You wouldn't know that unless you read ahead a little.

8. F. The original version is fine. It compares the current chili to the previous chili: "This chili is better than that chili." Choices (G), (H), and (J) compare two different (and therefore incomparable) things. They all compare chili to flavor. You have to compare chili to chili and flavor to flavor. It's a subtle difference, but get used to it because the ACT likes to test you on impeccably proper comparisons.

9. D. The first comma in the underlined portion is okay because it comes after an introductory phrase. The comma after *experimented*, though, isn't right. The information that comes after *experimented* is essential to the meaning of the sentence. For the sentence to be relevant, you need to know what kind of experimenting the author conducted. You use commas to separate nonessential elements from the rest of the sentence, but don't get commas involved with essential parts of a sentence. Semicolons join independent clauses, so you can cross out the answers that contain semicolons — Choices (B) and (C). Choice (D) is the only one left.

10. H. You don't talk *at*; you talk *to* or *with*. Cross out Choice (F) and look at the other options. All of them correct the preposition problem, but Choice (J) has needless repetition with its addition of *afterwards*. Choice (G) changes *several* to the wordier and more awkward "any number." The best answer is Choice (H).

Don't let *them* in Choice (H) scare you away. In this case, *them* clearly refers to the people because we're pretty sure the author didn't talk to the dishes, which is the only other possibility.

11. D. The underlined portion has two main problems. First, it has no verb, so the sentence is a fragment. Second, it uses *less* to describe the quantity of calories. Remember, you use *fewer* to describe plural nouns and *less* for singular concepts. All the choices fix the sentence fragment, but only Choice (D) changes *less* to *fewer*.

12. G. Before you try to place the sentence, notice that it talks only about salt and its effects on how people eat. Then use the answer choices to help you figure out the most logical position for it in the paragraph. Choice (F) suggests placement at the beginning of the paragraph. Sentence 1 already provides a nice transition from the previous paragraph, so you probably don't want to change it. Putting the sentence after Sentence 1, however, makes sense. Putting the new sentence, which makes the general statement that salt affects food intake, before Sentences 2 and 3 is logical because those sentences go on to give more detail about how salt actually affects food intake. You can eliminate Choice (H) pretty easily because you don't want to separate two sentences with specific information with a more general sentence. Putting the new sentence at the end of the paragraph seems redundant.

13. C. This question may have stumped you. You know that you use adverbs to describe how the action verb is carried out. At first glance, you may think the underlined portion uses the adverb *perfectly* correctly. However, *taste* isn't an action verb in this sentence. It's a linking verb. Therefore, you need to use the adjective *perfect* instead. "To taste perfectly" literally means to taste in a perfect way. Someone who tastes perfectly has perfect taste buds and an exquisite ability to taste. This sentence means to say that the food tastes perfect, and food doesn't have taste buds.

14. G. We're confident that you recognized that Choice (G) was the proper way to write the words in the underlined portion. The clause needs a subject and verb; "which is" satisfies this need. Choice (H) moves some words around and adds an ambiguous *too*, but it doesn't supply the clause with a subject and verb. Choice (J) comes through with a subject and verb — "that is" — but because it's worded so awkwardly, you can scratch it out.

15. **A.** The sentence just restates the information in the last two sentences of the passage. Because it doesn't add any relevant information, you should vote *no* on inserting it. Choices (A) and (B) give you that option. You can cross out Choice (B), though, because the problem isn't that the sentence is contradictory; the problem is that it's repetitive. Even if you weren't sure whether the sentence belonged, you could have eliminated Choice (C) because you know the information appears elsewhere in the passage. If the sentence says the same thing as the original ending sentence, it doesn't conclude the passage any better. So Choice (D) is also out.

16. **G.** The subject of the underlined clause is *who*, which means using the objective form *whom* is wrong and so is Choice (F). The other choices fix that problem, so the sentence must have other issues, too. Look carefully at Choice (J). This answer choice surrounds the phrase "who, governing themselves" with commas, so it shouldn't be essential to the sentence. In other words, the sentence should still make sense if you take it out. When you take it out, the question being asked is "how Native American tribes do so." Well, that's certainly confusing! Choose the construction that best identifies the real question being asked. Choice (G) gets the job done with "[how] tribes go about governing themselves." Choice (H) doesn't finish the thought and leaves you hanging, which is downright uncomfortable.

TIP

If you get confused about when to use *who* and *whom*, substitute *him* with an *m* for *whom* with an *m*. If *him* works, *whom* is proper. If *him* doesn't work, use *who*.

17. **B.** An adverb, which usually ends in *ly*, answers the question *how*. How are most tribal governments organized? Democratically. Choice (C) is grammatically correct, but it's unnecessarily awkward and prolix. (No, prolix isn't an expensive brand of watch. *Prolix* just means wordy.) Why say that a government is organized "in a democratic way" when you can say *democratically* instead? If you delete the underlined portion with Choice (D), you know that the government is organized but not how. The sentence would read, "Most tribal governments are organized, that is, with an elected leadership." That choice seems to say that the definition of organized is having an elected leadership, which isn't true.

REMEMBER

Many students fall into a bad habit on the ACT: They choose the DELETE answer every time they see it. But DELETE has no better or worse chance of being correct than any other answer choice.

18. **J.** The original is a comma splice, or two sentences (independent clauses) that are incorrectly joined. When you take out the subject of the second part of the sentence, that part of the sentence is no longer an independent clause; the simple conjunction *and* makes it part of the predicate of the main sentence. Choice (H) changes the meaning of the sentence and incorrectly puts a comma before the conjunction. The comma is only proper before the conjunction when an independent clause follows the conjunction. Choice (G) doesn't have any punctuation errors, but *however* indicates that the second sentence contradicts the first sentence, which isn't what the author is going for.

19. **A.** This question tests the distinction between *principal* and *principle*. *Principal* (with a *pal*) means main or primary. (You may have learned in about sixth grade that "the principal is your pal, your buddy.") *Principle* (with an *le*) is a rule. Knowing this distinction narrows your answers to Choices (A) and (B). You can cross out Choice (B) because you don't put a comma before the elements in a series.

20. **H.** If you missed this easy question, you probably read it too quickly. This sentence has a problem with subject/verb agreement. The subject of the sentence is *council*. *Council* is singular and requires the singular verb *has*. So Choice (H) is right.

REMEMBER

Did you let yourself get bamboozled by the prepositional phrase? The phrase "by the Secretary of the Interior and the people working for him" can't be the subject of the sentence because the nouns in the phrase are *objects* of the preposition *by*, and nouns can't be subjects and objects at the same time (see Chapter 5 for more grammar details).

21. A. *Tribe* is singular. (*Tribe* is a collective noun. Collective nouns look plural, but they're usually singular.) Because *tribe* is singular, it requires the singular pronoun *it* rather than *them.* So Choices (C) and (D) can't be right. Choice (B) avoids the pronoun agreement problem, but it creates a new error with its lack of parallel structure. Verbs in a series must be in the same grammatical form: to speak, act, and represent.

22. F. Giving the names for the presiding official of the council before you even mention the council and the presiding official doesn't make sense, so you know that Sentence 4 has to come after Sentence 3. Go ahead and cross out Choices (G) and (H). Sentence 3 mentions the presiding official. Talking about the various names for the presiding official right after the paragraph mentions the council itself makes more sense than waiting to do so a sentence or two later. Therefore, Choice (F) is the best option.

23. C. No need to break into a cerebral sweat for this pretty simple question. Verbs in a series must be in parallel form. This very long sentence has a number of verbs, and all are in the simple present: define, regulate, prescribe, levy, regulate, and control. The last verb must be in the same form as well — administer — so you can eliminate Choices (B) and (D) immediately. The original unnecessarily makes the last entry in the list a clause by adding the subject *they.*

24. J. The original sentence is a comma splice. You can't use a comma to join two sentences into one. You can't change the punctuation, so you have to do something to the underlined portion to change the first part of the sentence into an incomplete sentence (one that can't stand alone). Choices (G) and (H) don't cut it because both of them still contain a subject and a verb ("they did" and "it has"). The only choice that doesn't contain a verb and that, therefore, eliminates the independent clause is Choice (J).

25. C. You don't have to think too hard about Choice (A) because it doesn't form the possessive correctly. The sentence refers to more than one Native American, so you have to form a plural by putting the apostrophe after the *s.* Choice (B) sets up a nonrestrictive clause, "who demonstrated patriotism," but it doesn't have a comma after *patriotism,* so it doesn't work. The *when* in Choice (D) leaves you with an incomplete thought. You don't know what happened when the patriotism moved Congress. The correct answer needs to complete the proper construction of "it was not until . . . that . . . ." Choice (C) fits the bill and uses the proper possessive form.

26. G. The original sentence improperly contains both third and second person. One reads in one's history books or you read in your history books, but one doesn't read in your history books. Choices (H) and (J) change second person to third person but introduce a number problem in the process. *Their* is plural, and *one* is singular. So those answers don't work. Choice (G) has to be right.

27. B. Choice (A) makes no sense. It sounds like the Navajo Marines — rather than their language — were used as code. You have to find another option. Choice (C) is tempting, but it changes the meaning of the sentence. The Navajos didn't use the Marine language; they used the Navajo language. Choice (D) doesn't work either. The Navajo Marines' language didn't make up the code; the Navajo language did. Besides, *Marines* needs to be in posses- sive form. Even though it's in passive voice, Choice (B) is the best answer.

Sometimes the best answer of the four isn't the one you'd create if you had the chance. Sure, active voice is better than passive voice, but you don't have any other option in this case. You have to take what you can get.

28. F. In the original sentence, *such* is an adjective that correctly describes the noun *code*. Switching *code* and *such* in Choice (G) gives you "the only code such that the enemy could not break." In that construction, "such that" should describe how a verb acts. But the sentence doesn't have a verb for the phrase to describe. Cross out Choice (G) and the similar construction in Choice (H). As a general rule, eliminate any answer choices like Choice (J) that put a comma before *that*. *That* introduces a restrictive or essential clause that commas shouldn't set apart.

29. C. *Percent* is plural because it refers to *leaders,* which is a plural noun. So you need a plural verb, *are,* and a plural predicate noun, *veterans.*

REMEMBER

This question is an example of one of the rare instances when a prepositional phrase *does* affect subject/verb agreement. With *percent,* you have to look at the object of the preposition. For example, 50 percent of the *house* is infested with termites, but 50 percent of the *houses* in the neighborhood *are* infested with termites.

And speaking of termites, here's a quick joke: What did the termite say when he walked into the saloon?

"Is the bar tender here?"

30. G. The passage talks about what tribal governments do and what role Native Americans play in the political system, including their contributions to past wars, but nowhere does it predict the future. So you need to choose a *no* answer, either Choice (F) or (G). Between the two, Choice (G) is a better answer. (Notice how we used *between* and *better* to compare two choices?) Choice (F) isn't true. The passage doesn't focus mainly on tribal government; it talks equally as much about Native American contributions to military service.

31. C. The underlined portion contains a possessive form error. The great national parks belong to the country, so it should be "country's great national parks." The sentence refers to only one country (ours), so you can't choose the plural possessive form in Choice (B). Although both Choices (C) and (D) correct the possessive form of *country,* Choice (D) creates another possessive error by adding an apostrophe to *parks.* Nothing belongs to the park. The word was fine in plural form just the way it was.

32. H. The *as* in the sentence probably sounded strange to you when you first read it. It should have because it's not idiomatically correct to say "as we were there." You use *as* to indicate two events that happen at exactly the same time. The park ranger didn't give them information at the precise moment they got to the park. It happened at an indeterminate time during their stay or *while* they were there. Saying *whenever* seems to imply that the family had visited the park several times and that the park ranger gave them information whenever they were there. Choice (J) is redundant; the phrase "during our time" and the word *while* mean the same thing. Choice (H) is best.

33. D. The subject of the sentence is *theory,* not "plate tectonics." *Theory* is singular and needs a singular verb, *claims.* So you can narrow down the answers to Choices (C) and (D). You can eliminate Choice (C), though, because *whichever* makes no sense in the context of the sentence.

TIP

An underlined portion that features a verb often tests subject/verb agreement. Go back and identify the specific subject, and, in most cases, ignore the prepositional phrase.

34. J. When you compare two things, you use the *er* form rather than the *est* form. Cross out Choices (F) and (G). Choice (H) can't be right because it doesn't have commas on either side of the nonrestrictive clause that begins with *which.*

REMEMBER

Clauses that begin with *which* are nonrestrictive, or not essential, to the sentence. As nonrestrictive clauses, they should always have commas on both sides separating them from the rest of the sentence (or a comma and a period if they end the sentence).

35. B. You can't use a semicolon to join a dependent clause ("as the expanding oceanic crust . . . plate margins") and an independent clause ("it pierces deeply . . . to liquefy again"). So you know Choices (A) and (C) are out. Instead, you use a comma like the one in Choice (B) to separate a beginning dependent clause from the independent clause. Choice (D) takes away the independent clause at the end and creates an incomplete sentence that leaves you confused and frustrated. You don't need that kind of stress in the middle of a test! If you need to review dependent and independent clauses, look at Chapter 5.

36. F. The sentence is fine the way it is. The subject of the sentence is *components*, which is plural, so the sentence requires a plural verb, *result*. If you thought the subject was *rock*, you fell for the trap answer, Choice (H). If you picked Choice (G), your answer created a sentence fragment with no verb. Choice (J) unnecessarily changes the verb to past tense. Insert your answer into the original sentence to make sure it fits. *Result* fits because the rest of the paragraph is in the present tense.

37. D. The original is a fragment with no verb. Without the assistance of a helping verb, *building* isn't a verb. Alter the *ing* verb (which is often an indication of an error) to *built* to change the sentence to the simple past tense. Choice (B) is wordy and awkward and makes it sound like the mountain was built like you'd build a house.

We hope you didn't fall for Choice (C). The English language has no such word as *builded*. The past tense of *build* is *built*. (Come, come now, don't leave in a huff over that cheesy answer. As Groucho Marx would say, "Wait a minute and a huff!")

38. F. *Like* compares similar objects. That is, *like* usually connects two nouns. *As* compares situations or actions. So you can eliminate Choices (G) and (H). Choice (J) changes the meaning entirely. *Likely* means probably; *like* means similar to.

39. B. The possessive form of *it* is *its*, not *it's*. Choice (B) corrects the problem without changing the meaning of the sentence.

40. G. Sentence 4 begins with "These become the feeding chambers . . . ." So the sentence that comes before it must deal with something that could become feeding chambers. Sentence 3 ends with *eruptions*, but eruptions most likely don't become feeding chambers; therefore, you can cross out Choice (F). Look for another location for Sentence 4. Most paragraphs don't begin with an ambiguous concept like *these*, so you can eliminate Choice (H). By process of elimination, you know Sentence 4 comes after either Sentence 2 or Sentence 5. Sentence 5 just refers to a lake. A singular lake wouldn't become plural feeding chambers. Cross out Choice (J) and pick Choice (G). You don't even have to examine Sentence 2, but if you did you'd see that it refers to compartments of molten rock, which could become chambers.

41. B. You probably got a sense that something was wrong with this sentence when you read it, but exactly what was wrong may not have been obvious. Instead of spending a bunch of time trying to figure it out, just plug in answer choices to see which one works best. Say that the flora is a mix of species from the Sierra Nevadas *and* varieties from the Cascades. The other answer choices don't fit. So Choice (B) is your winner.

42. H. The subject is *park*, which is singular and requires a singular verb, like *boasts*. Therefore, you can eliminate Choices (F) and (J). Choice (J) changes *boast* to *have*, but *have* isn't singular either. *Boast* must be the verb that belongs in the sentence. Choice (G) doesn't cut it because it sounds as though the park is doing some boasting and also has 700 plant species. "To boast" simply means "to be proud to have" — as in you and your friends can boast some of the highest ACT scores around if you learn the tricks and the traps of the exam. Choice (H) is the right answer.

43. A. What do you think? Is a description of the types of plants that grow on Mount Shasta appropriate? Probably not. Besides being a little boring, a description of Mount Shasta's flora isn't really relevant to a passage about Mount Tehama in Lassen Park. Cross out Choices (C) and (D). Although Mount Shasta does have fewer plant types than Lassen Park, the smaller number of plant types isn't the reason that a description of them is inappropriate. You wouldn't want to see that description even if Mount Shasta had more plants than Lassen Park. The best answer is Choice (A).

44. G. You don't use a semicolon to introduce a series; instead, you use a colon or perhaps a dash. The punctuation marks in both Choices (G) and (J) work in the sentence, but Choice (J) replaces *of* with the wordy and unnecessary phrase "that are comprised by." Choice (G) is better. If you selected Choice (H), you created a comma splice, which is the result of joining independent clauses with a comma and no conjunction.

45. C. This last paragraph presents an entirely new topic about Lassen Park. So cross out Choice (A) and pick Choice (C). Previously, the passage gave a physical description of the land and discussed its plant life. This paragraph introduces you to the humans who inhabited the area. The paragraph doesn't contradict anything in the rest of the passage, and thinking that the author would say that the park only sustains life in the snowy winter months is just plain silly.

46. G. You may be surprised to find out that "having dreamed" doesn't function as a verb. It actually functions as a noun but looks like a verb. Therefore, the original sentence is a fragment and needs a change. Choice (J) doesn't help because *dreaming* is a noun, too. Because the writer is no longer a young boy, you're looking for a past tense verb. You find it in Choice (G).

REMEMBER

Remember that *ing* words often make complete sentences into incomplete sentences or fragments because they only look like verbs. Choose an *ing* word if you're looking for a noun, but don't expect it to work as a verb without a little help from a helping verb.

47. A. This question brings up the whole *who* versus *whom* dilemma. Use *who* for subjects and *whom* for objects. In this sentence, *who* is the subject of the clause "who has been my hero." So you know that *who* is the proper form. Cross out Choice (B). The objective form *whom* is okay in Choice (D) because it's the object of the preposition *of*, but if you change *who* to "of whom," the clause loses its subject and the sentence makes no sense. Choice (C) tries to separate "it's fair to say" as a nonessential clause, which would be fine except that the answer choice doesn't put a comma after *say*. You have to stick with Choice (A) here.

48. F. If you picked Choice (J), you answered too quickly. The simple subject and verb in Choice (J) may seem better than the original, but Choice (J) also puts a comma after *dream* and separates the verb from its object, which is a no-no in the grammar world. Choice (H) creates a sentence fragment, and Choice (G) incorrectly turns *boys* into a possessive.

49. A. This question tests the use of prepositions. You can't be fascinated at or captivated about something. "Apprehended with" in Choice (D) is an awkward word choice for the sentence. Going with Choice (A) is best here.

50. G. This question is an interesting one because all the answer choices are pretty bad. Your job is to choose the least awful among them. (Hmm, sounds rather like a mixer dance, doesn't it?) The original is in passive voice and is missing the comma after *Italy*. At first glance, Choice (H) may seem promising. It's in active voice and properly puts commas before and after *Italy*. Look at it carefully, though. A beginning phrase always describes the subject of the sentence. This answer literally states that *you* (not the city) are located a few miles past Naples. You probably wish you were in Naples rather than taking practice ACT tests, but, unfortunately, that's not the point of this sentence. Choice (J) has a whole mess of comma problems. You have to separate the country name (Italy) from the city name (Naples) with commas on either side. Choice (G) is in the passive voice (is found) rather than the active voice, but it doesn't have the punctuation or modifier errors that the other choices have, and passive voice isn't that big a problem in this sentence. It's really not important who exactly finds the city. The point is that it's found or located near Naples. Choice (G)'s the best of four rather lackluster choices.

51. B. Be wary of reflexive pronouns, such as *itself, himself, themselves,* and so on. The test makers often use them incorrectly on the ACT to make sure you're paying attention. They can't act as subjects the way that *himself* does in the underlined portion. The only answer that corrects the problem is Choice (B). Saying "cannot help but" is idiomatically correct.

52. G. The author shows Halliburton's sense of humor with this addition. He records how Halliburton makes light of the idea of being overcome by a volcano by imagining what it would be like for future explorers to excavate him and his typical tourist items. The only answer that demonstrates this lighthearted spirit is Choice (G). The passage isn't about hygienic practices or even a list of what the well-equipped explorer wouldn't leave home without. Cross out Choices (F) and (H), and, while you're at it, mark out Choice (J). The author seems to be interested in the effects of the volcano on Pompeii, but the list doesn't emphasize Vesuvius's devastation.

53. D. The original sentence doesn't have a verb. It's a fragment. The only answer choice that supplies a verb is Choice (D). None of the others makes the sentence complete.

54. F. *Anybody* is singular and requires the singular verb *invites*. Eliminate Choices (G) and (H) immediately. Choice (J) may be tempting, but the sentence doesn't have a comma before the underlined portion, which means it's a restrictive, or necessary, clause. Omitting a necessary clause would deprive the sentence of something that is, well, necessary. Choice (F) is the only way to go.

55. C. *Neither* always goes with *nor* (and *either* always goes with *or*). Whenever you see the word *neither*, make sure that *nor* follows hard on its heels. Choices (A) and (B) pair *neither* with *or*, so you can scratch them out right away. You can cross out Choice (D), too. It changes *or* to *nor*, but it changes the meaning of the sentence by replacing *too* with *enough*.

When you find a simple grammar or diction error, change only that part and leave the rest of the sentence alone. In general, changing as little of the sentence as possible is the way to go.

56. F. The underlined portion is fine the way it is. Choice (J) makes the sentence a fragment. The plural subject in Choice (H) doesn't agree with the singular verb. Choice (G) is awkward and changes the thing that's doing the appealing from the writing to the explorer.

57. D. The underlined verb is in the wrong tense. It refers to a past event, but *looks* is present tense. The only answer that's in the simple past tense is Choice (D): ". . . he sat in his hotel room . . . and looked out."

58. **J.** Whenever you see a pronoun in the underlined part of a sentence, make sure it has a clear reference. The only noun that *it* could refer to here is *landscape,* and you don't often refer to the summit of a landscape. So you can cross out Choice (F). Choice (G) doesn't solve the problem of the unclear pronoun, and Choice (H) compounds the problem by introducing an unclear plural pronoun. Only Choice (J) defines which summit the light flashes shoot from.

59. **C.** First, eliminate Choice (D). Even if you thought you should delete the sentence, references to volcanoes occur throughout the passage, so Choice (D) is wrong. Sentence 1 refers to "these chilling effects," so you know that it needs to go after a sentence that mentions some sort of chilling effects. You also need to know who *he* refers to. Nothing in the last sentence of the preceding paragraph provides a reference for either. So cross out Choice (A) and note that the remaining choices give you the option of putting the sentence before Sentence 4 or after Sentence 5. The best answer is Choice (C). The chilling effects can refer to the flashes of light from the volcano.

60. **H.** Given the tone of the passage, you can eliminate Choices (F) and (J). It's not objective and formal enough to be an encyclopedia or textbook entry. The passage doesn't express an editorial opinion, so by process of elimination, it must be the memoir of an older gentleman, which makes sense. The author reminisces about when he was young, which is perfectly appropriate for a memoir.

61. **D.** The sentence as it is doesn't express a complete thought; it's a fragment. Leaving out the word *that* makes the sentence complete.

62. **J.** A *routine* is something that's set and doesn't vary. Therefore, the original version is redundant and unnecessarily wordy. The author can make the point just as clearly with the one word *routines.*

63. **A.** The language used to compare warlike and romantic is fine the way it is. The proper construction is *more . . . than . . . .* Choices (B) and (C) improperly pair *as* with *than* and *more.* You can pair *as* with *as* to show similarity, but the original sentence doesn't show a similar relationship between warlike and romantic. So Choice (D) is out.

64. **H.** Because you're looking for the one word out of the four that doesn't work, find the answer choice that means something different from all the others. *Although, whereas,* and *even though* show contrast. *Because* shows cause and effect. Choice (H) is the one that doesn't belong with the others.

65. **D.** The underlined part needs to be a verb form that functions as a noun. One of the verb forms that can be a noun is the infinitive form, *to + verb.* You find the infinitive in Choice (D). Another form is the *ing* form of the verb without any helping words. In this case, the *ing* form would be *providing,* but it's not an option. The other choices are unnecessarily wordy and confusing.

66. **F.** The original version, with the aside set apart in commas, is correct. Choice (G) is inconsistent; to separate nonessentials in a sentence, you need two commas or two dashes but not one of each. Choices (H) and (J) don't include the whole aside within the commas.

67. **C.** Items in a series must be parallel in form. For example, you wouldn't say, "The ACT is thrilling, exciting, and a challenge." Instead, you'd say, "The ACT is thrilling, exciting, and challenging." Here, only Choice (C) eliminates the final clause and keeps the sequence of items in the same form — all nouns. (We cover parallelism in Chapter 6.)

68. G. You can safely assume that there are more than two types of birds and more than two types of bowers. Therefore, the correct superlative is *most*, which is used to compare three or more things, rather than the comparative form *more*, which is used to compare just two things.

69. B. The iris is the colored part of the eye. Saying "irises in the eye region" is redundant because you don't have irises in your ears or your tummy!

70. H. Saying that a pheasant "is with" eyes on its feathers doesn't make sense. Just as the peacock *has* eyes on its feathers, the pheasant *has* eyes as well. So Choice (H) is the winner here. Choice (J) is the trap. It creates unnecessary repetition. Inserted, it would make the sentence read, ". . . a pheasant also has them, too."

Be sure to reread the sentence with the answer you've chosen inserted. Doing so may take a few seconds, but it helps you prevent mistakes in questions like this one.

REMEMBER

71. B. The original version is wordy and awkward. Choose the simplest answer to make the point. Choices (C) and (D) are just as verbose as the original version. Also, in Choice (C), just who are *they?* Mysterious bird-naming people?

Although the shortest answer isn't always the best answer, it's always an answer worth checking out. We suggest plugging in the shortest answer first to see whether it works.

TIP

72. G. The original sentence uses passive voice, but it clearly states that the humans are the ones doing the action. Therefore, you need to find the option that changes the construction to active voice. Choice (H) makes things worse by keeping passive voice and creating a subject/verb agreement problem. Both Choice (G) and (J) make *humans* the subject of the sentence, and deciding which one does it best may be a little tricky. Choice (G) is in the present perfect progressive tense, and Choice (J) is in the present perfect tense. The distinction between the two tenses is subtle, and you probably won't be tested on it too often. The progressive tense in Choice (G) tells you that the emulation has occurred in the past and is still happening today. Choice (J) implies that humans have emulated birds in the past, but there's no indication that they still are. The next sentence tells you that humans in New Guinea are currently emulating birds, so the best answer is Choice (G). It tells you that bird emulating is still alive and well in present society.

73. D. The original version is a fragment, an incomplete sentence with no verb. Connecting it to the next sentence takes care of the problem. Just make sure you use the proper punctuation. You can use a semicolon to connect two groups of words only if both are complete sentences. And the colon's only appropriate when everything that comes before it is a complete sentence. You already know that first part is a fragment. Separate the beginning phrase from the rest of the sentence with a comma, Choice (D).

Bonus trivia: Speaking of New Guinea, birds aren't the only interesting creatures there. Did you know that Papua, New Guinea, has several types of kangaroos that live in the top layers of trees? Just imagine walking along through the trees and looking up to see a kangaroo! (You'd probably think you were hallucinating from studying too much for the ACT!)

74. G. The main idea of the paragraph is that humans try to dance like birds. The next sentence advances the idea by giving details about what humans in New Guinea wear to copy birds. To pick the best next sentence, cross out Choices (H) and (J). Both of them discuss topics that have nothing to do with the ways that humans emulate birds. Choosing between Choices (F) and (G) may be a little trickier. Both sentences provide more detail about how particular humans copy the birds. Choice (F), though, pretty much says the same thing as the sentence that comes right before it. To get more detail about how humans emulate birds in their dances, pick Choice (G). It stays on topic and adds new information.

75. A. The question just asks whether the essay contains a description of a bird courtship ritual. The first and second paragraphs contain several examples, so the answer has to be yes. You can cross out Choices (C) and (D). The author presents facts, not theories, so the best answer is Choice (A).

REMEMBER

Read carefully so you know exactly what the question asks. Notice that this question didn't ask you whether the main theme was about bird courtship rituals. If you picked Choice (C) or (D), you probably assumed the question was asking for the overall purpose of the essay rather than only one aspect.

Mathematics Test

1. D. The official, algebraic way to do this problem is to let the amount each cheerleader gave be c and the amount each football player gave be f. Then $c = 2f$. Because there are five cheerleaders, their total amount equals $5c$ or $10f$. The ten football players also gave $10f$. The final equation is

$$10f + 10f = 480$$
$$20f = 480$$
$$f = 24$$

After you finish the problem, double-check your answer by plugging it in and talking through the problem. Doing so takes only a few seconds and can save you from making silly mistakes. If each football player gave \$24, then the ten of them gave \$240. Each cheerleader gave twice as much as each football player, or \$48, so the five of them also gave \$240 $(5 \times 48 = 240)$ and $\$240 + \$240 = \$480$.

TIP

The ACT was nice enough to give you answer choices; why not take advantage of them? You can do this whole problem without algebra by simply plugging in the answer choices. Start with the middle value. If the middle value doesn't work, you'll know whether the number must be greater or less than that choice. First, $22 \times 10 = 220$ and $44 \times 5 = 220$ and $220 + 220 = 440$. Because 440 isn't enough, go to the next higher number, Choice (D). Plug in the numbers: $10 \times 24 = 240$, $5 \times 48 = 240$, and finally $240 + 240 = 480$.

2. H. Find the relationship between the first three terms: $2 + 3 = 5$, $5 + 3 = 8$, and $8 + 3 = 11$.

If you thought this question was too easy, keep in mind it's only Question 2. Questions tend to get harder as you move through the Math Test.

3. D. First, plug in -3 for x. So, $2x = 2(-3) = -6$ and $-3x = -3(-3) = 9$.

The minus sign outside the parentheses in the given equation $-(3y - 3x) + 4y$ changes the $+9$ to -9. (Remember that you have to distribute the minus sign through the parentheses.) You now have $-6 + -9 = -15$. Narrow the answers down to Choice (D) or (E). Next, solve for y: $-3y + 4y = y$. So the answer is $y - 15$, or Choice (D).

TIP

Make a habit of crossing out answers as you go. This method can prevent you from working through an entire problem and then choosing the wrong answer because you forgot the first part of the problem by the time you did the second part.

4. F. If two sides of a triangle are equal, their angles also are equal. Because all three angles of a triangle total 180 degrees, the two unmarked angles must be 60 degrees total $(180 - 120 = 60)$ or 30 degrees each $(60 \div 2 = 30)$. Angles along a straight line are *supplementary*, meaning they total 180 degrees. Therefore, $180 - 30 = 150$; the exterior angle measures 150 degrees.

TIP

The measure of an exterior angle is equal to the sum of the measures of its two remote interior angles. Here, the *remote* (in other words, "not next to") interior angles are *NLM*, which is 30, and *LNM*, which is 120, for a total of 150.

Did you notice that Choice (F) is the only possible answer? It's the only choice greater than 120. Because an exterior angle equals the sum of two remote interior angles, it must be $120 + x$; x isn't equal to 0. Therefore, the exterior angle is greater than 120.

5. B. First, use your common sense to eliminate Choices (C), (D), and (E). If Jarnelle can already assemble 300 widgets in one hour and is going to raise her rate and work eight hours, she certainly is going to assemble a lot more widgets than these answers show. That knowledge quickly narrows the answers down to Choices (A) and (B).

Next, find that 25 percent or one-fourth of 300 is 75, Choice (E), which you have already eliminated. (One good reason to eliminate choices as you go is to avoid falling for traps like this one.) If she increases her rate by 75, Jarnelle can now assemble 375 widgets in one hour — Choice (C). In eight hours, she can assemble $375 \times 8 = 3{,}000$ widgets.

Another way to estimate is to say that 375 is about 400 and $400 \times 8 = 3{,}200$. Only Choice (B) is remotely close.

6. H. To solve a proportion, first cross-multiply: $3 \times 25 = 75$ and $5 \times a = 5a$. Then make the products equal: $75 = 5a$. Finally, divide both sides through by 5: $a = 15$.

7. D. The sides of an isosceles right triangle are in the ratio $s : s : s\sqrt{2}$. The $s\sqrt{2}$ is the hypotenuse. (If you don't remember this formula, go to Chapter 9.) Each side or leg of the triangle, therefore, has to be 5. The area of a triangle is $\frac{1}{2}bh$. In an isosceles right triangle, the two legs are the base and the height, making the area of this triangle $\frac{1}{2}(5)(5) = \frac{1}{2}25 = 12.5$.

REMEMBER

Choice (B) traps students who forget to multiply the base and height by one-half. Choice (E) is the perimeter, not the area. Because answer choices often have such "variations" to trap a careless test-taker, circle what the question is asking for. Before you fill in the oval on the answer sheet, refer to that circled info again to be sure that you're answering the right question.

Did the phrase "square units in the area" confuse you? Not to worry. Just think of it as area.

8. K. Start by distributing the negative to the bracketed part of the equation. (To help you remember this principle, write a negative 1 in front of the parentheses.) Negative 1 times a is $-a$. Negative 1 times -3 is $+3$, which immediately eliminates Choices (G) and (H). Negative 1 times $-a$ is $+ a$. Combine like terms: $6a - a + a = 6a$.

REMEMBER

When the answers are all "variations on a theme" like Question 8's answers, double-check that you're keeping your positive and negative signs correct.

9. C. First, find 25 percent or $\frac{1}{4}$ of 18,000: $\frac{18{,}000}{4} = 4{,}500$. But don't pick Choice (E) because that's just the discount. Subtract it from \$18,000 to get \$13,500. Then take 5 percent of \$13,500, which is \$675. That's the luxury tax, so add it to \$13,500 to get \$14,175.

REMEMBER

If you chose Choice (A), you added the sales tax to the original cost, not to the sales cost. If you picked Choice (B), you assumed that a discount of 25 percent and a tax of 5 percent is the same as a discount of 20 percent. That logic is wrong because the percentages are percentages of different *wholes* (in the first case, the percent is of the original price; in the second case, the percent is of the sale price). Whenever you're dealing with percentages, keep in mind that a percentage is part of a whole and double-check that you have started with the correct whole.

10. **G.** This problem is easier than it looks. Draw a rectangle of width x and length $3x$ (because the problem tells you that the length is 3 times the width). Add all the sides to find the perimeter: $x + 3x + x + 3x = 8x$. The perimeter is 640, so $8x = 640$ and $x = 80$. If x, the width, is 80, then $3x$, the length, is 240. The area of a rectangle is length × width: $80 \times 240 = 19,200$.

11. **D.** Before you do any math, circle the words *closest approximation*. Those words are a clue that the problem is going to be a pain in the posterior — that you'll probably deal with some very weird numbers. More importantly, though, they're a clue that you don't have to work the problem through to the bitter end but that you can estimate a final answer.

Next, plug and chug. Put the numbers in and work the problem through, like so:

$$\frac{3 + 10(3-10)^2(9-10)}{10(9-10)}$$

$$\frac{3 + 10(49)(-1)}{190}$$

$$\frac{3 - 490}{190}$$

$$\frac{487}{190}$$

Here's where you estimate: 487 is close to 500 and 190 is almost 200 and $\frac{500}{200} = 2.5$. Just don't forget the negative sign!

TIP

This type of problem is great to do if word problems are hard for you. This question consists of numbers, numbers, and more numbers. However, this problem can also catch those who are prone to making careless errors. The more calculations you do, the greater the chance of a careless error. Double-check your answers to questions like this.

12. **K.** Angles along a straight line total 180 degrees. Forget about all the fraction stuff, and start off by plugging in nice, simple numbers that meet the requirements. Say, for example, that $x = 1$. That means that $y = 2x$ and $z = 3x$. See how neatly things work out? You're often rewarded for plugging in simple numbers. Then you have $x + 2x + 3x = 180$, $6x = 180$, and $x = 30$. If $8x = 640$, then $y = 60$ and $z = 90$. Yes, it works. Now just go back and answer the question: $z - x = 90 - 30 = 60$.

13. **A.** This problem looks a lot harder than it is; don't let yourself be intimidated. First, be sure that you get the wording straight. You're subtracting the first term from the second term. Think of this as "second term minus first term." If you overlooked this wording, you may have fallen for a trap and picked Choice (D) or (E).

Second, check that the variables are the same and are to the same power or you can't subtract them. For example, you can do $5a^3 - 3a^3$, but you can't do $5a^3 - 3a^2$ (unless, of course, you know the value of a). When the variables and *exponents* (or powers) are the same, you can ignore them and just subtract the *numerical coefficients* (the numbers in front of the variables): $1 - 5 = -4$. (Because no number is in front of the a^3b^4, you assume its coefficient is a 1.) Now your answer has to be Choice (A) or (B). Subtract the coefficients in front of the a^2b^3: $-2 - 3 = -5$.

14. **J.** The sides of a 30:60:90 triangle are in the ratio $s : s\sqrt{3} : 2s$, where s is the shortest side. (If this ratio doesn't sound familiar to you, flip to Chapter 9.) Draw the figure like this:

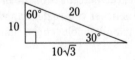

You know s is the height, opposite the 30-degree angle, and $s\sqrt{3}$ is the base, opposite the 60-degree angle. Apply the area of a triangle formula:

$$A = \frac{1}{2}(10)(10\sqrt{3})$$
$$A = 5 \times 10\sqrt{3}$$
$$A = 50\sqrt{3}$$

15. **E.** This question is as much vocabulary as it is math. A *mean* is the average of numbers: Add the numbers together (420) and divide by the number of numbers ($420 \div 5 = 84$). A *median* is the middle number when you put the numbers in order.

    If you picked Choice (D), you fell for the trap of thinking that 79 was the median because it was the "middle number." You have to put the numbers in sequential order first: 75, 79, 82, 91, 93. Now you can see that 82 is the median. Take the mean minus the median: $84 - 82 = 2$.

    Bonus trivia: While we're talking vocabulary, do you know what the mode is? A *mode* is the most repeated term, the one that shows up the most. For example, if the numbers were 2, 3, 2, 4, 5, the mode would be 2.

16. **J.** Draw a rectangle with a diagonal with a length of 6 that splits it into two 30:60:90 triangles. The ratio of sides of a 30:60:90 triangle is $s : s\sqrt{3} : 2s$. If the $2s$ side (the hypotenuse) is 6, then s (the shorter leg) is 3 and the longer leg is $3\sqrt{3}$.

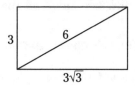

    Add the sides to find the perimeter: $3 + 3 + 3\sqrt{3} + 3\sqrt{3}$.

17. **E.** If you missed this relatively simple question, you probably got careless. In Choice (A), although 24 is indeed a common multiple of 4 and 6 (meaning that both terms divide evenly into it), 24 is not the least common multiple. The least common multiple is 12, Choice (E).

TIP

    To find a least common multiple quickly, list the multiples of the largest number: 6, 12, 18, 24 . . . . Then find the lowest number that both original numbers go into. In this case, both 6 and 4 go into 12.

    Choice (B) can't be right because 4 doesn't go into 6. Choice (C) isn't even logical. All numbers, except 0 and 1, can be factored down into prime numbers; that's what prime numbers are, the least positive integer factors. Choice (D) is wrong because the least prime factor of 4 is 2. (If you thought it was 1, you need to flip to Chapter 8. By definition, 1 isn't a prime number.)

18. **H.** First, remove the parentheses: $3x^2y + xy^2 - 2x^2y + 2xy^2$.

    The last term becomes positive because of the negative sign in front of the second set of parentheses. Remember to distribute the negative sign throughout the parentheses: $-1(-2xy^2) = +2xy^2$. Confusing signs is one of the most common careless errors you can make when solving algebra problems.

    Then combine like terms: $3x^2y - 2x^2y + xy^2 + 2xy^2 = x^2y + 3xy^2$.

19. E. Apply the formula for total surface area provided in the question note: $2\pi r^2 + 2\pi rh$.

The $2\pi r^2$ represents the areas of the top and bottom circles: Here, $4^2\pi = 16\pi$. Add the top and bottom areas: $16\pi + 16\pi = 32\pi$. The $2\pi r^2$ represents the circumference of the cylinder, which, if cut, would be the length of the base of a rectangle:

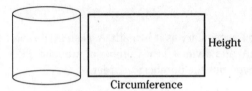

Circumference

Height

The area of a rectangle is lw. Here, that's $2\pi r^2$ times height, which is $2(4)\pi \times 10 = 80\pi$. Then all you have to do is add: $32\pi + 80\pi = 112\pi$.

20. J. Parallel lines have the same slope, so you can use the same formula for the parallel line. Isolate the y-value to get the slope-intercept form: $y = mx + b$ (where m is the slope of the line). Given that $2x + 3y = 6$, subtract $2x$ from both sides: $3y = 6 - 2x$. Then to get rid of the 3, divide everything by 3. You're left with $y = -\frac{2}{3}x + 2$. The slope is $-\frac{2}{3}$ because it's the value for m in the formula.

21. D. First, distribute the negative sign that's outside the parentheses, making the second expression $-3a^2 + 2ab - 8$. Then combine like terms: $2a^2 - 3a^2 = -a^2$. The answer has to be either Choice (D) or (E).

Next, $ab + 2ab = 3ab$. Between Choices (D) and (E), only Choice (D) works.

22. K. To find Jessica's missing test score, use the mean formula to create an equation with x representing the fifth missing test score: $\frac{93 + 92 + 90 + 100 + x}{5} = 95$. Solve the equation for x to find that $x = 100$.

Use the same method to find Josh's missing test score: $\frac{95 + 97 + 89 + 94 + y}{5} = 95$. Solve for y: $y = 100$. Subtract the two scores: 100 (Jessica's needed score) − 100 (Josh's needed score) = 0. The answer is Choice (K).

REMEMBER

If you picked Choice (F), you fell for the trap. The question doesn't ask for the difference between the score Josh needs and his current average score. Make sure you know exactly what information the question asks you for before you shade in your answer.

23. D. Remove the parentheses by distributing the negative sign; in other words, change the signs of the values in the parentheses: $2y - (4 - 3y) + 3$ becomes $2y - 4 + 3y + 3$. Combine the $2y$ and the $3y$ to get $5y$ and -4 and 3 to get -1. Put them together and you have $5y - 1$.

24. H. The value of the shaded area is what remains after you've subtracted the area of the unshaded portion (the circle) from the area of the entire figure (the square). The formula for the area of a square is s^2. The formula for the area of a circle is πr^2. Play Sherlock Holmes and do a little deducing. The radius of the circle is half the diameter, and the diameter is the same length as the sides of the square, which means the radius is half of s. Now you can set up an equation to find the length of each side of the square: $s^2 - \left(\frac{1}{2}s\right)^2 \pi = 144 - 36\pi$.

You could go through the process of solving for s, but it's faster to continue your powers of deduction: s^2 must equal 144 and 144 is the perfect square of 12. The square's side lengths are 12.

Draw the diagonal of the square. It creates two isosceles right triangles. The ratio of sides in an isosceles right triangle is $s : s : s\sqrt{2}$. If the side of the square is 12, the diagonal (which is the same as the hypotenuse of the triangle) is $12\sqrt{2}$.

25. **B.** First, find out the value of angle y inside the triangle. Because the angles of a triangle total 180 degrees, $y = 180 - (20 + 40) = 120$. Next, the three x angles and the y angle total 180 degrees because they form a straight line. Therefore, $120 + 3x = 180$ and $3x = 60$, so $x = 20$.

26. **H.** Sometimes the hardest part of a math problem is figuring out where to start. Use the test answers to help you with this one and work backward. If the machine is losing half the ball bearings every cycle, double the answer five times to track it down: 11 (end of fifth cycle) ×2 = 22 (end of fourth cycle); 22 × 2 = 44 (end of third cycle); 44 × 2 = 88 (end of second cycle); 88 × 2 = 176 (end of first cycle).

27. **B.** Note that the problem says each person wants to pay *under* $12, not exactly $12. This problem is relatively easy if you plug in the answer choices instead of trying to make equations. Start in the middle with Choice (C). Currently, if the 5 friends pay $22.20 each, the total cost of the time is $111.00. If 4 more friends join them, for a total of 9 people, divide $111 by 9 to get $12.33 — just *over* $12. You know you must have more people but probably just one more because you're so close. Plug in Choice (B). If you add 5 people, you have 10 people sharing the $111 cost. Divide 111 by 10 to get $11.10, which is under $12.

28. **J.** Cross-multiply to solve for a and b:

$$\frac{1}{a} = 4$$
$$4a = 1$$
$$a = \frac{1}{4}$$

And

$$\frac{1}{b} = 5$$
$$5b = 1$$
$$b = \frac{1}{5}$$

Therefore

$$\frac{1}{ab} = \frac{1}{\left(\frac{1}{4}\right)\left(\frac{1}{5}\right)} = \frac{1}{\frac{1}{20}} = 20$$

If you picked Choice (F), you forgot to divide by multiplying the reciprocal. If you answered with Choice (G) or (H), you added the 4 and 5 instead of multiplying them.

29. **D.** The circumference of a circle is $2\pi r$, so a circumference of 10π tells you that $r = 5$. The area of a triangle is $\frac{1}{2}bh$. The base, AC, is $2r$, or 10. The height, OB, is equal to r, or 5. So the area of the triangle is half of 5 times 10, which is 25.

30. **G.** You probably figured out that $4^3 = 64$, but don't get too excited and merrily pick Choice (J). If you substitute a positive 3 for x, you end up with $4^{-3} = -64$ because three negatives make a negative. That tells you that x has to be -3, such that $4^{-(-3)} = 4^3 = 64$ because two negatives result in a positive.

31. B. Do you remember that great saying you learned in right triangle trig: SOH CAH TOA ("soak a toe uh")? If not, review Chapter 9. To find tan Z, you need to use TOA or $\frac{\text{Opposite}}{\text{Hypotenuse}}$. The value of the side opposite of Z is 7; its adjacent side (the one that's not the hypotenuse) has a value of 24. The answer is $\frac{7}{24}$, Choice (B).

32. G. When you deal with percentages, start by plugging in 100. Say that the slow reader originally read at 100 words per minute. Then when she increased her speed by 25 percent, she read at 125 words per minute (because 25 is 25 percent of 100). If she reads at only 50 percent of, or half as fast as, the fast reader, the fast reader reads 250 words a minute. The fast reader's speed, 250, is what percent of the slow reader's original speed of 100? Create an equation (250 *is* what percent *of* 100):

$$250 = \frac{x}{100} \times 100$$
$$2.5 = \frac{x}{100}$$
$$250 = x$$

REMEMBER

If you picked Choice (D), you got careless and found what percentage the fast reader's speed is of the slow reader's increased speed rather than of her original speed. Circle precisely what the question is asking you so that you don't fall for traps like this one.

33. D. For every 2 yards (6 feet) that she swims, the swimmer actually progresses only 4 feet (because she loses 2 feet for every 2 yards). That means 1 yard swum = 2 feet covered. If 1 stroke is 5 yards, she goes 10 feet in that one stroke. The swimmer needs to cover 500 yards, or 1,500 feet, meaning that she has to take 150 (that is, $\frac{1500}{10}$) strokes.

34. K. One easy way to do this problem is to plug in numbers. Let $x = 5$ and $y = 10$. The farmer can plow 5 rows in 10 minutes or 1 row every 2 minutes. Therefore, the farmer can plow 30 rows in 1 hour (because 1 hour = 60 minutes). Let $w = 2$, such that the farmer works for two hours. If he can plow 30 rows in 1 hour, then he can plow 60 rows in 2 hours. The answer to the problem is 60. Go through all the answer choices, plugging in your values for x, y, and w, to find which one works out to 60. Choice (K) does the trick:

$$\frac{60(5)}{10} \times 2 = x$$
$$\frac{300}{10} \times 2 = x$$
$$30 \times 2 = x$$
$$60 = x$$

35. C. The only way to miss this problem is to intimidate yourself, to make the problem seem harder than it really is. Even if you haven't studied functions in school (that little *f* stands for *function*), you can solve this problem by following directions. Talk your way through the problem. Say to yourself, "I have something in parentheses. That means I cube the something, then add one." In this case, the *something*, the x, is given as −5. So cube −5 to get −125. Then add 1 to get −124. That's all there is to it!

REMEMBER

The answer choices are full of traps for the distracted student. If you incorrectly cubed −5 and got positive 125 and then added 1, you picked Choice (A). If you correctly cubed −5 and got −125 and then incorrectly added 1 and got −126, Choice (E) was waiting for you. And if you chose Choice (B), you combined both mistakes, cubing −5 to get the wrong answer of +125 and then subtracting rather than adding 1.

REMEMBER

Just because the answer you got is in front of you doesn't mean it's the right answer. The test makers are aware of commonly made mistakes and put them on the test to tempt you.

36. **K.** An octagon has 8 sides. The formula for the total interior angle measure of a figure is $(n-2)180$, where n stands for the number of sides. (We go over this formula in Chapter 9.) Here, $8-2=6$ and $6\times180=1{,}080$. Subtract 480 to get 600. An octagon has 8 angles. The question accounts for two of them, leaving the remaining 6 angles to sum up to 600 degrees. Divide 600 by 6 to get 100.

37. **B.** The four sides of a square are equal. Because square *RSTU* has a perimeter of 48, its sides measure $48 \div 4 = 12$. If points *A*, *B*, *C*, and *D* are midpoints, then each one divides the sides of the larger square into lengths of 6 units:

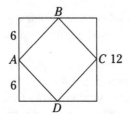

Each side of square *ABCD* is the hypotenuse of an isosceles right triangle. The ratio of the sides of an isosceles right triangle is $s:s:s\sqrt{2}$. That means the hypotenuse of each triangle is $6\sqrt{2}$. Multiply the side length by 4 to get a perimeter of $24\sqrt{2}$.

38. **K.** This problem is much easier than it looks. You don't have to find the lengths of each and every side. Just pretend you moved line *FE* to be at the same height as *DC*. That makes line *FC* the same length as *AB*. Then pretend you moved line *ED* to the left and put it on top of the short line *AF*. That makes line *AD* the same length as *BC*. Now take $16\times2=32$ and $9\times2=18$; then add them together for a total of 50.

39. **B.** You get the largest product by using the middle or median terms. Here, $13+13=26$ and $13\times13=169$, but 169 can't be the answer because *a* can't have the same value as *b*.

Therefore, you have to choose the next two largest terms, $12+14$. Multiply 12 and 14 to get 168.

40. **J.** Does this problem make you think of Egyptian hieroglyphics? Join the crowd. Instead of just saying, "That's history, Babe!" and guessing at this problem, make it easier to solve by plugging in numbers. Choose to substitute a value for *x* that doesn't equal 4 and is a perfect square; 9 works. Now solve the equation with 9 sitting in for *x*:

$$\frac{\left(\sqrt{9}+2\right)}{\left(\sqrt{9}-2\right)} = \frac{3+2}{3-2} = \frac{5}{1} = 5$$

Keep in mind that 5 is the answer to the computation. It isn't the value of *x*. Jot down the 5 to the side, draw a circle around it, put arrows pointing to it — do whatever it takes to remind yourself that the answer you want is 5. Now go through each answer choice, seeing which one comes out to be 5. Only Choice (J) works:

$$\frac{\left(9+4\sqrt{9}+4\right)}{9-4} = \frac{9+12+4}{5} = \frac{25}{5} = 5$$

Be very careful not to substitute 3 for *x* because $x=9$ and $\sqrt{x}=3$. Keep track of the values by writing "$x=9$" and "answer$=5$" in the margins of your test booklet.

When you plug in numbers, go through every single answer choice, *soporific* (sleep inducing) as it may be. If you started with Choice (K), for example, and made a careless mistake, you would assume that Choices (J), (H), and (G) didn't work either . . . and probably select Choice (F) by process of elimination. If you take just a second to work out Choice (F), though, you see that it too is wrong, alerting you to the fact that you made a mistake somewhere.

41. D. The cubed root of 64 is 4, and 4 squared is 16: $64^{\frac{2}{3}} = \left(\sqrt[3]{64}\right)^2$.

Questions with exponents and bases are among the easiest ones on the whole exam to answer correctly. If you're confused about how to work this problem, go to Chapter 8.

This type of problem, because it involves only numbers and no words, is perfect for students who get headaches just looking at some of those lengthy word problems.

42. H. A *prime number* has no positive integral factors other than 1 and itself. (We discuss prime numbers in detail in Chapter 8.) The prime numbers in Set A are 2, 3, 5, and 7, which add up to 17. (Did you forget 2? 2 is the only even prime number.) Note that 9 isn't prime because it factors into 3×3. The non-prime (also called *composite*) numbers from Set B are 6, 9, 12, and 15, which add up to 42. The sum of 17 and 42 is 59.

REMEMBER

Not all prime numbers are odd (2 is a prime number), and not all odd numbers are prime (9 is not prime).

43. B. To find probability, use this fraction:

$$\frac{\text{the number of possible desired outcomes}}{\text{the number of total possible outcomes}}$$

The cookie jar originally contained 19 cookies, but Paul ate 5 of them, leaving 14 total. That's the denominator. The jar originally contained 9 chocolate chip cookies, but Paul ate 2 of them, leaving only 7. That's the numerator. The fraction is $\frac{7}{14}$, which reduces to $\frac{1}{2}$ or 50%.

If you picked Choice (E), you fell for the trap. The question asks for the *percent* probability. Choice (E) would be saying one-half of one percent, not 50 percent.

44. H. You didn't need to make an equation to solve this problem. There's a much easier way. Draw a simple diagram that shows 13 marks so that the 13th dash has a *B* for billboard:

$$\underline{}\ \underline{}\ \underline{}\ \underline{}\ \underline{}\ \underline{}\ \underline{}\ \underline{}\ \underline{}\ \underline{}\ \underline{}\ \underline{}\ \underline{}\ \text{B}$$
$$\ \ 1\ \ \ 2\ \ \ 3\ \ \ 4\ \ \ 5\ \ \ 6\ \ \ 7\ \ \ 8\ \ \ 9\ \ 10\ \ 11\ \ 12\ \ 13$$

Then count backward from 1 and place the *B* on the 14th mark in a diagram like this one:

$$\text{B}\ \underline{}\ \underline{}\ \underline{}\ \underline{}\ \underline{}\ \underline{}\ \underline{}\ \underline{}\ \underline{}\ \underline{}\ \underline{}\ \underline{}\ \underline{}$$
$$14\ \ 13\ \ 12\ \ 11\ \ 10\ \ 9\ \ \ 8\ \ \ 7\ \ \ 6\ \ \ 5\ \ \ 4\ \ \ 3\ \ \ 2\ \ \ 1$$

Put the two diagrams together and count the marks:

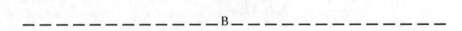

REMEMBER

If you thought that you could just add, you probably marked Choice (J), 27. Drawing the diagram shows you that you have to account for the billboard's spot from both ends of the street, so you have to subtract 1 from the sum, making the total 26.

45. **B.** Take this problem step by step. First, factor the expression. The product of the last terms has to be −8 and their sum has to be 7. The two values that have a product of −8 and a sum of 7 are −1 and 8. That means that $x^2 + 7x - 8$ factors into $(x+8)(x-1)$. Add the two expressions: $(x+8)+(x-1) = x+8+x-1 = 2x = 7$. If you need a refresher on how to factor trinomials, turn to Chapter 8.

46. **H.** The wording "in terms of" can be confusing, so ignore it. You're simply solving for b. Solve this problem the same way you solve other algebra problems. First, get all the b's on one side and all the non-b's on the other side. Subtract $3a$ from each side: $5b - 10 = 3a$. Next, divide both sides by what is next to the b:

$$\frac{5b}{5} = \frac{10 - 3a}{5}$$
$$b = 2 - \frac{3}{5}a$$

Notice that you must divide each term on the right side of the equation by 5.

47. **A.** Your goal is to get all the terms with x and y on one side of the equation and all the terms without x and y on the other side of the equation. To do so, first add $4mx$ to each side:

$$-4mx - \frac{3b}{c} = 4my$$
$$-4mx + 4mx - \frac{3b}{c} = 4mx + 4my$$
$$-\frac{3b}{c} = 4mx + 4my.$$

To solve for x and y, factor out $4m$ and divide:

$$-\frac{3b}{c} = 4m(x+y)$$
$$\frac{-3b}{4mc} = x + y$$

REMEMBER

The most common mistake students make on this type of problem is confusing their − and + signs. As soon as you get an answer, turn around and double-check it immediately. You can be pretty sure that the test makers will include in the answer choices whatever you get if you mess up the − and + signs.

48. **H.** You can solve this problem by distributing a through the parentheses to form a quadratic and then factoring the expression:

$$a(a+4) = 12$$
$$a^2 + 4a = 12$$
$$a^2 + 4a - 12 = 0$$
$$(a+6)(a-2) = 0$$

Set the factors equal to 0 and solve for a: $a = -6$ or $a = 2$.

TIP

A faster way to approach this question may be to backsolve. You can eliminate Choice (J) because when $a = 0$, the answer must be 0 instead of 12. Choice (K) is out because $4(4+4) = 32$. The remaining choices give you these possible values for a: 6, −6, 2, −2. Start easy. If a were 2, the equation would be $2(2+4)$, which is 12. Because 2 is a possible value for a, Choice (H) is a likely answer. Try −6: $-6(-6+4) = 12$. Choice (H) is your answer.

49. A. Follow the order of operations. First, multiply the parenthetical expressions: $(3+x)(4x)=3(4x)+4x^2=12x+4x^2$. Add 2 to get $4x^2+12x+2$. Next, multiply everything by the x outside the brackets: $x(4x^2+12x+2)=4x^3+12x^2+2x$.

TIP

This problem is great to do if you're running out of time. Figuring out what you have to do doesn't take much effort, and actually doing the work doesn't take much time. The only mistake you're likely to make is a careless one, so be sure to double-check your work.

50. J. Get rid of Choices (F) and (G) right away. These choices show that the distance equals 0 at one time beyond the starting time. But the car never moves back to the initial designated point. Choice (H) doesn't feature an interval when the car slows to 70 m/hr; instead, it shows that the car moved forward at a constant speed, stopped, and then resumed the constant speed. So it's out, too. Choice (K) is close, but the gas/lunch interval (horizontal line) lasts too long. Choice (J) is correct.

51. D. The two solutions of the equation result from factoring in the form of $(x\pm\_)(x\pm\_)=0$. The values that fill in the blanks are the ones that have a product of 6 and a sum of −5. The values that multiply to 6 and add up to −5 are −2 and −3, so the factored equation looks like this: $(x-2)(x-3)=0$.

To solve for x, make either expression inside the parentheses equal to 0:

$x-2=0$ when $x=2$
$x-3=0$ when $x=3$

The solutions are $x=2$ and $x=3$. Double-check your work:

$(2-2)(2-3)=0$
$(3-2)(3-3)=0$

Everything checks out. The sum of the solution is $2+3=5$, or Choice (D).

52. F. If $x+1$ is less than or equal to 8, then x is less than or equal to 7:

$x+1\le8$
$x\le7$

The graph that includes 7 and all numbers less than 7 is Choice (F).

If you chose Choice (G), you fell for the trap. You neglected to account for the "or equal to" portion of the inequality and left 7 out of the solution.

53. C. First, distribute the negative sign: $x+2y=4-x-y$. Add y to and subtract x from both sides: $3y=4-2x$. Then divide both sides by 3 to isolate the y: $y=\frac{4}{3}-\frac{2x}{3}$.

54. F. The key to answering this question is to remember the equation $\cos^2\theta+\sin^2\theta=1$. If you have trouble remembering this, think of a right triangle with a hypotenuse of 1, as in $x^2+y^2=1^2$ (think Pythagorean theorem).

Because $\cos\theta = \dfrac{adjacent}{hypotenuse} = \dfrac{x}{1} = x$ and $\sin\theta = \dfrac{opposite}{hypotenuse} = \dfrac{y}{1} = y$, you know that $x^2 + y^2 = 1^2$.

You can just rewrite this as $\cos^2\theta + \sin^2\theta = 1$.

Use this equation to solve the original problem: $\dfrac{\sin^2\theta + \cos^2\theta}{\sec^2\theta} = \dfrac{1}{\sec^2\theta}$. And because

$\sec\theta = \dfrac{1}{\cos\theta}$, $\sec^2\theta = \dfrac{1}{\cos^2\theta}$. Make the final substitutions:

$\sec^2\theta = \dfrac{1}{\cos^2\theta} = \dfrac{1}{\sec^2\theta} = \dfrac{1}{\dfrac{1}{\cos^2\theta}} = 1 \times \dfrac{\cos^2\theta}{1} = \cos^2\theta$.

TIP

These difficult trig problems aren't very common on the ACT; they usually appear only at the end of the math section. If you haven't studied a lot of trig, don't spend too much time trying to figure them out. If you get to one of these problems and you're running out of time, mark your best guess and move along to the next question. As long as you do well on most of the other problems, you don't have to answer these difficult questions correctly to get a good score.

55. **E.** Multiply both the top and the bottom of the fraction by $2 - \sqrt{3}$ (known as the *conjugate of the denominator*, just in case you care). Doing so makes the denominator equal to 1, so you can just ignore it from that point on: $\left(2 + \sqrt{3}\right)\left(2 - \sqrt{3}\right) = 2^2 + 2\sqrt{3} - 2\sqrt{3} - 3 = 4 - 3 = 1$. Multiply the numerator by $2 - \sqrt{3}$ and you have your answer: $7\left(2 - \sqrt{3}\right) = 14 - 7\sqrt{3}$.

This problem is great to do if you're short on time. It looks incredibly complicated, but all you have to do is multiply both the top and the bottom by the conjugate of the denominator.

56. **F.** The most straightforward way to approach this problem is to remember that slope is change in rise over change in run, or $\dfrac{y_2 - y_1}{x_2 - x_1}$. In this case, $y_2 - y_1 = -b - \left(-b\right)$, which comes out to be $-b + b$, and $x_2 - x_1 = a - 2a$, which comes out to be $-3a$. Substitute and you get $\dfrac{0}{-3a} = 0$.

You may have recognized that $y = -b$ in both points, which means y is constant and the line is horizontal.

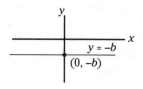

Horizontal lines have a slope of 0, reinforcing that Choice (F) is the answer.

If you did this problem upside down and got $\dfrac{-3a}{0}$, you thought it was undefined (because division by 0 is undefined) and chose Choice (K).

57. **D.** Choice (E) is a sucker bet. Just because the problem multiplied both the number of painters and the number of rooms by 3 doesn't mean that you multiply number of hours by 3.

If three times as many painters are working, they can do the job in one-third of the time one painter takes. If you're confused, reword the problem in your own terms. Suppose that you take three hours to mow a lawn. If your two friends chip in and help you, the three of you can work three times as fast and get the job done in just one hour. The same is true here. Three times the number of painters (from 3 to 9) means they can finish the job in one-third the time: $\dfrac{10}{3} = 3\dfrac{1}{2}$.

If you chose $3\frac{1}{2}$, you didn't finish the problem. Nine painters would do the same job — that is, paint four rooms — in $3\frac{1}{2}$ hours. But the number of rooms is three times what it was, so this factor triples the amount of time needed. Triple $3\frac{1}{2}$ to get ten hours. Yup, you're back to the original amount of time, which unfortunately was probably the first answer your "common sense" told you to eliminate.

TIP

Think about this problem logically. The painters take one-third the time, but they do three times the work. The one-third cancels out with the 3 to get you right back where you started.

58. **F.** First, write out each expression separately. $10.8\left(10^{-3}\right)$ means to move the decimal point three places to the left. (*Remember:* A negative power means the number gets smaller, shifting the decimal point to the left, not to the right.) The result is 0.0108. Do the same for the denominator. $400\left(10^{-5}\right)$ means to move the decimal point 5 places to the left, giving you 0.004. Next, divide 0.0108 by 0.004 to get 2.7. Finally, figure out which of the expressions is equal to 2.7. The expression $0.027\left(10^{2}\right)$ means to move the decimal point two places to the right (a positive exponent makes the number larger, meaning the decimal point shifts to the right, not the left), giving you 2.7.

REMEMBER

This question is probably the easiest one to make a careless mistake on in this whole exam. If you're going to do a problem of this sort, be sure that you can commit the time to do the problem carefully, double-checking your decimal point as you go and then triple-checking it after you're finished.

59. **D.** You can make this question easy, or you can make it hard. You want to do it the easy way, you say? Great: Plug in numbers. You can choose any numbers that your heart desires, but we suggest that you keep them small. Why waste time on a lot of multiplication? Let $q = 1$; Georgia buys 1 quart of milk. Let $d = 2$; the milk costs 2 dollars a quart. (Your numbers don't have to make fiscal sense; maybe it's rare yak's milk. You have better things to worry about.) Let $b = 3$. She buys 3 boxes of cereal at 3 dollars a box $(d + 1 = 2 + 1 = 3)$. Now you can easily figure the total. One quart of milk at 2 dollars a quart equals 2 dollars. Three boxes of cereal at 3 dollars a box equals 9 dollars. Add them up to get 11 dollars. Plug the values for q, d, and b into the answer choices and see which one equals 11. Choice (D) is your winner.

TIP

Keep two important concepts in mind when you plug in numbers: First, keep the numbers small and easy to work with. Second, jot down the numbers as you create them. That is, write to the side: $q = 1$, $d = 2$, and $b = 3$. Confusing the numbers (saying $d = 3$ or $b = 1$, for example) is super easy to do in the pressure of the exam. Take just a nanosecond to put down the assigned values and refer to them constantly.

Here's the algebraic way to solve this problem: The amount spent for milk is (q quarts) (d dollars/quart) = qd (when you cancel the quarts). Then the amount spent for cereal is (b boxes)($d + 1$ dollar/box) = b ($d + 1$) = $bd + b$ (when you cancel the boxes). Add these two expressions together: $qd + bd + b$. Factor out the d: $d\left(q + b\right) + b$.

If you think the algebra is straightforward, you're right . . . as long as you set up the original equation correctly. Unfortunately, too many people have no idea how to set up the equation and end up doing it upside down, inside out, or whatever. If you plug in numbers, you can talk your way through this relatively difficult problem in just a few seconds.

60. **K.** The interior angles of any triangle add up to 180 degrees. You're given two of the three angles of triangle *GFX*: 30° and 90°. Solve for the other angle: $180 - \left(30 + 90\right) = 60$. A 30:60:90 triangle has a special ratio for its sides: $s : s\sqrt{3} : 2s$, where s is the shortest side and $2s$ is the hypotenuse (the side opposite the 90-degree angle). Side *GX* is $2s$, the hypotenuse, which means that $s = 2$ and the other sides are 2 and $2\sqrt{3}$. If *FXS* is 2, then *XB* is 2 and *FB* is 4. The height of the rectangle is 4. If side *GF* is $2\sqrt{3}$, then *FE* is also $2\sqrt{3}$ and the length of the rectangle is $2\left(2\sqrt{3}\right)$ or $4\sqrt{3}$. The area of a rectangle is lw, so $4 \times 4\sqrt{3} = 16\sqrt{3}$.

Reading Test

1. **D.** To answer this question, focus on the first paragraph. The paragraph implies Choice (A) and comes right out and states Choice (B), but neither of these points is what the paragraph is all about. The answer that best summarizes the paragraph is Choice (D) because it includes all the paragraph's elements. The first paragraph doesn't compare Max's thought process with other people's thought processes, so you can eliminate Choice (C).

TIP

Cross out answers that mention only one part of the passage or paragraph in question. Remember that the best answer to a main-point question is the one that incorporates as much of the material as possible without making unreasonable assumptions.

2. **G.** You may know that *tangible* means capable of being perceived with the senses. If you don't, though, you can still answer this question correctly. Examine the sentence. *Tangible* describes something that Max's understanding is *not*. The next sentence elaborates. Max's understanding has come from "a voice in his head," but the voice seems to convey colors and vibrations rather than words. Sounds pretty fuzzy, doesn't it? Start plugging in the answer choices to see which one fits. Eliminate Choice (F) because it has an opposite meaning. It's not that his understanding *wasn't* vague. Choice (G) sounds good. Colors and vibrations don't provide something concrete. Check Choices (H) and (J) just to be sure. Neither works. The understanding did affirm Max's sense of purpose, and understanding that comes from something nebulous, such as inner voices without words, is probably able to change. Stick with Choice (G).

3. **C.** Cross out all the answers that appear in the passage. The second paragraph is all about Max's mathematical talent; Lines 88–89 tell you that he excelled in the 50-yard dash, which is a track event; and you read about his aptitude for football in Line 93. No part of the passage references gymnastics. Eliminate Choices (A), (B), and (D), and fill in the bubble for Choice (C).

4. **F.** Answers that aren't accurate or that cover only one part of the passage have to be wrong. The second-to-last paragraph says that Max expected to be perfect in everything and achieved perfection without being anxious about it. In other words, he didn't feel inadequate. Cross out Choice (G). Choice (H) implies a cause-and-effect relationship between Max's ability to hide his trauma and his academic and athletic successes. The passage doesn't say that Max tried to hide the trauma, so it definitely doesn't link his trauma to his successes. Nothing in the passage tells you that Max suffered socially. In fact, it tells you that he was student council president and captain of three athletic teams. Eliminate Choice (J). Choice (F) provides the best summary of the passage.

5. **B.** When you read the passage, you may have marked Lines 68–75 as Max's suicide thoughts. Go there to answer this question. The author clearly states that Max "seriously considered ending his life in order to escape his tormentor." Choice (C) contains no mention of Louis, Max's tormentor, so it has to be wrong. The paragraphs that discuss Max's suicide attempt don't mention his parents, so you'd have to assume too much to pick Choice (A). You're down to Choices (B) and (D). Both seem pretty good, but Choice (B) is better. It includes both his fear of his brother and his understanding of his purpose in life, the two elements the author gives in the 10th through 13th paragraphs. Choice (D) requires you to assume information that isn't stated in the passage about Max's reasons for considering suicide.

TIP

Eliminate answer choices that make assumptions that you can't justify with specific information in the passage.

6. **F.** The author's use of the word *such* before *exercises* means that he's referring to a previous thought. The prior paragraph talks about Max's ability to position imaginary shapes, not his ability to do physical exercises, so you can mark your pencil through Choice (G). Choice (J) is out because the author hasn't even mentioned Louis before this paragraph. The author mentions Max's ability to multiply large numbers when he was a baby, but he specifically states that the numbers were three-digit numbers rather than six-digit ones, so Choice (H) is out. Choice (F) correctly equates exercises with Max's mental movements of imaginary shapes.

7. **D.** Lines 91–94 tell you that Max displayed leadership skills even as a toddler by taking charge of any group. Choice (D) says exactly that. The other answer choices provide true statements about Max's attributes, but these characteristics aren't ones that the author specifically says provide proof of Max's early leadership tendencies.

8. **F.** Eliminate the answer choices that make true statements about Max and that describe qualities that aren't true of most other children. Choice (J) is an excellent paraphrase of Lines 34–37; Max did think he was exactly where he was supposed to be in life. Cross out (J). Most children don't go through the majority of their childhood without speaking, but Lines 52–53 and Lines 82–83 suggest that Max couldn't express himself verbally. Cross out Choice (G). Lines 100–102 say that, unlike other children, Max didn't get anxious about the expectations he had for himself. Choice (H) is out. By process of elimination, Choice (F) is the best answer. Nowhere in the passage does the author indicate that Max experienced a yearning for approval. On the contrary, it implies that Max wasn't worried about what other people thought of him.

TIP

Questions that require you to read through the whole passage to find out what's not in it can be very time-consuming. If you find that you're spending more than a minute to answer these types of questions, eliminate answers you know aren't right, guess from the remaining options, and move on.

9. **A.** This one should've been pretty easy. The question refers you directly to a line in the passage, so you know exactly where to go to find the answer. The paragraph before the one that mentions Max's obstacle says that Max considered ending his life to escape his tormenter. The tormenter is his obstacle. From the passage, you know that his tormenter is his brother, Louis. Fill in the bubble for Choice (A). If you want to be sure you're right, look at the other choices. Max recognizes that his intelligence is beneficial, and his lack of verbal communication doesn't seem to bother him. He seems to have no problem with general society, only his brother.

10. **J.** If you picked Choice (F), you probably did so because you didn't read the whole answer; the passage doesn't say that Max ever instilled fear in others. You can cross out Choice (H) because the author never suggests that Max lacked self-esteem or was self-absorbed. Choice (G) focuses just on social situations, and the passage covers more than Max's social development. The best answer is Choice (J) because it takes into consideration Max's overall life success and the cause of his early struggles.

11. **D.** You should have dumped Choice (C) right away. The ACT isn't going to write a passage whose primary purpose is to trash (*denounce* means to put down or to bad-mouth) someone, especially a professional such as a child psychologist. Main-idea, primary-purpose, or best-title answers are almost always positive or neutral, not negative.

Choice (B) is tempting. The passage does mention self-esteem (and if you're smart enough to look at the attribution, you'll see that the excerpt, in fact, comes from a book on self-esteem), but it never mentions anything about *low* self-esteem.

Choice (A) is also tricky. It just sounds so pompous and correct: "provides the foundation for life." La-di-da. However, the passage discusses children up to the age of 16, which is well beyond "early childhood." So by process of elimination, you know Choice (D) is the winner.

TIP

The primary purpose of many passages is to describe, discuss, or explain something. Those three words are so often the correct answer to a main-idea or primary-purpose question that you should immediately give them serious consideration. (They're not *always* right, of course — but almost always.)

12. **G.** This question is a gift to you. The answer is right there in the second sentence of the passage — selfhood.

If you chose Choice (J), you fell for the trap. Yes, children work to achieve competence at various tasks throughout the stages of childhood, but all the tasks lead to the ultimate goal of selfhood. Don't choose an answer simply because the passage mentions it. Be sure that the answer you choose refers to the specific question being asked.

13. **C.** The third paragraph mentions this cry of a child to make the point that he needs feedback and recognition of his achievements. So Choice (C) is right.

REMEMBER

Choice (A) is a true statement that the passage discusses; however, it isn't the answer to this specific question. Be careful that you don't choose a statement merely because it's true and appears in the passage. Doing so is like saying, "There are 360 degrees in a circle," when the teacher asks you for the capital of Romania. Sure, the statement is true, but what does it have to do with the matter at hand?

Choice (B) is tempting, but the passage discusses parent-pleasing behavior later in the fourth paragraph, not in conjunction with the given quotation.

14. **J.** This question traps rushed students who don't go back to see how the passage uses the statement in context. Lines 33–34 say that "the mother is the center of the child's world." True, the other answers mention games, but the phrase "the name of the game" was used metaphorically in this instance. To say that something is the "name of the game" means that it's the main idea, the point of the whole activity. For example, getting into college is the name of the game when you're studying for the ACT. If you didn't need a good ACT score to get into school, would you really go through all this mind-numbing studying? (You would? Just for our jokes? We're flattered, but whoa — get a life!)

15. **D.** The author states that this separateness is an important milestone in children's development, indicating that this separateness is vital. (A *milestone* is an event marking a significant stage in life. For example, getting a driver's license is a milestone to teenagers.)

TIP

Did you notice that all the wrong answers are negative and only the correct answer is positive? If you're guessing (the ACT has no penalty for wrong answers, so a guess is always worthwhile), dump the negative answers and go for the positive one. The ACT rarely trashes anyone or anything and is all sweetness and light.

16. **G.** The theme of the passage is the confusion between wanting two opposite things, such as demanding to have freedom from parents but being afraid to let go of them.

Obviously, every answer comes right from the passage itself, so they all look familiar and "sound right." For a question like this one, ignore the answer choices at first. Reread the passage and identify its main idea in your own words. Then go back and find which answer best expresses that idea. If you look at the answer choices first, they'll all look good. Try to predict the answer first.

17. D. This question should have been a pretty easy one. But you do need to examine more than just the indicated sentence; read the few sentences surrounding it. The next sentence says, "A child needs to ask what he is going to do with his life." Choice (D) is your answer.

You didn't fall for the cheap trick in Choice (A), did you? A *vocation* is not the same thing as a *vacation*. If you fell for Choice (B), you confused a *vocation* with a *location*.

18. J. The author talks about self-dependence in the last paragraph, so focus your attention there. The paragraph mentions three tasks a child has to accomplish to achieve self-dependence. If you were paying attention as you read through the passage, you probably underlined these tasks with your pencil.

Whenever a passage introduces a series, underline or star that part of the passage. The ACT often tests you on lists of information.

As you read each task in the paragraph, cross out the corresponding answer choice because you're looking for the answer choice that doesn't show up in the passage. The first task is to determine vocation, which is the same as figuring out what to do. Eliminate Choice (F). Next, the author mentions establishing values. As you continue to read through the paragraph, you see that the author equates values with moral concepts. You can cross out Choice (G). Choice (H) is a word-for-word copy of the third task, so you can mark through that answer. The remaining option is Choice (J). The passage suggests that the child needs to work through conflicts with his beliefs rather than avoid conflicts.

19. C. The passage discusses the various stages of children by their ages. *Chronological* means in order of time. If you didn't get this question right, you outsmarted yourself and tried to make matters more difficult than they really were. Believe it or not, not every single question on the ACT is out to get you.

20. H. You could answer this question based on either the last paragraph or the first paragraph. The final paragraph discusses how the final stage of development is establishing total independence. If total independence is the final stage, then the ultimate goal is that independence. The first paragraph also discusses how the purpose of childhood development is to achieve selfhood or self-knowledge.

21. D. Focus on the last two paragraphs in Passage A, which describe the Orgaz painting. All the choices are part of the picture except Choice (D). Tintoretto only appears in the first paragraph as one of the artists under whom El Greco apprenticed.

22. F. Get your pencil moving and mark straight through Choice (G). Beuys, not El Greco, studied at the Dusseldorf Academy. The first paragraph of Passage A says that El Greco received diverse artistic training, but it doesn't compare the level of diversity to other artists of his day. Choice (J) requires you to assume too much. You're down to Choices (F) and (H). Studying with Michelangelo gave El Greco the background for his unique style, but he continued to develop his style in Toledo. You don't have enough information to say that El Greco's training didn't go further after he apprenticed under Michelangelo. Process of elimination leaves you with Choice (F). The first two paragraphs in Passage A indicate that El Greco's training resulted from a combination of formal art studies and a variety of intellectual influences.

23. C. Passage A's third paragraph states that El Greco painted his masterworks in Spain, which is Choice (C). Although he trained in Italy, Choice (A), and Crete, Choice (B), he didn't paint his masterworks there. Passage B mentions that German artists influenced Beuys, but Passage A never makes a connection between El Greco and Germany. So cross out Choice (D).

24. G. The answer to this question is in the final sentence of Passage A, where the author states that the connections suggest that "the division between heaven and earth, spiritual and material, can only be transcended by the Spirit, symbolized by the flames." The paragraph mentions Saint Peter, the torches of the noblemen, and the petitions of the endless line of souls — Choices (F), (H), and (J) — but the author specifically designates Choice (G), the flame representing the Holy Spirit, as the thing that has the power to overcome the separation between the spiritual and material worlds.

25. C. You know Choice (A) is wrong because Byzantine mysticism and Italian Mannerism were El Greco's influences. The second paragraph of Passage B states that Beuys's art developed from his having to deal with the effects of World War II on the small German town where he grew up. That statement makes a good case for Choice (C). The passage touches on a few similarities between El Greco and Beuys, but it never suggests that El Greco influenced Beuys, which is what Choice (B) says. The fourth paragraph refutes Choice (D). Passage A discusses the religious factors that heavily influenced El Greco, but Passage B doesn't indicate the same influences on Beuys. Just because Beuys came from a predominantly Catholic town doesn't mean he had a Catholic upbringing.

REMEMBER

When a question asks you to find out what the passage implies or suggests, don't assume too much. You must be able to support all your assumptions with specific information from the passage.

26. J. The sentence states that the devastation of the war caused *schisms,* so it can't be a particularly positive word. So Choices (F) and (H) are out. When you replace the word with "religious beliefs," you say that the devastation of war created "political religious beliefs," which doesn't make sense. So Choice (G) doesn't work. The clear answer is Choice (J): Personal and political divisions are often a result of a devastating war.

27. B. If you're an artist or know anything about art, this question probably wasn't too hard for you. "Mixed media" refers to artworks that artists create using a mixture of techniques. If you don't know much about art, though, don't worry. Just use Passage B to answer the question. In the first paragraph, the author says that Beuys used pencil, colored ink, watercolor, and creased paper to create a work, which tells you that "mixed media" involves using more than one kind of artistic medium or technique. The paragraph describes original artwork rather than reproductions, so Choices (A) and (C) don't fit. Choice (D) is in there to catch test-takers who associate *media* only with journalism. The passage doesn't ever mention the way critics viewed the artists' works, so Choice (D) is irrelevant.

REMEMBER

Be sure to rely on information in the sentence to answer vocabulary-in-context questions. If you answer these questions based only on what you know about the word or phrases, you'll probably get them wrong. You need to do some detective work and look for clues in the passage.

28. F. The third paragraph of Passage A tells you that El Greco painted mostly religious themes because churches commissioned his work. Passage B's second paragraph reveals that Beuys wasn't limited by church sponsorship. Choice (F) seems likely. The first part of Choice (G) works, but the second part doesn't. The wishes of the churches he painted for — not his own passions — determined El Greco's subjects. The passage doesn't discuss the particular religious views of either painter, so you can cross out Choice (H). Likewise, the passage doesn't go into the socioeconomic backgrounds of the artists. Eliminate Choice (J). The best answer is Choice (F).

29. **B.** Passage B specifically states in the first paragraph that the artists painted different subjects with different media, so Choices (A) and (D) are out. Both passages indicate the two artists were influenced by earlier artists, but Passage A claims that El Greco was influenced by Cretan monks and Italian artists; Passage B indicates that Beuys had German influences. Cross out Choice (C). You can justify Choice (B) from both passages. Passage A in the second paragraph states that El Greco's paintings "portray the interplay between the spiritual world and the material world." It goes on to specify that *The Burial of the Count of Orgaz* illustrates these two worlds. Similarly, Passage B's last sentence clearly states that *Kadmon* portrays Beuys' "fascination with the relationship between the mystical and the tangible." Both paintings explore a similar theme, and Choice (B) is correct.

30. **F.** Keep in mind as you examine the answer choices that you're answering the question about Passage A. Passage A doesn't mention Beuys or *Kadmon*, so Choice (G) is unlikely. Both passages give a good amount of information about the artists' influences, but Passage A doesn't talk much about El Greco's materials, at least not more than Passage B does. Choice (J) is wrong. Although Passage A discusses the influences behind *The Burial of the Count of Orgaz*, it doesn't include the effect of El Greco's personal experiences. Rather, personal influences are emphasized in Passage B. Choice (H) is wrong. That leaves Choice (F). Passage A goes into great detail describing the way El Greco's painting shows the interchange between the spiritual and material. Passage B mentions the connection but doesn't describe *Kadmon* in a way that shows how the painting expresses the theme of the relationship between the two worlds. Choice (F) is best.

31. **B.** The first paragraph simply introduces blood clots, mentioning fixed and migratory clots. So Choice (B) is your answer.

Did you remember that *describe* is one of the Big Three? By Big Three, we mean the three words that are often (not always, but frequently enough to merit your attention) the correct answers to a primary-purpose question: discuss, describe, and explain.

32. **H.** The first paragraph tells you that a *thrombus* is a clot; an *embolus* is simply a migratory clot. Choice (H) is the winner here. The other answers may or may not be true. The passage doesn't give you enough information to decide.

33. **A.** Lines 33–35 state that, among pulmonary embolism patients, "the great majority suffer no serious symptoms or complications, and the disorder clears up without significant aftereffects." So Choice (A) is right.

Dramatic words, such as *invariably*, are usually (though not invariably) wrong. If you're making a guess (which is always worth doing because the ACT has no penalty for wrong answers), eliminate answers with strong, emphatic words (like *always* and *must*) and look for wimpy words (like *may* and *possibly*).

As for Choices (C) and (D), the passage doesn't discuss either children or diet.

34. **H.** Lines 13–14 state that the site of a pulmonary embolism is often a deep vein of the leg or pelvis. So you know Choice (H) is your answer.

A question that begins "According to the passage" is usually very straightforward. This type of question is worth an investment of your time. Go back to the passage and find the precise answer.

35. **B.** Although you may have been able to answer this question based on common sense, the theme of the first half of the passage is that thrombosis may turn into an embolism. Choice (A) is out in left field; the passage doesn't say anything about aiding others. Obviously, this is the cheap-trick answer, playing on the word *attendant*.

You have no information about the degree of risk, although the list of disorders is pretty daunting. So Choice (C) is out. And although women are classified according to childbirth status, the passage never contrasts women and men, so Choice (D) is wrong.

36. **J.** By citing a high percentage of patients who have venous thrombosis after recuperating from hip fractures, the passage implies that the risk of thrombosis worsens.

This passage uses *exacerbate* in its normal, everyday sense. (The ACT *exacerbates*, or makes worse, your tension headache.) This isn't always the case. A word may have a dozen meanings. Don't be surprised if the ACT uses the least common of those meanings in a passage.

37. **D.** The question directs you to the first sentence of the last paragraph, which gives you a short description of a pulmonary angiography. In that description, you find out that pulmonary angiographies are reliable but that their complexities prevent them from being performed routinely. Choice (D) provides an excellent paraphrase: The properties that prevent some patients from using it repeatedly or routinely are its complexities.

Choice (B) must be wrong because the paragraph doesn't mention anything about patient allergies. Choice (C) describes the simpler test rather than the pulmonary angiography. You may have had a harder time eliminating Choice (A), but the sentence says that the angiography — not the embolism it detects — is complex.

Every question in a section counts the same. A basic definition question like this one is easy to answer quickly. If you're short on time (and who isn't on the reading passages?), focus on this type of question.

38. **J.** The best title is often the broadest and most general statement offered. The passage mentions Choice (G) but only in one brief part. The passage never discusses Choices (F) and (H), so cross them out, too. You're left with Choice (J), which is broad and general.

You can often predict the answer to a main-idea or best-title question. Pretend that your buddy comes up behind you just as you finish reading the passage and asks you what it was about. Your first reaction is the best title: "Oh, I just read this dull passage about what blood clots are and how to recognize them." Bingo! Your prediction leads you right to Choice (J).

39. **C.** This question should have been very easy — if you remembered to expand your search. Often, when a passage sends you to specific lines, the answer isn't there. It's a little above or a little below those lines. Lines 66-67 at the end of the preceding paragraph state that ". . . other tests may be needed to confirm the diagnosis." The next few paragraphs describe such tests. Choice (C) is the answer you want here.

Choice (C) is the third correct answer in this passage that uses the word *describe* (see Questions 31 and 38). Many ACT passages, especially science passages, describe a problem or situation. Don't immediately choose *describe* every time you see it, but definitely give *describe* serious consideration. (You can think of *describe* as being "guilty until proven innocent." In other words, assume that *describe* is correct unless you can find something that's clearly better.)

To *lament* — Choice (A) — is to grieve over. Although you may lament having to take the ACT, few ACT passages themselves lament anything. Choice (B) has the dramatic word *prove*. Few ACT passages definitively prove anything. Also, you can probably eliminate Choice (B) by using common sense — Can *all* of anything be diagnosed?

40. **G.** The second-to-last paragraph (the *penultimate* paragraph, if you like to use pretentious language) mentions that pulmonary embolisms are difficult to diagnose on the basis of clinical symptoms alone.

You probably could have chosen Choice (G) based on its wimpy language alone. Dramatic or emphatic answers are rarely correct; hedging or wishy-washy answers are often correct. How can you go wrong saying something like, "should be done cautiously and in conjunction with other tests"? A physician makes a diagnosis cautiously and usually uses more than one test.

Did you fall for the trap answer, Choice (J)? Lines 96–97 mention a complex test that can't be done routinely on all patients — but these lines are talking about pulmonary angiography, not clinical symptoms. If you simply skimmed until you found familiar words, you probably let this cheap trick get the best of you. *Remember:* Just because the passage mentions an answer choice doesn't mean it's the correct answer.

Science Test

1. **B.** The answer to this question follows from the major relationship noted in the second-to-last paragraph of the analysis of this passage. Remember that the harder a spring is to stretch, the faster it will snap back to its regular position after it's released. Look at the two tables: Pole 3 requires the most force to bend but the least amount of time to snap back; Pole 1 requires the least force to bend but the greatest amount of time to snap back; Pole 2 is intermediate for both force and snap-back time. Choice (B) follows very cleanly from the numerical relationship shown in the two tables. The more force/less time relationship holds for all three poles, so you can't justify Choice (D).

2. **G.** As you see in Table 1, you have to use more force to bend a stiffer pole. In the introductory material before the tables, you find out that Poles 1 and 3 have the same mass (no, you don't have to calculate mass; the passage gives it to you right out, as a gift) and that Pole 2 has the greatest mass. Therefore, Pole 3, the carbon fiber pole, which is one of the least massive poles, is the stiffest. Eliminate Choice (F). On the other hand, when you compare fiberglass to carbon fiber, this smaller-mass-equals-stiffer-pole relationship doesn't hold. Eliminate Choice (H) because with Poles 1 and 2, the more massive pole is stiffer. To choose between Choices (G) and (J), look at Poles 1 and 2, the two fiberglass poles. Because the table indicates that the most massive pole is the stiffest, Choice (G) is the right answer.

3. **A.** This type of question is common in research-summary passages. This question requires you to understand some fundamentals of experimental design. A *controlled variable* (also known as an *independent variable*) is a factor that the experimenter can directly control (duh!). Because ACT questions often ask about controlled variables, you may want to identify those variables as you read through the experimental data upfront. In other words, as you read the problem, say to yourself, "Okay, what's different here?" In Passage 1, the experimenters are fiddling with two factors: the size of the pole and the material it's made of. Those factors are the controlled variables.

In this study, pole dimensions and material (fiberglass or carbon fiber) are controlled variables. The experimenter can easily change the diameter or length of a pole to a specific value, or he can change the pole's material. Choices (B), (C), and (D) mention factors that result from the experiment, not factors that the experimenters can change as part of the experiment.

4. **G.** Don't despair; this question isn't as tough as the terminology initially suggests. In fact, you can answer this question pretty much by using your common sense. What does *potential* mean? *Potential* is something that can happen but hasn't happened yet. (You have the potential to enjoy these questions . . . but that hasn't happened yet!)

The pole acts to transfer the energy produced while the vaulter runs into energy that lifts the vaulter upward. When bent, the pole has stored the energy gained from the running, but has not yet moved upward. At this point, the pole has the potential to move with much energy, but it isn't moving yet. Therefore, the pole has a lot of potential energy but no kinetic energy.

5. **D.** The question tells you that the vaulter needs a pole that isn't too massive when it's long. Focus on Choices (B) and (D) because they concern mass. Because low mass is the objective, Choice (D) is correct.

6. **G.** This passage's introduction tells you that beginning vaulters need poles that are relatively easy to bend. That means that Pole 1 is best for beginners.

7. **C.** The data suggests that a pole with a smaller diameter requires less force to bend into an 85-degree angle and more time to snap back from that angle. So this smaller carbon fiber pole will require less than the 6.3 N required to bend the 1.5 diameter carbon fiber pole and more than 591 msec to snap back from the 85-degree bend. Choice (C) is the answer that properly reflects the information in the tables.

8. **J.** Both tables reveal that as time in hours increases, the disintegration rate decreases. The only answer choice that conveys that relationship is Choice (J).

9. **C.** You can dump Choice (D) immediately. If the substance is down to 125 millicuries after 16 hours, how can it be up to 200 millicuries after 20 hours? Use your common sense to eliminate illogical answers.

   Choice (B) penalizes the careless reader who looks at Substance A rather than Substance B.

   The most important thing to notice is that the disintegration rate is cut in half every 4 hours. After 20 hours (which is only one 4-hour segment after 16 hours), you can expect that the rate will be half of what it was at 16 hours. Half of 125 is 62.5.

10. **G.** The disintegration rate goes down because the number of radioactive atoms goes down as the substance disintegrates. When fewer atoms are available to disintegrate, the disintegration rate naturally decreases.

    So what does all this information mean to you? The number of atoms decreases in the same way that the disintegration rate decreases. At 15 hours, the disintegration rate is only $\frac{25}{200}$ or $\frac{1}{8}$ of what the rate was when the measuring began. The number of atoms must be only $\frac{1}{8}$ of the original 10,000,000. You don't have a calculator, so apply some estimation: $\frac{1}{8}$ is close to $\frac{1}{10}$. And $\frac{1}{10}$ of 10,000,000 is 1,000,000. The closest answer is Choice (G).

11. **A.** Because wimpy or wishy-washy answers usually are better than dramatic or precise answers, eliminate Choices (B) and (D). Think about the choices as follows: If (B) is correct, the test maker also has to accept Choice (A), which really wouldn't be wrong. However, Choice (A) can be correct without Choice (B) being correct. The same thing is true for Choices (C) and (D). If you're going to make a guess, guess Choice (A) or (C), the safer answers.

    Just because 1,500 is halfway between 2,000 and 1,000 doesn't mean that the time has to be halfway between the times that are associated with 2,000 and 1,000. Take a look at Table 2. Notice that for every 4-hour interval, the decrease in millicuries is less. For example, the millicuries decrease 1,000 during the first 4 hours but decrease only 500 during the next 4 hours and decrease only 250 during the next 4 hours. You can conclude that more of a decrease occurs during the first 2 hours than during the second 2 hours. At 2 hours, the number of millicuries will be closer to 1,000 than to 2,000. You can conclude that the disintegration rate reached 1,500 a little before 2 hours, making Choice (A) the safe bet.

TIP

Although this question is tough, thinking logically about how the test makers construct the test can help you narrow the field. The test makers don't want to have to defend their answers. They're usually going to leave themselves some leeway by choosing less precise answers.

12. **H.** The key is to look for which substance took less time for the disintegration rate (which is directly related to the number of radioactive atoms) to fall to one-half of the original value. Substance A went from 200 to 100 in 5 hours, while Substance B went from 2,000 to 1,000 in only 4 hours. Therefore, Substance B has a shorter half-life, which narrows the field to Choices (H) and (J). Choice (J) is full of irrelevant garbage (the fact that the scientists decided to go home after 16 hours doesn't affect the half-life). Choice (H), on the other hand, actually reinforces the definition of half-life.

Choice (F) is misleading because the key isn't the absolute amount of substance present but the amount of substance present relative to the starting amount. Choice (G) is simply wrong. The amount present after 25 hours is half the amount after 20 hours; the amount doesn't completely disappear.

13. **B.** Hey, don't work too hard on this question. All you have to do is look at both tables and find the substance that has the lowest disintegration rate (which means a lower emission rate). You don't have to worry about the rate relative to the starting rate.

Because the disintegration rate is always lower after more time, knock out Choices (A) and (C) right away. Table 1 shows that the rate for Substance A after 20 hours is only 12.5 millicuries, and Table 2 shows 125 millicuries for Substance B after 16 hours.

14. **J.** Look at the first two sentences of Scientist 1's argument. She mentions a match between carbon dioxide and temperature variations and then uses the recent large change in carbon dioxide levels as evidence that significant changes in temperature will occur. Scientist 1 goes on to discuss how continued sharp increases in atmospheric carbon dioxide will lead to similar dramatic temperature increases. Scientist 1 implies that the recent carbon dioxide changes have been unprecedented. The data during the past 160,000 years show a correspondence between temperature and carbon dioxide fluctuations, but this correspondence has occurred in the absence of the dramatic changes the earth is now and soon will be experiencing. For Scientist 1 to use the fluctuation correspondence as evidence for what will soon happen, she must assume that the correspondence will continue in light of current and near-future sharp changes. So Choice (J) is right.

Scientist 2 discusses feedback factors in light of the computer models, which is a good reason to eliminate Choice (F) because the question asks about Scientist 1. You may infer from Scientist 2's discussion that the main difference between the two scientists regarding feedback factors is that Scientist 1 thinks that they'll increase the carbon dioxide-related warming and that Scientist 2 thinks that they'll minimize it.

Scientist 1 explains that the climate has changed, but she doesn't mention the exact causes of the climate changes. If she doesn't specify that there's a human contribution to the climate changes, you can't say that she assumes that humans can't limit their contribution. Eliminate Choice (G). Scientist 1 contradicts Choice (H) because she mentions that a 0.5°C rise is significant.

15. **C.** Choice (B) is tempting in that only Scientist 2 questions the models currently being used. He claims that a model that appropriately incorporates feedback factors will show that global surface temperatures won't rise as high as models currently predict. The problem with Choice (B) isn't that Scientist 2's viewpoint is inconsistent with the article but that

Scientist 1's viewpoint is also consistent. Scientist 1 relies on computer models, so an updated model could very well make Scientist 1's case even stronger. You don't know exactly how those feedback factors will contribute to global warming. Don't take as fact Scientist 2's opinion that the feedback factors will minimize warming. Although either scientist could turn out to be wrong in the face of a new model, both viewpoints are now consistent with the statement in the question. So Choice (C) is the right answer.

16. **F.** As mentioned in the analysis of the passage, the discrepancy in the temperature figures suggests that calculating global temperatures isn't a clear-cut process. Mean global temperature over 100 years entails gathering data from many sites for a long period of time. Some of these sites could have changed. You can also easily assume that scientists around the world don't agree on one accepted way to average all these sites together so they can represent what has happened around the entire world.

Choice (G) is wrong because a temperature measure is just that, a measure of temperature. The carbon dioxide is important only in that a change in carbon dioxide levels may account for why the temperature levels change. They're not included when numbers for temperature are taken and calculated.

Choice (H) is wrong because it's relevant only when the change in temperature occurred. Scientist 2 could very well also know about the hot years after 1980. The issue is simply how the present numbers compare to the numbers 100 years ago.

Choice (J) has to do with the consequences of increasing temperatures, not with the extent to which temperatures have risen.

17. **D.** The breakup of the ice sheet is indicative of global warming. Scientist 1 predicts greater global warming in the next hundred years, so she would expect there to be additional breaking up of Antarctic ice sheets. More breakup should lead to higher water levels and greater vulnerability to flooding.

Choice (A) is something that Scientist 2, who predicts minimal global warming in part because of feedback factors, would predict. Choice (B) is too exact. The passage discusses some numbers regarding the relationship between carbon dioxide and temperature, but it doesn't indicate that the relationship between the two is specifically that when one doubles, the other doubles. Choice (C) may tempt you if you think that ice means cooling, but remember that the ice is melting and melting involves heat. The main problem with Choice (C) is that, even if it were true, you'd have to have some specific science knowledge to say so.

REMEMBER

Keep in mind that choosing the correct answer on the ACT never requires you to know specialized scientific information.

18. **F.** Choice (F) is a nice, noncontroversial statement with which both scientists would agree. Scientist 1 stresses that rising carbon dioxide is linked to higher temperature (another factor), while Scientist 2 discusses *feedback factors*, which are factors that respond to carbon dioxide changes and will, in turn, affect the carbon dioxide. Scientist 2, who refers to improved energy technology, clearly disagrees with Choice (G), but so does Scientist 1, who mentions the possibility that carbon dioxide levels will stabilize. Choice (H) is out because Scientist 2 discusses a slowing down in the rate of carbon dioxide level increase. Choice (J) is also out because *directly* is too extreme. Plus, by discussing feedback factors, Scientist 2 certainly doesn't think any direct link exists.

TIP

Often, strong or extreme words are incorrect, so view them skeptically.

19. **C.** Scientist 1 asserts that a 0.6°C rise is significant because a 0.5°C change affected crop growth in the past. What if the 0.5°C change were a drop in temperature? Perhaps increased

temperatures will do nothing to the crops because the crops will do fine as long as temperatures stay above a certain level.

Eliminate Choice (A) because carbon dioxide has to do with what may cause global warming. It determines what significance increased temperatures will have. In addition, the 150-year figure in this choice doesn't challenge the 100-year figure Scientist 1 presents about temperatures. The time periods still overlap, and the passage discusses a general acceptance that both carbon dioxide and temperature are increasing. The big questions are to what extent the two are related and what the consequences will be.

Choice (B) isn't very important because higher temperatures have clearly occurred toward the end of the 100-year period. Exactly which years had these higher temperatures isn't important. Because relatively few years have passed since 1980, there isn't too much room for variation, anyway. So don't think less of Scientist 1 for omitting the exact years.

Choice (D) is out primarily because this choice has to do with the future, not the past hundred years. Also, Scientist 1 is free to predict a greater increase during the next hundred years because conditions are changing.

20. **G.** Scientist 2 mentions that water vapor and clouds make up 98 percent of the greenhouse effect, so it's reasonable to say that a change in water vapor will affect the greenhouse effect, which, in turn, will affect temperatures. In addition, Scientist 2 discusses how water vapor serves as a feedback factor, which contributes to temperature.

TIP

Choice (F) goes too far. Always be on the watch for answers that go beyond what you want, ones that are too extreme or continue past the point required. Scientist 2 mentions improved energy technology, implying that humans can handle some problems brought on by global warming, but you can't say whether Scientist 2 believes that humans can handle anything that comes their way.

Choice (H) picks up on the difference in figures mentioned at the end of the two scientists' passages, but watch out for the word *never*. Scientist 2 believes that the level will be below 1,100 parts per million in 2100, but he could feel that the level eventually will rise to 1,100.

Scientist 2 may believe Choice (J), but you can't say for sure. Scientist 2 believes that the rate of increase will slow and that the world will survive, but Scientist 2 could easily believe that such survival will occur even in the face of continually rising carbon dioxide levels.

21. **A.** The explanation for Experiment 4 states that the conditions of the two experiments were the same except that in Experiment 4 daytime temperatures were kept the same and nighttime temperatures varied. The only answer that conveys this distinction is Choice (A).

22. **J.** Experiments 1 and 2 show that only interruptions that occur during the night affect the flowering response. Eliminate Choices (F) and (H), which mention daytime hours. Choice (J) makes more sense than Choice (G) because, if the total number of hours were critical, a brief interruption would have very little effect. On the other hand, if the plants were somehow measuring the number of continuous nighttime hours, a brief interruption would affect the plant.

23. **C.** One major point of this passage is that SD and LD plants show opposite responses. This difference makes Choices (A) and (D) unlikely. You can make a good guess at this point by choosing between Choices (B) and (C). Remember, the ACT doesn't subtract points for wrong answers, so guessing is always justified. Having a 50-50 choice is a real treat.

When the experimenter presents light in the middle of the 16-hour night, the plants are exposed to only eight hours of uninterrupted night hours. The plant that flowers when nights are short will start flowering. Which plant meets this criterion? The LD plant, which is spinach in this passage, flowers when days are long and nights are short.

REMEMBER

You may be saying, "Yes, but what if . . ." Ah, Smart Students' Disease (in which you make things harder than necessary) is back. Don't be too concerned with the exact number of uninterrupted nighttime hours that spinach requires to flower. Although some LD plants may not flower until the number of uninterrupted night hours falls to, say, seven hours, the ACT won't pull this type of trick on you. The ACT doesn't expect you to memorize such obscure facts. What the ACT does test is your understanding that a nighttime interruption effectively shortens the night and, therefore, leads to LD flowering.

The information presented in the first part of the passage reinforces Choice (C). The passage mentions that cocklebur does not flower until day length is less than 15.5 hours. This statement means that nighttime must exceed 8.5 hours (24 − 15.5 = 8.5) for cocklebur to flower. When the experimenter flashes light in the middle of the 16-hour night, the night is effectively only 8 hours long, which means that the cocklebur won't flower.

24. **G.** The experimenter can easily choose different plants, keep the lights on or off at a certain time, or change the temperature. Whether the chosen plants flower, on the other hand, has to do with how the plants respond to the conditions presented in the experiment. Flowering depends on what happens to the other variables. Such dependent variables are a step removed from the direct control of the experimenter.

25. **C.** In both sets of experiments, changing the day conditions has no effect on the plants' responses, but changing the night conditions does affect the plants' responses. Choice (D) acknowledges this consistency, but the reason focuses on how the experiments are set up, not on the results. In many biological experiments, experimenters use the same organisms, but doing so doesn't guarantee similar results. (Imagine, for example, that you and your friend both have colds and are both given aspirin. No one can guarantee that both of you would have the same response to the medication just because you're both humans.)

Choices (A) and (B), besides being flat-out wrong from the start, also provide reasons that focus on the experimental conditions rather than the results. In addition, Choice (A) may not be correct because you have no information regarding the variety of plants used in Experiments 1 and 2. Choice (B) points out a key way that the sets of experiments differ, but the results are similar.

26. **G.** On the horizontal axes, day length increases to the right. The LD plant flowers during long days. This information means that high vertical values are associated with the right side of the graph. Eliminate Choices (H) and (J) because flowering doesn't increase with the increasing day length.

Choice (G) is better than Choice (F) because with LD plants, no flowering occurs until a critical day length is reached. (The experiments actually show that the LD plant responds when the length of night falls below a certain value, but associating an LD plant's flowering with long days is still okay.) In Choice (F), the graph continually rises, implying that flowering increases as day length increases from 0 hours. Choice (G) correctly shows that flowering doesn't occur when the day length is less than 15 hours.

27. **C.** So many questions are about SD and LD plants that you may have forgotten the third actor in this play, the DN plant. Look at the passage's introduction, which defines a DN plant as one that isn't sensitive to changes in day length. This type of plant should flower in any environment, including near the equator. (So you shouldn't be surprised that some weeds are DN plants.)

You can eliminate the other choices because the question tells you that around the equator the daylight and nondaylight hours are pretty much equal, which means the plants that require very long or very short days probably won't flower near the equator because the day length stays close to 12 hours and doesn't approach the number of hours necessary for flowering.

28. G. This straightforward question simply tests your ability to read a graph. Look at Figure 2, which deals with water. Locate 60°C on the horizontal axis and then go straight up until you're even with 1.00 atm (on the vertical axis). You're in the liquid region.

29. A. Look for a point on one of the figures where a solid is next to a gas. Choice (A) looks good. In Figure 1 (bromine), −20°C and 0.05 atm is near the lower-left corner, where a solid and a gas are next to each other. Liquid is out of the way, up and to the right.

Choice (B) is wrong because at 0°C and 0.80 atm, bromine is near the solid-liquid boundary. Water is also near that boundary at 0°C and 0.80 atm, so Choice (C) is also out. Choice (D) is way off because water is nowhere near a solid at 80°C and 0.50 atm.

30. G. The easiest way to answer this question is to use a straightedge (your answer sheet works great) to draw a vertical line from the 30°C mark on each figure. Now, for each figure, mark 0.6 atm and 0.3 atm on the line. On the bromine graph, 0.6 atm is in the liquid region and 0.3 atm is in the gas region when the temperature is 30°C, so Choice (G) is the answer. Don't be careless and pick Choice (F). The pressure is going down, so you're moving from a liquid to a gas, not from a gas to a liquid. The liquid region is generally higher than the gas region. On the water graph, you can see that both of your marks are in the liquid region, eliminating Choices (H) and (J).

31. D. Your gut instinct should attract you to Choices (B) and (D) because higher temperatures move particles farther apart. If you're running out of time, go ahead and make a guess. (50/50 odds aren't bad on this test because the ACT has no penalty for wrong answers.) Choice (D) is correct because water at 100°C and 0.60 atm is a gas, while bromine at 50°C and 0.80 atm — Choice (B) — is a liquid. Just to be certain, check Choices (A) and (C). In Choice (A), bromine is a solid. In Choice (C), water is also a solid.

32. H. You can probably eliminate Choice (F) by using common sense: Higher altitudes don't necessarily mean your pasta freezes! When an answer seems illogical or even amusing, put it aside for a moment. If none of the other answer choices are correct, you can always come back to it. (For those of you who love Sherlock Holmes, you'll recognize this strategy as a variation on his famous saying, which roughly goes, "When you have eliminated the impossible, whatever remains, however improbable, must be true.")

Go through the rest of the choices without wasting any time on Choice (F). Choice (G) is out because the water temperature, not the air temperature, is important (because the spaghetti is in the water). A look at Figure 2 confirms the first part of Choice (H): At 1.00 atm, water becomes a gas at about 100°C. At 0.80 atm, water becomes a gas at about 90°C. With the water boiling at a lower temperature, less heat is available to soften the spaghetti. The answer is probably Choice (H), but double-check Choice (J) just to be sure. Figure 2 contradicts Choice (J); think of how you analyzed Choice (H). Besides, in this problem, the water is already boiling, so the length of time required to boil water is irrelevant.

33. C. Neither of the two figures displays time, so you can eliminate Choices (A) and (B). When you compare the two figures, it's clear that at all points right of the curve defining the transition from liquid to gas, water is at a higher temperature. Choice (C) is correct.

34. H. Neither Choice (F) nor (G) is correct. The figures don't represent a clear direct relationship between magnitude and average differential. The earthquake with the lowest magnitude has the lowest average differential, but the site with the greatest magnitude doesn't have the greatest average differential. Choice (J) relates magnitude to wells and doesn't address the question's topic. Choice (H) is the best answer.

35. **B.** Choice (A) doesn't look right. All four sites had radon emissions that were greater than the normal amount found over the earth, making Choice (B) look good.

TIP

You should have leaned toward choosing Choice (B) as soon as you saw the wishy-washy, wimpy language in it. A correct answer often has language that isn't extreme or language that hedges a little bit. A conclusion that states that an association is *definitely* present is too strong unless scientists collected a lot more data.

None of the figures show wells that are 1,000 km (10 cm) away from the epicenter, so you can determine nothing about Choice (C).

The conclusion stated in Choice (D) is also unjustified. For the most part, wells near the epicenters show higher emissions, but the numbers aren't very close to 5 percent and scientists didn't take a measurement right at the epicenter.

36. **H.** The results of the studies indicate some association between earthquakes and radon emissions. Results that go along with the trend found in the studies strengthen the results and any claims derived from the results. You probably crossed out Choice (F) right away. Readings from earthquake sites in another location that aren't much different from average radon emission readings wouldn't provide more evidence for the claim that earthquakes and higher radon emissions are associated. In fact, the information may serve to weaken the claim. Likewise, Choice (G) tends to weaken the claim rather than strengthen it. Similar radon readings from 500 miles away from the earthquake site may indicate that something other than earthquakes is contributing to the high radon readings.

The finding cited in Choice (H) is more helpful. It produces a point that falls in line with the points from the other three sites, so it provides additional support for the claim. Choice (J) doesn't provide enough information. You need to see more earthquakes associated with high radon emissions. Simply having more earthquakes doesn't shed any light on the association between earthquakes and radon emissions.

37. **A.** You have to be careful when dealing with data that show an association (or *correlation*, in more mathematical terms). Just because two things go together doesn't imply that one causes the other. For example, the number of skyscrapers in a city and the number of children who live in that city have a correlation. That is, in general, cities that have more skyscrapers also have more young people. Does this correlation mean that young people are building the skyscrapers? Of course not. A more reasonable explanation is that when a city is large, it has many skyscrapers and youngsters. An underlying cause, namely overall city size, exists. Children don't cause skyscrapers, or vice versa.

This study simply measured a correlation. It wasn't designed to investigate any possible mechanism that would convert radon emissions into earthquakes, which knocks out Choices (C) and (D). Choice (B) is out because nothing in the study points to 4 percent as a magic number. (This particular point isn't true, anyway, but even if it were, you wouldn't have to know this information from some specialized outside study. You only have to know the info that the Science Test passages present.)

38. **J.** When scientists obtain a set of experimental results, the responsible factor is often difficult to isolate. For example, if a scientist wanted to study whether a new drug could increase ACT scores, he could give the drug to a group of students and then look at the scores. If the scores were high, the scientist could conclude that the drug had an effect. But what if the group studied included many people who had a history of scoring well on tests similar to the ACT? What if the students did better simply because they believed the drug would help them? By including a control condition, experimenters could rule out these possibilities. Experimenters could find a group that was equal to the drug group on previous test scores and then give these control students a *placebo* (a fake pill) but tell them that this pill is supposed to help raise ACT scores. If the drug group scored higher, experimenters could be more confident that the high scores aren't simply the result of using a high-achieving group or a psychological belief in the drug because the experimenters matched the two groups in terms of these factors. In this case, the chemicals in the drug more likely had something to do with the higher scores. The control condition helped rule out other possible factors.

In the earthquake studies, scientists measured radon emissions after earthquakes. They obtained high values, but such values could occur even in the absence of an earthquake. Scientists would need to know the radon emission level that normally occurs in the sites studied.

In a sense, Choices (F) and (H) mention conditions that are included in the studies. The studies compared the wells near the epicenters to worldwide values. Studying more wells from the same areas won't add anything new to the study, and the worldwide averages include virtually earthquake-free areas.

All Choice (G) would do is add more data to what has already been found. Clearing up the graph in Figure 5 would be particularly helpful, but the condition isn't a control condition.

39. **A.** Approach this question with good old common sense. If you want to predict an earthquake, you have to measure something *before* the earthquake occurs. The problem with the current studies is that scientists measured emissions after the earthquakes. Maybe the earthquakes caused the emissions, making radon pretty useless as a predictor. Choices (B), (C), and (D) wouldn't help unless researchers took measurements before the earthquake.

REMEMBER

You aren't required to have specific science knowledge to answer an ACT question, but the test makers do assume a level of common sense. The ACT doesn't teach or test false science (for example, you won't have an experiment with totally illogical results). This small act of kindness means that you can trust your common sense and general knowledge. The science portion of the ACT has very few traps or tricks in it. The science is pretty straightforward, as are the questions. Don't make these questions harder than they have to be.

40. **H.** Reading through the studies, you don't get a sense of any findings that are *conclusive*. The inclusion of this debatable word in Choice (F) is a big clue that the answer is wrong. Choice (G) is contrary to the findings of Study 2, which show a definite association between earthquake sites and higher radon emission readings. That leaves Choices (H) and (J). The scatter plot in Study 2 graphs the results of Study 1. The graph shows that, generally, as the magnitude of the earthquake increases so does the average differential of the radon emission readings. So Choice (H) is right. You can cross out Choice (J) because the graph shows a positive correlation rather than a negative one. A negative relationship would be if the differential went down as the magnitude increased.

REMEMBER

Be sure you know the definition of positive and negative correlations. You're bound to be asked about them on the test. If two factors have a *positive correlation*, they do the same thing (as one goes up, the other goes up, too). If they have a *negative correlation*, they do opposite things (as one goes up, the other goes down).

Writing Test

See the "Writing Test" section in Chapter 20 for general information on the features that your essay should contain.

Sample response

Whether ads promoting unhealthy foods should be allowed in a school setting is the issue at hand. With $200,000 in funding at stake for the school, the opinions vary. Those who argue that ads promoting poor eating habits are inappropriate for school property make a good point. Schools are supposed to educate students, whether that be about algebra and geometry or healthy choices. However, in the absence of other forms of funding, schools will have a better chance to provide a good education if they take advantage of the significant revenue available from advertisers.

No one will argue that soft drinks and chips are healthy substances for teens, and in an ideal world, schools should take the high road and prohibit the advertisement of junk food on their campuses. Our world is not ideal, though. Public schools are dependent on funds allocated by state governments. Many are funded by property taxes, and when tax revenues fall, schools suffer. Without proper funding, schools are unable to update their technology and pay quality teachers. Receiving payments from private companies allows schools to invest in resources that benefit students and enhance their future opportunities. Additionally, high school students don't live in a vacuum. Ads promoting all kinds of unhealthy options bombard them daily through TV ads, pop-ups in social media, and billboards along the roads and at bus stops. It isn't as though a lack of advertising at school will keep them from indoctrination. While soft drinks are indeed unhealthy, students will consume what they want to, whether they see an ad posted at school or somewhere else, so the school may as well reap the monetary benefits.

Ideally, schools should find advertisers that promote healthy living, but unless such companies are willing to pay the same fee as junk food promoters, schools should choose the companies that provide the most revenue. Until an alternative advertiser comes along, schools shouldn't suffer because some people fear their kids will be encouraged to drink soda. Parents with these concerns are able to choose to keep soda out of their homes, and schools can use some of the ad revenue to integrate programs that encourage healthy eating into the curriculum.

In short, allowing the ads to be posted isn't an ideal solution, but it may well be "the lesser of two evils." And at least this "evil" comes with an added benefit in the form of increased funding for the school.

Answer Key for Practice Exam 2

English Test

1.	C	16.	G	31.	C	46.	G	61.	D
2.	G	17.	B	32.	H	47.	A	62.	J
3.	C	18.	J	33.	D	48.	F	63.	A
4.	J	19.	A	34.	J	49.	A	64.	H
5.	B	20.	H	35.	B	50.	G	65.	D
6.	G	21.	A	36.	F	51.	B	66.	F
7.	C	22.	F	37.	D	52.	G	67.	C
8.	F	23.	C	38.	F	53.	D	68.	G
9.	D	24.	J	39.	B	54.	F	69.	B
10.	H	25.	C	40.	G	55.	C	70.	H
11.	D	26.	G	41.	B	56.	F	71.	B
12.	G	27.	B	42.	H	57.	D	72.	G
13.	C	28.	F	43.	A	58.	J	73.	D
14.	G	29.	C	44.	G	59.	C	74.	G
15.	A	30.	G	45.	C	60.	H	75.	A

Mathematics Test

1.	D	13.	A	25.	B	37.	B	49.	A
2.	H	14.	J	26.	H	38.	K	50.	J
3.	D	15.	E	27.	B	39.	B	51.	D
4.	F	16.	J	28.	J	40.	J	52.	F
5.	B	17.	E	29.	D	41.	D	53.	C
6.	H	18.	H	30.	G	42.	H	54.	F
7.	D	19.	E	31.	B	43.	B	55.	E
8.	K	20.	J	32.	G	44.	H	56.	F
9.	C	21.	D	33.	D	45.	B	57.	D
10.	G	22.	K	34.	K	46.	H	58.	F
11.	D	23.	D	35.	C	47.	A	59.	D
12.	K	24.	H	36.	K	48.	H	60.	K

Reading Test

1.	D	9.	A	17.	D	25.	C	33.	A
2.	G	10.	J	18.	J	26.	J	34.	H
3.	C	11.	D	19.	C	27.	B	35.	B
4.	F	12.	G	20.	H	28.	F	36.	J
5.	B	13.	C	21.	D	29.	B	37.	D
6.	F	14.	J	22.	F	30.	F	38.	J
7.	D	15.	D	23.	C	31.	B	39.	C
8.	F	16.	G	24.	G	32.	H	40.	G

Science Test

1.	B	9.	C	17.	J	25.	C	33.	C
2.	G	10.	B	18.	A	26.	G	34.	H
3.	A	11.	F	19.	H	27.	C	35.	B
4.	G	12.	C	20.	B	28.	G	36.	H
5.	D	13.	G	21.	A	29.	A	37.	A
6.	G	14.	D	22.	J	30.	G	38.	J
7.	C	15.	H	23.	C	31.	D	39.	A
8.	J	16.	A	24.	G	32.	H	40.	H

Chapter 23

Practice Exam 3

Here comes a chance to practice your ACT test-taking skills. You're probably pretty familiar with the exam format by now, but just in case you've had a momentary bout of amnesia (or you've skipped the first two practice exams in Chapters 19 and 21), we remind you what to expect. The following exam consists of four mandatory tests — a 45-minute English Test, a 60-minute Mathematics Test, a 35-minute Reading Test, and a 35-minute Science Test — and one optional 40-minute Writing Test.

For maximum benefit, take this test under the following normal exam conditions:

>> Sit where you won't be interrupted (even though you'd probably welcome any distractions).

>> Use the answer sheet provided to mark your answers.

>> Set your timer for the time limits indicated at the beginning of each test in this exam.

>> Do not go on to the next test until the time allotted for the test you're taking is up.

>> Check your work only for the test you're taking; don't look at more than one test at a time.

>> Do not take a break in the middle of any test.

>> Give yourself one ten-minute break between the Math Test and the Reading Test.

TIP

When you've completed the entire practice exam, turn to Chapter 24, where you'll find detailed explanations of the answers as well as an abbreviated answer key. Go through the answer explanations to all the questions, not just the ones you missed. We include a bunch of useful information that provides a good review of everything we cover in the other chapters of this book. We've tried to keep your attention by inserting a little corny humor every now and then.

Note: The ACT Writing Test is optional. If you register to take the Writing Test, you'll take it after you've completed the other four tests. For information about the optional Writing Test, see Part 6.

Answer Sheet

English Test

1. Ⓐ Ⓑ Ⓒ Ⓓ	51. Ⓐ Ⓑ Ⓒ Ⓓ
2. Ⓕ Ⓖ Ⓗ Ⓙ	52. Ⓕ Ⓖ Ⓗ Ⓙ
3. Ⓐ Ⓑ Ⓒ Ⓓ	53. Ⓐ Ⓑ Ⓒ Ⓓ
4. Ⓕ Ⓖ Ⓗ Ⓙ	54. Ⓕ Ⓖ Ⓗ Ⓙ
5. Ⓐ Ⓑ Ⓒ Ⓓ	55. Ⓐ Ⓑ Ⓒ Ⓓ
6. Ⓕ Ⓖ Ⓗ Ⓙ	56. Ⓕ Ⓖ Ⓗ Ⓙ
7. Ⓐ Ⓑ Ⓒ Ⓓ	57. Ⓐ Ⓑ Ⓒ Ⓓ
8. Ⓕ Ⓖ Ⓗ Ⓙ	58. Ⓕ Ⓖ Ⓗ Ⓙ
9. Ⓐ Ⓑ Ⓒ Ⓓ	59. Ⓐ Ⓑ Ⓒ Ⓓ
10. Ⓕ Ⓖ Ⓗ Ⓙ	60. Ⓕ Ⓖ Ⓗ Ⓙ
11. Ⓐ Ⓑ Ⓒ Ⓓ	61. Ⓐ Ⓑ Ⓒ Ⓓ
12. Ⓕ Ⓖ Ⓗ Ⓙ	62. Ⓕ Ⓖ Ⓗ Ⓙ
13. Ⓐ Ⓑ Ⓒ Ⓓ	63. Ⓐ Ⓑ Ⓒ Ⓓ
14. Ⓕ Ⓖ Ⓗ Ⓙ	64. Ⓕ Ⓖ Ⓗ Ⓙ
15. Ⓐ Ⓑ Ⓒ Ⓓ	65. Ⓐ Ⓑ Ⓒ Ⓓ
16. Ⓕ Ⓖ Ⓗ Ⓙ	66. Ⓕ Ⓖ Ⓗ Ⓙ
17. Ⓐ Ⓑ Ⓒ Ⓓ	67. Ⓐ Ⓑ Ⓒ Ⓓ
18. Ⓕ Ⓖ Ⓗ Ⓙ	68. Ⓕ Ⓖ Ⓗ Ⓙ
19. Ⓐ Ⓑ Ⓒ Ⓓ	69. Ⓐ Ⓑ Ⓒ Ⓓ
20. Ⓕ Ⓖ Ⓗ Ⓙ	70. Ⓕ Ⓖ Ⓗ Ⓙ
21. Ⓐ Ⓑ Ⓒ Ⓓ	71. Ⓐ Ⓑ Ⓒ Ⓓ
22. Ⓕ Ⓖ Ⓗ Ⓙ	72. Ⓕ Ⓖ Ⓗ Ⓙ
23. Ⓐ Ⓑ Ⓒ Ⓓ	73. Ⓐ Ⓑ Ⓒ Ⓓ
24. Ⓕ Ⓖ Ⓗ Ⓙ	74. Ⓕ Ⓖ Ⓗ Ⓙ
25. Ⓐ Ⓑ Ⓒ Ⓓ	75. Ⓐ Ⓑ Ⓒ Ⓓ
26. Ⓕ Ⓖ Ⓗ Ⓙ	
27. Ⓐ Ⓑ Ⓒ Ⓓ	
28. Ⓕ Ⓖ Ⓗ Ⓙ	
29. Ⓐ Ⓑ Ⓒ Ⓓ	
30. Ⓕ Ⓖ Ⓗ Ⓙ	
31. Ⓐ Ⓑ Ⓒ Ⓓ	
32. Ⓕ Ⓖ Ⓗ Ⓙ	
33. Ⓐ Ⓑ Ⓒ Ⓓ	
34. Ⓕ Ⓖ Ⓗ Ⓙ	
35. Ⓐ Ⓑ Ⓒ Ⓓ	
36. Ⓕ Ⓖ Ⓗ Ⓙ	
37. Ⓐ Ⓑ Ⓒ Ⓓ	
38. Ⓕ Ⓖ Ⓗ Ⓙ	
39. Ⓐ Ⓑ Ⓒ Ⓓ	
40. Ⓕ Ⓖ Ⓗ Ⓙ	
41. Ⓐ Ⓑ Ⓒ Ⓓ	
42. Ⓕ Ⓖ Ⓗ Ⓙ	
43. Ⓐ Ⓑ Ⓒ Ⓓ	
44. Ⓕ Ⓖ Ⓗ Ⓙ	
45. Ⓐ Ⓑ Ⓒ Ⓓ	
46. Ⓕ Ⓖ Ⓗ Ⓙ	
47. Ⓐ Ⓑ Ⓒ Ⓓ	
48. Ⓕ Ⓖ Ⓗ Ⓙ	
49. Ⓐ Ⓑ Ⓒ Ⓓ	
50. Ⓕ Ⓖ Ⓗ Ⓙ	

Mathematics Test

1. Ⓐ Ⓑ Ⓒ Ⓓ Ⓔ	31. Ⓐ Ⓑ Ⓒ Ⓓ Ⓔ
2. Ⓕ Ⓖ Ⓗ Ⓙ Ⓚ	32. Ⓕ Ⓖ Ⓗ Ⓙ Ⓚ
3. Ⓐ Ⓑ Ⓒ Ⓓ Ⓔ	33. Ⓐ Ⓑ Ⓒ Ⓓ Ⓔ
4. Ⓕ Ⓖ Ⓗ Ⓙ Ⓚ	34. Ⓕ Ⓖ Ⓗ Ⓙ Ⓚ
5. Ⓐ Ⓑ Ⓒ Ⓓ Ⓔ	35. Ⓐ Ⓑ Ⓒ Ⓓ Ⓔ
6. Ⓕ Ⓖ Ⓗ Ⓙ Ⓚ	36. Ⓕ Ⓖ Ⓗ Ⓙ Ⓚ
7. Ⓐ Ⓑ Ⓒ Ⓓ Ⓔ	37. Ⓐ Ⓑ Ⓒ Ⓓ Ⓔ
8. Ⓕ Ⓖ Ⓗ Ⓙ Ⓚ	38. Ⓕ Ⓖ Ⓗ Ⓙ Ⓚ
9. Ⓐ Ⓑ Ⓒ Ⓓ Ⓔ	39. Ⓐ Ⓑ Ⓒ Ⓓ Ⓔ
10. Ⓕ Ⓖ Ⓗ Ⓙ Ⓚ	40. Ⓕ Ⓖ Ⓗ Ⓙ Ⓚ
11. Ⓐ Ⓑ Ⓒ Ⓓ Ⓔ	41. Ⓐ Ⓑ Ⓒ Ⓓ Ⓔ
12. Ⓕ Ⓖ Ⓗ Ⓙ Ⓚ	42. Ⓕ Ⓖ Ⓗ Ⓙ Ⓚ
13. Ⓐ Ⓑ Ⓒ Ⓓ Ⓔ	43. Ⓐ Ⓑ Ⓒ Ⓓ Ⓔ
14. Ⓕ Ⓖ Ⓗ Ⓙ Ⓚ	44. Ⓕ Ⓖ Ⓗ Ⓙ Ⓚ
15. Ⓐ Ⓑ Ⓒ Ⓓ Ⓔ	45. Ⓐ Ⓑ Ⓒ Ⓓ Ⓔ
16. Ⓕ Ⓖ Ⓗ Ⓙ Ⓚ	46. Ⓕ Ⓖ Ⓗ Ⓙ Ⓚ
17. Ⓐ Ⓑ Ⓒ Ⓓ Ⓔ	47. Ⓐ Ⓑ Ⓒ Ⓓ Ⓔ
18. Ⓕ Ⓖ Ⓗ Ⓙ Ⓚ	48. Ⓕ Ⓖ Ⓗ Ⓙ Ⓚ
19. Ⓐ Ⓑ Ⓒ Ⓓ Ⓔ	49. Ⓐ Ⓑ Ⓒ Ⓓ Ⓔ
20. Ⓕ Ⓖ Ⓗ Ⓙ Ⓚ	50. Ⓕ Ⓖ Ⓗ Ⓙ Ⓚ
21. Ⓐ Ⓑ Ⓒ Ⓓ Ⓔ	51. Ⓐ Ⓑ Ⓒ Ⓓ Ⓔ
22. Ⓕ Ⓖ Ⓗ Ⓙ Ⓚ	52. Ⓕ Ⓖ Ⓗ Ⓙ Ⓚ
23. Ⓐ Ⓑ Ⓒ Ⓓ Ⓔ	53. Ⓐ Ⓑ Ⓒ Ⓓ Ⓔ
24. Ⓕ Ⓖ Ⓗ Ⓙ Ⓚ	54. Ⓕ Ⓖ Ⓗ Ⓙ Ⓚ
25. Ⓐ Ⓑ Ⓒ Ⓓ Ⓔ	55. Ⓐ Ⓑ Ⓒ Ⓓ Ⓔ
26. Ⓕ Ⓖ Ⓗ Ⓙ Ⓚ	56. Ⓕ Ⓖ Ⓗ Ⓙ Ⓚ
27. Ⓐ Ⓑ Ⓒ Ⓓ Ⓔ	57. Ⓐ Ⓑ Ⓒ Ⓓ Ⓔ
28. Ⓕ Ⓖ Ⓗ Ⓙ Ⓚ	58. Ⓕ Ⓖ Ⓗ Ⓙ Ⓚ
29. Ⓐ Ⓑ Ⓒ Ⓓ Ⓔ	59. Ⓐ Ⓑ Ⓒ Ⓓ Ⓔ
30. Ⓕ Ⓖ Ⓗ Ⓙ Ⓚ	60. Ⓕ Ⓖ Ⓗ Ⓙ Ⓚ

Reading Test	Science Test
1. Ⓐ Ⓑ Ⓒ Ⓓ	1. Ⓐ Ⓑ Ⓒ Ⓓ
2. Ⓕ Ⓖ Ⓗ Ⓙ	2. Ⓕ Ⓖ Ⓗ Ⓙ
3. Ⓐ Ⓑ Ⓒ Ⓓ	3. Ⓐ Ⓑ Ⓒ Ⓓ
4. Ⓕ Ⓖ Ⓗ Ⓙ	4. Ⓕ Ⓖ Ⓗ Ⓙ
5. Ⓐ Ⓑ Ⓒ Ⓓ	5. Ⓐ Ⓑ Ⓒ Ⓓ
6. Ⓕ Ⓖ Ⓗ Ⓙ	6. Ⓕ Ⓖ Ⓗ Ⓙ
7. Ⓐ Ⓑ Ⓒ Ⓓ	7. Ⓐ Ⓑ Ⓒ Ⓓ
8. Ⓕ Ⓖ Ⓗ Ⓙ	8. Ⓕ Ⓖ Ⓗ Ⓙ
9. Ⓐ Ⓑ Ⓒ Ⓓ	9. Ⓐ Ⓑ Ⓒ Ⓓ
10. Ⓕ Ⓖ Ⓗ Ⓙ	10. Ⓕ Ⓖ Ⓗ Ⓙ
11. Ⓐ Ⓑ Ⓒ Ⓓ	11. Ⓐ Ⓑ Ⓒ Ⓓ
12. Ⓕ Ⓖ Ⓗ Ⓙ	12. Ⓕ Ⓖ Ⓗ Ⓙ
13. Ⓐ Ⓑ Ⓒ Ⓓ	13. Ⓐ Ⓑ Ⓒ Ⓓ
14. Ⓕ Ⓖ Ⓗ Ⓙ	14. Ⓕ Ⓖ Ⓗ Ⓙ
15. Ⓐ Ⓑ Ⓒ Ⓓ	15. Ⓐ Ⓑ Ⓒ Ⓓ
16. Ⓕ Ⓖ Ⓗ Ⓙ	16. Ⓕ Ⓖ Ⓗ Ⓙ
17. Ⓐ Ⓑ Ⓒ Ⓓ	17. Ⓐ Ⓑ Ⓒ Ⓓ
18. Ⓕ Ⓖ Ⓗ Ⓙ	18. Ⓕ Ⓖ Ⓗ Ⓙ
19. Ⓐ Ⓑ Ⓒ Ⓓ	19. Ⓐ Ⓑ Ⓒ Ⓓ
20. Ⓕ Ⓖ Ⓗ Ⓙ	20. Ⓕ Ⓖ Ⓗ Ⓙ
21. Ⓐ Ⓑ Ⓒ Ⓓ	21. Ⓐ Ⓑ Ⓒ Ⓓ
22. Ⓕ Ⓖ Ⓗ Ⓙ	22. Ⓕ Ⓖ Ⓗ Ⓙ
23. Ⓐ Ⓑ Ⓒ Ⓓ	23. Ⓐ Ⓑ Ⓒ Ⓓ
24. Ⓕ Ⓖ Ⓗ Ⓙ	24. Ⓕ Ⓖ Ⓗ Ⓙ
25. Ⓐ Ⓑ Ⓒ Ⓓ	25. Ⓐ Ⓑ Ⓒ Ⓓ
26. Ⓕ Ⓖ Ⓗ Ⓙ	26. Ⓕ Ⓖ Ⓗ Ⓙ
27. Ⓐ Ⓑ Ⓒ Ⓓ	27. Ⓐ Ⓑ Ⓒ Ⓓ
28. Ⓕ Ⓖ Ⓗ Ⓙ	28. Ⓕ Ⓖ Ⓗ Ⓙ
29. Ⓐ Ⓑ Ⓒ Ⓓ	29. Ⓐ Ⓑ Ⓒ Ⓓ
30. Ⓕ Ⓖ Ⓗ Ⓙ	30. Ⓕ Ⓖ Ⓗ Ⓙ
31. Ⓐ Ⓑ Ⓒ Ⓓ	31. Ⓐ Ⓑ Ⓒ Ⓓ
32. Ⓕ Ⓖ Ⓗ Ⓙ	32. Ⓕ Ⓖ Ⓗ Ⓙ
33. Ⓐ Ⓑ Ⓒ Ⓓ	33. Ⓐ Ⓑ Ⓒ Ⓓ
34. Ⓕ Ⓖ Ⓗ Ⓙ	34. Ⓕ Ⓖ Ⓗ Ⓙ
35. Ⓐ Ⓑ Ⓒ Ⓓ	35. Ⓐ Ⓑ Ⓒ Ⓓ
36. Ⓕ Ⓖ Ⓗ Ⓙ	36. Ⓕ Ⓖ Ⓗ Ⓙ
37. Ⓐ Ⓑ Ⓒ Ⓓ	37. Ⓐ Ⓑ Ⓒ Ⓓ
38. Ⓕ Ⓖ Ⓗ Ⓙ	38. Ⓕ Ⓖ Ⓗ Ⓙ
39. Ⓐ Ⓑ Ⓒ Ⓓ	39. Ⓐ Ⓑ Ⓒ Ⓓ
40. Ⓕ Ⓖ Ⓗ Ⓙ	40. Ⓕ Ⓖ Ⓗ Ⓙ

English Test

TIME: 45 minutes for 75 questions

DIRECTIONS: Following are five passages with underlined portions. Alternate ways of stating the underlined portions come after the passages. Choose the best alternative; if the original is the best way of stating the underlined portion, choose NO CHANGE.

The test also has questions that refer to the passages or ask you to reorder the sentences within the passages. These questions are identified by a number in a box. Choose the best answer, and shade in the corresponding oval on your answer sheet.

Passage 1

Hockey Season

The coolness of the ice rink and the hum of the <u>Zamboni means only</u> one <u>thing; it's hockey</u> time!
$\overline{}$
1
$\overline{}$
2
<u>All signs pointing toward a successful season</u> for
$\overline{}$
3
the Clement Cougars.

Clement's hockey team <u>is not just made up of</u>
$\overline{}$
4
Clement players. Rounding out the team are
players from St. Thomas High School and Our
Lady High School, too. Though three schools
<u>are represented; the</u> vast majority of the players
$\overline{}$
5
are from Clement.

<u>Here's a little bit about the players from</u>
$\overline{}$
6
<u>Clement.</u> Returning to Clement for his senior
<u>year, the position of goalie is played by Brendan</u>
$\overline{}$
7
<u>Sanchez.</u> For the past two years Brendan has been
playing hockey in a special league in Washington
State. Sanchez's unmatched skills will be an
excellent addition to an already great Clement team.
Sanchez is surrounded by a great supporting cast
that includes such star players <u>as Clement center,</u>
<u>Taylor Poldale, St. Thomas senior, Don Silver, Our</u>
<u>Lady senior, Nick Woodson, and Clement junior,</u>
$\overline{}$
8
<u>Justin Frank.</u> Look for <u>the upperclassmen, to step</u>
<u>up and take over</u> the roles vacated by graduated
$\overline{}$
9
players, Brad Hunt and Steve Wilson. [10]

[1] Some of the players, like Sanchez, have
been preparing for the rigorous season by joining
fall hockey teams. <u>Him and Poldale</u> are currently
$\overline{}$
11
playing for local AA league teams. [2] <u>It is hoped</u>
<u>that this extra practice</u> will give the team the edge
$\overline{}$
12
to overcome its rival, Apple River High School. [3]
Last year, the Clement Cougars won nine games
and lost <u>five and played good enough</u> to make the
$\overline{}$
13
playoffs. [4] The Cougars hope to rebound this
season and take home the state championship. [5]
Unfortunately, they were dealt a devastating two to
one loss in the final seconds at the hands of Coach
Jim Quinlan and the Apple River team. [14]

This year will be an exciting one. So grab
your jackets, buy your tickets, and come support
the Cougars on their way to high school hockey
stardom. [15]

1. **(A)** NO CHANGE

    (B) Zamboni only means

    (C) Zamboni mean only

    (D) Zamboni, means only

2. **(F)** NO CHANGE

    (G) thing; its hockey

    (H) thing. Its hockey

    (J) thing, it's hockey

3. **(A)** NO CHANGE

    (B) All signs points toward a successful season

    (C) All signs point toward a successful season

    (D) All signs have pointed toward a successful season

4. **(F)** NO CHANGE

    (G) are not just made up of

    (H) isn't just made up of

    (J) isn't made up of just

5. **(A)** NO CHANGE

    (B) are represented, the

    (C) are represented: the

    (D) were represented the

6. Which of the following would be the best way to introduce the paragraph?

    (F) NO CHANGE

    (G) The team has many players.

    (H) Some of the team is the same as last year.

    (J) DELETE the underlined portion.

7. **(A)** NO CHANGE

    (B) year, the goalie position made up of Brendan Sanchez.

    (C) year, Brendan Sanchez plays goalie.

    (D) year; Brendan Sanchez plays the position of goalie.

8. **(F)** NO CHANGE

    (G) as: Clement center Taylor Poldale, St. Thomas senior Don Silver, Our Lady senior Nick Woodson, and Clement junior Justin Frank

    (H) as Clement center: Taylor Poldale, St. Thomas senior: Don Silver, Our Lady senior: Nick Woodson, and Clement junior: Justin Frank

    (J) as, Clement center, Taylor Poldale, St. Thomas senior, Don Silver, Our Lady senior, Nick Woodson, and Clement junior, Justin Frank

9. **(A)** NO CHANGE

    (B) the upperclassmen to step up

    (C) the upperclassmen, to take over

    (D) the upperclassmen to step up and take over

10. At this point in the story, the author is considering including a list of the entire team roster. Would it be appropriate to include that list here?

    (F) Yes, because the primary purpose of the essay is to let the reader know who is on the hockey team.

    (G) Yes, because providing a list of players would make the essay more interesting.

    (H) No, because putting a complete list of players in the middle of the essay would interrupt its flow and interfere with its focus.

    (J) No, because the focus of the essay is how the hockey team performed last year, so knowing this year's roster is irrelevant.

11. **(A)** NO CHANGE

    (B) Poldale and him

    (C) Him, and Poldale,

    (D) He and Poldale

12. **(F)** NO CHANGE

    (G) Hopefully, this extra practice

    (H) This extra practice, hopefully,

    (J) Everyone is hopeful that with this extra practice

GO ON TO NEXT PAGE

13. (A) NO CHANGE

    (B) five games and played sufficiently good enough

    (C) five and played well enough

    (D) five games, and then played sufficiently well enough

14. The most logical position for Sentence 4 is:

    (F) where it is now.

    (G) after Sentence 5.

    (H) after Sentence 2.

    (J) before Sentence 1.

15. This article was written in response to an assignment to provide an article for the high school newspaper that would entice students to attend hockey games. Did the writer fulfill the assignment?

    (A) Yes, because the essay is written in a casual, enthusiastic style that promotes the excitement of following the hockey team's season.

    (B) Yes, because the essay provides detailed information about all of the players so that readers will get to know them better.

    (C) No, because the essay focuses too much on the disappointing season the team experienced the year before.

    (D) No, because the essay is written in a style and uses language that is too formal for a high school newspaper.

Passage 2

Promoting Easy Recycling

It is commonly agreed that recycling being a
                        16
critical step, in both maintaining a clean and green
       17
environment and sustaining America's quest for

autonomous independence. The secondary markets
  18
for recycled paper, cardboard, aluminum, asphalt,
               19
copper, plastic, and glass are at all-time highs and

have never been greater. Public education regard-
     20
ing the moral and ethical responsibilities to keep

the environment clean has increased. 21 Their is

now a large supply and an increasingly strong
    22
demand for recycled goods. But we still have

problems in one area; the ability to collect and sort
                    23
recyclables.

[1] Recycle bins have seemingly become

depositories for strictly any type of trash, recyclable
             24   25
or not from a tattered mattress and last weeks' TV
                          26
dinner. [2] The recycle bins that newspaper

publishers, grocery stores, and big box department

stores have traditionally placed in their parking

lots have become trash magnets that produce

increasingly determined complaints from patrons

and neighbors. [3] Part of the reason that the

stores are so willing to remove the bins is because

of the significant expense involved in having to

separate trash from newsprint and other recycla-

bles, including aluminum, cardboard, plastic, and

glass. [4] Neighbors frequently ask stores to

remove their recycle bins largely because they

become displeasing to the eye and unsightly. 28
                          27

One solution to the problem has come from

entrepreneurs who has begun charging for
              29
monthly pick-ups of recyclable materials, like

paper, aluminum, plastic, and glass, from custom-

ers' curbsides. The monthly fee for this service

usually pays for the costs incident to collection

and separation of the materials. Additionally,

these businesses sell the materials for a profit on the secondary recyclable market after they separate them. This practice is generally viewed as a "win-win" situation for the businesses and their contented customers, who have to pay only a small fee to contribute toward a cleaner, more energy-independent America. 30

16. **(F)** NO CHANGE
   (G) could have been
   (H) had been
   (J) is

17. **(A)** NO CHANGE
   (B) step in both maintaining
   (C) step, in maintaining both
   (D) step, both in maintaining

18. **(F)** NO CHANGE
   (G) autonomously
   (H) autonomous,
   (J) DELETE the underlined portion.

19. **(A)** NO CHANGE
   (B) recycled paper; cardboard; aluminum; asphalt; copper; plastic;
   (C) recycled paper: cardboard and aluminum, asphalt, copper, plastic,
   (D) recycled paper and cardboard and aluminum, asphalt, copper, plastic

20. **(F)** NO CHANGE
   (G) are at all-time highs
   (H) have never been greater and are at all-time highs
   (J) have never been at such an all-time high

21. At this point, the author wants to add this sentence about recycling education:

   While the increase in public education has inspired people to partake in recycling programs, many only do so for a short period of time before reverting to old habits.

   Should the author insert this addition?
   (A) No, because the insertion breaks up an existing cause-and-effect relationship in the paragraph.
   (B) No, because the sentence brings up a topic that is completely different from information covered in the rest of the paragraph.
   (C) Yes, because the insertion provides information that is necessary to understand the relationship between public education and increased recycling practices.
   (D) Yes, because the sentence adds interesting information about human nature.

22. **(F)** NO CHANGE
   (G) There is now a large
   (H) There's now a super huge
   (J) Theirs is now a large

23. **(A)** NO CHANGE
   (B) in one area: the ability to collect and sort recyclables.
   (C) in one area. The ability to collect and sort recyclables.
   (D) in one area which is the ability to collect and sort recyclables.

24. **(F)** NO CHANGE
   (G) rigorously
   (H) mainly
   (J) virtually

25. **(A)** NO CHANGE
   (B) trash, recyclable or not,
   (C) trash recyclable or not,
   (D) trash, recyclable, or not,

GO ON TO NEXT PAGE

26. (F) NO CHANGE
    (G) to last week's TV
    (H) and last weeks TV
    (J) to last weeks' television

27. (A) NO CHANGE
    (B) unsightly and displeasing to the eye
    (C) unsightly
    (D) displeasingly unsightly

28. The most logical and coherent placement for Sentence 4 is:
    (F) where it is now.
    (G) before Sentence 1.
    (H) before Sentence 3.
    (J) at the beginning of the next paragraph.

29. (A) NO CHANGE
    (B) whose begun
    (C) they have begun
    (D) who have begun

30. Given that all of the following sentences are true, which one would most effectively conclude this passage?
    (F) As more people enroll in these recycle programs, the country will become much closer to achieving a greener and more sustainable future.
    (G) More public education would only help further America's sustainability goals.
    (H) If neighbors would stop complaining about recycle bins' being eyesores, the greater public would benefit as a result.
    (J) If more big businesses would step up their game, more small businesses would be likely to follow suit.

Passage 3

The Bill of Rights

The first amendment to the United States Constitution provides that "Congress shall make
                                          31
no law respecting or prohibiting the free exercise thereof; or abridging the freedom of speech, or of the press, or the right of the people peaceably to assemble, and to petition the Government for a redress of grievances." Constituting the Bill of Rights are ten amendments, nine others and this
                              32
one in the Constitution. The Bill of Rights does protect more than thirty liberties and rights. The
                              33
Fourteenth Amendment made most of the Bill of Rights applicable to the states, through a process
                                                34
called incorporation.

Originating the Bill of Rights are the English
                    35
Magna Carta of 1215, the English Bill of Rights of 1689, various other English precedents and acts, and the experience of people in England and America. Once the Bill of Rights was ratified by
         36
three-fourths of the fourteen states, virtually all opposition to the U.S. Constitution quickly disappeared.

[1] The effect of the Bill of Rights are deeply
                                      37
embedded in our daily lives. [2] For example, the Bill of Rights by prohibiting most attempts to
                        38
censor certain types of art or music. [3] It also protects speech, which means you can pretty much
                  39
say whatever you want about a government official in the editorial section of a newspaper or in a blog on the Internet. [40] [4] The Bill of Rights protects our often heated debates on abortion, and school prayer, and the death penalty. [5] And the speech
                                      41
you hear police officers give on TV shows when
  42
they tell someone who has been arrested that he has "the right to remain silent" is also a Bill of Rights issue. [6] This practice is known as reading someone the Miranda rights. [43] [7] The first

amendment protection of the rights of extremist groups to peacefully assemble means that any group can stage a protest <u>as long as they are not violent.</u> [8] By protecting the civil liberties of even extreme groups the police and courts seek to preserve the right to freedom of expression for all Americans. 45

31. **(A)** NO CHANGE
(B) that provides
(C) that says
(D) provides, that,

32. **(F)** NO CHANGE
(G) Constituting the Bill of Rights are ten amendments: nine others and this one in the Constitution.
(H) This amendment and nine others constitute the Bill of Rights, which is comprised of the first ten amendments to our Constitution.
(J) Constituting the Bill of Rights are ten amendments; nine others and this one in the Constitution.

33. **(A)** NO CHANGE
(B) Rights does protect more than thirty liberty's and rights
(C) Rights protects more than thirty liberties and rights
(D) Rights, which does protect more than thirty liberties and rights

34. **(F)** NO CHANGE
(G) states through a process called incorporation.
(H) states; through a process called incorporation.
(J) states: through a process called incorporation.

35. **(A)** NO CHANGE
(B) The Bill of Rights originate in
(C) The Bill of Rights that originate from
(D) The origins of the Bill of Rights include

36. All of the following would be an acceptable alternative to the underlined portion EXCEPT:
(F) When
(G) As soon as
(H) While
(J) After

37. **(A)** NO CHANGE
(B) The affect of the Bill of Rights are deeply embedded
(C) The effects of the Bill of Rights is embedded deep
(D) The effects of the Bill of Rights are deeply embedded

38. **(F)** NO CHANGE
(G) prohibits
(H) prohibit
(J) that prohibits

39. **(A)** NO CHANGE
(B) speech, that means
(C) speech that means
(D) speech. Which means

40. The author is considering deleting Sentence 3. Without this sentence, the paragraph would primarily lack:
(F) an irrelevant point.
(G) an example of how the Bill of Rights protects freedom of speech in the daily lives of Americans.
(H) a thorough explanation of the concept of Freedom of Speech.
(J) its main idea.

41. **(A)** NO CHANGE
(B) abortion, school, prayer, and the death penalty.
(C) abortion and school prayer, and the death penalty.
(D) abortion, school prayer, and the death penalty.

GO ON TO NEXT PAGE ➤

42. **(F)** NO CHANGE

 (G) The speech you hear

 (H) Hearing the speech

 (J) But the speech you hear

43. The author is considering including in Sentence 5 the full text of the Miranda speech rather than the short quote provided. Should the author make this change?

 (A) No, because current television shows do not contain as many instances of police officers reading the Miranda rights as past television programs have.

 (B) No, because the paragraph provides practical examples of more than just one right.

 (C) Yes, because it is difficult to grasp the content of the Miranda rights speech from the short quote provided.

 (D) Yes, because the full text of the speech would provide readers with a better understanding of the pervasiveness of the Bill of Rights in daily life.

44. **(F)** NO CHANGE

 (G) provided that they are not violent.

 (H) as long as they are nonviolent.

 (J) as long as it is not violent.

45. Suppose the writer had intended to write an essay that thoroughly details the freedoms granted to Americans by the Bill of Rights. Would this essay successfully fulfill the writer's goal?

 (A) Yes, because the author offers real life examples that exemplify how the Bill of Rights apply to daily life.

 (B) Yes, because in explaining its origins, the author implies that the Bill of Rights gives Americans all of the freedoms provided for by various other English precedents and acts.

 (C) No, because the essay fails to include an explanation of the Right to Bear Arms.

 (D) No, because the author describes some freedoms in detail but doesn't deal with all components of the Bill of Rights.

Passage 4

Jackson's Relationship with the Cherokee

[1] Andrew Jackson President signed the Indian
46
Removal Act in 1830, which appropriated $500,000
47
for the U.S. military to force the Cherokee tribes to
48
march from their homes in Florida and southern

Georgia to Oklahoma. [49] [2] In 1832, the Native

Americans, who won a victory supported by most
50
Northern leaders in the U.S. Supreme Court case of

Worchester v. Georgia. The decision held that Native

American nations were independent and not

subject to state regulation. [3] However, after the
51
case decision, President Jackson, provoking,
52
asserted that Chief Justice John Marshall, the

longest serving Chief Justice in Supreme Court
53
history, had made his decision and "now let's see
54
him enforce it." [4] Although Jackson professed to

having what he called the kindest feelings, his

actions and subsequent statements belied his
55
words toward the Cherokees.
56

In 1835, Jackson entered into treaty negotia-

tions with the Cherokee, that ended up in the
57
relinquishment of all of their land east of the

Mississippi River. Jackson gave the Cherokees until
58
1838 to leave the area. Some left voluntarily, but
59
most did not. Those who remained were forced by

the U.S. military to walk the 1,200 mile "Trail of

Tears" from Georgia to lands in Oklahoma, usually

with only the clothes they were wearing. The brutal

journey in 1838 to 1839 resulted in the deaths of

about one-fourth of the Cherokee population from

disease, starvation, exposure, and exhaustion. [60]

46. **(F)** NO CHANGE

(G) President Andrew Jackson

(H) Andrew Jackson, President

(J) Andrew Jackson, who was president,

47. **(A)** NO CHANGE

(B) that appropriated

(C) which is appropriating

(D) that is appropriating

48. All of the following would be an acceptable alternative to the underlined portion EXCEPT:

(F) coerce

(G) command

(H) help

(J) compel

49. The author is considering placing a period after 1830 in Sentence 1 and deleting the rest of the sentence. If the author did this, the paragraph would primarily lose:

(A) detail about an act that is unrelated to the rest of the information in the passage.

(B) descriptive detail that provides background information that is key to understanding the struggle set forth in the remainder of the passage.

(C) irrelevant details that are repeated later in the paragraph.

(D) information that contradicts the notion later in the passage that Jackson might not have had the best intentions of the Cherokees at heart.

50. **(F)** NO CHANGE

(G) the Native Americans, winners of

(H) the winning Native Americans

(J) the Native Americans won

51. **(A)** NO CHANGE

(B) Consequently,

(C) Additionally,

(D) Therefore,

52. **(F)** NO CHANGE

(G) Jackson provokingly

(H) Jackson, provokingly

(J) Jackson, provoking

53. At this point, the author is considering eliminating this underlined portion. Should the author make this change?

(A) Yes, because the information is irrelevant and detracts from the focus of the paragraph.

(B) Yes, because the information would be more logically placed in the next paragraph.

(C) No, because the phrase gives the reader background information on John Marshall necessary to an understanding of the significance of the decision.

(D) No, because the information in the phrase provides an important fact in the history of the United States.

54. Which of the following would be an appropriate way to rephrase the underlined portion?

(F) and now he had to live with it.

(G) and now would be singlehandedly responsible for its enforcement.

(H) and that Jackson would play a major role in its enforcement.

(J) but that enforcement would prove nearly impossible.

55. Which of the following would be a suitable substitution for the underlined word?

(A) backed up

(B) contradicted

(C) reiterated

(D) echoed

GO ON TO NEXT PAGE

56. The best placement for the underlined portion would be:

   (F) where it is now.

   (G) after *the kindest feelings* (but before the comma).

   (H) after the word *professed*

   (J) after the word *belied*

57. (A) NO CHANGE

   (B) Cherokee that

   (C) Cherokee that,

   (D) Cherokee, that,

58. The author is considering deleting the underlined sentence. If this is done, the passage would primarily lose:

   (F) interesting but irrelevant detail about a specific date.

   (G) information that is repeated elsewhere in the passage.

   (H) a portion of the passage that reveals the true character of Andrew Jackson.

   (J) a relevant point that adds to the progression of the timeline explained in the paragraph.

59. (A) NO CHANGE

   (B) voluntarily: but

   (C) voluntarily, however

   (D) voluntarily,

60. Suppose the author's intent was to dispute the argument that Andrew Jackson was an enemy of the Cherokees. Would this passage fulfill the writer's goal?

   (F) Yes, because the passage quotes Jackson's affirmation that he only has the "kindest feelings" toward the Cherokees.

   (G) Yes, because the passage reveals that Jackson showed animosity toward Chief Justice John Marshall rather than the Cherokees.

   (H) No, because the passage talks primarily about Jackson's relationship with Native Americans in general rather than his feelings toward the Cherokees specifically.

   (J) No, because the passage focuses on the methods Jackson used to move the Cherokees out of Georgia.

Passage 5

Silent Films

[1]

Because it's hard to reveal character without conversation, silent film personalities are essentially one-dimensional. Bad guys are all bad and good guys, all good. Supporting characters are often stereotypes included just to show the theme or add humor.

[2]

What silent films lack in subtlety; they make up for in exaggeration. Without assistance from dialogue, other means are applied in silent films to get their points across. One-dimensional characters, exaggerated movements, ceaseless action, and expressive musical scores compensate for the lack of words.

[3]

Silent film characters can't tell the audience what their thinking, so they must show it. Therefore, physical actions and gestures are exaggerated and overacted far beyond normal movement. 66 Without the use of words, silent film stars must talk with their bodies.

[4]

To maintain the attention of its audience, the silent film is a frenzy of perpetual activity. Scenes change by the second, and the transitions between them are choppy. Silent films may contain car chases, foot chases, jail breaks, roller skating

escapades, and there is lots of dancing, all occur-
68
ring in a matter of minutes. When action cannot
clarify the story, placards expressing dialogue,
thoughts, and the passage of time fill the void.

[5]

Complementing this frenetic motion is an
expressively musical score. Unlike modern film,
69
the musical score provides much more than
background accompaniment. 70 The music plays as
large a role in the silent film than does dialogue in
71
the "talkies." Ominous chords signal danger,
fast-paced jingles heighten chase scenes, and
72
singing violins encourage romance. In the absence
of words, silent films employ creativity and
ingenuity to tell their stories. 74 75
73

61. **(A)** NO CHANGE
  (B) Bad guys are all bad; good guys good.
  (C) Bad guys are all bad, good guys are all good.
  (D) Bad guys are all bad, which means good guys end up being all good.

62. **(F)** NO CHANGE
  (G) What silent films make up for in sub-tlety, they lack in exaggeration.
  (H) Silent films make up for what they lack in subtlety and exaggeration.
  (J) What silent films lack in subtlety, they make up for in exaggeration.

63. **(A)** NO CHANGE
  (B) dialogue assistance, other means were applied in silent films
  (C) dialogue assistance, silent films applied other means
  (D) assistance from dialogue, silent films apply other means

64. **(F)** NO CHANGE
  (G) there
  (H) they're
  (J) they've been

65. **(A)** NO CHANGE
  (B) exaggerated
  (C) overacted and exaggerated
  (D) exaggeratedly overacted

66. At this point, the author is considering insert-ing this sentence:

For example, a character could demonstrate puzzlement by aggressively scratching his head.

Should the author make this insertion?

  (F) Yes, because the sentence provides the reader with an image to describe more specifically the point made in the previ-ous sentence.
  (G) Yes, because the sentence gives the reader important insight into human behavior.
  (H) No, because the sentence contradicts information that the author states else-where in the passage.
  (J) No, because the sentence conveys a humorous tone that is inappropriate for the passage.

67. **(A)** NO CHANGE
  (B) and additionally
  (C) because
  (D) furthermore

68. **(F)** NO CHANGE
  (G) escapades, and many dance numbers
  (H) escapading, and there is lots of dancing
  (J) escapades, dancing from many actors

69. **(A)** NO CHANGE
  (B) expressively, musically score
  (C) expressive musical score
  (D) musically expressive score

70. At this point, the author wants to add another sentence that compares the role of the musical score in modern films and silent films. Which of the following sentences would best accomplish this goal?

- **(F)** While the musical score in modern day films is used to enhance viewers' emotional experiences, without music, the silent film audience has no way to identify with the characters other than through visual cues.
- **(G)** In modern day films, the use of dialogue often offers a clear-cut look into the characters' intents and emotions.
- **(H)** Silent films, if lacking a musical score, are at a bit of a loss in guiding the audience toward the feelings and emotions the filmmaker and the actors are trying to convey.
- **(J)** In modern day films, the musical score can help in not only using various chords to signal different emotions, but also through the lyrics in the music chosen for a given scene.

71. (A) NO CHANGE
- **(B)** the silent film as dialogue,
- **(C)** the silent film, more than dialogue
- **(D)** the silent film as dialogue

72. The author is considering deleting the underlined sentence. If the author were to make this deletion, the essay would primarily lose:

- **(F)** superfluous detail that detracts from the main idea of the paragraph.
- **(G)** examples of the various musical accompaniments that advance one's understanding of the critical role that musical scores play in modern films.
- **(H)** an understanding of the most frequent emotions silent filmmakers try to convey through musical scores.
- **(J)** examples of specific musical accompaniments and how they contribute to advancing the story in silent films.

73. (A) NO CHANGE
- **(B)** and originality
- **(C)** and also inventiveness
- **(D)** DELETE the underlined portion.

74. The most logical and coherent position for Paragraph 2 is:

- **(F)** where it is now.
- **(G)** before Paragraph 1.
- **(H)** before Paragraph 4.
- **(J)** before Paragraph 5.

75. The writer wants to retitle this essay with a more descriptive and appropriate title. Which of the following would best replace the current title?

- **(A)** Musical Scores Play a Big Role in Silent Films
- **(B)** The Evolution of Film in the Twentieth Century
- **(C)** How Silent Films Tell Their Stories
- **(D)** Why Films Contain Car Chases

DO NOT TURN THE PAGE UNTIL TOLD TO DO SO **STOP** DO NOT RETURN TO A PREVIOUS TEST

Mathematics Test

TIME: 60 minutes for 60 questions

DIRECTIONS: Each question has five answer choices. Choose the best answer for each question and shade the corresponding oval on your answer sheet.

1. Angela has half as much money as Holly, who has three-fourths as much as Dolores. If Angela has $60, how much money does Dolores have?

- **(A)** $120.00
- **(B)** $90.00
- **(C)** $150.00
- **(D)** $160.00
- **(E)** $360.00

2. If $y \neq 0$, what is the value of $\dfrac{3}{\left(\dfrac{4}{y}\right)}$?

- **(F)** $\dfrac{12}{y}$
- **(G)** $\dfrac{3y}{4}$
- **(H)** $\dfrac{4}{3y}$
- **(J)** $\dfrac{y}{12}$
- **(K)** $\dfrac{3}{4y}$

3. A sailboat has a sail that is 16 ft high. The base of the sail measures 12 feet. What is the measurement in feet from the bottom-left point of the sail's base to the top of the sail?

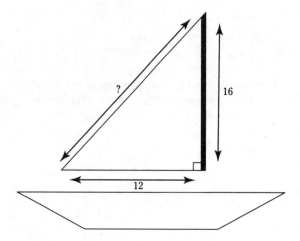

- **(A)** 18
- **(B)** 19
- **(C)** 20
- **(D)** $\sqrt{2}$
- **(E)** 28

4. A total of 11 students took an exam, and their average score was 84. If the average score for 6 of the students was 79, what was the average score of the remaining 5 students?

- **(F)** 88
- **(G)** 89
- **(H)** 90
- **(J)** 91
- **(K)** 92

GO ON TO NEXT PAGE

5. What is the value of x if $x + y = 6$ and $x - y = 4$?

   (A) 1

   (B) 5

   (C) 0

   (D) −1

   (E) −5

6. When adding the fractions $\frac{u}{2}, \frac{x}{4}, \frac{y}{16}$, and $\frac{z}{24}$, what would you find as the least common denominator?

   (F) 24

   (G) 32

   (H) 48

   (J) 96

   (K) 768

7. In the figure, $\overline{OB}$ is perpendicular to $\overline{OA}$ and $\angle AOC$ is 8° greater than $\angle AOB$. What is the measure of $\angle AOC$?

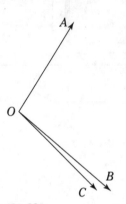

   (A) 82°

   (B) 90°

   (C) 98°

   (D) 172°

   (E) 188°

8. Consider all statements below to be true.

   All Dingbats are blue.

   Homer is a Dingbat.

   Prudence is blue.

Which of the following statements has to be false?

   (F) Prudence is a Dingbat.

   (G) Homer is blue.

   (H) Prudence could be a Dingbat.

   (J) Prudence is not a Dingbat.

   (K) Homer is not blue.

9. To raise money for a local charity, Bonnie sets up a lemonade stand in her busy neighborhood. Her parents donated the cups, so Bonnie's only costs were her purchase of x pounds of lemons for p dollars per pound and s pounds of sugar at d dollars per pound. Which of the following expresses Bonnie's total cost, in dollars, of producing the lemonade for her sale?

   (A) $(x + s)(p + d)$

   (B) $x + p + s + d$

   (C) $xd + sp$

   (D) $sd + xp$

   (E) $(xp)(sd)$

10. Which of the following expressions is equal to $(x + y)^2$?

   (F) $2x + 2y$

   (G) $x^2 + y^2$

   (H) $x^2 + 2xy + y^2$

   (J) $x^2 - y^2$

   (K) $2xy$

11. If $x^2 = 144$ and $y^2 = 81$, which of the following could be a value for $x + y$?

   (A) −24

   (B) −21

   (C) −18

   (D) 2

   (E) 25

12. Jan has a necklace on which she strings exactly 3 charms and only 3 charms in no particular order. One of these charms always contains a blue stone, one is always made of silver with no stones, and one is always made of gold with no stones. Jan owns 4 charms with blue stones, 5 charms made of silver with no stones, and 3 charms made of gold with no stones. How many different combinations of 3 charms can Jan string on her necklace?

   (F) 12

   (G) 23

   (H) 60

   (J) 120

   (K) 360

13. Which of these expressions is equal to $9ab\left(3a^3b^2 + 5ab\right)$?

   (A) $27a^4b^3 + 45a^2b^2$

   (B) $27a^4b^3 + 5ab$

   (C) $27a^3b^2 + 45ab$

   (D) $9ab\left(15a^4b^3\right)$

   (E) $135a^5b^4$

14. Evan has earned \$230, \$50, and \$120 at his last 3 garage sales. He plans to hold one more garage sale next Saturday. If Evan wants to earn an average of exactly \$160 on the 4 sales, his earnings for Saturday's garage sale must be:

   (F) \$220

   (G) \$230

   (H) \$240

   (J) \$250

   (K) \$260

15. If $20^c = 4^3 \times 5^3$, the value of c is:

   (A) 3

   (B) 6

   (C) 9

   (D) 27

   (E) 60

16. At what point does $3x + 7y = 21$ intersect the x-axis?

   (F) $(0, 3)$

   (G) $(3, 0)$

   (H) $(8, 0)$

   (J) $(7, 0)$

   (K) $(0, 7)$

17. If $1 - \dfrac{2}{a} = 3 - \dfrac{4}{a}$, then $1 - \dfrac{2}{a} =$

   (A) -1

   (B) 0

   (C) 1

   (D) $\dfrac{2}{3}$

   (E) $\dfrac{3}{4}$

18. If $a^2 = -1$ and $\left[\left(a^2\right)^5\right]^x = 1$, what is the least positive integer value of x?

   (F) 0

   (G) 1

   (H) 2

   (J) 3

   (K) 4

19. If $ABCD$ in the figure is reflected across line l, the coordinates of the reflection of point D are:

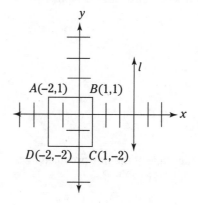

   (A) $(1, -2)$

   (B) $(3, -2)$

   (C) $(4, -2)$

   (D) $(7, -2)$

   (E) $(10, -2)$

GO ON TO NEXT PAGE

20. The population of Boomtown doubles every 50 years. The number of people in Boomtown this year is 10^3. What will the population of Boomtown be in 3 centuries?

(F) $3(10^3)$

(G) $6(10^3)$

(H) $(10^6)(10^3)$

(J) $(2^6)(10^3)$

(K) $(10^3)^6$

21. If $(x-4)$ is a factor of $(x^2 - kx - 28)$, then the value of k is:

(A) −11

(B) −7

(C) −3

(D) 3

(E) 7

22. What are all values for z for which $|z - 3| < 4$?

(F) $z < 7$

(G) $z > 7$

(H) $0 < z < 6$

(J) $-1 < z < 7$

(K) $-6 < z < 0$

23. Which of these expressions is equivalent to $\left(-3x^2 y^5\right)^3$?

(A) $-27x^5 y^8$

(B) $-27x^6 y^{15}$

(C) $-9x^5 y^8$

(D) $9x^5 y^8$

(E) $27x^6 y^{15}$

24. What is the slope of the line provided by the equation $32x + 5y + 12 = 0$?

(F) −32

(G) $-\dfrac{32}{5}$

(H) $-\dfrac{5}{32}$

(J) $\dfrac{32}{5}$

(K) 12

25. An old lighthouse on a remote part of the coast of Maine can provide a boat that is 4.5 miles away with a flash of light every 20 seconds. The light flashes every time it makes a full rotation. How many degrees does the light rotate in 2 seconds?

(A) 8

(B) 9

(C) 18

(D) 36

(E) 81

26. In the figure, $\triangle ACE$ is equilateral and $\overline{FB}$ is parallel to $\overline{EC}$. Point G is the midpoint of $\overline{FB}$. If $\overline{AB}$ measures 4 units and $\overline{AB}$ measures 6 units, what is the measurement in units of the perimeter of the trapezoid formed by points F, B, C, and E?

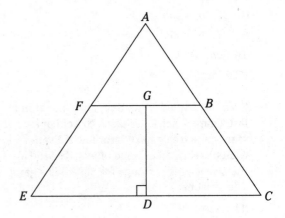

(F) 18

(G) 19

(H) 24

(J) 26

(K) 28

27. If $x + 2x + 3x = y$, then $2x - y = ?$

(A) $-8x$

(B) $-6x$

(C) $-4x$

(D) $-3x$

(E) $4x$

28. Which of these is a value of x that satisfies $\log_x 27 = 3$?

(F) 3

(G) 9

(H) 12

(J) 21

(K) 27

29. The Swift Express and Douglas Dependable are two trains that travel the same route in opposite directions on parallel tracks. The two trains started at the same time from opposite ends of the 900-mile route. They travelled toward each other at constant rates. The Swift Express completed the 900-mile journey in 3 hours; the Douglas Dependable finished the same trip in 5 hours. How many miles had the Swift Express travelled when it met the Douglas Dependable?

(A) 300

(B) 360

(C) 544.5

(D) 562.5

(E) 600

30. In the coordinate plane, point O is the origin, point A has coordinates of $(2, -2)$, point B has coordinates of $(6, 0)$, and point C has coordinates of $(4, -6)$. Any two points can be connected to form a line segment. Which of the following is true about the line segments formed by connecting any two points?

(F) $\overline{OA} = \overline{AB}$

(G) $\overline{OC} = \overline{BC}$

(H) $\overline{AC} = \overline{AB}$

(J) $\overline{OA} = \overline{OB}$

(K) $\overline{OB} = \overline{BC}$

31. In the figure, $\triangle MNO$ and $\triangle OPQ$ are similar. The length of $\overline{NM}$ is $\frac{5}{8}$ inch; the length of $\overline{PQ}$ is $\frac{5}{6}$ inch. Which of the following is the value of $\frac{b}{a}$?

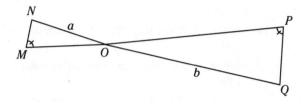

(A) $\frac{1}{4}$

(B) $\frac{1}{3}$

(C) $\frac{3}{4}$

(D) 1

(E) $\frac{4}{3}$

32. In 2010, Esteban invested $1,000 in a 10-year certificate of deposit (CD) that pays him interest at an annual percentage rate (APR) of 2.5% compounded annually, which means that the interest he earns each year is added to the principal amount in advance of the next year. The informational brochure that Esteban received provided him with a standard formula he can use to determine the growth of his money: $NV = IV \times (1 + P)^Y$. He read that NV stands for the value of his money at the end of the term of his CD, IV stands for the value of his money at the beginning of the term of his CD, P stands for the percent his money increases, and Y is the number of years in the term of his CD. Rounded to the nearest dollar, what will his accumulated balance be in 2020 when the CD reaches maturity?

(F) $1,025

(G) $1,280

(H) $1,290

(J) $1,300

(K) $9,313

GO ON TO NEXT PAGE

33. Line l has a negative slope and a positive x-intercept. Line m is parallel to line l and has a negative x-intercept. The y-intercept of line m must be:

(A) negative and greater than the y-intercept of line l.

(B) negative and less than the y-intercept of line l.

(C) positive and greater than the y-intercept of line l.

(D) positive and less than the y-intercept of line l.

(E) zero.

34. The roots of a quadratic equation have a sum of 3 and a product of 2. Which of the following could be the equation?

(F) $x^2 + 3x + 2$

(G) $x^2 - 2x - 3$

(H) $x^2 + 4x + 3$

(J) $x^2 + 2x - 3$

(K) $x^2 - 3x + 2$

35. For the number sequence $2, 6, 10, 14 \ldots$, which of the following represents the value of the nth term?

(A) $2n$

(B) $2n^2$

(C) $n(n-1)$

(D) $n(n+1)$

(E) $2n(2n-1)$

Use the information that follows to answer Questions 36 through 38.

C and O are the centers of the bases of the right circular cylinder in the figure. The height of the cylinder is 6 inches and $\overline{XY}$ is 4 inches.

36. Which of these, in inches, is closest to the perimeter of $\triangle XYO$?

(F) 6.32

(G) 10.32

(H) 17

(J) 16.65

(K) 20

37. Given that $\triangle XYO$ has no mass, which of these, in cubic inches, is nearest to the volume of the cylinder?

(A) 38

(B) 75

(C) 224

(D) 301

(E) 1,000

38. Which of the following must be true about the angles in the figure?

(F) $\angle OXY = \angle XYO$

(G) $\angle XYO < \angle XOY$

(H) $\angle XOY = \angle OYX$

(J) $\angle XOY > \angle OXY$

(K) $\angle OXY < 45°$

39. Which of the following has the least value?

(A) $\left(100 \times 10^5\right)^{10}$

(B) $1,000,000,000,000,000$

(C) 1000^{100}

(D) $\left(10 \times 10^{10}\right)^{10}$

(E) 100^{1000}

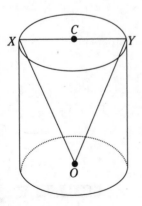

40. The figure shows a square prism. Which of the given vertices is located in the plane determined by the vertices S, U, and X?

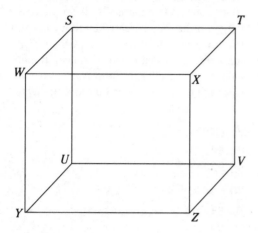

(F) W

(G) Z

(H) Y

(J) T

(K) V

41. To create a more refreshing beverage, the snack stand at the beach mixes lemonade with iced tea. The proprietor has found that the best mixture results when the final product is 15 percent lemonade. How many liters of lemonade should the employees mix with 2 liters of iced tea to achieve the best mixture?

(A) $\frac{3}{10}$

(B) $\frac{17}{50}$

(C) $\frac{6}{17}$

(D) $\frac{13}{20}$

(E) $\frac{13}{10}$

42. A line with equation $x = 6$ is graphed on the same xy-coordinate plane as a circle with a center point of $(3, 5)$ and a radius of 4. What are the y-coordinates of the points where the line and the circle intersect?

(F) 8 and 2

(G) 7 and −1

(H) 10 and 0

(J) 7.65 and 2.35

(K) 6.87 and −0.87

43. In an attempt to win a pizza baking contest, the employees of Guido's Italian Eatery prepared a crust that was 122 feet in diameter. They cut pepperoni slices from 1-foot pepperoni logs, and they placed the pepperoni slices on the crust so that there were exactly 10 slices per square foot of pizza crust. If they cut exactly 50 slices from each pepperoni log, how many pepperoni logs did they need to fill the pizza?

(A) 77

(B) 2,338

(C) 4,842

(D) 7,345

(E) 9,352

44. All the sides of the right triangle in the figure are measured in the same units of length. What is the value of $\dfrac{(\sin A)}{(\cos B)}$?

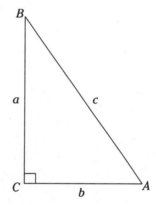

(F) $\dfrac{a}{c}$

(G) $\dfrac{c}{a}$

(H) $\dfrac{a^2}{c^2}$

(J) $\dfrac{ac}{b^2}$

(K) 1

45. Two positive integers r and s satisfy the relationship $r \dagger s$ only when $q = r^2 + 2$. If s, t, and u satisfy the relations $s \dagger r$ and $t \dagger u$, what is the value of s in terms of u?

(A) $u^2 + 2$

(B) $u^2 + 2$

(C) $u^4 + 4u^2 + 4$

(D) $u^4 + 4u^2 + 6$

(E) $u^4 + 8u^2 + 16$

GO ON TO NEXT PAGE

46. Points D, E, and F lie on a circle. A line drawn from D to F passes through the center of the circle. Which of the following is true about the measurement of the angle formed by points D, E, and F?

(F) $\angle DEF = 90°$

(G) $0° < \angle DEF < 90°$

(H) $90° < \angle DEF < 180°$

(J) $\angle DEF = 180°$

(K) $180° < \angle DEF < 360°$

47. Given that $\begin{bmatrix} a & b \\ c & d \end{bmatrix}$ is $cd\left(b^2 - a^2\right)$, what is the value of $\begin{bmatrix} 4x & 2y \\ 7y & 3y \end{bmatrix}$ when $x = 4$ and $y = -2$?

(A) $-20{,}160$

(B) -168

(C) 0

(D) 168

(E) $20{,}160$

48. In the figure, $z\left(\sin\theta\right) = ?$

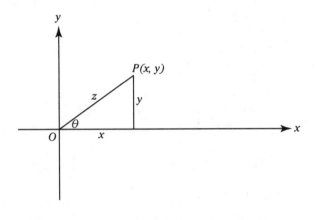

(F) x

(G) y

(H) z

(J) $\dfrac{y}{z}$

(K) $y + z$

49. Parasailing is much like water-skiing, except that the rider is connected to a parachute rather than water-skis and trails the boat in the air rather than directly behind it. If the rope attached to a parasailer is 50 meters long and the angle created by that rope and the surface of the water is 53°, which of the following is closest to the distance, in meters, from the parasailer to the surface of the water? (Assume that the rope is taut and the water surface is level.)

(A) $\left(\tan 53°\right)50$

(B) 50

(C) $\left(\sin 53°\right)50$

(D) $\left(\cos 53°\right)50$

(E) 53

50. Which of the following expressions is equivalent to $2x\left(\dfrac{3}{y} + \dfrac{4}{z}\right)$?

(F) $\dfrac{24x}{yz}$

(G) $\dfrac{24x}{y+z}$

(H) $\dfrac{14x}{y+z}$

(J) $\dfrac{8xy + 6xz}{yz}$

(K) $\dfrac{14x}{yz}$

51. The average salary of the 14 employees of Simon's Crougar Industrial Smoothing, Inc., is \$51,000. When a new employee, George, is hired, the average salary increases to \$51,200. What is George's salary?

(A) \$51,400

(B) \$51,700

(C) \$52,000

(D) \$53,000

(E) \$54,000

52. If $\sqrt{5p} = 3.67$, then what is the value of p?

(F) 0.73

(G) 1.64

(H) 2.69

(J) 8.21

(K) 18.35

53. Recently, on a day when many Congress members were either ill or attending to matters in their home states, 410 members of the House of Representatives and 90 Senate members voted on a tax increase. A total of 350 members from the two government bodies voted "no" on the tax measure. If the same percentage of members gave a "no" vote in the House of Representatives as gave a "no" vote in the Senate, how many members of the House of Representatives voted "no" on the tax increase?

(A) 63

(B) 70

(C) 206

(D) 287

(E) 349

54. The figure shows one cycle of the graph of the function $y = \sin x$ for $0 \le x \le 2\pi$. If the maximum value of the function occurs at point A, what are the coordinates of A?

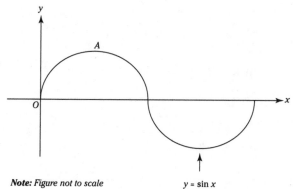

Note: Figure not to scale $y = \sin x$

(F) $\left(\dfrac{\pi}{4}, 1\right)$

(G) $\left(\dfrac{\pi}{4}, \pi\right)$

(H) $\left(\dfrac{\pi}{2}, 0\right)$

(J) $\left(\dfrac{\pi}{2}, 1\right)$

(K) $\left(\dfrac{\pi}{2}, \pi\right)$

55. The solution set for a quadratic equation is 4 and −3. The equation must be which of the following?

(A) $x^2 - 12$

(B) $x^2 + x + 12$

(C) $x^2 + x - 12$

(D) $x^2 - x + 12$

(E) $x^2 - x - 12$

56. If a, b, and $c \ne 0$ and if $a^3 b^5 c^6 = \dfrac{a^2 c^6}{3b^{-5}}$, what is the value of a?

(F) $\dfrac{1}{3}$

(G) $\dfrac{b^{10}}{3}$

(H) $3b^{10}$

(J) $\dfrac{c^{12}}{3}$

(K) 3

57. Janet is filling in a patch of lawn with sod. The patch is in the shape of a parallelogram. The length of the patch is 8 feet and its width is 6 feet. One of the interior angles measures 120°. How many square feet of sod will Janet need to completely fill the patch?

(A) 48

(B) $24\sqrt{3}$

(C) $18\sqrt{3}$

(D) 24

(E) 18

58. Which of the following represents the graph of the solution set of $|x| - 1 \le 3$?

(F)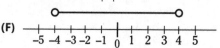

(G)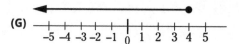

(H)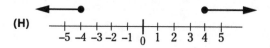

(J)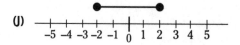

(K)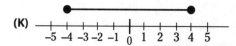

GO ON TO NEXT PAGE

59. The figure shows a cube with a side length of 5 cm. If points W and Z are midpoints of the edges of the cube, what is the area in square centimeters of $WXYZ$?

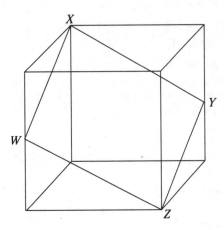

(A) 5.59

(B) 11.18

(C) 22.36

(D) 31.25

(E) 976.56

60. In the figure, the area of the shaded region bound by the graph of the parabola $y = f(x)$ and the x-axis is 5. What is the area of the region bound by the graph of $y = f(x-3)$ and the x-axis?

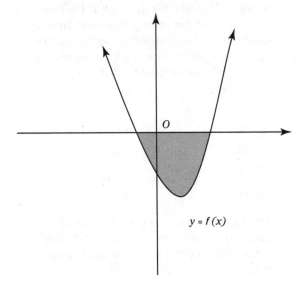

(F) 2

(G) $\dfrac{5}{3}$

(H) 5

(J) 8

(K) 15

Reading Test

TIME: 35 minutes for 40 questions

DIRECTIONS: Each of the four passages in this section is followed by ten questions. Answer each question based on what is stated or implied in the passage and shade the corresponding oval on your answer sheet.

Passage I — Prose Fiction

This passage is adapted from *A Happy Boy* by Bjørnstjerne Bjørnson, who was a Norwegian poet, novelist, and dramatist.

Line

It was a cloudy evening, not cold; no stars were to be seen; the morrow might bring rain. A drowsy breeze blew over the snow, which was swept clear in patches on the white uplands, while
(05) in other places it had formed deep drifts. Along by the roadside where now snow happened to lie there was a margin of slippery ice; it lay blue-black between the snow and the bare ground, and could be seen glimmering here and there as far as the
(10) eye could reach. On the mountainsides there had been snow-slips; their tracks were black and bare, while on each side of them the snow lay smooth and white, except where the birch-trees clustered together in dark patches. There was no water to be
(15) seen, but half-naked moors and bogs stretched up to rivers and lowering mountains.

The farms lay in large clusters in the midst of the level ground; in the dusk of the winter evening they looked like black masses from which light
(20) shot forth over the fields, now from one window, now from another; to judge by the lights there was a great deal going on inside. Young people, grown-up and half-grown up, flocked together from various quarters. Very few kept to the road; almost
(25) all, at any rate, left it when they drew near the farms, and slipped away, one behind the cowhouse, a pair under the store-house and so forth; while some rushed away behind the barn and howled like foxes, others answered farther off like cats.
(30) One stood behind the wash-house and barked like an old angry dog. The girls came marching along in large bands; they had a few boys, mostly little boys, with them, who skirmished around them to show off. When one of the gangs of girls came near
(35) the house and one or other of the big boys caught sight of them, the girls scattered and fled into the passages or down the garden, and had to be dragged out and into the rooms one by one. Some were so extremely bashful that Marit had to be

sent for, when she would come out and positively (40) force them in. Sometimes one would come who had not been invited and whose intention it was not to go in, but only to look on, until in the end she would be persuaded just to have one single dance. Those guests whom she really cared for, Marit (45) invited into a little room where the old people sat and grandmother did the honors; they were kindly received and treated. Eyvind was not among the favored ones, and he thought that rather strange.

The best player of the village could not come (50) until late, so they had meanwhile to manage with the old one, a cottager called Grey Knut. He knew four dances, two spring dances, a halling and an old so-called Napoleon waltz. He struck up, and the dancing began. Eyvind did not dare to join in (55) at first, for there were too many grown-up people; but the half-grown ones soon banded together, pushed each other forward, drank a little strong ale to hearten them, and then Eyvind also joined in. The room grew very hot, the fun and the ale (60) mounted to their heads.

Marit danced more than anyone else that evening, probably because the party was in her grandparents' house, and so it happened that Eyvind caught her eye, but she always danced with some- (65) one else. He wanted to dance with her himself, so he sat out one dance in order to run to her directly when it ended, and this he did; but a tall, swarthy fellow with bushy hair pushed in front of him.

"Get away, youngster," he cried and gave (70) Eyvind a shove, so that he nearly fell backwards over Marit. Never had such a thing happened to him, never had anyone been other than kind to him, never had he been called "youngster" when he wanted to join in anything. He reddened to the (75) roots of his hair, but said nothing, and drew back to where the new musician, just arrived, had taken his seat and was tuning up. Eyvind looked at Marit dancing with the bushy-haired man, she laughed over the man's shoulder so that her white teeth (80) showed, and Eyvind, for the first time in his life, was aware of a strange, tingling pain in his breast.

GO ON TO NEXT PAGE ➔

He looked at her again and again, and the more he looked the clearer it seemed to him that
(85) Marit was quite grown-up.

1. The passage is most likely part of a:
   (A) fable.
   (B) romance novel.
   (C) coming-of-age tale.
   (D) tragic poem.

2. The character of Marit can best be described as:
   (F) gregarious and influential.
   (G) extremely bashful.
   (H) cold and callous.
   (J) kind and grandmotherly.

3. When the author states in Line 82 that Eyvind experienced a "strange, tingling pain in his breast," he is inferring that Eyvind:
   (A) had drunk too much ale.
   (B) was feeling embarrassed that he had been called "youngster."
   (C) was physically injured by the tall, swarthy fellow's shove.
   (D) was experiencing his first feelings of disappointment.

4. The author suggests that Eyvind is a rather timid individual in all of the following instances EXCEPT:
   (F) when he fails to join in the dancing at first because all of the dancers were older than he.
   (G) when he said nothing in response to the bushy-haired man.
   (H) when he continued to watch Marit dance with the bushy-haired man.
   (J) when he failed to respond to the grandmother's invitation to enter the little room.

5. The author most likely provides the description in the first paragraph to:
   (A) place the events of the house in perspective within the larger realm of the natural world.
   (B) demonstrate how the party attendees braved harsh, cruel conditions in order to reach their destination.
   (C) provide a glimpse into typical Scandinavian life.
   (D) highlight the frigid and potentially dangerous conditions the characters faced every day.

6. The best way to describe Marit's feelings for Eyvind is that she:
   (F) pitied him.
   (G) was secretly in love with him.
   (H) felt repulsed by him.
   (J) was indifferent toward him.

7. The author mentions the little room where the old people sat (Line 46) in order to:
   (A) describe the room where Marit took the timid girls to persuade them to dance just one dance.
   (B) show that Marit cared more for old people than for people her age.
   (C) offer a glimpse of the true nature of the relationship between Marit and Eyvind.
   (D) provide insight into the character of the grandmother.

8. As it is used in Line 32 *bands* most likely refers to:
   (F) gangs of ruffians.
   (G) groupings of young girls.
   (H) members of a parade organized to celebrate a village holiday.
   (J) groups of musicians headed to play at the dance.

9. It can be reasonably inferred from the passage that Eyvind's attendance at the dance:

(A) consisted primarily of sitting and watching Marit dance with others.

(B) resulted in the realization that his life was changing.

(C) was spent sitting with the grandmother and having conversations with older people.

(D) ended with his sulking in the corner because the admonishment from the swarthy fellow was the first time he had ever experienced rejection.

10. It is reasonable to conclude that the people who live in Eyvind's village:

(F) experience cloud cover and cold almost every day because they live very far north.

(G) engage in activities that involve participation by a variety of age groups.

(H) are generally fearful of traveling on the designated roads and prefer to move through the countryside by running from farmhouse to farmhouse.

(J) prefer to dance to music performed by young musicians.

Passage II — Social Science

Passage A

This passage is adapted from *The Rise and Fall of the U.S. Mortgage and Credit Markets: A Comprehensive Analysis of the Market Meltdown*, by James R. Barth (John Wiley & Sons, Inc.).

Line   The economy has been engaged in a massive wave of deleveraging since 2007, a scramble to reduce debt and sell assets as well as an attempt to obtain new capital from any willing source, includ-
(05) ing the government. Unfortunately, this process has caused a major credit crunch and sent asset prices further downward. Even solid companies with no connection to the real estate and finance sectors have been affected as credit markets seized
(10) up. In the process, a rush to liquidity has created severe difficulties for individuals, small businesses, large corporations, and even state and local governments as they try to obtain short-term funding simply to meet payrolls and cover ongoing operating expenses. (15)

In many cases, the government has now become the buyer of last, if not first, resort, intervening in the market in ways not seen since the New Deal. To contain the damage, the government invoked some existing but seldom-used pow- (20) ers and created others out of whole cloth. As the financial sector continued to lurch from crisis to crisis in 2008, the government's response has been marked by an improvisational quality that has failed to restore confidence in the financial system. (25)

The government has attempted to shore up mortgages directly. In July 2008, the Housing and Economic Recovery Act authorized the Federal Housing Authority to guarantee up to $300 billion in new 30-year fixed-rate mortgages for subprime (30) borrowers. But the guarantees were conditional on lenders voluntarily writing down principal loan balances to 90 percent of current appraisal value. At the same time, the Treasury announced a temporary program to purchase Fannie Mae and Fred- (35) die Mac mortgage-backed securities to help make more mortgage financing available to home buyers.

When all of these government interventions failed to stem the growing crisis, even bolder action was undertaken in October. The Fed, in ad- (40) dition to several other new and historic programs, took steps to force down home mortgage rates by agreeing to buy up to $600 billion of housing-related securities issued and guaranteed by Fannie Mae, Freddie Mac, Ginnie Mae, and Federal Home (45) Loan Banks as well as creating a $200 billion program to lend money against securities backed by car loans, student loans, credit card debt, and small-business loans.

Passage B

This passage is adapted from *Place, Exclusion, and Mortgage Markets*, by Manuel B. Aalbers (John Wiley & Sons, Inc.).

The summer of 2007 marked the beginning (50) of the subprime mortgage crisis. What started as a subprime mortgage crisis quickly developed into a general mortgage and housing crisis. A few

months later it was clear that there was a credit
(55) crunch, and one by one, commentators suggested
this was the worst crisis since the stock market
crash of 1929 and the subsequent crisis of the
early 1930s. Several of them even claimed that the
subprime meltdown of 2007 would soon make the
(60) stock market crash of 1929 look like a small crisis.
It also became clear that the credit crunch was not
limited to the United States; investors and financial
institutions around the globe were affected by what
seemed at first a very specific and limited problem.
(65) Since financial institutions are a crucial corner-
stone of the economy, the crisis spread not only
from the U.S. to the rest of the world, but also from
credit markets to all kinds of markets. Globaliza-
tion implied a greater interconnectedness not only
(70) between different places, but also between different markets.

In society, people are excluded not only on
the basis of class and race, but also on the basis of
place. The mortgage market is no different; in fact,
(75) it is exactly highly developed and institutional-
ized markets like the mortgage market that have
a tendency to exclude. Mortgage redlining is the
identification of an area, usually a neighborhood
or ZIP code area, where no mortgage loans are to
(80) be issued, which is a form of place-based financial and social exclusion. Mortgage applicants are
excluded *from* obtaining housing by being denied
mortgages in redlined neighborhoods. Current
homeowners are excluded *through* housing be-
(85) cause they are unable to sell their house, becoming trapped in their neighborhood. In the case of
mortgage financing, the supply side (i.e., the lenders) has the power to exclude part of the demand
side (i.e., the customers). Financial institutions can
(90) provide the essential underpinnings for positive
social development, but they also have destruc-
tive power — the power to deny credit loans. One
possible method is to put certain neighborhoods on
a black list. A financial institution might black-
(95) list a neighborhood if it is already considered or
expected to develop into a "slum." Almost without
exception it is a self-fulfilling prophecy.

11. According to Passage A, one purpose of the
Housing and Economic Recovery Act was to:

(A) allow home buyers more access to
mortgage loans.

(B) force lenders to write down principal
loan balances to 90 percent of their
current appraisal value.

(C) restore the public's confidence in the
Federal Housing Authority.

(D) reduce the influence of the federal
government in the financial crisis.

12. As it is used in Line 39, *stem* most likely
means to:

(F) originate.

(G) grow slowly.

(H) remove.

(J) stop.

13. It is reasonable to infer that the author of
Passage A would agree with which of the following statements about Americans' lack of
confidence in the financial sector?

(A) The lack of confidence resulted from a
lack of attention to borrowers of government funds.

(B) Americans' confidence was completely
restored when the bailout plan guaranteed up to $300 billion in new 30-year
fixed-rate mortgages for subprime
borrowers.

(C) The government's seemingly unplanned
response to the economic crisis and a
series of additional crises continues
to erode the public's confidence in its
leaders.

(D) The actions of the Federal Housing
Authority created a sense of stability in
the United States economy.

14. According to Passage A, all of the following
are components of deleveraging the economy
EXCEPT:

(F) offering lower mortgage rates to new
homebuyers.

(G) reducing debt.

(H) selling assets.

(J) attempting to gain new capital from any
willing source.

15. When the author of Passage B refers to *redlining* in Lines 77, he most nearly means:

(A) the government practice of trapping people in their neighborhoods.

(B) the practice of discriminatory loans based solely on class and race.

(C) denying a mortgage loan based on the ZIP code of the dwelling.

(D) granting exclusive access to subprime loans to wealthy homebuyers.

16. The primary purpose of the first paragraph in Passage B is to:

(F) reveal the author's anti-government perspective.

(G) summarize the effects of a specific and limited problem.

(H) present an overview of what the government has chosen to do to combat a growing financial crisis.

(J) describe the pervasiveness of a past financial crisis as well as its national and global effects.

17. The author of Passage B mentions the economic concepts of supply and demand to:

(A) demonstrate that financial institutions use economic principles for positive social development.

(B) identify the participants in a mortgage financing relationship.

(C) illustrate how mortgage lenders decide which neighborhoods to blacklist.

(D) explain how a global economy works during a financial crisis.

18. The authors of both passages would likely agree with which of the following statements about the state of the U.S. economy in 2007 and 2008?

(F) The financial crisis decreased an individual's ability to obtain loans.

(G) The government had intervened in the U.S. market in ways not seen since the New Deal.

(H) The crisis was the worst one since the stock market crash of 1929.

(J) The only way the economy would return to normal was through government intervention.

19. The author of Passage B would most likely respond to the temporary program mentioned in Lines 34–35 of Passage A in which of the following ways?

(A) The program would be more effective if the government allocated more money to it.

(B) Individuals in certain neighborhoods would be more interconnected as a result of the program.

(C) The public would gain increased confidence in the country's financial stability as a result of the program.

(D) The program would likely be ineffective in certain ZIP codes.

20. Which of the following is true regarding the two passages?

(F) Passage A views the financial crisis as fundamentally a national issue, whereas Passage B is primarily concerned with the global effects of the crisis.

(G) Passage A is much more optimistic regarding homeowners' ability to buy houses during the crisis than Passage B is.

(H) Passage A is primarily critical of government practices, while Passage B is primarily critical of those of financial institutions.

(J) Both passages imply that greater government involvement in the financial crisis would create a better position for homebuyers and sellers in redlined neighborhoods.

GO ON TO NEXT PAGE ▶

This passage is adapted from *A Guide to Early Printed Books and Manuscripts*, by Mark Bland (John Wiley & Sons, Inc.).

Line   When we look at books as books, we are conscious of more than simply shape, colour, and weight. Imagine, for instance, that on the table is a copy of an early eighteenth-century poem, printed
(05) in folio and set in large type with obvious spaces between the lines. If a literary person was asked "What is the most obvious thing about what you are looking at?" their first reply might be something like "It is a poem." To the extent that a poem
(10) involves the layout of type on a page in a way that distinguishes it from prose, the answer would have some cunning, but to distinguish the text as 'a poem' is to invite a literary reading of the words as *words*. The most obvious thing about the page
(15) (before anything had been 'read') is, in fact, the size of the type and the space between the lines, and that is the step that is often overlooked: large type and extra space meant more paper was used, more paper meant more expense, and someone
(20) had to pay the bill — quite possibly not the printer, or publisher. The difference between looking at a page and seeing "a poem," or seeing a relationship between type, paper, and space is the difference between "being literary," and thinking like a bibli-
(25) ographer. The physical aspects of a text are always determined by the economics of book production ('Who paid for this?' is a useful question, if one not always possible to answer), as well as the materials and methods combined to create the document.

(30)   There is a second point to the example as well, and it has to do with the relationship between form and meaning. To recognize that the text is "a poem" is to recognize something about its form, its conventions, and its readership. In the first
(35) instance, the text does not matter. If, to make the point clear, we were to discover that the text was, in fact, a prayer, we would want to know why the conventions of one textual form had been applied to another; and we would want to know who made
(40) that decision, why, and whether the text was, in some way, verse. What the text actually said would still be of secondary importance, and would only come into play once we had understood the way in which the formal criteria had been reapplied. Over
(45) time, this is how the conventions of textual design evolve: slight adjustments are made to the formal aspects of presentation that cumulatively affect the appearance of the page in quite radical ways.

Furthermore, texts get presented in new ways to reflect the changing history of their use: an early (50) edition of Shakespeare was printed according to the conventions of seventeenth-century casual reading; a modern edition is usually designed for the classroom with its accompanying introduction, illustrations, notes, and a list of textual variants.

One of the most obvious ways to trace the (55) evolution of a text is to study its typography, or its manuscript equivalent, script. The history of letterforms, and the way in which they are laid out on a page, reflect social conventions as well as individual choice. This is why it is possible, simply (60) by looking at a document, to estimate when it was made to within a period of five or ten years. Bindings similarly reveal periods and tastes, as do the apparently incidental features of format, ornament stocks, and the use of ruled borders. Each of (65) these elements has required a conscious decision by someone at some time, and for this reason it is as necessary to see the text as to read it. Indeed, sometimes it helps not to read the text at all — certainly it helps to read the text only after these (70) other aspects of the book have been taken into consideration.

Bibliography is a historical and analytical discipline concerned with literature in the broadest meaning of that word. Hence, it is an appreciation (75) of literary texts and historical facts that usually shapes a desire to recover more accurately the history of a text through the processes of its making and the ways in which it was read. The point, however, is that in order to understand printed books (80) and manuscripts, the approach to literary documents cannot be limited to 'high' literature.

21. The primary purpose of the passage is best explained as an attempt to:

(A) discredit other authors who define early literary works only by observing their form.

(B) illustrate that the best way to trace the evolution of a text is to examine its typography.

(C) argue that a study of the physical aspects of books is more important to an analysis of early literature than reading its content and observing its form.

(D) show that an analysis of historical literature involves paying attention to more factors than merely what the works actually say.

22. As it is used in Line 12, *cunning* is best defined as:

(F) slyness.

(G) wisdom.

(H) folly.

(J) danger.

23. The author describes all of the following as means of estimating a book's age EXCEPT:

(A) examining its binding.

(B) paying attention to the way it observes social conventions in its ornamentation.

(C) observing whether it is written in the form of a poem, prayer, or other literary type.

(D) looking at the way the letters and words are formed.

24. The author would argue that the primary difference between the quality of "being literary" and that of "thinking like a bibliographer" is:

(F) one requires an appreciation for literary texts and historical facts, and the other ignores altogether the texts and their place in history.

(G) one considers the financial components of book making, and the other does not.

(H) one looks at the written page and sees a poem, and the other looks at a page and sees the relationship between type, paper, and space.

(J) one recognizes the relationship between form and meaning, and the other considers only the financial aspects of creating a literary work.

25. Which of the following statements about tracking the development of a text is supported by the passage?

(A) It is possible to determine the approximate age of a text just by looking at the way its letters are formed.

(B) Often, the most obvious way to establish a book's age is by examining how its story line reveals social conventions.

(C) It is possible to estimate the age of a text within a period of five to ten years by observing the kind of paper the bookbinder used.

(D) The best way to determine the age of a book is by reading the text for content and meaning.

26. *Bibliography*, as it is used in Line 73, most likely refers to:

(F) a list of books and articles that appears at the end of a publication that references the resources the writer used to develop a thesis on a particular subject.

(G) a list of publications that the author of this passage used to understand printed books and manuscripts.

(H) the study of the way texts were created and read in an attempt to comprehend their historical context.

(J) the ornamental script that early publications used to adorn the text.

27. The author would argue that the style of letterforms in a given document reflects the:

(A) standard practices of the time when the document was written.

(B) socioeconomic status of the document's creator.

(C) exact age of the document.

(D) document's literary genre.

GO ON TO NEXT PAGE

28. The mention of "'high' literature" in the final paragraph (Line 82) most likely refers to:

(F) works that can be categorized as having deep meaning.

(G) works that were costly to produce.

(H) poems or prayers.

(J) works that were produced by royalty or high-ranking government leaders.

29. In the second paragraph, the passage cites that a common component of literature designed for modern classrooms is:

(A) an accompanying test bank to assess students' learning.

(B) the use of computerized technology to produce brilliantly colored illustrations.

(C) a record of variations of the text.

(D) an extensive biography of the author.

30. Which of the following would the author say best describes the way that the conventions of textual design evolve over time?

(F) Printers and publishers find more cost-effective strategies of reproduction that result in ever-changing font style and line spacing options.

(G) Bibliographers' appreciation of literary texts and historical facts produces a system that helps to record more accurately the history of a text's popularity.

(H) Creators make small alterations to texts' appearances that eventually result in noticeably different page presentations.

(J) As printers and publishers become more aware of what components are aesthetically pleasing to readers of a given type of text, they develop new ways to format text.

Passage IV — Natural Science

Line   When people hear the word "prehistoric," they think of animals, especially dinosaurs. But there were prehistoric plants as well, and they were just as unusual to modern sensibilities as the animals
(05) of those ancient times. Evidence of early plant life comes from fossils. Fossils may have resulted from leaves and stems that fell into a lake and stuck in the mud at its bottom. The plants avoided decay because they were buried quickly in the sedi-
(10) ment and were not exposed to oxygen. As the mud turned into rock the carbon films and impressions of the plant parts were preserved. Pieces of wood, sometimes whole trees, became fossilized when water filled all their pores with silica, which
(15) is a hard mineral like quartz. Eventually the wood turned into stone, through a process called petrification.

This fossil record shows scientists how plants have evolved over time. During the Jurassic Period
(20) the dominant plants were cycads, gingkoes, conifers and ferns. There is no evidence of flowering plants until the next period, known as the Cretaceous Period. One of the oldest known flowers has been discovered in rocks that are over 115 million
(25) years old.

Among the most interesting of prehistoric plants are the cycads, which flourished 65 million to 240 million years ago. Cycads are sometimes called "living fossils" because they reached their
(30) peak around 200 million years ago. Cycads are a member of the order Cycadales, which contains the most primitive seed-bearing plants. Cycads are not conifers, but they are related to conifers because cycads are also cone bearing.

(35)   The plants are extant today, in areas as widely scattered as South America, Africa, Australia and Malaysia. Although they primarily live in the wet tropical or semi-tropical habitats, some species can not only survive but thrive in arid regions as
(40) well. Scientists long considered the widespread distribution of the cycad a mystery, as the seeds were too large to be carried by wind or ocean currents or birds. One popular theory connects the migration of cycads to the theory of Continental
(45) Drift. Briefly, Continental Drift hypothesizes that at one point millions of years ago, there existed just one continent, a supercontinent named Pangaea. Over the years, the continents separated, drifting apart and taking their flora and fauna with them.
(50) Thus, the plants that otherwise would be not as widely dispersed are found in far-flung areas.

If these plants provided sustenance to the gargantuan animals of that time (several times as large as any animals alive today), the plants
(55) must have been huge as well. Today's cycads have trunks that can grow up to 50 feet tall. But it is the cones that are perhaps the most impressive. There are two different types of cones, pollen cones (which grow on the male plants) and seed cones
(60) (which grow on the female plants), and these can be as long as 36 inches and weigh up to nearly 100 pounds. One variety of seed pods produces

bright red seeds. These seeds are ground into flour and used as foodstuffs by people in Africa. Some
(65) Japanese cooks mix brown rice with the powdered seeds of some cycads and ferment the mixture into a miso. In America, the Seminole Indians of Florida used the pith of cycads to make bread. Unfortunately, some ground cycad seeds have been found
(70) to be carcinogenic (cancer-causing) if not properly prepared.

There are also leaves on the cycad plant, which grow into a sort of crown and thus make many people who merely glance at a cycad think it is
(75) a palm tree. The trunks may occasionally grow underground, leaving an impression that the leaves are growing directly out of the ground. In fact, many parts of the cycads are underground. Inside the roots of the cycad are blue-green algae. The
(80) conversion of atmospheric nitrogen into ammonia is one way the cyanobacteria supply the cycad with inorganic nitrogen. It is fascinating to note that even though the cyanobacteria are in the dark underground, they have the same membrane struc-
(85) ture and pigments of other bacteria that thrive in the sunlight. Why does this strange structure remain? One theory is that evolution has not yet had sufficient time to change the portions that at one point had been essential to the plant's survival.

(90) Despite its longevity, the cycad, according to the World Conservation Union's Cycad Specialist Group, is one of the most threatened groups of plants in the world. Of the more than 320 species in existence, over half are threatened or endan-
(95) gered. Groups like the Cycad Society devote themselves to funding education and scientific research efforts to promote cycad conservation and ensure this prehistoric plant's survival for another 200 million years.

31. The main purpose of the passage is to:

(A) discuss similarities between prehistoric animals and prehistoric plants.

(B) refute the theory that cycads were spread via birds.

(C) contrast and compare prehistoric and current plant life.

(D) provide an overview of cycads.

32. In Line 35, the word *extant* most nearly means:

(F) extinct.

(G) prehistoric.

(H) narrowly distributed.

(J) still existing.

33. The passage mentions that scientists have had difficulty coming up with a definitive explanation for:

(A) why the cycad is found in so many different locations.

(B) what caused the continents to drift apart.

(C) why prehistoric plants were so much larger than current plants.

(D) why the supercontinent separated in the first place.

34. Which of the following is true about the fossil record of early plant life?

(F) It provides less information about plants than the fossil record of animals provides about animals.

(G) It provides an explanation of how earlier plant life has developed into modern flora.

(H) It shows evidence of flowering plants in all known prehistoric periods.

(J) It was created by decayed plants that had never been exposed to oxygen.

35. The author's purpose in mentioning Pangaea is to:

(A) provide a possible reason for why the cycad is extinct today.

(B) prove the cycad was once the largest plant on earth.

(C) suggest one cause for the cycad's widespread distribution.

(D) refute the theory that the continents were once connected.

GO ON TO NEXT PAGE ➤

36. The passage suggests that the Jurassic Period:

(F) contained only non-flowering plants.

(G) was the period in which cycads, gingkoes, conifers, and ferns became extinct.

(H) occurred about 115 million years ago.

(J) existed immediately after the Cretaceous Period.

37. The author includes mention of all of the following EXCEPT:

(A) a difference between seed cones and pollen cones.

(B) some medicinal properties of cycad seeds.

(C) a danger involved in using the seeds of the cycad.

(D) what kinds of cycad seeds are used in cooking.

38. The author claims that people confuse a cycad with a palm tree because:

(F) they produce similar types of seeds.

(G) the cycad grows in the same tropical regions as does the palm tree.

(H) the cycad's leaves may resemble the fronds of a palm tree.

(J) both plants are approximately the same size.

39. According to the passage, one function of cyanobacteria is to:

(A) allow the cycad to live underground.

(B) supply the cycad with inorganic nitrogen.

(C) help the cycad reproduce.

(D) enable the cycad to live long periods without water.

40. The primary purpose of the last paragraph (Lines 90–99) is most likely to:

(F) describe a potential reality and mention what steps are being taken to prevent it.

(G) reveal that most species of cycad plants will become extinct within 200 million years.

(H) promote the efforts that the World Conservation Union has made in cycad conservation.

(J) explain what scientific research has revealed about how to best ensure the longevity of cycad species.

Science Test

TIME: 35 minutes for 40 questions

DIRECTIONS: Following are seven passages and then questions that refer to each passage. Choose the best answer and shade in the corresponding oval on your answer sheet.

Passage I

Buoyancy is a force that acts in the upward direction on objects which are fully or partially submerged in a fluid. The two laws of buoyancy, which were discovered by Archimedes in the third century B.C., are as follows:

1. For fully submerged objects, the upward buoyant force is equal to the weight of the fluid displaced.

2. For floating objects, the weight of the object is equal to the weight of the fluid displaced.

In general, denser objects are less buoyant, and denser fluids provide more buoyancy to objects submerged in them. A more buoyant object will be able to float and carry more weight before it sinks, while a less buoyant object will sink with less weight applied. The shape of the object also has an effect on buoyancy, particularly for floating objects.

A student performed two studies to investigate how material and fluid type affect buoyancy. In each study, miniature boats were constructed with identical size and dimensions. The masses of the boats were not identical because of the varying material densities. The boats were placed in fluid, and 1 kilogram weights were incrementally placed inside of the boats until the boats no longer floated.

Study 1

In the first study, three different boats with the exact same size and dimensions were constructed from wood, aluminum, and concrete. Each of the boats was placed in pure water, and weights were placed in the center of the boats until the boats sunk. The results are shown in Table 1, indicating the maximum weight that each boat was able to hold before sinking.

Study 2

In the second study, a single boat made of wood was placed in three different liquids, and weights were placed in the center of the boat until it no longer floated. The three fluids tested were oil, pure water, and sea water. The results are shown in Table 2, indicating the maximum weight the boat was able to hold before sinking in each fluid.

TABLE 1

Boat Material	Maximum Weight Supported before Sinking (kg)
Wood	13
Aluminum	7
Concrete	8

TABLE 2

Fluid Used	Maximum Weight Supported before Sinking (kg)
Oil	11
Pure water	13
Sea water	14

1. Which of the following material and fluid combinations was used in both of the two studies?

(A) concrete and pure water

(B) wood and oil

(C) wood and pure water

(D) aluminum and sea water

GO ON TO NEXT PAGE

2. If a trial had been conducted using an aluminum boat with oil as the fluid, what would have been the maximum weight supported before sinking?

(F) 7 kg

(G) greater than 7 kg

(H) less than 7 kg

(J) The data from the two studies does not provide enough information to predict the results of that combination.

3. Which of the following conclusions is not supported by the data?

(A) Pure water provides more buoyancy to floating objects than sea water.

(B) Oil provides less buoyancy to floating objects than pure water.

(C) A boat made of concrete is less buoyant than one of the same size made of wood.

(D) A boat made of wood is more buoyant than one of the same size made of aluminum.

4. Based on the data in Tables 1 and 2, which of the following appears to have the greatest effect on buoyancy?

(F) boat material

(G) boat size

(H) fluid

(J) The data does not provide enough information to make a conclusion.

5. According to Table 1, which of the following are likely to have similar densities?

(A) wood and aluminum

(B) aluminum and concrete

(C) concrete and wood

(D) wood and pure water

6. According to Table 2, which of the following fluids is the densest?

(F) oil

(G) pure water

(H) sea water

(J) gasoline

7. Which of the following is true about the two studies?

(A) In Study 1, the fluid used was held constant and the boat material was varied.

(B) In Study 2, the fluid used was held constant and the boat material was varied.

(C) In both studies, the fluid used and the boat material were varied.

(D) In both studies, the fluid used and the boat material were held constant.

Passage II

Suppose that a 50-kg block is placed on an incline as shown in Figure 1 below. A cable running over a frictionless pulley connects the 50-kg block to another block which is hanging off the edge of the ramp. The coefficient of friction between the block and the ramp, μ_k, is unknown.

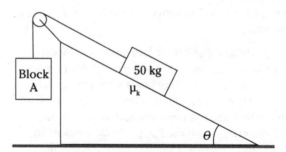

FIGURE 1: Configuration of blocks.

When the blocks are placed in the configuration shown in Figure 1, the 50-kg block slides up the ramp as Block A moves downward and eventually contacts the ground. Table 1 shows the results of 12 trials where Block A was released from rest in the position shown in the figure. The amount of time it took for Block A to reach the ground was recorded. For each trial, the mass of Block A was varied, as well as the angle θ of the ramp.

TABLE 1

Mass of Block A (kg)	Angle of Ramp (degrees)	Time for Block A to Reach the Ground (seconds)
40	10	0.62
	20	0.78
	30	1.13
	40	6.38
50	10	0.57
	20	0.66
	30	0.78
	40	1.00
60	10	0.54
	20	0.60
	30	0.68
	40	0.78

8. Across all ramp angles tested, as Block A's mass increased, the time for Block A to reach the ground:

(F) increased only.

(G) decreased only.

(H) increased then decreased.

(J) decreased then increased.

9. At which ramp angle did Block A reach the ground fastest?

(A) 10 degrees

(B) 20 degrees

(C) 30 degrees

(D) 40 degrees

10. Suppose an additional trial is performed with the mass of Block A as 70 kg and a ramp angle of 30 degrees. How long will it take for Block A to reach the ground?

(F) 0.74 seconds

(G) 0.62 seconds

(H) 1.15 seconds

(J) 0.68 seconds

11. Table 1 best supports which of the following statements about the time for Block A to reach the ground?

(A) If the ramp angle is increased and the mass of Block A is increased, Block A will reach the ground more slowly.

(B) If the ramp angle is increased and the mass of Block A is decreased, Block A will reach the ground faster.

(C) If the ramp angle is decreased and the mass of Block A is increased, Block A will reach the ground faster.

(D) If the ramp angle is decreased and the mass of Block A is decreased, Block A will reach the ground more slowly.

12. Based on Table 1, which combination of Block A mass and ramp angle would most likely produce equilibrium (no movement) of the blocks?

(F) 50 kg, 24 degrees

(G) 40 kg, 8 degrees

(H) 60 kg, 32 degrees

(J) 40 kg, 41 degrees

GO ON TO NEXT PAGE

13. Which of the following graphs best represents the relationship between ramp angle and amount of time for Block A to reach the ground?

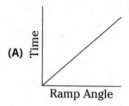
(A)

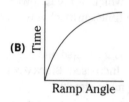
(B)

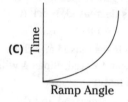
(C)

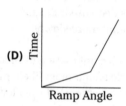
(D)

Passage III

Poor vision is a relatively widespread problem among humans. The most common vision defects include myopia, hyperopia, astigmatism, and presbyopia. Myopia is commonly called "nearsightedness" and is characterized by the ability to see only nearby objects while far-away objects appear blurry. The opposite of myopia is hyperopia, commonly called "farsightedness." This is where the lens of the eye focuses images behind the retina, making nearby objects difficult to see. Astigmatism is a condition caused by an irregular cornea or lens where the eye cannot focus an image properly on the retina, resulting in blurry vision. Presbyopia occurs with increased age and results in the inability to focus on nearby objects, often making reading difficult. Figure 1 below depicts the basic anatomy of the human eye.

There are multiple viewpoints on the causes and proper treatment of poor vision, two of which are explained below.

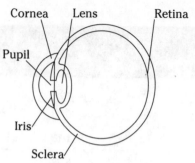

FIGURE 1: Anatomy of the human eye.

Genetic Theory

Vision problems in humans are hereditary and occur regardless of environmental factors. Vision exams should be conducted on children beginning at a young age so that issues can be identified early. The best solutions available to treat vision errors include eyeglasses, contact lenses, and eye surgery. These treatments quickly correct the majority of vision issues and have been used for centuries in the past, as shown in artwork and literature. More recently, contact lenses have been used as a convenient solution for vision correction, providing an additional treatment option to those with poor vision. Additionally, laser eye surgery has been shown to be a long-lasting solution for refractive vision errors.

Environmental Theory

Poor vision is a result of improper use of the human eye. When one focuses for too long on nearby objects, such as books, televisions, or computers, the eye is weakened, and this leads to vision errors. When these issues are corrected through artificial vision correction devices, such as eyeglasses and contact lenses, the eyes adapt to this handicap and are allowed to degenerate further, causing the vision problem to worsen. Human children who spend a great deal of time focusing their eyes on nearby objects rather than playing outside are much more likely to develop vision defects early on in life. Humans who make a habit of not focusing on nearby objects experience much fewer cases of poor vision.

A more natural and healthier solution to vision problems is learning to properly exercise the eyes and to reduce time spent focusing on nearby objects. Many people with vision errors such as myopia and astigmatism have been able to correct or greatly reduce their refractive error through exercising the muscles around their eyes. This exercise, combined with giving the eyes proper amounts of relaxation, serves to prevent as well as reverse common vision errors.

14. According to the genetic theory, which of the following humans is most likely to have a vision error?

 (F) an adult who spends time focusing on nearby objects

 (G) a human who regularly practices eye exercises

 (H) a child whose parents have poor vision

 (J) a child who spends a great deal of time outdoors

15. Which of the following statements about vision errors would be most consistent with both theories?

 (A) Vision errors are caused by a lack of reading.

 (B) Vision errors can be corrected at a young age.

 (C) Vision errors have existed for centuries.

 (D) Vision errors are more common among children than adults.

16. According to those who espouse the environmental theory, which of the following beliefs held by those who follow the genetic theory creates the most significant drawback to correcting vision problems?

 (F) Vision errors are hereditary.

 (G) Humans have experienced vision errors for centuries.

 (H) There are multiple ways to correct vision errors.

 (J) Vision errors should be corrected at a young age with eyeglasses.

17. Those who follow the environmental theory assume that:

 (A) vision problems can develop at any time during life.

 (B) children's vision is not affected by watching television.

 (C) laser eye surgery is a permanent solution to vision errors.

 (D) vision problems cannot be reversed, only prevented.

18. Which of the following is consistent with the genetic theory but not with the environmental theory?

 (F) Eyeglasses allow humans to see correctly.

 (G) Focusing on nearby objects causes vision errors.

 (H) Exercising eye muscles has no effect on vision.

 (J) A child with vision errors is likely to have a sibling who has vision errors.

19. Which of the following would be accepted by advocates of either theory?

 (A) Vision errors may be identified early in life.

 (B) Eye exercises are a healthy alternative to eyeglasses.

 (C) Vision deterioration is less likely in those who wear eyeglasses.

 (D) Children who play outside are less likely to develop vision errors.

20. Evidence suggests that vision errors are more common in some societies in the world and less common in others. Which of the following theories is supported by this evidence?

 (F) the genetic theory

 (G) the environmental theory

 (H) both theories

 (J) neither theory

Passage IV

An electrical circuit is essentially a circular path in which electrons can flow. Typically, a voltage source, such as a battery, will provide the necessary power to keep the electrons flowing through the circuit. The rate of flow of electron charge in the circuit is called electrical current. Electrical current is measured in amperes (A). A student constructed a simple electrical circuit using a battery, resistors, and wire. The potential of a battery is measured in volts (V), and the resistance of resistors is measured in ohms (Ω). Figure 1 represents the electrical circuit configuration.

GO ON TO NEXT PAGE

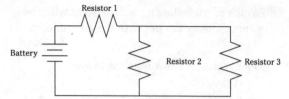

FIGURE 1: A simple electrical circuit configuration.

The student conducted two studies on the electrical circuit to examine the effect of changing components in the circuit. Each of the studies is described below, followed by the results obtained in the study.

Study 1

In the first study, the battery used to power the circuit was changed, and the voltage across each resistor was measured using a voltmeter by placing the voltmeter in parallel with each resistor. The resistances of Resistors 1, 2, and 3 were 100Ω, 1000Ω, and 5000Ω omega, respectively. Table 1 shows the results.

Study 2

In the second study, the resistance of Resistor 1 was changed, and the current through each resistor was measured using a digital multimeter. In order to take the measurements, the multimeter was placed in series with each of the resistors. The current measurements taken were very small in magnitude, so they are shown in milliamperes (mA), which are one-thousandth of an ampere. The 9.0 volt battery from the first study was used in the circuit. Table 2 shows the results.

TABLE 1 Voltage Measured across Resistor (Volts)

Battery Used (V)	Resistor 1 (Ω)	Resistor 2 (Ω)	Resistor 3 (Ω)
1.5	0.16	1.34	1.34
3.0	0.32	2.68	2.68
4.5	0.48	4.02	4.02
6.0	0.64	5.36	5.36
9.0	0.96	8.04	8.04

TABLE 2 Current Measured through Resistor (mA)

Resistor 1 Resistance (Ω)	Resistor 1	Resistor 2 (Ω)	Resistor 3 (Ω)
100	9.64	8.04	1.61
200	8.71	7.26	1.45
300	7.94	6.62	1.32
400	7.30	6.08	1.22
500	6.75	5.63	1.13

21. How many different batteries did the student use in both studies?

(A) 1

(B) 5

(C) 6

(D) 10

22. Study 1 suggests that the voltage measured across Resistor 2 is smallest when the battery voltage is:

(F) 1.5 V.

(G) 3.0 V.

(H) 6.0 V.

(J) 9.0 V.

23. Which of the following best describes the difference between Studies 1 and 2?

(A) In Study 1, the Resistor 3 resistance was varied; in Study 2, the battery voltage was varied.

(B) In Study 1, the battery voltage was varied; in Study 2, the Resistor 2 resistance was varied.

(C) In Study 1, the battery voltage was varied; in Study 2, the Resistor 1 resistance was varied.

(D) In Study 1, the Resistor 2 resistance was varied; in Study 2, the Resistor 1 resistance was varied.

24. In Study 2, as the Resistor 1 resistance was increased, the current through:

(F) Resistor 2 increased and the current through Resistor 3 increased.

(G) Resistor 3 increased and the current through Resistor 1 decreased.

(H) Resistor 1 decreased and the current through Resistor 2 decreased.

(J) Resistor 3 decreased and the current through Resistor 2 increased.

25. Which circuit configuration was used in both studies?

(A) battery voltage of 1.5 V, Resistor 1 resistance of 100Ω

(B) battery voltage of 9.0 V, Resistor 1 resistance of 100Ω

(C) battery voltage of 1.5 V, Resistor 1 resistance of 500Ω

(D) battery voltage of 9.0 V, Resistor 1 resistance of 500Ω

26. In Study 1, if a 12.0 V battery had been used, the voltage measured across Resistor 2 would have been closest to:

(F) 10.71 V.

(G) 8.04 V.

(H) 1.29 V.

(J) 0.96 V.

27. Which of the following conclusions about the electrical circuit is best supported by Studies 1 and 2?

(A) The voltage across Resistors 1 and 2 is always equal, and the current through Resistor 1 is always greater than the current through Resistor 3.

(B) The voltage across Resistors 2 and 3 is always equal, and the current through Resistor 2 is always greater than the current through Resistor 1.

(C) The voltage across Resistors 2 and 3 is always equal, and the current through Resistor 3 is always equal to the current through Resistor 2.

(D) The voltage across Resistors 2 and 3 is always equal, and the current through Resistor 1 is always equal to the sum of the currents through Resistors 2 and 3.

Passage V

When astronauts travelled to the Moon during the Apollo Program, they collected samples of the lunar surface and brought them back to the Earth to be studied. If a long-term colony were ever to be constructed on the Moon, there would have to be resources available that could be used for construction materials, fuel, and food. The lunar samples that were brought back to Earth were analyzed and their compositional elements were determined.

Samples from the Moon are categorized depending on where they were collected. Those taken from the dark-colored low-lying areas are considered to be from the lunar lowlands, while those taken from the light-colored elevated areas are considered to be representative of the lunar highlands. Figure 1 is a graph showing the most common elements by weight percent that are typically present in the Earth and how these compare to the elements found in the lunar highlands and lowlands.

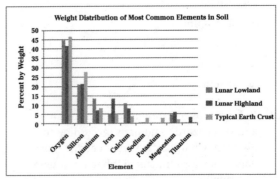

FIGURE 1: Comparing the elements found in the Earth's surface to those found in the Moon's surface.

Additional elements are found in the Earth's crust as well as on the Moon, but they are present in much smaller weight percentages. Figure 2 compares these less common elements in the lunar highlands and lowlands with typical Earth crust.

GO ON TO NEXT PAGE

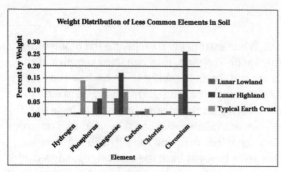

Weight Distribution of Less Common Elements in Soil

Lunar Lowland
Lunar Highland
Typical Earth Crust

FIGURE 2: Comparing less common elements in the lunar surface to those in the Earth's crust.

28. Which of the following elements was most common in the Moon soil samples?

  (F) carbon

  (G) manganese

  (H) chromium

  (J) titanium

29. Which of the following elements comprises the largest percent by weight in the lunar highlands?

  (A) aluminum

  (B) iron

  (C) calcium

  (D) sodium

30. In larger concentrations, chromium can pose a health hazard to humans. According to Figure 2, what location would be the most dangerous for humans to inhabit because of chromium?

  (F) lunar lowlands

  (G) lunar highlands

  (H) Earth landmasses

  (J) Earth oceans

31. Which of the following elements are found in higher concentrations in the Earth's crust than in the lunar lowlands?

  (A) silicon and aluminum

  (B) iron and calcium

  (C) sodium and potassium

  (D) chlorine and chromium

32. Hydrogen, carbon, and oxygen are important in the production and use of fuel, an essential resource. Which of the following conclusions about the data causes the most concern for prospective lunar inhabitants?

  (F) Oxygen is present in soil on the Moon and on the Earth in roughly similar concentrations.

  (G) Hydrogen is present in higher concentrations in the lunar lowlands than in the lunar highlands.

  (H) Oxygen is present in soil on the Earth in higher concentrations than carbon.

  (J) Hydrogen is present in smaller concentrations on the Moon than on the Earth.

33. Which of the following correctly lists elements in the lunar lowlands from lowest to highest concentration?

  (A) iron, calcium, aluminum

  (B) aluminum, calcium, iron

  (C) iron, aluminum, calcium

  (D) calcium, iron, aluminum

Passage VI

A scientist performed two studies to determine the factors affecting the spiciness of jalapeño peppers. Chili peppers like the jalapeño are spicy because of a chemical compound contained within them called capsaicin. To quantify the spiciness, the Scoville heat unit scale is used, which is a measure of the amount of capsaicin in the pepper. Higher capsaicin results in a higher measure of Scoville heat units, which corresponds to a spicier pepper.

The plants used in the studies were grown from a single group of seeds and planted in the same type of soil and given the same amount of light each day. Test groups were designed to vary the watering frequency and soil temperature of the plants to determine the resulting effects on spiciness. There were five plants in each test group, with all plants in a test group being subjected to identical conditions. Multiple peppers from each plant were tested, and the average measured Scoville heat units for all of the peppers from each plant are shown in the tables.

Study 1

In the first study, the watering frequency was varied for each test group. The soil temperature was kept at 25° for all plants in Study 1. The results of the study are shown in Table 1.

Study 2

In the second study, the temperature of the soil was varied for each test group by placing the pots on heating mats and adjusting the heat to keep the soil at the desired temperature. The plants were watered every three days. The results of the study are shown in Table 2.

TABLE 1

Days between Watering	Average Measured Scoville Heat Units of Each Jalapeño Plant in the Test Group					Average of Test Group
1	3,900	3,800	4,300	4,100	4,000	4,020
2	4,400	4,500	4,200	4,300	4,900	4,460
3	5,100	5,100	5,200	4,500	5,100	5,000
4	5,500	5,300	5,700	5,600	5,800	5,580
5	6,300	5,600	6,700	5,200	6,100	5,980

TABLE 2

Temperature of Soil (°)	Average Measured Scoville Heat Units of Each Jalapeño Plant in the Test Group					Average of Test Group
15	4,700	4,200	4,300	4,100	4,400	4,340
20	4,800	4,600	4,200	4,700	4,800	4,620
25	5,000	5,100	4,900	4,900	5,400	5,060
30	5,100	5,300	4,800	5,300	4,900	5,080

34. As soil temperature increases, average measured Scoville heat units:

(F) increase only.

(G) decrease only.

(H) increase then decrease.

(J) stay the same.

35. According to Study 1, if a jalapeño plant has a soil temperature of 25° and produces peppers with an average of 4,500 Scoville heat units, how often is it most likely watered?

(A) every day

(B) every two days

(C) every week

(D) every two weeks

36. If a jalapeño plant is kept in soil with a temperature of 30° and is watered every three days, what is the best estimate for the average amount of Scoville heat units contained in its peppers?

(F) 3,800

(G) 4,400

(H) 5,100

(J) 5,600

GO ON TO NEXT PAGE

37. According to Study 1, as a jalapeño plant is watered more often, the spiciness of its peppers:

(A) increases.

(B) decreases.

(C) stays the same.

(D) is indeterminate.

38. If a scientist wanted to conduct another study on a factor affecting jalapeño spiciness that was not examined in Studies 1 and 2, she should:

(F) vary the soil composition.

(G) vary the soil temperature.

(H) hold constant the frequency of watering.

(J) hold constant the light provided to the plants.

39. Based on the studies, which of the following combinations of soil temperature and watering frequency would likely produce the widest variation in spiciness from plant to plant?

(A) water every 5 days and 25°C soil temperature

(B) water every 3 days and 25°C soil temperature

(C) water every 3 days and 30°C soil temperature

(D) water every 3 days and 20°C soil temperature

40. According to Studies 1 and 2, what conditions are most likely to produce spicy jalapeño peppers?

(F) lower soil temperature and more frequent watering

(G) higher soil temperature and more frequent watering

(H) lower soil temperature and less frequent watering

(J) higher soil temperature and less frequent watering

Writing Test

TIME: 40 minutes

DIRECTIONS: Respond to the following prompt in a logical, clear, and well-organized essay that follows the rules of Standard English. Write your essay on a separate sheet of lined paper.

A state politician believes that it is becoming increasingly obvious that the preoccupation with a liberal arts curriculum in higher education is misplaced as the unemployment rate and student loan delinquency rate reach new highs. The politician cites statistics from the U.S. Department of Labor that state that the demand for graduates trained in trades, like plumbers, electricians, mechanics, and other technicians, has never been greater than in the last century. Similarly, unemployment rates for vocational grads, who often attend private trade schools rather than state public universities, are also at an all-time low. Based upon these facts, the politician claims it is time for the state legislature to allocate more funding for vocational educational programs instead of for schools that focus on a liberal arts curriculum. A group of professors from the local state college opposes the measure stating that a liberal arts education prepares students for more than just a trade; it provides them with the means to make informed decisions for a lifetime.

Read and carefully consider these perspectives. Each suggests a particular way of thinking about the current degree of emphasis America places on a liberal arts education.

Perspective 1: The state politician has made some very important points that are worthy of careful consideration. When it comes to higher education, the primary goal is to help students adopt the skills necessary for establishing a profitable and fulfilling career. As far as providing them with "the means to make informed decisions," well, that ability should be established long before one reaches higher education.

Perspective 2: A liberal arts education teaches valuable skills, such as problem-solving, critical thinking, and communication, and these are traits that lend themselves to *any* potential career path. That is why a liberal arts education is so critical. Ask many employers what they value most in a job candidate, and they'll likely say things like writing and communication skills, and the ability to work well in a team. That's why a liberal arts education is so inherently valuable.

Perspective 3: While a liberal arts education helps students build key skills that will help them as they forge their own post-college careers, those skills will be entirely useless if there are no jobs available in which to utilize them. Thus, more funding does need to be allocated to schools and programs that teach "trades," although alternative fundraising solutions, such as say, a cigarette tax, should be utilized to reduce the strain felt by liberal arts schools.

Essay Task

Write a unified, coherent essay in which you evaluate multiple perspectives as to whether funding for liberal arts education should be diverted to vocational education programs. In your essay, be sure to:

- Clearly state your own perspective on the issue and analyze the relationship between your perspective and at least one other perspective.

- Develop and support your ideas with reasoning and examples.

- Organize your ideas clearly and logically.

- Communicate your ideas effectively in standard written English.

Your perspective may be in full agreement with any of the others, in partial agreement, or wholly different.

Chapter 24

Practice Exam 3: Answers and Explanations

O kay. You've completed the practice exam in Chapter 23. We realize that you've had your nose to the grindstone for a long time. You probably need a break. Go ahead. Take a time out. But come right back and read through all the answer explanations we provide in this chapter — yes, even the ones you got right. Along the way, we offer tons of tips and traps — valuable information that you'll be able to use when you face the real ACT on test day.

After you read through the explanations, turn to Chapter 20 to determine approximately what score you would've received if this practice test were real. If you're short on time, skip to the end of this chapter, where we provide an abbreviated answer key.

English Test

1. **C.** At first glance, you may not think the subject of this sentence is plural, but it is: coolness *and* hum. That means you need a plural verb. Believe it or not, *mean* is plural, and the only answer that contains *mean* is Choice (C).

2. **F.** The words before the punctuation mark create a complete sentence, and the words after the punctuation create a complete sentence. Because no conjunction joins the two clauses, a semicolon does. So the sentence is fine as is. Choice (J) makes the sentence a comma splice.

    Choice (H) may have tempted you because, of course, you can punctuate two independent clauses with a period. Hold on, though. Choice (H) uses *its* (the possessive form) to mean *it's* (the contraction of "it is").

3. **C.** The underlined part isn't a complete sentence. *Pointing* without any assistance from another helping verb doesn't work as a verb. You have to change it to a word that functions as a real verb. The paragraph is in simple present tense, so pick Choice (C) rather than Choice (D). Choice (B) creates a new error by pairing a singular verb with a plural subject.

4. J. This question may have been a little tricky because the misplaced modifier is hard to spot at first. But after you see that *just* is in the wrong place, you can fix the sentence in a jiffy. *Just* refers to the kinds of players — they weren't just from Clement. It doesn't refer to "made up," so you can't say that the hockey team was "just made up" (unless perhaps the players had all recently painted on clown faces).

REMEMBER

Modifiers, words that describe other words, need to be as close to the words they describe as possible.

The answer that puts *just* in its place is Choice (J). Don't worry that it changes "it is" to *it's.* The tone of the essay is casual, so contractions are okay.

5. B. Semicolons separate independent clauses. Whenever you see a semicolon in a sentence, the words that come before it and the words that come after it have to make complete sentences. The words that come before the semicolon in this sentence don't create a complete sentence. They make a dependent clause. You separate a beginning dependent clause from the rest of the sentence with a comma. So Choice (B) is the right answer.

6. J. The paragraph is about more than just the players from Clement, so the underlined sentence doesn't provide an accurate idea of what the paragraph is about. Cross out Choice (F) and check out your other options. Eliminate Choice (H) because the paragraph is primarily about Sanchez, who wasn't on the team last year. Plus, Choice (H) awkwardly compares *team* to *year*. Choice (G) is vague and uninformative and would be better introducing a paragraph about the number of players on the team rather than the characteristics of individual members. The best answer is Choice (J). The last sentence of the previous paragraph sets up that the next paragraph is about the players.

7. C. This sentence begins with a description of someone who's returning to Clement, but the subject of the sentence is *position.* The position isn't returning. Brendan Sanchez is. Choose the answer that makes Sanchez the subject of the sentence without creating a new error. Choices (C) and (D) correct the error. Choice (D) changes the comma to a semicolon, though. A semicolon doesn't work in this sentence because the information that comes before it isn't a complete sentence. Choice (C) corrects the error and deletes unnecessary words.

REMEMBER

Whenever you see a beginning phrase with a comma after it, check the subject of the sentence. The beginning phrase should describe the subject of the sentence. If it doesn't, you have to change it.

8. F. This question tests you about comma usage. Commas correctly separate elements in a series from one another and appositives from the nouns they describe. This sentence has both a series and a few appositives. Each player's name needs to be surrounded by commas, just the way it appears in the original sentence. The colon in Choice (G) isn't proper because the words that come before a colon must be a complete sentence. You don't use colons to set apart appositives, so Choice (H) is out. The problem with Choice (J) is that comma with no purpose in between *as* and *Clement.*

9. D. You don't have any reason to insert a comma anywhere in the underlined words, so cross out Choices (A) and (C).

REMEMBER

Whenever you see a comma in the underlined words, check it carefully to make sure it's used properly and has a definite reason for being there.

Choice (B) gets rid of the comma, but it also cuts out "and take over," which changes the message of the sentence. So (D) is the answer you want here.

10. H. The passage is a casual article designed to get readers psyched about the hockey team. Sticking a list of players right in the middle of the article probably wouldn't be appropriate. If a list is necessary, which is debatable, it would work better at the end of the article so that it doesn't interrupt the information in the passage. Because the answer is no, cross out Choices (F) and (G). Then all you have to do is pick the right reason for not including the list. The focus of the essay isn't last year's performance, so the answer has to be Choice (H).

11. D. Always check an underlined pronoun to make sure it's used properly. "Him and Poldale" is the subject of the sentence. *Him* is the objective form. You can't use an objective pronoun to fill the position of sentence subject. The only answer that changes *him* to *he* is Choice (D).

12. F. As weird as it may sound, "it is hoped" is the proper way to say this expression. *Hopefully* is an adverb and is almost always used incorrectly on the ACT. In Standard English (the way it's written in formal books, not the way most high schoolers speak it), you use *hopefully* only to describe the way you did something. For instance, "I entered the ACT test center hopefully, anticipating an awesome score after many diligent hours of careful preparation." "Everyone is hopeful" in Choice (J) isn't improper, but the addition of the preposition *with* doesn't work with the remainder of the sentence.

REMEMBER

Always reread the sentence with your answer inserted to check that it makes sense and to verify that you haven't missed something in your eagerness to make a choice.

13. C. *Good* is an adjective. *Well* is an adverb. This sentence uses *good* to describe how the Cougars played. You use adverbs to describe the action of verbs, which means *good* doesn't belong here. The proper construction is "played well." Cross out Choices (A) and (B). Choice (D) is redundant. *Sufficiently* and *enough* mean the same thing. The best answer is Choice (C).

14. G. Saying that the Cougars have to rebound before you talk about their previous losses doesn't make a whole lot of sense. Sentence 5 mentions last year's losses, so Sentence 4 needs to come after Sentence 5. Choice (G) is the winner here.

15. A. You can eliminate Choice (D) because the tone of the passage isn't formal. The essay mentions last season's losses but doesn't dwell on them, so cross out Choice (C). Choice (A) is a better answer than Choice (B) because the essay doesn't provide details about all the players.

16. J. This deprived sentence has no verb, which means it's really not a sentence. *Being* can't function as a verb unless it's paired with a helping verb. Choose the answer that gives the sentence a verb. Make sure to use the proper tense. The rest of the paragraph is in present tense. Choice (J) follows that trend. The other two choices suggest that recycling was good in the past.

TIP

Use the verbs in the other sentences in the paragraph to figure out what tense the verb should be in the sentence with the underlined words.

17. B. The comma in the underlined words has no purpose. Take the poor, aimless punctuation mark out of its misery by removing it from the sentence. The only choice that completes this noble task is Choice (B). Choices (C) and (D) try to move the position of *both* around, but *both* is fine just where it is. Recycling is a step in both maintaining and sustaining.

18. J. This sentence provides a classic case of redundancy. *Autonomous* and *independence* mean the same thing, so you don't need both of them. Omit *autonomous* by choosing Choice (J) and move on.

19. A. The underlined series is punctuated correctly. A comma comes after every item in the list. Semicolons are overkill in this case, so cross out Choice (B). The colon in Choice (C) suggests that everything that comes after it is an example of recycled paper. And Choice (D) is wrong because you need to replace those extra *ands* at the beginning of the list with commas.

20. G. The problem with this sentence is another additional redundant repetition. Yikes! It's contagious. If markets are at all-time highs, they've never been greater. You don't need to say it twice. Choice (G) cures the malady. Choice (J) eliminates *greater* but remains repetitious because "have never been" conveys the same message as *all-time*.

21. A. The proposed insertion flows fairly well from the sentence before it, but it doesn't work with the sentence after it. If people tend to discontinue participating in recycle programs, the next statement about increased supply and demand for recycled goods doesn't make sense. So the answer is no. Cross out Choices (C) and (D). Now you just have to decide between Choices (A) and (B). The topic isn't *completely* different from the information in the rest of the paragraph. It's about public education and recycling. Choice (A) is better. Inserting the sentence would break up the information that public education has caused increased supply and demand for recycled goods.

REMEMBER

After you determine the short answer to a "no, no, yes, yes" question on the English Test, you've got a 50 percent chance of picking the right answer. If you can't determine the short answer right away, you often can eliminate at least two answers because the rest of the answer choices aren't true. These questions are often less time-consuming than they appear.

22. G. If you noticed that the underlined words contain the wrong version of *their*, give yourself a strong pat on the back. *Their* is the possessive form of *they*, and a noun always has to follow it. But a noun doesn't come after *their* in this sentence. Choice (G) presents the correct version, and it doesn't change *large* to "super huge," a choice of words that doesn't fit with the relatively formal tone of the rest of the passage.

23. B. Check the words that come before and after the semicolon. The words after it aren't a complete sentence, so you know the semicolon isn't right. If a semicolon doesn't work, a period certainly won't either. Cross out Choice (C). Deciding between Choices (B) and (D) may be a little more challenging. *Which* introduces a nonrestrictive (or nonessential) clause, so it needs to be separated from the rest of the sentence by a comma. Cross out Choice (D). The best way to punctuate the sentence out of the four options is with the colon in Choice (B).

24. J. In this sentence, *strictly* describes "any type of trash." But the right use of *strictly* is to narrow down something to a specific type rather than the more general *any* type. You need to replace *strictly* with a more accurate word. Cross out Choice (G) because referring to types of trash as rigorous just doesn't make sense. In the context of this sentence, *mainly* means mostly and *virtually* means almost. It makes more sense to say "almost any type of trash" than "mostly any type of trash."

25. B. One look at the answer choices tells you exactly what kind of error to focus on. All the choices are the same except for the commas. So your job for this question is to figure out where the commas go. Don't waste time looking for any other error. "Recyclable or not" is a phrase that provides more information about the type of trash. You separate it from the rest of the sentence by surrounding it with commas. The only choice that properly puts commas on either side of the phrase is Choice (B). There's no reason for the comma between "recyclable" and "or" in Choice (D).

Notice that the question doesn't ask you to determine whether the phrase is essential or not. All you have to know is how to punctuate a nonessential phrase.

26. **G.** Examining the answer choices helps you focus on the errors in the underlined words. First, you notice that Choices (G) and (J) change *and* to *to*. The proper construction is "from . . . to," which means that *to* is correct. Mark through Choices (F) and (H) with your No. 2 pencil and take a closer look at the remaining options. Choice (J) changes TV to television, and Choice (G) changes *weeks'* to *week's*. *TV* is fine here. The dinners the passage refers to are commonly called "TV dinners" rather than "television dinners." The answer must be Choice (G). It properly changes *weeks'* from the plural possessive to the singular possessive *week's*. There's only one "last week."

27. **C.** *Unsightly* is a more concise way of saying "displeasing to the eye." Including both in the sentence is needlessly repetitious. The answer that corrects the issue is Choice (C).

28. **H.** Sentence 4 provides more detail about the complaints that neighbors make. Therefore, it makes the most sense to put it right after Sentence 2 (and before Sentence 3) because it's the sentence that states that neighbors complain about the "trash magnets" that recycle bins have become. Eliminate Choice (G) right away because Sentence 4 would be out of place without knowing the information in Sentence 2. It works better before Sentence 3 because it refers to removing the recycle bins, and Sentence 3 further explains why stores are willing to engage in the removal. Choice (J) would put Sentence 4 in a paragraph about a different topic, the recycling entrepreneurs. Picking Choice (H) provides the best flow of information in the paragraph.

If this question takes you more than half a minute to sift through the answer options, eliminate answer choices you know have to be wrong — such as Choices (G) and (J) — and guess from the remaining choices. You don't want to waste precious time on this question when you could use the time to answer easier questions later in the section.

29. **D.** The underlined words have a subject/verb agreement issue. *Who* refers to *entrepreneurs*, which is a plural noun. Therefore, the verb has to be plural — "have begun." Choice (C) creates a run-on sentence, and Choice (B) incorrectly changes *who* to the possessive form *whose*.

30. **F.** Eliminate answers that mention topics that were only covered in other paragraphs. Choice (G) is about public education, which appears only in the first paragraph. Choice (H) talks about neighbor complaints, which appears only in the second paragraph. The last paragraph doesn't distinguish between small and big businesses, so Choice (J) addresses a topic that hasn't been discussed. The best conclusion for the passage is Choice (F) because it refers to the programs discussed in the last paragraph and relates them to the general passage theme of promoting a greener future that's introduced in the first paragraph.

31. **A.** The sentence is fine the way it is. *That* isn't nonessential and shouldn't be separated by commas. Choice (D) is wrong. If you picked Choice (B) or (C), you created an incomplete sentence that leaves you waiting for more information.

Always reread the sentence with your answer choice inserted. This step alerts you to problems with your answer that you may miss otherwise. When you read this sentence with Choice (B) or (C), you immediately notice that something is wrong.

32. **H.** The sentence is unclear and awkward. The reference to "this one" is vague, and it sounds like only "this one" is in the Constitution. Choice (H) changes the reference from "this one" to "this amendment" and clarifies that all ten amendments are in the Constitution.

When a whole sentence is underlined, look for an unclear reference or modifier error. You'll probably have to rewrite the sentence to fix the error.

33. **C.** Cross out Choice (B) because you don't need to change *liberty* to the possessive form; in fact, doing so is wrong. You can also eliminate Choice (D) because it deletes the main verb and makes the sentence incomplete. Between the remaining choices, Choice (C) is more direct and, thus, is the better answer. The emphasis provided by the phrasing in the original sentence is unnecessary.

34. **G.** Knowing how the Fourteenth Amendment made the Bill of Rights applicable is essential to the idea of the sentence. Therefore, you can't separate the underlined portion from the rest of the sentence by any form of punctuation.

35. **D.** The original wording of the sentence is strange. The listed items didn't originate the Bills of Rights. People did. The list includes elements that form the origins of the Bill of Rights. Choice (D) most properly conveys this idea.

36. **H.** Eliminate the answer choice that doesn't show that opposition disappeared soon after the Bill of Rights were ratified. Examine each option by reading it in the sentence. "When the Bill of Rights was ratified," "as soon as the Bill of Rights was ratified," and "after the Bill of Rights was ratified" convey the same general idea as "once the Bill of Rights was ratified." *While* is the same as *during,* which would mean that the opposition decreased at the same time that the Bill of Rights was ratified.

37. **D.** This sentence has a subject/verb agreement problem. The subject (*effect*) is singular and the verb (*are*) is plural. One of them has to change. Cross out Choice (A). *Affect* is almost always used as a verb rather than a noun, so Choice (B) is wrong. Both of the remaining choices change *effect* to the plural, but Choice (C) incorrectly makes the verb singular. Choice (D) corrects the problem without creating a new error.

38. **G.** The phrase "by prohibiting" isn't a verb, so the sentence has no verb and is a fragment. Choice (J) inserts a verb, but *prohibits* goes with *that* rather than "Bill of Rights," which means the sentence is still a fragment. The best answer is Choice (G). It provides a singular verb for the singular subject.

39. **A.** The original sentence correctly uses *which* to introduce a descriptive clause that's not essential to the main point of the sentence, which is that the Bill of Rights protects speech. Choice (D) retains the *which* but creates a sentence fragment. So Choice (A) is the answer here.

Choose *that* to introduce clauses that are essential (or restrictive) and *which* to introduce clauses that aren't essential. Always use a comma to separate clauses that begin with *which* from the rest of the sentence. Don't separate clauses that begin with *that* by inserting a comma.

40. **G.** Approach this question by eliminating answers you know aren't right. The sentence provides an explanation of free speech, but it doesn't go into enough detail to be thorough. Cross out Choice (H). The main idea of the paragraph is that the Bill of Rights affects daily life. Eliminating Sentence 3 wouldn't take away this idea, so Choice (J) can't be right. The sentence introduces the concept of free speech and explains how it affects daily life, so it isn't irrelevant. The answer has to be Choice (G). The sentence gives the specific examples of the editorial section and Internet blogs to show how free speech plays out in daily life.

41. **D.** You need to separate a list of three or more items with commas. The only *and* is the one that comes before the last item. The only answer that follows these rules is Choice (D).

Choice (B) looks like it corrects the problem, but *school* and *prayer* aren't separate issues, so you shouldn't separate them with a comma. The issue is school prayer. (Americans may debate about education or school issues but not about school itself.)

42. **G.** Eliminate Choice (J) right away. *But* signals a contrasting idea, but this sentence just expands on the ideas in the sentence that come before it. Choice (H) tells you that *hearing* the Miranda speech is a rights issue. The Bill of Rights doesn't particularly give you the right to hear the speech on TV. (Although that would be a great argument to offer your parents when they tell you to turn off the television and get studying for the ACT. "But Mom, watching this cop show is my Constitutional right!")

The problem with the original sentence is the presence of *and.* You may have been told that you never begin a sentence with *and.* Although that's usually a good practice, it's not a hard and fast rule of Standard English. The issue isn't that the sentence begins with *and.* It's that the *and* is redundant. The sentence later includes *also.* Saying "and the speech is also a *right*" is repetitive. Ditch the *and* and pick Choice (G).

43. **B.** The paragraph provides a series of examples of free speech. Its main idea isn't the Miranda speech, so the full quote would be not only unnecessary but also pretty boring. Eliminate the yes answers, Choices (C) and (D). How many instances of Miranda speeches appear on TV is irrelevant. The best answer is Choice (B). Because the paragraph explores more rights than just Miranda rights, a copy of the full speech would be major overkill.

44. **J.** Pay attention to underlined pronouns. Make sure that they have clear references and that their references agree in number. This sentence says a group can stage a protest as long as the protest is not violent. *They* is plural, but it renames the singular noun *protest.* The proper singular pronoun to refer to *protest* is *it.* The only choice that corrects the problem is Choice (J).

REMEMBER

Don't let answer choices that make irrelevant word changes distract you from the real problem in the sentence. In this question, "as long as" and "not violent" aren't improper constructions that require changing.

45. **D.** The essay gives a pretty thorough explanation of the First Amendment, but the author tells you that the Bill of Rights is more than just the First Amendment. Because the essay doesn't go into detail about the freedoms granted by the other amendments, the answer to this question is no. Cross out Choices (A) and (B). Your task is to choose the best answer of the two remaining. Choice (D) is better than Choice (C) because it's more comprehensive. Even if it included an explanation of the Right to Bear Arms, the essay probably wouldn't fulfill the intended goal.

REMEMBER

Only one answer can be right. Sometimes you find yourself choosing between two answers that could be right. Pick the one that's "more right" than the other.

46. **G.** When a title follows a person's name, you have to surround it with commas. Choice (F) is wrong. Choice (H) isn't any better. Because the title comes before the name in Choice (G), no commas are necessary. Choice (J) is also technically correct; commas surround the nonessential clause. But Choice (G) is less wordy, so it's a better choice than Choice (J).

47. **A.** Because a comma comes after 1830, the clause that comes after it must be nonessential. You introduce nonessential clauses with *which*, not *that.* The sentence is fine as it is. Choices (C) and (D) use the progressive tense, which makes it sound like the Act is still in the process of appropriating.

48. H. Pick the answer that's not like the others. Choices (F), (G), and (J) all imply force without the other's consent. Choice (H) is gentler and more benevolent than the others. It doesn't belong and is, therefore, the correct answer.

49. B. The question asks you to determine what the result would be if the author deleted the description of the Indian Removal Act. This description provides relevant information about the event that precipitated the issues between Jackson and Native Americans. You can cross out Choice (C) because the description is definitely relevant. You have to know the ramifications of the Act to understand what the Native Americans fought to win a victory over. Therefore, the information is related to the rest of the passage, and Choice (A) can't be right. Choice (D) is clearly wrong. The information supports rather than contradicts the idea that Jackson didn't care about the interests of the Native Americans. The answer has to be Choice (B).

TIP

At first, you may be tempted to hurry through this question or skip it altogether because it seems to require a lot of reading. Give it a chance, though. The incorrect answer choices are pretty easy to eliminate.

50. J. The original sentence is a fragment. It doesn't have a main verb. Read each answer choice in the sentence. The only option that gives the sentence a verb is Choice (J).

51. A. Pick the appropriate transition word for this sentence. The right answer is the one that shows the relationship between the sentence with the underlined word and the information in the sentence before it. The previous sentence talks about the victory of the Native Americans over Jackson's coercion. The sentence that follows the underlined word is about Jackson's determination to thwart the decision. The two pieces of information contrast each other. Therefore, Choice (A) is the best answer because *however* shows contrast. *Additionally* would work if the sentences had similar ideas, but they don't. Eliminate Choice (C).

The words in Choices (B) and (D) mean the same thing; they both show cause and effect. They can't both be right, so both must be wrong.

52. G. The error you need to correct here has to do with the word *provoking*. The word tells you how Jackson asserted, and words that tell how someone performs an action verb need to be adverbs. The adverb form is *provokingly*. Cross out Choices (F) and (J). Choice (H) contains the adverb, but it also sticks in an unjustified comma. The answer that corrects the adverb problem and punctuates the sentence properly is Choice (G).

53. A. The passage isn't about Chief Justice Marshall. Although the underlined portion provides you with an interesting tidbit of history, it's not pertinent to the message of the sentence. It actually keeps you from honing in on the main idea of the sentence. Therefore, the best answer is Choice (A).

REMEMBER

Even if you aren't sure whether the answer is yes or no, you can eliminate answer choices based on the explanations they give. Information about Chief Justice Marshall definitely doesn't belong in the next paragraph. That paragraph doesn't even mention the Supreme Court. Cross out Choice (B). Knowing that Marshall was the longest-serving Chief Justice doesn't provide a better understanding of the importance of the Court decision presented in the passage, so Choice (C) is out. Eliminating these two choices gives you a 50 percent chance of guessing correctly.

54. J. The idea conveyed in the underlined words is that Jackson wouldn't allow the Court decision to be enforced. The answer that best paraphrases that concept is Choice (J). Choice (H) conveys the opposite thought. So does Choice (F), and it's unclear who *he* refers to. Choice (G) doesn't convey that Jackson doesn't want the decision to be enforced.

55. B. If you don't know what *belied* means, just reread the sentence with each answer choice inserted. The one that makes sense is the right answer. *Although* at the beginning of the sentence means that the second part of the sentence opposes the idea in the first part. Jackson wasn't kind to the Cherokees. His actions *contradicted* his profession that he had the kindest feelings, so Choice (B) is right. The other choices show similarity between the two ideas in the sentence rather than opposition.

56. G. You have kind feelings *toward* someone, but you speak words *to* or *about* someone. Therefore, the underlined portion fits better after feelings. Cross out Choice (F) and pick Choice (G). You don't know who Jackson professed to, and *toward* doesn't work with *professed,* so Choice (H) is out. Likewise, Choice (J) is wrong because you don't belie toward someone.

57. B. Here's another question that deals with restrictive and nonrestrictive clauses. *That* introduces restrictive clauses and shouldn't be separated from the rest of the sentence with a comma. Choice (B) takes away the comma.

When you see a comma before *that,* it's almost always wrong.

REMEMBER

58. J. If you don't know the conditions of the treaty, you don't know why the brutal journey mentioned at the end of the paragraph took place from 1838 to 1839. The information in the sentence isn't irrelevant, and it doesn't appear anywhere else in the passage. You can cross out Choices (F) and (G). Other sentences in the passage are about Jackson's character, but this one isn't. The best answer is Choice (J).

59. A. The punctuation in this sentence is correct. The words that come before the comma form a complete thought, and the words that come after it form a complete sentence. The conjunction *but* joins them, which means the comma before *but* is proper. Choice (D) makes the sentence a comma splice because it takes out the conjunction. *However* is a conjunctive adverb, which is a fancy way of saying it needs a semicolon before it and a comma after it. Choice (C) can't be right.

60. J. The passage doesn't paint a positive picture of Jackson's relations with the Cherokees, so you can eliminate the yes answers. Then cross out Choice (H) because the passage deals with specific ways that Jackson dealt with the Cherokees. The best answer is Choice (J).

61. A. Strangely enough, this sentence is okay the way it's written. Commas can replace missing words in balanced expressions. In this case, the comma takes the place of *are* in the second expression. If you're unsure, you can check the other answers and cross out ones that contain errors. Choice (C) is a comma splice. Choice (D) is wordy and adds a cause–and–effect relationship the original doesn't suggest. Choice (B) deletes a word from the second expression but doesn't replace it with a comma. The best answer is Choice (A).

62. J. The problem with this sentence isn't the wording. It's the punctuation. The first clause isn't a complete sentence, so you can't use a semicolon to separate it from the rest of the sentence. Choices (G) and (H) change the meaning of the sentence. Choice (J) properly separates the beginning dependent clause from the rest of the sentence with a comma.

63. D. Change the passive voice to active voice and you can also correct the modifier problem. Dialogue isn't assisting "other means"; it's assisting silent films. "Silent films" needs to be the subject of the sentence. Both Choices (C) and (D) make silent films the subject, but Choice (C) is in past tense. The rest of the paragraph is in present tense, so Choice (D) is better.

TIP

If the underlined portion of a sentence is in passive voice, pick an answer that changes it to active voice unless that change creates another error. Passive voice isn't necessarily wrong, but active voice is almost always better.

64. **H.** *Their* is the possessive form of *they*. The construction that makes sense in this sentence is *they're*, which is the contraction of "they are." The characters can't tell the audience what they are (or they're) thinking. Choice (H) corrects the error and maintains the simple present verb tense that the rest of the paragraph uses.

65. **B.** *Exaggerated* and *overacted* mean the same thing, so you don't need both of them. Choice (B) takes care of the redundancy.

66. **F.** You may not know right away whether the inserted sentence would be appropriate, but you can apply POE (process of elimination) to help narrow down the choices. Cross out Choice (H). The sentence doesn't contradict anything in the passage. A humorous tone wouldn't be inconsistent with the causal language in the passage. Besides, the sentence isn't particularly humorous. Choice (J) is out. Through POE, you know the answer is yes. Choose the answer that provides the best reason. The sentence provides an example, not a behavioral study. Choice (F) is the best answer.

67. **A.** The sentence seems fine the way it is, but check the other options to be sure. Choice (B) is redundant. Choice (D) doesn't have the right punctuation. (You need a semicolon before *furthermore* and a comma after it.) Choice (C) suggests a cause-and-effect relationship in the sentence that the passage doesn't justify. Keep the status quo with Choice (A).

68. **G.** The underlined series lacks parallel structure. All the elements in a series have to be in the same grammatical form. Everything in the list is a noun except the last item, which is an independent clause. Pick the answer that changes the independent clause to a noun form. Choice (H) keeps the clause, so it's wrong. Choice (J) omits the *and* from the series, so it can't be right. Choice (G) corrects the problem by changing the clause to the noun "dance numbers."

TIP

Often, underlined words that are part of a series signal a parallelism issue. When you see a series, check the punctuation and make sure all the elements are in the same grammatical form.

69. **C.** This sentence uses the adverb *expressively* to describe the noun "music score." Adverbs describe actions verbs, not nouns. Choice (C) changes the adverb to an adjective. Choice (B) makes the situation worse by changing musical to musically and inserting an unjustified comma. Choice (D) changes the meaning of the sentence.

70. **F.** Eliminate answers that aren't about the effects of the musical score. Choice (G) talks about dialogue and doesn't mention music. Cross out answers that don't compare the modern film experience to the silent film experience. Choice (H) talks only about silent films. Choice (J) discusses only modern films. The only answer that deals with music and compares the two kinds of films is Choice (F).

TIP

When you remember to use POE (process of elimination, that is), this question suddenly gets much easier.

71. **D.** This sentence has a bad case of comparisonitis. The words it uses to compare music to dialogue are simply wrong. To cure the problem, realize that the proper construction is "as large as" rather than "as large than." Choice (C) doesn't add the *as*. So cross it out. Choices (B) and (D) include *as*, but Choice (B) slips in an incorrect comma after dialogue. The best answer is Choice (D).

REMEMBER

If you picked Choice (B), you probably read it too quickly and failed to see the comma. If you reread the sentence with Choice (B) inserted, you can see right away that it has a problem comma. Always reread the sentence with your answer inserted before you move to the next question.

72. **J.** The underlined sentence has a bunch of examples of how music conveys information in silent films. The right answer probably has the word *examples* in it. That knowledge leads you to Choices (G) and (J). Choice (G) is about modern films, so eliminate it. The answer is probably Choice (J), but check the others just to be sure. The examples aren't *superfluous* (or unnecessary fluff), so cross out Choice (F). They help you understand the concept in the previous sentence. The examples aren't of emotions, so Choice (H) isn't accurate. Choice (J) is the answer.

73. **D.** *Creativity* and *ingenuity* mean the same thing. To correct the redundancy, pick Choice (D). *Originality* and *inventiveness* are other synonyms of creativity, so Choices (B) and (C) don't fix the problem.

74. **G.** You knew this one was coming. The test warned you about it from the beginning of the passage. As you read through the passage, you may have been looking for paragraphs that seemed out of place. The question tells you that the paragraph to consider is Paragraph 2. As you read through the paragraph, you may notice that it summarizes the points that the other paragraphs make. This summarizing feature may indicate that it's an introduction or conclusion paragraph. The choices don't give you the option of ending with Paragraph 2, so it probably belongs at the beginning, before Paragraph 1.

    The paragraph doesn't belong before Paragraph 5 because the first sentence of Paragraph 5 refers to the "frenetic motion" in Paragraph 4. If you put Paragraph 2 between them, that reference wouldn't make sense. Nothing in Paragraphs 3 and 4 tells you that Paragraph 2 should go between them, either. Therefore, the best answer is Choice (G).

REMEMBER

    This question comes at the end of the section when you're probably running out of time. If you're pretty sure the answer is Choice (G), save time by marking it on your answer sheet and moving on to the next question. If you have time at the end of the section, go back to this question to check the other answer options.

75. **C.** Pick an answer that summarizes a majority of the passage and isn't too general or too specific. The passage talks about musical scores in only one paragraph, so Choice (A) is wrong. Choice (B) is about film in general rather than silent films. Cross it out. Choice (D) is both too general (it's about all films) and too specific (just car chases). The best answer is Choice (C).

Mathematics Test

1. **D.** Keep in mind that the question asks for the amount Dolores has. But to figure out Dolores's amount, you have to know what Holly has. That Angela has half as much money as Holly is the same as saying that Holly has twice as much as Angela. Make an equation. Let A = Angela and H = Holly. That gives you $2A = H$; $2(\$60) = H$; $\$120 = H$. Holly has $120.

Next, if Holly has $\frac{3}{4}$ as much as Dolores, then Dolores has $\frac{4}{3}$ as much as Holly (let D = Dolores):

$$D = \frac{4}{3}H$$

$$D = \frac{4}{3}\$120$$

$$D = \$160$$

Dolores has $160.

If you picked Choice (A), you mixed up Holly and Dolores. Choice (B) is what you get if you multiplied $120 by $\frac{3}{4}$ rather than $\frac{4}{3}$. If you chose Choice (C), you correctly doubled $60 to get $120, but then you mistakenly figured that if Holly's $120 was $\frac{3}{4}$ of Dolores's amount, you just had to add $\frac{1}{4}$ of $120 to it. Finally, Choice (E) is just wishful thinking on Dolores's part.

2. **G.** You remember how to divide by a fraction, right? You just multiply by the reciprocal. In this case, change the first division bar to a multiplication symbol and then flip the fraction underneath from $\frac{4}{y}$ to $\frac{y}{4}$. Then multiply. You get $\frac{3y}{4}$.

REMEMBER

Don't let the $y \neq 0$ throw you. Just ignore it. It's just there to let you know that the answer isn't an undefined number.

If you picked Choice (F), you spaced the reciprocal rule and multiplied by $\frac{4}{y}$. Choice (H) flips the numerator rather than the denominator. Choice (J) results from flipping $\frac{4}{y}$ and leaving the 3 on the bottom rather than on the top. Finally, Choice (K) is wrong because it uses the wrong division bar for the problem. The parentheses clearly indicate that you're not supposed to divide $\frac{3}{4}$ by y.

3. **C.** The problem tells you that the height of the sail is perpendicular to its base, which means the sail forms a right triangle. The question asks you to find the measurement of the hypotenuse of that triangle. Before you call on Pythagoras and his theorem, check the ratio of the triangle. It's 12:16: x. Notice that 12 is 4 times 3 and 16 is 4 times 4. Looks like a 3:4:5 right triangle to us! Multiply 5 by 4 to complete the proportion. The answer has to be 20, which is Choice (C). If you chose any other answer, you were just guessing.

If you forget the common ratios of right triangles, you can rely on the Pythagorean theorem to find the measurement. The theorem states that the hypotenuse squared is equal to the sum of the squares of the other sides: $a^2 + b^2 = c^2$. Plug in the two side lengths and solve for c:

$$a^2 + b^2 = c^2$$
$$12^2 + 16^2 = c^2$$
$$144 + 256 = c^2$$
$$400 = c^2$$
$$\sqrt{400} = c$$
$$20 = c$$

4. **H.** You need to find the average score of several members of a larger group. Use the average formula.

REMEMBER

By definition, an *average* equals the sum of all the scores divided by the number of scores:

$$\text{Average} = \frac{\text{Sum of scores}}{\text{Number of scores}}$$

For a detailed discussion of averages and means, check out Chapter 8. Set up the equation and plug in what you know. On the left of the equation is the average of the scores, which the problem tells you is 84. On the right is the sum of all 11 scores divided by the total number of scores, which is 11. Put 11 as your denominator.

Figuring what goes in the numerator is a little trickier. You don't know each individual score, but you do know a little about their averages. The problem tells you that the average of the first 6 scores is 79. If you apply the average formula to this information, you know that their sum is 474:

$$79 = \frac{\text{Sum}}{6}$$
$$79 \times 6 = \text{Sum}$$
$$474 = \text{Sum}$$

Similarly, the sum of the last 5 scores can be represented by 5*x* (meaning 5 times *x*), with *x* representing the average score of the 5 remaining students. The equation looks like this:

$$84 = \frac{474 + 5x}{11}$$

Solve for *x* to get your answer: $972 = 474 + 5x; 450 = 5x; 90 = x$.

The answer is Choice (H). If you picked any of the other options, you either guessed or made a math error. Be careful with your calculations.

5. **B.** You can solve simultaneous equations two ways. The faster way is by elimination; just stack them and add. The $+y$ and $-y$ cancel out and you're left with $2x = 10$. You can quickly see that $x = 5$.

The other way is to solve the first equation for *y* "in terms of *x*" (which is a fancy way of saying solve for *y* with *x* still in the equation) and then substitute what you get for *y* into the second equation. When you solve for *y* in the first equation, you get $y = 6 - x$. Substitute $6 - x$ for *y* in the second equation: $x - (6 - x) = 4; x - 6 + x = 4$. Combine like terms: $2x - 6 = 4$. Solve for *x*: $2x = 10$. What a coincidence! $x = 5$.

6. **H.** The *least common denominator* is the smallest number that all denominators go into.

The fastest way to solve this problem is by examining the answer options. Because you're looking for the smallest number, start with the smallest answer. Choice (F) is smallest, but 16 isn't a factor of 24. The next value is 32. 16 goes into 32, but 24 doesn't. Choice (G) is out. Try Choice (H): 2, 4, and 24 are definitely factors of 48. And 16 goes into 48 an even 3 times. You have your winner!

You don't have to test the other two options, because they're larger than 48 and you're looking for the lowest value.

7. **C.** If ray *OB* and ray *OA* are perpendicular, they form a right angle measuring 90 degrees. If angle *AOC* is 8 degrees greater than angle *AOB*, then it must measure 98 degrees.

Choice (A) is incorrect because it subtracts 8 degrees from 90 degrees instead of adding it. Choice (B) doesn't work because it's the measure of right angle *AOB*. If you picked either Choice (D) or (E), you mistakenly thought perpendicular lines formed an angle that measures 180 degrees (the measure of a straight angle or a straight line).

8. **K.** This question may not seem like a math question at all. But don't panic! The ACT may throw a few logic questions into the Math Test.

Sometimes drawing diagrams can help you keep things straight in logic problems. A simple Venn diagram is good for problems that group information as this one does.

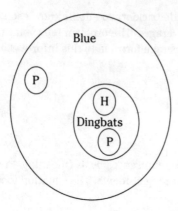

The first statement says that all Dingbats are blue. That tells you that a smaller circle, Dingbats, fits into a larger circle, blue. Homer (H) is an even smaller category. He fits into the Dingbats circle. That tells you that Homer must be blue. Prudence (P) isn't so cut and dry. She's blue alright, but that means she can fit anywhere in the big blue circle. She can be a Dingbat like Homer, but she doesn't have to be.

Now before you rush right into the answer choices with your new-found knowledge, check the question. It asks you for what must be *false*. Use your diagram to eliminate options that must be or could be true. Prudence could be a Dingbat or not. Cross out Choices (F), (H), and (J). Homer is indeed always blue. (Poor guy!) So Choice (G) is wrong. The right answer has to be Choice (K).

9. D. The problem tells you that Bonnie's only costs were the lemons and sugar she had to buy to make the lemonade. The correct formula is the one that shows how much she paid for the lemons and sugar.

If the proper formula isn't immediately obvious to you, you could spend a whole bunch of time trying to figure it out. Or you could save some time and substitute numbers for the variables in the problem to see which answer works out. We vote for saving time!

When you're substituting numbers for variables, pick easy numbers to work with. Say that she bought 10 pounds of lemons for $2 a pound and 5 pounds of sugar for $3 a pound. That means that $x = 10$, $p = 2$, $s = 5$, and $d = 3$. Write this information in your test booklet. Bonnie spent $20 on lemons (10 times $2) and $15 on sugar (5 times $3) for a total cost of $35. Plug your made-up numbers into the answer choices to see which one equals 35.

Choice (A) works out to 75: $(10 + 5)(2 + 3) = (15)(5) = 75$. Cross it out and check Choice (B): $10 + 2 + 5 + 3 = 20$. That can't be right. For Choice (C), multiply 10 and 3 to get 30 and 5 and 2 to get 10. Then add them together to get $30 + 10$ or 40. Keep looking. Choice (D) has you multiply 5 and 3 to get 15 (which is what Bonnie spent on sugar) and 10 and 2 to get 20 (which was her cost for lemons) and add the sums: $15 + 20 + 35$. That works! If you have time, check Choice (E): $xp = 10$ and $sd = 15$. If you multiply them, you end up with 150.

10. H. First, recognize that $(x + y)^2$ is the same as $(x + y)(x + y)$. As you may remember from algebra class (or Chapter 10), the product of two identical added terms is always the square of the first term (x) plus the square of the last term (y) plus 2 times the product of both terms (xy). In this case, that works out to be Choice (H): $x^2 + 2xy + y^2$. If you forgot the rule, you could use the FOIL method to multiply the expressions. The product of the First terms is x^2, the product of the Outer terms is y^2, and the products of the Inner terms are xy and xy. Put them all together and you get $x^2 + 2xy + y^2$.

You know you can eliminate Choice (J) because the product of positive values can't result in an expression that contains a negative.

11. **B.** This one isn't too hard. You should've immediately noticed that 144 and 81 are perfect squares. You remember from those dreaded memorized multiplication tables that 12 times 12 is 144 and 9 times 9 is 81. You can easily see that $x = 12$ and $y = 9$. All you have to do is add them together, right? $12 + 9 = 21$, But wait! 21 doesn't appear in the answer choices. Because the product of two negative values is positive, x could be 12 or –12 and y could be either 9 or –9. Therefore, $x + y$ could be 21, –21, 3, or –3. The only one of these answers that appears is –21, Choice (B).

12. **H.** You could write out all the possibilities, but you don't have all day! The order of the charms doesn't matter. All you have to do is multiply together the number of charms in each category: $4 \times 5 \times 3 = 60$. That means there are 60 possible 3-charm combinations for Jan's necklace. If you picked Choice (F), you added the number of charms instead of multiplying them.

13. **A.** All this question takes is a little distributing. Multiply $9ab$ by the first term: $9ab \times 3a^3b^2 = 27a^4b^3$. Eliminate Choices (C), (D), and (E) because they have a different first term. You can take the time to multiply $9ab$ by the second term, but you already know the answer has to be Choice (A) because the second term can't still be $5ab$ after you multiply it by $9ab$.

If you picked Choice (D) or (E), you forgot that you can't add terms that aren't exactly alike.

REMEMBER

14. **H.** You know the formula for finding an average. You just have to arrange it to fit the question. You know the average amount per sale ($160), the number of sales Evan has (4), and the amount he's made at the first 3 sales ($230, $50, and $120). You just don't know the amount of Saturday's sale because it hasn't happened yet. Let x equal the amount he has to make at the fourth sale. Now you can set up the equation and solve for x:

$$\text{Average} = \frac{\text{Sum of amounts}}{\text{Number of sales}}$$
$$160 = \frac{230 + 50 + 120 + x}{4}$$
$$640 = 230 + 50 + 120 + x$$
$$640 = 400 + x$$
$$240 = x$$

Evan needs to make $240 on Saturday's sale, which is Choice (H). If you picked anything other than Choice (H), you either guessed or miscalculated.

15. **A.** You could solve this problem by figuring out the value of the right side of the equation and then playing with your calculator until you find out what power of 20 that equals. How tedious!

The faster way to solve this problem is to notice that $20^c = (4 \times 5)^c$, which is the same as $20^c = 4^c \times 5^c$. All the exponents must be the same, and c must be 3. (Review the rules for multiplying bases and exponents in Chapter 8.)

16. **J.** The y-coordinate of a point where a line intersects the x-axis is 0, and the y-coordinate is always listed last. Eliminate the choices that list 0 first: Choices (F) and (K). Because you know that $y = 0$, all you have to do now is substitute 0 for y in the equation: $3x + 7(0) = 21$. This simplifies to $3x = 21$. Divide both sides by 3, and you get $x = 7$. The point's coordinates are (7, 0).

Another (but more time-consuming) way to approach this question would be to put the equation in the slope-intercept form by getting y by itself on the left side of the equation:

$$3x + 7y = 21$$
$$7y = -3x + 21$$
$$y = -\frac{3}{7}x + 3$$

This equation tells you that the line intercepts the y-axis at $(0, 3)$ and the line has a slope of $-\frac{3}{7}$. Now you can graph the line on the coordinate plane. Begin at $(0, 3)$ and draw a line with a negative slope. That means to find the next point on the line, you count 3 points down and 7 points to the right (because lines with negative slope fall from left to right). What do you know? This point lies on the x-axis at point $(7, 0)$.

17. **A.** Just solve the first equation for a:

$$1 - \frac{2}{a} = 3 - \frac{4}{a}$$
$$1 + \frac{2}{a} = 3$$
$$\frac{2}{a} = 2$$
$$2 = 2a$$
$$1 = a$$

Wait, you're not done yet! You know that $a = 1$, but that's not what the question asks. You need to come up with the value of $1 - \frac{2}{a}$. Substitute 1 for a and you get $1 - \frac{2}{1} = 1 - 2 = -1$.

18. **H.** This one is easier than it looks. Start out by substituting -1 for a^2 in the second equation:

$$\left(-1^5\right)^x = 1$$

Simplify: $-1^5 = -1$, which means the equation is now $-1^x = 1$.

To make -1 a positive number, its exponent has to be even. The value of x has to be an even number; the least positive integer that is also an even number is 2.

Choice (A) may have tempted you. By definition any number raised to the zero power $= 1$, but don't be fooled! 0 can't be right because 0 is neither negative nor positive and the question asks for a positive integer.

REMEMBER

19. **E.** For this problem, you need to know what it means to reflect a figure.

TIP

When you reflect a shape, it flips over at one of its ends to form a kind of mirror image. The problem tells you that the shape is reflected across line l. That means the shape flips and flies across line l until its left side is the same distance from line l as its right side was before. Line l forms a center line between the edge of the original shape and the edge of the reflected shape. The following figure can help you picture the reflection.

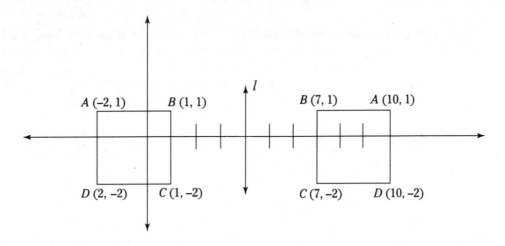

$$A\,(-2, 1) \qquad B\,(1, 1) \qquad\qquad B\,(7, 1) \qquad A\,(10, 1)$$

$$D\,(2, -2) \qquad C\,(1, -2) \qquad\qquad C\,(7, -2) \qquad D\,(10, -2)$$

As you can see from the answer choices, the y-coordinates stay exactly the same. You're only concerned with the x-coordinate of point D. In its new position, point D holds the spot 10 spaces away from the y-axis. Its new coordinates are $(10, -2)$, Choice (E).

REMEMBER

Don't let the y-axis confuse you; line l is the critical center line in this problem. And don't worry if you weren't particularly fond of this question. Problems about reflected shapes crop up only every once in a while on the ACT.

20. **J.** If the population doubles every 50 years, in 3 centuries (300 years) the population will double 6 times. You can express this value as 2^6. The 2 stands for the fact that the population doubles (or multiplies by 2), and the 6 shows that it happens 6 times. All you have to do is multiply the 10^3 people by 2^6 to find the total population. You don't actually have to multiply the value out because Choice (J) states the answer simply as $\left(2^6\right)\left(10^3\right)$.

Before you spend a lot of time performing calculations, check the answer choices to see what form they're in. Sometimes you don't have to figure things out completely.

21. **C.** The quadratic expression in the problem $(x^2 - kx - 28)$ has two factors. The problem tells you that $(x - 4)$ is one of them. To determine what the other factor is, focus on the last term in the expression (-28). Ask yourself what value multiplied by -4 produces -28. Well, $28 \div -4 = 7$. So the other factor of the quadratic expression has to be $(x + 7)$. When you use the FOIL method to multiply $(x - 4)$ and $(x + 7)$, you get $x^2 + 3x - 28$. That's not exactly the same as the original expression, though. The middle term of the original expression is $-3x$ rather than $3x$. To make the middle term negative as it is in the original expression, k must equal -3: $x^2 + (-3)x - 28 = x^2 - 3x - 28$.

REMEMBER

Be careful when you choose a value for k. In the problem, the quadratic expression specifically shows that k is negative. So, k must be -3.

22. **J.** When you solve the inequality for z, you discover that $z < 7$, which means you can cross out Choices (G), (H), and (K). Don't stop there and pick Choice (F), though. Because the value has to be positive (because it's an absolute value), there's a lower limit to the values that can equal z. Eliminate Choice (F) and mark Choice (J) as your answer.

REMEMBER

The *absolute value* of a number is always positive. It simply refers to how far the number is from 0. No matter what, the expression $z - 3$ is positive. As long as you realize that the possible values for z have a lower limit, you don't have to figure out what that lower limit is to solve the problem. To verify your answer, though, substitute -1 for z: $|-1 - 3| < 4$. The absolute value of -4 is 4, which equals 4. Therefore, -1 doesn't satisfy the conditions and z must be greater than -1. The possible values for z are 0, 1, 2, 3, 4, 5, and 6.

23. B. You can write $\left(-3x^2y^5\right)^3$ as $(-3)^3\left(x^2\right)^3\left(y^5\right)^3$. As long as you remember that you multiply the exponents, you're smooth sailing on this problem. $-3^3 = -27$, which means you can cross out Choices (C), (D), and (E) because none has a coefficient of -27. The difference between Choice (A) and Choice (B) is that Choice (A) adds the exponents instead of multiplies them. Choice (A) has to be wrong. So Choice (B) has to be right.

24. G. Aren't you glad you know the slope intercept form for the equation of a line? (If you need a refresher, check out Chapter 10.) Just isolate y on the left side of the equation by subtracting 12 and $32x$ from both sides and then dividing by 5:

$$32x + 5y + 12 = 0$$
$$5y = -32x - 12$$
$$y = -\frac{32}{5}x - \frac{12}{5}$$

The resulting coefficient of x $\left(-\frac{32}{5}\right)$ is the slope! What could be easier? Just make sure you keep your negative and positive signs straight and you'll breeze right through these types of questions.

25. D. This question may have you daydreaming of quaint New England lighthouses and ocean landscapes. Snap out of it! Sit forward in your uncomfortable chair, take up your No. 2 pencil, and realize that this is just a standard circle problem.

As it rotates, the light in the lighthouse moves full circle, or 360 degrees. Because the light takes 20 seconds to complete one full rotation, the lighthouse rotates 18 degrees per second: $\frac{360}{20} = 18$.

Hold it! Don't stop there and pick Choice (C). The question asks for the number of degrees the light rotates in 2 seconds, not 1. Multiply 18 by 2 seconds and you get 36 degrees.

WARNING

If you marked Choice (E), you tried to work the 4.5 miles into the problem and multiplied 18 by 4.5. The number of miles that the lighthouse projects its light has no bearing on its rotation speed. The ACT question creators just put that information in there to test your ability to weed out unnecessary information. Impress them with your gardening skills (weed out — get it?) and focus only on the information that's relevant to answering the question.

26. J. To determine the perimeter of trapezoid *FBCE*, you have to figure out the lengths of segments *FB*, *BC*, *EC*, and *FE* so you can add them together. The problem gives you the length of two of the sides. $BC = 6$ units and the left and right sides of the trapezoid are equal because the triangle is equilateral, which means that $FE = 6$ units, too. Find the measurements of *FB* and *EC* and you're done!

Apply what you know about triangles. If triangle *ACE* is equilateral, all angles measure 60 degrees and the side lengths are equal. *EC* has to be 10 units. *AB* added to *BC* forms one side of triangle *ACE* (side *AC*). $AB = 4$ units and $BC = 6$ units. That means that *AC* is 10 units ($4 + 6 = 10$), and $AC = EC$. So far the perimeter is $6 + 6 + 10$, or 22, units. You can eliminate Choices F and G.

Your remaining task is to find the length of *FB*. Accomplish this task by recognizing that triangle *ABF* is also equilateral. You know that *FB* and *EC* are parallel. You should note that lines *AE* and *AC* are transversals that cut through these parallel lines. That means that the corresponding angles these lines form are equal. Angles *AEC*, *AFB*, *ACE*, and *ABF* all equal 60 degrees, which means that triangle *ABF* is also equilateral and has equal side lengths. Because $AB = 4$, $FB = 4$. Add 4 to 22 to get 26, and you know that Choice (J) is the perimeter of the trapezoid.

Note that the fact that point *G* is the midpoint of *FB* is irrelevant to the problem. We hope you didn't spend too much time trying to use that useless information to solve the problem.

27. **C.** Because you're supposed to solve for $2x - y$ and the equation contains the terms $2x$ and y, all you have to do is get $2x - y$ on one side of the equation and the rest of the terms on the other side. To accomplish this task, just subtract x and $3x$ from the left side of the equation and subtract y from the right: $x + 2x + 3x = y$; $2x - y = -x - 3x$; $2x - y = -4x$.

REMEMBER

You can solve many ACT math problems in more than one way. You could also solve this problem by solving the first equation for y and substituting that value for y in the second equation: $x + 2x + 3x = 6x$, so $6x = y$. When you substitute $6x$ for y in the second equation, you get $2x - 6x$, which equals $-4x$.

28. **F.** Questions that involve logarithms are scarce on the ACT, which probably suits you just fine, but they're also pretty simple. Even if you've never studied logarithms in your life, you can handle these questions. All you have to know is that $\log_x 27 = 3$ means that it takes 3 *x* times to get 27. Therefore, $x = 3$. You multiply 3 three times to get 27. That's all there is to it!

29. **D.** This word problem is a distance problem. The formula for finding distance (*d*) is rate (*r*) × time (*t*).

To find out how many miles the Swift Express travels before it meets up with the Douglas Dependable, first determine the rate of each train by applying the distance formula and plugging in numbers you know. If Distance = Rate × Time, then Rate = $\frac{\text{Distance}}{\text{Time}}$. Swift Express's rate is $\frac{900}{3}$, or 300 miles/hour. The Douglas Dependable travels at a rate of $\frac{900}{5}$, or 180 miles/hour.

To continue with the solution, ask yourself which of the three elements of the formula (rate, time, or distance) both trains have in common when they meet in the middle. It's not rate, because you know from your calculations that the rates are different. It's not distance, because the faster train must travel more miles than the slower train. It must be time. Don't let the 3 hour and 5 hour designations fool you. These tell you the total time each train took to travel the entire distance. But you're looking for the time it takes them to meet in the middle. Both trains travel the same amount of time before they meet.

Modify the distance formula to solve for time. Then set up an equation that makes the two trains' times equal to each other. You can let 1 stand for the Swift Express and 2 stand for the Douglas Dependable:

$$T = \frac{D}{R}$$

$$\frac{d_1}{r_1} = \frac{d_2}{r_2}$$

Plug the values you know into the equation with *x* standing for the distance the Swift Express has travelled when the two trains meet. If Swift Express has travelled *x* miles when they meet, Douglas Dependable will have travelled $900 - x$ miles, or the difference between the total 900 miles and the *x* miles that Swift Express has travelled. Here's what your equation looks like:

$$\frac{x}{300} = \frac{900 - x}{180}$$

Cross-multiply to solve for x:

$$180x = 300(900 - x)$$
$$180x = 270,000 - 300x$$
$$480x = 270,000$$
$$x = 562.50$$

The answer is Choice (D).

30. **H.** When you look at the answer choices, you realize that you need to find out which line segments are equal. Approach this problem by using the distance formula to figure out the length of each line segment: $d = \sqrt{(y_2 - y_1)^2 (x_2 - x_1)^2}$.

TIP

If you have a hard time envisioning this question without a picture of the points on the coordinate plane, sketch out a quick graph, like this one:

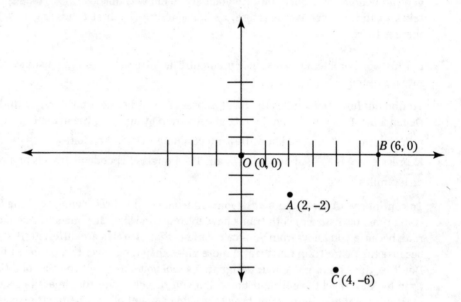

When you look at the graph, you may think that lines AB and AC have similar lengths. Don't rely on your eye to answer this question, but start your calculations with these points. Find the length (distance) of line AC:

$$d_{AC} = \sqrt{\left[-6 - (-2)\right]^2 + (4 - 2)^2}$$
$$d_{AC} = \sqrt{(-4)^2 + 2^2}$$
$$d_{AC} = \sqrt{16 + 4}$$
$$d_{AC} = \sqrt{20}$$

Follow the same process for line AB:

$$d_{AB} = \sqrt{\left[0 - (-2)\right]^2 + (6 - 2)^2}$$
$$d_{AB} = \sqrt{2^2 + 4^2}$$
$$d_{AB} = \sqrt{4 + 16}$$
$$d_{AB} = \sqrt{20}$$

Lines AB and AC are the same length. Choice (H) is the correct answer. If you calculate the length of the other lines, you'll find that OA is $\sqrt{8}$, OC is $\sqrt{52}$, BC is $\sqrt{40}$, and OB is 6.

31. E. When two triangles are similar, one is an enlargement of the other with the same angles and respective sides in the same proportion to one another. You can set up a proportion to solve this problem.

You know that lines *NM* and *PQ* are similar sides of the two triangles because they're across from equal angles. Likewise, *a* and *b* are similar sides because they're across from equal angles. So the ratio of *b* to *a* is the same as the ratio of line *PQ* to line *NM*, or $\frac{5}{6} : \frac{5}{8}$.

A ratio is like a division problem: $\frac{5}{6} : \frac{5}{8} = \frac{\frac{5}{6}}{\frac{5}{8}}$. Solve the problem to find the ratio of the two triangles: $\frac{\frac{5}{6}}{\frac{5}{8}} = \frac{5}{6} \times \frac{8}{5} = \frac{40}{30} = \frac{4}{3}$. Because the ratio of the two triangles is $\frac{4}{3}$, the value of $\frac{b}{a}$ is also $\frac{4}{3}$. So Choice (E) is right.

WARNING

If you picked Choice (B), you found the ratio of the small triangle to the large triangle rather than the other way around. Order matters with ratios, so work carefully.

32. G. This problem gives you the formula for figuring out exponential growth. All you have to do is fill the missing information into the equation and solve for *NV*. The initial value of the loan was $1,000, so *IV* = $1,000. *P* = 2.5% (which you can convert to 0.025) and *Y* = 10 because the investment grew from 2000 to 2010. Here's the resulting equation:

$$NV = 1,000 \times (1 + 0.025)^{10}$$
$$NV = 1,000 \times 1.025^{10}$$

Use your calculator to determine that $1.025^{10} = 1.280084544$. When you multiply by 1,000, you just move the decimal point to the right three spaces, but you already know that because all the answer choices are in thousands. *NV* = 1.280084544, which rounds to $1,280. This question is an easy one as long as you keep track of your decimal points.

33. B. Drawing a diagram is probably your best strategy for this problem.

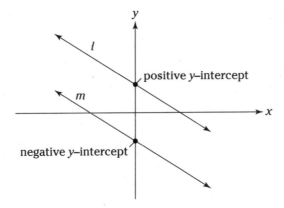

Line *l* has a negative slope and a positive *x*-intercept (meaning it's to the right of the *y*-axis). Its *y*-intercept is positive as well (meaning it's above the *x*-axis). If line *m* is parallel to line *l* and line *l* has a negative slope, line *m* also has a negative slope. A line with a negative slope falls from left to right. So if a line with a negative slope has a negative *x*-intercept, that line has to also have a negative *y*-intercept. Eliminate Choices (C), (D), and (E) because they say that the *y*-intercept of line *m* is positive or zero. If the *y*-intercept of line *m* is negative and the *y*-intercept of line *l* is positive, the *y*-intercept of line *m* has to be less than the *y*-intercept of line *l*, so Choice (B) must be the correct answer.

34. K. The values that add up to 3 and multiply to 2 are 2 and 1. Be careful, though, these values are the roots of the equation, not the factors. The factors that result in roots of 2 and 1 are $(x-2)(x-1)$. Now all you have to do is FOIL. (No, we didn't say FOLD. Hang in there. You still have 26 questions to go. Check out Chapter 8 if you don't remember how to FOIL.)

The quickest way to move through the problem is to exert a little POE (that's short for process of elimination). All choices have the same first term, so you don't have to figure that out. The last term should be $+2$ because $-2x \times -1 = 2$. Feel free to cross out Choices (G), (H), and (J). The outer terms equal $-1x$, and the inner terms result in $-2x$. The answer has to be Choice (K) because it has a negative middle term.

TIP

You can also approach this problem by simply factoring each answer choice to see which one has roots of 2 and 3. The process goes more quickly when you recognize that factoring Choices (F) and (H), which have all positive terms, will give you only negative roots. In that case, the last term will be positive, but the middle term will be negative. That way you'd only have to try Choices (G), (J), and (K). The roots of Choice (G) are 3 and -1. Choice (J)'s roots are -3 and 1.

35. E. Just using a quick number substitution for each possible answer is the fastest way to solve this problem. You can eliminate answers that fail to give you 2, 6, and 10 when you substitute 1, 2, and 3 for n. For instance, you can cross out Choice (A) because, although $2(1) = 2$, $2(2)$ isn't 6 and $2(3)$ isn't 10. Choices (B), (C), and (D) don't work for all three of the first terms in the sequence. Choice (E) is the ticket: $2[2(1)-1] = 2(1) = 2$; $2[2(2)-1] = 2(3) = 6$; and $2[2(3)-1] = 10$.

36. J. To find the perimeter of the triangle, you have to know its side lengths. You know the length of one side. Line *XY* measures 4 inches. The other two sides are equal. When you find the value of one, you'll know the value of the other.

Your job is much easier after you notice that the side you need to know is also the hypotenuse of a right triangle that's formed when you draw a line through point *0* that joins the sides of the cylinder as shown in the following figure.

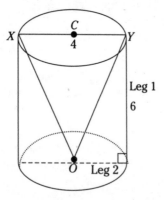

Leg 1 of the triangle is 6 inches. Leg 2 is 2 inches because it's the radius of a circle with a diameter that measures 4 inches and the radius is half the diameter.

The side lengths aren't in one of those handy Pythagorean triples we talk about in Chapter 9, so you have to apply the Pythagorean theorem:

$$c^2 = a^2 + b^2$$
$$c^2 = 6^2 + 2^2$$
$$c^2 = 36 + 4$$
$$c^2 = 40$$
$$c = \sqrt{40}$$

The square root of 40 is a little more than 6, but don't pick Choice (F). You're not done yet. You have to add up the sides of the original triangle to find its perimeter. The sum is $\sqrt{40} + \sqrt{40} + 4$. You can calculate the value on your calculator or determine that it's a little more than $6 + 6 + 4$, or 16. The closest answer is Choice (J).

37. **B.** The language of the question tells you that you're supposed to find the volume of the cylinder and ignore the triangle inside. The formula for the volume of a cylinder is $V = \pi r^2 h$. If you've memorized the formula, the rest of the question is simple. The height is 6 inches and the radius is 2 inches. Substitute the values in the formula and solve for V: $\begin{aligned} V &= \pi(2)^2 6 \\ V &= \pi 24 \end{aligned}$.

The answers don't contain the π sign, so use your power of estimation. π is about 3.14, which is just a little over 3, and 24 times a little over 3 is a little more than 72. The answer choice that's closest to a little more than 72 is 75, Choice (B).

38. **F.** Because O is the center of the base, the lines that connect it to opposite sides of the top have to be equal. (You figured that out in Question 36.) If the sides are equal, the angles opposite them are also equal. The answer has to be Choice (F).

If that seemed too easy, you may want to check the other options. You know that Choices (G), (H), and (J) are untrue. Line XY is shorter than the other two sides of the triangle, so its angle also must be smaller than the other angles.

Note: Because you know that Choice (F) is true, don't spend too much time considering Choice (K). You know from working out Question 36 that the angle next to angle OXY in one of the right triangles you drew is the smallest of the three angles in the right triangle. One of the other angles is 90 degrees. That means the other two angles have to add up to 90 degrees. If the two angles were equal, they'd both measure 45 degrees. They're not equal, so the smaller angle has to be less than 45 degrees. That small angle and angle OXY form a 90-degree angle. If the small angle is less than 45 degrees, angle OXY must be more than 45 degrees.

39. **B.** This problem focuses on the rules of bases and exponents. The easiest way to solve this problem is to reduce each expression to a single power of $10(10^x)$. Then you can compare the quantities in a similar format. Choice (E) is already in that format. The next easiest answer to evaluate is Choice (B). Count the zeros to find the exponent. 1,000,000,000,000,000 is the same as 10^{15}, which is less than 10^{100}. Cross out Choice (E).

Eliminate Choice (C), too: 1000^{100} has to be greater than 10^{15}. Don't work out Choice (A). As soon as you notice that you have to multiply 10^5 ten times, you know it can't be less than 10^{15}. The same goes for Choice (D): 10^{10} ten times has to be greater than 10^{15}. Choice (B) has the least value.

When you compare the answer choices, this problem becomes less time-consuming than it originally seemed. You don't have to calculate all the options to eliminate some wrong answers, which is the case for many ACT math questions. So don't give up on a question before you look for shortcuts in the answer choices.

40. **G.** The plane that contains vertices S, U, and X cuts diagonally through the square prism from back-left to front-right.

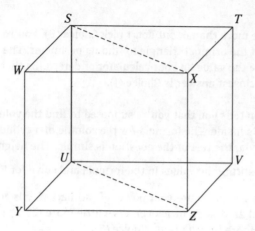

As shown in the figure, that plane also contains vertex Z in the lower-right corner. None of the other vertices falls in this plane. So Choice (G) is the winner.

41. **C.** Lemonade has to end up being 15 percent of the total beverage, so the best way to solve the problem is to set up a proportion with lemonade on the top and total liquid on the bottom.

On the left side, put $\frac{15}{100}$ to represent that lemonade will be 15 percent of the total or 15 parts per 100. On the right side of the proportion, make the numerator the total amount of lemonade that ends up in the beverage; call that x because it's what the problem asks you to figure out. The denominator is the total amount of combined liquid. You can represent that with $2 + x$, which is the two liters of iced tea plus x amount of lemonade. The proportion is $\frac{15}{100} = \frac{x}{2+x}$.

Cross-multiply and solve:

$$15(2+x) = 100x$$
$$30 + 15x = 100x$$
$$30 = 85x$$
$$\frac{30}{85} = x$$
$$\frac{6}{17} = x$$

If you picked Choice (A), you incorrectly multiplied the 2 liters of iced tea by 15 percent. Doing so doesn't account for the additional liquid required to create the combination.

42. **J.** Drawing a graph may help you visualize the problem, but you can't solve it visually and graphing eats up precious time. So working out the necessary calculations is a better way to go. This problem involves two equations and substitution.

The first equation you know is the equation of the line: $x = 6$. The second equation is the equation of the circle. The general equation for a circle is $(x - h)^2 + (y - k)^2 = r^2$, where h and k are the x- and y-coordinates of the center of the circle and r is its radius. Thus, the equation for this specific circle is $(x - 3)^2 + (y - 5)^2 = 4^2$. Remember it because almost every ACT Math Test has at least one question regarding the equation of a circle.

The first equation tells you that $x = 6$, so substitute 6 for x in the equation and solve for y:

$$(6-3)^2 + (y-5)^2 = 4^2$$
$$9 + (y-5)^2 = 16$$
$$(y-5)^2 = 7$$
$$y - 5 = \pm\sqrt{7}$$
$$y = 5 \pm \sqrt{7}$$

Use the square root key on your calculator to find that the y-coordinates are 7.65 and 2.35, or Choice (J).

If you picked Choice (F), you probably sketched out a rough graph and tried to eyeball the right answer.

REMEMBER

Reading through this question may have inspired you to guess and run, which may not be a bad idea if you're pressed for time by this point in the exam and haven't memorized the equation of a circle. Bubble in something for this time-consumer and move on to the next problem. Be sure to mark it so that you'll know to come back to it if you have time at the end of the section.

43. **B.** Use the formula for the area of a circle $A = \pi r^2$ to find the pizza's area. Divide the diameter of 122 feet by 2 to get the correct radius in square feet of 61 feet:

$$A = \pi(61)^2$$
$$A = \pi(3{,}721)$$
$$A = 11{,}689.87$$

You need 10 pepperoni slices per square foot, so multiply that number by 10 to get 116,898.70 total slices of pepperoni on the pizza. Then divide that large number by 50 to figure out how many pepperoni sticks the pizza makers need. The answer is 2,337.97 sticks. Don't forget to round up to 2,338 so you don't run out of pepperoni! If you picked Choice (A), you used the formula for circumference instead of area.

If this problem doesn't give you real incentive to do well on the ACT so you can go to college and get a good education so you don't have to cut up 2,338 pepperoni sticks at a pizza restaurant for a living, we don't know what will!

44. **K.** You just need to know a few basic trig rules to answer this question. Don't worry. No prior trigonometry class is required. Merely memorize SOH CAH TOA. (Review Chapter 9 if you can't remember what this acronym means.) All you have to do is divide sin A by cos B. To determine sin A, find angle A on the figure. The opposite side of angle A is a, and the hypotenuse of the triangle (the side opposite the 90-degree angle) is c. Therefore, $\sin A = \frac{a}{c}$. To find cos B, work with angle B on the figure. The side adjacent (or next) to it is a. The hypotenuse is still c. That means $\cos B = \frac{a}{c}$. What do you know? The value of sin A is the same as the value of cos B. Any number divided by itself is 1. The answer is Choice (K). That wasn't so bad!

45. **D.** Making sense of this problem requires a little language interpretation.

Two positive integers r and s satisfy the relationship r † t only when $r = s^2 + 2$. The funny symbol between r and s means that whenever you have two values with the symbol between them you create the given equation with those values inserted.

So this problem results in two equations: s†t gives you $s = t^2 + 2$, and t†u means $t = u^2 + 2$. Because you're solving for s in terms of u, you have to make the t's disappear. The second equation solves for t in terms of u. Substitute $u^2 + 2$ for t in the first equation: $s = \left(u^2 + 2\right)^2 + 2$. Use FOIL to square the first expression: $\left(u^2 + 2\right)\left(u^2 + 2\right) = u^2 + 4u^2 + 4$. Add 2 and combine: $s = u^4 + 4u^2 + 6$. After you get past the language barrier, this problem practically solves itself.

46. F. This problem describes an inscribed angle in a semicircle. Here's what it looks like:

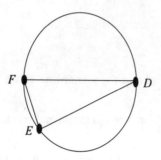

Thales's theorem states that an inscribed angle in a semicircle is a right (90-degree) angle. That's all the information you need to pick Choice (F) and eliminate the others.

47. A. If you know how to substitute, you can solve this problem. The *determinant* tells you how to determine which values constitute a, b, c, and d. The equation shows you where to put the values when you know what they are. This is all just a fancy way of saying that $a = 4x$, $b = 2y$, $c = 7y$, and $d = 3y$. Insert these values into the equation: $(7y \times 3y)\left[(2y)^2 - (4x)^2\right]$. Finish up by substituting 4 for x and -2 for y and solving the equation:

$$\left(7(-2) \times 3(-2)\right)\left[(2(-2))^2 - (4(4))^2\right] = ?$$
$$(-14 \times -6)(-4^2 - 16^2) = ?$$
$$84(16 - 256) = ?$$
$$-20{,}160 = ?$$

48. G. Find the value of $\sin\theta$, multiply it by z, and you're done. Remember that SOH tells you $\sin\theta = \dfrac{\text{opposite}}{\text{hypotenuse}}$. The opposite side is y. The hypotenuse is z. The final answer is $z\sin\theta = z \times \dfrac{y}{z} = y$, Choice (G). If you picked Choice (F), you were thinking cosine, not sine.

49. C. It's arts and crafts time. Sketch the little boat. Add the water. Draw the rope. Draw a person in the air. Behold! Your masterpiece reveals a right triangle. Its vertices are the boat, the parasailer, and the point in the water directly beneath the parasailer:

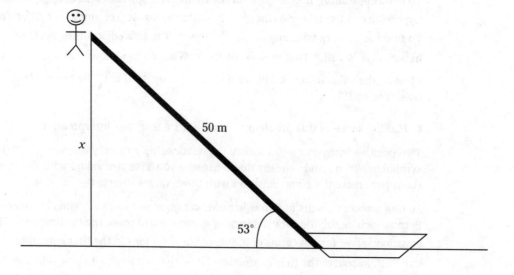

You know that Choice (B) isn't right even before you do any calculating. After all, the hypotenuse of a right triangle is always longer than either of the other two sides.

As the problem explains, the angle that the rope makes with the surface of the water is 53 degrees. You know the length of the hypotenuse (50 meters), and you want to know the length of the side that's opposite the 53-degree angle (x). Sounds like you need to apply sine: SOH or $\sin 53° = \dfrac{\text{opposite}}{\text{hypotenuse}}$. Delete Choices (A) and (D) because they use tangent and cosine. Plug in the values and solve for x:

$$\sin 53° = \frac{x}{50}$$
$$x = (\sin 53°)50$$

50. **J.** To evaluate the expression, engage in a little distribution. Multiply $2x$ by both terms inside the parentheses:

$$2x \times \frac{3}{y} = \frac{6x}{y}$$
$$2x \times \frac{4}{y} = \frac{8x}{z}$$

The new expression is $\dfrac{6x}{y} + \dfrac{8x}{z}$. Unfortunately, that's not an answer option, so you must press on.

Fractions have to have the same denominator before you can add them. To find the lowest common denominator of two variables, just multiply them. The product of y and z is yz. Convert each fraction so its denominator is yz. Multiply the top and bottom of the first term by z. That gives you $\dfrac{6xz}{yz}$. Multiply the top and bottom of the second fraction by y and you get $\dfrac{8xy}{yz}$. When you add the two fractions together, you get $\dfrac{8xy + 6xz}{yz}$, or Choice (J). If you picked Choice (F), you multiplied the fractions instead of adding them.

51. **E.** The formula for finding average is simple. It's just the sum of all the salaries divided by the number of salaries. The trick for this question is to figure out where to put what you know in the equation. The question gives you the average of all the salaries: $51,200. Insert that value for *average* in the equation. The total number of salaries is 15. That's the number you divide by. The tricky part is determining how to represent the sum of all salaries. You know that the first 14 salaries average $51,000. Apply the average formula again: $51,000 times 14 must be the sum of the other 14 salaries. Let x stand for George's salary and add that to the sum of the other salaries. Your equation looks like this: $51,200 = \dfrac{(6 \times 51,000) + x}{15}$.

Solve for x and you're through:

$$768,000 = 714,000 + x$$
$$54,000 = x$$

George's salary is above average. If you chose Choice (A), you probably made the mistake of adding George's salary (x) to just one $51,000 salary rather than 14 of them.

52. **H.** Don't let the square root sign throw you. Solve this equation in the same way you would any other equation. For this problem, you have to "break out" the variable p from the square root "jail" it's trapped in.

Get the variable by itself on one side of the equation by performing the opposite function to both sides of the equation. The opposite of taking the square root of something is to square it. Square everything on both sides of the equation. You end up with $\sqrt{5p} \times \sqrt{5p} = 3.67 \times 3.67$, or $5p = 13.4689$. When you divide both sides by 5, you get 2.69, Choice (H).

53. D. This word problem has you working with percentages. Make sure you're clear about what you're supposed to figure out and what you know. The answer you're looking for is the number of Representatives who voted no. You know that the percentage of no votes is the same in both groups, but you don't know what that percentage is. You can set up an equation to figure out the percentage of no votes. Make x the percentage of members that voted no in each group: $410(x) + (90)x + 350$. This means that a certain percentage of 410 Representatives and the same percentage of Senators adds up to a total of 350 members who voted no. Solve for x: $500x = 350$; $x = 0.7$, which is 70%.

Don't get all excited and select Choice (B). The question doesn't ask you for the percentage of no votes. It wants you to figure out the number of no votes in the House of Representatives.

Multiply 410 by 70% (or 0.7) to get 287 naysayers. If you picked Choice (A), you figured out the number of Senators who voted no.

54. J. The information you need to help you find the answer is hidden in the problem. It helps to know that $\sin \pi = 0$ (or use your calculator to figure it out). Read through the problem and add information to the figure it provides.

Following the x-axis from left to right; you have three x-intercepts (where the graph of the function crosses the x-axis and $y = 0$). The first x-intercept is the origin (0, 0). According to the function, the last x-intercept has coordinates of ($\sin \pi$, 0). When you know that $\sin \pi = 0$, you can deduce that the middle x-intercept has coordinates of (π, 0). Point A then must have x-coordinates between 0 and π and a y-coordinate greater than 0. The range of values for sine lies between -1 and 1 ($-1 \le \sin x \le 1$). Because point A represents the maximum y-value of $\sin x$, the y-coordinate is 1.

The figure states that it's not drawn to scale, so you can't assume by looking at it that point A is $\left(\frac{\pi}{2}, 1\right)$ even though the x-coordinate appears to be halfway between 0 and π. To confirm your answer, use your calculator to determine the sine of $\frac{\pi}{2}$. Sure enough, it equals 1.

If you guessed Choice (A) or (B), you incorrectly approached the graph as though it represented $0 \le x \le \pi$. Choice (C) can't be right because clearly y doesn't equal 0. You can eliminate Choice (E) right off the bat because $\sin x$ can't equal π because π is approximately 3.14 and the sine of a number can't be greater than 1. If this explanation seems like Greek to you, don't worry. You don't need to learn a new language. These types of questions appear rarely on the ACT. Spend your time and effort on questions you understand instead.

55. E. If 4 and -3 are the solution set of a quadratic equation, the factors must be $(x - 4)(x + 3)$. Use FOIL to multiply the expressions. You end up with $x^2 - x - 12$, Choice (E).

56. F. This question is about multiplying and dividing bases with exponents.

Keep these rules in mind as you solve this problem:

REMEMBER

>> You can multiply and divide exponents only when the bases are the same.

>> When you see a base raised to a negative exponent, it equals the reciprocal of the base raised to the positive version of the exponent.

To get a by itself, divide both sides of the equation by c^6. That gives you $\frac{1}{b^5}$. Convert b^{-5} into $\frac{1}{b^5}$. To divide by a fraction, multiply by the reciprocal $\frac{a^2}{3} \times \frac{b^5}{1} = \frac{a^2 b^5}{3}$. This gives you $a^3 b^5 = \frac{a^2 b^5}{3}$. Divide both sides by b^5 to eliminate that term. To isolate a, divide both sides by a^2. This gives you $a = \frac{1}{3}$.

57. B. The number of square feet of sod is the area of the parallelogram. The area of a parallelogram is *bh*. The base of the garden is the length of one of its sides (let's say the longer one measures 8 feet.) Because the garden is shaped like a parallelogram, you can't assume that the measure of its width is the 6-feet measure on the other side. To find the width measure, draw a parallelogram that slants to the right and create a right triangle by drawing a line from its top left corner that's perpendicular to the base.

The angle your new line extends from measures 120 degrees. Opposite angles in a parallelogram have the same measurements, and all four angles add up to 360 degrees. That means the two smaller angles of the garden measure 60 degrees and the other large angle measures 120 degrees.

REMEMBER

The right triangle you've created is a 30:60:90 right triangle. The side ratio of a 30:60:90 triangle is $s : s\sqrt{3} : 2s$.

The smaller side (the one opposite the 30-degree angle) is equal to half the hypotenuse, and the longer side (the one opposite the 60-degree angle) is equal to the smaller side multiplied by $\sqrt{3}$. The smaller side is half of 6, which is 3, and the longer side, the height of the parallelogram, is $3\sqrt{3}$. Multiply that value by the base of 8. The number of square feet of sod that Janet needs is $24\sqrt{3}$.

58. K. The absolute value of *x* is the number of spaces *x* is from 0 on the number line. When you solve the inequality by adding 1 to both sides, you learn that $|x| \leq 4$. That means that *x* includes −4 and 4 and all numbers between them on the number line. Eliminate Choices (G) and (H) because they show that values for *x* are unlimited in at least one direction. Choice (J) results from subtracting 1 from both sides of the inequality instead of adding it. If you picked Choice (F), you forgot that *x* includes −4 and 4. The best answer is Choice (K). The solid points at −4 and 4 indicate that the two values are included in the solution set.

59. D. To find the area of *WXYZ*, you have to know the length of its sides. As it turns out, all four sides are the hypotenuses of equal right triangles. Each triangle has one leg that measures 5 cm (the length of one edge of the cube) and a second leg that measures 2.5 cm (half the length of one side of the cube). Apply your trusty friend the Pythagorean theorem to find the length of the hypotenuse (which is the length of each side of *WXYZ*):

$$c^2 = a^2 + b^2$$
$$c^2 = (5)^2 + (2.5)^2$$
$$c^2 = 25 + 6.25$$
$$c^2 = 31.25$$

Note: You could figure out the square root of 31.25 to discover the length of the hypotenuse, but then you'd just have to square it again to get the area of *WXYZ*. Because the sides of *WXYZ* are equal, it's a square. The area of a square is the square of one of its side lengths. The side length of *WXYZ* is the square root of 31.25, and, therefore, 31.25 is the area of the square.

If you chose Choice (A), you didn't finish the problem, and Choice (E) incorrectly squares 31.25 a second time.

60. H. Replacing $f(x)$ with $f(x-3)$ does nothing more than shift the parabola over 3 units to the right. That move has no effect on the area. The area remains 5, or Choice (H).

REMEMBER

The last three questions in this section were probably easier for you than some of the questions that come before them. Don't spend too much time on really difficult questions that may prevent you from getting to easier questions later in the test. If it takes you more than a minute to answer a question, mark your best guess and move along.

Reading Test

1. **C.** The passage is clearly not a poem, so cross out Choice (D). A *fable* tells a story with a moral lesson and often uses humanized animals as its main characters. That definition is too specific to apply to this passage. So you can narrow down your options to Choices (B) and (C). You may have noticed a hint of romance in the story, but it's mostly about an instance when the young protagonist, Eyvind, has experiences, such as watching Marit outgrow him and experiencing embarrassment at being called a *youngster*, that mark his development from a child to a young man. Choice (C) is the best answer.

2. **F.** Marit is the one who coaxes the bashful children into the party. She dances more than anyone else. You can hardly describe her as bashful. Cross out Choice (G). You probably wouldn't use the adjective *grandmotherly* to describe a tireless dancer, either. Choice (J) is out. Marit doesn't pay much attention to Eyvind, but that doesn't categorize her as callous. The best answer is Choice (F). *Gregarious* means social and outgoing.

3. **D.** The tingling sensation occurs in the last line of the paragraph that describes the scene in which the tall fellow pushes Eyvind away. The tingling doesn't occur right after the fellow calls him a youngster, though. It happens after he sees Marit laughing and dancing. The line says that this is the first time Eyvind has experienced this feeling, and it implies that he's disappointed that Marit has outgrown him. The best answer is Choice (D). The passage doesn't say that Eyvind drank ale. Nor does the paragraph give any indication that Eyvind experienced physical injury from the push.

4. **J.** Cross out the answers that express a legitimate time when Eyvind was timid. Start with Choice (F) because Lines 58–59 say that he didn't dare join in the dancing at first. He didn't stand up for himself when the bushy-haired man pushed him, so you can cross out Choice (G), too. The passage says that Eyvind moved back away from the dance floor when he watched Marit dance, which suggests timidity. Choice (H) is out. The passage says that Eyvind didn't get an invitation to enter the little room, so he definitely didn't fail to respond to it. Choice (J) describes the one time when Eyvind wasn't timid because it didn't happen.

5. **A.** The description doesn't portray particularly harsh or dangerous conditions, which means that Choices (B) and (D) aren't right. The first paragraph doesn't mention anything about Scandinavian life. The answer has to be Choice (A). The introductory paragraph sets the natural backdrop for the main events of the story.

REMEMBER

Using the power of POE (process of elimination) can really help you out on the Reading Test. When you first look at the answer choices, you may feel a bit overwhelmed. They may all look right or all look wrong, or they may seem like they're about a completely different subject than the passage you read! Cross out answers that are obviously wrong. Soon, you'll be able to focus on the best option.

6. **J.** Marit doesn't pay much attention to Eyvind. The answer that best describes this fact is Choice (J). Nothing in the passage implies that she loves Eyvind, and her feelings toward him aren't strong enough to be repulsion or pity.

REMEMBER

Unless something in the passage specifically suggests a strong answer choice, the right answer is probably fairly neutral.

7. C. The author describes the little room to point out that Eyvind didn't get invited to Marit's family's inner circle. You don't have to make any inferences to cross out Choice (A). No one danced in the little room. The grandmother isn't a major figure in the passage, so the purpose of the scene probably isn't to learn more about her. Eliminate Choice (D). Old people were in the room but not necessarily because Marit invited them. Choice (B) isn't right. The best answer is Choice (C). The passage says that Marit invited guests she really cared for to the room. She didn't invite Eyvind. So she must not really care for Eyvind, something that Eyvind finds strange. From this little scene, you realize that Eyvind makes more of his relationship with Marit than she does.

8. G. *Bands* refers to the groups of girls that walked together to the party. The passage also refers to them as *gangs*, but it doesn't give a negative impression of them. They aren't ruffians. Keep Choice (G) in mind and cross out Choice (F). The passage says they marched along, but that doesn't mean they were in a parade. Choice (H) is wrong. If you picked Choice (J), you probably tried to answer the question without looking at the passage. A *band* is often a group of musicians, but that's not the case in this passage.

REMEMBER

Don't answer reading questions based on your outside knowledge. Use the passage to answer every question.

9. B. POE to the rescue! Cross out choices that make you think beyond the scope of the passage or that are just plain wrong. Choice (C) is one of the just plain wrong ones. Eyvind wasn't invited to the grandmother's room, so he couldn't have spent all his time there. The passage says that Eyvind danced, so he didn't just sit and watch Marit. Cross out Choice (A). The passage doesn't specifically state that Eyvind was in the corner or that he sulked. He seemed to be in a state of shock rather than depression. Cross out Choice (D). The fact that he was experiencing new feelings and noticing changes in Marit implies that he realized his life was changing. Choice (B) is best.

10. G. You can't make assumptions about everyday weather in the village from the description of one evening. Choice (F) makes you infer way beyond the information in the passage. Likewise, just because groups of children make their way to the party by running from farmhouse to farmhouse doesn't mean that all villagers travel that way. Lines 53–55 suggest that the villagers prefer dancing to the new musician rather than the old one, but that's because he's a better player and knows more songs. The passage doesn't say that he's necessarily older. Cross out Choices (H) and (J) and consider Choice (G). Because the passage tells you that people of different ages attended the dance, you can reasonably assume that the villagers participate in activities with different age groups, even if those activities include just this one dance.

11. A. The act appears in the third paragraph of Passage A. Compare each answer choice to the information in the paragraph to see which one is a result of the act's passage. Choice (A) paraphrases the last sentence of the paragraph, which says that one provision of the act was a temporary program to help make more mortgage financing available to homebuyers. Choice (B) may seem right at first, but the passage says that the condition on lenders to write down loan balances was voluntary, so the act didn't force actions on lenders. The passage doesn't include information on how the public viewed the FHA, so Choice (C) is wrong. Choice (D) is clearly wrong; the act is providing for more federal government intervention in the financial situation. Choice (A) is the answer.

12. **J.** To answer vocabulary-in-context questions, replace the original word with each answer choice to see which one makes sense. The original sentence says that the interventions failed to *stem* the growing crisis. The interventions didn't fail to *originate* the growing crisis, so Choice (F) doesn't fit. Choice (G) sounds way too awkward. You're down to Choices (H) and (J). You may be able to say that the interventions failed to *remove* the growing crisis, but the better answer is Choice (J). It sounds better to say that interventions failed to *stop* the growth rather than *remove* it.

WARNING

Don't choose an answer to a vocabulary-in-context question based on what you think the word's definition is. The ACT often tests you on words that have several alternative definitions.

13. **C.** Look in Passage A's second paragraph where it says that the government's improvisational (or unplanned) response to the crisis has contributed to the public's failing confidence in its ability to restore the financial system. Choice (C) provides a nice paraphrase of this idea. Choice (D) is wrong because although the passage summarizes some of the actions of the Federal Housing Authority, it doesn't indicate how the economy responded to those actions. Choice (B) contains one of those debatable words — *completely* — that raises a red flag. Nothing in the passage suggests that anyone's confidence has been completely restored. Choice (A) is out because the passage doesn't associate lack of confidence with lack of attention to borrowers. In fact, much of the passage is about how the government attempted to address issues related to borrowing.

14. **F.** This question was a pretty easy one. "Deleveraging" appears in the first sentence, so you don't have to look deep in the passage to find it. The first passage says that it means to reduce debt, sell assets, and obtain capital from any source. So you can cross out Choices (G), (H), and (J) with confidence. The only answer left is Choice (F). Home mortgage rates aren't part of the definition.

15. **C.** Passage B defines redlining as "the identification of an area, usually a neighborhood or ZIP code area, where no mortgage loans are to be issued." Choice (C) paraphrases this definition best. Choice (A) is wrong because the passage indicates that redlining is a financial institution practice rather than a government one. While the passage implies that the effect of redlining is to discriminate against certain classes and races, the actual practice is based on identifying certain neighborhoods to deny mortgage loans to. So Choice (B) is incorrect. You can't justify Choice (D); redlining regards denying loans rather than granting them. You can't assume that because the practice of redlining denies loans to certain neighborhoods, it therefore limits loans (and particularly subprime loans) to only the wealthy.

16. **J.** The first paragraph in Passage B explains the subprime lending crisis and its effects. The author doesn't express anti-government opinions nor does he mention government actions to combat the crisis, so Choices (F) and (H) are out. You can also cross out Choice (G). The paragraph specifically states that the crisis seemed at first to be specific and limited, but it grew to have global ramifications. The best answer is Choice (J). The paragraph starts with a quick history of the subprime lending crisis and ends with its global effects.

17. **B.** Although Passage B claims that financial institutions can promote positive social development, the discussion of supply and demand in Lines 87-89 introduces the power that lenders use to exclude borrowers, a practice that is negative rather than positive. Choice (A) is wrong. Passage B mentions ways in which lenders choose blacklisted neighborhoods later in the paragraph, but not in the context of supply and demand. The second paragraph concerns domestic lending practices and not the global economy, so you can't justify Choice (D). Choice (B) is best. The author defines supply and demand as "lenders" and "customers" to identify who controls what elements of the lending relationship and clarify that lenders have the power to control the supply of mortgage financing.

18. **F.** Passage A is critical of government intervention and Passage B doesn't discuss government's involvement in the crisis experienced in 2007 and 2008, so Choice (J) is clearly wrong. Choice (G) is stated by Passage A but not Passage B, and Choice (H) is stated by Passage B but not Passage A, so neither choice provides a statement that both passages would agree with. Passage A talks about the difficulty individuals have obtaining short-term funding and the government's largely unsuccessful attempts to remedy the problem, and Passage B spends the entire second paragraph discussing the difficulties homebuyers have in getting mortgage loans. Choice (F) is best.

19. **D.** The temporary program mentioned in Passage A is designed to make mortgage loans more easily available to homebuyers. Passage B claims that certain neighborhoods are redlined, meaning they're denied mortgages, so these neighborhoods wouldn't likely benefit from the program. Choice (D) is correct. Passage B isn't concerned with government spending or public confidence in the economy, so Choices (A) and (C) are out. The author's discussion of interconnectedness regards the spread of the financial crisis and not the issue of certain ZIP codes being denied loans, so eliminate Choice (B).

20. **H.** Passage A mentions the effect of the crisis on individuals, corporations, and state and local governments in addition to the national economy, and although Passage B mentions global effects, its primary concern is with the ability of certain homebuyers to secure mortgages. Choice (F) doesn't work. Passage A emphasizes the difficulty in securing funding in the first paragraph and indicates that government programs have failed, so it would be a stretch to say the author is much more optimistic about the housing market than the author of Passage B is. Choice (G) is out. Choice (J) is clearly incorrect. Passage A suggests that government intervention has largely failed, and Passage B doesn't mention government help at all. Choice (H) is the best option. Passage A says the government's attempts to stem the crisis have failed, and Passage B blames the discriminatory practices of financial institutions on the inability of those in certain neighborhoods to secure mortgages to buy homes.

21. **D.** You can begin eliminating answer choices just by reading the first word in each option. The passage is more informative than argumentative, so you can make a pretty good bet that its purpose isn't to discredit or argue. You may not want to cross out Choices (A) and (C) based on this observation alone, but you should definitely examine the other two choices more closely. Choice (B) is too specific for a main-idea question. The passage discusses more elements than just typography. Choice (D) sounds right. It's general enough to encompass the whole passage and is a good summary of the last paragraph, which says that *bibliography* requires attention to many aspects of the text.

TIP

If you're pressed for time, mark Choice (D) on your answer sheet and press on. If you're on track time-wise, take a couple of seconds to consider Choices (A) and (C). The passage doesn't talk about authors, so Choice (A) can't be right. When you read through Choice (C), you see that it's wrong, too. The passage doesn't get into what elements of study are most important. It just says that analyzing many aspects is important. Now you can be confident that Choice (D) is the best answer.

22. **G.** Don't try to answer this question based on your own definition of *cunning*. Substitute each choice for *cunning* in the passage and pick the one that makes the most sense. The sentence before the reference presents what would be a logical answer to a question. Then the author says that this answer would have some *cunning* (or correctness) given certain circumstances. Choices (F), (H), and (J) don't convey the same meaning. The answer that's most similar to *correctness* is Choice (G): The answer would have some wisdom given certain circumstances.

If you tried to answer this question based on what you know *cunning* means, you may have picked Choice (A). One of the definitions of *cunning* is slyness, but that meaning doesn't fit in this context. Always analyze the answers to vocabulary-in-context questions by putting them in the passage.

23. **C.** This question is pretty easy after you figure out which part of the passage gives you the answer. If you skim the questions before you read the passage, you know that you'll encounter a question about estimating a book's age. When you get to the third paragraph and read about estimating the age of a book within five to ten years, you know to mark that particular sentence.

Don't actually try to answer the question while you read the passage. Just mark the information in the passage so you know where to return later when you're in question-answering mode.

Lines 57–60 say that the way letters are laid out on a page reflects social conventions. The next sentence says that this is why you can estimate a document's age by looking at it. The answer that paraphrases this information is Choice (D), so you can cross it out. Binding and ornamentation appear in Lines 63–66 as additional ways that documents reveal their age. Cross out Choices (A) and (B). Choice (C) must be the answer, which makes sense. The author talks about literary types in another paragraph, and all periods produce different types of literature.

24. **H.** The quotes in the question appear in Lines 20–23 in the first paragraph. From this sentence, you know that "being literary" means looking at a page and seeing a poem. Someone who thinks "like a bibliographer" sees the physical aspects of the document, such as type (meaning the style of the letters), paper, and space on the page. Choice (H) is almost a word-for-word copy of the passage.

If you picked Choice (G) or (J), you read too much into the passage. The passage says that physical aspects are determined by economics, but that fact doesn't mean that the bibliographer is especially concerned with the financial aspects of creating a document. The bibliographer's primary focus is on the physical aspects themselves. The debatable word *altogether* in Choice (F) should have raised a red flag.

25. **A.** If you answered Question 23 correctly, you probably got this one, too. The third paragraph states that looking at a document's physical aspects reveals its age. Choices (B) and (D) concern style and story rather than physical elements. Cross out both of them. The paragraph specifically mentions letterforms, bindings, format, ornament stocks, and ruled borders as revealing age but not paper type. Choice (A) is a better answer than Choice (C).

26. **H.** The last paragraph defines *bibliography*. Pick the answer that best summarizes the last paragraph. Its gist is that bibliography is the broad study of texts, including the history of how the text was made and how it was read. Choice (J) focuses on one specific element of the way a text was made. Cross it out. Choice (H) is the best summary.

If you picked Choice (F) or (G), you relied on the definition of bibliography that you're familiar with — the list of resources your teachers make you include at the end of your research papers. The result of that tedious task isn't what the author of this passage is talking about.

27. A. A discussion of letterforms appears in the third paragraph. The author says they reflect the social conventions of the time they were created. "Social conventions" and "standard practices" have pretty much the same meaning. Pick Choice (A). Beware of Choice (C): It contains the debatable word *exact*. The passage says you can estimate a document's age from its letterforms. Estimating isn't the same as knowing its exact age. The passage never says that the way letters are formed in a work reveals whether it's a poem, prayer, or other type of literature, so Choice (D) is wrong. If you picked Choice (B), you probably read in the first paragraph that the physical aspects of a document are always determined by the economics of book production. That's not enough information to say that the style of letterforms reveals the creator's specific socioeconomic status.

REMEMBER

Don't choose an answer that makes you read too much into what the passage actually says. For this question, you have to take too big of a stretch to say that the economics of book production is related to the socioeconomic status of an individual.

28. F. The best way to answer this question is to begin with POE. The passage isn't clear about exactly what high literature is, so you have to figure out what it is not. Choice (J) can't be right because the passage doesn't say anything about works produced by royalty. The passage talks about poems and prayers specifically, but it doesn't suggest that these two genres form a separate kind of literature. So cross out Choice (H). Choice (G) is probably wrong, too. The point of the last paragraph is that analyzing literature should include the way it was made as well as whatever is traditionally done with "high" literature. The passage associates costs of production with the physical aspects of a document (the way it's made), so the cost of production doesn't distinguish "high" literature. The only answer choice left standing is Choice (F). The author advocates examining the physical aspects of a work as well as its literary value. The first sentence of paragraph two refers to the relationship between form and meaning, suggesting that those who are literary focus more on meaning than form. *Bibliography*, then, takes into consideration form and meaning and isn't limited to analyzing just meaning in the way that those who study only "high" literature are.

REMEMBER

This question requires you to engage in a lengthy thought process. Don't waste too much time trying to answer it. Eliminate answers that are obviously wrong, guess, and go on to questions that are easier to answer.

29. C. The passage lists the common components as the introduction, illustrations, notes, and list of textual variants. Eliminate answers that don't relate to these components. The passage doesn't mention test banks, so cross out Choice (A). Choice (B) refers to illustrations, but the passage doesn't get specific enough for you to say that the illustrations are computerized. So Choice (B) is wrong. An author's biography could be part of an introduction, but the passage doesn't say so. Choice (D) is out. Textual variants refer to different variations of the text. The best answer is Choice (C).

30. H. The second paragraph tells you how the conventions of textual design evolve. The answer that paraphrases this sentence is Choice (H). The passage doesn't discuss what makes a text more aesthetically pleasing or popular, so Choices (G) and (J) aren't right. Choice (F) doesn't work because although the passage mentions that costs affect style, it doesn't say anything about how costs concern the way texts evolve.

31. D. A *main purpose* or *main idea* is by definition broad and general. So an answer with the word *overview* is often correct because it encompasses nearly everything. Hence, Choice (D) is your winner here. Choice (A) is wrong because the passage barely mentions prehistoric animals. In Choice (B), *refute*, which means to disprove, is rarely a correct answer. (Passages discuss or describe; they don't often refute or criticize. Chapter 13 covers this concept in more detail.)

The fact that Choice (B) may be a true statement is irrelevant (the cycad seeds were too large to be spread by birds). The mere fact that an answer is true doesn't mean it's the correct answer to the question.

Choice (C) is overly broad. The passage includes little discussion of current plant life, and what's there is limited to cycads, not to plants in general.

32. **J.** The line implies that the plants, although prehistoric, still exist today and goes on to tell you where they may be found. Choice (F) is exactly backward; the plants are *not* extinct. Choice (G) is illogical in the context of the passage. Choice (H) contradicts the rest of the sentence, which tells you how widespread the plants are.

33. **A.** This question is about pure detail. Lines 40–43 state that scientists considered the widespread distribution of the cycad a mystery.

34. **G.** The answer to this specific-information question comes right out of the passage. The first sentence of the second paragraph says that this fossil record (referring to the early plant life fossils discussed in the first paragraph) shows how plants have evolved over time. Choice (G) is a nice paraphrase of this statement. The passage doesn't compare plant fossils to animal fossils, so Choice (F) is out. The word *all* in Choice (H) indicates that it's probably not right. The first paragraph says that the fossils develop from plants that haven't decayed, so cross out Choice (J).

35. **C.** A passage often suggests; it rarely refutes (to *refute* is to disprove). Pangaea, which appears in paragraph four, was the one large supercontinent that later broke into smaller continents, taking the cycad seeds and plants with them. The author mentions this idea as a possible way to explain the seeds' widespread distribution. Choice (A) is wrong because the cycad is not extinct today; it's *extant* (still in existence). Choice (B) is going too far. Although the passage says that the plants in prehistoric times were huge, it doesn't mention or imply that the cycad was the largest plant.

36. **F.** You know that Choice (G) can't be right. Cycads still exist, so they didn't become extinct in the Jurassic Period. The second paragraph says that the Cretaceous Period came after the Jurassic Period, so cross out Choice (J). If you picked Choice (H), you focused on the age of rocks that contain fossils of flowers rather than the age of the Jurassic Period. The best answer is Choice (F). If no evidence of flowers exists until the period after the Jurassic Period, the Jurassic Period probably didn't have any flowering plants.

37. **B.** Paragraph five tells you that the seed cones are female and the pollen cones are male. The paragraph also warns of the cancer-causing properties of the seeds, but it never mentions any medicinal properties.

A question like this one requires an investment of time. Unless you're a reader who retains everything after one quick reading, you're probably wise to go back and double-check your memory. Look for the precise answer; don't depend on remembering everything.

38. **H.** Paragraph six states that the leaves of the cycad plant grow into a crown that makes people think the plant is a palm tree.

39. **B.** A question that begins "according to the passage" is often a gift to you. It's usually a simple detail-related question that requires little thought. All you have to do is go back and find the answer in the passage, usually stated very clearly and directly. Here, paragraph five says that "the conversion of atmospheric nitrogen into ammonia is one way the cyanobacteria supply the cycad with inorganic nitrogen."

40. F. The last paragraph focuses on the possible extinction of cycads and the steps groups are taking to prevent it. Hey, that's exactly what Choice (F) says! The passage doesn't include enough specific information to verify Choice (G) or (J). The article is more informative than persuasive, so Choice (H) isn't the primary purpose of the paragraph.

Science Test

In each of the following sections, we explain how to interpret the tables and figures that accompany each passage in the Science Test. Then we go into more detailed explanations of the specific questions and their answers. This isn't a suggestion that you spend time examining the passage material before you attempt the questions.

REMEMBER

Don't spend precious seconds evaluating science passages before you tackle the questions. Use clues from the questions and answer choices to determine where to focus your attention in the passage.

1. C. Study 1 used pure water for all three trials. Study 2 used wood for all three trials. This info immediately leads you to the correct answer: wood and pure water. Only Study 1 used Choice (A), concrete and pure water, while only Study 2 used Choice (B), wood and oil. Neither study used Choice (D), aluminum and sea water.

2. H. For this question, you have to understand what both tables are telling you and then combine the information. Aluminum is the densest of the three materials and, therefore, has the least buoyancy, as shown in Table 1. By looking in Table 2, you can see that oil is the least dense of the fluids, and thus, provides the least buoyancy. The combination of the least buoyant material and the least buoyant fluid would mean that the maximum weight supported would be less than any of the other combinations given and, therefore, less than 7 kg.

REMEMBER

Be sure to look at all the information provided, and don't assume that you'll be able to answer each question using only a single table.

3. A. You're looking for the answer that the passage *doesn't* support. Pay careful attention to what the statements say. If you confuse more buoyant and less buoyant, you'll quickly reach the wrong conclusion. Even if you pick Choice (A) right away as the correct answer, check the others to make sure you haven't missed something important.

Choices (A) and (B) refer to Table 2. Choices (C) and (D) refer to Table 1. From the tables, you can see that sea water provided the most buoyancy because it supported the maximum weight before the wood boat sank. Oil provided the least buoyancy. From Table 1, you can conclude that wood was the most buoyant boat material. Aluminum was the least. Choices (C) and (D) are true because wood was the most buoyant.

4. F. This question involves looking at the weights supported and evaluating the effect of varying boat material and fluid type. Table 1 tells you that the wooden boat was significantly more buoyant than the other materials. It supported a weight of nearly twice that of the aluminum boat. Table 2 shows you that the range of weight supported by the different fluids was small, varying only from 11 to 14. This small range indicates that fluid type had a smaller effect on buoyancy than material type.

Cross out Choice (G) right away. The question clearly states that you should base your answer on the data in Tables 1 and 2. Boat size isn't a part of the studies, so you can't conclude anything about it.

5. B. The text that comes before the tables tells you how density relates to buoyancy and how buoyancy relates to the weight applied to the object before it sinks. After you figure out that substances with similar densities have similar buoyancies, you can look in the tables to find which boat materials had a similar amount of weight applied to them before the boat sank. In Table 1, aluminum and concrete were very similar, whereas wood was much different. Go ahead and eliminate Choices (A) and (C) because you know that the density of wood isn't similar to aluminum or concrete. Pick Choice (B).

WARNING

Choice (D) is a trick. You can't tell from the data whether wood and pure water have similar densities. Don't let this bother you, though, because the question asks you to answer according to Table 1, which gives information only about boat materials.

6. H. To answer this question correctly, make sure you understand that denser fluids provide more buoyancy to objects submerged in them and that a more buoyant object can float and carry more weight before it sinks. Armed with this knowledge, you can go to Table 2 and see that sea water provided the most buoyancy to the boat because it supported the maximum weight. Therefore, sea water is the densest. Choice (J) is obviously wrong because the studies don't address gasoline at all.

7. A. Study 1 involves three boats of different materials, and each is placed in water. So, it's true that the liquid used was the same for each boat and the material was different. Study 2 involves one boat placed in different liquids, so the material used remained constant and the liquids changed. Choice (A) is the only answer that correctly states the study set up.

8. G. Look at the figures for a ramp angle of 10 degrees. At a mass of 40 kg, the block's time is 0.62 seconds. When the block's mass is 50 kg, its time is 0.57 seconds. A 60kg block resulted in a time of 0.54 seconds. It appears that time decreases only as mass increases. The same is true for other ramp angles. The answer is Choice (G).

9. A. You can look at any of the three masses for Block A to answer this question. For each mass, the ramp angle of 10 degrees produced the smallest time for Block A to reach the ground. So Choice (A) is your answer.

You can also think about this question logically to check your answer. Based on Figure 1, you see that as the ramp angle was reduced, the 50-kg weight hung by the cord less and less and was supported by the ramp more and more. Therefore, as the ramp angle decreased, the friction between the ramp and the 50-kg block became more significant and the weight of the 50-kg block became less significant in slowing the fall of Block A. The friction force was smaller in magnitude than the weight of the 50-kg block, which means that as the ramp angle decreases, Block A reaches the ground in a smaller amount of time.

10. G. For this question, pay attention to the trends shown in Table 1. One of the trends is that as the mass of Block A increased, the time for Block A to reach the ground decreased. This trend makes sense logically because a heavier block would more easily overcome the frictional and gravitational forces exerted on the cable by the 50-kg block. Look at Table 1 at a ramp angle of 30 degrees and a Block A mass of 60 kg. You see that Block A took 0.68 seconds to reach the ground. So if the mass of Block A were increased to 70 kg, you know that the time for Block A to reach the ground would have to decrease. Therefore, the answer has to be something less than 0.68 seconds. The only choice that's less than 0.68 seconds is Choice (G).

11. C. Consider the trends in Table 1 to help you with this question. A lower ramp angle made Block A reach the ground faster. So did a higher mass of Block A. Armed with this knowledge, you can quickly pick Choice (C). Rule out Choice (B) because none of the data supports it.

WARNING

Choices (A) and (D) may trick you if you look only at specific instances in the table. When the ramp angle was increased from 20 to 30 degrees and the mass of Block A was increased from 50 to 60 kg, Block A did reach the ground more slowly. But when the ramp angle was increased from 30 to 40 degrees and the mass of Block A was increased from 40 to 50 kg, Block A reached the ground faster. Choice (A) isn't consistently true for every case. The question asks for the answer that's best supported. Choices (A) and (D) have to be incorrect because they're not always true; the data always supports Choice (C).

12. J. For this question, think about what the amount of time it takes for Block A to reach the ground means. A small amount of time means that the block slid quickly and wasn't at all in equilibrium. A large amount of time means that the block was moving slowly and wasn't far from being in equilibrium. In other words, as the amount of time to reach the ground increased, the system came closer to equilibrium. If the system were perfectly at equilibrium, then the time for Block A to reach the ground would be infinitely large. From Table 1, you can see that the largest time occurred with a ramp angle of 40 degrees and a Block A mass of 40 kg. Based on the trends in the table, you know that as the ramp angle was increased, the time for Block A to reach the ground also increased. Therefore, with a mass of 40 kg and a ramp angle larger than 40 degrees, you'd expect the system to be close to equilibrium. Hence, Choice (J) is the winner here.

Using the same logic, you can eliminate the other choices. From the table, you'd expect Choice (A) to yield a time somewhere between 0.66 seconds and 0.78 seconds, which wouldn't indicate equilibrium. Similarly, you'd expect Choice (D) to yield a time between known data points in the table. For Choice (G), you'd expect a time faster than 0.62 seconds based on the trends, meaning that Choice (J) is the only possible answer.

13. C. This question asks you to apply your knowledge of the trends shown in the table to a graphical representation. All the choices indicate that as the ramp angle increases, time also increases, so you have to look more closely at the numbers shown in the table to determine the correct answer. Increasing the ramp angle from 10 to 20 degrees increased the time a small amount. You can look at any of the masses used to verify this trend. Increasing the ramp angle from 20 to 30 degrees increased the time by a larger amount, and increasing it from 30 to 40 degrees increased the time by an even larger amount. After you see this trend, you can determine that the time for Block A to reach the ground grows exponentially with ramp angle. In other words, the graph's curve gets steeper as it moves up to the right, just as the one shown in Choice (C) does. For Choice (A) to be right, the relationship between ramp angle and time would have to be steady. The line in Choice (B) becomes less steep as it moves to the right. Choice (D) may be tempting, but it would work only if the data increased linearly between three data points.

14. H. The genetic theory supports the idea that vision problems are hereditary and can't be changed by using eyes in a certain way. Choices (F), (G), and (J) all talk about a specific use of one's vision, which isn't part of the genetic theory. Choice (H) is the only possible answer here.

REMEMBER

Generalizing the gist of the answer choices makes associating them with one theory or the other much easier to do. According to the genetic theory, the only way vision errors occur is if they're passed on from parents to their children. Any answer that says you can correct error through eye use can't be part of the genetic theory.

15. B. Both theories discuss correcting vision at a young age, but the method of correction differs. You can eliminate all the choices besides Choice (B) by noticing that they're either referenced by only one or none of the theories. Neither theory supports Choice (A) (though the environmental theory would say that a lot of reading affects vision). Only the genetic theory discusses Choice (C), and neither theory discusses Choice (D).

16. **J.** To answer this question, you need to identify the belief that the environmental theory discusses negatively and that the genetic theory supports. The environmental theory doesn't specifically address any negative effects of thinking that vision problems are hereditary. People who assume that vision errors are hereditary can still correct their vision by using the methods of the environmental theory. So cross out Choice (F). Choice (G) is wrong for the same reason. Thinking that vision problems have been around for awhile doesn't create more vision problems. Both theories suggest that you can correct vision errors through multiple ways, so Choice (H) isn't right, either. Environmental theorists talk about the negative effects of wearing glasses at an early age, which is a practice endorsed by the genetic theory folks. The environmental theorists say that the practice of wearing glasses promotes more vision problems. Choice (J) is the correct answer.

17. **A.** For this question, just look closely at the environmental theory to see which choice it supports. Choice (A) is correct because the environmental theory says that vision errors result from focusing too long on nearby objects, which is something that could happen at any time in life. Choice (B) is incorrect because the environmental theory makes the exact opposite claim, stating that watching television affects vision. Choice (C) is incorrect because the environmental theory doesn't support laser eye surgery. The theory also supports the idea that vision problems can be both prevented and reversed, which makes Choice (D) incorrect.

18. **H.** Skim through the choices to see which ones are inconsistent with the environmental theory. From the remaining answers, choose the one that's consistent with the genetic theory.

    Cross out Choice (F) because the environmental theory never claims that eyeglasses don't allow humans to see well. It just argues that glasses aren't a strong solution to underlying vision errors. The environmental theory states that focusing on nearby objects creates vision problems, so eliminate Choice (G). This leaves you with Choices (H) and (J) as possibilities. Choice (J) is consistent with both theories because siblings have similar genetic makeups and are brought up in similar environments. The correct answer has to be Choice (H). Exercising eye muscles promotes vision according to the environmental theory but isn't helpful according to those who hold to the genetic theory.

19. **A.** Look at the choices to find one that both theories support. Choice (A) works because both theories say that vision errors can be identified in children. The genetic theory doesn't support Choices (B) and (D), and Choice (C) doesn't go along with the environmental theory's premise that glasses make vision problems worse.

20. **H.** Think about what traits people who come from the same societies may have in common. In many cases, people in the same society have shared genetics because their families and ethnicities have lived near each other for generations. They may also share similar environmental factors, such as hobbies and lifestyles, because of societal customs. Therefore, societies that are more prone to vision errors could be that way because of genetic factors or environmental factors. So evidence that vision errors are more common in certain societies and less common in others supports both the genetic theory and the environmental theory.

21. **B.** Study 1 used five batteries of different voltages. Study 2 used the same 9.0 volt battery from Study 1. Across both studies, the student used five different batteries. Choice (B) is correct.

WARNING

The percentage amounts on Figure 2 are considerably lower than those on Figure 1, so don't base your answer on which elements have the tallest bars.

22. F. This question asks you to look at Table 1, which portrays the data for Study 1, and find when the voltage across Resistor 2 was smallest. The column labeled "Resistor 2 (1000Ω)" shows you that the smallest voltage measured was 1.34 V and that this voltage occurred when the battery used was 1.5 V. Choice (F) is the correct answer. You can also figure this one out simply by knowing the trends from Study 1. The voltage across each resistor increased when the battery voltage increased. Therefore, you know that the smallest voltage across any of the resistors occurred with the smallest battery voltage, which was 1.5 V.

23. C. You have to look at the text for each study to find the answer to this question. The first study varied the battery voltage and measured the voltage across each resistor. The second study varied the Resistor 1 resistance and measured the current through each resistor. This information corresponds with Choice (C).

TIP

Keeping in mind that Resistor 1 was the only resistor that was changed allows you to eliminate Choices (A), (B), and (D) right away because they mention varying Resistors 2 and 3.

24. H. This question is about Study 2, so look at Table 2. As you can see, the current through each of the three resistors decreased as the Resistor 1 resistance increased. This trend tells you to jump straight to Choice (H) because it's the only one that says that both currents decreased. Even if you didn't recognize this overall trend, you can look at Table 2 and find the decreasing trend for each individual resistor. Choices (F), (G), and (J) are incorrect because they say that the current through one of the resistors increased as Resistor 1 resistance increased.

25. B. The two main components of the circuit examined in these studies were the battery used and the resistance of Resistor 1. For both studies, one of these components was varied while the other was held constant. In Study 1, battery voltage was varied, while Resistor 1 resistance was held constant at 100Ω. In Study 2, Resistor 1 resistance was varied and battery voltage was held constant at 9.0 V. Therefore, the configuration used in both studies was a battery voltage of 9.0 V and a Resistor 1 resistance of 100Ω. You can tell that Choices (A) and (C) are incorrect because Study 2 didn't use a battery voltage of 1.5 V. Similarly, Choices (C) and (D) are incorrect because Study 1 didn't use a Resistor 1 resistance of 500Ω.

26. F. To answer this question, you have to extrapolate the data given in Table 1. The table tells you that the voltage measured across Resistor 2 increased as the battery voltage increased. The question asks you to extrapolate out to a battery voltage of 12.0 V, which would mean that the voltages across each of the resistors would increase. With a 9.0 V battery, the voltage across Resistor 2 was 8.04 V, so you know the answer you're looking for has to be greater than 8.04 V. Choice (F) is the only one greater than 8.04 V, so it's the correct answer.

WARNING

Did you pick Choice (G) because it was the highest voltage given in the table for Resistor 2? Don't think that the choice you're looking for will always be exactly one of the numbers provided in the table. You may have to extrapolate or use logic to predict what might happen if certain aspects of an experiment are altered.

27. D. From Table 1, you can see that the voltage across Resistors 2 and 3 was always the same; that's because they were arranged in parallel in the circuit. Armed with this info, you can eliminate Choice (A). When you look at Table 2, you may notice that the current through Resistor 1 was always equal to the sum of the currents through Resistors 2 and 3. This trend leads you to the correct answer of Choice (D). Even if you didn't notice this trend, though, you can go ahead and determine that the other choices are incorrect. The current through Resistor 2 was never greater than the current through Resistor 1, so Choice (B) is wrong. The current through Resistors 2 and 3 was never equal, so Choice (C) is also incorrect.

28. J. You find the answer to this question by reading the figure titles. Figure 1 provides information about the most common elements, and Figure 2 provides information about the less common elements. The only answer choice that appears on Figure 1 is Choice (J), titanium. The other answers are on Figure 2, so they must be less common then titanium.

29. B. Look for the largest percent by weight but focus only on the elements listed in the answer choices. Figure 1 provides what you need to get the right answer. The largest concentrations overall are oxygen and silicon, but neither of those are choices, so you have to keep going to the right to find the next highest element.

Did you put down aluminum because it comprises the largest concentration in the typical Earth crust of the four choices given? The question asks specifically about the lunar highlands, so Choice (A) is incorrect. In the lunar highlands, the element with the next highest percent by weight is iron, so Choice (B) is the correct answer. Choices (C) and (D) are incorrect because calcium and sodium are present in smaller concentrations than iron.

30. G. You need to look at Table 2 to answer this question. The question states that chromium is dangerous in larger concentrations, so locate the place with the highest percent by weight of chromium. That place is the lunar highlands, Choice (G). Choice (F) is incorrect because the lunar lowlands have lower concentrations than the lunar highlands (although the percent by weight in the lowlands is also potentially hazardous). Choices (H) and (J) are wrong because the graph shows that the concentrations of chromium on the Earth are the smallest.

31. C. To answer this question, you just need to find which elements are present in higher concentrations in the Earth's crust than in the lunar lowlands. The elements that fit this description are oxygen, silicon, sodium, potassium, hydrogen, phosphorus, manganese, carbon, and chlorine. This information leads you to Choice (C) because both sodium and potassium are present in higher concentrations on the Earth than in the lunar lowlands. Choice (A) is wrong because aluminum is present in higher concentrations in the lunar lowlands than in the Earth's crust. The same applies to Choices (B) and (D).

32. J. The question says that hydrogen, oxygen, and carbon are all important for fuel, which lets you know that they're desirable on the Moon. So, ideally, they'd be in at least as high of a concentration on the Moon as they are in the Earth's crust. Choice (F) isn't an issue because it says that the oxygen levels in the soil are satisfactory. Choice (G) might cause enough concern to prevent an outpost construction in the lunar highlands, but if you look at the graph, you see a more pertinent issue with hydrogen. Choice (J) causes a lot of concern because hydrogen is necessary for fuel, yet it's present in much smaller concentrations on the Moon than on the Earth. Choice (J) is the correct answer. Choice (H) talks only about the Earth, so it isn't particularly relevant to prospective lunar inhabitants.

33. A. This question requires you to look at three elements and list them in order from lowest to highest concentration according to their presence in the lunar lowlands. You can answer this one pretty quickly just by looking at Figure 1. Of calcium, iron, and aluminum, iron has the lowest percent by weight. Calcium comes next, and aluminum has the highest percent by weight. Choice (A) is the correct answer.

34. F. Table 2 shows the relationship between soil temperature and Scoville heat. As the soil temperature increases, the heat for each plant and the average heat of the test group increases only. The correct answer is Choice (F).

35. B. To answer this question, go to Table 1 to find out which watering frequency would result in an average of 4,500 Scoville heat units. The test group that had the closest to this number of heat units was the group with two days between watering. It had an average of 4,460 Scoville heat units. Choice (B) is the best answer.

WARNING

Make sure you pay attention to the units. If you just saw the number 2 and didn't look to see that it was being measured in days, you might have mistakenly put down Choice (D), every two weeks, which is an incorrect answer.

36. H. To answer this question, focus on Table 2, which shows the results of Study 2, which consisted of watering the plants every three days. When you look at the data for 30°, you see that the average number of Scoville heat units for the test group was 5,080. This is very close to Choice (H), which is the correct answer. None of the other choices are very close to 5,080. Choice (F) is so low that it doesn't seem at all likely to occur in Study 2, in which the plants received water every three days.

37. B. For this question, focus on the trends that the data present. Table 1 shows that when the scientist watered the plants every five days, the average number of Scoville heat units was 5,980. However, when the scientists watered the plants more often, such as every day, the average number of Scoville heat units was only 4,020. These results indicate that the increase in watering frequency resulted in less spicy peppers. Therefore, when a jalapeño plant is watered more often, the spiciness of its peppers decreases. Choice (B) is the correct answer.

TIP

Observe trends in the data whenever you can. Even though the measured Scoville heat units varied quite a bit from plant to plant, the overall average of the test group showed a clear trend.

38. F. The correct answer to this question conveys the element that wasn't tested in either of the studies. Choice (F) is the correct answer because neither study varied the soil composition. Choice (G) is incorrect because the point of Study 2 was to vary the soil temperature and observe the effects. Choice (H) is incorrect because the frequency of water was held constant in Study 2, and holding a variable constant doesn't generate more data. Eliminate Choice (J) because the light provided to the plants was held constant in both studies.

39. A. You have to look up each of the answer choices individually in the tables to answer this question. Choice (A) appears in Table 1 and shows the Scoville heat units ranging from 5,200 to 6,700, which is a range of 1,500. Choice (B) appears in both Table 1 and Table 2; it shows a range of 700 in Table 1 and 600 in Table 2. Choice (C) is present in Table 2 and shows a range of 500 Scoville heat units. Choice (D) appears in Table 2 and shows a range of 600. Choice (A) has the largest range by a long shot, which makes it the correct answer.

REMEMBER

This question takes longer to answer than some others because you have to look through both tables and examine each answer choice. Spotting the wide variation recorded in Table 1 with five days between watering may be fairly easy to do. But if you're running out of time at the end of the section, mark a guess for time-consuming questions like this one and move on to the remaining questions. If you have time, you can go back and spend more time working out the answer.

40. J. The key to answering this one correctly is recognizing the trends shown in Tables 1 and 2. Table 1 shows that the spiciest peppers were produced with the least frequent watering (every 5 days), and Table 2 shows that the spiciest peppers were produced with the highest soil temperature (30 degrees Celsius). The combination of these factors should result in the spiciest jalapeño peppers, assuming that the plants survive the hot and dry conditions.

Writing Test

See the "Writing Test" section in Chapter 21 for general information on the features that your essay should contain.

Sample response

As more high school graduates head for college than have in past decades, fewer pursue trade careers, resulting in a decrease in the number of plumbers, electricians, mechanics, and other technicians. Part of the issue may be that government funding for education is extended to four-year colleges rather than vocational training. If more federal funding were allocated to vocational training, more graduates would probably use those funds to gain skills to meet the high demand for expert technicians. Federal funding should be allocated to liberal arts programs, but more funds than the current allocation should be directed to trade training and education. Many of today's most popular careers may not exist in ten years, and the skills gained during preparation for a specific career may become obsolete. The communication and problem-solving skills gained in studying the liberal arts are also skills that translate well to whatever the job market may have in store for the future. So investing in liberal arts degrees may have a greater long-term impact than funding vocational programs. Graduates with important critical-reasoning skills may be more adaptable to a fluctuating job market and may be better positioned to move into high-paying careers or creating businesses that provide job opportunities for others. Studies have shown that over decades, those who major in English, history, philosophy, and other liberal arts areas may achieve higher salaries than those who work in tech fields. Scrapping an investment in liberal arts to fund vocational programs may have severe long-term effects.

Therefore, the government should find ways to subsidize both educational avenues. Funding should be allocated to vocational training at a rate proportional to the demand for trade positions in society. Rather than simply taking money from liberal arts to give to trade-based education, alternative funding solutions should be sought. Then, society will benefit in both the short and long term.

Answer Key for Practice Exam 3

English Test

1.	C	16.	J	31.	A	46.	G	61.	A
2.	F	17.	B	32.	H	47.	A	62.	J
3.	C	18.	J	33.	C	48.	H	63.	D
4.	J	19.	A	34.	G	49.	B	64.	H
5.	B	20.	G	35.	D	50.	J	65.	B
6.	J	21.	A	36.	H	51.	A	66.	F
7.	C	22.	G	37.	D	52.	G	67.	A
8.	F	23.	B	38.	G	53.	A	68.	G
9.	D	24.	J	39.	A	54.	J	69.	C
10.	H	25.	B	40.	G	55.	B	70.	F
11.	D	26.	G	41.	D	56.	G	71.	D
12.	F	27.	C	42.	G	57.	B	72.	J
13.	C	28.	H	43.	B	58.	J	73.	D
14.	G	29.	D	44.	J	59.	A	74.	G
15.	A	30.	F	45.	D	60.	J	75.	C

Mathematics Test

1.	D	14.	H	27.	C	40.	G	53.	D
2.	G	15.	A	28.	F	41.	C	54.	J
3.	C	16.	J	29.	D	42.	J	55.	E
4.	H	17.	A	30.	H	43.	B	56.	F
5.	B	18.	H	31.	E	44.	K	57.	B
6.	H	19.	E	32.	G	45.	D	58.	K
7.	C	20.	J	33.	B	46.	F	59.	D
8.	K	21.	C	34.	K	47.	A	60.	H
9.	D	22.	J	35.	E	48.	G		
10.	H	23.	B	36.	J	49.	C		
11.	B	24.	G	37.	B	50.	J		
12.	H	25.	D	38.	F	51.	E		
13.	A	26.	J	39.	B	52.	H		

Reading Test

1.	C	9.	B	17.	B	25.	A	33.	A
2.	F	10.	G	18.	F	26.	H	34.	G
3.	D	11.	A	19.	D	27.	A	35.	C
4.	J	12.	J	20.	H	28.	F	36.	F
5.	A	13.	C	21.	D	29.	C	37.	B
6.	J	14.	F	22.	G	30.	H	38.	H
7.	C	15.	C	23.	C	31.	D	39.	B
8.	G	16.	J	24.	H	32.	J	40.	F

Science Test

1.	C	9.	A	17.	A	25.	B	33.	A
2.	H	10.	G	18.	H	26.	F	34.	F
3.	A	11.	C	19.	C	27.	D	35.	B
4.	F	12.	J	20.	J	28.	J	36.	H
5.	B	13.	C	21.	B	29.	B	37.	B
6.	H	14.	J	22.	F	30.	G	38.	F
7.	A	15.	A	23.	C	31.	C	39.	A
8.	G	16.	H	24.	H	32.	J	40.	J

8

The Part of Tens

Chapter **25**

Ten Wrong Rumors about the ACT

They're whispered in the bathrooms and written in notes passed in the classroom. What are they? They're the vile and vicious rumors about the ACT — rumors that seem to grow with each telling. One of our jobs as test-preparation instructors is to reassure students and their parents that the latest rumors they've heard about the ACT are likely false. Here, we address ten of the rumors you may have heard. Quick hint: They're all wrong!

You Can't Study for the ACT

If you really believed this rumor, you wouldn't have bought this book (and we're really glad you did!). Of course you can study for the ACT!

The ACT tests grammar; you can certainly refresh your memory of the grammar rules. The ACT tests algebra, geometry, and arithmetic; you can definitely study formulas and rules in those areas. In addition, a little preparation can make you very comfortable with the format and timing of the test, which reduces your test-taking anxiety and ultimately improves your score. This book, in particular, discusses tricks and traps that the test-takers build into the exam; by knowing what they are ahead of time, you can avoid falling into them on test day.

Different States Have Different ACTs

This rumor is based on the fact that the score sheet compares your performance to that of other students who have taken the ACT in your state. When you receive your ACT score, you find out your percentile rank nationally and within your state. However, all students in all states take the exact same ACT on any one test date. (Of course, the ACT changes from one date to the next; otherwise, you could keep retaking the same test. You'd be surprised how many students don't realize this little nuance and merrily say to us, "Oh, I remember the questions from last time, so I'll do great next time.") If you take the ACT internationally, you do have different test questions from those on paper tests — and a different format. International tests are offered online, but most U.S. students take paper tests.

The ACT Has a Passing Score

The ACT has no such thing as a passing or failing score. By looking at the college websites of the schools you're interested in attending, you can get a pretty good idea of the score you need to get based on your GPA. If you have a high GPA, your ACT score can be lower than if you have a low GPA. In fact, you may be pleasantly surprised how low your ACT score can be. Scoring on the ACT isn't like scoring on high school exams, for which a 65th percentile is failing. If your score is in the 65th percentile on the ACT, you've actually done above average, better than 65 percent of the others who've taken the test.

The ACT Tests IQ

The ACT is a college entrance exam. It tests your potential for doing well in college. If you're the type who normally studies hard for an exam, you'll probably study hard for the ACT and do well on it and then study hard for college exams and do well on them, too. The key is in the preparation. You have the same opportunity to do well on the ACT regardless of whether you're a Super-Brain or as cerebrally challenged as the rest of us. With this book, you find out how to improve your ACT scores with all sorts of tricks, tips, and techniques — something that's much harder to do on IQ exams.

You Can't Use a Calculator on the ACT

Back when your parents took the ACT, you couldn't bring a calculator. Nowadays, though, using a calculator is perfectly acceptable, and recommended, for the Mathematics Test. You can't use it on any other section, however. Just make sure your calculator meets the specifications listed on the official ACT website (www.actstudent.org). The ACT's requirements for calculators are a little more stringent than the SAT's.

You Should Never Guess on the ACT

Wrong, wrong, wrong. You should always guess on the ACT. This exam has no penalty for guessing. Never leave an answer blank. Fill in something, anything, on the chance that you may get lucky and get the question correct.

REMEMBER

Random guessing on the ACT can only help you.

The ACT Is Easier Than the SAT

Maybe. Maybe not. The exams test similar subjects. Both have grammar, reading, and math questions. The ACT reading passages — both in the Reading Test and in the English Test — tend to be at a slightly easier reading level than the reading, writing, and language passages on the SAT. The math questions on the ACT are straightforward and all mulitple-choice, with none of the grid-in questions featured on the SAT. However, the ACT does feature a few advanced math concepts that may not appear on the SAT.

TIP

The SAT and ACT present questions in slightly different ways, so we suggest that you practice taking both tests to see which one fits you better.

Selective Colleges Prefer the SAT to the ACT

All colleges accept both the ACT and SAT. It's true that years ago the SAT was more popular on the two coasts and the ACT flourished in the middle of the country, but the ACT has grown in popularity to the point that the number of students who take the ACT is about equal to those who take the SAT. In fact, some selective colleges don't require SAT Subject Test scores from students who provide ACT scores.

You Have to Write an Essay

Wrong. You don't have to write an essay during the ACT. It's optional, and the number of colleges that want to see an essay score from either the ACT or SAT has been decreasing over the years. Even so, to be sure your bases are covered, taking this portion of the test is a good idea even though you probably don't want to.

You Shouldn't Take Both the SAT and the ACT

Many students take both exams. Usually, the ACT is offered a week or two after the SAT. You may get burned out taking two exams this close together or have trouble studying for both of them, but you certainly may take both tests. Colleges accept either your SAT or ACT score. When we counsel students, we suggest that they take full-length practice exams for both tests. You may do better on one than you do on the other, and you won't know which one you're better at until you try them both.

Chapter **26**

Attention, Parents! Ten Ways You Can Help Your Child Succeed on the ACT

As a parent, you may wonder what you can do to help your student study for the ACT. Well, wonder no longer! This chapter has ten specific steps for helping your child do their best.

Give Awesome Test-Prep Materials

If you bought this book, you did your child a huge favor. Reading this book and taking the full-length practice tests in Chapters 19, 21, and 23 give your child an edge over other juniors and seniors who haven't prepared. Nicely done!

Encourage Studying

Possessing this book is one thing; actually using it is another. Help your child work out a study schedule and give incentives to stick to it, such as picking out the family's dinner menu for one week or allotting more screen time.

Supply a Good Study Environment

Make sure your child has a quiet study area where they can concentrate without being disturbed by siblings, pets, friends, TV, cellphones, or the computer. Quality study time is time spent without distractions.

Take Practice Tests Together

You'll be better able to discuss the questions and answers with your child if you take the practice tests, too. Pretend you're a test proctor and be the official timer when they take the full-length practice tests. When finished, read through the answer explanation chapters (Chapters 20, 22, and 24) together and discover which question types they may need to improve on. Then look up those particular topics in earlier chapters for a refresher on the rules that govern them.

Model Good Grammar

Help your children recognize mistakes in English usage questions by speaking properly with them and *gently* correcting grammar mistakes in your conversations. Before you know it, they'll be correcting you!

Help Memorize Math Formulas

The online Cheat Sheet for this book has a list of tips your student needs to know for the math test; check it out at www.dummies.com and search for the ACT Cheat Sheet. Quiz them to make sure they remember them.

Encourage Reading

One of the best ways to improve reading scores is to actually read. Go figure! Incorporate reading into your family's schedule and set up times to read short passages together and discuss their meanings.

Explore Colleges Together

Your child's ACT scores become more important to them when they realize what's at stake. Taking them to college fairs and campus visits can foster enthusiasm for college and make taking the ACT more relevant.

Arrive at the Test Site on Time

If the test site is unfamiliar to you, take a test drive before the exam date to make sure you don't get lost or encounter unexpected roadwork on the morning of the test. That day, make sure the alarm is set properly so they rise with plenty of time to get dressed, eat a healthy breakfast, and confirm they have the items they need to take with them to the exam.

Help Keep a Proper Perspective

Remind your students that although the ACT is important, it isn't more important than their schoolwork or being good to their family. An exam score isn't a reflection of their worth (or your parenting skills). It's just one of the many tools colleges use to assess students' skills and determine whether they're a proper fit for their freshman classes.

Index

About the Authors

Lisa Zimmer Hatch, MA, and **Scott A. Hatch, JD,** have been preparing teens and adults to excel on standardized tests, gain admission to colleges of their choice, and secure challenging, lucrative professional careers since 1987. For more than 30 years, they have administered their award-winning standardized test-preparation and professional career courses for live college lectures, online forums, and other formats through more than 300 universities worldwide.

Lisa and Scott have taught students internationally through live lectures, online forums, and independent study opportunities. They have written the curriculum for all formats, and their books have been translated for international markets. Together they have authored numerous law and standardized test-prep texts, including *GMAT for Dummies, LSAT For Dummies, 1,001 Practice Problems For Dummies, SAT II U.S. History For Dummies, SAT II Biology For Dummies, Catholic High School Entrance Exams For Dummies,* and *Paralegal Career For Dummies* (John Wiley & Sons, Inc.).

Lisa is currently an independent educational consultant and the president of College Primers, where she applies her expertise to guiding high school and college students through the testing, admissions, and financial aid processes. She dedicates herself to helping students gain admission to the colleges or programs that best fit their goals, personalities, and finances. She graduated with honors in English from the University of Puget Sound and received a master's degree in humanities with a literature emphasis from California State University. She has completed the UCLA College Counseling Certificate Program and is a member of the Higher Education Consultants Association (HECA).

Scott received his undergraduate degree from the University of Colorado and his Juris Doctor from Southwestern University School of Law. He is listed in *Who's Who in California* and *Who's Who Among Students in American Colleges and Universities* and was named one of the Outstanding Young Men of America by the United States Junior Chamber (Jaycees). He was also a contributing editor to the *Judicial Profiler* and *Colorado Law Annotated* and has served as editor of several national award-winning publications. His current books include *A Legal Guide to Probate and Estate Planning* and *A Legal Guide to Family Law,* which are the inaugural texts in B & B Publication's Learn the Law series.

Dedication

We dedicate *ACT 2022 For Dummies,* to our children and their families. Our family demonstrated patience, understanding, and assistance while we wrote this book, and we're very blessed to have them in our lives.

Authors' Acknowledgments

This book wouldn't be possible without the contributions of Jackson Springer, Julia Brabant, Zachary Hatch, Zoe Hatch, Hank Zimmer, and Jennifer Seeley, who provided practice test material and helpful input. We also acknowledge the input of the thousands of students who've completed our test-preparation courses and tutorials over the last 30 years. The classroom and online contributions offered by these eager learners have provided us with lots of information about what areas require the greatest amount of preparation.

Our project organization and attempts at wit were greatly facilitated by the editing professionals at Wiley. Our thanks go out to Elizabeth Stillwell and Chad Sievers for their patience and guidance throughout the process and to tech editor Karen Berlin Ishii for her attention to detail and helpful suggestions during the editing process.

Finally, we wish to thank our literary agent, Margo Maley Hutchinson, at Waterside Productions in Cardiff for her support and assistance and for introducing us to the innovative *For Dummies* series.

We thrive on feedback from our students and encourage our readers to email their comments and critiques to info@hatchedu.com.

Publisher's Acknowledgments

Acquisitions Editor: Elizabeth Stillwell

Editorial Project Manager and Editor: Chad R. Sievers

Technical Editor: Karen Berlin Ishii

Production Editor: Tamilmani Varadharaj

Cover Image: © kali9/Getty Images